TO THE STUDENT: A Study Guide for this textbook is available through your college bookstore under the title *Study Guide — Principles of Marketing* by Martin S. Myers and Robert F. Lusch. The Study Guide can help you with course material by acting as a tutorial, review, and study aid. If the Study Guide is not in stock, ask the bookstore manager to order a copy for you.

Principles of Marketing

KENT PUBLISHING COMPANY

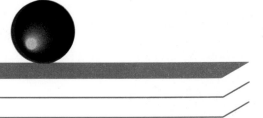

Principles of Marketing

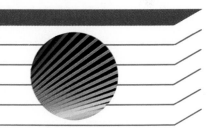

Robert F. Lusch
Arizona State University

Virginia N. Lusch
Market Concepts

BOSTON, MASSACHUSETTS
A Division of Wadsworth, Inc.

To Heather . . . yesterday's child, today's woman, tomorrow's hope.

Editor: Read Wickham
Production Editor: Marianne L'Abbate
Interior Designer: Carol H. Rose
Interior Illustration: Boston Graphics, Inc.
Photo and Ad Researcher: Carole Frohlick
Cover Art: Visual Graphic Services
Cover Design: Lehman Millet Incorporated
Manufacturing Manager: Linda Siegrist

KENT PUBLISHING COMPANY
A Division of Wadsworth, Inc.

© 1987 by Wadsworth, Inc., 10 Davis Drive, Belmont, California 94002.

Printed in the United States of America

1 2 3 4 5 6 7 8 9 — 91 90 89 88 87

LIBRARY OF CONGRESS CATALOGING-IN-PUBLICATION DATA

Lusch, Robert F.
  Principles of marketing.

  Includes indexes.
  1. Marketing.   I. Lusch, Virginia, 1949–
II. Title.
HF5415.L82   1987   658.8   86–18490
ISBN 0-534-03897-2

PREFACE

This book is designed and written for the student who wants a basic solid understanding of the critical concepts and phenomena in marketing. *Principles of Marketing* will help the student achieve this understanding by 1) using many examples from the exciting and dynamic world of marketing, 2) clearly and concisely defining new terms when they are first introduced, and 3) providing logical and illustrative explanations of marketing phenomena. All the pedagogical devices in this book were designed with these objectives in mind.

The reader of this book is assumed to have no prior knowledge of marketing. We realize that most students will take only one marketing course and that they therefore need to acquire in this one course an appreciation of the role of marketing in society and in the organization. The book is suitable for a wide variety of instructional formats because it is divided into eight parts that can be reordered or selectively deleted where necessary. This book is written primarily for the undergraduate introduction to marketing course, but it could also be conveniently used as an introductory text for MBA students who have had no formal coursework in marketing.

STATEMENT OF PURPOSE

Principles of Marketing is written in a modular format. Part I, "An Introduction to Marketing," contains important key concepts to be used throughout the remainder of the book and discusses why marketing is important to individuals and organizations. Chapter 1 reveals that marketing is an exchange process and highlights the rapid growth of marketing by nonprofit, service, and international organizations. Chapter 2 discusses the firm's external environments—social, competitive, economic, technological, physical, legal/political, ethical—and the opportunities they present. Chapter 3 discusses how firms capitalize on environmental trends to formulate strategic marketing plans that help achieve their objectives.

The primary focus of Part II, "Understanding the Marketplace," is on the dynamic setting in which marketing occurs. Chapter 4 discusses the need for marketing research and information to understand the marketplace. Chapter 5 focuses on the sociological, psychological, and economic factors that influence consumers' purchasing decisions. Chapter 6 identifies different organizational markets and shows how organizational buyers make purchasing decisions. Chapter 7 explains several approaches used to segment markets and discusses how to select a target market.

Parts III through VI focus on the four primary decision variables in marketing—product, place, promotion, and price—which are often referred to as the marketing mix. Part III, "Product Planning and Decisions," focuses on the product component. Chapter 8 introduces, defines, and explains numerous product concepts, such as product positioning, product mix,

ORGANIZATION AND CONTENTS

product life cycle, branding, packaging, and product warranties. In Chapter 9, methods for systematically developing new products are discussed.

"Distribution Planning and Decisions," Part IV, details the "place" component of the marketing mix. Chapter 10 reveals what marketing channels are and why they develop, and their importance, characteristics, and legal considerations. Chapter 11 introduces the physical distribution system, its management, and its relation to the management of customer service activities. Chapter 12 discusses the most popular types of retailing, retailer classifications, store atmosphere, the evolution of retail competition, the structure of wholesaling, and ways to market products more effectively through wholesalers.

Part V, "Promotion Planning and Decisions," concerns the third component of the marketing mix. Chapter 13 focuses on understanding the marketing communication process, which is critical to developing successful promotion strategies. The role of advertising in our economy, different types of advertising, the advertising decision-making process, and publicity are covered in Chapter 14. Chapter 15 describes career opportunities in personal selling and the different types of salespeople, explains the selling process and sales force management, and discusses sales promotion.

Price is the final element of the marketing mix and it is discussed in Part VI, "Price Planning and Decisions." Chapter 16 discusses how price is influenced by the firm's external environments, and how managers develop price objectives and policies. Chapter 17 discusses the price strategies a firm can establish and explores the economic approach to price setting, how prices are set, and different pricing tactics.

Part VII, "Special Growth Opportunities," describes the rapid growth of international, services, and nonprofit marketing. Chapter 18 discusses the different orientations a firm can have toward international marketing, the importance of understanding foreign environments, and foreign market entry strategies. Chapter 19 discusses the rapid growth of the service sector in many countries and explains how services differ from goods, the competitive forces service marketers confront, and how to understand the service customer. Chapter 20 describes the differences between nonprofit and conventional marketing, how to develop a marketing plan for a nonprofit firm, and the ethics of nonprofit marketing.

Part VIII, "Execution, Evaluation, and the Future of Marketing," concludes our discussion. Chapter 21 describes the two major steps in executing a marketing plan: implementation and control. Chapter 22 reflects on the performance of marketing on a societal level, the ethical behavior of marketers, and what marketing might be like in the mid 1990s.

PEDAGOGICAL DEVICES

This book is intended to be "user friendly" and includes many learning aids to make the material more meaningful, comprehensible, and interesting. Each chapter begins with a set of Learning Objectives that tells the student what should be accomplished in the chapter. Next, a profile of a leading marketer is provided. These Marketer Profiles give the student role models by discussing people who have succeeded in marketing. All Key Concepts are boldfaced and their definitions italicized at their first mention in the text. Other important terms are also italicized. Each chapter has two Marketing in Actions. These are boxed inserts that elaborate on and explain key concepts. Each Marketing in Action provides the reader with an inside view of how organizations and industries practice marketing.

Numerous four-color photographs, advertisements, and figures accompany the text and graphically depict the concepts under discussion. A number of tables enable the student to readily grasp the relationships among complex data and key concepts.

Each chapter ends with a narrative Summary; a list of Key Concepts that were boldfaced within the chapter, together with the page numbers on which the terms were defined; ten to twenty Review and Discussion Questions; and three to five Action Problems. The Review and Discussion Questions will help students think about the material in the chapter and test the comprehension of what they have just read. The Action Problems will get students involved in experiential learning exercises, which will help them to better understand the concepts presented in the chapter.

At the conclusion of each of the eight parts are cases. These cases allow students to apply important concepts and marketing principles that were learned in each of the eight parts. A total of 44 cases are included, and the following are based on real-life company marketing situations or problems:

- "The Marketing and Distribution of Trade Books"
- "Motor Carriers Face Drastically Altered Environments"
- "Mineral Water and Natural Soda"
- "Chrysler Corporation and Its Publics"
- "Publix"
- "Hewlett-Packard: Strategies for Leadership"
- "Quality Travel Agency"
- "Firestone Masterminds the Auto Repair Market"
- "Consumer Research, Shopper Needs, and Market Segmentation"
- "Trinity Memorial Hospital"
- "MCI Mail Expands Product Mix"
- "Competition Encourages Product Modification in Soft Drink Industry"
- "Marriott Hotel Corporation Plans for Growth"
- "New Coke"
- "Film Distribution"
- "Ensuring Product Availability at Whirlpool"
- "The Kroger Company"
- "Management of Software Inventory"
- "Negative Publicity for the Alcohol Industry"

- "Improving Sales Force Productivity at Avis"
- "Price Competition in the Rental Car Business"
- "Longchamp Stemware"
- "The Motorcycle Glut"
- "Political Uncertainty on Hong Kong Island"
- "Henry and Richard Block of H & R Block, Inc."
- "Willoughby Realty Inc. and Willoughby/Gendell Commercial Real Estate Services"
- "R. J. Reynolds Tobacco Company: Advertising, Children, and Smoking"
- "Nestle's Infant Formula"

All of these preceding, real-life company cases were prepared as a basis for class discussion rather than a way to illustrate appropriate or inappropriate handling of marketing situations by the company. The fictitious cases were prepared with the same intention.

Appendix A, "Marketing Math, Finance, and Accounting," should be helpful to students who need a review of income statements, balance sheets, markup percentages, and other important accounting and finance terms— terms that marketing managers may need to understand. Appendix B, "Marketing Careers and Marketing Professionalism," will help students learn about the many career opportunities in marketing. A discussion of the fundamental qualifications of a marketing professional are also presented. Over 300 important concepts are defined in the Glossary. A Subject Index and a Name and Company Index conclude the book.

SUPPLEMENTAL ITEMS

Study Guide

The Study Guide is comprehensive and should be a significant learning aid to the serious student. Each chapter has a review of the learning objectives, a chapter summary, definitions of key concepts, matching exercises, true/false questions, and multiple-choice questions. The Study Guide also has a detailed exercise in each chapter, where students must apply what has been learned, and a case study, where key concepts for the chapter are put into a realistic setting for more action-oriented learning.

Instructor's Manual

The Instructor's Manual offers numerous suggestions for preparing classroom presentations. Each chapter of this manual includes: 1) chapter overview, 2) learning objectives, 3) key concepts, 4) chapter outline, 5) suggestions on use of Marketer Profile and Marketing in Actions, 6) lecture outline, 7) answers to Review and Discussion Questions, and 8) answers or guidelines for Action Problems. The Instructor's Manual also provides analyses of the forty-four cases in the book. Each case is analyzed and brief teaching notes are provided. Also a list of three to four important concepts each case covers and suggested chapter(s) where it may be used are offered. Analyses for the forty-three cases in the Study Guide are also provided, as well as teaching notes for these cases. The final part of the Instructor's Manual provides over 100 transparency masters. Also thirty-five of the transparency masters offer definitions of the thirty-five most important concepts in *Principles of Marketing.* These allow the instructor to prepare an overhead of a Key Concept definition, which will enable students to take class notes easily.

Overhead Acetates

A package of 100 overhead acetates of the most important figures, tables, and advertisements in the book is provided to adopters. Fifty of these are in full color and enable the instructor to illustrate key points.

Test Bank

The Test Bank includes more than 2300 objective test items. Each chapter has approximately sixty multiple-choice questions and forty-five true/false questions. A computerized Test Bank is also available for personal computers in the IBM and Apple families.

Marketing Showcase (Software Package)

The software package, *Marketing Showcase,* was developed by Cognitive Development Company. It is an interactive analysis program packaged with several data sets. This software is not just a "simulation," but allows analysis of real marketing data, such as magazine subscription rates, sales of many specific products, and demographic characteristics of sales areas. Using lively, color graphics, *Marketing Showcase* also allows instructors to present classroom demonstrations that illustrate particular points in this textbook. *Marketing Showcase* runs on the IBM PC or compatibles with one disk drive and color graphics capacity.

Videotapes

There are five videotapes to accompany *Principles of Marketing.* The first is "Marketing Concepts," which provides an overview of marketing and marketing functions. It describes the evolution of marketing, identifies the basic characteristics of consumer and industrial markets, explains target marketing, and provides insight into the four elements of the marketing mix.

"Marketing Product Strategy" covers the nature of a product and the importance of product development. Special emphasis is placed on the critical impact of the life cycle of a product.

"Marketing Promotional Strategy" emphasizes the importance of promotion in marketing strategy. Attention is focused on the blending of advertising, personal selling, sales promotion, and publicity.

"Marketing Distribution" considers the factors in and the channels available for distributing goods to the ultimate consumer. The components of an organization's physical distribution system and the importance of its proper management are discussed.

"Marketing Pricing Strategy" describes the importance of pricing. It focuses on the potential pricing objectives of a business, the role of supply and demand, costs, and market analysis for determining prices, as well as potential price strategies to reach the consumer.

A STATEMENT OF GRATITUDE

This book and all the supplements became a manageable project with the outstanding assistance of Read Wickham and Marianne L'Abbate, both at Kent Publishing Company. Our developmental editor, Carlyle Carter, offered invaluable assistance at all stages of manuscript development. We also wish to thank Al Kagan for his assistance on the Instructor's Manual, Martin Meyers at the University of Wisconsin at Stevens Point for providing cases in the textbook and for his assistance on the Study Guide, and Melvin Stith for his assistance on the Test Bank and computer simulation. The understanding support of our daughter, Heather, made this four-year undertaking possible. Finally, we wish to thank the companies and individuals that granted us permission to use their words, thoughts, exhibits, photos, advertisements, and data.

ROBERT F. LUSCH
VIRGINIA N. LUSCH

Craig Kelley
California State University at Sacramento

J. Ford Laumer
Auburn University

Eldon Little
Drake University

James Littlefield
Virginia Polytechnic Institute

George Lucas
Texas A & M University

Eric Lynn
Philadelphia College of Textiles and Science

Maurice Manner
Marymount College

Stephen Miller
Oklahoma State University

Emerson Milligram
Carlow College

H.J. Mitchell
Culver-Stockton College

John Morris
University of Toledo Community and Technical College

Charles Patton
Pan American University

Richard Pesta
Frostburg State College

Winston Ring
University of Wisconsin at Milwaukee

Therese Riordan
St. John Fisher College

W. Daniel Rountree
Middle Tennessee State University

William Sekely
University of Dayton

David Shani
Baruch College of the City University of New York

Eric Shaw
Florida Atlantic University

Mark Speece
Central Washington University

George Sztajer
Augustana College

Richard Tead
Georgia Institute of Technology

Melvin Tick
Bluefield State College

Margaret Trossen
Mount Vernon College

Cameron Williams
University of South Alabama

Richard Wozniak
Northeastern Illinois University

George Yohanek
Mary Washington College

BRIEF CONTENTS

CONTENTS

PART **II**   **UNDERSTANDING THE MARKETPLACE**   **89**

Chapter **4**   **The Marketing Research Process and the Marketing Information System   91**

Chapter **5**   **Consumer Buying Behavior   120**

Chapter 6   Organizational Markets and Buying Behavior   148

Chapter 7   Market Segmentation and Target Marketing   180

PART III   PRODUCT PLANNING AND DECISIONS 233

Chapter 8   Product Concepts 235

MARKETER PROFILE   *King Karpen of Aireloom*   *235*

Chapter **17** Price Determination 518

CASES FOR PART VI 542

PART **VII** SPECIAL GROWTH OPPORTUNITIES 547

Chapter **18** International Marketing 549

PART **VIII**   **EXECUTION, EVALUATION, AND THE FUTURE OF MARKETING**   **643**

Chapter **21** **Executing the Marketing Plan 645**

Chapter **22** **Evaluation, Ethics, and the Future of Marketing 676**

Principles
of
Marketing

AN INTRODUCTION TO MARKETING

The first three chapters of *Principles of Marketing* introduce the topic of marketing and discuss why marketing is important—to you and to any type of organization. Chapter 1, "Marketing: An Overview," reveals that marketing is an exchange process consisting of buyers and sellers and highlights the rapid growth of marketing by nonprofit, service, and international organizations. Chapter 2, "The Marketing Environments," discusses the firm's external environments and the opportunities and threats they present. Chapter 3, "Marketing Management and Strategic Planning," discusses how firms capitalize on environmental trends to formulate strategic marketing plans that help achieve their objectives.

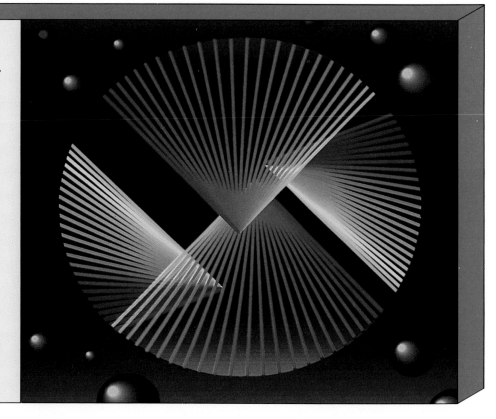

## CHAPTER 1

LEARNING OBJECTIVES

LEARNING OBJECTIVES

After you complete this chapter, you should be able to:

- **Define** and **explain** what marketing is

- **Identify** and **discuss** four reasons why the study of marketing should be important to you

- **Define** the marketing concept and **describe** its three pillars

- **List** three sectors of the economy where the practice of marketing is growing rapidly and **discuss** the reasons for this growth

MARKETING: AN OVERVIEW

MARKETER PROFILE

Lee A. Iacocca of Chrysler Corporation

Lee A. Iacocca began his career in the automobile industry in 1946 with Ford Motor Company. Iacocca rose rapidly to the top at Ford and became president in 1970; however, in 1978 he was fired. Iacocca could have received up to $1.1 million in deferred bonuses from Ford if he had not gone to work for another automobile company. Instead, he accepted an offer to be president of the almost bankrupt Chrysler Corporation.

In 1978, when Chrysler was close to bankruptcy, Iacocca faced the almost impossible challenge of making the company profitable again. He immediately responded to this challenge by attempting to transform Chrysler into a marketing-oriented firm. Chrysler was still a production-oriented company, and its rationale for existence was superior engineering. Former Chrysler president Townsend said it best, "What this company had in all of its products was more engineering differences than any other products being offered [to] the American people." Iacocca decided to change this orientation by giving the American car-buying public what they wanted instead of what Chrysler engineers liked to design. He began to give them smaller cars with fuel economy, good styling, better quality, low cost maintenance, and lower prices. He also brought back the convertible, which was an instant success, and introduced a minivan geared toward today's smaller families.

One successful strategy that Iacocca introduced at Chrysler was production of several cars from interchangeable parts. Iacocca took two successful K-cars—the Plymouth Reliant and the Dodge Aries—and created the Chrysler LeBaron, Dodge 400, Chrysler E class, Dodge 600, and Chrysler New Yorker. The cost of these transformations and other new product development ran about $6 to $7 billion between 1980 and 1985.

Iacocca also realized that Chrysler needed more than the consumer's patronage to succeed, so he also developed good exchange relationships with other key publics including the federal government. He obtained major wage and salary reductions from the United Auto Workers, received $1.2 billion in guaranteed government loans, obtained discounts from

key suppliers, and borrowed money from its dealers. Under the direction of Iacocca, Chrysler succeeded not only in becoming highly profitable, but also in paying back all of its government-guaranteed loans by early 1984.

Sources: Chrysler Corporation annual reports and selected news releases; Peter Vanderwicken. "What's Really Wrong at Chrysler," *Fortune* (May 1975), pp. 176–179, 274, 276; "Off to the Races Again," *Fortune* (December 4, 1978), pp. 15–16; "It Won't Be Easy," *Forbes* (November 27, 1978), p. 130; Andy Pas. "Chrysler's Iacocca Believes He Will Find $500,000,000 Interim Financing to April," *Wall Street Journal* (December 24, 1979), p. 3; "Can Chrysler Keep Its Comeback Rolling?" *BusinessWeek* (February 14, 1983), pp. 132–136; Lee A. Iacocca. "The Rescue and Resuscitation of Chrysler," *Journal of Business Strategy* 4(Summer 1983), pp. 67–69; Marjorie Sorge. "Iacocca Complains and Explains in His Life Story," *Automotive News* (October 22, 1984), p. 3.

INTRODUCTION

As the preceding Marketer Profile on Lee Iacocca and Chrysler Corporation suggests, good marketing can be the savior of an organization. In the United States, those firms that develop good marketing programs often prosper and those that do not often falter. It is also true that countries with superior marketing talents tend to grow more rapidly than others. For example, the economic growth of Japan since World War II has been due largely to excellence in the area of international marketing.

The purpose of this chapter is to introduce you to marketing. We want you to know what marketing is and why it is an important subject to study. We also wish to familiarize you with the practice and rapid growth of marketing in business today.

WHAT IS MARKETING?

Marketing is an activity that surrounds our daily lives. Everywhere you look on your way to school or work you will see the impact of marketing. You will undoubtedly pass billboards advertising goods or services, you will pass retail establishments, or you may see trucks or trains transporting merchandise. Each of these is an important part of the marketing system.

This book is the result of marketing activity. Someone had to decide to produce this book to fill a need in the marketplace, and once it was developed and produced, the book had to be sold. To accomplish this, a considerable amount of marketing activity occurred. For example, research had to be conducted to determine what students and professors desired in a principles of marketing textbook; paper and other raw materials had to be purchased; the services of a typesetter had to be obtained; artists and photographers had to be hired; the price had to be set; the books needed to be stored in warehouses; the book had to be promoted to college professors; and trucks were needed to transport the books to hundreds of college bookstores.

Marketing is a complex process, and marketing experts often disagree on what marketing is and what it consists of. To avoid this controversy,[1] we will use the official American Marketing Association definition of marketing:

> **Marketing** *is the process of planning and executing the conception, pricing, promotion, and distribution of ideas, goods, and services to create exchanges that satisfy individual and organizational objectives.*[2]

Note several things about this definition. First, marketing is viewed as a process of planning and executing, which suggests that marketing is a managerial process. Second, this managerial process involves conception (i.e., thinking of or deciding what idea, good, or service to market) and the pricing, promotion, and distribution of ideas, goods, and services. Third, the managerial process is directed at creating exchanges that satisfy individual and organizational objectives.

A key point about this definition of marketing is that it views marketing as an exchange process. For exchange to occur, five conditions are necessary[3]:

1. There must be two parties.
2. Each party must have something that could be of value to the other.
3. Each party must be capable of communication and delivery.
4. Each party must be free to accept or reject the offer.
5. Each party believes it is appropriate or desirable to deal with the other party.

When these five conditions are met, a potential exchange relationship has been established. For example, suppose you neglected to bring a pen to class today and your instructor announced a pop quiz to be completed in ink. You may be able to borrow a pen from the person sitting next to you, but you may have to resort to buying one from the enterprising student two rows back. For this exchange to occur, the student must have a pen available for you and you must have something to trade for it. In addition, each of you must believe it is desirable to deal with each other and each of you must be free to accept or reject the offer. Finally, you must communicate with each other in order to complete the transaction and take delivery. Whether an exchange actually occurs will depend on a variety of other factors that we will explore throughout this book.

WHY STUDY MARKETING?

Marketing is part of the fabric of U.S. society. Thus, it is important to understand marketing and its role in our society. To help you understand marketing, we will examine why marketing is integral to our society and why it is important to three groups, (1) society, (2) organizations, and (3) individuals.

Marketing and Society

From a societal perspective, marketing is important because approximately one-third of the U.S. labor force is employed in marketing-related activities and approximately 50 percent of the price the consumer pays for products is for marketing-related activities. The influence of marketing on society is more than economic; however, marketing also has a cultural influence on society.

Marketing's influence on culture can be understood by examining the new products that marketing has brought into our lives: MTV, chocolate chip granola bars, air conditioning, microwave ovens, frozen pizza, personal computers, electronic banking, credit cards, laser disks, four-wheel-drive sports cars. Essentially the products we enjoy and consume are part of the cultural fabric of our society. Witness Pepsi's creation of the Pepsi generation.

Marketing as a cultural phenomenon can help shape our wants and desires. Consider the influence of the large, regional shopping center (one with several department stores and hundreds of specialty stores selling clothing, toys, furniture, appliances, sporting goods) on your desires. During a visit to a shopping mall you can view thousands of products from the corners of the world. You can see stereos, televisions, and cameras from Japan and Korea, crystal from Ireland, perfume from France, shoes from Italy, furniture from Denmark, stuffed animals from Taiwan, diamonds from Africa, furs from Canada, and cheese from Wisconsin. You will also be exposed to the dress and mannerisms of people from all strata of society—wealthy and poor; educated and uneducated; old and young; fat and trim. The regional shopping center is a giant melting pot, which influences our goals: the poor, deprived child decides she wants to be successful so she can have the things other people are purchasing; the aging executive decides he wants to look young like the fashionable young adult shoppers; the fat man or lady is encouraged to diet by seeing trim and fit shoppers.

Marketing and Organizations

Developing Successful Exchanges. Marketing is important to an organization because it helps that organization create successful exchange relationships with potential buyers. For this to take place, the right products must first be produced and then correctly distributed, promoted, and priced. Note that these tasks directly relate to our definition of marketing. Lee Iacocca saved Chrysler Corporation from bankruptcy because he focused on each of these four key marketing areas. On the other hand, DeLorean built stylish automobiles, but sales were dismal due to poor distribution and poor product quality. RCA videodisks were taken off the market because, although comparably priced, they were not as versatile as videocassette players. Think of all the personal computers—Adam, Osborne, 4A—that were dropped from the market because of inappropriate marketing programs and not because of production problems. Similar examples also exist in the international arena. In 1979, Gerber was forced to sell its Venezuelan operation after major losses because government price controls forced Gerber to sell its merchandise at 1968 prices. Sales of International Harvester farm tractors dropped substantially in Turkey because a lack of qualified repairmen in that country forced the company to initiate an extensive training program.

Financial Investment.   Marketing is a major cause of financial investment and expenditures in an organization.[4] In fact, marketing accounts for approximately 50 percent of the price of most products. For example, Procter & Gamble spends over $700 million annually on advertising, while General Motors spends over a billion dollars a year on transportation. If only 5 percent of these transportation dollars are wasted, the negative impact on GM's profits amounts to over $50 million a year. Campbell Soup spends over $500 million annually on marketing activities. International Business Machines spends over 3 billion dollars annually in research and development to help improve existing products and create new products. Similar figures could be cited for other marketing activities, such as personal selling, public relations, packaging, and warehousing. As you can see, marketing is a major user of the organization's financial resources. Because these expenditures and investments help the organization create and cement successful exchanges with customers, they are generally dollars well spent.

Marketing and Individuals

Freedom to Specialize.   Marketing is important to each of us because it allows us to specialize. To better appreciate this, imagine a society in which each person must hunt, cook, and make his or her own clothing, shelter, and tools. Predictably, not everyone in this society would be equally proficient at all these activities. In fact, if the best hunter concentrated on hunting, the best toolmaker on making tools, and so on, then the society could create a higher level of wealth. However, this system would only work if everyone could exchange their surpluses for the goods and services they needed. By establishing a marketing system, people are given the freedom to specialize.

Here is the yearly food consumption of a typical American family of four.

Utility Creation. Marketing is also important because it adds to the value of products. The production system creates form utility. **Form utility** is created when *separate materials are combined and transformed into a finished product that has higher value than the separate materials composing it.* Assembling copper, plastic, glass, and other materials into the form of a stereo creates something of higher value. Marketing also creates utility—time, place, and possession utility. **Time utility** is *the value created from having a product available at the time you desire it*; for example, being able to go to a 7-11 convenience store late at night to purchase a bag of potato chips. **Place utility** is *the value created by having a product at the place you desire it*, such as having a lobster dinner at a Red Lobster restaurant in Tucson, Arizona. **Possession utility** is *the value created from having the legal right to possess and freely use a product.* Marketing by the exchange process helps to convey legal title, or the right to use products. Marketing institutions, such as wholesale and retail businesses, offer a forum for transacting business and transferring title to merchandise and thus help people possess products by offering to sell items on credit purchase agreements or on lease or rental contracts. For example, by renting tuxedos, a formal wear store helps people enjoy the utility of possessing a tuxedo.

Higher Purchasing Power. Marketing is also important to you as an individual because it helps you to become a better consumer. Buying, like selling, is part of the marketing process. If you learn how to be a better buyer, then the income that you earn will stretch further. All of us probably have met people with different standards of living who earn approximately the same income. Typically, individuals with the higher standard of living are wiser purchasers: they avoid buying on impulse; avoid excessively costly credit buying; engage in comparative shopping to get the best value for their dollar; and in general, engage in good purchasing practices. You can increase your standard of living not only by earning more but also by buying "right."

Career Opportunities. Marketing is an area of significant and varied career opportunities, all of which can be very rewarding. There are marketing careers in advertising, sales, marketing research, retailing, wholesaling, product management, international marketing, public relations, and transportation or distribution. These careers are in industries that produce goods ranging from technologically sophisticated items such as computers and artificial limbs to less complex items such as paper clips or nuts and bolts. You can have a career in a service industry, such as banking, insurance, or health care, or in a nonprofit organization, such as an art museum, an orchestra, a political party, or a chamber of commerce. There are marketing careers all over the world and in all sectors of the economy. Appendix B provides you with more information on careers in marketing.

Salaries for top marketing executives compare favorably with salaries of other top executives (Table 1.1). Because entry level salaries in marketing for college graduates vary greatly, we will not give any figures here. However, your college placement bureau should be able to provide figures based on what recent graduates from your college have been offered.

THE MARKETING CONCEPT

Now that we have introduced you to what marketing is and why you should study it, let's examine how organizations should practice marketing. During the 1950s, a philosophy for the practice of marketing emerged known as the marketing concept. The marketing concept viewed the consumer as the focal point of all marketing activities.[5] Organizations that practice the **marketing concept** *study the consumer to determine consumer needs and wants and then organize and integrate all activities within the firm toward helping the consumer fulfill these needs and wants while simultaneously achieving organizational goals.* There are three pillars to the marketing concept: (1) consumer orientation, (2) integrated or total company effort, and (3) achievement of organization goals.

Table 1.1 The Ten Best Paid Sales and Marketing Executives in 1984

Executive's Name	Employer	Position	Total Compensation
Robert A. Bardagy	Comdisco	Senior vice president marketing	$1,237,681
Irving L. Rousso	Russ Togs	Executive vice president sales	$ 864,879
George A. Levine	Quotron	Vice president marketing and secretary	$ 861,841
Richard C. Bartlett	Mary Kay Cosmetics	Vice president marketing	$ 785,035
David R. Mackie	Tandem Computers	Vice president U.S. marketing	$ 565,154
John J. Shields	Digital Equipment	Vice president sales and service	$ 561,906
Norman A. Myers	Browning-Ferris	Vice chairman and chief marketing officer	$ 514,025
James W. Crook	First Mississippi	Senior vice president sales	$ 508,775
Richard F. Polhemus	Xidex	Vice president, general manager domestic sales	$ 487,194
Frank E. Mosier	Sohio	Senior vice president marketing	$ 428,500

Source: *Sales & Marketing Management* (August 12, 1985), p. 53. Reprinted by permission of *Sales & Marketing Management* magazine. Copyright August 12, 1985.

Consumer Orientation

The **consumer orientation** *dimension of the marketing concept argues that a firm can be more successful if it determines what the consumer needs and wants before it decides what product to produce and/or sell.*[6] In the past, many firms would produce what they were good at producing. This practice allowed them to turn out numerous products, many of which were of extremely high quality; however, these products often were difficult to sell because they did not meet a consumer need. For example, many manufacturers continued to produce manually operated adding machines after the advent of the electronic calculator in the late 1950s. Although much of the output was of a good quality, a need no longer existed. Consequently, the firms that did not adapt and begin to make a product for which there was a demand eventually faced bankruptcy.

To successfully practice the principle of consumer orientation, firms need to regularly conduct marketing research. **Marketing research** is *the systematic collection, recording, and analyzing of data that deal with the marketing of goods and services.* The tools of marketing research allow the firm to assess consumers' needs and wants. Marketing research will be discussed more thoroughly in Chapter 4.

Regardless of how much marketing research is conducted, no organization can be certain of consumers' wants and needs. This is especially true with new product development or anticipatory manufacturing. For instance, Firestone Tire Company must produce snow tires in the summer for the coming fall and winter season. No matter how much research Firestone conducts, it will still face some uncertainty about the weather and therefore may overproduce or underproduce snow tires for the coming season. Consequently, the role of good executive judgment in marketing decision making cannot be ignored. Since marketing is not a precise science, good subjective judgment resulting from years of "hands on" experience is also a key to successfully implementing the marketing concept.

Integrated Effort

A second pillar of the marketing concept is the principle of **integrated effort**, in which *departments within the organization work together toward the common goal of satisfying the customer.* Integrated effort is a systems point of view, in which all departments recognize they are interdependent parts of an organization. Because they are interdependent, they must cooperate to enable the firm to achieve its objectives. Cooperation is often difficult because one department's goals may conflict with those of another department and with the organization's overall objectives.

Several types of conflicts can develop between departments within an organization. One type is the inherent conflict between low unit production costs and high consumer satisfaction. For example, if Sony were to standardize all its television production processes to produce a single size black and white television in a single style, then it could achieve significantly lower costs per television produced. However, this would hurt Sony's marketing efforts because most consumers want variety and selection when purchasing a new television.

Another type of conflict can occur between the finance and the marketing departments. The finance department would like to be tough in granting credit to customers to minimize the risk of default. Conversely, the marketing department would like to be generous in granting credit to enhance the product's appeal to the customer.

Organizational Goals

The final pillar of the marketing concept states that the organization should engage in exchanges based on their potential for helping the organization achieve its goals. Organizations do not participate without expecting something in return, and what they receive should help them achieve their objectives.

Most U.S. organizations are profit oriented and thus only plan to sell their output if it is profitable to do so. A firm may increase its sales, but this does not necessarily mean that its profits will increase. If the transaction costs more to complete than the product is priced, then total company profitability is harmed. Although an organization can increase its sales by more intense advertising and personal selling, if costs rise quicker than sales revenue, then the firm will be worse off.

The many television sets available today is an example of how organizations strive toward the goal of customer satisfaction.

Evolution of the Marketing Concept

Although many firms practice the marketing concept introduced in the 1950s, many others do not. You can probably name a few in each category. If an organization is not practicing the marketing concept, it probably has either a production or a sales orientation. In the history of U.S. commerce, these two orientations generally preceded the consumer orientation that is characteristic of marketing today. We will briefly survey the U.S. history of production orientation and sales orientation.

Production Orientation.   Before 1920, most firms in our economy had a **production orientation**, that is, *their primary concern was to produce as much as possible, with high efficiency.* This orientation is not surprising, since there was a large unmet demand for the basic necessities of life. The name of the game was to produce necessities, such as textiles to make clothing, transportation, food, and shelter, at the lowest possible cost. Firms that prospered during this period were those that made major advances in production technology and could lower production costs as a result. For example, the success of Ford Motor Company was largely due to its superior assembly techniques, which enabled the production of a low cost auto-mobile. This was the technology that Iacocca brought to Chrysler. Although Henry Ford could get by with selling only black Model Ts, this philosophy doesn't work once production outstrips demand.

Sales Orientation.   By 1920, the U.S. economy was producing more than the consumer really wanted or needed. Thus, the major concern of most firms soon became selling, and they adopted a sales orientation. With a **sales orientation,** *firms aggressively use promotional tools, such as advertising and salespeople, to convince the customer to purchase the firm's prod-uct(s)*, regardless of whether the customer wants or needs the product(s). During the 1920s, firms added significantly to marketing expenditures in the areas of personal selling and advertising.

Firms with a sales orientation, however, did not have a consumer ori-entation. They were concerned with the consumer, but only in terms of how to get them to buy what the firm produced. This is the major difference between the sales orientation and the consumer, or market, orientation, which is part of the marketing concept. A sales-oriented firm considers the consumer only after the product has been produced, while a consumer-oriented firm consults the consumer and studies the market *before* the product is produced (Figure 1.1). Because the company produces what the consumer needs or wants, the marketing and selling process becomes much easier and more efficient. In the Marketing in Action on page 14, you will learn how Polaroid recently abandoned its production and sales orientation and adopted the marketing concept.

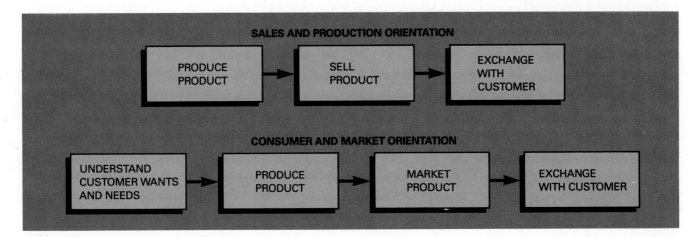

Figure 1.1
Sales and Production Orientation Versus Consumer and Market Orientation

Problems in Implementing the Marketing Concept

Although intuitively appealing, the marketing concept creates certain implementation problems, which we will discuss, by adhering too closely to the philosophy of consumer orientation.

Societal Considerations. What may be best for individual consumers, may not be best for society.[7] For example, individual consumers may like 400-horsepower automobiles; however, too many of these monsters on the road can cause excessive air pollution. Alternatively, some consumers may like the convenience of nonreturnable bottles, but returnables may better conserve our natural resources and preserve the environment.

Because of such societal concerns, some marketing scholars have proposed a societal marketing concept.[8] *Organizations* that adopt the **societal marketing concept** *determine consumer needs and wants and then integrate all activities in the firm to serve these needs while simultaneously enhancing societal well-being and achieving organizational goals.* Thus, the marketing executive operating under the societal marketing concept must balance the interests and desires of three groups: consumers, society, and the firm's owners.

The major problem with the societal marketing concept is that the marketing executive usurps the democratic process by attempting to decide what is best for society. Marketers neither have the right nor the expertise to decide public policy.[9] Critics of the societal marketing concept, for example, argue that if a consumer wants nonreturnable soda containers then

MARKETING IN ACTION

Polaroid Adopts Marketing Concept

Some companies such as Polaroid have only recently adopted the marketing concept. Edwin H. Land, the inventor of the Polaroid instant camera and founder of Polaroid Corp., believed that marketing success was based on the development of innovative products that consumers would then be persuaded to purchase. Under his leadership and direction, Polaroid used little or no marketing research. This production and sales orientation worked as long as Land could improve his instant camera and as long as use of traditional cameras was complicated and the delay in developing pictures was long. When easy to use, computer-controlled 35-mm cameras were invented and 1-hour photo processing centers began to spring up around the country, however, the market for instant photography faltered.

Land left Polaroid in 1980, after the company lost approximately $300 million on Polavision—an instant home movie camera. Industry analysts acknowledged that Polavision was a technological success, but there was just no market for the product. With the departure of Land, William J. McCune became president and brought the marketing concept to Polaroid.

Under McCune's direction the company's approach to product development became more pragmatic.

Now Polaroid begins by targeting a market need; for example, the need to convert graphic computer displays to color slides, for which the company developed Palette, which sells for $1,499. The product development efforts at Polaroid now involve the integrated efforts of the engineering, marketing, and manufacturing operations. Under Land's direction, these three domains were independent and had little or no contact with each other.

Sources: Authors' knowledge of Polaroid Corp.; Polaroid corporate annual reports to stockholders; "Polaroid Sharpens its Focus on the Marketplace," *BusinessWeek* (February 13, 1984), pp. 132, 134, 136; Alex Beam, "A Troubled Polaroid Is Tearing Down 'the House that Land Built,'" *BusinessWeek* (April 29, 1985), pp. 51, 52.

---

the soda marketer should provide them as long as such containers are legally permissible.

Technological Innovation. Undue consideration of consumer needs and wants may create technological nearsightedness.[10] Marketing research techniques can only reveal what needs and wants consumers can express, while many of our most successful innovations have resulted from technological breakthroughs rather than marketing research. The jet engine, Teflon cookware, nylon, television, radio, and many other innovations that spurred growth industries were not the result of consumer demand, as most people cannot envision products beyond their own experience. Therefore, limiting research and development to those areas specified by consumers would indeed stifle innovation.

Interorganizational Behavior. Although the marketing concept encompasses integrated effort within the firm, almost all marketing activity in the United States involves distinct organizations working together to deliver goods and services to the consumer.[11] **Interorganizational behavior** involves *the process of human interaction between organizations, such as how a representative from Eli Lily (a pharmaceutical company) interacts with the pharmacist at a local Walgreens drugstore.* A manufacturer must understand not only how to get departments within the firm to work together, but also how to develop cooperation among wholesalers, retailers, advertising agencies, trucking companies, and other organizations that it needs in the marketing process.[12] More discussion concerning interorganizational behavior can be found in Part IV of the text.

Firms that do not recognize the needs of these other organizations will be at a competitive disadvantage in the long run. Procter & Gamble, for example, has been accused of concentrating its efforts on the consumer and not giving priority to amiable relations with its store and wholesaler

Procter & Gamble recognizes the need for—and the competitive advantages of—developing cooperation among its important retailer and wholesaler accounts.

At P&G, we hear you.

Photograph by Michael Maloney, Cincinnati, Ohio.

There must have been times in the past when it seemed to some of you that we at P&G were not willing to listen.

But we are listening now. Since we're dependent on you for the sale of our products, we simply cannot thrive—or even survive—unless our brands, promotions and ideas are truly good for your business as well as for ours.

We've already put many of your ideas into action. To name just a few:

- ☐ Our price lists have been changed so customers have an incentive to buy full truckloads.
- ☐ You have the option of picking up selected brands at our producing plants in full truckloads for an additional allowance.
- ☐ Inventories are assembled into unit loads which fit the pallets used by most customers.

And this is just the beginning. If we didn't know it before, we certainly do now: it *pays* to listen.

All of us at P&G want to learn and to earn your continuing support so we can establish an even stronger working partnership in the future.

Brad Butler

O.B. Butler
Chairman, Procter & Gamble

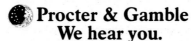 **Procter & Gamble
We hear you.**

accounts. One million-dollar customer said, "P&G has always treated us as a necessary evil."[13] The company is now attempting to overcome this insensitivity to its wholesalers and retailers. Recently, P&G's chairman, Owen B. Butler, said to members of the Food Marketing Institute, "I know there are times when it seems to some of you that we are not willing to listen. I hope we can reverse that feeling because we are at least as anxious to listen to you as we are to our millions of individual customers."[14]

THE GROWTH OF MARKETING

Nonprofit Marketing

Marketing has grown rapidly in the nonprofit as well as the profit-oriented sector of the U.S. economy. **Nonprofit marketing** is *the application of marketing principles to nonprofit organizations.* Nonprofit organizations (e.g., churches, political parties, government agencies, schools, universities, zoos, museums, and charitable organizations) may sell traditional economic goods and services; for example, art museums often have gift shops. In addition, they often attempt to market people, places, and ideas or causes. Political parties largely market people (i.e., political candidates), a local chamber of commerce tries to market a place (i.e., a city such as Dallas), and social action groups try to market an idea or cause (i.e., the equal rights amendment).

Nonprofit organizations use marketing principles and tools to help them achieve their objectives.[15] In this sense, they are similar to traditional profit-oriented firms. The major difference is in their objectives—they are *nonprofit.* Consider, for example, the marketing activity that the U.S. Army has engaged in over the last ten years. It has tried to improve its product (a career in the military) by giving enlistees more job options and by improving military pay, and it has heavily promoted these benefits in the media. The nonprofit objective is to increase voluntary enlistment in the Army.

Given the tremendous growth in nonprofit marketing over the last decade, we will devote Chapter 20 to the topic.

Marketing of Services

Until recently, most marketing in the United States dealt with tangible products. In fact, most of the companies that pioneered marketing, such as Procter & Gamble, General Foods, General Motors, and Whirlpool, manufactured goods. Today, however, the U.S. economy is dominated by service industries, and as a result the service sector is experiencing rapid growth in marketing techniques. Banks, insurance firms, health clubs, dental offices, airlines, and major industries that sell services (intangible products) have employees and executives who are marketing specialists. **Services mar-**

> TODAY'S WOMAN HAS A WILL OF HER OWN
>
> Time was when a woman didn't feel she needed to have a will. Her husband or father or some other male member of the family took care of such things. But today many women prefer to handle things themselves—to make their own decisions. They want to decide who gets the teaspoons, the stock, the real estate or the antiques.
>
> The best way for you to be sure that your wishes will be carried out is to make a will of your own. And the first step is to see your attorney. After you have remembered those close to you, we ask you to remember the American Cancer Society. We promise to use anything you leave us carefully and prudently in research, in public and professional education and to improve the quality of life of cancer patients.
>
> If you or your attorney want to know more about the Society and what we do, call your local ACS Unit or write to the American Cancer Society, 4 West 35th Street, New York, NY 10001.
>
> AMERICAN CANCER SOCIETY

The American Cancer Society, a non-profit organization, applies marketing tools and principles to encourage women to include the Society in their wills.

keting is *the application of marketing principles to the development, distribution, and sale of products that are primarily intangible (services).*

Some firms are beginning to diversify into services in the hopes of obtaining a significant share of this growth sector. For example, Bally Manufacturing (the king of slot machines and video game machines) acquired Six Flags Corp. (a mix of entertainment and amusement parks) in 1982 and Health & Tennis Corp. of America (the largest chain of health clubs in the world) in 1983 and opened Bally's Park Place Casino Hotel in Atlantic City in 1985.[16] Sears Roebuck and Company, the largest retailer in the country, decided to diversify into services in the early 1980s and concentrate its energies in financial services.[17] It bought Dean Witter Reynolds, which propelled it into the stockbrokerage business, and Coldwell Banker, which specializes in real estate investment and banking. Sears has owned Allstate Insurance for a number of years.

The growth in the service sector is shown in Figure 1.2. Because of the

MARKETING IN ACTION

The application of marketing principles to health services can be found in "Operation Outreach," a marketing program developed by the American Dental Association. The marketing objective of the program will be "motivating and influencing the public to seek dental care." A major part of the program is the development of "how to" materials and workshops for dentists that will instruct them in how to market their dentistry. Materials available for purchase or rental by dentists include:

● A dental market planner workbook offering a step-by-step approach to developing a tailored, personalized marketing plan.

Marketing by the American Dental Association

● Marketing starter kits containing sample recall cards, patient audit forms, staff questionnaires, patient newsletters, practice brochures.

● Target marketing packages including marketing tools and promotional ideas to reach the more than 100 million Americans who do not regularly visit the dentist.

● Marketing idea files, a collection of the latest literature on specific marketing techniques and topics

described in the dental market planner.

● Practice-building seminars in selected locations throughout the United States, as well as a national videoteleconference on dental practice promotion.

● A quarterly marketing newsletter covering developments in dental marketing, resource materials, literature, abstracts, interviews with experts, and information on other health care activities.

Source: Based on "Operation Outreach Seeks to Expand Dental Market," *Marketing News* (February 18, 1983), pp. 1, 27.

rapid growth in services and the high proportion of personal consumption expenditures on services, we will devote Chapter 19 to an expanded discussion of the principles of services marketing.

The Marketing in Action on this page provides an example of services marketing: the American Dental Association applies marketing tools to motivate and influence the public to seek dental care.

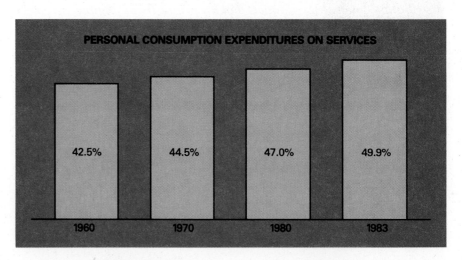

Figure 1.2

Growth in the Service Sector

Source: U.S. Bureau of the Census. *Statistical Abstract of the United States: 1982–1983,* 103rd edition (Washington, DC, 1982), p. 421; and same source, 105th edition, p. 435.

The tremendous growth in the service sector of the U.S. economy has spurred retail firms such as Sears, Roebuck and Company to diversify into services and services marketing.

International Marketing

International marketing is *the marketing of goods and services between foreign countries.* International marketing consists of **exporting**—*when a firm, government, or individual from one country sells a product to a firm, government, or individual in another country*—and **importing**—

when a firm, government, or individual in one country purchases a product from a firm, government, or individual in another country.[18]

The United States is heavily involved in both exporting and importing, although less so than some other countries such as Japan. Exporting is about 9 percent of the U.S. gross national product (GNP; the total national output of goods and services valued at market price) and 14 percent of Japan's; importing is approximately 10 percent of the U.S. GNP and 15 percent of Japan's.[19]

As the U.S. economy reaches maturity due to stabilizing population levels and moderate growth in real income (income adjusted for inflation), more organizations are attempting to increase their emphasis on international marketing. In fact, international marketing represents a significant percent of total sales for some U.S. firms; this is true of Boeing, with 35 percent of its sales in exports, Caterpillar Tractor (27%), Hewlett-Packard (23%), Northrop (22%), Ingersoll-Rand (16%), and Motorola (19%).[20] Because of the increasing importance of international marketing, Chapter 18 will be devoted to this topic.

Much of China's need for better transportation is being met with imported construction equipment, such as this Caterpillar Wheel Loader at work on a railroad tunnel.

SUMMARY

This first chapter introduced you to the field of marketing. We discussed the role of marketing in society and why marketing is important to you and to organizations that you might someday work for.

Marketing was defined as the process of planning and executing the conception, pricing, promotion, and distribution of ideas, goods, and services to create exchanges that satisfy individual and organizational objectives. The core of marketing is the exchange process, and five conditions are necessary for exchange to occur: (1) there must be two parties, (2) each party must have something that could be of value to the other, (3) each party must be capable of communication and delivery, (4) each party must be free to accept or reject the offer, and (5) each party must believe it is appropriate or desirable to deal with the other party.

The marketing concept, which is widely practiced today, espouses that firms should study consumer needs and integrate the efforts of all departments in the firm toward serving consumer needs while simultaneously achieving organizational objectives. Although intuitively appealing and widely practiced, this philosophy has certain weaknesses, including its neglect of what is good for society, its tendency to create technological nearsightedness, and its neglect of interorganizational behavior. As a result of this neglect of what is good for society, some marketing scholars have proposed the societal marketing concept, which recommends that firms not only serve the consumer and achieve organizational goals, but also enhance society's well-being. The problems with this philosophy were also reviewed.

This chapter also introduced you to the rapid growth in the practice of marketing. Marketing principles and tools are being applied to nonprofit organizations to market people, places, and causes. In addition, the marketing of services is growing rapidly. Finally, international marketing is receiving increased interest from U.S. firms.

This chapter also briefly discussed the large number and variety of careers in marketing. A separate appendix on marketing careers is provided at the end of the book.

KEY CONCEPTS

marketing (p. 5)
form utility (p. 8)
time utility (p. 8)
place utility (p. 8)
possession utility (p. 8)
marketing concept (p. 9)
consumer orientation (p. 10)
marketing research (p. 10)
integrated effort (p. 10)
production orientation (p. 12)
sales orientation (p. 12)
societal marketing concept (p. 13)
interorganizational behavior (p. 14)

nonprofit marketing (p. 14)
services marketing (pp. 16–17)
international marketing (p. 19)
exporting (p. 19)
importing (pp. 19–20)

REVIEW AND DISCUSSION QUESTIONS

1. How is the definition of marketing provided in this text different from the view of marketing you had before you read this chapter?

2. What are the five conditions necessary for exchange to occur?

3. Why is marketing an important area of study?

4. Define the four types of utility. Which of these is uniquely associated with marketing?

5. How does marketing create value? Give an example using a product you are familiar with.

6. Define and discuss the three pillars of the marketing concept.

7. How might a university or college practice the marketing concept?

8. Why should the vice president of finance of a corporation be knowledgeable about marketing?

9. Before 1920, most firms in the United States had a production orientation rather than a sales orientation. Why?

10. Identify and briefly discuss some of the problems involved in implementing the marketing concept.

11. Should marketing managers be concerned with the societal consequences of their decisions?

12. Explain why services marketing, nonprofit marketing, and international marketing are becoming more important in the United States. How can the marketing concept be applied to these areas?

13. In 1985, a new Aston Martin V-8 coupe was priced at $100,000, or $24.39 per pound, while a new two-door Chevrolet Chevette sold for $5,470, or $2.61 per pound. The raw materials (glass, plastic, steel, rubber, textiles, and so on) used to manufacture these two cars are approximately the same. Explain or give several possible reasons why the Aston Martin cost almost ten times more per pound than the Chevette.

ACTION PROBLEMS

1. Select a firm that you believe is not practicing the marketing concept. Explain why you think the firm is not practicing it and then suggest how it could implement the marketing concept. If possible, obtain a copy of the firm's annual report to see how profitable it has been and how it spends its money.

2. One of your friends, who is a sociology major, has asked why you are studying marketing. Write a 300-word essay describing the benefits you expect to receive from studying marketing.

3. How well does the college that you are attending provide time and place utility to its students? Write a list of suggestions for improving the provision of time and place utility.

4. Identify some of your needs and wants that are not being met in the marketplace and explain why they are not being met.

NOTES

1. Many additional definitions as well as the nature and scope of marketing itself are discussed in Shelby D. Hunt, "The Nature and Scope of Marketing," *Journal of Marketing* 40(July 1976), pp. 17–28; Shelby D. Hunt and John J. Burnett, "The Macromarketing/Micromarketing Dichotomy: A Taxonomical Model," *Journal of Marketing* 46(Summer 1982), pp. 11–26.

2. "AMA Board Approves New Marketing Definition," *Marketing Educator* (Spring 1985), p. 1.

3. Philip Kotler, *Marketing Management: Analysis, Planning, and Control* (Englewood Cliffs, NJ: Prentice-Hall, 1984), p. 8.

4. A good discussion of the financial aspects of marketing is provided in Frank H. Mossman, W.J.E. Crissy, and Paul M. Fischer, *Financial Dimensions of Marketing Management* (New York: John Wiley & Sons, 1978).

5. F.J. Borch, "The Marketing Philosophy as a Way of Business Life," *Marketing Series No. 99* (New York: American Management Association, 1957), pp. 3–16; J.B. McKitterick, "What's the Marketing Management Concept?" *The Frontiers of Marketing Thought and Action* (Chicago: American Marketing Association, 1957), pp. 71–82.

6. Some authors also argue that the consumer needs to have an operative philosophy; see James T. Rothe and Lisa Benson, "Intelligent Consumption: An Attractive Alternative to the Marketing Concept," *MSU Business Topics* (Winter 1974), pp. 29–34; George Fisk, "Criteria for a Theory of Responsible Consumption," *Journal of Marketing* 37(April 1973), pp. 24–31.

7. Martin L. Bell and C. William Emory, "The Faltering Marketing Concept," *Journal of Marketing* 35(October 1971), pp. 37–41; William Lazer, "Marketing's Changing Social Relationships," *Journal of Marketing* 33(January 1969), pp. 3–9; Laurence P. Feldman, "Societal Adaptation: A New Challenge for Marketing," *Journal of Marketing* 35(July 1971), pp. 54–60.

8. Kotler, *Marketing Management,* p. 29.

9. John F. Gaski, "Dangerous Territory: The Societal Marketing Concept Revisited," *Business Horizons* (July–August 1985), pp. 42–47.

10. Roger C. Bennett and Roger C. Cooper, "Beyond the Marketing Concept," *Business Horizons* (June 1979), pp. 76–83; Peter C. Riesz, "Revenge of the Marketing Concept," *Business Horizons* (June 1980), pp. 49–53; Robert H. Hayes and William J. Abernathy, "Managing Our Way to Economic Decline," *Harvard Business Review* (July–August 1980), pp. 67–77.

11. Johan Arndt, "Toward a Concept of Domesticated Markets," *Journal of Marketing* 43(Fall 1979), pp. 69–75.

12. Principles of interorganizational behavior are discussed in Gary L. Frazier, "Interorganizational Exchange Behavior in Marketing Channels: A Broadened Perspective," *Journal of Marketing* 47(Fall 1983), pp. 68–78.

13. "Why P&G Wants a Mellower Image," *BusinessWeek* (June 7, 1982), p. 60.

14. Ibid.

15. Philip Kotler and Sidney Levy, "Broadening the Concept of Marketing," *Journal of Marketing* 33(January 1969), pp. 10–15. Some authors have opposed the application of marketing to these nontraditional areas; see David J. Luck, "Broadening the Concept of Marketing—Too Far," *Journal of Marketing* 33(July 1969), pp. 53–55.

16. Faye Rice, "Guess Who's the Sultan of Sweat," *Fortune* (April 16, 1984), pp. 52–56; "Bally's: Living High off Low Rollers," *BusinessWeek* (May 27, 1985), pp. 118, 120.

17. "The New Sears, Unable to Grow in Retailing, It Turns to Financial Services," *BusinessWeek*

(November 16, 1981), pp. 140–146; "The Synergy Begins to Work for Sears' Financial Supermarket," *BusinessWeek* (June 13, 1983), pp. 116–117.

18. An excellent text on the topic of international marketing is Philip R. Cateora and John M. Hess, *International Marketing* (Homewood, IL: Richard D. Irwin, 1979, 4th ed.).

19. Statistical Office of the United Nations, *Monthly Bulletin of Statistics* (New York: United Nations, July 1982).

20. "The 50 Leading Exporters," *Fortune* (August 5, 1985), pp. 60–61.

## CHAPTER 2

LEARNING OBJECTIVES

After you complete this chapter, you should be able to:

- **Identify** and **discuss** the seven major external environments

- **List** and **define** the six publics of an organization

- **List** and **explain** how the publics of an organization can affect its performance

- **Describe** the job of an environmental scanner and give two reasons why organizations employ them

THE MARKETING ENVIRONMENTS

MARKETER PROFILE

Henry Henderson of Henderson Industries

Henry Henderson (one of America's most successful entrepreneurs) owes his success in business to his awareness of changes in the technological environment. He is president and sole owner of Henderson Industries, an innovative high technology company in West Caldwell, New Jersey. Henderson is an engineer by training, and on graduation from the State University of New York, he went to work for Richardson Scale Co., a manufacturer of industrial scales. In 1954, when Richardson Scale Co. was looking for subcontractors to assist with a heavy production schedule, Henderson applied for the job. Richardson accepted Henderson's offer, and for the next thirteen years, Henderson not only headed his own business (which had Richardson Scale as a key customer) but also continued to work at Richardson Scale.

In 1967, Henderson decided to devote 100 percent of his energies to Henderson Industries. He recognized the growth potential in national defense and robotics and began to compete for government contracts that would provide the resources to develop product innovations in these growth areas. For example, the company was a subcontractor on NASA's space shuttle project and designed and manufactured a materials-handling system. In a later contract, Henderson was able to take knowledge the company gained in the shuttle project and move into the design of nuclear reactor control panels. Similarly, knowledge gained in designing and manufacturing control panels gave the company machine language software development skills that it is using to develop its own programming language to control robots in a contract for the Watervliet Army Arsenal in Albany, New York.

Henry Henderson sees phenomenal future growth potential in international markets. After four years of selling effort and many trips to the People's Republic of China, he has closed a deal to design and manufacture tire control consoles and materials handling equipment for the Ta Chung Hau Rubber Tire Plant.

INTRODUCTION

As you saw in the preceding Marketer Profile, Henry Henderson succeeded because he was aware of the technological environment, where he identified market opportunities and developed plans to exploit these opportunities. The purpose of this chapter is to help you better understand the host of external environments that provide the organization and its publics with opportunities and threats. Once you develop an appreciation for the nature and scope of these external environments, we can move on to Chapter 3, where we will learn how to translate environmental trends into strategic marketing plans that capitalize on these trends and help the organization achieve its objectives.

THE FIRM AS AN OPEN SYSTEM

A business organization can be viewed as a **system**—*a set of interacting and interrelated elements that forms an entity.* An organization is a system composed of a set of interacting departments and/or work groups, each of which performs different functions. Typical departments are finance, accounting, production, marketing, legal, and research and development.

A business firm is an **open system**, *one that is affected by outside forces.*[1] For example, consider a locally owned and operated day care center. Some of the outside forces that would affect it include national and state laws regarding the building, safety precautions, health and sanitation standards; competition from a local church-operated day care center; the number of unemployed and working parents in the neighborhood; the weather; and local beliefs and attitudes about childrearing. The day care center would also be influenced by the many publics with which it deals. The day care center needs to interact with suppliers of food, linens, cleaning supplies, and so on; employees, stockholders or owners, who provide financial capital; and customers, who provide the demand for child care to make the business economically feasible. Most businesses are affected by these outside forces and are thus open systems (Figure 2.1).

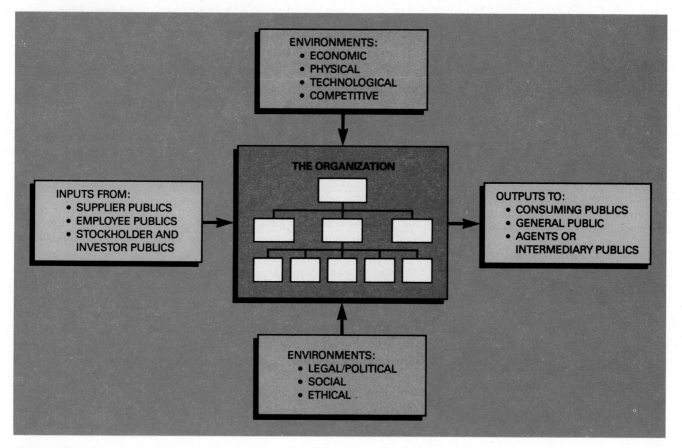

Figure 2.1
The Organization As an Open System

A **closed system**, on the other hand, is *one that is not affected by outside forces.* Closed systems are theoretical for the most part because most entities are affected by some outside force. The sun is the usual example of a closed system because it affects other entities without being affected by them.

External Environments

The **external environments** of a business firm are *the set of forces outside the organization that affect the survival potential of the organization and influence its decision-making process.*[2] There are seven external environments which we list on the following page and discuss in more detail later in the chapter.

1. The **social environment**, which *consists of the behavior of individuals and groups of individuals in society.*

2. The **competitive environment**, which *consists of all other sellers who are vying for the patronage of the same consumers or market the firm is seeking.*

3. The **economic environment**, which *includes the factors that determine the income and wealth-generating ability of the economy.*

4. The **technological environment**, which *consists of the application of science to develop new methods or ways of doing things.*

5. The **physical environment**, which *consists of the geographic and raw material characteristics of the country or part of the country where a firm operates.*

6. The **legal/political environment**, which *consists of the rules and regulations society has imposed on business firms and the political interest groups that affect it.*

7. The **ethical environment**, which is *composed of the norms or moral behavior that society imposes on business and marketers.*

Since the external environments are generally uncontrollable, the marketing manager must develop plans that are consistent with the external environments and changes in these environments. The examples in Table 2.1 help dramatize the point that external environments influence marketing planning and decision making.

Multiple Publics

A **public** of an organization is *"any group that has an actual or potential interest or impact on an organization's ability to achieve its objectives."*[3] As we discussed in Chapter 1, an organization that practices the marketing concept directs its activities and efforts toward satisfying the needs and wants of its customers. Although the firm should be concerned primarily with the consuming public, it also must interact with and develop good relations with the following publics:

❑ **Consuming publics** are *those groups in a society that use or consume a firm's output (also called customers).*

❑ **Supplier publics** are *other organizations that provide a firm with raw materials, services, machinery, and other items needed to produce a product and operate its business.*

❑ **Employee publics** are *the individuals who perform jobs and activities within the firm.*

❑ **Stockholder and investor publics** *provide the firm with the financial resources it needs to operate.*

Table 2.1   External Environments Affect Marketing Decision Making

External Environment	Corporate Example
Social environment	The increase in working women and two-career families prompted McDonald's to open earlier and add a breakfast menu.
Competitive environment	The acceleration of Japanese auto competition forced U.S. auto makers to improve product quality and produce smaller, more fuel efficient autos.
Economic environment	High interest rates and declining real income in the early 1980s forced home builders such as U.S. Homes to build smaller, more affordable homes.
Technological environment	The development of microcomputer technology made the computer a household good and spawned such companies as Apple, Compaq, and Kaypro.
Physical environment	Increased pollution in metropolitan areas in the 1970s resulted in more environmental legislation and thus the need for products to clean up the environment, such as smokestack filters for factories.
Legal/political environment	The deregulation of the motor carrier industry in the early 1980s forced motor carriers such as Lee Way to become more marketing oriented.
Ethical environment	Increased concern by the general public that alcoholic consumption was becoming excessive among teenagers prompted Anheuser-Busch to provide substantial financial support for the Alcoholic Beverage Medical Research Foundation at Johns Hopkins University School of Medicine and for Students Against Driving Drunk (SADD).

❑ **Agent or intermediary publics** are other organizations that *help the firm sell and distribute its output.*

❑ **General public** is *the totality of society on which a firm is dependent for support and freedom to function or operate.* If the general public develops a negative attitude toward an organization, then patronage of the firm could be harmed and laws could be passed to constrain the organization.

If a firm is not able to obtain the support of its other publics, then marketing efforts directed at its consuming publics may be hampered. For example, when employees at American Airlines strike for higher wages, the airline's ability to provide customer service is hampered. When a firm like Revlon fails to develop good relations with wholesalers and retailers (its agent publics), its exchanges with consuming publics will be harmed.[4] Firms can develop strategies to influence the attitudes of multiple publics toward the firm.[5]

Reacting to Environmental Change

The marketing process and, especially, marketing planning help organizations cope with the constantly changing external environments and publics. A change in an external environment rarely affects the firm *directly*. Typically, such a change will first affect one of the firm's publics, which will cause a change in that public's behavior toward the firm, which in turn will cause a change in the firm's behavior or performance. (This chain is illustrated in Figure 2.2.) For example, a rise in interest rates from around 10 percent to 16 percent would affect at least four publics—suppliers, customers, stockholders/investors, and agents/intermediaries—causing the following reactions:

- ❑ *Suppliers* would demand quicker payment from the firm.
- ❑ *Customers'* purchasing power would decline because the cost of credit would rise.
- ❑ Some *stockholders* might decide to sell their stock and put the proceeds into bonds, money market funds, or treasury bills.
- ❑ *Intermediaries,* such as wholesalers or retailers, might decide to carry smaller inventories because of the higher cost of financing inventories.

THE EXTERNAL ENVIRONMENTS

The preceding section points out two fundamental facts about changes. *First,* identifying and analyzing changes in external environments are prerequisites to effective planning. Firms know that changing environments will affect their key publics and thus their firm, so they must scan these environments, anticipate changes, and plan for these changes. *Second,* firms are largely masters of their own destiny. They (and only they) can decide how and when to respond to changing environments. We will now discuss additional aspects of each of these external environments.[6]

Social Environment

Although generalizing the state of the social environment on a national basis is difficult, marketers must recognize certain trends.

The Changing U.S. Household.   Increasingly, the husband is no longer the sole breadwinner.[7] In 1984, an estimated 69 percent of married U.S. households had both husband and wife employed in the labor force.[8] This dual-income phenomenon is having a dramatic impact on household purchasing power and is helping create a market for many luxury goods, such as second cars, boats, and vacation homes.

Families are becoming smaller. The family with three or more children has almost disappeared, many couples are choosing to remain childless, and

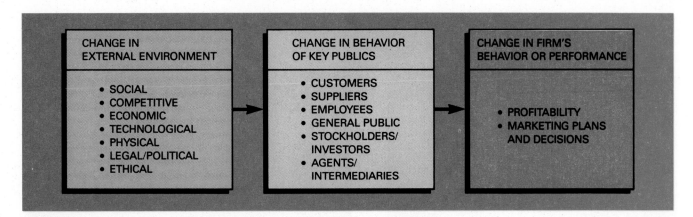

Figure 2.2
The Impact of Changing Environments

the norm has become one or two children. With fewer children, the couple can spend more time working outside the home and can spend their money to purchase non-child-related items.[9] Because children represent a major long-term investment in the range of $75,000 to $200,000 (from birth through college), families with fewer children are likely to spend more on the items they purchase for those children.

The number and percentage of persons over 18 years of age who are married has declined in the last twenty years for two reasons (see Figure 2.3). First, the number of people getting divorced has risen dramatically. Second, people are waiting longer to get married. As a result more households are being headed by singles, and one source estimates that by 1990 approximately 45 percent of all households will be headed by singles.[10] The needs of singles are characterized by smallness. Single people purchase smaller cars, smaller houses, smaller appliances, and single-serving food packages. Their life-style reflects more mobility, a greater fashion awareness, affluence, and increased leisure time. Keep in mind, however, that the singles life-style is also age-related: a twenty-three-year-old man or woman lives differently than a sixty-year-old.[11]

The retired or senior citizen market is experiencing explosive growth and will continue to grow over the next several decades. In 1950, only 8.1 percent of the population was over 65 years old; by 1978, the proportion had risen to 11 percent, and by 2025, approximately 19.5 percent of the population will be over 65 years old.[12] Today's senior citizens are healthier and wealthier than in past decades. Social security payments tied to inflation, Medicare, and company pension plans have increased the discretionary income of many senior citizens, especially because most don't have home mortgage payments.[13] They are an attractive market for restaurants, drugs, travel, motor homes, labor-saving appliances, planned retirement communities, jewelry, art, and other collectibles.

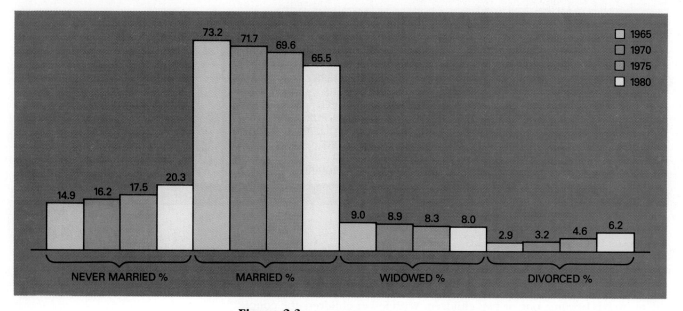

Figure 2.3

Changing Marital Status in the United States[a]

[a]Population over 18 years of age.
Source: U.S. Bureau of the Census. *Statistical Abstract of the United States: 1982–1983,* 103rd edition (Washington, DC, 1982), Table 47, p. 38.

Shifting Geographic Patterns.   Over the last twenty-five years, there has been a profound and dominant shift in the places where people choose to live and work. The southern, West Coast, and mountain states experienced rapid population growth in the 1980s, and this trend is expected to continue. On the other hand, population growth in the Midwest and Northeast is stagnating.

Another geographic shift that has occurred in the past 25 years is a return to the cities. In the 1960s, when many cities were torn apart by riots, people flocked to the suburbs. Today, cities such as Detroit, Dayton, Tulsa, and Baltimore are enjoying a rebirth due to redevelopment efforts and the excitement and convenience of city living.

Countering the movement to the center city is the growth of nonmetropolitan markets. Between 1970 and 1980, the population of nonmetropolitan areas grew 15 percent while that of cities grew only 9 percent.[14] Many people view small towns as attractive places to raise families. The cost of living tends to be lower than that in large metropolitan areas, and crime and congestion are also less prevalent. To serve the needs of this expanding market, retailers such as Wal-Mart, K mart, and Sears are building new stores in markets as small as 10,000.

The Renaissance Center (left) in Detroit is a focus of center city activity and an example of the geographical shift back to urban areas. Retailers such as Wal-Mart (right) recognize the growth of nonmetropolitan areas and meet those market needs with new stores.

A Culture in Transition.   The U.S. culture is in a state of transition because some of our basic societal beliefs, attitudes, and values are changing. Let's briefly explore some of the changes that have occurred over the last few decades.

In the 1970s, *casualness* increased dramatically as people attempted to reduce their stress level. For example, pickup trucks, vans, and jeeps became more popular; children in all social classes began wearing jeans to school; some professors taught class in cutoff jeans and T-shirts; house designs encouraged living and entertaining centered around the kitchen, family room, and outdoors. By 1980, this trend included a component of neatness, so that the life-style was casual but not shabby. Jeans and T-shirts maintained their popularity, but they were tidied up, often with designer labels. Pickups and vans continued to proliferate but became as comfortable and luxurious as automobiles. The outdoor movement grew, as did the appeal of stylish $300 hiking outfits and $500 bicycles.

The distinction between *male and female sex roles* in American society has become blurred as indicated by the proliferation of unisex clothing and hairstyles. Women have entered jobs or careers traditionally held by men; witness the increase in female bus drivers, sanitation workers, executives, physicians, lawyers, and police officers. At the same time, some men took jobs and careers traditionally held by women. The number of male nurses and secretaries rose dramatically; more men took jobs as sales clerks, cooks, and flight attendants; and some husbands decided to stay at home and take care of the household as their wives became the breadwinners. Overall, this change has altered consumer purchasing patterns, as more men shop for groceries and more women purchase cars, lawn mowers, tools, and other traditionally "male" purchases.

Over the last two decades, the influence of the *protestant work ethic* has declined dramatically in the United States. Many lower-level workers intentionally skip a day of work each week, and fewer executives are willing to work sixty-hour weeks. Physicians are refusing to see patients after-hours because they want more time to be with their families. The work force increasingly demands more rewards for less output. Recognizing this trend, marketers must recruit, train, and motivate human resources to become loyal, productive employees.

In the 1970s and 1980s, the American public exhibited substantially *less confidence in large institutions,* especially large businesses and government institutions. Skepticism regarding business and government was based mainly on feelings that these institutions were self-centered and ignored the public's wants and needs. This attitude underscores the need for firms to recognize that the general public is a key public and that all firms need this public's trust if they are to survive and prosper in the long run.

Many households, especially dual-income households and single professionals, are becoming more concerned with *time* rather than money *management.* For example, a two-income household may be more concerned with whether they can afford the time from their busy schedules for a Hawaiian vacation than with the trip's actual expense.

Voluntary simplicity is a value system in which people seek a balance between an outwardly simple but inwardly rich way of life: material simplicity and ecological awareness are stressed.[15] A person who practices voluntary simplicity is often a home gardener and an active do-it-yourselfer. This value system has been fueled by an increasing awareness of the depletion of natural resources and by the desire to become more self-reliant.

Another trend you should recognize is the increased concern for *wellness,* which is the realization that life can be extended by the proper mix of work, diet, and exercise. This new orientation attempts to prevent illness rather than fight illness once it occurs. In fact, some physicians are now opening wellness clinics where they don't treat disease but guide individuals in developing a program for overall physical and mental well-being. The wellness movement has had a dramatic effect on the demand for sportswear, exercise equipment, low sugar and low sodium foods, and health clubs.

Ethnicity.   Although the U.S. is known as the great melting pot, a considerable degree of ethnic identity persists. Such ethnic groups as Hispanics, blacks, and Asians can be viewed as subcultures within the United States, each of which shares many values with the overall U.S. culture but also has distinguishing values and beliefs that influence their tastes in food, clothing, personal care products, music, and a host of other products. Ethnic subcultures tend to be geographically concentrated, which makes it easier for the marketer to focus on them. For example, Los Angeles–Long Beach has

With the wellness movement came the growing demand for aerobics classes and the market needs that go with it—an example of how cultural changes and trends affect market demands.

2.5 million Hispanics and 1 million blacks; New York City has 1.6 million Hispanics and 2.1 million blacks; and Chicago has 1.4 million blacks and more than 500,000 Hispanics.[16]

Competitive Environment

Market competition in the U.S. has intensified since the early 1970s for several reasons: a decline in population growth; a decline in the growth of household incomes; and intensified foreign competition, especially from Japan and the four Asian tigers (Hong Kong, Taiwan, Singapore, and South Korea). Consequently, the only way for a business to grow at an above-average rate is to take business from competitors. Since competitors will not willingly allow their customers to be taken, intensified competition results. In the latter half of the 1980s and early 1990s, marketing managers will need to monitor the competitive environment very closely.

The Marketing in Action on page 36 illustrates how GTE's Sylvania Division monitors the activities of its competitors.

Economists have traditionally assessed competition by counting the number of companies that sell a particular product: the more sellers, the greater the competition. Depending on the number of sellers, four types of competitive structures exist: pure competition, monopolistic competition, oligopoly, and monopoly. Table 2.2 presents some general characteristics of these four competitive structures, which we will discuss briefly.

Pure Competition. In **pure competition**, *a large number of sellers sell an undifferentiated product, such as wheat, corn, or hogs.* Each seller controls a very small percentage of the total market, and since the product is homogeneous, it must be sold at the market price. If corn is selling for

MARKETING IN ACTION

GTE's Computer Records Secrets of 51 Competitors

GTE's Sylvania Division has succeeded in an area few other companies have even begun to explore: it has constructed a computer data base which continuously tracks the activities of 51 competitors. The two-year-old system, Management Information of Competitor Strategies (MICS), combines information gleaned from standard Securities and Exchange Commission filings and articles from industry publications with reports and analyses submitted by GTE's field staff.

For the most part, according to system manager James Roden, MICS has succeeded. "Updating, though, has become a real problem," he said. "Because of the number of companies we are tracking and the amount of data we have to input, we are considering dividing the system into several parts. One data base will monitor our competitors in the hardware end of our business and another will track competition in long-distance carrying services."

Each competitor record, Roden said, monitors up to 17 strategic categories such as background of officers, management strategy, marketing strategy, regulatory updates, pricing, production, distribution strategy, R&D, and new technology. MICS receives its data from GTE's 30 Strategic Business Units scattered throughout the company. Marketing and sales staff members feed the MICS system with "hearsay, rumor, and grapevine-intelligence" from the field, filling out 20-page forms. Then they route the forms to GTE's headquarters in Stamford, Conn., where a staff analyst sifts through the papers for useful data. Before entering the information, the analyst will interview the employees who submitted the forms to check for accuracy.

MICS operates on a time-sharing computer system in Florida owned by GTE. While an authorized staff member anywhere in the company can tap into MICS from an on-line terminal, no one can enter data from a remote location (for security reasons). Additional security measures are planned to prevent tampering and illegal data manipulation.

"There are still three areas we feel need refining," Roden said. "We need a better updating procedure. We also have to determine which person will do the interpreting and analysis. Certain divisions or those with different line functions see the analysis from different angles and require broader or narrower interpretations."

Source: Reprinted by permission from "Intelligence Update," a newsletter published by Information Data Search Inc., 80 Trowbridge St., Cambridge, MA 02138.

Table 2.2   Characteristics of Four Dominant Competitive Structures

Characteristic	Pure Competition	Monopolistic Competition	Oligopoly	Monopoly
Number of sellers	Very large	Large	Few	One
Product uniqueness	None; homogeneous products	Some perceived by buyers	Some, but easily substitutable	High; no easy substitutes
Price competition	Must sell at market price	Very important and common	Firms try to avoid it	Unnecessary
Nonprice competition	Unnecessary	Important and common	A priority	Some amount used to expand total market

$2.91 a bushel, a farmer who tries to get $2.95 will be unsuccessful. Similarly, selling at $2.86 would be unwise since the farmer could sell all of his output at $2.91. With pure competition, nonprice competition, such as heavy advertising, doesn't pay, since each seller is selling an undifferentiated and easily substitutable product. Some firms have turned basically undifferentiated products, such as chickens and fruits, into branded products, such as Perdue chickens, Sunkist lemons, Ocean Spray cranberries. When this happens, the products enter monopolistic competition.

Monopolistic Competition. In the case of **monopolistic competition,** *many sellers sell similar but not necessarily identical products. Each firm has differentiated its product somewhat and thus has some degree of control over the price it can charge.* Firms facing monopolistic competition find that both price and nonprice competition are important. Jordache tries to develop an image of uniqueness for its jeans and also engages in price competition to compete with other brands of jeans. Other examples of products facing monopolistic competition are men's and women's apparel, magazines, shoes, and cosmetics.

Oligopoly. In an **oligopoly,** *there are only a few sellers and thus each firm's sales are a high percentage of the total market. Each brand has unique characteristics but can be substituted easily. Sellers cannot ignore each other's actions.* There is an attempt to avoid price competition, but nonprice competition is intense, especially in the areas of advertising, personal selling, unique product attributes, and customer service. The U.S. auto industry is an oligopoly. Fords, Chevrolets, and Chryslers are easily substitutable and similarly priced, especially in a given size and quality range. Although the price and features of a Cadillac El Dorado and a Lincoln Mark may be comparable, we are faced with a daily onslaught of commercials trying to differentiate them.

Monopoly. A **monopoly** exists when *there is only one seller of a product.* Monopolies are almost nonexistent in the United States, but when they do exist, they usually are regulated by the government. For example, Amtrak has a monopoly on passenger train service in the United States, and the Bell Company had a monopoly on telephone service until the government ruled that Bell was violating federal antitrust laws.

Although there is only one seller of the product in a monopoly, all products face competition from products in different categories. For example, Amtrak faces competition from buses, airplanes, and cars. Since monopolists do not face direct competition, they do not need to engage in price competition. Nonetheless, since a price decrease will increase unit sales, monopolists may decide to charge lower prices. Also, monopolists do not need to advertise or engage in other nonprice competition, but they may do so to expand total demand. The De Beers Company controls most

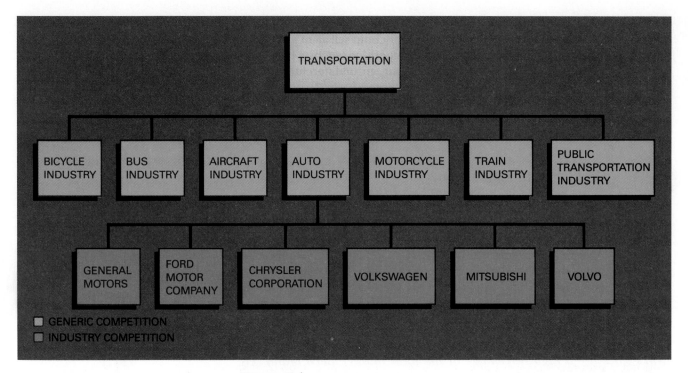

Figure 2.4
Generic and Industry Competition

of the world's diamond supply, but their advertising attempts to expand the total demand for diamonds.

Generic Competition.   The economists' view of competition, which we just reviewed, is constraining because it focuses on products rather than need satisfaction. Companies compete to fulfill customers' needs and not to sell products. For example, IBM is in the information business, not the computer business. The concept of generic competition recognizes this subtle, yet important distinction. **Generic competition** consists of *competition between all products capable of satisfying the same basic need.* When firms define their competition generically, they are not blind to significant competitive threats from supposedly unrelated products. Figure 2.4 shows the difference between the generic and industry-based competition for transportation.

Competitive Intensity.   In yet another nontraditional view of competition, Harvard University Professor Michael Porter argues that competitive intensity comes from four sources, illustrated in Figure 2.5.[17] The higher

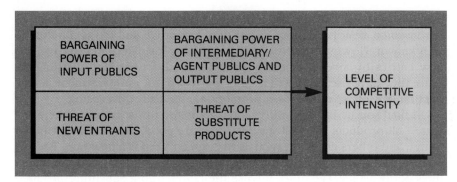

the bargaining power of input publics, especially suppliers, the higher is the competitive intensity. If a firm is purchasing supplies or labor services from suppliers that control a large share of the input market, then the suppliers will be able to exercise a large amount of control over input prices. If a firm needs to pay unrealistically high input prices, then competition in the end markets it serves will intensify. Given the indisputable fact that high bargaining power among input publics will intensify competition, a firm may develop a plan that reduces its dependence on certain input publics. For instance, the Southland Corporation, which owns and operates over 7,000 convenience stores and is the largest independent retailer of gasoline in the United States, created a gasoline supply division in 1981 to reduce its dependence on petroleum distributors. This division sells over $700 million of gasoline to 7-11 stores and over $500 million of gasoline to unrelated gasoline retailers.[18]

A second influence on competitive intensity is the bargaining power of intermediary or agent publics (discussed in Chapters 10 through 12) and output publics. Again, high concentration affects bargaining power; for example, in the tire industry, the auto manufacturers are a major intermediary for new tires because new cars come equipped with new tires. Since the auto industry is highly concentrated, the manufacturers can largely set the price at which the tire manufacturers will sell to them. Faced with this scenario, a company like Firestone may decide to develop or focus on other means of distribution, such as its 1982 decision to lease hundreds of J.C. Penney automotive centers and convert them to Firestone automotive centers.[19]

A third influence on competitive intensity is the threat of new entrants. If entry barriers are low (i.e., the cost of starting a new business), new competitors can easily enter the market and competition will intensify. Predictably, therefore, a firm may try to develop such a strong competitive advantage that it would be difficult for new competitors to attack the firm's business without a major expenditure of human and financial resources. For instance, beer production is not very expensive and the technology is well known. However, the major brewers have insulated themselves from new entries by investing heavily in national advertising and distribution. Thus, they have created barriers to entry, based not on investment in production, but on investments in promotion, especially advertising.

A final source of competitive intensity is the threat of substitute products.[20] All products have substitutes; some are good, such as margarine for butter, and others are poor, such as a recapped tire for a new one. The key point is that the greater the number of substitute products and the higher their performance, the more intense the competition. Substitute products also can create a ceiling on prices. For example, as fuel costs rose in the 1970s people lowered their thermostats in the winter, switched to heavier clothing, and bought wood-burning stoves.

These examples show only some of the ways firms can insulate themselves from competitive intensity.[21] The key point is that although the firm should insulate itself from competitive intensity, it does not want to eliminate the competition. If this were accomplished, the firm would be a monopolist and the federal government (i.e., the Justice Department and the Federal Trade Commission) does not allow monopolies.

Economic Environment

Our economy goes through **business cycles**, which are *the changing patterns of economic growth over time. A business cycle consists of three stages: (1) prosperity, (2) recession, and (3) recovery.* A firm's marketing effort varies depending on the current stage of the business cycle.

Prosperity. During a period of prosperity, relatively few people are unemployed and total income and purchasing power are high. After adjusting for inflation, there should be real economic growth for the total economy. This suggests that consumer incomes will rise faster than the prices for goods and services, so that consumers will feel optimistic and spend more freely, thus further stimulating the economy.

Marketers also spend more freely during prosperity: they are more willing to conduct marketing research studies, add to their sales force, increase advertising expenditures, enlarge the product mix, and carry larger inventories. One of the biggest problems marketers face during prosperity, however, is that they overexpand, creating a lot of waste in the marketing organization. As long as prosperity continues, they can get away with this behavior, but problems occur if they are not able to spot a downturn in the economy in time to "cut the fat." Inevitably, firms get caught with excess inventory and marketing overhead as the economy begins to falter.

Recession.   During a recession, unemployment rises and total income and purchasing power decline. Consumers try to get by with less, making their dollars stretch further. Price awareness increases, purchases of durables such as cars and appliances are postponed, and money is put into savings whenever possible. People who haven't lost their jobs adopt more conservative spending patterns because they fear they may lose them. During a recession, the marketing manager basically confronts reluctant consumers. There are exceptions, however. Since consumers are trying to spend less, firms that sell money-saving products will experience increased demand during recession. For example, manufacturers of do-it-yourself products, discount food stores, and breakfast cereal companies can all expect strong demand during a recession.

How do marketers respond to a recession? When a marketing manager realizes the economy is in a recession (and this is usually sometime after it has actually started), he or she will cut back marketing effort, because the organization starts to encounter serious cash-flow problems caused by declining sales volume. Consequently, budgets are cut for all departments in the organization, and marketing is not spared. In part, this is unfortunate. Obviously, some fat was built up during prosperity, so that some costs can be cut without affecting marketing effort. At some point, however, cutting marketing costs becomes counterproductive. Marketing expenditures are demand-stimulating expenditures. Cutting the advertising budget and sales force will only serve to further erode the firm's sales. The consumer may be reluctant during a recession, but this is exactly why the firm should expend extra marketing efforts (not less): to persuade the consumer to purchase.

Recovery.   During recovery, the economy begins its move from recession to prosperity and the unemployment rate drops as laid-off workers are recalled to their jobs. Consumers slowly regain their confidence in the economy and begin to acquire the goods they postponed purchasing during the recession.

As with the other stages, the biggest challenge marketing managers face during a recovery is being able to identify the start of the recovery and respond rapidly. At the depth of the recession, inventories will be at a minimum. As soon as the economy turns around, a large, pent-up demand will begin to be unleashed and the firms with good product selection and large inventories will be able to grab a large share of this market. In addition, since most firms will be caught with inadequate inventories, there will be little price competition and the firm with adequate inventories can experience a rapid growth in profitability. If the forecasted recovery does not materialize, however, there is a risk of getting stuck with excess inventory. Few firms are willing to take this gamble and prefer to wait until the recovery is clearly underway.

Technological Environment

Technology is the application of science to develop new methods or ways of doing things. Technology has always had a major impact on society, and no economic sector is immune from its impact. Refrigeration allows us to eat shrimp in August in Iowa; jet airplanes allow us to fly to Paris in a few hours; computers enable us to pay bills without handling cash; and modern kitchen appliances free us of household chores, giving us more leisure time.

Major developments in technology can have enormous marketing implications because they can drastically alter industries. For example, a new vaccine currently is being developed that will help prevent tooth decay.[22] If this new product finally reaches the market and is successful, it will have a profound impact on the dental industry. Genetic engineering also promises to create major changes in agribusiness.[23] Both Heinz and Campbell Soup are attempting to apply genetic engineering techniques to produce a "supertomato,"[24] which will have less water and more solids (most tomatoes are 95% water). The water is costly since ripe, water-laden tomatoes need to be transported from field to packing plant, where most of the fluid is cooked away. Other researchers are attempting to develop a square tomato that can be easily packed into cans. The potential applications of genetic engineering are even more phenomenal: some scientists are working on building organic computer chips—computer chips that are actually living organisms.

Despite the technological promise of these new products, the process of technological innovation is lengthy and complex. Firms often must gamble on technology to attain success, but many companies have gambled and lost. For example, RCA spent over a decade developing its videodisk player and, after several years of dismal sales, withdrew the product from the market in early 1984 at a cumulative loss of $580 million.[25] Xerography took nearly twenty years to move through the seven stages shown in Table 2.3.

The marketer's job in relation to technology is twofold. First, marketing managers should monitor the technological environment in conjunction with the other environments in an effort to develop ideas for new products. An awareness of technological possibilities combined with a good understanding of customer needs and the economic and competitive environments can help marketing managers to spot potential new products. Second, marketing managers should bring technology to market by convincing the consumer or buyer that a new way of doing something is preferable to the old way. Adoption of a technological innovation from the customer's perspective is risky, and the marketer must alleviate this sense of insecurity. For example, many banks have run special promotions and contests to get their customers to use automatic teller machines, and supermarkets equipped with automatic scanning machines are encouraging customers to double check their receipts for errors in an effort to convince them that the machines make fewer errors than do humans.

Table 2.3   Steps in the Process of Technological Innovation

Stage	Identified By	Comment
Research	1. Scientific suggestion, discovery, recognition of need or opportunity	The latter source (need recognition) seems to be the origin of the majority of contemporary innovations.
	2. Proposal of theory or design concept	Trial and error results in crystallization of a successful theory or design concept.
	3. Laboratory verification of theory or design concept	The operational validity of the concept suggested in previous stage should be demonstrated. This is often difficult for the manager because the thing or concept demonstrated is a phenomenon rather than an application.
	4. Laboratory demonstration of application	The principle is embodied in a laboratory model of the device (or sample material or its equivalent) to demonstrate that the theory in stage 2 can create a product that performs a useful and intended function.
Development	5. Full-scale or field trial	The concept moves from the laboratory bench to trial in a realistic environment. Succession of prototypes follows, leading eventually to a marketable product.
	6. Commercial introduction or first operational use	First sale of an operational system; may be deliberate or unconscious premature application of previous stage and so be replete with debugging problems and subsequent changes in technology.
Mass production and mass marketing	7. Widespread adoption as indicated by substantial profits, common usage, and significant impact	The sharp delineation of this stage is difficult. An individual firm might choose to classify it as recovering its research and development investment through profits on the sale of the innovation or simply achievement of profitability.
	8. Proliferation	The technical device is applied to other uses such as using computer microprocessors in autos to control fuel/air mix and engine emissions. This stage may begin much earlier.

Source: Adapted from James R. Bright and Milton E.F. Schoerman (eds.). *A Guide to Practical Technological Forecasting* (Englewood Cliffs, NJ: Prentice-Hall, 1973), p. 7. Used by permission.

Physical Environment

The physical environment constrains us all and cannot be ignored, although products have been developed that reduce these constraints (e.g., air conditioners, furnaces, umbrellas, irrigation systems, interstate highways, and even artificial snow so that we can ski when the weather doesn't cooperate). Since all products rely, either directly or indirectly, on natural resources, marketers must take the physical environment into consideration when planning their marketing strategies. Even a service marketer relies on the physical environment. A lawyer, for example, needs an air-conditioned office to work effectively in the hot summer, and air conditioning requires energy such as coal, oil, or hydropower.

Our natural resources are not unlimited and must be protected, or else they will be exhausted. Conservation and environmentalist groups, such as the Sierra Club and the National Wildlife Federation, are attempting to preserve the delicate balance between humans and the environment. Industry and the general public are recognizing the need to conserve; witness the growth in the use of recycled paper, aluminum cans, returnable bottles, phosphate-free detergents, and nonaerosol cans to protect the ozone layer in the atmosphere.[26]

As natural resources become scarcer, their price will rise dramatically. This has occurred with oil prices and will someday occur with all other resources. Countries that control large shares of these resources will eventually capitalize on the monopoly they have and attempt to control prices, as the OPEC countries did with oil. Marketing managers must recognize this eventuality and develop contingency plans for using less expensive substitutes. The development of these substitute materials, such as super strength plastics, synthetic fuels, and synthetic fibers, will represent a major growth market.

Marketing managers must also recognize that the quality of the physical environment is directly related to the quality of life. Clean air, lakes, and rivers improve our life-styles. Trees and wildlife promote a sense of tranquillity. Using a handmade product from 100 percent natural materials brings many people considerable enjoyment.

Legal/Political Environment

The United States as well as most countries has government regulations on business firms and their marketing activities. In general, these regulatory laws attempt to make the process and impact of marketing fairer to both buyers and sellers.[27] As will be illustrated throughout this book, marketing decisions are regulated at the local, state, or federal government levels. The major pieces of federal legislation that constrain marketing will be discussed in the chapters that discuss product, price, promotion, and distribution decisions. Because laws are continually changing, marketers must keep abreast of changes in the legal environment and regularly consult lawyers to ensure the legality of their marketing programs.

The marketer must also recognize the constraints imposed by the political environment. The *political environment* consists of interest groups (other than government regulatory bodies) that attempt to influence a firm's or an industry's conduct. For instance, the *consumerism movement,* which is a social movement that seeks to protect the rights and safety of consumers, has been responsible for spawning public interest groups such as Ralph Nader's Public Citizen organization. This organization was instrumental in getting laws passed to improve auto safety standards.

Many interest groups look after the rights of particular segments of the

As raw materials become more scarce and their prices rise accordingly, companies such as Budweiser become actively involved in recycling their aluminum beverage containers.

population. The National Organization of Women (NOW) attempts to promote women's rights; the National Association for the Advancement of Colored People (NAACP) works to improve black rights; and the American Association of Retired Persons (AARP) hopes to improve and protect the rights of the elderly. Each of these groups and many others may influence a firm's marketing conduct through the use of product boycotts of firms that do not support their causes.

The Better Business Bureau, which is supported by local businesses, also tries to influence business conduct. The Better Business Bureau uses the media to inform the public of businesses in the community that employ unfair business practices.

Finally, political activity can have international dimensions. For example, Saudi Arabia will not import products from U.S. firms that sell to Israel.

Ethical Environment

Marketers must be aware of the ethical environment in which they conduct business. Some practices that are legal may be unethical and vice versa. Also, ethics vary by culture; thus, although it may be proper to bribe government officials in some countries, it is unethical as well as illegal for U.S. businesses to do so. The concluding chapter of this book discusses the role of ethics in marketing.

THE ENVIRONMENTAL SCANNER

Because of the constant change in external environments, numerous firms are beginning to employ environmental scanners. An **environmental scanner** is *a person who collects and analyzes data on the firm's external environments.* This person monitors changes in:

1. The social environment, as reflected in changing demographics and social values.
2. The economic environment, as delineated by changes in economic indicators such as unemployment, interest rates, inflation, incomes, inventories, money supply.
3. Technology, as reflected by industry newsletters, trade shows, and scholarly journals.
4. The physical environment, as assessed by gathering statistics on prices and availability of raw materials and the public's attitude about the quality of their physical environment.
5. The legal/political environment, tracked by government publications, trade association newsletters, and the popular business press.
6. Competitors' tactics, as reflected by their strategies, new product introductions, and methods of doing business.

The environmental scanner performs a useful role because no marketing plan should be developed without an explicit awareness of what is occurring or likely to occur in the firm's external environments. In fact, changes in the external environments provide an early warning system to the firm. Generally, it will take some time before a change in the external environment exerts the maximal impact on one or more of the firm's publics and thus on the organization. For example, when unemployment rates drop or rise, the firm will not feel the impact for several weeks or even months because it takes time for any change to ripple through the economy.

Once a firm is notified of changes in its external environments, it can develop plans to cope with good or bad trends. Say a baby food business accurately monitors the declining birth rate and projects this trend to continue. This is obviously not encouraging news, but because the firm can confront the news head-on, it can develop plans to introduce new products, modify existing products, or make other changes in its marketing activities. It is not true that "no news is good news"—it is better to receive bad news and react appropriately than to receive no news when something may be undermining the basic structure of the marketplace.

The environmental scanner's role is also important because it can help a firm identify opportunities emerging from trends in the external environments. The Marketing in Action on page 47 shows how four environmental forces created a market opportunity for home health care services.

MARKETING IN ACTION

New markets emerge when the proper environmental factors come together to create an opportunity. A contemporary example of this is the explosive growth in the home health care business. Although home health care has been around for centuries, it is now becoming a major business because of factors in the social, technological, economic, and legal environments.

In general, health care tends to be concentrated on the over-65 age group, and this segment of the U.S. population is rapidly increasing. The U.S. Census Bureau projects that by 1990, 13 percent of our population, or 32 million persons, will be over 65 years of age. This over-65 age group wants to be active and do things on their own, and this includes caring for their own health at home. Coupled with these trends is a

The Emergence of an Opportunity: Home Health Care

revolution in medical technology which has produced home intravenous feeding machines, home chemotherapy equipment, and in-home kidney dialysis. For example, Baxter Travenol Laboratories has a home dialysis machine that can treat the patient in his or her home for $14,000 annually as compared with up to $25,000 annually for traditional dialysis. Thus, economic savings is a major reason for home health care. Hospital charges for even the most basic services can exceed $300 per day, whereas in-home care usually costs $50 per day.

The legal and political environ-

ment has also spurred the growth of home health care. A 1980 change in federal law allowed more Medicare reimbursement for home treatment. Consequently, from 1979 to 1982, Medicare reimbursements for home health care rose 146 percent.

The home health care market, which was $2 billion in 1982, is expected to grow 40 percent annually for the next five to ten years. Predictably, this has enticed companies such as Upjohn, American Hospital Supply, and Foremost-McKesson, to expand their efforts in this rapid growth market.

Source: Based on authors' experiences and in part on "The Robust New Business in Home Health Care," *BusinessWeek* (June 13, 1983), pp. 96–100.

SUMMARY

This chapter's purpose was to help you better understand that good planning in marketing cannot occur until a firm analyzes its external environments. The external environments (which are largely uncontrollable) will affect the organization's publics, which the firm must influence to gain their support.

There are seven external environments: (1) the social environment, (2) the competitive environment, (3) the economic environment, (4) the technological environment, (5) the physical environment, (6) the legal/political environment, and (7) the ethical environment. The publics affecting the business firm include consumers, suppliers, agents or intermediaries, employees, stockholders or investors, and the general public. When a change occurs in one of the external environments, it usually affects one or more of the firm's publics, which causes the firm's behavior or performance to change.

In a discussion of the social environment, we learned how the U.S. household is changing, how geographic patterns of living are changing, and how the U.S. culture is in transition. Our discussion of the competitive environment examined the traditional economic view of four competitive structures: pure competition, monopolistic competition, oligopoly, and monopoly. In addition, we took a nontraditional view of competition by defining generic competition as competition between all products capable of satisfying the same basic need. Another nontraditional view discussed suggested that there are four sources of competitive intensity: bargaining power of input publics, bargaining power of intermediary/agent publics and output publics, threat of substitute products, and threat of new entrants.

The economic environment was discussed in terms of business cycles. Marketing was discussed during times of prosperity, recession, and recovery. We learned that the marketer has two tasks in regard to the technological environment. First, marketing managers should monitor the technological environment in an effort to develop new product ideas. Second, the marketer must be able to bring technology to market by convincing the consumer or buyer that a new way of doing something is preferable to the old way.

We also discussed the physical environment because all products, either directly or indirectly, rely on natural resources. The need for conservation and recycling of materials was stressed as was the need to develop a clean physical environment. Because of the rising price of many natural resources, a growth market exists for developing lower cost substitute materials.

The legal environment was not discussed in detail because the legal constraints on marketing will be illustrated throughout this text. However, we did learn that marketing decisions are regulated at the local, state, and federal government levels. The marketer must also recognize the constraints imposed by the political environment, which consists of interest groups (other than government regulatory bodies) that attempt to influence a firm's or an industry's conduct. Finally, we mentioned the ethical environment, which will be treated in detail in the concluding chapter of this text.

Because of the ever changing nature of the external environments a firm must perform regular research to keep abreast of changes in the external environments. This research is often done by an environmental scanner. Research of this type will help forewarn the company of threats and opportunities, which will be major inputs into the strategic marketing management process to be discussed in Chapter 3.

KEY CONCEPTS

system (p. 26)
open system (p. 26)
closed system (p. 27)
external environments (p. 27)
social environment (p. 28)
competitive environment (p. 28)
economic environment (p. 28)
technological environment (p. 28)
physical environment (p. 28)
legal/political environment (p. 28)
ethical environment (p. 28)
public (p. 28)
consuming publics (p. 28)
supplier publics (p. 28)
employee publics (p. 28)

stockholder and investor publics (p. 28)
agent or intermediary publics (p. 29)
general public (p. 29)
pure competition (p. 35)
monopolistic competition (p. 37)
oligopoly (p. 37)
monopoly (p. 37)
generic competition (p. 38)
business cycles (p. 40)
environmental scanner (p. 46)

REVIEW AND DISCUSSION QUESTIONS

1. Explain why a business organization should be viewed as an open system.

2. List and briefly describe the external environments of a business firm. How controllable are these external environments?

3. List the six major publics of an organization and explain why a firm must be concerned with more than consuming publics.

4. Discuss how the American household of today is different from the typical household of 20 years ago. What are the marketing implications of this change?

5. Define and describe the characteristics of the four dominant competitive structures.

6. Distinguish between generic competition and industry competition. Give examples of each.

7. What are the four primary sources of competitive intensity?

8. Discuss how the behavior of consumers and marketers changes over the three stages of a business cycle.

9. What is a marketer's job in relation to technology?

10. Why should a marketer be concerned with the physical environment? Give examples to illustrate your key reasons.

11. All legal marketing decisions are ethical. Agree or disagree with this statement. For example, there is nothing illegal about a physician setting fees without regard to whether some segments of the population can afford them; thus, there is nothing unethical about this practice.

12. Explain how an environmental scanner plays an important role in a firm.

ACTION PROBLEMS

1. Assume you are the marketing manager of a company that you are familiar with and discuss the ways in which external environments would have the most impact on your firm.

2. Assume you are the owner of a 300-acre citrus farm in the Rio Grande Valley of Texas. You sell your output of grapefruit in a purely competitive market. Discuss how you could change your product so that you do not need to sell it in a purely competitive market.

3. A major trend in the world today is the move toward an information society, in which all homes, businesses, schools, and other organizations are linked by computer terminals. Part of this information age includes the development of sophisticated software that will allow robots to see, hear, smell, feel, and be more agile. What is the influence of such a scenario on a television manufacturer's publics and speculate on the potential marketing implications.

4. Write a short essay (around 300 words) on how trends regarding the American family and the changing U.S. culture influence your life-style and the products you consume.

NOTES

1. The open systems nature of marketing is discussed in Eric R. Reidenbach and Terence A. Oliva, "General Living System Theory and Marketing: A Framework for Analysis," *Journal of Marketing* (Fall 1981), pp. 30–37.

2. For a counterview that argues that the environment can be managed or controlled, see Carl P. Zeithaml and Valarie A. Zeithaml. "Environmental Management: Revising the Marketing Perspective," *Journal of Marketing* 48(Spring 1984), pp. 4–53.

3. Philip Kotler, *Marketing Management: Analysis, Planning and Control* (Englewood Cliffs, NJ: Prentice-Hall, 1984), p. 84.

4. The idea that a firm is dependent on many different publics is discussed in Paul F. Anderson, "Marketing, Strategic Planning and the Theory of the Firm," *Journal of Marketing* 46(Spring 1982), pp. 15–26; Jeffrey Pfeffer and Gerald R. Salancik, *The External Control of Organizations* (New York: Harper and Row, 1978).

5. Bernie Whalen, "Kotler: Rethink the Marketing Concept," *Marketing News* (Sept. 14, 1984), pp. 1, 22, 24.

6. One of the first marketing textbooks that espoused a strong environmental orientation was Robert J. Holloway and Robert S. Hancock, *Marketing in a Changing Environment* (New York: John Wiley & Sons, 1964).

7. The dual-income household is discussed in detail in Bruce Steinberg, "The Mass Market Is Splitting Apart," *Fortune* (November 28, 1983), pp. 76–82.

8. U.S. Bureau of the Census, *Statistical Abstract of the United States: 1985* (Washington, DC, 1984), p. 399.

9. The economics of fertility is discussed in Richard P. Bagozzi and M. Frances Van Loo, "Fertility as Consumption: Theories from the Behavioral Sciences," *Journal of Consumer Research* 4(March 1978), pp. 199–228.

10. Walter Guzzardi, Jr., "Demography's Good News for the Eighties," *Fortune* (November 5, 1979), pp. 92–106.

11. For a more complete discussion of the singles market, see Ronald D. Michman, *Marketing to Changing Consumer Markets* (New York: Praeger Publishers, 1983), pp. 38–42.

12. U.S. Bureau of the Census, *Statistical Abstract of the United States: 1982–1983* (Washington, DC, 1982), p. 8; U.S. Bureau of the Census, *Statistical Abstract of the United States: 1979* (Washington, DC, 1979), pp. 8–9.

13. Michman, *Marketing,* pp. 44–47.

14. Michman, *Marketing,* p. 64.

15. Duane S. Elgin and Arnold Mitchell, "Voluntary Simplicity: Life Style of the Future?" *The Futurist* (August 1977), pp. 200–206; Ronald D. Michman, "New Directions for Lifestyle Behavior Patterns," *Business Horizons* (July–August 1984), pp. 59–64.

16. "1985 Survey of Buying Power," *Sales & Marketing Management* (July 22, 1985), pp. A-24, A-54.

17. Michael E. Porter, "How Competitive Forces Shape Strategy," *Harvard Business Review* (March–April 1979), pp. 137–145.

18. *The Southland Corporation 1982 Annual Report.*

19. "The J.C. Penney Company (A): Marketing and Financial Strategy," in William R. Davidson, Daniel D. Sweeney, and Ronald W. Stampfl, *Retailing Management,* 5th edition (New York: John Wiley & Sons, 1984), pp. 541–547.

20. An article that takes a broad view of substitute products is George S. Day, Allan D. Shocker,

and Rajendra K. Srivastava, "Customer-Oriented Approaches to Identifying Product-Markets," *Journal of Marketing* (Fall 1979), pp. 8–19.

21. For some additional insights on insulation from competitors, see Bruce D. Henderson, "The Anatomy of Competition," *Journal of Marketing* 47(Spring 1983), pp. 7–11.

22. "The Race for Miracle Drugs," *BusinessWeek* (July 22, 1985), pp. 92–96.

23. Richard C. Davids, "Here Comes the Next Green Revolution," *World* 4 (1982), pp. 4–13.

24. "The Race to Breed a 'Supertomato,'" *BusinessWeek* (January 10, 1983), p. 33.

25. Joel England and Amy Orlan, "RCA Scratches Video Disk," *Home Furnishings Daily* (April 16, 1984), pp. 76, 77; "RCA: Will It Ever Be a Top Performer?" *BusinessWeek* (April 2, 1984), pp. 52–56.

26. "Reverse Vending Machines Turn Recycling into Profit for Retailers," *Marketing News* (November 25, 1983), p. 4.

27. An excellent book on the legal dimensions of marketing decision making is Louis W. Stern and Thomas L. Eovaldi, *Legal Aspects of Marketing Strategy* (Englewood Cliffs, NJ: Prentice-Hall, 1984).

CHAPTER **3**

LEARNING OBJECTIVES

After you complete this chapter, you should be able to:

- **List** the seven steps in the strategic marketing management process

- **Explain** the elements of marketing strategy

- **Enumerate** and **explain** the three levels of multilevel strategic planning

- **Discuss** the types of growth and retrenchment strategies a firm can pursue

- **Construct** the General Electric business screen and the BCG product portfolio matrix and **discuss** how each relates to strategic planning

MARKETING MANAGEMENT AND STRATEGIC PLANNING

MARKETER PROFILE

Ken Chenault of American Express

Ken Chenault, senior vice president of American Express Travel Related Services Company and general manager of the firm's merchandise services unit, grew up in Hempstead, Long Island, in New York. After graduating from Bowdoin College and Harvard Law School, he worked first as a corporate lawyer and then as a consultant involved in forming and implementing strategies for a variety of Fortune 500 companies. He joined American Express in 1981 and was promoted to vice president of marketing for the division in 1983.

He has seen his division's earnings triple since 1983, and they are expected to triple again by 1988. Much of the division's growth has been attributed to the marketing strategy Chenault helped to develop, which directed the unit to a customer-oriented marketing focus, shifting it from its product-oriented focus of previous years.

Chenault compares his role to that of a coach trying to give the team a competitive edge: he not only has to keep the ball rolling but must keep it rolling faster and faster in an environment of increasingly sophisticated competition. For Chenault, staying ahead of the competition means meticulous planning, fostering a creative atmosphere, and keeping a pulse on the business by meeting regularly with lower-level managers.

"American Express has a great deal of [trustworthiness] in the minds of the public, and in the marketing of our products we cannot abuse that trust." Chenault goes on to say, "If you buy a product from us and you don't like it, you might have second thoughts about purchasing a financial service from us or have second thoughts about using your card. So there is a tremendous corporate responsibility to make sure that we're selling high-quality products."

Source: Based on David Squires. "Success in the Cards," *Black Enterprise* (December 1985), pp. 77, 78, 96.

INTRODUCTION

The preceding marketer profile focused on Ken Chenault and how he developed a marketing strategy for American Express Travel Related Services Company, shifting the orientation from the product to the customer, and how he stayed ahead of the competition with careful planning.

Progressing from our discussion of the external environments in Chapter 2, in this chapter we will consider the process of managing marketing activity in the organization, with special emphasis on the process of *planning* and *executing* marketing strategies. You will recall from Chapter 1 that marketing was defined as the process of planning and executing the conception, pricing, promotion, and distribution of ideas, goods, and services to create exchanges that satisfy individual and organizational objectives. This chapter focuses on planning for marketing at multiple levels in the organization; Chapter 21 details the execution of these plans.

Strategic marketing management is *the analysis, strategy, implementation, and control of marketing activities to achieve the organization's objectives.* The two main components of the strategic marketing management process, which is illustrated in Figure 3.1, are planning and execution—key terms in our definition of marketing. **Planning** is *deciding today what to do in the future* and *consists of analysis and strategy.* **Execution** is essentially *making things happen* and *consists of implementation and control.*

SWOT ANALYSIS

As shown in Figure 3.1, the first step in the strategic marketing management process is analysis. Analysis consists of identifying the firm's *Strengths* and *Weaknesses* as well as *Opportunities* and *Threats.* Note that the first letters in each of these words compose the acronym SWOT.[1] Figure 3.2 outlines the components of a **SWOT analysis,** which consists of *studying a firm's performance trends, resources, and capabilities to assess a firm's strengths and weaknesses, explicitly stating a firm's mission and objectives, and scanning the external environments to identify opportunities and threats* facing the organization.

Strengths and Weaknesses

A firm's strengths and weaknesses can be identified and analyzed by studying performance trends, resources, and capabilities. Past performance typically is measured in financial terms, such as sales and profits. Profits act as proph-

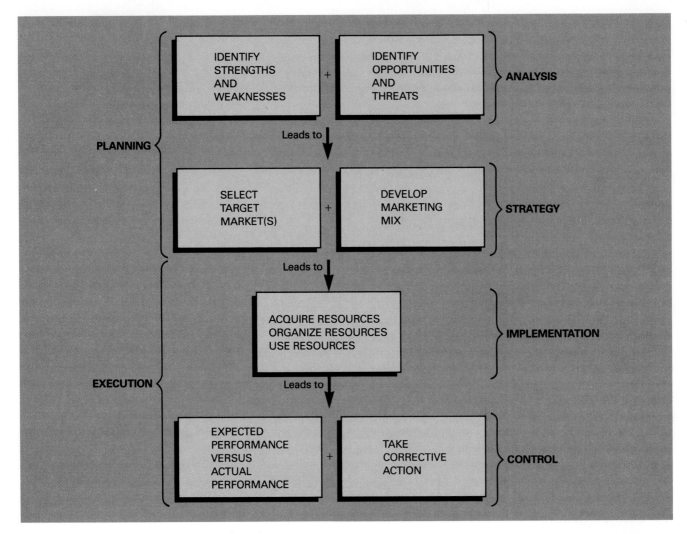

Figure 3.1

The Strategic Marketing Management Process

ets, in a sense. For example, yearly increases in profits are a sign of strength, while a steady decline in profits indicates that the firm has a problem. Current resources and capabilities also help to determine a firm's strengths and weaknesses. Resources and capabilities refer to various things: special talents (i.e., the company has one of the most creative advertising departments in the country), areas of expertise (i.e., the company is a beer producer and is the industry leader in developing new brewery technologies), unique assets (i.e., the company holds 12 patents on new products or has

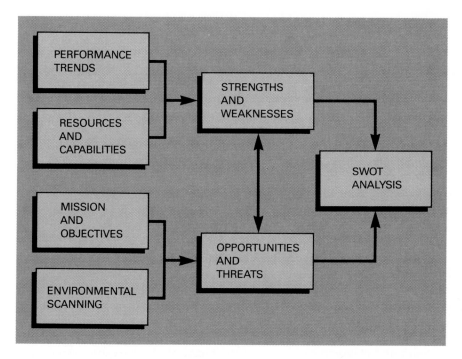

Figure 3.2
SWOT Analysis

$50 million in available cash), or any other advantage that can be drawn on for support (i.e., a pharmaceutical company may have excellent working relationships with retail druggists).

Opportunities and Threats

Opportunities and threats can be identified by stating the organization's mission and objectives and engaging in the process of environmental scanning discussed in Chapter 2.

Mission and Objectives.   A **mission** is *a firm's overall justification for existing.* The marketer can more easily identify opportunities and threats when the firm's mission has been clearly stated, because the mission provides a lens through which the external environments can be viewed. For example, the outlawing of gene splicing would pose a threat to firms such as Genex Corporation (a company that manufactures products using biotechnology) but not to firms such as Parker Pen Company. Defining what constitutes a threat—and an opportunity—depends on the nature of the firm's mission.

The firm's mission should not be time or product line specific; it should be broad to be as applicable five, ten, or twenty years from now as it is today. The concept of generic competition discussed in Chapter 2 is useful in this regard. Generic competition recognizes that a customer does not engage in an exchange of money for goods and services, but in an exchange of something of value for need fulfillment. For example, Black and Decker sells quarter-inch holes, not quarter-inch drills; Revlon does not sell lipstick to keep lips moist, but to offer buyers the feeling of beauty; and Safeway and Kroger are not patronized to purchase food, but to provide substance to satisfy physiological and often psychological needs.

Table 3.1 provides several examples of how marketing-oriented organizations might state their missions. Note that these missions are broad, so that the organization need not change its mission whenever the environments change. Thus, the mission will provide a long-term perspective and guiding force for all planning in the organization.

By its very nature, an organization's mission is broad, providing general direction for the firm. More specific direction is obtained by the statement of a firm's objectives, since **objectives** are *specific, quantifiable results that a firm wants to achieve in a given period.* Most firms, even nonprofit enterprises, develop financial objectives, which are objectives stated in monetary or economic terms. Appendix B, "Marketing Math, Finance, and Accounting," elaborates on some of the financial objectives that firms may have.

Environmental Scanning.   Once the mission and objectives have been established, the marketer needs to engage in environmental scanning to identify opportunities and threats. The types of opportunities the marketer is attempting to identify are market opportunities. A **market opportunity** exists *when there is an unmet or unsatisfied need or want in the marketplace that the firm has an interest in and capability of satisfying.*[2] There are several things you should note about this definition. First, opportunities exist in terms of markets. A **market** consists of *all potential*

Table 3.1   Mission Statements

Our mission is to help make ordinary women feel beautiful.

—Cosmetics Manufacturer

Our mission is to help support the marketing efforts of our customers.

—Food Wholesaler

Our mission is to help people better express their feelings toward others.

—Greeting Card Manufacturer

Our mission is to help people of all ages experience and enjoy literature.

—Retail Book Store

buyers with a similar need and the purchasing power to fill this need and all firms or sellers offering to satisfy that need. Second, by suggesting that the firm must have an interest, we mean that the firm's mission and objectives should be consistent with filling the unmet need.[3] For example, you would not expect Quaker Oats to develop a portable kidney dialysis machine, even though there is a significant need for this type of product. However, developing a portable kidney dialysis machine may be an opportunity for a firm such as Eli Lilly or American Hospital Supply. Third, the firm must have the capability to satisfy the unmet need or want. This explains why the SWOT analysis diagram shows an arrow between strengths and weaknesses and opportunities and threats (see Figure 3.2).[4]

Threats As Opportunities. Every market opportunity that an organization encounters originates in the firm's external environments. A marketing opportunity evolves from a change in the social, technological, competitive, legal/political, ethical, economic, or physical environments. Quite often, these changes are viewed as threats to the organization, but resourceful marketers can sometimes turn potential threats into opportunities. For example, toy industry marketing managers should view the decline in birth rates as an opportunity to broaden their market base to appeal to adults by developing more sophisticated toys and games for the adult population. Grocery store managers should see the rise in eating away from home as an opportunity to develop in-store delis and restaurants, expanded frozen food departments, and an increased assortment of easy-to-prepare, high-quality food items.

Threats As Negative Forces. Ideally, threats are translated into opportunities, but this may not always be possible since some threats may represent negative forces in terms of their influence on the firm's success. In fact, some threats may represent such a strong negative force that withdrawal from or avoidance of a particular market may be the most profitable strategy.

Four types of threats should be viewed as negative forces.[5] The first of these is a threat that impedes a strategy's implementation. Say, for example, that Babcock and Wilcox is developing a new type of nuclear reactor for public utilities, but antinuclear power legislation is passed in many states. Even if the company successfully designs a new reactor, it may not be able to implement its new product strategy. A second type of threat that can be a negative force is one that increases a strategy's risks. For example, a firm may be planning to double its production capacity for dishwashers in order to increase sales. It recognizes that most dishwashers are purchased with new homes, but the economic forecasts for new home construction has become more volatile each month because of the economy's increasing unpredictability. Consequently, the riskiness of doubling capacity and seeking higher sales is increased. A third type of threat occurs when the resources needed to implement a strategy increase. For example, a company developing a new drug may be hampered by government legislation that requires two additional years of premarket testing before the drug can be commercially produced and marketed. A fourth type of threat reduces profitability or financial performance expectations. For example, a company that produces microchips could be threatened by the announcement that large Taiwanese and South Korean firms plan to enter this market and concentrate their selling efforts on U.S. and European markets.

DEVELOPING A MARKETING STRATEGY

Referring back to Figure 3.1, you can see that strategy is the next step after analysis in the strategic marketing management process. In this step, the marketer develops a marketing strategy to pursue a market opportunity. The two primary elements of a marketing strategy are the selection of a target market and the development of a marketing mix.

Selecting a Target Market

A total market is generally too large and consists of buyers who are too heterogeneous to be a viable target for an organization's marketing efforts. Consequently, a firm should select a **target market**, which is *a portion of the total market and consists of a group of buyers with similar traits that the organization wants to attract.* In order to select a target market, an organization must first segment the market. **Market segmentation** is *the division of a heterogeneous group of buyers or potential buyers into more homogeneous groups with relatively similar product needs.* By segmenting the market, marketers can better serve the needs of their customers. For example, the market for adult clothing has been segmented by size and sex. Women's World caters to the large woman; various shops devote themselves to the big and tall man; 5-7-9 Shops and special departments within traditional department stores focus on the petite female; and stores such as Casual Corner, Chess King, and County Seat cater to average size figures. The cola market is another example of market segmentation. Among other things Coca-Cola has segmented this market according to buyers' preference for sugar or sugar-free and caffeine or caffeine-free cola.

Selecting a target market is a major marketing decision and a competitive necessity in the U.S. marketplace. By targeting marketing efforts on selected market segments, the firm can better serve the consumer and increase profits or better achieve some other objective. Consequently, the firm is better able to practice the marketing concept. Market segmentation and target marketing will be discussed in more detail in Chapter 7.

Developing the Marketing Mix

Once the target market has been selected, the marketing mix must be determined. The **marketing mix** consists of *the four controllable marketing variables: product, distribution (or place), promotion, and price.*[6] These marketing elements must be blended appropriately to achieve the maximum response from the target market. The marketing mix is controllable because firms usually have a high degree of freedom in making product, distribution, promotion, and price decisions.

Figure 3.3 illustrates the links between environments, publics, and the marketing strategy. Chapter 2 discussed how changes in the external environments and the behavior of a firm's publics can influence marketing decision making. More explicitly, the company copes with these changes by altering its marketing strategy (i.e., by adjusting its marketing mix or target market). For example, between 1979 and 1983, Ireland's Waterford Glass Group lost customers (a key public) because it did not respond to changes in the social environment. Increasingly, the U.S. buyer was more interested in fashion than in conservative styling. Once Waterford recognized this trend in the social environment, it began to develop new products

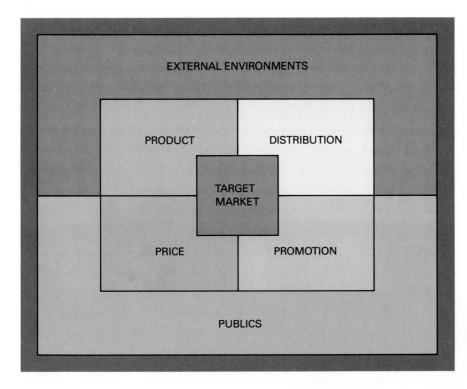

Figure 3.3

External Environments, Publics, and Marketing Strategy

(i.e., it altered its marketing mix) to capitalize on these growth opportunities emanating from the changing social environment.

We will now discuss briefly each element of the marketing mix; these areas will be detailed in Parts III through VI of the text.

Product. As a marketing manager, you must first decide what products to offer your target market. A **product** is *a bundle of tangible and intangible attributes that a seller offers the potential buyer and that satisfies the buyer's needs or wants.* Note that a product is more than its tangible attributes. For instance, a Christian Dior sweater offers more than its ability to keep you warm; it also offers the intangible attribute of prestige or status to the wearer. A new Sony or Hitachi television comes with a warranty and a promise that the dealer will service your set when and if needed, which are the product's intangible attributes.

Some products are referred to as **services**, which are *intangible tasks that satisfy buyer or user needs.* Some popular services are insurance, dry cleaning, psychological counseling, hairstyling, and credit cards.

Figure 3.4 illustrates a continuum of products ranging from purely tangible to purely intangible. At the purely tangible end are such products as Morton Salt, and at the purely intangible end of the spectrum are products such as Allstate Insurance or American Express credit cards. In between are products such as restaurants, which sell both tangible (food) and intangible products (waiter/waitress service and convenience).

Products that are primarily tangible can be classified as durable or nondurable goods. A **durable good** is *a manufactured product capable of a long, useful life, such as furniture, household appliances, and automobiles.* Durable goods are often referred to as *hard goods.* A **nondurable good** is *a manufactured or processed product with a relatively short life span, such as food, clothing, gasoline, beverages, and paper goods.*

Figure 3.4
The Product Continuum

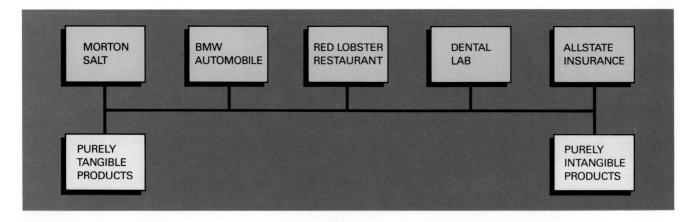

Distribution. Distribution is essential to marketing decision making because the final consumer/buyer and manufacturer usually are separated by physical distances. Recall from our earlier discussion that for marketing to occur, the seller must be capable of delivery. **Distribution** is *the marketing channel used and the physical delivery of a product to market.* The **marketing channel** is *the set of institutions or people that participate in moving goods and services from their source or production to point of final consumption or use.* The most common institutions are manufacturers, wholesalers, and retailers. For example, the Kellogg Company, which is located in Battle Creek, Michigan, sells Kellogg's Corn Flakes to food wholesalers throughout the United States—Super Valu in Minnesota, Fleming Companies in Pennsylvania, Malone and Hyde in Tennessee, and so on. The food wholesalers in turn sell to retail stores such as Safeway, Food Giant, A&P, Alpha Beta, and Kroger. This marketing channel is pictured in Figure 3.5.

Firms that specialize in physically transporting merchandise are also necessary. Motor carriers, such as Lee-Way, rail carriers, such as Southern Pacific, and air carriers, such as Flying Tiger, are notable examples.

The distribution decisions and activities that you as a marketing manager will need to be familiar with are discussed in Chapters 10, 11, and 12. Some of the distribution decision areas you will learn about are marketing channel design, transportation mode selection, warehousing, and physical distribution service levels.

Promotion. Marketing cannot occur unless communication exists between the buyer and the seller. **Promotion** is *communication by marketers that attempts to inform, persuade, and influence potential buyers of a product in order to elicit a response.* Promotion activities can be grouped into advertising, personal selling, sales promotion, and public relations. Different organizations use various mixes of these promotional activities. A firm like Miller Brewing uses advertising as its primary means of communication with its target market, but it will also use sales promotion in retail stores with such things as end-of-aisle displays. A firm such as Avon, on the other hand, will use both advertising and personal selling via its door-to-door representatives.

A major activity of marketers is promotion management; some of the decision areas and activities include establishing advertising objectives, developing an advertising budget, recruiting salespeople, training salespeople, designing sales promotions such as contests and end-of-aisle displays, and developing a media plan. Chapters 13 through 15 will address these decisions.

Price. As a marketing manager, you will also need to establish the price of your product. A **price** is *something of value that is exchanged for something else.* Prices are usually stated in monetary terms, such as, "This Texas Instruments calculator is priced at $18.95." However, prices can be expressed in nonmonetary terms, and this is especially true for nonecon-

Figure 3.5

A Common Marketing Channel in the United States

Filene's demonstrates a well-rounded mix of marketing communications between buyer and seller, using the key promotion vehicles—advertising, personal selling, sales promotion, and public relations.

Courtesy of Filene's.

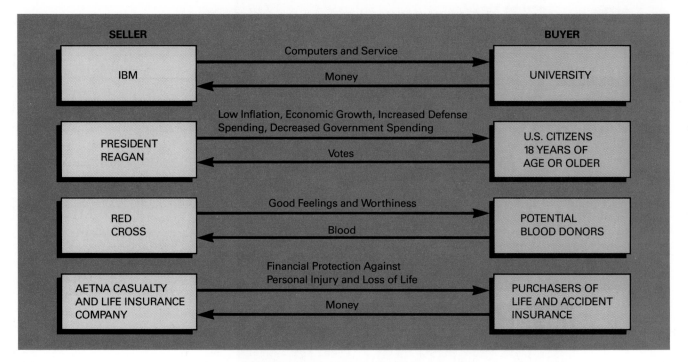

Figure 3.6
Prices Exchanged for Products

omic goods and services. During the 1984 presidential campaign, Ronald Reagan offered a platform consisting of increased defense spending, decreased government spending, lower inflation, and higher economic prosperity. This was his product, which he offered to the voting-age population in return for their votes. Their votes were the price they paid, or what they exchanged for his platform. Consider the other examples shown in Figure 3.6.

Pricing requires the marketing manager to make a series of complex decisions, such as developing an overall price strategy, setting price objectives and price tactics, and deciding whether to raise or lower prices. These and many other price decisions are discussed in Chapters 16 and 17.

Blending

As we mentioned earlier, the marketing mix must be blended to achieve the maximum response from a target market. For example, a large promotion budget or a high-priced marketing channel has implications for price setting. Product attributes will influence the selection of advertising themes and,

MARKETING IN ACTION

Wendy's "Old Fashioned" Hamburgers

The success of Wendy's International is due in part to its successful blending of marketing mix components to reach a well-defined target market. Wendy's target market is 18 to 49 year olds. This market segment desires a higher quality burger than McDonald's offers and wants more selection in their burgers. Wendy's developed a product to fill this need. The chain makes "old fashioned" hamburgers with fresh—never frozen—100 percent beef that is made fresh into patties each morning in every restaurant. In addition, eight condiments are available and the firm offers three different sizes of burgers; thus, a customer can have a burger 256 different ways. To cater to adults who don't like hamburgers, the chain also offers chili and a salad bar. Consistent with high-quality food, prices are somewhat higher than McDonald's, Burger King, and other fast-food restaurants.

Wendy's distribution system focuses on convenient retail locations located on one-half to three-quarter acre sites. The outlets have thirty to forty parking spaces and a pickup window that remains open in some locations several hours after the inside dining area has closed. Convenience in distribution is important because the 18- to 49-year-old adult generally is very busy. The interiors of the restaurants are cheerful and feature turn-of-the-century decor with table tops printed with early twentieth-century advertisements. This decor reinforces the "old fashioned" image.

Wendy's promotion is blended to be consistent with its product, price, and distribution decisions. Advertising stresses the "old fashioned" way to make hamburgers, the pickup window service to provide take-home convenience, a menu of top-quality products, and a warm, inviting family dining room.

Source: Wendy's International annual reports.

---

consequently, price setting. In later chapters, you will learn more about the blending process. The Marketing in Action on this page illustrates the marketing mix in action.

Until now our discussion has focused on the marketer's role in developing a firm's marketing strategy, which consisted of defining a target market and developing a marketing mix for the target market. If a firm is relatively small, it can concentrate on only this type of strategic planning. Frequently, however, strategic planning is used in multimillion and multibillion dollar firms, and because of these firms' tremendous size, it actually occurs at multiple levels in the organization. The president or chief executive officer of a large corporation, such as Carnation, General Foods, John Deere, and Xerox, does not have the time to do strategic planning for the hundreds of products and markets the firm handles. He or she must delegate some planning to lower-level managers.

In large corporations, strategic planning occurs at three different levels: (1) the corporate level, (2) the strategic business unit level, and (3) the product market level. Corporate level strategic planning concerns the organization as a whole and deals with the basic question of whether the firm should pursue a strategy of growth or retrenchment. As we will soon see, these growth and retrenchment strategies have profound implications for

MULTILEVEL STRATEGIC PLANNING

marketers at all levels in the organization. The next level concerns planning for **strategic business units (SBUs)**, which are *profit centers in an organization that serve broad customer needs.* A **profit center** is *the part of an organization that is responsible for sales, expenses, and investments and is accountable for the profits it generates.* The third level concerns strategic planning for **product markets**, which are *product groups that serve narrow customer needs.*

Figure 3.7 illustrates the concept of multilevel strategic planning at

Figure 3.7

Multilevel Strategic Planning at General Foods

Source: Adapted from Henry Assael, *Marketing Management: Strategy and Action* (Boston: Kent Publishing Company, 1985), p. 96. © 1985 by Wadsworth, Inc. Reprinted by permission of Kent Publishing Company, a division of Wadsworth, Inc.

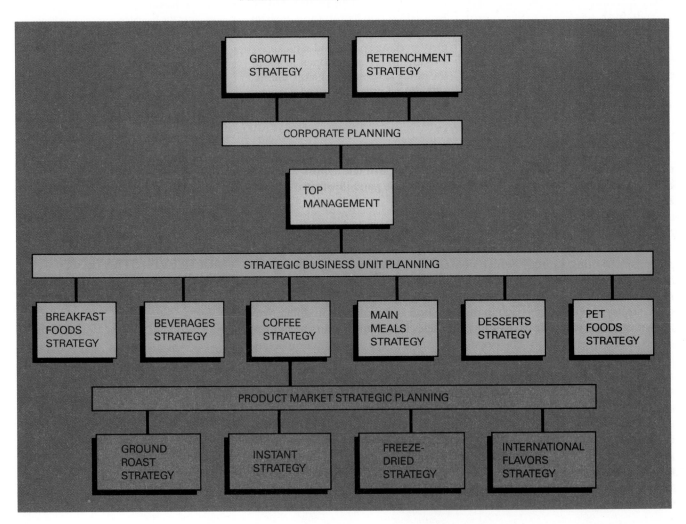

General Foods. Top management is responsible for corporate planning and strategic business unit planning. The six SBUs at General Foods are breakfast foods, beverages, coffee, main meals, desserts, and pet foods. Obviously, overall corporate growth or retrenchment strategies will influence SBU planning. After top management completes SBU planning, each SBU manager (who is often a vice president) must conduct the product market strategic planning. For example, in Figure 3.7 we see that the coffee SBU is composed of four product markets: ground roast, instant, freeze-dried, and international flavors. General Foods has multiple brands within each of these markets (e.g., ground roast brands include Maxwell House, Yuban, and Maxwell House Decaffeinated). Product market strategic planning will concern the mix and the marketing strategies for these products.

The SWOT analysis concept introduced at the outset of this chapter will be used at all levels of planning in the organization. This reinforces the importance of identifying a firm's strengths, weaknesses, opportunities, and threats before plans are developed for any organizational level.

Corporate Strategic Planning

The corporate level strategic planner should first conduct a SWOT analysis (Figure 3.8). Since the concept and meaning of SWOT analysis have already been discussed, there is no need to review it again; however, two elements of the SWOT analysis can be very helpful in corporate level strategic planning: performance trends and objectives. Strategic gaps can be identified by examining past performance trends, projecting them into the future, and then comparing them with the firm's objectives. A **strategic gap** is *the extent to which a firm's required financial performance for some future period is greater than the projected financial performance.*

The strategic gap concept is illustrated in Figure 3.9. Note that the projected financial performance assumes that no change in strategy occurs; it assumes status quo. On the other hand, the required financial performance reflects what a firm would like to see occur in terms of financial performance in forthcoming budget periods. This figure shows that the longer the time horizon, the larger the strategic gap, because the firm's external environments are constantly changing, causing old strategies to become outdated.

Once the corporate strategic planner has conducted the SWOT analysis and identified any strategic gap, he or she can formulate corporate strategies. All firms have two broad strategic options: growth and retrenchment. **Growth strategies** *attempt to close a strategic gap by sales growth*, and **retrenchment strategies** *attempt to close a strategic gap by a planned reduction in the size of the organization.*

Growth Strategies. Several standard growth strategies can be adapted for any business and will become more specific and fine-tuned when they are company specific. Figure 3.10 shows a product/market expansion matrix,

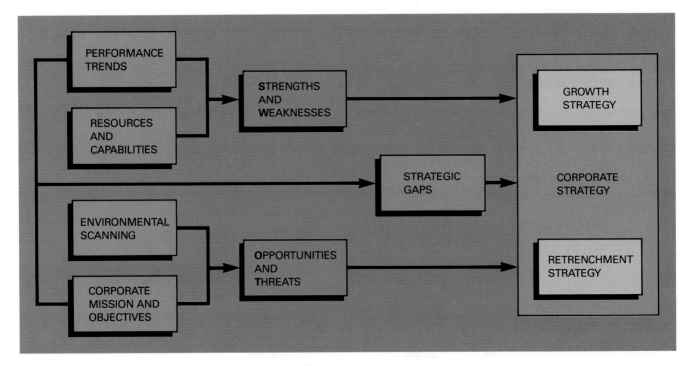

Figure 3.8
SWOT Analysis for Corporate Strategic Planning

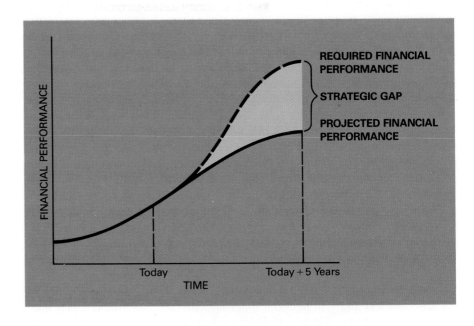

Figure 3.9
The Strategic Gap Concept

	EXISTING PRODUCTS	NEW PRODUCTS
EXISTING MARKETS	MARKET PENETRATION	PRODUCT DEVELOPMENT
NEW MARKETS	MARKET DEVELOPMENT	DIVERSIFICATION

Figure 3.10

Growth Strategy Matrix

Source: Adapted from H. Igor Ansoff. "Strategies for Diversification" *Harvard Business Review* (September–October 1957), pp. 113–124.

which is the basis of all growth strategies.[7] This matrix classifies strategies by existing markets or new markets and by existing products or new products. Four basic strategies are shown: market penetration, market development, product development, and diversification.

Market penetration is *a growth strategy that involves concentrating on existing markets and products.* Generally, a company focuses on intensifying its marketing efforts in order to increase market share. **Market share** is *a firm's sales in a particular market divided by total market sales.* This strategy can elicit a fierce retaliation in a highly competitive market, especially if overall growth in the industry is stagnant. An example is MCI's attempt to penetrate the long-distance phone calling market with low prices and AT&T's retaliatory actions, such as lowering its prices, offering discount coupons on merchandise, and increasing advertising.

Gaining market share in a no-growth market causes competitors' sales to drop, which inevitably elicits a competitive response. A market penetration strategy works best in industries with rapid growth and relatively low competition. Importantly, if the firm successfully penetrates the market, it can achieve significant cost savings because of its large volume and thus increase its financial performance. This was essentially Commodore's strategy in the early 1980s with its Commodore 64 home computer.

Market development is *a growth strategy in which the firm attempts to sell existing products in new markets.* This can be done by expanding into new geographic markets, as Walt Disney did when it opened Walt Disney World in Florida and Disneyland in Japan. The company currently has plans to open a Disney Entertainment Park in Europe.[8] Market development may also involve directing marketing efforts at new market segments. For example, American Motors Corporation recently began to concentrate more of its efforts on the leasing segment of the new car market.

A big advantage of market development is that the firm doesn't need to expend any additional resources on the development of new products. A market development strategy is especially attractive if the company has excess production capacity. Even if no excess capacity exists, however, when the firm does build new capacity, it is dealing with a familiar production technology.

Market development involves relatively little risk at the production end of the business; the risk is on the marketing side. Developing a new market can require considerable market research and expenditures of promotion resources, such as advertising and personal selling. Because none of these marketing investments represents fixed capital investments with resale or salvage values, a large loss could be incurred if this strategy is unsuccessful.

Product development is *a growth strategy in which the firm develops new products or modifies existing products to better serve its existing markets.* For example, Tandy Corporation has continuously modified and added new models to its line of personal computers to better serve the household and small business market.

Often, minor product changes will enable a company to reach certain market segments more effectively. For instance, Whirlpool frequently adds features to its home appliances, such as ice makers to its refrigerators or energy and water-saving features to its dishwashers. Some home builders add features to their new houses to appeal to the more upscale home buyer, such as whirlpool baths, fireplaces, and ceramic tile. When relatively minor product changes are made, a product development strategy is not very risky; the biggest payoff from a product development strategy usually comes from a major product innovation, which is naturally a high-risk venture. For example, Searle invested over $20 million to develop NutraSweet, a low calorie sweetener made from protein components. NutraSweet is now used by many major food and beverage manufacturers in the United States and Canada.[9]

A **diversification** *growth strategy involves taking a company into new products and new markets.* This is the most risky growth strategy and should only be pursued after the firm has exploited growth opportunities that capitalize on existing markets, existing products, or both. Diversification involves new production and marketing methods.

One less risky type of diversification strategy is **convergent diversification**. With convergent *(sometimes called concentric) diversification, a firm attempts to diversify into products and markets that use a firm's existing production or marketing knowledge.* For example, an electrical and plumbing wholesaler may diversify into grocery wholesaling since the techniques of inventory management, warehousing, transportation and selling would be similar. The Marketing in Action on page 71 illustrates how NCR Corp. is pursuing a convergent diversification strategy.

The most risky diversification strategy is **conglomerate diversification**, which *consists of adding products and serving markets that are totally unrelated to the firm's current business.* Often this is accomplished by a merger or outright purchase of another firm in an unrelated business. For example, the Quaker Oats Company has diversified into specialty retailing and now owns four specialty retailers: Jos. A. Bank Clothiers, a retail and direct mail marketer of traditional men's and women's apparel and accessories; Brookstone, a marketer of hard-to-find tools and housewares sold through mail-order catalogs and retail stores; Herrschners, a mail-order marketer of needle crafts in the United States and Canada; and Eyelab, an

MARKETING IN ACTION

Historically, NCR Corp. (National Cash Register) concentrated its efforts on equipment that processes transactions for retailers and financial institutions. However, competition in this market has intensified, and this market is reaching maturity. In 1982, NCR shipped only 10.6 percent of bank-teller terminals in the United States, and sales of retail terminals have been flat since the late 1970s.

The company's response has been to develop a convergent, or concentric, diversification strategy; that is it is developing new products to sell to

Convergent Diversification at NCR

new markets so that its customer base can be expanded. These new products are personal computers, word processors, semiconductors, and telephone communication systems, whose development allows NCR to use existing technological skills and manufacturing processes. NCR can also capitalize on its marketing and service skills because the

NCR brand is widely recognized and because a national and international service network already exists.

All diversification strategies require financial capital. Luckily, NCR was sitting on cash balances of $527 million with a debt of only 16 percent of its total capital.

Source: Based on corporate annual reports and "NCR: Trying to Expand its Customer Base with a Batch of New Products," *BusinessWeek* (December 19, 1983), pp. 68, 72, 73.

eyewear department store chain that sells prescription and nonprescription products.[10]

One of the few advantages of conglomerate diversification is that it allows a firm to spread its risks by operating in multiple unrelated lines of business. Because they are unrelated, it is unlikely that they would grow or decline at the same rate when the economy changes. The strategy is similar to an investor who has a diversified portfolio of stocks, bonds, and money market funds to reduce risk.

The available evidence suggests that successfully managing unrelated businesses is indeed difficult. There appears to be some advantage in cash management and transferring cash across divisions or businesses as needed, but beyond that, there appears to be no positive effect of conglomerate diversification. Recognizing this harsh reality, Pepsico divested itself of Lee Way Motor Freight in 1984, which it had purchased in the mid 1970s.

Retrenchment Strategies.   Retrenchment strategies involve liquidation of parts of the business or cost containment, or both. A firm may decide that the best way to close a strategic gap is to liquidate one portion of the business that is losing money or not performing up to par. The organization resources and capabilities may be so weak and the threats so severe, or opportunities so unpromising, that getting out of the business may be wise. Notable and well-recognized firms have pursued this option. For example, in 1985, General Mills decided to sell its toy group, which included Parker Brothers, a General Mills possession for 17 years and a leading toy company (sales of over $700 million) that makes Monopoly, Sorry, and other games and toys.[11]

Marketing managers often overlook the possibility of closing strategic gaps by developing strategies for cost containment. Robert A. Fox, president and chief operating officer of the Del Monte Corporation, has identified cost containment as a major strategic opportunity for the 1980s.[12] Costs can be contained by cutting wasteful expenses, such as excessive expense allowances for salespeople, using an excessive amount of air freight to ship last-minute orders, or using too much overtime for warehouse forklift drivers because of poor scheduling of inbound and outbound freight.

Cost containment strategies can be in promotion, distribution, and product areas. One of the advantages of cost containment strategies is that they are internal to the firm and thus can be hidden from competitors, reducing the likelihood of being copied or imitated. Consider the following cost containment strategies practiced by well-known firms:

❑ Between 1980 and 1983, Western Auto Supply Company, which supplies over 2,000 Western Auto stores, reduced its number of distribution centers from ten to six. This strategy improved distribution productivity, lowered distribution costs, and generated significant financial resources on the sale of the unnecessary distribution centers.[13]

❑ In 1983, Allis-Chalmers Corporation pursued cost containment strategies directed at three key publics. In regard to intermediary publics, it attempted to better control agricultural equipment dealer inventories by closely matching production with retail demand to reduce equipment carrying costs. In terms of supplier publics, they sought price concessions from material suppliers. Finally, employee publics were successfully asked to exercise restraints in wage demands during contract negotiations.[14]

❑ In 1983, Owens-Illinois, one of the leading manufacturers of packaging products, successfully used computer design techniques to reduce by 10 percent the weight of one-liter plastic beverage bottles. They also devised a cost-saving method of prelabeling their bottles.[15]

SBU Level Planning

As we mentioned earlier, SBU level planning is constrained by overall corporate strategy. For example, if a company decides to diversify as an avenue for growth, then it may stringently allocate funds to existing SBU managers for business growth. Conversely, if top management decides on a cost containment strategy, then each SBU manager will be required to cut costs. Basically, corporate level planning sets the tone for planning at all other levels.

Typically, SWOT analysis at the SBU level is conducted with the aid of a business screen. A **business screen** is *an analytical device used to evaluate the strengths, weaknesses, opportunities, and threats of each SBU in order to determine if it is a candidate for growth or retrenchment.*

General Electric has developed the business screen shown in Figure

3.11. On the vertical dimension of this business screen is market, or industry, attractiveness. **Market attractiveness** is *an uncontrollable dimension that includes market size, market growth rate, competitive intensity, legal constraints, and a host of other factors that represent the opportunities and threats emanating from the SBU's external environments.* On the horizontal dimension is business strength, which is a controllable dimension. **Business strength** is *the firm's ability to compete effectively in its industry or market* and includes factors such as the firm's knowledge of an industry, market, or customers; its market share or financial performance; the quality of its marketing personnel; production capabilities; its ability to be price competitive; and other factors that represent the SBU's resources, capabilities, and performance.

Note in Figure 3.11 that both the horizontal and vertical dimensions are divided into three categories: the SBU can be low, moderate, or high in attractiveness, and the business strength can be weak, moderate, or strong. This breakdown results in nine cells, colored green, yellow, or red. An SBU is deemed attractive if it falls into the green area, and a growth strategy is appropriate for it. To be in the green area, the SBU must be either high in

Figure 3.11

SWOT Analysis and the General Electric Business Screen

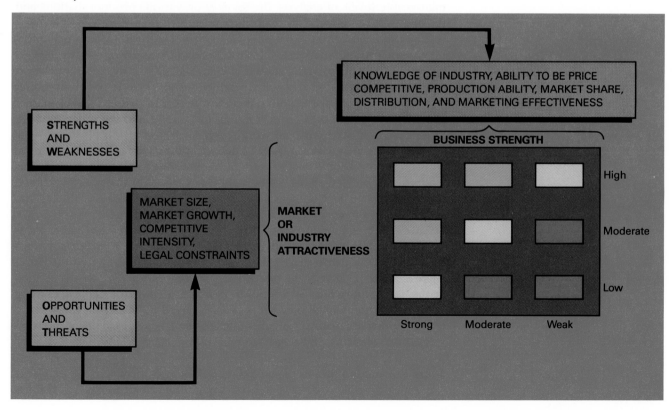

business strength or industry attractiveness and no less than moderate in the remaining dimension. An SBU in the yellow area is considered moderately attractive, and the firm should proceed with caution. If the firm has sufficient growth opportunities with SBUs in the green cells, the yellow SBUs may be candidates for retrenchment. SBUs in the yellow cells are characterized by either moderate business strength and industry attractiveness or are strong in one of these dimensions but weak or low in the other. The SBUs in the red cells should be liquidated as soon as possible. Top management should not allocate valuable resources to these SBUs. The industry's attractiveness and the business strength in these SBUs are moderate at best and typically weak.

This GE business screen also can be used to evaluate potential new SBUs. In this case, the planner would attempt to project business strength and industry attractiveness. Only new SBUs that are projected to fall into the green cells should be pursued, and then only if they are consistent with the firm's mission and objectives.

Product Market Level Strategic Planning

As we work our way down the organizational ladder to more specific and manageable levels of analysis, the focus is on various product markets and the brands that compose these product markets. Once again, SWOT analysis will be used. One of the most popular frameworks for doing strategic planning at the product market level is the **Boston Consulting Group (BCG) product portfolio matrix**, shown in Figure 3.12.[16] At the product market level we are dealing with specific product brands that compose a product market, so that we are mainly concerned with the overall rate of market growth as an indicator of opportunities and threats and with market share as a measure of strengths and weaknesses.

The vertical axis in Figure 3.12 depicts the *market growth rate,* or the annual real (inflation-adjusted) rate of growth for the product market. This is arbitrarily divided at the 10 percent rate for a cutoff between high and low growth. The horizontal axis depicts *relative market share,* which is the market share for your brand relative to that of your largest competitor. A relative share of 0.25 indicates that a company has a market share that is 25 percent of its leading competitor's (i.e., the competitor's share is 4 times greater than the firm's share). A relative share of 2.5 means that the firm's share is 2.5 times that of the next-strongest competitor. This axis is divided at the 1.5 point, which is the point at which a company achieves strong competitive dominance or what is often referred to as critical mass.

The portfolio matrix is divided into four cells, stars, cash cows, question marks (or wildcats), and dogs. We will discuss each briefly.

Stars.　A star is a product in a high growth market for which the company has a high relative market share and competitive dominance. Often these

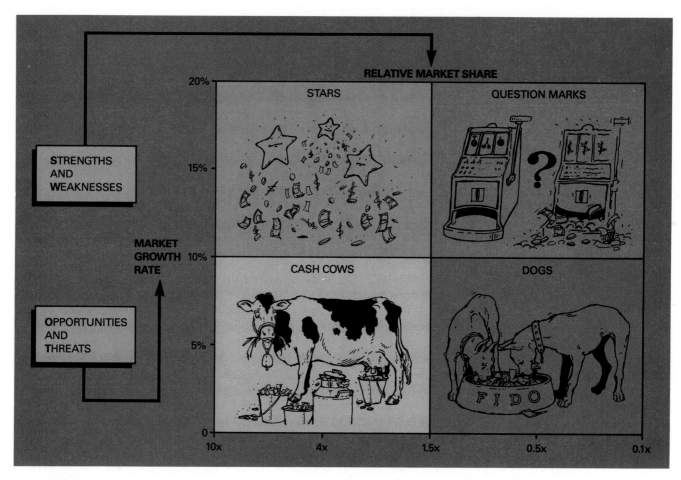

Figure 3.12
SWOT Analysis and the BCG Product Portfolio Matrix

are the products for which a company was an innovator and grabbed a large market share early. Since the market is growing rapidly, the marketing strategy is to hold on to this market share through regular product refinement and heavy promotion expenditures. Consequently, stars require a large and continuing commitment of financial capital to fuel their growth.

Cash Cows.   Products that fall in the cash cow quadrant are in a low growth market but have a dominant share of that market. Since growth is low, the capital needed to support these products is minimal. In fact, these cash cows, as the name implies, tend to generate more cash than they can use. This cash will be used to fund other products such as stars or question marks. Note that today's stars will be tomorrow's cash cows.

Question Marks.   Question marks are often referred to as wildcats or problem children. They represent products that have a low relative market share in a high growth market. The firm can take a gamble with these products, investing large amounts of capital in hopes of increasing relative market share and thus moving them toward the star quadrant, or the firm can simply try to maintain their market share, which will still be costly because of the highly competitive nature of growth markets and the resultant costs of maintaining market share. A third option is to drop these products.

Dogs.   Dogs are products with a low market share in a low growth market. They are self-supporting but do not help support other products in terms of cash flow. Trying to increase market share in a low growth market is an exercise in negative cash flow—it is not worth the effort. Dogs are usually excellent candidates for deletion.

Cash Flow.   In our discussion of the BCG matrix, we often referred to cash flow, which is an important part of strategic planning at the product level. Some products will be net users of cash, and others will be net providers of cash. Two basic relationships can be stated based on the portfolio matrix. First, the higher the relative market share, the higher is a product's cash-generating ability, because high market share is related to higher profits.[17] Second, the higher the market rate of growth, the higher is the product's cash-using needs. Cash is needed to increase sales and maintain market share. The objective of strategic planning at the product market level should be to maintain a balanced portfolio, where cash cows can support the question marks and stars. The process is dynamic: as time passes, stars will become cash cows and some question marks will become stars. This scenario dramatizes the importance of adding new products over time—to give birth to the stars and cash cows of the future—and also underscores the importance of deleting products that do not generate cash and have a low likelihood of ever doing so. Importantly, cash cows should not become sacred cows; once they can no longer help finance other products, they should be considered candidates for deletion.[18]

A RECAP AND PERSPECTIVE

This chapter completes the first part of this book. Chapter 1 defined marketing and explained why it is an important area of study. We introduced the marketing concept as a philosophy for the practice of marketing and highlighted the rapid growth of marketing in nonprofit firms, service firms, and international business. Chapter 2 explained that the firm is an open system that is constrained by external environments and participates in exchanges with multiple publics. Since the publics that interact with a firm are influenced by external environments, the organization must systematically scan the external environments for opportunities and threats. Chapter 3 used the knowledge gained in the first two chapters to explain marketing management and strategic planning. Marketing management and strategic planning should be preceded by a SWOT analysis to identify the strengths and weaknesses of a firm and the opportunities and threats it faces. This is an important aspect of marketing strategy development and consists of selecting a target market and developing a marketing mix. It is also an important aspect of corporate strategic planning and is directed at determining whether a firm should pursue growth or retrenchment strategies. In addition, SWOT analysis is used in SBU level planning to determine which SBUs are in need of further growth and which should be liquidated or retrenched. Finally, SWOT analysis can be used in product market level planning to identify products that are stars, cash cows, question marks, and dogs.

With this background knowledge we can now proceed to the remaining parts of this book. Part II will explain the marketplace, since marketing strategies cannot be developed effectively unless the buyer in the marketplace is understood and a target market is identified. Parts III through VI will show you how to plan the marketing mix. Part III will focus on product planning and decisions; Part IV will cover distribution planning and decisions; Part V will discuss promotion planning and decisions; and Part VI will concentrate on price planning and decisions.

This book clearly is oriented toward planning and decision making; we want you to assume the role of a marketing manager as you read this book. With the solid understanding of planning marketing strategy provided in Parts III through VI, we will discuss special growth opportunities in marketing in Part VII. Separate chapters will focus on international marketing, marketing of services, and nonprofit marketing. The last part of the book will discuss the execution of marketing plans, which requires the acquisition, organization, and utilization of resources and the control of the marketing strategy. Control will be accomplished by comparing actual with expected performance and taking corrective action to modify the marketing strategy where necessary. The final part of the book also evaluates the performance of marketing on a societal level and speculates on the future of marketing.

SUMMARY

This chapter introduced the concept of strategic marketing management, which is the analysis, strategy, implementation, and control of marketing activities in order to achieve the organization's objectives. Planning is deciding today what to do in the future and consists of analysis and strategy, whereas execution is making things happen and consists of implementation and control of the strategy. This chapter focused on planning—the analysis and strategy elements of strategic marketing management.

Analysis can be accomplished by conducting a SWOT analysis, which consists of studying a firm's performance trends, resources, and capabilities to assess strengths and weaknesses, stating a firm's mission and objectives, and scanning the external environments to identify opportunities and threats facing the organization. The marketer wants to identify market opportunities that exist because there is an unmet or unsatisfied need or want in the marketplace and for which the firm has an interest in and capability to satisfy. At the same time the marketer should try to convert threats into opportunities.

Once the SWOT analysis has been completed, the marketer can develop a marketing strategy to pursue a market opportunity. The two primary elements of a marketing strategy are selection of a target market and development of a marketing mix to offer to the target market. A marketing mix consists of product, distribution, promotion, and price decisions.

In large organizations, strategic planning occurs at three different levels: (1) the corporate level, (2) the SBU level, and (3) the product market level. Planning at each of these levels uses the concept of SWOT analysis. The purpose of corporate level planning is to arrive at growth or retrenchment strategies. Four alternative growth strategies are market penetration, market development, product development, and diversification. Retrenchment strategies can involve liquidation of parts of the business or cost containment, or both. Typically, SBU level planning uses a business screen to evaluate each SBU and determine which to expand and which to retrench. In this regard, the GE business screen, which examines market attractiveness and business strength for each SBU, is very helpful. This screen categorizes SBUs into three types: (1) green SBUs are deemed attractive, and a growth strategy is appropriate for them; (2) yellow SBUs are considered moderately attractive, and the firm should either cautiously expand or, if the firm has sufficient green SBUs, retrench them; (3) red SBUs are unattractive and should be liquidated as soon as possible.

Product market level strategic planning focuses on various product markets and the brands that compose these product markets. One of the more popular frameworks for doing strategic planning at the product market level is the BCG product portfolio matrix. This matrix incorporates the concept of SWOT analysis because it examines the overall rate of market growth, which is an indicator of opportunities and threats, and market share, which is an indicator of strengths and weaknesses. The BCG matrix categorizes all of the firm's products into stars, cash cows, question marks, and dogs. Stars are products in growth markets for which the firm has a high relative market share and are candidates for a growth strategy. Cash cows are products in low growth markets for which the firm has a high relative market share. These products are candidates for neither growth nor retrenchment but are used to generate cash to support other products. Question marks are products with a low relative market share in a high growth market. Predictably, the question marks are gambles and can be candidates for either growth or, if the risk is too high in relation to the possible returns, liquidation (i.e., retrenchment strategy). Products that are dogs are in a slow growth market and are low in relative market share and therefore are usually excellent candidates for liquidation.

KEY CONCEPTS

REVIEW AND DISCUSSION QUESTIONS

1. Define strategic marketing management and discuss its relation to the definition of marketing provided in Chapter 1.

2. What is SWOT analysis? How is it used in strategic marketing management?

3. How can threats in the external environments be translated into opportunities? Name the four situations in which threats should be viewed as negative forces.

4. What are the elements of a marketing strategy?

5. Describe the various levels in the organization that are involved in strategic planning and give examples of the types of strategic planning done at each level.

6. What is a strategic gap? How are strategic gaps closed?

7. Strategic plans should always result in the development of some form of growth strategy. Agree or disagree with this statement and defend your position.

8. Name the four standard growth strategies that a firm can develop.

9. Explain the circumstances in which a market penetration strategy would be most applicable.

10. Explain why organizations should consider both growth strategies and retrenchment strategies.

11. Draw the GE business screen and discuss how it can be used in strategic planning.

12. Explain why the BCG product portfolio matrix is a useful tool in product planning and in determining a firm's cash-flow situation.

ACTION PROBLEMS

1. Scan your local daily newspaper for several days (preferably Friday, Saturday, and Sunday) and clip all the advertisements for either women's or men's apparel. Categorize these advertisements into groups that you believe reflect similar target markets. Try to label the target market for each group of advertisements.

2. You and a good friend plan to open a restaurant and cocktail lounge that has a target market of 21-to-35-year-old professionals. Develop the marketing mix for this proposed business.

3. An industrial robot manufacturer wants to begin producing and marketing robots for the home. What environmental factors may arise that make this market more attractive? What might occur in the environment that threatens this market from developing?

4. A manufacturer of stereo components is confronted by the following three environmental trends: (1) increasing competitive pressures from foreign manufacturers, (2) increased application of computer technology to stereo components, and (3) rapid growth in discretionary income among two-income households aged 25 to 44 years. Develop a list of possible strategies the company might consider in order to increase its sales to twice the industry average.

5. As a strategic planning analyst, you are in the process of identifying strategic gaps for your employer, a lawn mower manufacturer. Sales over the last five years have been (in millions of dollars) $5.6, $6.2, $7.3, $7.4, and $7.3. The company's goal is to increase sales at a compound annual growth rate of 10 percent. On the other hand, current trends suggest that sales may be flat over the next five years. If sales do not grow, what will be the dollar amount of the strategic gap in five years?

NOTES

1. George S. Day, *Strategic Market Planning: The Pursuit of Competitive Advantage* (St. Paul, MN: West Publishing Co., 1984), p. 52.

2. For a more complete discussion of opportunity analysis, see Martin L. Bell, *Marketing Concepts and Strategy* (New York: Houghton-Mifflin, 1972); Derek F. Abell, "Strategic Windows," *Journal of Marketing* (July 1978), pp. 21–26.

3. For more information on developing a mission and objectives, see H. Igor Ansoff, *Corporate Strategy* (New York: McGraw-Hill, 1965); Derek F. Abell, *Defining the Business* (Englewood Cliffs, NJ: Prentice-Hall, 1980).

4. The process of identifying opportunities that are consistent with the firm's mission, objectives, and resources is often called strategic planning; see Derek F. Abell and John S. Hammond, *Strategic Marketing Planning* (Englewood Cliffs, NJ: Prentice-Hall, 1979).

5. George S. Day, *Strategic Market Planning*, p. 53.

6. For a further discussion of the marketing mix, see Neil Borden, "The Concept of the Marketing Mix," *Journal of Advertising Research* (June 1964), pp. 2–7; William Lazer, James D. Culley, and Thomas A. Staudt, "The Concept of the Marketing Mix," in E.J. Kelley and William Lazer (eds.), *Managerial Marketing: Policies, Strategies, and Decisionmaking* (Homewood, IL: Richard D. Irwin, 1973), pp. 27–37.

7. H. Igor Ansoff, "Strategies for Diversification," *Harvard Business Review* (September–October 1957), pp. 113–124.

8. *Walt Disney Productions Annual Report 1984.*

9. *Searle Annual Reports 1982 and 1983.*

10. *The Quaker Oats Company Annual Report 1984,* pp. 26–27.

11. Alex Beam and Judith H. Gorzynski, "General Mills: Toys Just Aren't Us," *BusinessWeek* (September 16, 1985), pp. 105–109.

12. R.A. Fox, "Putting Marketing on a 'Business' Basis," *The Nielsen Researcher* (No. 1, 1983), pp. 2–10.

13. *Beneficial Corporation Annual Report 1983.*

14. *Allis-Chalmers Corporation Annual Report 1983.*

15. *Owens-Illinois Annual Report 1983.*

16. *The Product Portfolio* (Boston: The Boston Consulting Group, 1970), Perspectives No. 66.

17. Sidney Schoeffler, Robert D. Buzzell, and Donald F. Heany, "Impact of Strategic Planning on Profit Performance," *Harvard Business Review* 52(March–April 1974), pp. 137–145; Robert D. Buzzell, Bradley T. Gale, and Ralph G.M. Sultan, "Market Share—A Key to Profitability," *Harvard Business Review* 53(January–February 1975), pp. 97–106.

18. For a discussion of how to analyze the product portfolio, see George S. Day, "Diagnosing the Product Portfolio," *Journal of Marketing* 41(April 1977), pp. 29–38; Yoram Wind and Vijay Mahajan, "Designing Product and Business Portfolios," *Harvard Business Review* (January–February 1981), pp. 155–165.

CASES FOR PART 1

1.

The Marketing and Distribution of Trade Books

In 1982, sales by U.S. book publishers exceeded $7 billion and approximately $1 billion of this amount was spent on trade books. Trade books are those books published for the general adult market. Because the market potential for trade books has been estimated at several billion dollars, sales were lower than they should have been.

One reason sales are low is that current practices of distribution and marketing of trade books are rather cumbersome. Publisher representatives visit bookstores semiannually to take orders. A small retail bookstore may deal with 100 to 150 publishers, receiving 200 to 300 sales visits annually; however, a large retail bookstore may deal with about 400 publishers and receive around 800 sales calls per year. Despite all this activity, about 20 percent of the publishers account for 80 percent of a typical store's sales volume.

Publishers have trouble forecasting demand for a new title. An estimated 25 percent of a trade publisher's stock must be dumped at a fraction of the investment in the stock because of overproduction. Retailers also have great difficulty in estimating demand for a specific title (over 20,000 new trade titles are published annually). They often end up returning about one-third of the books they have ordered. Most publishers allow retailers to return books for up to twelve months after they were initially purchased.

If you frequent bookstores, you probably know that many patrons walk out of a bookstore empty-handed. Obviously, a typical bookstore can only stock a fraction of the available titles, and sometimes, even when a title is stocked, the customer cannot find it. Of the 220 million visits that U.S. consumers make to bookstores annually, approximately half leave the stores without making a purchase.

Questions

1. Why do you think it is difficult for the trade book publishing industry to practice the marketing concept?
2. Identify any emerging technologies that you believe could help improve the distribution system for books.

Sources: Kevin Higgins. "Trade Publishing Suffers from Insufficient Marketing," *Marketing News* (December 24, 1982), pp. 1, 5; Kevin Higgins. "Inadequacies in Distribution System Blamed for Book Publishing Malaise," *Marketing News* (December 24, 1982), pp. 1, 10.

2.

Motor Carriers Face Drastically Altered Environments

Until the Motor Carrier Act of 1980 (and related legislation), for-hire truckers in the United States were highly regulated by the Interstate Commerce Commission (ICC). There were two types of truckers: private and for-hire. Private carriers were owned by the organizations for which they transported freight and were not regulated by the ICC. For instance, K mart owned several hundred trucks to transport merchandise from its warehouses to its stores. For-hire carriers, on the other hand, were regulated by the ICC and were either common carriers that hauled freight for the general public or contract carriers that had on-going agreements to haul freight for one or more firms. Contract carriers could design services to meet each customer's needs. For-hire carriers also were restricted in terms of the types of commodities they could transport and the routes they could travel.

The Motor Carrier Act of 1980 and related legislation substantially reduced regulations. Entry into the motor carrier industry is now relatively easy. For example, the number of regulated motor carriers grew from 23,054 in August 1981 to 32,968 in April 1983. Also, private carriers can now operate on a for-hire basis without being regulated by the ICC as long as they haul freight for a wholly owned subsidiary. In addition, carriers are free to cover more routes and haul a wider variety of products.

Predictably, this drastic change in the legal and competitive environments for motor carriers has resulted in intensified competition and declining profits. For instance, between 1976 and 1979, rate of return on equity in the industry averaged 14.3 percent; in 1980 to 1981, it fell to 4.5 percent; and in 1982, it was 0 percent. The consensus among industry analysts is that to survive in this type of competitive environment, motor carriers need to increase their productivity and enhance their marketing skills.

Questions

1. Explain how changes in the external environments influenced competition in the motor carrier industry. What is the generic competition that motor carriers face?
2. How can motor carriers increase their productivity and become more marketing oriented?

Source: Based in part on Donald M. Hill and Richard K. Ross, Jr. "Good Buddy, Can You Spare a Dime?" *Management Focus* (July–August 1983), pp. 6–11.

3.

Mineral Water and Natural Soda

Bottled mineral water has been a popular drink in Europe for centuries. Leonardo da Vinci and Michelangelo regularly drank mineral water to aid their health. Other notable mineral water devotees include the French scientist Louis Pasteur and Russia's Peter the Great.

The continuing popularity of bottled water is evidenced by the fact that the typical French person drank 14.5 gallons of bottled water in 1984 and West Germans drank an average of 12 gallons each. These figures compared to an average per capita consumption of 4 gallons in the United States (which, incidentally, is 3 times what it was in 1976). In 1984, U.S. bottled water sales were $800 million.

The bottled water market in the United States began to experience rapid growth in 1977 when the president of Société Anonyme Source Perrier mounted a successful $4 million promotional campaign. Soon owners of other springs began to market their beverages more aggressively. In fact, by 1984, there were over fifty brands of bottled water being marketed in the United States.

The U.S. consumer has a different motive for drinking bottled waters than does the European consumer. Europeans drink bottled water for its mineral content, whereas Americans drink it for its lack of salt, caffeine,

sugar, and other additives and preservatives. U.S. purchasers are the same ones who have quit smoking, have cut down on salty products and caffeine, and are stocking their pantries with herbal teas and juices.

Now, a new beverage category is emerging in the United States—natural soda. One of the entrepreneurs in this market is Sophia Collier, who used her kitchen to develop a mixture of mineral water and natural fruit extract. Sophia and a friend, Connie Best, started American Natural Beverage Corp. By 1984, the firm was selling ten flavors of Soho Natural Soda in twenty-three states.

The natural soda business has captured less than 1 percent of the $26 billion soft drink industry in the United States; however, rapid growth is forecast over the next five years, as it is for bottled water. Recently, Shasta Beverages jumped on the bandwagon with its new line of Spree Natural Sodas, and Sunkist is planning an entry in the natural soda field. Also, Perrier has added a citrus taste to its mineral water.

Questions

1. What trends in the external environment may favorably influence the bottled water and natural soda market?
2. As a result of the growth trends for bottled waters and natural sodas and factors in the external environments, should Pepsi and Coca Cola generate a product development strategy?

Source: Based in part on information in Timothy Green. "Apostles of Purity, Mineral-Water Buffs Swear By the Stuff," *Smithsonian* (October 1984), pp. 105–114; "Natural Soda: From Health-Food Fad To Supermarket Staple," *BusinessWeek* (January 14, 1985), p. 72.

4.

Chrysler Corporation and Its Publics

The operating philosophy of the Chrysler Corporation and its chief executive officer, Lee A. Iacocca, is best illustrated by the following series of quotations from the 1983 report to stockholders:

Labor

- "Chrysler employees realize that the best job security comes from making high quality cars that people will buy."

- "We intend to remain lean and tightly staffed, but we also plan to have the people we need to meet the challenges of the future."

- "As we install new technology in our factories and offices, we are making sure that our employees can use the new equipment and techniques efficiently. In our rebuilt plant in Windsor, for example, Chrysler employees spent over 900,000 manhours, or 450 manyears, in training."

- "Rapidly increasing use of computers and robotics is of paramount importance to the achievement of Chrysler's goals of higher quality and productivity. We had only 16 robots in 1975, now we have 375, and the number is increasing rapidly. By 1988, we will have well over 1,000."

Suppliers

- "Our new inventory system is based in part on Chrysler's team approach with suppliers. To assure high quality parts at reasonable prices, we are working more closely with our suppliers on both quality and cost. We're developing new cooperative relationships, and many suppliers are becoming involved very early in our design and production plans."

- "Our aim is to integrate supplier operations with our own, thereby enabling them to reduce their inventories, invest in modern equipment, and share the benefit of the resulting savings. In a number of instances, we have negotiated larger contracts that assure suppliers of a stronger business relationship with us."

Dealers

- "Chrysler's strengthened product line and sales performance meant record profits for our dealers in 1983."

- "Chrysler aims to improve owner loyalty, reduce warranty costs, and increase sales and profits for Chrysler Corporation and our dealers. In 1983, we increased our dealer service support and training by 77 percent."

- "We are making sure our dealers provide best-in-class service for our best-in-class products. Dealer mechanics need the skill to service our high technology cars and trucks, and dealer service management people must be able to diagnose customer product problems accurately and handle them effectively."

Stockholders and Investor Publics

- "We repaid the $1.2 billion in loans guaranteed by the federal government. This action was taken seven years early, saving $392 million in interest and government fees. It strengthened our balance sheet and helped facilitate our access to traditional credit markets."

- "We cleaned up our balance sheet by reclassifying $1.1 billion of preferred stock into common stock and by exchanging common stock for lender warrants."

- "We placed the winning bid of $311 million for the 14.4 million Chrysler warrants held by the U.S. government. We retired those warrants—and with them the uncertainty about their potential dilution and stock-price effect."

- "In December (1983), we resumed preferred dividend payments, and paid all arrearages, on the 10 million shares of preferred stock held by the public."

- "In April 1984, we will resume dividend payments on our common stock, with a quarterly payment of 15 cents per share payable to stockholders of record as of March 15, 1984."

Customers

- "Our 1984 models are technically advanced, high quality products offering what the public wants: front-wheel drive, fuel efficiency, good looks, high technology, and the best warranty protection on the market."

- "By 1990, half of all car buyers will be under 40. To appeal to this growing young family market, we are investing $650 million to design and build an entirely new line of four-door sedans for the 1985 model year."

- "Because we use galvanized steel so extensively in our pickup trucks and sport utility vehicles, we're now able to offer the industry's first five-year/ 100,000 mile rust perforation warranty."

Questions

1. Does Chrysler practice the marketing concept?
2. What conflicts may arise between the multiple publics (labor, consumers, stockholders, suppliers, dealers) that Chrysler must work with?

Source: *Chrysler Corporation 1983 Report to Shareholders.*

5.

Publix

Florida, one of the most heavily populated Sunbelt states, has attracted many competitors in the food business, and as competition intensifies, some firms are choosing to leave the market. Surprisingly, however, other firms continue to enter this intensely competitive market.

Consider these changes that occurred in 1984 in the Florida market:

- Grand Union (a New Jersey–based firm) shut down close to fifty supermarkets and warehouse stores and headed north.

- Pantry Pride closed fifty-six stores but acquired five closed Grand Unions and opened eight warehouse-style Sun Supermarkets.

- Piggly Wiggly reentered the Florida market with three new stores after staying away for a half century.

- Winn-Dixie acquired eleven closed Grand Unions.

- Kash N' Karry (owned by Lucky Stores of California), acquired fifteen of the closed Grand Union stores.

- A&P opened two superstores.

- Pueblo International opened a prototype 85,000 square foot warehouse market.

- Safeway entered the Florida market with an 84,000 square foot Pak N' Save.

Publix is one of the oldest and dominant food store chains in Florida. In 1984, it had sales of $3.2 billion in its 278 stores, all of which are located in Florida. In 1984, Mark Hollis became president of Publix after working his way up the organization ladder from clerk to store manager to director of warehousing and then to public affairs. Despite the intense competition in the Florida market and the entry of dominant out-of-state chains, Hollis is bullish on Publix.

He cites the Golden Rule, "the principle upon which George Jenkins founded the company 54 years ago," as the reason he thinks Publix flourishes and will continue to do so. "Our purpose is to operate the finest food stores in America, where customers find it a pleasure to shop and employees find it a pleasure to work. If we do that, we'll be just fine."

Questions

1. Evaluate Publix's mission. Is it as applicable today as it was fifty-four years ago?
2. How will Publix's mission influence its marketing strategy?

Source: Based in part on Robert E. O'Neill. "Publix: New Face, New Challenge," *Progressive Grocer* (January 1985), pp. 55–58.

6.

Hewlett-Packard: Strategies for Leadership

Hewlett-Packard Company is in one of the most dynamic periods of its forty-four-year history. It is a time of change in the needs of customers, in the technologies available to meet those needs, and in the size and shape of HP itself.

When a company changes as rapidly as HP, there is a possibility of it growing apart, of its product lines and operations diverging. For HP, the opposite is true. Its organization and products have become better integrated to shape and support the company's purpose.

Although HP's 6,400 products serve many different markets, their common purpose is to provide customers with the information needed to solve technical and business problems. HP's strength lies not only in its wide spectrum of products, but also in its ability to merge technologies to provide comprehensive solutions to a variety of specific problems. HP products are information tools in a three-tiered strategy.

Tier One

HP is continuing a strategy that has served it well over the years: offering products that represent state-of-the-art technology and that are useful on a stand-alone basis. Each product is a tool that provides information to help solve a problem, such as the measurement of an electronic function, the analysis of a chemical compound, the monitoring of a vital life sign, or the computation, analysis, display or transmission of data.

Tier Two

Joining individual products to create systems is a second way HP is making information an effective decision making tool. Increasingly, HP is designing its products as modules that can interact with other HP equipment or with products of other vendors. HP's systems may consist of test and measurement instruments, data-processing equipment, instrumentation for chemical analysis or medical monitoring, or combinations of these product groups.

This ability to combine product groups is one of HP's main strengths and is manifested in many ways. Networks of computers and personal workstations help organizations create, move, store and use information effectively. Measurement systems linked to computers translate what is happening on the factory floor into information that managers can use in decision making. In laboratories, analytical instruments and computers combine to computerize and automate the preparation and analysis of chemical compounds. In health care fa-cilities patient-monitoring and critical-care equipment, data management, financial and order-entry systems combine to improve care while helping control costs.

Tier Three

The third tier of HP's strategy is to provide software packages that further integrate HP equipment in order to solve customer problems. *Productivity networks* is the term HP used to describe its integrated software packages. Just as a system represents linked equipment, productivity networks represent software programs that are linked to provide total business solutions.

Some of these networks are designed to meet the needs of a wide variety of customers. For example, HP's Information Productivity Network allows any organization to effectively use word processing, data base management and electronic mail. Other productivity networks serve specific kinds of organizations, such as manufacturers, retail trade and distribution industries, laboratories, hospitals and educational and financial institutions.

HP's Manufacturer's Productivity Network (MPN) illustrates the combination of products, systems and software applications. MPN's goal is to build on a manufacturer's existing base of HP hardware and software and integrate the information used in activities such as computer-aided engineering, materials management and financial accounting. Individually, these application programs already offer powerful solutions to business problems. However, the MPN concept recognizes that the effectiveness of all software applications will be greatly enhanced when they "talk" to each other.

For example, computer-aided design products linked to automated test equipment will allow a manufacturer's engineering section to directly transmit its requirements and process constraints to the design team. Input from the marketing department—customer preferences and order forecasts—will be transmitted to both the engineering and manufacturing areas.

Whether in a manufacturing environment or a service organization, the possibilities for a constructive coupling of information are numerous. It is this linkage of software programs that is called for in HP's productivity network strategy.

State-of-the-art products, systems linking them together, and productivity networks to maximize their usefulness to customers—these are some of the ways HP is working to provide customers with the information they need to make their organizations more productive.

Questions

1. What is Hewlett-Packard's mission? How does this mission influence the firm's marketing strategy?
2. Evaluate Hewlett-Packard's three-tiered strategy. Could the three tiers be set up as strategic business units?

Source: *Hewlett-Packard Company 1983 Annual Report,* pp. 5, 7. Courtesy of Hewlett-Packard Company.

7.

Establishing a Dental Practice

In 1977, the U.S. Supreme Court ruled that advertising professional services and prices was legal. The Court held that this type of marketing effort was protected by the First Amendment of the U.S. Constitution. Since 1977, retail dentistry has grown rapidly. In retail dentistry, a dental clinic is opened in a discount or department store or as a separate operation in a retail shopping mall. Both Sears and Montgomery Ward are opening dental clinics in their stores. In addition, many retail dentistries are franchised operations.

Retail dentists tend to advertise heavily and offer attractive prices. They also tend to have long operating hours, often staying open until 9 P.M. and on Saturdays and Sundays.

Julie Foreman, a recently graduated dentist, is planning to open a practice in Tucson, Arizona. Although Tucson is oversupplied with dentists, Foreman wishes to establish a practice there anyway because the warm, dry desert climate is good for her serious arthritic condition. This is very important because she needs flexibility in her hands to perform good dental work. Tucson has many traditional dental clinics, both private and group practices, and also has several retail dentistries. She realizes that she cannot compete on a price basis with the 20 to 40 percent lower fees that retail dentistries charge.

Although retail dentistries do have some strong competitive advantages, they also have some drawbacks. Most important is that most retail dentistries have high turnover in their professional staff, which encourages a poor doctor-patient relationship. Also, retail dentistries tend to rush patients through the clinic and often provide a poor explanation of the work being performed.

Tucson, Arizona, is a city with many different types of households and neighborhoods. There are neighborhoods in the northwest and northeast foothills with extremely high income households. Many of these areas have homes in the $200,000 to $500,000 price category. On the other hand, areas in South Tucson have neighborhoods with very low household incomes, as well as educational levels. Many houses in this area are valued at less than $40,000. These households are predominantly of Spanish origin and are Spanish speaking. Other areas of Tucson contain households that fall between these two extremes.

Questions

1. How can Dr. Foreman compete if she cannot compete on a price basis?
2. How could Dr. Foreman go about developing a marketing strategy that centered around the three utilities that marketing provides?

UNDERSTANDING THE MARKETPLACE

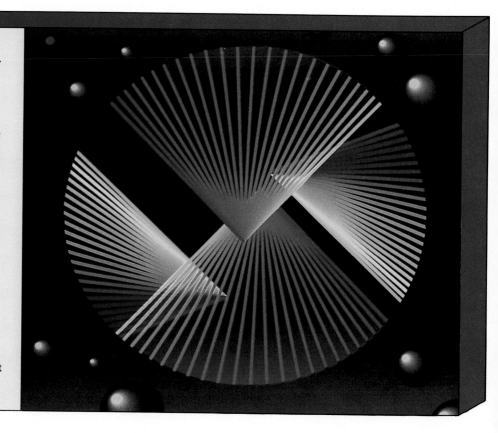

Part II of *Principles of Marketing* explores the dynamic arena in which marketing occurs. Chapter 4, "The Marketing Research Process and the Marketing Information System," discusses the role of marketing research and information in designing successful marketing programs. Chapter 5, "Consumer Buying Behavior," focuses on the factors that influence consumers' purchasing decisions. Chapter 6, "Organizational Markets and Buying Behavior," identifies different organizational markets and shows how they make purchasing decisions. Chapter 7, "Market Segmentation and Target Marketing," explains several approaches used to segment consumer and organizational markets and discusses how to select a target market.

## CHAPTER 4

THE MARKETING RESEARCH PROCESS AND THE MARKETING INFORMATION SYSTEM

MARKETER PROFILE

John Malec, William Walter, and Gerald Eskin of Information Resources, Inc.

John Malec had dreams of being a winner. He felt certain that his idea for a new kind of market research was a winner, but it took several years of searching for start-up capital and the right technology to prove it.

After studying marketing in college and spending three years in the U.S. Navy, Malec took a job with a research consulting firm. He later became owner in charge of the Chicago office of NPD Research Corp. (now NPD Group Inc.). Malec left his job at NPD in 1974 because of a difference of opinion about where the company should concentrate and expand. Malec was pushing for putting capital into electronic data-gathering equip-ment, but his partners at NPD did not agree.

Shortly thereafter, Malec met and formed a working relationship with Gerald Eskin and Penny Baron, both marketing professors at the University of Iowa. The three formed a partnership based on their vision to create the "perfect marketing research instrument." This revolutionary new device gathers data through electronic monitoring equipment connected through cable television and supermarket checkout scanners and then correlates the data with a computer. Because none of the three partners had the necessary background in designing computer systems, another partner was recruited. It was Bill Walter's job to develop the computer programs that would catalog all the items in a grocery store and tie the purchase of those items to the television monitoring results. The system that evolved from all this planning and hard work is called BehaviorScan.

Information Resources Inc. (IRI) uses BehaviorScan to collect data from 24,000 households, 3,000 in each of eight representative markets. In each of these markets, supermarket scanning and cable TV are predominant. Each of these households has a plastic identification card that is presented to the cashier when the household members go through the checkout lane at local supermarkets. This allows IRI to maintain a computer file on the purchases of each

household. In each participant's home, a microcomputer on the back of the TV set tracks viewing habits. In return for participating, each household is given a $20 annual prize and a chance to win weekly prizes ranging from $15 items to a one-week trip for two to Mexico.

Some of IRI's clients are Procter & Gamble, Campbell Soup, General Foods, and Ralston Purina. The IRI technology allows these clients to replace existing commercials with new ones and to test these in the homes of the BehaviorScan participants. However, IRI can only change advertisements for time slots the client has already purchased. This facility allows IRI to test the effectiveness of new ads because the shopping pat-

terns of the households viewing the new ads can be monitored through supermarket scanning.

Penny Baron left the company in 1981 to return to her teaching career. When IRI went public in March 1983, its shares traded at eighty-eight times their 1982 earnings and each of the founders became a multimillionaire. IRI was truly a winner.

Source: Fern Schumer. "The New Magicians of Market Research," *Fortune* (July 25, 1983), pp. 72–74; Gian M. Fulgoni and Gerald J. Eskin. "The BehaviorScan Research Facility for Studying Retail Shopping Patterns," in William R. Darden and Robert F. Lusch (eds.), *Patronage Behavior and Retail Management* (New York: Elsevier Science Publishers, 1983); Richard Kreisman. "Buy the Numbers," *Inc.* (March 1985), pp. 104–112.

INTRODUCTION

Marketing managers need adequate information to make good decisions, although the nature of this information may vary considerably. Consider the area of retail marketing. Information Resources used the BehaviorScan to monitor consumers' shopping and viewing habits. Another marketer might obtain information by regularly reading the advertisements of competing retailers and occasionally visiting their stores. Still another retailer might conduct quarterly price audits of major competitors to obtain information on its price competitiveness.

Many firms use the marketing research process to aid their managers in making good decisions. The marketing research process is actually a subsystem of the larger marketing information system, but since it is the most widely used part, we will discuss it first. Then we will deal with the other subsystems of the marketing information system: the accounting system, the marketing intelligence system, and the marketing models system.

THE MARKETING RESEARCH PROCESS

Marketing research, as defined by the American Marketing Association, is *"the systematic gathering, recording, and analyzing of data about problems related to the marketing of goods and services."*[1] The five most common types of research activities are (1) determination of market characteristics, (2) measurement of market potentials, (3) market share analysis, (4) sales analysis, and (5) studies of business trends. Table 4.1 profiles the research activities of 599 companies involved in manufacturing consumer or industrial products, financial services, marketing research and consulting, pub-

Table 4.1 Research Activities of 599 Companies

Research Activities	Percent Doing	Percent Done by Marketing Research Dept.	Percent Done by Another Dept. in Firm	Percent Done by Outside Firm
Determination of market characteristics	97	88	3	6
Measurement of market potentials	97	88	4	6
Market share analysis	97	85	6	6
Sales analysis	92	67	23	2
Studies of business trends	91	68	20	3

Source: Dik Warren Twedt (ed.). *1983 Survey of Marketing Research* (Chicago: American Marketing Association 1983), p. 41.

lishing and broadcasting, advertising, health services, retailing, and whole-saling.

The marketing research process is a tool that helps managers wisely or adequately resolve marketing problems.[2] A simple model of the marketing research process called **SELECT** shows the steps in solving a marketing problem. **SELECT** is an acronym for *the six steps in marketing research:*

1. *Situation analysis.*
2. *Explicitly stating the problem.*
3. *Laying out the research design and collecting data.*
4. *Evaluating research results and making a decision.*
5. *Creating a plan to implement the decision.*
6. *Testing the correctness of the decision.*

We will explain these six steps in the following sections.

Situation Analysis

At the initial stage of the marketing research process, a problem confronts the company or marketing department; usually, this problem is not specifically defined or is incorrectly defined. The marketing manager often begins to realize a problem exists when organizational objectives are not met. For example, the organization may have anticipated a 10 percent sales gain last quarter, but sales only grew 3 percent, or the company may have had a target of filling and shipping 95 percent of its orders within 24 hours, but it may have only filled 88 percent in that time. These are only *symptoms* of the problem, however. The actual problem is determining why sales only grew 3 percent, not that sales grew only 3 percent rather than 10 percent. Was it due to noncompetitive pricing? Foreign competition entering the market? A recession in the industry?

To help identify the true problem(s) rather than the symptoms, a firm should conduct a situation analysis. A **situation analysis** is *an investigation of the factors internal and external to the firm that potentially relate to the problem area.* In a situation analysis, the marketing manager or researcher relies on secondary data about the firm or the external environments and its publics. **Secondary data** is *data that has already been collected or published for purposes other than the one immediately at hand.* The secondary data could come from sources inside the firm, in which case they are usually accounting data such as invoices or charge accounts, data from prior research studies, or other regularly collected data such as warranty cards. The secondary data could come from outside sources as well, which means that another organization collected and published the data for other purposes.

To continue with the prior example, perhaps the marketing researcher locates a study conducted by a trade association that shows that total industry sales have fallen two quarters in a row and that last quarter they fell 2 percent. Since the firm's sales actually grew 3 percent, the situation is not so bad despite the fact that the company had a 10 percent sales growth goal. Perhaps the real problem was that the 10 percent growth goal was unrealistic given the fact that industry sales were actually declining.

Secondary data should be used whenever possible because they are readily available (i.e., timely), and are relatively low cost compared with primary data. **Primary data**, *data collected explicitly to solve a particular problem,* often need to be collected, since secondary data frequently are not sufficient to solve the problem at hand. Table 4.2 presents a partial list of potentially useful outside sources of secondary data.

Explicitly Stating the Problem

Once the situation has been analyzed, the marketing manager or researcher should be in a good position to explicitly state what he or she *believes* to be the problem. This problem statement is then followed by a *hypothesis,* which attempts to identify the *cause* of some event. Technically, a hypothesis does not need to state a causal relationship, it merely needs to state what one expects to occur or to be the true situation. A hypothesis is an educated guess or hunch based on the situation analysis and the manager's experience. The following are some examples of hypotheses that marketing managers or researchers might develop:

Table 4.2   External Sources of Secondary Data Important to Marketers

External Source	Brief Description
Government data	Most federal government agencies will provide secondary data. Perhaps most important to marketers is the Bureau of the Census. The housing and population census is conducted every 10 years, in years ending in zero. The following census studies are conducted every 5 years, in years ending in two and seven: retail trade, wholesale trade, manufacturing, agriculture, transportation, services, and local governments.
Trade associations	Every major industry has its own professional trade association. These associations, such as the National Association of Wholesalers, National Tire Dealers and Retreaders Association, Retail Hardware Association, regularly conduct research on industry trends and disseminate this information to member firms.
Commercial publications	Many magazines that focus on particular industries or functional areas in business conduct special research studies that are included in special issues of the magazine. Some of these magazines are *Sales and Marketing Management, Fortune, Advertising Age, BusinessWeek, Chain Store Age, Automotive News,* and *Progressive Grocer.*
Syndicated research houses	Some private research firms produce syndicated data—standardized data collected and sold to many customers. Some of the more popular firms are A.C. Nielsen, Daniel Starch Co., Arbitron, and SAMI.
Nonprofit research foundations and academic associations	Numerous nonprofit organizations often sponsor marketing research projects, including the Marketing Science Institute and the Institute of Retail Management. Also, associations such as the American Marketing Association publish research journals such as the *Journal of Marketing* and the *Journal of Marketing Research.*

1. Sales declined because consumers became dissatisfied with our product quality.
2. Sales declined because our advertising effectiveness declined.
3. Sales decined because our retailers devoted less shelf space to our product and more shelf space to competitor products.

Note that each of these hypotheses identifies a purported cause of the sales decline. When an explicit cause is stated, it is easier to design a research study to determine whether to accept or reject the hypothesis. The Marketing in Action on page 96 shows how the U.S. Army used marketing research to develop a new recruiting plan.

Laying Out Research Design and Collecting Data

With a specific hypothesis or hypotheses in mind, the market researcher can lay out the research design and then proceed to collect the necessary data. A **research design** is *a blueprint or map for obtaining and collecting*

MARKETING IN ACTION

Switching to an all-volunteer enlistment policy created a major problem for the U.S. Army in 1973. The army needed 780,000 enlistments or reenlistments annually, and such a large need for human resources put the army "in direct competition with civilian businesses and universities." The army decided to use marketing research in order to help identify factors that could improve recruiting efforts. Consider the following examples:

- "A 1981 study showed that the over-21 age group consistently scored higher in mental aptitude tests than younger recruits." Advertisements appealing to this age group could be used to improve the quality of recruits.

Marketing Research Helps U.S. Government Develop Volunteer Army

- "A 1982 study measured youth attitudes toward recruiting incentives. As a result, the army modified its enlistment bonuses. To appeal to those who wanted to pursue a higher education, a $15,200 continuing education benefit for two-year enlistees was instituted. To encourage longer term enlistments, a $5,000 bonus for four-year enlistees was put in place."

- Another recent study predicted that a policy of "leaner and meaner"

weight requirements would result in a 20 percent drop in new recruits.

One of the most successful uses of marketing research was the development of the U.S. Army's "Be all that you can be" campaign. Marketing research findings "indicated the need to deemphasize the militaristic aspects of the service and instead promote the job training opportunities, particularly in high technology fields." This campaign ranks as the most recognizable of all military advertising campaigns.

Source: Based on "Today's Army Relying on Marketing Research to Attain Recruitment Goals," *Marketing News* (July 6, 1984), pp. 1, 16.

the primary data needed to test a hypothesis. There are five sequential steps in the research design process: (1) design a list of data requirements, (2) design a method for collecting data, (3) design data collection forms, (4) design a sampling plan, and (5) design a data analysis plan.

Designing a List of Data Requirements. The first step in the research design process is to identify the data that need to be collected to test a hypothesis. For each concept in the hypothesis, the researcher must identify the specific data that will be used to measure that concept.[3] This step appears to be obvious but is often overlooked. Consider the following hypothesis developed by the research director of a chain of women's apparel stores:

> **Women with a high fashion orientation will patronize our store more regularly.**

This hypothesis states that a cause of patronage at this store is high fashion orientation. The more fashion oriented a customer is, the more likely she is to patronize this store. Fashion orientation and patronage need to be measured, but first they must be defined. Does *patronage* mean (1) the number of times a month a customer shops at the store, (2) the amount of money a customer spends per month at the store, or (3) the percentage of her apparel expenditures that she makes at this store? Each of these is a measure of patronage, but what specific data or measure is needed? Are all three measures needed? The answer often depends on the problem's importance and the amount of time and money available for the study. In this example, it probably would be quite easy to obtain at least two of the patronage measures.

Trying to measure fashion orientation might be more difficult than measuring patronage. The excerpted questionnaire in Table 4.3 shows how one retailer tried to do this.

Designing a Method for Collecting Data. A variety of methods can be used to collect primary data, and each method has certain situations for which it is most appropriate. The three principal methods for collecting primary data are (1) the observation method, (2) the survey method, and (3) the experimental method.

With the **observation method**, *data are obtained by watching human behavior.* The prime advantage of this method is that no one is questioned directly, and ideally, the people being observed are unaware or unaffected

Table 4.3   Excerpt from Telephone Survey on Fashion Orientation

HELLO, this is —————— with Colt Research. I am conducting a market research survey about consumer shopping habits.

1. *Is this/May I speak to* the lady of the house?
    IF THERE IS NO FEMALE HEAD OF HOUSEHOLD, TERMINATE.
    IF NEW PERSON, REPEAT INTRODUCTION.
2. I am going to read you some statements about shopping and other activities. Using a scale from one to ten, tell me how true the statement is for you. A one means that the statement is *never* true for you. A ten means that the statement is *always* true for you. If it is true *about half of the time,* you would say five. You may choose *any number* from one to ten. Do you understand the scale?
    Using *any number* from one to ten, how true is this statement for you? CONTINUE FOR EACH STATEMENT.

	Never			Sometimes						Always
2.1 I go to more social events than most people do.	1	2	3	4	5	6	7	8	9	10
2.2 I usually buy new products before my neighbors do.	1	2	3	4	5	6	7	8	9	10
2.3 I am very concerned about clothing fashions.	1	2	3	4	5	6	7	8	9	10
2.4 When selecting clothing, I like to be ahead of the crowd, among the first with a new look.	1	2	3	4	5	6	7	8	9	10
2.5 I look and dress the way I want regardless of whether others like it.	1	2	3	4	5	6	7	8	9	10
2.6 When shopping for clothing, I often buy at stores where I can get name brands for less.	1	2	3	4	5	6	7	8	9	10

by the observer. As the observers often are paid for "waste time" when there is nothing to observe, this method can be expensive.

To illustrate the observation method, consider a K mart store that has had a six-month decline in sales. A few years ago, when the store was doing well, a research study found that over 40 percent of the K mart customers lived more than four miles from the store. Last year, two additional discount department stores opened in the area; one located two miles to the east, and the other four miles to the west. Thus, the manager hypothesized that store sales dropped because the number of shoppers living more than four miles from the store declined as a result of this new competition.

To test this hypothesis, someone was stationed in the parking lot at random hours of the day over several weeks, to write down shoppers' car license numbers. The researcher then went to the county motor vehicle department and, by tracing these license numbers, obtained the addresses of the shoppers. These addresses were then plotted on a map so that the researcher could observe whether less than 40 percent of shoppers live more than four miles from the store.

Some other techniques of the observation method of data collection involve taking pictures or films of people shopping; connecting devices to their television or radios to monitor their media habits; and simply observing people in a consumer setting. For example, toy manufacturers often observe children at play with toys in an attempt to determine the appeal of certain toys.

In the **survey method** of data collection, *people are questioned directly by telephone, mail, or personal interviews.* The *telephone method* involves answering questions posed by an interviewer over the phone. The *mail method* requires the respondent to answer and return a printed questionnaire. The *personal interview method* occurs face-to-face, with the interviewer recording responses on some type of form. Each of these three methods of surveying has advantages and disadvantages, which are profiled in Table 4.4.

The **experimental method** is *a procedure in which the researcher assesses how changes in manipulated variables affect other variables; the factor to be assessed is called the dependent variable, and the factors that affect it are called the independent variables.* To ascertain the effect of the independent variables on the dependent variable, the experimenter holds most of the independent variables constant while varying (i.e., manipulating) one or two and watching the resulting impact on the dependent variable.[4] Suppose, for example, you hypothesize that retail shelf space affects your product's sales. To test this hypothesis you could randomly vary the amount of shelf space devoted to your product and then investigate the impact on sales. If you had thirty stores to use in your experiment, you could randomly assign ten of them to have 40 linear feet of shelf space, ten to have 50 linear feet, and ten to have 60 linear feet. By holding advertising, prices, and store hours constant at each of the stores, you could isolate the impact of shelf space on sales. This experiment is illustrated in Figure 4.1.

Table 4.4   Advantages and Disadvantages of Different Surveys

Survey	Advantages	Disadvantages
Telephone	Quick to execute	Length of time you can keep people on phone limits the amount of data that can be collected
	Moderately expensive	Often phone numbers are unlisted or a list of phone numbers of target group may not be available
	Good control of sample	
Mail	Inexpensive	Slow in getting responses
	Good for sensitive questions	Poor control of sample (high nonresponse)
	Allows collection of fair quantity of data	Cannot clarify question if it is not understood by respondent
Personal interview	Good control of sample	Expensive
	Allows collection of large quantity of data	Interviewer cheating possible
	Can clarify confusing questions	Biased responses for sensitive questions

Manufacturers will often conduct experiments when introducing new products. For instance, the company might select four cities to *test market* (i.e., have a trial marketing program) a product. The four cities selected would be relatively equal demographically and competitively. The new product would be priced high in two of the test cities and low in the other two cities. In a few months, sales could be analyzed across the four cities to assess the impact of price on sales volume.

Designing Data Collection Forms.   All methods for collecting data require some type of data collection form. For an observation study, the observer may simply place check marks on a pad of paper when a certain type of behavior is seen. In an experiment, a form may be used to record results. The survey method uses the most sophisticated data collection form because usually a specific set of questions must be asked and answered. Since an adequate discussion of the considerations in questionnaire design is beyond the scope of this text, you may want to consult some additional sources.[5] We will focus our discussion on types of questions and the criteria of a good question.

Basically, two types of questions can be asked: open-ended and closed-ended. With an *open-ended question,* no possible response categories are suggested to the interviewee; for example:

Why did you purchase a new car?

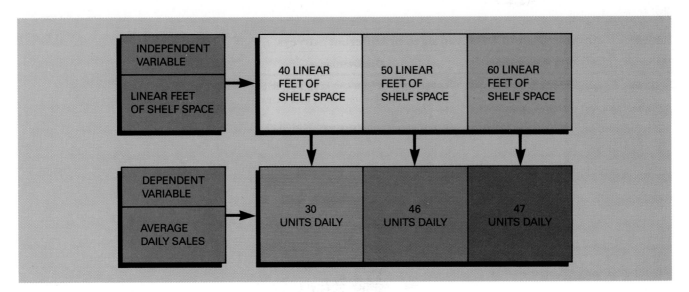

Figure 4.1
The Experimental Method

The respondent is given maximum freedom of response with an open-ended question, which can have both advantages and disadvantages. The major advantage is that no researcher bias is built into the question. The respondent can answer without being forced to check certain well-established response categories. As a result, open-ended responses can be quite insightful and allow the researcher to uncover areas he or she had not anticipated. The major disadvantage of an open-ended question is that the responses are difficult to categorize and analyze because they take so many different forms. Consider the following four answers to the preceding question:

Why did you purchase a new car?
1. "Because my existing car was too old."
2. "Because the new car was on sale."
3. "Because I thought it was a good idea and I really wanted a new car."
4. "I am not sure. . . . It sure does get good mileage, and it even performs well . . . but I guess it was because of the special interest rate. I certainly couldn't have purchased it unless I got that salary raise last month."

Now, consider asking this question to 500 people and all the possible responses that might be obtained and the difficulty in categorizing those varied responses. For this reason, closed-end questions are often preferred.

The possible responses or answers are supplied in a *closed-ended question*. This requires the researcher to identify the possible answers before the data are collected. As a result, the data collection will only provide information on the frequency of certain responses to a question. Closed-

Survey research is becoming a popular method of collecting data on international markets.

ended questions can be dichotomous (only two responses possible) or multichotomous (more than two answers possible).

An example of a dichotomous question is:

"Would you consider purchasing a new television in the next six months?"
___ yes
___ no

An example of a multichotomous question is:

"Would you consider purchasing a new television in the next six months?"
___ **definitely yes**
___ **probably yes**
___ **not sure**
___ **probably not**
___ **definitely not**

The major advantage of closed-ended questions is that the results are easy to categorize and analyze because all answers must fit into prescribed categories. The major disadvantage is that the response categories may not include one for the respondent's true feelings. Consider the preceding dichotomous question. The respondent could answer yes or no, but perhaps most respondents are undecided and would prefer to say *maybe.* Without that possibility, however, they may tend to answer *no* more frequently than truly represents their underlying feeling or belief.

When designing a questionnaire, it is not easy to develop effective questions. Effective question construction is an art form that takes years to develop. There are, however, six criteria to consider for an effective question; it must be (1) relevant, (2) clear, (3) brief, (4) unoffensive, (5) unbiased, and (6) specific.[6]

A *relevant* question is pertinent to the particular research objectives; it furthers the search for needed information. Often, questionnaire designers get carried away with their own interests and include a question because it would be interesting to know how people would respond to it. Questions should not be included merely because the results would be interesting. By only asking questions that pertain to the research objective, the questionnaire length can be kept to a minimum, and this will help ensure that a larger number of people will complete the questionnaire.

A good question should also be *clear* in its meaning. Each word in the question must be understandable to the respondents. Therefore, the respondents' education and background should be kept in mind so that the proper vocabulary can be used. You do not want to use words that people cannot understand, and you do not want to use words that have different meanings to different people. For example, say you are researching shopping patterns and ask people if they would travel a long distance to buy their favorite brand of beer. A long distance may be a mile to a New York City dweller, but it may be 25 miles to someone in Wyoming.

Questions should be *brief*—generally twenty words or less—and clearly stated. Respondents get less confused by brief questions than by excessively wordy ones.

Questions should never be asked in an *offensive* manner. For example, if you are asking people about their income, you would not ask them if their income was above $40,000 or below $40,000. This kind of question puts most respondents in an embarrassing position because they need to say "below $40,000." A better alternative would be to give them several ranges with the lowest one well below what most people would earn—say, $7,500.

Questions should not be worded so that they *bias* the respondent. For example, you wouldn't ask, "Don't you think the U.S. president is doing a good job handling foreign affairs?" Rather, you would ask, "Is the U.S. president doing a good job in handling foreign affairs?"

Finally, questions should be *specific* and deal with only one particular topic at a time. You would not ask, "Do you think that BMWs are safe and fuel-efficient automobiles?" To be able to interpret your results, you should break this into two questions: "Do you think that BMWs are safe automobiles?" and "Do you think BMWs are fuel-efficient automobiles?"

As the preceding discussion has illustrated, writing effective questions for questionnaires is difficult. Since even the experienced marketing researcher can make mistakes, many firms insist on *questionnaire pretesting*, which consists of administering the questionnaire to a small group before using it to gather information from the entire survey group. This added step is relatively inexpensive and can help identify questions that are irrelevant, unclear, too wordy, offensive, biased, or too general.

Designing a Sampling Plan. Almost all marketing research projects require a sample of the population because it is too costly in terms of time and money to contact all the people in the study population. For example, if ABC wanted to research the media habits and preferences of U.S. households, it could not afford to interview over 70 million households. Instead, it would take a sample of this population—perhaps 2,000 households. If these 2,000 households are to be used to draw conclusions about the total population, they must be representative of the total population. A representative sample can be obtained using a good sampling plan.[7]

There are two basic types of sampling plans: a probability sampling plan and a nonprobability sampling plan. In a **probability sample**, *each individual in the population has a known probability of being selected.* Say,

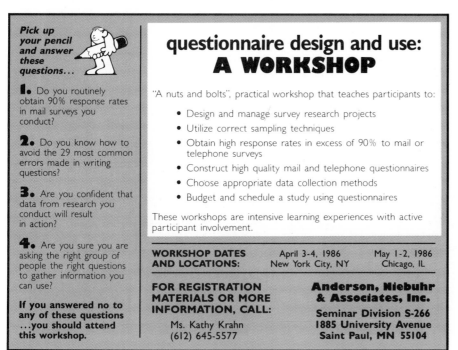

Attending workshops and seminars on questionnaire design helps the marketer develop better research skills.

for example, that your classroom has 58 students and that each of you writes your name on a card and puts it into a hat. If one name is drawn from the hat, then you have a known probability of 1 in 58 of being the drawn name. Because there is a known probability for each individual, the researcher can estimate what is known as *sampling error.* Sampling error is a measure of the extent to which the sample can be expected to mirror the population on the characteristics or phenomena being studied. On the other hand, in a **nonprobability sample**, *the probability of a person being included in the sample is unknown;* thus, sampling error cannot be assessed. For obvious reasons, the researcher usually prefers a probability sample. The major types of sampling plans are shown in Figure 4.2.

The three most common types of probability sampling are (1) simple random sampling, (2) cluster sampling, and (3) stratified sampling. With *simple random sampling,* every element in the population has an equal chance of being selected as part of the sample. Recall the example in which ABC decided to interview 2,000 households. A simple random sample would require that ABC have a list of all households in the United States (the population to be studied) from which 2,000 households would be selected at random. This could be accomplished by numbering the households consecutively and then allowing ABC's computer to generate a random list of 2,000 numbers to determine which households to interview.

As you might expect, simple random sampling can become quite time

Figure 4.2

Major Sampling Plans

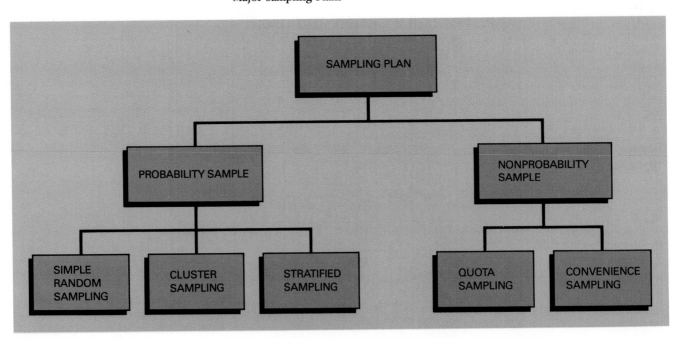

consuming because of the effort typically required to develop a list of the population elements. Consequently, cluster sampling may be used instead. With *cluster sampling,* the total population can be broken down into a number of mutually exclusive groups (usually geographic areas) where each element in the population belongs to one and only one group. A random sample of these groups is then selected, and if necessary, a random sample of elements in the selected clusters could be chosen. For example, the total households in the United States could be clustered into 90,000 groups according to the census track. If ABC wanted to interview 2,000 households, it could randomly select 200 census tracks and then randomly select ten households to interview in each census track.

A third form of probability sampling is stratified sampling. In *stratified sampling,* the population is broken down into more homogeneous segments according to a common characteristic and a random sample of each of these segments is conducted. For instance, ABC might believe that media habits are different for households in communities with less than 50,000 people, 50,000 to 500,000 people, and over 500,000 people. If stratified sampling were used, ABC would group the population by community size and then randomly sample the individuals within each group. This would ensure that ABC had a representative sample from each of these strata (in this case, community size). The difference between cluster and stratified sampling is that in cluster sampling not every cluster or group is selected for sampling, whereas in stratified sampling, all strata or groups are selected for sampling.

Most nonprobability samples are of two types: (1) a convenience sample or (2) a quota sample. A *convenience sample* is based on obtaining respondents who are convenient or easily accessible. For example, friends, relatives, or acquaintances may be interviewed, or the researcher may simply stand on the street corner of a busy intersection and interview pedestrians while they wait for a traffic light to change. A *quota sample* involves interviewing people who meet certain criteria regardless of where they are located or how they are contacted. For instance, the researcher may decide to interview 100 people; thirty-five white men, thirty-five white women, fifteen black men, and fifteen black women, all over the age of 18 years. The interviewer would find this quota of people and interview them. Once fifteen female blacks over 18 years of age had been interviewed, the interviewer would not interview any more black women.

The advantage of nonprobability sampling over probability sampling is that it is less expensive. Its drawback is that the individuals chosen in nonprobability sampling may not be representative of the relevant population. Therefore, the market researcher must determine the need for precise research results and choose the sampling plan accordingly.

Designing a Data Analysis Plan. Once the data have been collected, the marketing researcher must be able to analyze them. For example, Table 4.5 shows the results of a survey in a large southwestern city on the radio programming preferences of the population. Table 4.5 shows a one-way

Table 4.5   Radio Programming Preferences

Radio Programming Format	Frequency of Responses (%)
Beautiful music	12
Classical	8
Country	28
Middle-of-the-road	16
Rock	30
Soul	6
Total	100

frequency distribution; from it, you can discern the popularity of different radio formats. The most popular formats are rock music and country music. Now, if you refer to Table 4.6, you will see how a two-way analysis of the data tells a richer story. In a two-way analysis, responses are cross-tabulated by two variables; in this case, radio program preferences are cross-tabulated by respondents' age. Rock music is the most popular format for respondents aged 13 to 24 years, whereas middle-of-the-road music is most popular for respondents over 45 years of age.

There are many techniques for analyzing data, and it is fair to say that there is no single best technique for all situations. Marketing researchers and the decision makers who use marketing research data should become familiar with the advantages and disadvantages of the many alternative statistical techniques for data analysis. The statistical analysis is beyond the scope of this text; however, many excellent books are available on this topic.[8]

Evaluating Research Results and Making a Decision

After the data have been collected and analyzed, the results must be evaluated and the decision made. In order for decision makers to properly evaluate research, the researcher must clearly communicate the results in a written and/or oral report.[9] (Table 4.7 provides some guidelines for developing a good written research report.)

With the research report in hand, management can now make a decision. As we said before, the marketing researcher is not the decision maker. The marketing researcher is a staff person who advises management, but he or she does not decide on the course of action the firm will take. However, the researcher can and often does play a key role in suggesting which decisions the data strongly support. In this sense, the researcher is a key influencer of decisions.[10]

Table 4.6   Radio Programming Preferences by Age Category

Radio Programming Format	Age Category (yr)			
	13–24	**25–35**	**36–44**	**45 +**
Beautiful music	6 %	10 %	16 %	17 %
Classical	2	4	11	18
Country	20	35	28	18
Middle-of-the-road	14	16	24	28
Rock	48	30	17	15
Soul	10	5	4	4
Total	100 %	100 %	100 %	100 %

Creating a Plan to Implement the Decision

After a decision has been made, a plan must be developed stating how and when to implement the decision. Since this may involve more marketing research, we consider it part of the research process. Assume that a firm does some research and decides, based on the results, to change a product's name. How should the firm go about changing the name? What time of year should the change take place? Should it notify its distributors of the anticipated change, or wait and let them know at the same time the consumer is informed? The marketing researcher usually does not develop the imple-

Some firms such as SDR specialize in providing data analysis and data processing services.

Table 4.7   Guidelines for Developing an Effective Research Report

Know your audience	A research report must effectively communicate relevant information to decision makers. You should know who the decision makers are and use a vocabulary appropriate for them. Use only familiar words and avoid slang and technical jargon. Keep in mind that all research has objectives; try to communicate how the research findings meet these objectives and relate to the information needs of the decision makers.
Get to the point, but be complete	Remember that the decision makers have time constraints and only want the information that will help them make a decision. Consequently, try to cover the important points and exclude the trivial aspects, even if they are interesting.
Objectivity is essential	The researcher is only a reporter of facts and should avoid conveying any value judgments. It is not the researcher's role to sell the results. Also, if the results are likely to disappoint the decision makers or conflict with their views of the world, the researcher should not try to soften the impact by cleverly writing around the issue. In short, the researcher must objectively report the results and objectively assess their validity. The decision makers can then either accept or reject the findings based on their experience.

mentation plan, but the researcher does make recommendations and may suggest that more research is needed in specific areas of the plan. With the research results and the market researcher's recommendations, the advertising manager or product manager (or whatever manager is responsible for the decision) can make and implement the decision.

Testing the Correctness of the Decision

The last step in the SELECT model is testing the correctness of the decision. This is an important part of a manager's and a researcher's learning process; you can better learn about the validity of your theories and judgments if you systematically observe the results of your decisions to see if they bring the anticipated results. For example, if you conduct research that leads you to raise your product quality as a means of increasing sales only to find after implementing this decision that product sales did not change, then you have learned something about the relationship between product quality and sales volume. When a decision produces an unintended consequence, a hypothesis should be developed to explain this result. In the preceding example, you might hypothesize that increased product quality will only increase sales if the customer perceives the increase in product quality. If this hypothesis is found to be true, then in the future when you increase product quality, you will also advertise to the customer that the product quality has risen so that the customer will become aware of the change.

Now that you have become familiar with the marketing research process, you can appreciate the value of the information it can provide. This valuable information is not without cost, however. Even a modest survey can cost $5,000, and some large-scale surveys cost in excess of $100,000.

Essentially, marketing research is conducted to help the organization better practice and implement the marketing concept. Marketing research will help the firm select better target markets and offer them the right product with the right promotion at the right place and the right price. Thus, research is intended to improve the quality of decision making. Nonetheless, a firm must always make a tradeoff between the cost of the research and its value. Its value is the expected increase in profits or, in the case of nonprofit organizations, some other objective resulting from improved decision making. Marketing research should only be done if its expected value exceeds its costs.

Many firms do not conduct marketing research, but instead rely on the expertise and judgment of their marketing managers. In a study of 261 firms, one marketing professor found that over 50 percent allocated none of their marketing budget to marketing research. In fact, only about 10 percent of the firms allocated more than 5 percent of their marketing budgets to research. Some of the firms that decided to spend nothing on research obviously made a "deliberate management decision not to engage in marketing research, based on careful and objective evaluation of the potential benefits and costs of marketing research."[11] Other possible explanations for the absence of marketing research are (1) a lack of management support for, or trust in, marketing research; (2) a misunderstanding, or maybe even lack of knowledge, about the potential benefits of marketing research; (3) an erroneous belief that a firm cannot afford marketing research because of the circumstances under which it operates.

The preceding discussion illustrated that marketing research can be an important source of information that can help managers make better marketing decisions. However, many organizations have gone beyond conducting marketing research to get marketing information and have developed marketing information systems.

THE MARKETING INFORMATION SYSTEM

A **marketing information system (MIS)** is *a blueprint for the continual and periodic systematic collection, analysis, and reporting of relevant data about any past, present, or future developments that could or already have influenced the firm's marketing performance.* Several prominent features of the MIS should be highlighted:

1. Both *continual* and *periodic* collection of *relevant* data should occur. Data should be collected *continually* on those activities that are always in a state of flux, such as the organization's sales and profits or competitor behavior. Data should be collected *periodically* when a nonrecurring problem arises, such as the level of advertising to place on a new product or how to set up a new marketing channel to reach a new market segment. Only the information that is pertinent to the decision-making process should be collected.

2. *Analysis and reporting* of data are important parts of the MIS. You cannot give a marketing manager a computer tape with 500,000 bits of data; the information is not useful until it is analyzed and placed in a reportable and understandable format.

3. The data can be about *past, present,* and *future* developments, all of which can be relevant for marketing decision making. Most accounting information is historical; it tells how the marketer has performed. However, retail point-of-sale (POS) terminals provide data on what is happening now (present), and six-month monetary projections by the Federal Reserve Board tell what interest rates are likely to do in the future.

Figure 4.3 outlines an MIS and its major subsystems: (1) the marketing research system, (2) the accounting system, (3) the marketing intelligence system, and (4) the marketing models system.[12] This diagram also shows that data are collected from both the firm's external environments and the publics that it serves (see Chapter 2). After the data have been processed and analyzed in one or several of these subsystems, they are reported to marketing decision makers. Let's examine each of the major subsystems of the MIS in more detail.

Marketing Research System

The market research process, detailed earlier in the chapter, is part of the larger MIS. Aided by the marketing models system, it is specifically concerned with problem solving. The accounting system and the marketing intelligence systems, on the other hand, are primarily concerned with identifying potential problems and reporting what has happened and what is happening in the marketplace.

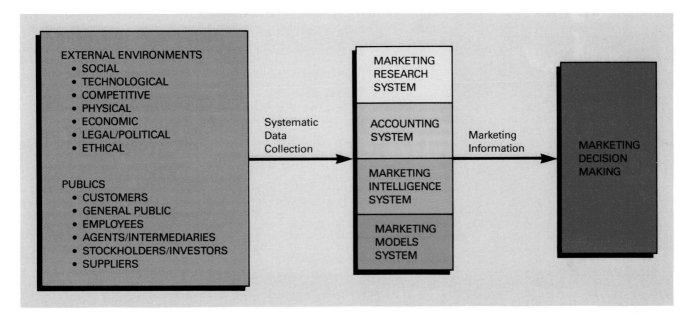

Figure 4.3
The Marketing Information System

Accounting System

A firm's *accounting system* is the set of procedures developed for recording monetary transactions and is a valuable source of information to marketing managers.[13] An example will help illustrate this point. Assume that you are the marketing vice president of the XYZ Drill and Lathe Company. Your company sells two major lines of industrial machinery, industrial power drills and lathes, and these products are sold in the northeastern and midwestern United States. The year 1986 has ended, and sales for your company fell from $25,000,000 in 1985 to $22,000,000 in 1986. This information alone does not tell you much; however, Figure 4.4 separates the sales of the XYZ Drill and Lathe Company by territory and product line for 1985 and 1986. You see that sales in the Northeast actually rose from $15,000,000 to $16,000,000 during that period. On the other hand, sales in the Midwest declined 40 percent from $10,000,000 to $6,000,000. The problem is clearly in the Midwest. Next, you should note that sales of industrial drills in the Midwest stayed at $3,000,000 each year, whereas sales of lathes dropped from $7,000,000 in 1985 to $3,000,000 in 1986. You can see that your major problem is with lathes in the Midwest.[14]

There are many other uses of accounting data besides the one just

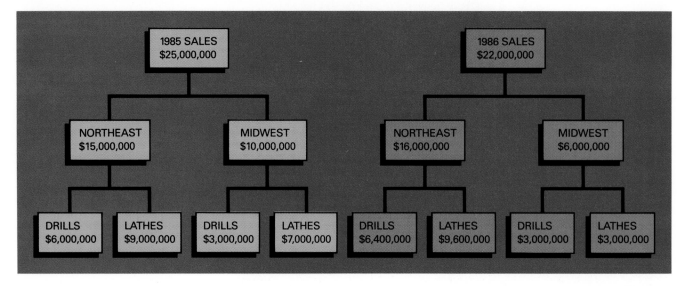

Figure 4.4
XYZ Drill and Lathe Company: 1985 Versus 1986 Sales

illustrated, and these will be discussed in Chapter 21. For the time being, you should recognize that the accounting system can be very helpful in identifying a firm's strengths and weaknesses—important ingredients in the strategic planning process discussed in Chapter 3.

Marketing Intelligence System

The accounting system deals with data and information on past occurrences, while the marketing intelligence system tends to focus on current events or occurrences that may affect a firm's future performance. The **marketing intelligence system** continually *monitors relevant data about an organization's external environments and publics.*[15] Recall from our discussion of strategic planning in Chapter 3 that it was important to monitor external environments and the firm's publics so that opportunities and threats could be identified. Following are some examples of how a firm can get an inexpensive, regular flow of data on the external environments and its publics:

1. Subscriptions to trade news publications, such as *Retail Home Furnishings, Progressive Grocer, Hardlines Wholesaling, Building Supply News,* and *Automotive News.*
2. Subscriptions to general business publications, such as *Fortune,* the *Wall Street Journal,* and *BusinessWeek.*
3. Annual reports to stockholders and news releases of competitors.
4. Salespeople's information.

5. Subscription research services, such as A.C. Nielsen Company, Daniel Yankelovich, Inc., and Information Resources Inc.

6. Industry trade shows.

7. Computerized literature search, which is the use of the firm's computer system to scan the national news for articles on specified subjects.

Marketing Models System

Increasingly, marketing managers are using models to assist them in making decisions.[16] A *model* is an abstraction of reality. A **marketing model** is *an abstraction of some real marketing phenomena to be used as a frame of reference to facilitate decision making.* We will introduce three major types of marketing models: decision tree models, mathematical function models, and theory-in-use models.

Decision Tree Models.   A **decision tree model** is *a graphical model in which the alternative decisions a manager can select from are portrayed as branches of a tree.*[17] Figure 4.5 shows two decision trees, one more complex than the other. The one on the top depicts a simple decision tree and shows that the marketer is faced with a decision of raising or lowering a product's price. The sales and profitability of the product will depend on whether the price stays the same, is raised, or is lowered. As a marketing manager who espouses the marketing concept, you would want to select the action that would result in the highest profit.

You are probably saying to yourself that the preceding decision tree is too simple to be of much use. Recall that models are not the real thing but merely abstractions of reality. To make the decision tree more realistic, you could add more branches by taking into account such factors as changes in the competition (bottom panel of Figure 4.5), changes in the economy, or some combination of factors.

Mathematical Function Models.   A **mathematical function model** *specifies quantitative relationships between a dependent variable and independent variable(s).* The dependent variable is the phenomena we are attempting to explain, and the independent variable(s) is used to explain the phenomena.

Figure 4.6 shows some graphical examples of mathematical function models. The linear demand curve model in the left-hand panel of the figure correlates the variable quantity demanded with the variable price. As price declines, the quantity demanded rises.

Many mathematical models of marketing phenomena are nonlinear, as shown in the right-hand panel of Figure 4.6, which graphs the relationship between sales and advertising expenditures.[18] As advertising increases, sales rise, but at a declining rate of growth, and ultimately plateau at some saturation level. There are other types of marketing models, but they are beyond the scope of this text.[19]

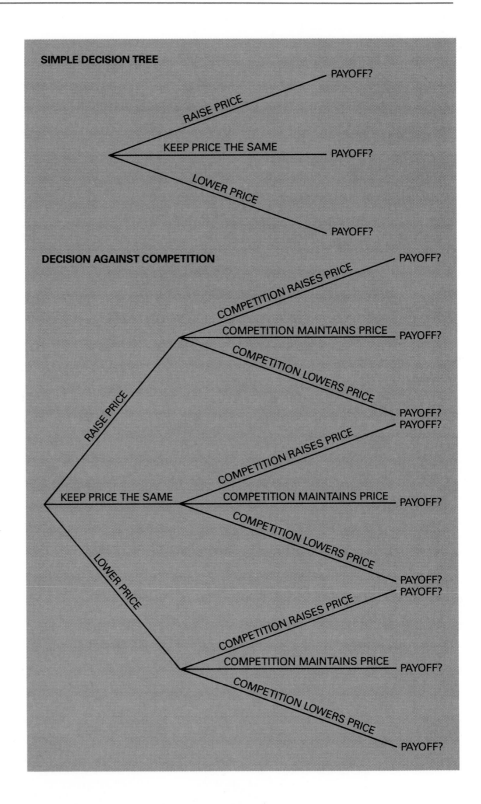

Figure 4.5
Decision Tree Models

MARKETING IN ACTION

With the explosive growth of computer technology, many companies, such as Abbott Labs, are building a decision support system (DSS) as the backbone of their MIS. The DSS consists of an integrated package of computer hardware and software that can be used to highlight a firm's strategic marketing opportunities and tactical marketing problems. In 1983/1984, the Hospital Products Division at Abbott Labs purchased and implemented a DSS. The need and potential benefit of a DSS for the division were large because of the scope of its business—it produces and markets over 2,000 products for thousands of hospitals across the United States and has annual sales in excess of $3 billion.

One of the primary tasks of this DDS is to organize its accounting data so that managerially useful reports can be generated. Within 60 minutes the DSS can generate a detailed sales and profit report on any

Building a Decision Support System at Abbott Labs

segment or piece of the Hospital Products Division's business. For example, the manager can get a report on the sales and profit performance of a product, group of products, geographic region, or a particular customer (i.e., hospital). Before the Hospital Products Division built their DSS, it took a clerical worker two days to generate a single report.

In addition to sophisticated accounting analysis, the DSS has the following capabilities (some of which are not fully operational and implemented at Abbott Labs):

● **Sales forecasting.**

● **Monthly reports on actual sales versus planned sales.**

● **Analysis of the profitability of promotional programs.**

● **"What if" analysis, such as what will happen to sales and profit if prices are changed?**

● **Optimal bids to make to win new hospital supply contracts.**

● **Generation of detailed customer segmentation profiles.**

Mr. Hulsy, manager for hospital fluids, summarizes Abbott's experience in developing a state-of-the-art DSS, "The system's hurdles are sizable, but the bang for the buck when we're there is stupendous. It can do things we've only dreamed about."

Source: Based on Daniel C. Brown. "The Anatomy of a Decision Support System," *Business Marketing* (June 1985), pp. 80–86. With permission from *Business Marketing.* Copyright Crain Communications, Inc.

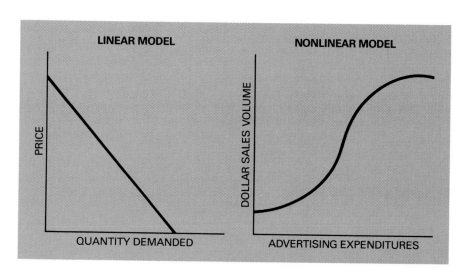

Figure 4.6

Mathematical Function Models

Theory-in-Use Models.   Marketing decision makers use theory to make decisions.[20] The theory may be based on what they learned in college, results of past decisions, hunches and educated guesses, or some combination of these. In any case, a *theory* can be thought of as a series of interconnected propositions of the "if, then" form. A **theory-in-use model** *includes a set of "if I do A, then B will occur" statements.* For instance, based on economic principles and what the marketer has experienced in the past, he or she may conclude that *if* the price is lowered, *then* the quantity sold will increase, or that *if* we do a 12-month test market, *then* competition will steal our idea and beat us to full-scale marketing of the product.

The Marketing in Action on page 115 explains how Abbott Labs has developed an integrated computer hardware and software system as part of its MIS.

SUMMARY

In this chapter, we discussed the marketing information system (MIS) with special emphasis on the marketing research process. The marketing research process consists of those techniques and procedures that are used to systematically gather, record, and analyze data about problems related to the marketing of goods and services. The SELECT model represents the marketing research process and shows the steps to follow in arriving at and implementing a solution to a marketing problem. SELECT is an acronym for: (1) *S*ituation analysis, (2) *E*xplicitly stating the problem, (3) *L*aying out the research design and collecting data, (4) *E*valuating research results and making the decision, (5) *C*reating a plan to implement the decision, and (6) *T*esting the correctness of the decision. We emphasized step 3, research design, by discussing designing data requirements, data collection methods, data collection forms, sampling plans, and data analysis plans.

After discussing marketing research, we described the three other subsystems of the MIS. The accounting system is the set of procedures the organization has developed for recording monetary transactions. Because many of these monetary transactions are with the firm's customers, the accounting system can be used to identify and analyze trends in the sales and profitability of selling to different customer groups. The marketing intelligence system is used to continually monitor the organization's external environments and the multiple publics it interacts with. The marketing models system consists of a group of abstract representations that managers can use to organize marketing data and view the world of marketing in order to make better decisions. We introduced decision tree models, mathematical function models, and theory-in-use models.

KEY CONCEPTS

marketing research (p. 92)
SELECT model (p. 93)
situation analysis (p. 94)

secondary data (p. 94)
primary data (p. 94)
research design (p. 95)

observation method (p. 97)
survey method (p. 98)
experimental method (p. 98)
probability sample (p. 103)
nonprobability sample (p. 104)
marketing information system (MIS)
  (p. 110)

marketing intelligence system (p. 112)
marketing model (p. 113)
decision tree model (p. 113)
mathematical function model (p. 113)
theory-in-use model (p. 116)

REVIEW AND DISCUSSION QUESTIONS

1. Name the four subsystems of the marketing information system and give a brief definition of each.

2. What is the SELECT model?

3. Why should a situation analysis be conducted before a hypothesis is formulated?

4. What is the difference between primary and secondary data? State the primary advantage and primary disadvantage of secondary data.

5. What are the five steps in a research design and why is research design important to the process of marketing research?

6. How are data obtained with the observation method?

7. What are the advantages and disadvantages of the different survey methods— mail, telephone, and personal interview?

8. Why do you think the experimental method is used less frequently in marketing than in the hard sciences such as chemistry?

9. Distinguish between open-ended and closed-ended questions. Cite the major advantage and disadvantage of each.

10. What are the criteria for writing good questions for a questionnaire?

11. What are the two major categories of sampling plans? Which type do market researchers prefer? Why?

12. What role does the market researcher play in a firm's decision making?

13. Why do some firms choose to conduct market research? Why do some firms choose not to?

14. What is the purpose of the marketing intelligence system?

15. What relationship does accounting data have to marketing decision making?

16. What role can salespeople play in a firm's marketing information system?

17. Define *model* and explain why marketing models are no substitute for marketing decision makers.

ACTION PROBLEMS

1. Marketing researchers often conduct research that deals with consumer satisfaction. How would you define and measure consumer satisfaction? Assume that you are the marketing manager for Yamaha motorcycles. Develop five closed-end, multichotomous questions to measure customer satisfaction.

2. Visit a major library in your community to determine how much secondary information is available on an industry you want to learn more about. Some sources you should definitely consult are *Business Periodicals Index, Accountants Index, Standard and Poors Industry Reports,* and *Census of Business.*

3. Locate and read recent annual reports to stockholders of two or three competing firms. What information could each competitor learn from the other's annual report?

4. Develop a decision tree model for a local sporting goods retailer considering raising or lowering its advertising budget.

5. Pick a business venture to open in your campus area. Design a ten-question survey to be mailed to students at your school that will discover their views and habits associated with your proposed venture. Use at least two types of questions and explain what kind of sampling you would use.

6. Your position is marketing manager (a recently created position) of Community Symphony. Community Symphony knows nothing about their patrons. Prepare a memo to the symphony's board of directors requesting $10,000 for a market research study. Be sure to identify the objectives of the research and the benefits that can be expected.

NOTES

1. Committee on Definitions, *Marketing Definitions: A Glossary of Marketing Terms* (Chicago: American Marketing Association, 1960), p. 17.

2. The marketing research process is discussed in more detail in Harper W. Boyd, Jr., Ralph Westfall, and Stanley F. Stasch, *Marketing Research: Text and Cases,* 4th edition (Homewood, IL: Richard D. Irwin, 1977); Ben Enis and Keith Cox, *The Marketing Research Process* (Pacific Palisades, CA: Goodyear Publishing Company, 1972).

3. The importance of developing good measures in marketing is discussed in Gilbert A. Churchill, Jr., "A Paradigm for Developing Better Measures of Marketing Constructs," *Journal of Marketing Research* (February 1979), pp. 64–73; Roger M. Hesler and Michael L. Ray, "Measure Validation in Marketing," *Journal of Marketing Research* (November 1972), pp. 361–370.

4. To obtain more insight into the use of the experimental method in marketing, see Seymour Banks, *Experimentation in Marketing* (New York: McGraw-Hill, 1965); Keith K. Cox and Ben M. Enis, *Experimentation for Marketing Decisions* (Scranton, PA: International Textbook Company, 1969); John R. Nevin, "Using Experimental Data to Suggest and Evaluate Alternative Marketing Strategies," in Subhash C. Jain (ed.), *Research Frontiers in Marketing* (Chicago: American Marketing Association, 1978), pp. 207–211; Chem L. Narayana and James F. Horrell, "Evaluation of Quality Factors in Marketing Experiments," *Journal of the Academy of Marketing Science* (Summer 1976), pp. 599–607; Alan G. Sawyer, Parker M. Worthing, and Paul E. Senoak, "The Role of Laboratory Experiments to Test Marketing Strategies," *Journal of Marketing* (Summer 1979), pp. 60–67.

5. R.F. Barker and A.B. Blankenship, "The Manager's Guide to Survey Questionnaire Evaluation," *Journal of the Market Research Society* (October 1975), pp. 233–241; Patricia Labaw, *Advanced Questionnaire Design* (Cambridge, MA: ABT Books, 1981); Abraham N. Oppenheim, *Questionnaire Design and Attitude Measurement* (New York: Basic Books, 1966).

6. This list was adapted from Robert A. Peterson, *Marketing Research* (Plano, TX: Business Publications, Inc., 1982), pp. 234–243.

7. For some recent developments and trends in sample design, see William P. Dommermuth, *The Use of Sampling in Marketing Research* (Chicago: American Marketing Association, 1975); Martin R. Frankel and Lester R. Frankel, "Some Recent Developments in Sample Survey Design," *Journal of Marketing Research* (August 1977), pp. 280–293.

8. James A. Davis, *Elementary Survey Analysis* (Englewood Cliffs, NJ: Prentice-Hall, 1971); Frederick Mosteller and John W. Tukey, *Data Analysis and Regression* (Reading, MA: Addison-Wesley Publishing, 1977); Paul E. Green, *Analyzing Multivariate Data* (Hinsdale, IL: Dryden Press, 1978); Jagdish N. Sheth (ed.), *Multivariate Methods for Market and Survey Research* (Chicago: American Marketing Association, 1977).

9. Some good hints on how to write a good research report are found in Stewart H. Britt, "The Writing of Readable Research Reports," *Journal of Marketing Research* (May 1971), pp. 262–266.

10. For a discussion of whether the researcher is a decision maker, see R.J. Small and L.J. Rosenberg, "The Marketing Researcher as a Decision Maker: Myth or Reality?" *Journal of Marketing* (January 1975), pp. 2–7.

11. A. Parasuraman, "Research's Place in the Marketing Budget," *Business Horizons* (March–April 1983), pp. 25–29.

12. To obtain a more complete understanding of marketing information systems, you might refer to Richard H. Brien and James E. Stafford, "Marketing Information Systems: A New Dimension for Marketing Research," *Journal of Marketing* (July 1968), p. 21; Donald F. Cox and Robert E. Good, "How to Build a Marketing Information System," *Harvard Business Review* 3(May–June 1967), pp. 145–156; David B. Montgomery and Glenn L. Urban, "Marketing Decision Information Systems: An Emerging View," *Journal of Marketing Research* (May 1970), pp. 226–234.

13. Leland L. Beik and Stephen L. Buzby, "Profitability Analyses by Marketing Segments," *Journal of Marketing* (June 1973), pp. 48–53.

14. Sales analysis is discussed further in Donald W. Jackson, Jr., and Lonnie L. Ostrom, "Grouping Segments for Profitability Analysis," *MSU Business Topics* (Spring 1980), pp. 33–44.

15. David B. Montgomery and Charles B. Weinberg, "Toward Strategic Intelligence Systems," *Journal of Marketing* (Fall 1979), pp. 41–52.

16. Textbooks that specifically deal with marketing models include Philip Kotler, *Marketing Decision Making: A Model Building Approach* (New York: Holt, Rinehart and Winston, 1971); David B. Montgomery and Glenn L. Urban, *Management Science in Marketing* (Englewood Cliffs, NJ: Prentice-Hall, 1969); and L.J. Parsons and R.L. Schultz, *Marketing Models and Economic Research* (New York: Elsevier North-Holland, 1976).

17. A good discussion of decision trees in marketing decision making can be found in Harper W. Boyd, Jr., Ralph Westfall, and Stanley F. Stasch, *Marketing Research: Text and Cases* (Homewood, IL: Richard D. Irwin, Inc., 1977), pp. 184–206.

18. The mathematical function characterizing the relationship between sales and advertising has been modeled often, and this research is summarized in Gert Assmus, John U. Farley, and Donald R. Lehmann, "How Advertising Affects Sales: Meta-analysis of Econometric Results," *Journal of Marketing Research* 21(February 1984), pp. 65–74.

19. For an example, see L.J. Parsons and R.L. Schultz, *Marketing Models and Economic Research* (New York: Elsevier North-Holland, 1976).

20. For a more complete discussion of theory in use, see David T. Wilson and Morry Ghingold, "Building Theory from Practice: A Theory-in-Use Approach," in Charles Lamb, Jr., and Patrick Dunne (eds.), *Theoretical Developments in Marketing* (Chicago: American Marketing Association, 1980), pp. 236–239; Gerald Zaltman and Melanie Wallendorf, *Consumer Behavior: Findings and Management Implications* (New York: John Wiley & Sons, Inc., 1983), Chapter 2.

CHAPTER 5

CONSUMER BUYING BEHAVIOR

MARKETER PROFILE

Ira N. Bachrach of Name Lab

Ira N. Bachrach wrote a college graduate degree thesis on patterns that form words in the English language. The thesis gathered dust while Bachrach pursued a successful career in marketing and advertising. After selling his own advertising agency and subsequently engaging in the venture capital business, he decided to retire and enjoy the fruits of his labor.

This inactivity did not last for long, in part because his wife kept pleading with him to find something to do. Bachrach decided to apply the principles he had developed in his graduate thesis to the naming of products. He started a company called Name Lab, which has become so successful that clients are now being turned away because the demand for its services is too great.

Developing successful product names requires a good understanding of consumer behavior and linguistics. With over 130 jobs to its credit, one of Name Lab's biggest successes occurred with a company entering the portable computer business. The company's founders initially wanted to call the product Gateway and the company Gateway Technologies. However, one of the key investors urged the founders to consult Name Lab for advice. One of Name Lab's guiding principles is that a product name should denote its attributes and describe the product—Bachrach calls these "attributive nouns." For example, the name *Sentra* was developed to connote safety and security for a new car introduced into the U.S. market by Nissan Motors. In the case of Gateway Technology, the new word had to denote portableness and computers.

Name Lab finally came up with *COMPAQ*, which sends two messages—one indicating "computer and communications" and the other "a small, integral object." Subsequently, the company named itself and its portable computers *COMPAQ*. The corporation had first-year sales

of $111 million—a U.S. record. By using the same name for the company and its first product introduction, consumer acceptance increased because of the learning effects of repetition. Furthermore, the *paq* suffix "fits neatly into what could become a product family name: Printpaq, Datapaq, Wordpaq, and the like."

Source: Based on Robert A. Momis. "Name-Calling," *INC.* (July 1984), pp. 67–74. Direct quotes are from this article. David Holmstrom. "A Man of His Words," *American Way* (February 1984), pp. 173–176.

INTRODUCTION

This chapter details how people make purchasing decisions in the so-called consumer market. The **consumer market** *consists of all buyers and potential buyers for goods and services that are acquired for personal or household use,* such as food, clothing, textbooks, transportation, and housing. You were part of a consumer market when you purchased this textbook.

Consumers are constantly involved in decision making, whether the products they purchase are consumed quickly, such as food and gasoline, or consumed slowly over time, such as a house or a car.

Consumers do not make decisions in a vacuum—they are influenced by three broad factors: (1) sociological factors, (2) psychological factors, and (3) economic factors. **Sociological factors** *deal with the influence of other persons and groups on the consumer's decisions.* **Psychological factors** are *variables such as attitudes, learning processes, motivation, and perceptual processes that are internal to the individual's thought processes.* Ira Bachrach's Name Lab, discussed in the Marketer Profile, uses psychological principles and concepts to develop product and company names. **Economic factors** *are concerned with the influence of a person's income and other economic resources on purchasing behavior.*

THE CONSUMER AS DECISION MAKER

Problem Recognition

The decision-making process begins when the consumer recognizes a problem. *Problem recognition* occurs when the consumer's desired state of affairs departs sufficiently from the actual state of affairs to place the consumer in a state of unrest so that he or she begins thinking of ways to resolve the difference. Recall from Chapter 1 that problem recognition usually is tied to the fulfillment of needs. Consider a few examples. While driving across town you notice that your car's gas tank is almost empty; you hear an advertisement for a new Panasonic stereo and realize that your ten-year-old stereo needs replacing; you will be graduating from college shortly and do not own any suitable clothes for your new career.

Not all problems will stimulate the same level of problem-solving activity. "The level of one's desire to resolve a particular problem depends upon two factors; the magnitude of the discrepancy between the desired and existing states and the importance of the problem."[1] Consider the example about the gas tank. If a quarter of a tank remained, the problem would be less urgent than if the gas gauge were on empty. Next, compare your recognition of the problem about replacing your old stereo with your recognition of the problem of acquiring a career wardrobe. In all probability, one of these problems would be more important to you, and thus you would be more motivated to solve it first.

Degree of Problem Solving

The amount of problem-solving activity consumers engage in varies considerably depending on their prior experience. Consumers learn quickly, and once they find the product brands and retail stores that are good at satisfying their needs, the degree of problem solving regarding buying and consumption decreases. Table 5.1 illustrates three levels of consumer problem solving. Note that these levels are determined by whether or not the consumer has a strong preference for a specific brand and retail store.

Habitual Problem Solving. With **habitual problem solving**, *the consumer relies on past experience and learning to convert the problem into a situation in which no decision is required.* The consumer has a strong preference for the brand to buy and the store from which to purchase it. Using past experience, the consumer has arrived at an adequate solution for many consumer problems. Frequently purchased products of relatively low cost and low risk tend to belong in this category (e.g., toothpaste, milk,

Table 5.1 Three Types of Consumer Problem Solving

Brand Preference	Store Preference	
	Strong	**None or Weak**
Strong	Habitual problem solving	Limited problem solving
None or weak	Limited problem solving	Extended problem solving

bread, soda pop); however, products of higher value may also be in this category. For example, while traveling, some people can be loyal to both a particular brand and a specific retailer. When confronted with the need to travel, they may go to their favorite travel agent (store loyalty) and book a flight on American Airlines (brand loyalty) because they have had good experience with both in the past.

Limited Problem Solving.   **Limited problem solving** occurs when *the consumer has a strong preference for either the brand or the store, but not both.* The consumer may not have a store choice in mind but may have a strong preference or may even have decided on the brand to purchase. Since the brand has been determined, the consumer has, in a sense, restricted the problem-solving process to deciding which store among those that carry the brand to patronize. Because the consumer may not know all the stores that carry the item, some searching may be required. To illustrate, assume the picture tube on your TV fails and you decide to get a new set rather than repair the old one. You know that you want an RCA portable color set, but since you are new in town, you do not know where to get the best buy. Although we refer to this category as limited problem solving, there may be extensive decision making in regard to deciding which brand or store to select. Problem solving should be viewed as a continuum.

Extended Problem Solving.   **Extended problem solving** occurs when *the consumer recognizes a problem but has decided on neither the brand nor the store.* For example, a woman in her early twenties has just received a promotion and a 25 percent raise from the bank that employs her. Over the last year, she has put off purchasing several major durable goods that she wants—a car, living room furniture, and a laser disk player. With the 25 percent raise, she can afford some, but not all, of these items. She has little prior information and experience regarding alternative brands and retailers for these products; therefore, she must engage in extensive problem solving to select the products she should buy, to determine which are the appropriate brands, and to learn which retail outlets carry what she wants. Extensive problem solving typically involves infrequently purchased, expensive products of high risk. Here, the consumer desires a lot of new information, which implies a need for extensive problem solving.

Figure 5.1 is a basic model of consumer behavior showing that the stages of problem recognition are influenced by sociological, psychological, and economic factors. We will discuss sociological factors first.

SOCIOLOGICAL FACTORS

Four sociological factors have a major impact on a consumer's purchasing decisions: one's culture, social class, family, and reference groups. A brief discussion of each of these will help familiarize you with how they influence consumer purchasing decisions.

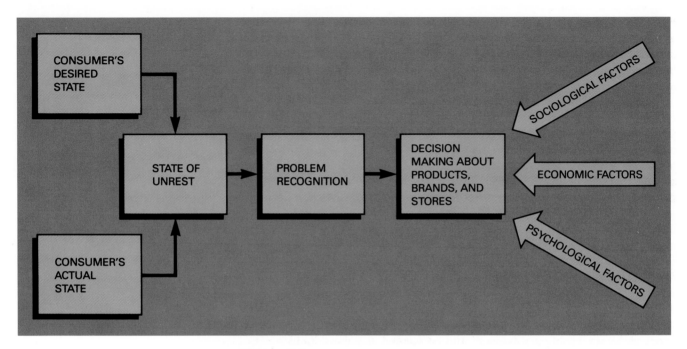

Figure 5.1

A Basic Model of Consumer Behavior

Culture

We take for granted that the culture in the United States differs from that in Brazil or Japan, but what do we mean specifically by the term *culture?* We will define **culture** as *a set of beliefs, attitudes, customs, and institutions created by people to help them explain and cope with their environment.* Included in our definition are work ethics, rites of passage, biases, churches, police departments, art museums, libraries, hospitals, automobiles, houses, air conditioning, and universities—those things that help people adjust or cope with the world that surrounds them. Chapter 18 will examine how understanding foreign cultures is critical to successful international marketing. Our discussion in this chapter will focus on the United States.

Culture prescribes behavior through norms and values. By *norms* we mean "rules that specify or prohibit certain behaviors in specific situations and are based on or derived from cultural values."[2] For example, the way we dress and the way we speak usually are governed by where we are and to whom we are speaking. Our behavior in church, a fine restaurant, the theater, or the classroom may be different from that at home, at the beach, at a rock concert, and at an informal restaurant. Norms tell us that this difference in behavior is acceptable as long as we are acting properly for the specific situation. *Cultural values* are widely held beliefs that state what is desirable and have some influence on behavior.[3] Cultural values influence our consumption decisions. The Marketing in Action on page 128 illustrates how the cultural values of the Hispanic consumer shape his or her buying decisions.

Competitiveness and freedom of choice are two major American cultural values. We believe we should be able to purchase the best products at the best prices regardless of whether they are made in the USA, Japan, or somewhere else. When shopping for a watch, for example, we can choose from similar products made in the United States, Japan, and Switzerland and make our final selection based on the best value. Some other American core cultural values and their influence on consumption are shown in Table 5.2.

Throughout the 1950s, the American people generally strived to conform with their peers. There was a great desire to "keep up with the Joneses," or to have and do what friends and neighbors did. In the late 1960s and early 1970s, however, consumers began expressing a desire to stand out from the crowd. They expressed this shift many ways: styles of dress, art forms, housing, leisure-time activities, diet, work, and so on. This trend, which continues today, suggests to marketers the need to offer consumers the opportunity to individualize and enhance their self-image by offering them distinctive products. For example, builders of tract homes offer consumers a wide variety of floor and wall coverings, light fixtures, and exterior elevations to enable the new home owner to have a unique home. Many auto dealers offer the auto purchaser dealer-installed options such as pin-striping, mag wheels, and custom stereos to help differentiate the purchaser's car from the thousands of other new cars just like it. Specialty retail apparel stores are employing fashion consultants to assist customers in assembling a wardrobe that gives them a distinctive and individual look.

Social Class

Social class can be defined as "a *group of people with similar levels of prestige and esteem who also share a set of related beliefs, attitudes, and values that they express in their thinking and behavior.*"[4] Most researchers who study social class have broken down the U.S. population into five or six social classes based on variables such as occupation, education, income, and housing.[5] Occupation usually is rated the most important variable in determining social status, followed by income, education, and housing. Approximately 2 percent of the U.S. population is upper class, 10 percent is upper middle class, 30 percent is middle class, 40 percent is lower middle class, and 18 percent is lower class.[6]

Table 5.3 shows an analysis of the consumption of food items as a function of social class. Note some of the significant findings: tonic water, frozen juice, and imported wine are consumed more frequently by members of higher social classes than by the lower classes. On the other hand, bologna,

Table 5.2   American Core Cultural Values

Value	General Features	Relevance to Consumer Behavior
Achievement and success	Hard work is good; success flows from hard work	Acts as a justification for acquisition of goods ("You deserve it")
Activity	Keeping busy is healthy and natural	Stimulates interest in products that save time and enhance leisure-time activities
Efficiency and practicality	Admiration of things that solve problems (e.g., save time and effort)	Stimulates purchase of products that function well and save time
Progress	People can improve themselves; tomorrow should be better	Stimulates desire for new products that fulfill unsatisfied needs; acceptance of products that claim to be "new" or "improved"
Material comfort	"The good life"	Fosters acceptance of convenience and luxury products that make life more enjoyable
Individualism	Being one's self (e.g., self-reliance, self-interest, and self-esteem)	Stimulates acceptance of customized or unique products that enable a person to "express his own personality"
Freedom	Freedom of choice	Fosters interest in wide product lines and differentiated products
External conformity	Uniformity of observable behavior; desire to be accepted	Stimulates interest in products that are used or owned by others in the same social group
Humanitarianism	Caring for others, particularly the underdog	Stimulates patronage of firms that compete with market leaders
Youthfulness	A state of mind that stresses being young at heart or appearing young	Stimulates acceptance of products that provide the illusion of maintaining or fostering youth

Source: Leon Schiffman and Leslie Kanuk. *Consumer Behavior,* © 1978, p. 359. Reprinted by permission of Prentice-Hall, Inc., Englewood Cliffs, NJ 07632.

potato chips, and Tang are consumed more heavily by the lower social classes.

Another example is provided in Table 5.4, which shows how AT&T used social class research to gain insights into its customers' needs and preferences. The research revealed that upper social class users were very interested in phones that were modern in design and came in a variety of styles.

Social class has also been shown to determine patronage at retail stores. It has been found that the higher a woman's social status, the more she prefers to shop at a conventional department store, such as Dayton-Hudson's, Dillards, Rich's, Sanger Harris, Gimbles, or Macy's, rather than a discount department store, such as K Mart, Wal-Mart, or Target.[7] This is especially true for products of high social risk (i.e., high risk that other people will

Table 5.3   Frequency of Consumption Differences Across Hollingshead Index of Social Position Strata

Food Item	Upper	Upper Middle	Middle	Lower Middle	Lower
			Social Strata[a]		
Ground coffee	4.07	**4.79**	4.17	3.93	*2.61*
Frozen juice	5.48	**6.00**	5.35	4.83	*3.58*
Tang	*1.63*	1.74	1.77	1.64	**2.82**
Tonic water	**3.07**	2.31	1.79	1.69	*1.58*
White domestic wine	1.85	2.15	**2.25**	2.08	*1.52*
White imported wine	**3.41**	2.87	2.56	2.08	*1.42*
Scotch	**2.85**	2.18	2.08	1.61	*1.55*
Bologna	*2.04*	2.28	3.13	3.50	**3.88**
Potato chips	*1.96*	2.58	3.15	3.08	**3.30**
Canned meat	*1.37*	1.91	**2.40**	2.12	2.03

[a]Differences across the social classes are significant at the 0.01 level except frozen juice, which is significant at the 0.10 level. Boldface indicates the highest. Italic indicates the lowest.

Source: Reprinted from C. Schaninger. "Social Class Versus Income Revisited: An Empirical Investigation," *Journal of Marketing Research* (May 1981), pp. 197–201, published by the American Marketing Association. Used by permission.

disapprove of the purchase) such as jewelry and clothing.[8] Social class also is related to the use of in-home shopping (i.e., mail, telephone, and catalog shopping). In-home shopping is more likely to occur in the higher social classes.[9]

Family

The family is the most immediate and continuous source of group influence on consumer decision making. Most people will belong to two families in their lifetime: the family into which they are born and the family they create when they get married and/or have children. Families influence our consumption decisions in many areas. For example, your choice of college may have been influenced by your family, and, in most cases, the house or apartment you live in when you create your own family will be chosen based on input of family members. In fact, most consumption decisions are not individual decisions, but household or family decisions because all or most family members will share in the consumption process and in the decision-making process.

Research on family decision making has focused on the relative influ-

MARKETING IN ACTION

The 1980 U.S. Census of Housing and Population reported that 14.6 million Hispanics reside in the United States. The growth of this ethnic group is phenomenal: it grew 60 percent during the 1970s compared with a 6 percent rise in the white population and a 17 percent rise in the black population. Hispanics have a unique culture that they often maintain after they immigrate to the United States. American marketers are beginning to realize the importance of the Hispanic consumer and to apply different marketing strategies to appeal to this large cultural group.

Research conducted by Professors Bellenger and Valencia has profiled the Hispanic consumers as considerably different from their white counterparts. A synopsis of their findings follows.

Hispanics are *more* likely to:

- **Prefer to shop at smaller stores.**

Appealing to the Hispanic Consumer

- **Dislike impersonal ("no heart or soul") stores.**

- **Be ecology-minded—they agree that products that pollute should be banned.**

- **Be cautious—they do not buy unknown brands to save money.**

Conversely, Hispanics are *less* likely to be:

- **Skeptical of ads—they believe that advertising represents a true picture of products.**

- **Venturesome—they do not like to be the first to try new products.**

- **Impulse buyers—they plan their purchases.**

- **Apathetic about shopping—they do not consider it to be a terrible waste of time.**

- **Credit card holders.**

Research of this type on the Hispanic consumer is helping U.S. firms to fine tune their marketing strategies. For example, these findings reinforce the fact that Hispanics like stores with personal attention. To them "shopping is an emotional and personal experience. They like to know who they are buying from. Therefore, there is a need to personalize, especially in advertising. A&P for example, used the 'Amigo del Pueblo' (friend of the people) campaign successfully to reinforce their Hispanic customer franchise."

Source: Based on Danny N. Bellenger and Humberto Valencia. "Understanding the Hispanic Market," *Business Horizons* (May–June 1982), pp. 47–50. Adapted with permission.

---

ence of the husband and wife. One research team identified four types of family decision-making structures[10]:

1. *Autonomic.* Husband and wife make approximately equal numbers of decisions, but each decision is made by one partner or the other.
2. *Husband dominant.* The husband makes the majority of the decisions with little or no input from the wife.
3. *Wife dominant.* The wife makes the majority of the decisions with little or no input from the husband.
4. *Syncratic.* Each partner has roughly equal influence on each decision.

It is unrealistic, however, to categorize a family into one of these particular types for all their decision making because a family's method of making purchase decisions varies depending on the product and situation. For example, life insurance may be a husband-dominant decision, schooling may be a wife-dominant decision, vacations may be syncratic, and garden tools and clothing may be autonomic.[11] When planning a marketing strategy,

Table 5.4   AT&T's Use of Social Class to Understand Differences in Customer Needs[a]

Product-Specific Statements	Percent Agreeing with Statement[b]			
	Upper	Upper Middle	Lower Middle	Lower
1. Phones should come in patterns and designs as well as colors.	58	63	**80**	60
2. A telephone should improve the decorative style of a room.	77	73	**82**	47
3. Telephones should be modern in design.	**89**	83	85	58
4. A home should have a variety of telephone styles.	**51**	39	46	8
5. You can keep all those special phones, all I want is a phone that works.	56	68	67	**83**
6. The style of a telephone is unimportant to me.	51	58	54	**86**

[a]Differences between the classes are significant at the 0.05 level.
[b]Highest percentages are in bold type.

Source: Adapted with permission of the publisher from A. Marvin Roscoe, Jr., Arthur LeClaire, Jr., and Leon G. Schiffman. "Theory and Management Applications of Demographics in Buyer Behavior," in Arch G. Woodside, Jagdish N. Sheth, and Peter D. Bennett (eds.), *Consumer and Industrial Buying Behavior* (New York: American Elsevier, 1977), pp. 74–75. Copyright 1977 by Elsevier Science Publishing Co., Inc.

the marketing manager should know which member is the primary decision maker for that product so that promotion can be directed at that individual.

Children also influence household consumption decisions. They may influence such things as selection of a restaurant and family vacations.[12] In addition, children often ask their parents for products such as candy, toys, bicycles, stereos, and even cars, and as you are well aware, parents will sometimes yield to these requests.

Reference Groups

In addition to your culture, social class, and family, you are influenced by your reference groups. **Reference groups** are *those groups with which an individual identifies, and thus the group becomes a standard, a norm, or a point of reference for the consumer.*[13] Reference groups can be divided into three categories:

1. *Membership groups.*   Groups to which a person belongs (e.g., churches, clubs, and political parties).

BALLY® OF SWITZERLAND

The difference between dressed, and well dressed.

Shoes   Handbags   Small Leather Goods   Accessories

Bally presents itself as having products to satisfy upper-class tastes.

2. *Aspiration groups.* Groups that an individual does not currently belong to but that he or she aspires to belong to or be associated with. For example, social cliques and rock music groups are aspiration groups for many teenagers.

3. *Dissociative groups.* Groups that the person does not belong to and does not desire to be associated with. For example, a presidential candidate probably would not want to belong to or be associated with the Ku Klux Klan.

Each type of reference group can influence consumption patterns, but reference group influence will be strongest when the product is visible in usage situations.[14] For example, consumers' use of products such as alcoholic beverages, home furnishings, cars, or clothing will be more susceptible to reference group influence than will their use of products such as laundry soap, canned vegetables, or coffee.

The following examples should reinforce the impact of reference groups on consumption. If you belong to a cycling club, then the members of that club will, to some degree, influence the type and brand of bicycle you purchase. For example, they may influence you to buy a Pinarello, Moser, Rossin, or Cinelli. If you aspire to join a college fraternity or sorority, then you may purchase clothing to help you be identified as the type of person they want as a member. On the other hand, if you do not want to be associated with a fraternity or sorority, you may go out of your way to dress in a manner that is the direct opposite of how they dress.

PSYCHOLOGICAL FACTORS

We will now focus on four psychological factors that influence consumer decision making: motivation, attitudes, learning processes, and perceptual processes. Unlike sociological factors, which are external to the individual, psychological factors are internal to the individual.

Motivation

Motivation can be viewed as *an internal force that directs people to act in a particular way to satisfy a particular need.* Motivation is goal-directed behavior—the goal is to satisfy a need. As we discussed in Chapter 1, marketers attempt to satisfy consumer needs with products. Predictably, therefore, marketing managers must understand how motives direct consumers toward need-satisfying behavior. One of the most well-known theories of human motivation is Maslow's need motive hierarchy. The theory is very general and is intended to explain a broad range of behavior. Maslow's hierarchy is based on four premises[15]:

1. All humans acquire a similar set of motives through genetic endowment and social interaction.
2. Some motives are more basic or critical than others.
3. The more basic motives must be satisfied to a minimum level before other motives are activated.
4. As soon as the basic motives are satisfied, more advanced motives come into play.

Figure 5.2 presents Maslow's hierarchy of the five human needs: physiological, safety, belongingness, esteem, and self-actualization. The first two are the basic, or lower order, needs, and the next three are the advanced, or higher order, needs. Physiological needs are the things you require for survival to satisfy hunger and thirst and to shelter you from the elements of nature. Once these needs are met, you can begin to satisfy your safety needs, or those that keep you healthy and protect you from enemies. The belongingness needs are next and are for those things that bring you friendship and love. Once belongingness needs have been attained, you can start seeking to fill your esteem needs, which include gaining power, prestige,

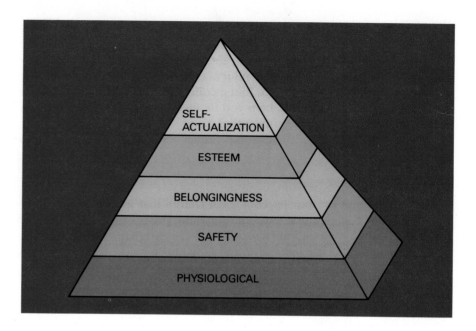

Figure 5.2

Maslow's Hierarchy of Needs

and importance in the eyes of others. The highest order need is for self-actualization, the need to feel that you have accomplished, to the best of your abilities, all you have set out to do.

We can all think of exceptions to Maslow's hierarchy, but it does explain general behavior patterns. Marketers have recognized the value of this need hierarchy in the design of promotional appeals. The marketing manager should also recognize that several different need levels may create motivation in any given purchase situation.

Attitudes

An **attitude** can be viewed as *"a learned predisposition to respond in a consistently favorable or unfavorable manner with respect to a given object."*[16] The object could be a product, brand, salesperson, or retail store. Attitudes have traditionally been viewed as being composed of three dimensions: cognitive, affective, and behavioral. The *cognitive dimension* refers to the understanding of the attitude object (i.e., do you know the product's purpose?). The *affective dimension* concerns the feelings of like or dislike toward the object (i.e., do you have a positive feeling toward the product?). The *behavioral dimension* refers to the action tendencies toward the attitude object (i.e., do you have a predisposition to purchase that product?).

Attitude models can be used to study and understand purchasing behavior. An *attitude model* shows how attitudes are formed in a consumer's mind. One popular attitude model shows that an attitude is formed by beliefs about the brand's characteristics or attributes and the importance you put on those characteristics or attributes.

Let's consider an example in the political arena. Remember that political candidates can be viewed as products that need to be marketed. In assessing two candidates for the U.S. Senate race in your state, you feel that leadership ability and conservatism are crucial attributes. Candidate A is highly conservative and has excellent leadership abilities, while candidate B is only moderately conservative but has excellent leadership abilities. Based on the beliefs you hold, you would have a more favorable attitude toward candidate A and thus would be more likely to vote for this candidate.

Learning Process

Consumers learn from their experiences in the marketplace, and this knowledge influences consumption decisions. **Learning** can be defined as *the "more or less permanent acquisition of tendencies to behave in particular ways in response to particular situations or stimuli."*[17]

There are four basic components in the learning process. **Stimulus,** *the first component of the learning process, is often called the cue.* It refers to *any object or phenomenon in the environment that is capable of eliciting a response.* Examples of marketing stimuli are advertisements, point-of-purchase displays, coupons, salespeople, and free samples.

The second component is **drive,** which is *a motivating force that directs behavior.* Drives can be physiologically based (hunger and the need to stay warm in the cold) or learned (the desire for a mink coat or a summer vacation in Colorado). A stimulus will only be capable of eliciting a response if it taps a drive. The stronger the drive, however, the less of a stimulus is needed to elicit a response. If you are hungry, then even the poorest or shortest television or newspaper advertisement for food will prompt you to take time to eat. The old adage "never go grocery shopping when you are hungry" also illustrates the link between stimulus and drive.

The third component of the learning process, *response,* is simply your reaction to the stimulus and drive. In a marketing framework, this would consist of your purchasing a new pair of jeans because you desire status (drive) and have seen a commercial portraying jeans as a status symbol (stimulus).

The last component is *reinforcement,* which is the reward or punishment you receive as a result of your response. *Rewards* are positive reinforcements and encourage you to behave in a similar way in future situations. *Punishments* are negative reinforcers and teach you not to repeat a certain behavior. For example, if you see a TWA advertisement like the one on page 135, which implies that flying Ambassador Class will reduce your drive for comfort and self-esteem, then you might purchase an Ambassador Class ticket the next time you need to travel. If flying Ambassador Class made you feel more comfortable and relaxed and made you feel good about your position in life (esteem), then you were rewarded and probably will fly TWA Ambassador Class in the future. On the other hand, if the flight was noisy and crowded, and the food and drink poor, then you would receive negative reinforcement, since your drives were not reduced satisfactorily, and the likelihood of your purchasing a TWA Ambassador Class ticket in the future is low.

The learning process is illustrated in Figure 5.3. The stimulus portrayed is the Golden Arch, which triggers the hunger drive, which in turn elicits the response of buying a Happy Meal, followed by positive reinforcement of fast service, good food, and a surprise in the Happy Meal box.

Perceptual Process

The behavior of consumers is strongly influenced by how they perceive the environment around them, including products and other marketing stimuli. **Perception** can be defined as *the process of receiving and deriving meaning from stimuli present in the environment.*[18] Although perception is a complex process, one thing that is known is that perception depends on both external stimuli and personal factors.[19]

Figure 5.3
The Learning Process

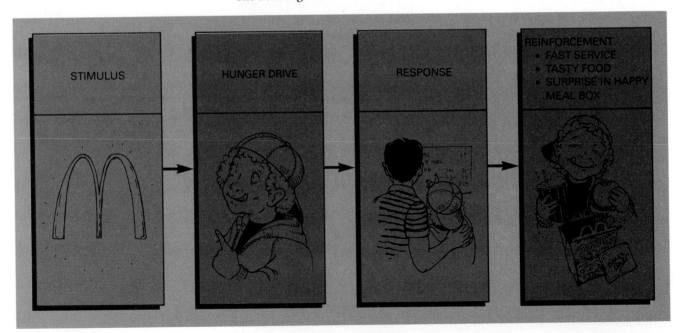

IT'S A SMALL PRICE
TO PAY FOR COMFORT.

TWA's Ambassador Class.® A separate business class that's only $10-$30 more than coach.

A seat in TWA's business class has all the characteristics of luxury. Except one.

The expensive price.

For only $10-$30 more than coach,* you can reap the many benefits of our business class—a separate, roomy cabin that has fewer seats per row. So there's never more than one seat between you and the aisle.

You don't have to look hard to find

TWA's Ambassador Class, either. Because TWA has it on *every* widebody we fly in the U.S. And we're the only airline that does.

Sitting in the lap of luxury.

Imagine this. Settling back into a wider seat. Relaxing with complimentary headsets and drinks. And on longer flights, you'll enjoy appetizers and a gourmet meal served on fine china.

And that's not all. If you're enrolled in TWA's Frequent Flight Bonus℠ program, you'll earn 125% of your miles flown just by flying in our business class.

One more thing. Call your travel agent, corporate travel department or TWA now and ask for Ambassador Class on your next flight.

Because at this price, it pays to go in style.

You're going to like us TWA

*Lowest unrestricted domestic coach fare.

TWA, with its Ambassador Class, appeals to the consumer's drives for comfort and esteem.

External Stimuli. You may recall from our discussions of learning that external stimuli in a marketing context can be such things as advertisements, point-of-purchase displays, coupons, salespeople, and free samples. For example, consider the magazine advertisement for Signal mouthwash on page 136. The consumer's perception of this advertisement will depend on things related to the advertisement itself. Since this advertisement is in color, it will stand out more often than the same ad in black and white. Because it usually appears as a full-page ad, it will be noticed more often than would a quarter-page ad. If the advertisement appears inside the front cover, it will be perceived more often than if it is in the middle of the magazine. If the advertisement has appeared in this magazine every month for the last year, it will be perceived more readily than if this is its first appearance.

Personal Factors. Personal factors, such as attitudes, motives, and prior experience also influence consumer perceptions. For example, if you have a positive attitude toward personal hygiene, you will be more likely to

"Kiss me, I got the Signal."

"Kiss me, I got the Signal."

"Kiss me, I got the Signal."

"Kiss me, I got the Signal."

"Kiss me, I got the Signal."

"Kiss me, I got the Signal."

"Kiss me, I got the Signal."

"Kiss me, I got the Signal."

"Kiss me, I got the Signal."

"Kiss me, I got the Signal."

"Kiss me, I got the Signal."

"Kiss me, I got the Signal."

"Kiss me, I got the Signal."

"Kiss me, I got the Signal."

"Kiss me—"
  "I know. You got
  the Signal."

Signal® mouthwash fights the strongest mouth odors. Even onions. Even garlic.

A consumer's perception of this ad depends on both external and personal stimuli.

notice the mouthwash advertisement than would a person who is unconcerned with personal hygiene. Motives (in this case, sex appeal) or past experiences influence perceptions. If you are currently using Signal mouthwash, then you will be more likely to perceive the advertisement.

Selective Exposure.   Consumers do not perceive all the stimuli that confront them daily. Have you ever been in your room reading a book with the radio or television on and found that you were unaware of the broadcast—or the book? This is called **selective exposure**—*the process of screening out excessive stimuli so that they don't reach our awareness level.* Obviously, this situation creates a major challenge for the marketer who is trying to attract your attention.

The marketing manager should be aware of three criteria that help consumers perceive marketing stimuli. First, a stimulus that *provides information that helps satisfy a present need* is more likely to be perceived. For instance, if you have hay fever, then in the spring months, you will be more likely to notice ads for hay fever and allergy medication. Second, a stimulus that *relates to an anticipated event* is more likely to be perceived. For example, you are more likely to perceive political advertising a week or a few days before an election because the anticipated event (election day) is nearby. Third, a *major change in the intensity of a stimulus* will be more likely to be perceived. If a beer brewer triples its advertising budget, then you will be more likely to perceive its ads, or if the brewer cuts its price on a six-pack of beer from $3.49 to $2.49, you will be more likely to perceive the price cut than if the price were lowered to $3.29.

Selective Distortion.   Another aspect of perception, **selective distortion,** is *the alteration or modification of the information received by consumers to make it consistent with their values, beliefs, attitudes, and prior experiences.* Thus, stimuli may not be perceived as the marketer intended. For example, when exposed to an advertisement in favor of the equal rights amendment, someone who opposed it would try consciously or unconsciously to distort the message to be consistent with his or her own views.

Selective Retention.   One last perception-related concept with which you should be familiar is selective retention. In **selective retention,** *some or most of the information received is forgotten and thus what is retained is selective.* For example, if you are pro-nuclear energy, then you are likely to forget any articles, brochures, or other messages that are antinuclear.

Our discussion of perceptual processes has basically shown that consumers generally perceive what they wish to perceive: reality largely exists only in the mind of the consumer. If a manufacturer refines its production technology and improves its labor force in order to increase product quality, and if the consumer does not perceive this change, then all is wasted. Part of the job of marketing is to get the consumer to perceive the seller's offer in the same vein as does the seller.

ECONOMIC FACTORS

The most important economic influence on consumption is consumer income. Wise marketers have long recognized that population growth does not automatically mean increased market opportunities, for the population must have purchasing power. There are over one billion Chinese, but they are not the most lucrative market in the world because their per capita income in U.S. dollars is only $566. Conversely, the population of Switzerland is just over 6 million people, but they represent an attractive market because their average per capita income equals $15,698 U.S. dollars.

Some of the most common ways to measure consumer income are:

1. **Personal income**, which is *an individual's total before-tax income* (about 3 trillion dollars in the United States in 1985).

2. **Disposable personal income**, which is *personal income less taxes and social security levies* (about $2.5 trillion in 1985).
3. **Discretionary income**, which is *the income remaining after the basic necessities of life and fixed commitments, such as auto and house payments or rent, are paid.* This is usually 35 to 40 percent of disposable income.

An added dimension to each of the preceding measures of income is *real income,* which is income adjusted for the effects of inflation. Real income is an accurate gauge of actual purchasing power. Figure 5.4 shows the changes in real disposable personal income since 1960, while Table 5.5 illustrates how Americans spend their income.

Consumer incomes are certainly an economic constraint. A person cannot purchase products without the necessary purchasing power. Possession of purchasing power does not mean that the person will buy; a willingness to buy is also necessary.[20]

Perception plays a role in economic factors.[21] For example, you may have the economic resources to purchase a new car or take a European summer vacation, but as mentioned in our discussion of the economic environment in Chapter 2, if you perceive the economic environment as uncertain and unstable, you may decide not to buy the car or take the

Figure 5.4

Per Capita Income Trends[a]

[a]Data from 1960–1983.

Source: U.S. Bureau of the Census. *Statistical Abstract of the United States: 1982–1983* (Washington, DC, 1982), p. 421; and same source, (1985), p. 438.

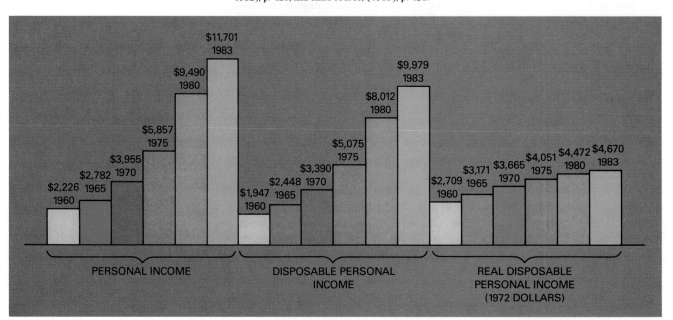

Table 5.5   Consumer Spending Patterns[a]

Item	Complete Reporting of Income				
	Lowest 20 Percent	Second 20 Percent	Third 20 Percent	Fourth 20 Percent	Highest 20 Percent
Income before taxes	$3,901	$9,838	$16,594	$24,560	$42,767
Average weekly expenditure					
Food, total	$30.20	$40.79	$52.77	$66.03	$81.20
Food at home, total	22.87	29.33	36.04	44.61	50.61
Food away from home	7.33	11.46	16.73	21.42	30.59
Alcoholic beverages	2.30	3.87	5.66	6.93	9.82
Tobacco products and supplies	1.76	2.62	3.71	3.66	3.38
Personal care products	2.15	3.00	3.87	5.07	6.96
Housekeeping supplies	2.32	3.30	3.98	5.77	7.33
Energy, total	18.97	28.16	33.99	41.21	51.14
Electricity and natural gas	8.69	11.20	12.35	14.92	18.41
Fuel oil and other fuels	2.63	2.92	3.20	3.37	3.47
Gasoline, motor oil, and additives	7.65	14.04	18.44	22.92	29.26
Nonprescription drugs and supplies	1.12	1.63	1.70	1.76	2.35

[a]Weekly expenditures of urban households, less students, 1980–1981.

Source: U.S. Department of Labor Statistics. Consumer Expenditure Survey: Diary Survey, 1980–81 (Washington, DC, September 1983), Bulletin 2173, p. 13.

vacation. Because of the importance of economic expectations and perceived economic conditions, the Institute for Social Research at the University of Michigan has developed the *index of consumer sentiment.* This index is constructed quarterly and is used to predict changes in the economy three to six months before they occur.[22] The index of consumer sentiment is based on a survey of people's opinions on their personal financial expectations, the overall economy, and the buying environment. The index has been quite useful for predicting the demand for consumer durables such as automobiles.

Price inflation has a major impact on purchasing behavior. When the rate of inflation is high and is expected to continue, consumers typically respond in two ways. First, they may go out and spend more today (and save less) because they expect goods will cost more in the future. This actually helps to further fuel inflation because more dollars are chasing a limited supply of goods. Second, consumers may delay purchasing and put more money into savings. This may occur because consumers believe the economy is unhealthy as a result of high inflation and therefore they tend to save for an uncertain future. They may also expect that sooner or later, this unhealthiness will result in a depression, at which point prices will return to normal levels.

Throughout the 1970s, the United States experienced high inflation, often above 10 percent per year. Consumers basically developed three coping strategies to deal with this situation[23]: (1) increasing their income by working more or having their spouses join the labor force, (2) curtailing expenditures, and (3) increasing their efficiency in the marketplace. Table 5.6 shows the results of one study that examined how consumers increased their efficiency.

POSTPURCHASE EVALUATION

The consumer decision-making process does not end when a consumer purchases a product: the final stage in the process is evaluation of the purchase decision. This stage, called **postpurchase evaluation,** *assesses how satisfied or dissatisfied the consumer is with the purchase.*

Satisfaction/Dissatisfaction

Since the consumer decides on a brand as well as a retail outlet, four states of postpurchase satisfaction are possible, and these are shown in Table 5.7. One possible state of affairs is the consumer who is satisfied with the brand purchased and the retail outlet patronized. This consequence reinforces future loyalty to the brand and retailer. In each of the other cells in Table 5.7, however, some degree of dissatisfaction with the brand or retail outlet, or both, has occurred.

Why does dissatisfaction occur? Before a consumer purchases a product and selects a retail outlet, he or she will have some expectations of the product and the retail outlet. After visiting the retailer and using the product, the consumer will have first-hand experience about performance. If per-

Table 5.6   Ways of Increasing Consumer Efficiency

Method	Percentage of Consumers Using
Becoming more energy conscious	72.8
More comparative shopping	64.6
Becoming less wasteful	61.4
Value fuel economy in cars	58.0
Shopping for specials and bargains	56.3
Buying more products through wholesale outlets	51.3
Looking for cheaper products (e.g., private labels)	34.6

Source: Avraham Sharma. "Coping with Stagflation: Voluntary Simplicity," *Journal of Marketing* (Summer, 1981). Reprinted from the *Journal of Marketing,* published by the American Marketing Association.

MARKETING IN ACTION

Tracking Auto Purchasers' Behavior

The firm, J.D. Power and Associates, regularly conducts major surveys on the satisfaction of auto purchasers. These customer satisfaction surveys are conducted at three points in time: (1) soon after the purchase, (2) three to four months after the purchase, and (3) thirteen to fourteen months afterward. By this later date, customers have had time for the romance of the new car to wear off and to have made several visits to the dealership for service and warranty matters. Questions are asked in the following areas:

- **Problems at delivery.**

- **Problems during first year of operation.**

- **Warranty and service experience at dealership.**

- **Dealer evaluation.**

- **Future purchase intentions.**

- **Overall level of satisfaction.**

In addition to consumer satisfaction research, three times a year the firm surveys 5,000 driving-age consumers about their auto usage, intentions to purchase a new auto, and their attitudes toward cars. A part of the attitudinal research asks the respondents to rate automobile attributes in terms of importance for their next auto purchase. For example, recent surveys have shown that increasingly important attributes to the U.S. auto buyer are "dependability and trouble-free operation."

Source: Based on information in "How Do You Measure Satisfaction?" *Automotive News* (September 17, 1984), p. 10; Joseph Bohn. "How Power Rates Owner Satisfaction," *Automotive News* (September 17, 1984), pp. 29–34.

formance is less than expected, dissatisfaction will occur.[24] Marketing managers should realize that consumers tell their acquaintances and friends about their likes and dislikes with products and stores. If several friends tell

Table 5.7   Results of Postpurchase Evaluation

Brand of Product	Retail Outlet Patronized	
	Satisfied	**Dissatisfied**
Satisfied	Consumer's behavior is strongly positively reinforced—HIGH SATISFACTION	Consumer is dissatisfied with retailer that was patronized.
Dissatisfied	Consumer is dissatisfied with brand purchased.	Consumer's behavior is strongly negatively reinforced—HIGH DISSATISFACTION

you that a particular brand of product is terrible, then you may not purchase that brand based on the experiences of others. This illustrates the importance of having satisfied consumers.

Cognitive Dissonance

Discomfort also may ensue if consumers feel that they did not shop around enough before making a choice. **Cognitive dissonance** is the *doubt that occurs when the consumer becomes aware that unchosen alternatives have desirable attributes,*[25] *leading the consumer to wonder whether he or she made the right decision.* Say, for example, that you just purchased a new cordless telephone and you are very satisfied with its range and performance. After owning it for a week, however, you see the same phone advertised by another local retailer for $15 less. You therefore experience dissonance because you did not shop around before making your purchase.

How do consumers reduce dissonance? Consumers can reassess the attractiveness of unchosen alternatives, or they can search for information to validate the choice made. For example, after experiencing dissonance over the cordless phone, you may ask friends about the reputation of the retailer you did not patronize. You may find that this dealer offers poor service and tends not to stand behind the factory warranty. Hence, you rationalize that the added $15 you paid was probably worth it in the long run since the patronized dealer is reputed to offer excellent service.

Complaint Behavior

How do consumers react when they are dissatisfied with a product or retail outlet?[26] One reaction—to take no action—occurs more often for products of low unit value because the time and effort required to complain may not be worthwhile. For major durables, however, the consumer usually takes some form of private or public action, as illustrated in Figure 5.5.

Manufacturers of major durables encourage consumers to voice their complaints. General Motors, for example, has established toll-free or call-collect numbers in the fifty states for GM car owners with unresolved engine or transmission problems.[27] The legal/political climate also prompts complaint behavior; the Maryland Attorney General's office has prepared a kit to help consumers who are seeking to resolve complaints with General Motors. The kit gives helpful tips on how to reach higher settlements with the company.[28] In addition, numerous studies have researched consumer satisfaction and complaint behavior. One company performing surveys in this area is highlighted in the Marketing in Action on page 141.

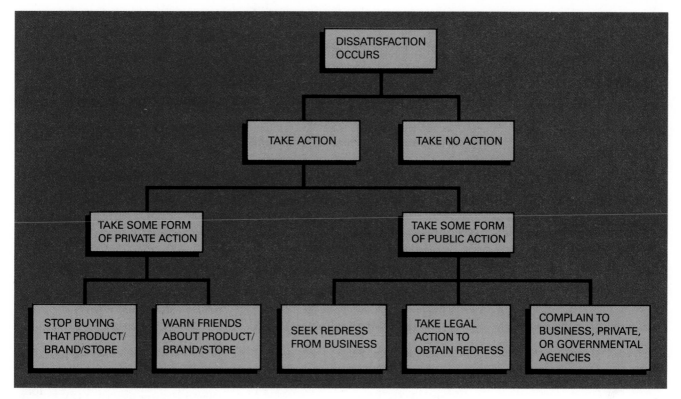

Figure 5.5

Actions Consumers Take in Response to Product Dissatisfaction

Source: R. Day. "Extending the Concept of Consumer Satisfaction," in W.D. Perreault, Jr. (ed.), *Advances in Consumer Research,* Vol. 4, (Chicago: Association for Consumer Research, 1977), p. 153. Used by permission.

SUMMARY

This chapter acquainted you with how consumers make purchasing decisions. You learned that a useful way to view consumer behavior was as a decision-making process, initiated when the consumer recognizes a problem. Problem recognition occurs when the consumer's desired state of affairs departs sufficiently from the actual state so as to place the consumer in a state of unrest. The consumer then tries to decide which products, brands, and retail stores can help reduce this state of unrest and solve the problem.

Three types of consumer problem solving were discussed: habitual problem solving, limited problem solving, and extended problem solving. Consumer decision making is influenced by three broad factors: sociological, psychological, and economic. Sociological factors deal with the influence of culture, social class, family, and reference groups on the consumer's decisions. Psychological factors are variables that are internal to the consumer's thought processes and include such factors as motivation, attitudes, learning processes, and perceptual processes. Finally, economic factors are concerned with how a person's economic resources and economic expectations influence consumer behavior.

Consumer behavior does not end once a purchase has been made since purchase experiences will be evaluated. This postpurchase evaluation can result in satisfaction, dissatisfaction, or both. A consumer could be satisfied with a product, but not with the retailer from whom it was purchased, or vice versa. Dissatisfied consumers may complain either privately or publicly, but in any event, dissatisfied consumers are less likely to purchase the same product or patronize the same store in the future.

KEY CONCEPTS

consumer market (p. 121)
sociological factors (p. 121)
psychological factors (p. 121)
economic factors (p. 121)
habitual problem solving (p. 122)
limited problem solving (p. 123)
extended problem solving (p. 123)
culture (p. 124)
social class (p. 125)
reference groups (p. 129)
motivation (p. 131)
attitude (p. 132)

learning (p. 133)
stimulus (p. 133)
drive (p. 133)
perception (p. 134)
selective exposure (p. 136)
selective distortion (p. 137)
selective retention (p. 137)
personal income (p. 137)
disposable personal income (p. 138)
discretionary income (p. 138)
postpurchase evaluation (p. 140)
cognitive dissonance (p. 142)

REVIEW AND DISCUSSION QUESTIONS

1. List and explain the three different degrees of consumer problem solving.

2. Which of the four sociological factors that were discussed have had the greatest impact on your clothing purchasing behavior? Explain.

3. A marketing manager only needs to understand "culture" when products are being marketed internationally. Agree or disagree with this statement and state your reasons.

4. Which social class (i.e., upper, lower, middle, and so on) do you think represents the largest consumer market in the United States? Please state your reasons.

5. What are the major types of family decision making with respect to consumer purchases? Which type best characterizes your family?

6. Are family pets (cats, dogs, birds, and so on) family members? Can they influence household purchases?

7. Define *reference groups* and discuss how they influence consumer behavior.

8. Briefly explain Maslow's hierarchy of human needs. How might a company such as Kellogg use Maslow's theory of motivation in selling breakfast cereal?

9. Define *attitude* and explain the three dimensions of an attitude.

10. If a person likes a brand, he or she is more likely to purchase that brand. Why might this statement be incorrect?

11. Explain the steps in the learning process and illustrate with an example of your choice related to consumer behavior.

12. Discuss the relationship between habitual problem solving and learning processes.

13. Define and give examples of selective exposure, selective distortion, and selective retention.

14. How are perceptual processes related to the economic environment? How does this influence consumer decision making?

15. What is cognitive dissonance? How might a company such as Chrysler reduce the dissonance that customers have after they purchase a new Chrysler automobile?

16. In the early 1960s, people in their twenties consumed 3.4 cups of coffee per day. By the early 1980s, consumption among this group was 1.3 cups per day. What behavioral concepts in this chapter can help explain this change?

17. Parents can purchase fruit (e.g., apples, oranges, cherries) for their children for $0.50 to $1.00 a pound, or they can buy Fruit Rolls (flattened, sweetened, and rolled-up fruit) for over $7 per pound. Why do they purchase the higher priced product?

18. Name the four possible states of postpurchase satisfaction.

ACTION PROBLEMS

1. Make three columns and list the following products under the appropriate heading: lower, middle, or upper social class.

a. Scotch
b. Yacht
c. *True Romance* magazine
d. Mercedes-Benz Auto
e. Budweiser beer with dinner
f. above-ground swimming pool in backyard
g. *National Geographic* magazine
h. Curlers in hair (women)
i. Fake fur coat
j. Artichokes for dinner
k. Collards for dinner
l. Room air conditioner
m. Wine with dinner
n. White socks (men)
o. Central air conditioning
p. Polyester suit (men)
q. Orthodontic treatment
r. Interior design service
s. Membership in the Democratic party
t. Heineken beer with guests

2. Hard work is one of the core American cultural values, and it is believed to result in achievement and success. Find some examples of particular products and brands that are promoted as rewards for adhering to this core value.

3. In selecting a new apartment, what attributes would you consider? Rank these attributes in terms of their importance. Is there an apartment complex in your community that performs well on the attributes that are most important to you? What is your attitude toward this apartment complex?

4. Two families each win $20,000 in the state lottery. Each family has two young children under 6 years old, and both parents work in each family. One family is in the upper middle class, and the other is in the lower class. How might you expect each family to spend the $20,000 prize?

5. Interview a foreign college student on your campus about how he or she perceives U.S. consumers to be different from those in his or her home country. Try to identify the influence of sociological factors—family members, culture, social class, reference groups—in the purchasing process.

6. List the advertisements you recall seeing over the last several days. Explain how the perceptual processes of selective exposure, selective distortion, and selective retention influenced this list.

7. Develop a list of the membership groups, aspiration groups, and dissociative groups that are your reference groups. Give an example of how each of these groups has recently influenced your consumption and shopping behavior.

8. You and a close friend are considering opening a restaurant. One site you have in mind has 4,000 households within two miles, most of which are in the top 40 percent income brackets. Another site has 4,800 households within two miles, most of which are in the bottom 40 percent income brackets. Using the data in Table 5.5, estimate the total amount the households within a two-mile radius of each site will spend on food away from home. Estimate sales at each potential site assuming a 4 percent market share for the first site and a 6 percent market share for the second site.

NOTES

1. Del I. Hawkins, Roger J. Best, Kenneth A. Coney, *Consumer Behavior: Implications for Marketing Strategy* (Plano, TX: Business Publications, Inc., 1983), p. 454.

2. Ibid., p. 63.

3. F.M. Nicosia and R.N. Mayer, "Toward a Sociology of Consumption," *Journal of Consumer Research* (September 1976), p. 67.

4. Gerald Zaltman and Melanie Wallendorf, *Consumer Behavior: Basic Findings and Management Implications* (New York: John Wiley & Sons, 1983), p. 114; Pierre Martineau, "Social Classes and Spending Behavior," *Journal of Marketing* 23(October 1958), pp. 121–141; Richard P. Coleman, "The Significance of Social Stratification in Selling," in Martin L. Bell (ed.), *Marketing: A Maturing Discipline* (Chicago: American Marketing Association, 1961), pp. 171–184.

5. A.B. Hollingshead and F.C. Redlich, *Social Class and Mental Illness* (New York: John Wiley & Sons, 1958); W.L. Warner, M. Meeker, and K. Eels, *Social Class in America: Manual of Procedure for the Measurement of Social Status* (Chicago: Science Research Associates, 1949).

6. W. Wells, *Lifestyle and Performance* (Chicago: American Marketing Association, 1974), p. 241; R.P. Coleman, *Social Status in the City* (San Francisco: Josey-Bass, 1971), p. 59; and the computations and experience of this text's authors.

7. Rachael Dardis and Marie Sandler, "Shopping Behavior of Discount Store Customers in a Small City," *Journal of Retailing* 47(Summer 1971), pp. 60–72.

8. V. Kanti Prasad, "Socio-Economic Product Risk and Patronage Preferences of Retail Shoppers," *Journal of Marketing* 39(July 1975), pp. 42–47.

9. Peter L. Gillett, "A Profile of Urban In-Home Shoppers," *Journal of Marketing* (July 1970), pp. 40–45.

10. P.G. Herbst, "Conceptual Framework for Studying the Family," in O.A. Aeser and S.B. Hammond (eds.), *Social Structure and Personality in a City* (London: Routledge, 1954).

11. Harry L. Davis and Benny P. Rigaux, "Perception of Marital Roles in Decision Processes," *Journal of Consumer Research* 1(June 1974), p. 57.

12. G.J. Szybillo and A. Sosanie, "Family Decision Making: Husband, Wife and Children," in W.D. Perreault, Jr. (ed.), *Advances in Consumer Research* (Chicago: Association for Consumer Research, 1977), pp. 46–49.

13. James H. Myers and William H. Reynolds, *Consumer Behavior and Marketing Management* (Boston: Houghton Mifflin, 1967), pp. 173–174.

14. Francis S. Bourne, "Group Influence in Marketing and Public Relations," in R. Likert and S.P. Hayes, Jr. (eds.), *Some Applications of Behavioral Research* (New York: UNESCO, 1961).

15. A.H. Maslow, *Motivation and Personality,* 2nd edition (New York: Harper & Row, 1970).

16. M. Fishbein and I. Ajzen. *Belief, Attitude, Intention and Behavior: An Introduction to Theory and Research* (Reading, MA: Addison-Wesley, 1975), p. 6.

17. Michael L. Ray. "Psychological Theories and Interpretations of Learning," in Scott Ward and Thomas S. Robertson (eds.), *Consumer Behavior: Theoretical Sources* (Englewood Cliffs, NJ: Prentice-Hall, 1973), p. 47.

18. David Loudon and Albert Dela Bitta, *Consumer Behavior: Concepts and Applications* (New York: McGraw-Hill, 1979), p. 319.

19. Thomas Robertson, *Consumer Behavior* (Morristown, NJ: Scott, Foresman, 1970), pp. 14–16.

20. George Katona, "Understanding Consumer Attitudes," in Richard T. Curtin (ed.), *Surveys of Consumers 1974–1975: Contributions to Behavioral Economics* (Ann Arbor, MI: Institute for Social Research, 1976), pp. 203–219.

21. Fred Van Raaij, "Economic Psychology," *Journal of Economic Psychology* 1(March 1981), pp. 1–24.

22. George Katona, *Surveys of Consumers,* pp. 203–219.

23. David Caplovitz, "Making Ends Meet: How Families Cope with Inflation and Recession," *Annals of the American Academy of Political and Social Science* (July 1981), pp. 88–98.

24. R. Anderson, "Consumer Dissatisfaction: The Effect of Disconfirmed Expectancy of Perceived Product Performance," *Journal of Marketing* (February 1973), pp. 33–44; Richard L. Oliver, "A Cognitive Model of the Antecedents and Consequences of Satisfaction Decisions," *Journal of Marketing Research* (November 1980), pp. 460–469; Robert A. Westbrook, "Sources of Consumer Satisfaction with Retail Outlets," *Journal of Retailing* (Fall 1981), pp. 68–85; John E. Swan and I. Fred Trawick, "Disconfirmation of Expectations and Satisfaction with a Retail Service," *Journal of Retailing* (Fall 1981), pp. 49–67.

25. Carl E. Block and Kenneth J. Roering, *Essentials of Consumer Behavior: Concepts and Applications,* 2nd edition (Hinsdale, IL: Dryden Press, 1979), p. 517.

26. Consumer complaint behavior is further discussed in J. Jacoby and J.J. Jaccard, "The Sources, Meaning and Validity of Consumer Complaining Behavior: A Psychological Analysis," *Journal of Retailing* (Fall 1981), pp. 4–22; A. Andreasen and A. Best, "Consumers Complain—Does Business Respond?" *Harvard Business Review* (July–August 1977), pp. 93–101; Claes Fornell and Robert A. Westbrook, "The Vicious Circle of Consumer Complaints," *Journal of Marketing* (Summer 1984), pp. 68–78.

27. "Numbers Listed for GM Complaints," *Automotive News* (October 8, 1984), p. 24.

28. "Kit Is Designed to Aid in Claims," *Automotive News* (October 22, 1984), p. 33.

CHAPTER 6

LEARNING OBJECTIVES

After you complete this chapter, you should be able to:

- **Distinguish** between producer, government, and reseller markets

- **List** and **explain** the two major determinants of organizational buying behavior

- **Describe** the three major types of decision situations in organizational buying

- **Identify** the four types of members in the organization who have an impact on the buying decision

- **Relate** open-to-buy, forward buy, and off-premise buying to retail and wholesale buying

- **Explain** systems selling and value analysis and relate them to organizational buying behavior

ORGANIZATIONAL MARKETS AND BUYING BEHAVIOR

MARKETER PROFILE

Moreton Binn, the King of Bartering

All organizations must secure goods and services from other organizations to conduct their operations. Some organizations, though, may use barter as a noncash way to acquire the needed goods and services. Bartering is the trading of goods and services without the exchange of money. Over one-half of the largest U.S. corporations engage in bartering to some extent.

Moreton Binn (his friends call him "Mort") is a world-class expert in bartering between organizations. He serves as a broker in bringing together organizations that have excess inventory or services they need to liquidate. Binn likes to make deals, and in 1982, he put together $365 million in barter-

ing deals for various firms. Some of the products Mort has dealt in are automobiles, airline space, tennis rackets, and industrial chemicals.

Binn's deals are often quite complex. One involved trading $3.5 million in Spaulding tennis rackets and golf equipment to a resort hotel in Miami. Spaulding used some of the rooms at the hotel for a sales conference, and Mort traded the remainder to BSR, a producer of sophisticated stereo turntables. These turntables were then traded to radio stations to use as promotional giveaways in return for radio advertising spots. The radio spots were then traded to a retail chain in exchange for small appliances and cash.

Bartering can be thought of as a

grown-up version of trading bubble gum cards. It requires "a flexible mind not bound by conventional notions of money or price tags, plus a quick eye for spotting profit opportunities other people might not see." Obviously, Moreton Binn possesses those qualities. As Moreton Binn says, "Who needs money? You can-	not eat it or wear it." From his perspective, it is strictly a measurement that can sometimes get in the way of a good business deal.
	Source: Based in part on William G. Shepherd Jr. with David M. Paine. "The Baron of Barter," *United Airlines Inflight Magazine* (March 1983), pp. 79–85.

INTRODUCTION

Mort Binn has made his living matching the needs of organizational buyers. This chapter will explore several aspects of organizational markets and buying behavior. The types of organizational markets, the determinants of organizational buying decisions, decision makers, and the process of organizational buying will all be explained. In addition, specific types of organizational buying behavior, such as open-to-buy and forward buying, will be examined. Finally, some of the similarities and differences between consumer buying behavior, which was discussed in Chapter 5, and organizational buying behavior will be elucidated.

ORGANIZATIONAL MARKETS

Organizational markets are *composed of business units and organizations that purchase goods and services to be used, directly or indirectly, in the production of other goods and services or to be resold to governments, resellers (retailers and wholesalers), and producers.* The organizational market (sometimes called the business market) in the United States is larger than the consumer market, primarily because for every consumer product you purchase, several organizational transactions must occur. Consider your purchase of a pair of shoes, for example. A leather tanner bought hides that were then sold to a shoe manufacturer. The shoe manufacturer in turn sold the shoes to a wholesaler, who sold them to retailers. Finally, one of the retailers sold you a pair of shoes. All of the transactions except the last one are examples of organizational buying.

In the United States, there are over 4 million organizations of every imaginable type that are potential buyers of goods and services.[1] For example, there are over 51,000 hotels and motels in the United States, each of which needs to purchase items such as bed linens, cleaning supplies, and furniture. The United States also has over 275,000 restaurants, 20,000 funeral homes, and 30,000 new-car dealers. Consider the many goods and services, such as those shown in the RCA advertisement on page 150, that organizations need to purchase to operate their businesses. Buying organizations also include government units. There are roughly 15,000 public school districts in the United States that buy such things as books, computers, buses, furniture, and paper goods.

Organizations purchase all types of products from other businesses.

Although there are many organizations in the United States, a small proportion accounts for a disproportionate amount of economic activity. In 1984, the top 500 U.S. industrial manufacturing organizations had sales of $1,759 billion and the top fifty retail organizations had sales of $297 billion.[2]

The federal government has developed the **standard industrial classification (SIC)** system, which is *a system for categorizing all U.S. businesses by product or market segment.[3] The system has seven digits; the first four deal with industry groups, the fifth shows the product class, while the sixth and seventh denote specific products.* This system is an important market segmentation tool because it enables companies to pinpoint specific areas, industries, and markets with relative ease. A number of publications, both government and private industry, use the SIC codes to report data.

The SIC system starts with eleven basic categories, which make up all industrial markets:

1. Agriculture, forestry, and fisheries
2. Mining
3. Construction
4. Manufacturing
5. Transportation, communication, and electric, gas, and sanitary utilities
6. Wholesale trade
7. Retail trade
8. Finance, insurance, and real estate
9. Services
10. Public administration
11. Not elsewhere classified

The SIC system gets quite detailed. Based on their primary activity, organizations can be categorized by two- to seven-digit codes. Figure 6.1 presents a blueprint of the one- to four-digit SIC system for durable goods wholesale trade.

For market analysis purposes, organizational markets can be conveniently categorized as producer markets, government markets, and reseller markets. Let's examine each of these in more detail.

Producer Markets

Producer markets *consist of firms that purchase goods and services for the production of other goods and services.* For example, Nestle (a leading worldwide manufacturer of processed foods headquartered in Switzerland) needs to purchase over $20 billion Swiss francs (roughly $10 billion U.S. dollars) of goods and services annually to operate its business. These purchases include such diverse items as computers, paper clips, grain, assembly line machinery, coffee beans, legal services, and toilet paper.

Types of Products. The producer market handles many different types of products, as the preceding Nestle example illustrates. These products can be classified by the following categories: raw materials, major equipment, accessory equipment, component parts, process materials, supplies, and organizational services.[4] These products are generally referred to as industrial products.

Raw materials are unprocessed products from mines, farms, forests, and oceans. A firm purchases raw materials, which usually are processed to become part of a manufactured product. Oscar Mayer, for example, buys live hogs, which are butchered and processed to make bologna. Raw materials usually are purchased in large quantities and typically are bought according to grade and specification. For example, Coors Brewery in Golden,

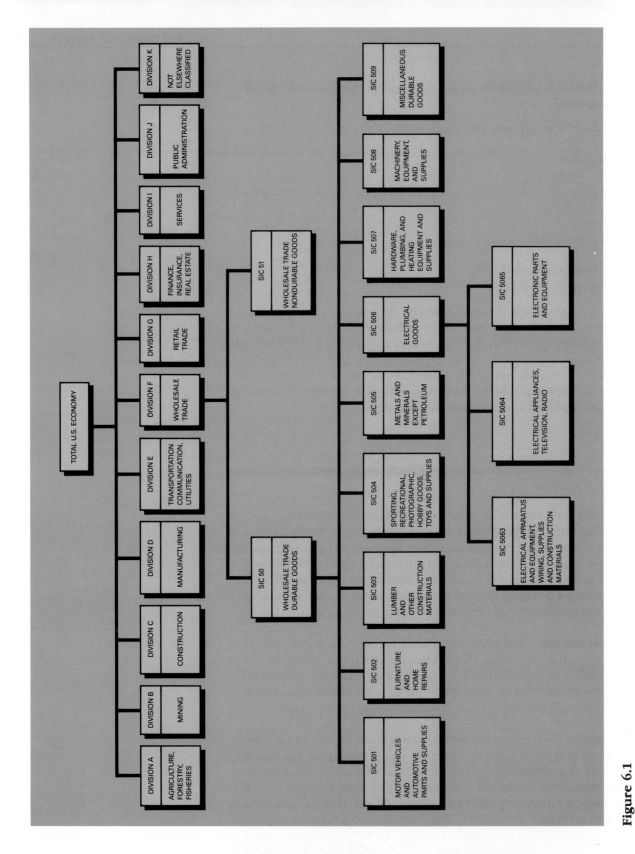

Figure 6.1

The SIC System

Source: *1972 Standard Industrial Classification Manual* (Washington, DC: Office of Management and Budget, 1972).

Colorado, buys grain by the carload, but it only purchases grain that meets certain quality standards.

Major equipment consists of machinery and large tools used to manufacture goods. Ford Motor Company annually purchases over $1 billion in stamping machines, lathes, and robots to make automobiles. Major equipment is expensive and usually involves extensive decision making by the purchasing organization. Also, since major equipment usually is technologically sophisticated, the sellers of this equipment must offer good service. Services such as training and installation, repair and maintenance, and financing are an important part of the product offering.

Most major equipment is custom designed rather than mass-produced. For instance, all of the equipment and machinery in the INTERCERAMIC tile plant in Chihuahua, Mexico, was custom designed and produced in Italy.

Accessory equipment is used to facilitate production, administrative, clerical, or marketing activities, but it is not directly used in the manufacture of the final physical product. Some examples are calculators, filing cabinets, and fire extinguishers. Accessory equipment is usually standardized and less expensive than major equipment. Also, the sellers of accessory equipment do not need to offer as many services as do sellers of major equipment.

Component parts are incorporated directly into the physical product being produced. These items either are fully assembled or require little processing before assembly into the final product. For instance, auto manufacturers purchase tires, batteries, spark plugs, and wiring harnesses from other companies.

Process materials are directly incorporated in manufactured products, but cannot be physically identified in the final product. For example, Shell and most other oil companies purchase platinum to use as a catalyst in the cracking process of gasoline production. The Coca-Cola Company uses corn syrup to produce its soft drinks.

Like accessory equipment, *supplies* help facilitate production and op-

General Electric robots are major equipment used by the company to manufacture goods.

erations but have a relatively short life. Cleaning products, pens, pencils, paper, and pulley belts are examples. Sometimes supplies are referred to as *MRO items*—*m*aintenance, *r*epair, and *o*perating (or overhaul) supplies.

Organizational services, also called *industrial services,* are services that organizations buy, such as legal services, telecommunications services, and marketing research, to conduct their business. Most of these services could be performed internally, if desired, but often outside consultants or service organizations are hired.

The Marketing in Action on page 155 illustrates how international competition is increasingly taking over the market for industrial services. Thus, U.S. firms must become good international marketers not only of tangible goods, but also of services.

Special Market Characteristics.   Producer markets have certain unique characteristics that create special marketing problems.[5] As a potential marketing manager, you should be familiar with these characteristics.

The demand for products in producer markets is a **derived demand** since it *is based on or derived from the demand for consumer products.* The demands for textile machinery in the apparel industry, steel in the auto industry, lumber in the furniture industry, and oil in the petroleum industry are all based on final consumer demand.

Derived demand creates a marketing problem because the manufacturer of products for producer markets must anticipate future consumer demand. A textile machinery manufacturer cannot wait to see how much apparel consumers will buy two years from now; it must anticipate that demand today so that the supply of textile machinery will be sufficient when demand materializes. Obviously, this situation is risky for the textile machinery producer, but risk taking is always part of marketing activity.

Joint demand occurs *when the demand for two or more products is interdependent because the products must be used together.* For example, the demand for machinery and the demand for lubricants is a joint demand. Joint demand creates problems because the demand for one product cannot increase without increasing the demand for the other product. If a producer of industrial lubricants wants to sell more lubricants, the use of machinery must also increase—an element over which there is little control.

Postponability of demand occurs when a manufacturer can get by without purchasing additional major equipment even though demand for a product increases. The manufacturer may decide instead to work existing equipment harder or longer. The production facility may, for example, go from one to two or even to three shifts before new equipment is purchased. Producers may prefer this alternative, even though it increases overtime and repair costs, because they may feel uncertain about how long demand for their output will stay high.

Most producers have inventories of goods and materials, such as raw materials, component parts, process materials, and supplies. Inventory fluctuations occur when the producer adjusts the inventory levels to conform

MARKETING IN ACTION

Firms in the United States historically have held a commanding lead in the international marketing of industrial services. The U.S. firms were clear leaders in banking, insurance, advertising, telecommunications, construction services, and business consulting. Now, an increasing number of foreign firms are taking the lead in the lucrative markets for industrial services.

Consider the following examples of increased foreign competition:

- France, with the Ariane rocket, is now able to launch their own telecommunications satellites and is also selling their launching services to other countries. Several other nations probably will have their own launching systems within a decade, which will increase competition in the satellite launching market.

- Korea's Hyundai Engineering and Construction Co. is aggressively going after foreign construction contracts, especially in Saudi Arabia,

International Competition Intensifies in Industrial Services Markets

where U.S. firms such as Bechtel traditionally had a stronghold.

- Canada's Olympia & York Developments Ltd. has become the second largest real estate developer in the United States.

- The British advertising agency Saatchi & Saatchi has acquired two U.S. advertising agencies and is now among the top ten advertising agencies in the world. Saatchi & Saatchi started from nowhere in 1970 and now has offices in forty countries.

- The Evergreen Marine Corp. and Yangming Marine Transport, both of Taiwan, are now respectively the

fifth and tenth largest shipping firms in the world. Both firms regularly undercut the prices of shippers from other countries by 5 to 10 percent.

- The Japanese bank Sumitomo is tackling world financial markets and has even entered Switzerland.

U.S. firms will have to fight aggressively to hold their share of industrial services markets as more and more foreign countries move from smokestack industries to a service economy.

Source: Based in part on "The Next Trade Crisis May Be Just Around the Corner," *BusinessWeek* (March 19, 1984), pp. 48–55; Paul Hemp, "Saatchi & Saatchi Agrees to Acquire Ad Agency in U.S., " *The Wall Street Journal* (April 17, 1986), p. 12; and "Ariane Three-Year Launch Schedule Averages Seven Missions Annually, Includes Initial E LA-2 Operations," *Aviation Week and Space Technology* (December 17, 1984), p. 53.

to present or anticipated future economic conditions. In the early 1980s, for example, when the prime interest rate was 21 percent, many producers cut back on inventories because of the high costs of carrying them. Conversely, in the mid-1970s, when the United States witnessed many raw material shortages and rapid price inflation, producers built up inventories, in part to shelter themselves against future price increases.

Because the demand for major equipment and many other industrial goods is derived, the demand for these goods is subject to a *multiplier effect.* With the multiplier effect, a small change in consumer demand will create a more than proportionate change in industrial demand.

The following example illustrates the multiplier principle. In 1981, the ABC Shoe Company produced 500,000 pairs of shoes. To accomplish this, it had a factory with five shoe machines, each capable of producing 100,000 pairs of shoes per year. The life expectancy of a shoe machine is five years, and given the age distribution of existing machines, ABC replaces one machine each year. Thus, in 1981, it had a demand for one new machine (see

Table 6.1). In 1982, demand went up to 600,000 pairs of shoes—a 20 percent increase—so that the company had to buy two new machines; one for replacement and one to increase capacity from 500,000 to 600,000 shoes annually. Machine demand went up 100 percent. In 1983, demand jumped to 800,000 shoes, which meant the company needed to buy three new machines; one for replacement and two for added capacity. Note shoe demand went up 33 percent, but machine demand increased 50 percent. Finally, shoe demand dropped to 700,000 pairs in 1984, so that ABC did not need to buy any new machines. Since they had eight machines and only needed seven at year-end 1983, even after they retire one machine in 1984 they will have sufficient capacity. Note that shoe demand fell 12.5 percent, but new machine demand totally vanished.

For many types of industrial equipment, changes in technology create new demands. Often, existing equipment is not worn out, but new equipment is technologically superior and may be more cost effective. For instance, there is nothing physically wrong with a standard office typewriter; however, they pale in comparison to the newer electronic typewriters and word processors with all their built-in features. Thus, companies are scrapping their old typewriters in favor of the new machines. The old machines, although not worn out, are becoming technologically obsolete.

Still another facet of the producer markets are government-created markets, which are new producer opportunities brought about because of governmental regulations. For example, the Occupational Safety and Health Administration (OSHA) stimulated demand for protective clothing, which created an opportunity for Vallen Corporation (a wholesaler of industrial safety equipment). Similarly, the Environmental Protection Agency (EPA) has helped to create demand for pollution control equipment. Most of the governmental agencies have been created for the protection of people, places, or resources, and some parties become dissatisfied when agencies and new laws concerning them are created. For example, although the Vallen Corporation was pleased with OSHA's rulings on protective clothing, the factories where this clothing needs to be worn were unhappy because their costs were increased.

Table 6.1   Multiplier Principle: ABC Shoe Company

Year	Consumer Demand		Machines Needed				
	Units	% Change	Total Machines	For Replacement	For Growth in Consumer Demand	Total New Machines	% Change
1981	500,000	—	5	1	—	1	—
1982	600,000	20	6	1	1	2	100
1983	800,000	33.3	8	1	2	3	50
1984	700,000	−12.5	7	0	0	0	—

The Glass Packaging Institute realizes the demand for glass is derived, and thus encourages manufacturers and retailers to produce and sell soft drinks in glass bottles.

Government Markets

The **government market** *consists of federal, state, and local government agencies and the goods and services they purchase to conduct operations and serve the public.*[6]

Types of Products. Opportunities exist for almost all business organizations in the government markets because the government buys all types of products, from ice cream to nuclear reactors, and because purchasing is spread out geographically over local, state, and federal agencies. Federal buying, however, is not always done on a national level. In fact, the FBI and the U.S. Border Patrol occasionally purchase automotive maintenance and repair services locally. Most federal purchasing of standard, nonmilitary items occurs through the General Services Administration (GSA). Many of the products purchased by the government are similar to the types of producer goods defined earlier in the chapter.

Special Market Characteristics.   Government agencies purchase on a competitive basis through bid solicitation. Two types of bidding are popular: open bidding and negotiated contract bidding.

In an **open bid** *the government procurement office invites bids from qualified suppliers.* An interested supplier must meet certain specifications and apply to be a qualified supplier in order to be placed on the bidders' list. The supplier then will be sent invitations for bids whenever the government agency has a purchasing need. The invitation for bids carefully describes the materials or products the government desires to purchase in terms of technical specifications, quality, and so on. The terms of the contract are also carefully stated (i.e., delivery dates and timing of payment). Open bidding occurs for standardized and mass-produced items such as tires, office equipment and supplies, lawn mowers, and shampoo.

Increasingly, the federal government is encouraging life cycle costing bids where appropriate. *Life cycle cost* is the cost of the product over the expected life of the product based on energy, repair, and maintenance costs. This estimate enables the agency to determine which product will be the better buy over the life of the product. For example, a $5 engine bearing that is estimated to last five years with little or no maintenance might be a better long-range buy than a similar product costing $3 but with a life of two years. Recognizing the importance of life cycle costing has helped Lawson Products (a wholesaler of MRO supplies) secure the Air Force as a customer. Salesperson Donnie Richards gives an example, "The costs of their hydraulic hose consumption has been cut in half by the substitution of Lawson's products for less expensive items."[7] An Air Force base is a heavy user of hydraulic hoses for cranes, aircraft lowering, and ground maintenance equipment.

In **negotiated contract bidding,** *a government agency directly negotiates a contract with a limited number of firms and then awards the contract to one of them.* The award does not necessarily go to the lowest price bidder, since the government usually considers other factors, such as the supplier's reputation and their ability to complete the project on schedule and to control costs. Negotiated contract bidding usually occurs with custom-designed, non-mass-produced items, such as Minute Man Missiles or a hydroelectric dam. There is little effective competition for these types of items; thus, negotiated contract bidding is preferable to open bidding.

The U.S. government market is large—and growing rapidly—despite politicians' attempts to limit the growth in government spending. Government spending has grown for a variety of reasons. First, the government is providing more services to the public than it has in the past. Second, the number of government agencies has increased over the years. Every time a new agency such as OSHA or the EPA is created, the amount of government

Government agencies use negotiated contract bidding as an effective means of obtaining products from companies on whom they feel they can rely.

spending and, hence purchasing, rises. Third, inflation has caused the costs of goods and services the government purchases to rise, just as the cost of consumer goods has risen drastically over the last fifteen years.

Despite the vast selling opportunities created by the government, many businesses do not sell to the government for a number of reasons: too much paperwork, too many negotiated contracts, not knowing whom to contact, special product specifications, and the government's slow decision-making process.[8] The General Services Administration, for example, buys such common items as garbage cans, tableware, loose-leaf binders, facial tissue, table napkins, and pencils, but it is often unable to find at least three firms willing to submit a bid to sell these items despite the fact that the minimum purchase is $50,000.[9]

Most business firms need to recognize that despite the problems in selling to the government the effort can have sizable payoffs. Donnie Richards of Lawson Products states, "It's the only type of customer I know of that will purchase everything in your catalog after you have met the necessary qualifications and gained the necessary approvals."[10] Hermon E. Valentine (founder of Systems Management American Corp., one of the largest black-owned businesses in the United States) has also discovered the value of selling to the government. In 1982, his firm landed a government contract for an estimated $150 million to assist in the development of the U.S. Navy's shipboard nontactical automated program, which involves the installation of computer systems on approximately 450 U.S. Navy ships. In May 1984, the company received a $55 million contract extension, and Valentine expects sales to the navy to reach $250 million by the end of the 1980s.[11]

The Marketing in Action on page 161 provides another example of selling to the government. Table 6.2 provides several sources of additional information on this lucrative business.

Reseller Markets

The **reseller market** *consists of business organizations that purchase products for resale to other business organizations or individuals.* Two major types of resellers are wholesalers and retailers. **Wholesalers** *purchase from manufacturers or other wholesalers and in turn sell to retailers, manufacturers, service organizations, or other wholesalers.* **Retailers** *purchase from wholesalers or manufacturers and in turn sell to the final consumers.* Chapter 12 will discuss retailing and wholesaling in more detail.

Table 6.2   Sources of Information on Government Purchasing Practices

Publication	Description
GSA Supply Catalog (Washington, DC: U.S. Government Printing Office)	Lists 20,000 products commonly purchased by the GSA
U.S. Government Purchasing and Sales Directory (Washington, DC: U.S. Government Printing Office)	Provides information on all federal purchasing offices and their product needs
Federal Buying Directory (available without cost at all GSA Business Service Centers)	Who's who of federal purchasing officials based in Washington
Commerce Business Daily (Washington, DC: U.S. Commerce Department)	A newspaper that invites bids for civilian agency procurement for goods and services over $5,000 and for military items over $10,000
Herman Holtz, *Government Contracts: Proposalmanship and Winning Strategies* (New York: Plenum Press, 1979)	Explains how to write contract proposals and how the government evaluates proposals and bids

MARKETING IN ACTION

Selling Brushes to the Army

During the Vietnam War, many U.S. soldiers found themselves in danger when the M-16 rifles they were using jammed in combat. Investigations were launched to determine the source of the problem, and it was discovered that mud, sand, dirt and other debris were causing the rifles to jam. During this period, Owens Brush Co. of Iowa City, Iowa, began to receive large orders from post exchanges in Vietnam. These orders far exceeded the quantity of toothbrushes needed for oral hygiene: the brushes were being used to clean the M-16 rifles.

Richard Hyman, vice president and sales manager at Owens Brush, immediately recognized the potential demand that this situation created. He decided to modify an existing brush to suit the task of rifle cleaning. He "selected a fairly large, multituft brush, changed the texture to a stiffer version, and cut a large, V-shaped notch across the short axis of the brush head. This notch facilitated cleaning around corners and certain hidden surfaces that otherwise could not be reached."

The modified brushes were sold through the post exchange system for the purposes of cleaning rifles. There were two shortcomings to Hyman's approach, however: the brush was *not* designed from scratch to do the best job, and selling through post exchanges was a back-door approach to selling to the army. What was needed was a brush engineered to do the job and that would be sold directly to the army. Mr. Hyman set out to accomplish this task. Fifteen months of visiting Pentagon and legislative representatives ensued before Hyman finally located the person responsible for such a purchase decision—the commanding officer of the Rock Island Arsenal. After a series of meetings, the brush was designed to meet a long list of criteria the army had developed and Richard Hyman closed the sale!

Source: Based on Richard M. Hyman. "Try, Try Again," *Sales and Marketing Management* (June 8, 1981), pp. 39–40. Copyright 1981. Used by permission.

Types of Products. Although resellers primarily purchase products for resale, they also must purchase goods and services to conduct their operations. In this regard, they buy many of the producer items mentioned earlier in the chapter. Following is an example of a reseller purchasing items not for resale, but instead to enable it to conduct its operations. Fleming Companies (the second largest food wholesaler in the United States) recently built a 500,000 square foot automated warehouse in Houston, Texas. To construct this building, Fleming purchased construction materials and services, computers, forklifts, pallet jacks, trucks and trailers, refrigerated lockers, office equipment, conveyors, electric motors, and metal racks at a cost in excess of $20 million.

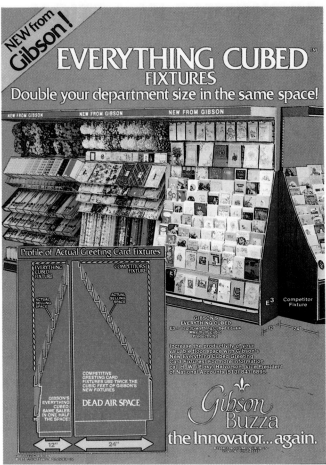

Retailers can purchase 3M's Merchandise Monitoring System (left) to improve their store operations by reducing shoplifting. Buzza shows retailers how to increase space productivity with their "everything cubed" fixtures (right).

Photo at left from Mark Joseph—Chicago.

Special Market Characteristics. Retailers and wholesalers are primarily concerned with three things: gross margins, space productivity, and inventory productivity.[12] **Gross margin** *shows how much gross profit (sales less cost of goods sold) the reseller makes as a percentage of sales.* Retailers and wholesalers must receive a fair gross margin because they must be able to pay for handling costs, such as labor, storage, damage, and transportation.

Retailers and wholesalers also prefer to handle products that offer the potential of high space productivity. **Space productivity** typically is defined in terms of *sales or gross profit per square foot of retail or wholesale space.* Because floor space is a scarce resource, the reseller wants to get as much return on it as possible. If a reseller wants to handle a new product, it often must drop or devote less space to an existing product.

About 50 percent of a reseller's investment is in inventory. Since inventory is such a high proportion of investment, resellers prefer to handle products with good inventory productivity. **Inventory productivity** can be defined as *sales or gross profit divided by average inventory investment.* The higher the inventory productivity, the more attractive a product is to resellers and the higher the probability they will handle it.

Now that we have explained the different types of organizational markets, let's examine how organizations buy. The **organizational buyer** is *a professional who is employed solely to buy goods and services for the organization.* Although the professional buyer is more rational than the consumer buyer when making purchasing decisions, he or she is only human; thus, emotional factors, such as friendships with suppliers and personality conflicts between the supplier's salesperson and the purchasing agent, can influence purchasing decisions.

    Table 6.3 contrasts the organizational buyer with the consumer buyer. By carefully examining the information in this table, you will see that the

WHAT DETERMINES ORGANIZATIONAL BUYING BEHAVIOR?

Table 6.3   Contrasting Behavior of the Organizational and the Consumer Buyer

Buying Stage	Organizational Buyer	Consumer Buyer
Recognition of problem or need	Purchases are *planned* and needs are anticipated	Purchasing occurs when need arises
Determination of product characteristics	Systematic, cost-benefit analysis	What is affordable
Description of product characteristics	Technical specifications	User benefits
Search for suppliers	Regional or national in scope	Immediate trade area or community of residence
Acquisition and analysis of proposals	Proposals and bids formally solicited	Usually occurs after the consumer decides from whom to purchase
Evaluation of proposals and selection of supplier	Extensive comparison and ranking of suppliers	Limited evaluation and very subjective
Selection of an order routine	Time and place of delivery and frequency of order specified as part of the contract	Informally agreed on
Performance feedback and evaluation	Active file maintained on supplier and product performance	Informal evaluation, which results in general feeling of satisfaction or dissatisfaction

Source: Buying stage information adapted from Patrick J. Robinson, Charles W. Faris, and Yoram Wind. *Industrial Buying and Creative Marketing* (Boston: Allyn & Bacon, Inc., 1967), p. 14. Used by permission.

organizational buyer exercises a more professional and systematic approach to the buying process.

Figure 6.2 presents a basic model of the organizational buying process. You will see from this model that the organizational buyer uses one set of criteria to evaluate products and another set to evaluate suppliers. These criteria are influenced by the decision situation, the product, and the buying center. The **buying center** consists of *all members of the organization who have an impact on the buying decision (e.g., users, influencers, buyers, deciders, and gatekeepers).* The evaluative criteria are combined with expectations about alternative products and alternative suppliers and culminate in a decision about which product to purchase *and* which supplier to patronize. The results of this purchasing decision are added to the buyer's storehouse of experience and will affect future organizational buying decisions. The following sections will discuss evaluative criteria, buyer expectations, and the process of organizational buying.

Evaluative Criteria

Types of Evaluative Criteria.   As we said before, an organization uses two sets of criteria to make a purchasing decision—one to evaluate products and one to evaluate suppliers. Some of the more common evaluative criteria are displayed in Table 6.4. For each decision situation, the criteria can be ranked in terms of their relative importance: depending on the problem that needs to be solved, some criteria will be more important than others. For example, if energy consumption is an evaluative criterion for the purchase of a farm tractor, then one of the first things the buyer must determine is which brand—John Deere, Ford, or Massey Ferguson—gets the best fuel consumption for similar size tractors. The buyer must also try to decide which tractor dealer has the best service facilities and service personnel.

Business firms that sell to organizations might find an importance-performance analysis helpful.[13] In **importance-performance analysis,** *customers rate the job the organization is doing (i.e., performance) based on a set of evaluative criteria; it also shows how important these criteria are to customers in their purchasing decisions.* Figure 6.3 shows the results of an importance-performance analysis for a supplier. The selling organization needs to improve its performance for those evaluative criteria in the upper left quadrant, which represent criteria of above average importance to the customer for which the supplier's performance is below average. Criteria in the upper right quadrant represent those that are important to the customer and for which the supplier is performing well. The message here is to keep up the good work. The lower right quadrant contains the criteria that the customer deems relatively unimportant, but for which the supplier is doing a good job. The supplier should consider deemphasizing these criteria and devoting resources to a more important area. Finally, the lower left quadrant contains criteria that are relatively unimportant and for

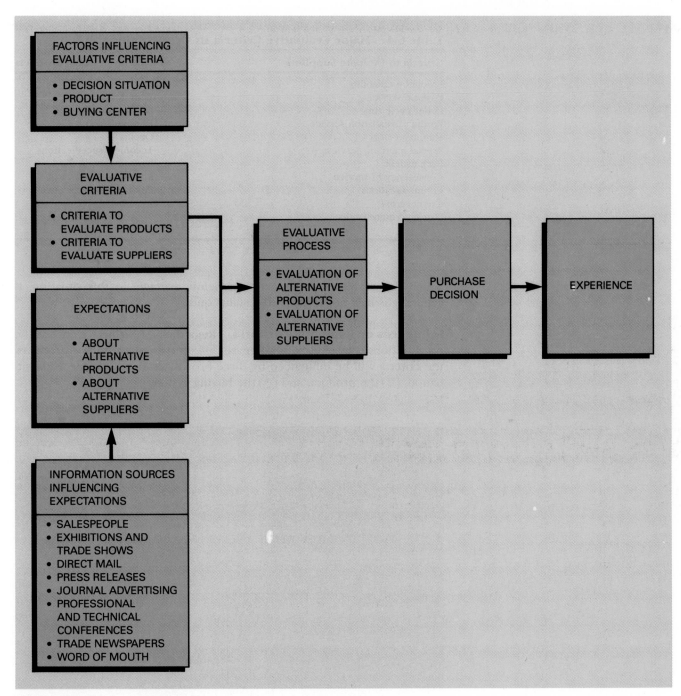

Figure 6.2

A Basic Model of Organizational Buying

Source: Adapted by permission of the publisher from David W. Cravens and David W. Finn. "Supplier Selection by Retailers: Research Progress and Needs," in William R. Darden and Robert F. Lusch (eds.), *Patronage Behavior and Retail Management* (New York: Elsevier North-Holland, 1983), p. 227.

Table 6.4   Major Evaluative Criteria in Organizational Buying

Criteria to Evaluate Suppliers	Criteria to Evaluate Products
Product Availability	Price
Postsale service	Warranty
Order cycle time	Energy consumption
Product installation service	Durability
Shipping errors	Quality
Special handling services	Technical specifications
Back orders	Performance in use
Consistency of service	Appearance
Communications	Physical characteristics
Credit terms	
Damaged merchandise	

which the supplier's performance is below average. In this situation, it generally is best not to upset the status quo.

Influences on Evaluative Criteria.   Regardless of evaluative criteria the organizational buyer uses to compare different suppliers and/or products, the criteria will be influenced by three broad factors: (1) the decision situation, (2) the product, and (3) the buying center.

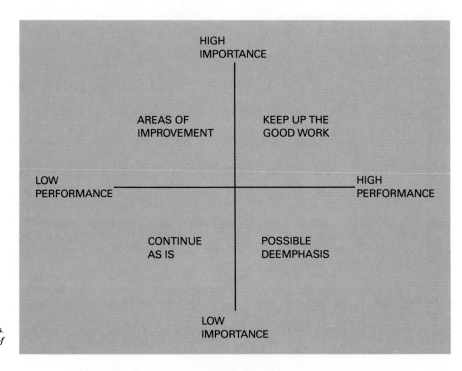

Figure 6.3

Importance-Performance Analysis

Source: Based on John A. Martilla and John C. James. "Importance-Performance Analysis," *Journal of Marketing* 41 (January 1977), pp. 77–79.

When we discussed consumer buyer behavior in Chapter 5, we examined three types of decision situations: habitual problem solving, limited problem solving, and extended problem solving. A similar set of decision situations exists in organizational buying: straight rebuy, modified rebuy, and new task buying.[14]

Straight rebuy occurs when *the prior purchase of a product was satisfactory and no new information is needed for subsequent purchases.* Straight rebuy is common for frequently purchased items; as long as the favored supplier continues to perform well, the organization will buy from the same supplier and select the same brand. In this situation, it is difficult for another supplier to sell to the organization. Often a competitive supplier will try to demonstrate to the organizational buyer that the favored supplier is not performing well with respect to certain evaluative criteria, such as price and delivery time.

With **modified rebuy,** *the organizational buyer is dissatisfied because the current supplier and/or product is not performing up to standard with respect to some evaluative criteria. Therefore, the buyer must reevaluate the supplier and/or product.* The evaluative criteria could be altered in several ways. For instance, more criteria could be added, a different level of importance could be attached to the criteria, or the criteria could remain unchanged, but new suppliers or products could be added to the list under consideration.

As an example of modified rebuy, suppose that the board of directors of a large corporation was upset with the accounting firm that audits the firm's financial statements because its audit took too long. The board could respond in several ways. First, more criteria could be added for evaluation, so that the accounting firm would be evaluated in terms of cost, accuracy, and prestige as well as speed. Therefore, the accounting firm has a chance to obtain a high overall rating, even if it is slow. Second, the board of directors could decide to deemphasize the time it takes to perform the audit and emphasize the accounting firm's prestige. Since its current accounting firm is internationally recognized and respected, the board could decide to continue to use their audit services. Third, the board could decide not to change its evaluative criteria and to contact other major accounting firms to see if they can offer faster service.

New task buying occurs when *the organization has a new problem to solve and is not certain which product and/or supplier to use.* As might be expected with new task buying, a considerable amount of information must be gathered about both suppliers and alternative products that can solve the problem. Also, since the buying situation is new, the organizational buyer must establish the appropriate evaluative criteria to use. An example of new task buying is a manufacturer deciding for the first time to convert one of its assembly lines to robotics.

The particular good or service being purchased will influence the criteria for evaluation and the level of importance placed on each criterion. For instance, if the product is technically sophisticated, such as a computer, then warranty and postsale service probably will be given major importance.

On the other hand, if the product is a standardized, nondifferentiated good (i.e., grade #2 corn), then price may be the sole important evaluative criterion.

Buying center members can influence the evaluative criteria used in making a purchase decision and the relative importance placed on these criteria. The members of the buying center can be categorized as follows[15]:

1. *Users* are the members of the organization who will actually use the product being purchased. For example, a secretary may help establish the evaluative criteria for the purchase of a new word processing system (i.e., whether it is user friendly, number of special features, printer speed).

2. *Influencers* are members of the organization who do not use the product but can influence the evaluative criteria, either directly or indirectly. They can also provide information or opinions about the alternatives. For example, a firm's maintenance personnel could influence the type of carpet selected to redecorate an office because they know which carpets are easier to clean and maintain.

3. *Buyers,* who are usually in the purchasing department, are those organizational members who have the formal authority to make the purchase decision. They normally are involved in negotiating with suppliers.

4. *Deciders* are organizational members who possess the power, either formally or informally, to decide which product and supplier to select. Buyers are usually the deciders; however, there may be other deciders. The purchasing agent may be the buyer and decider, but the purchasing agent's decision could be reversed if top management disagrees. There may also be multiple deciders, such as groups and committees who make recommendations to top management.

5. *Gatekeepers* are organizational members who control the flow of information to other members of the buying center. By controlling the flow of information, they can prevent some suppliers or products from being considered. Purchasing department employees are usually gatekeepers, as are personnel such as secretaries and engineers.

The number of members in the organization influencing the purchase decision will vary depending on the type of buying decision under consideration. For a relatively routine purchase, such as staples or paper clips, only the users and buyers may be important. For a complex purchase, such as a new computer system, the number of parties making the decision may increase and involve users, buyers, influencers, gatekeepers, and deciders. This basic principle is illustrated in Figure 6.4.

One of the most important things to recognize about the five types of organizational members who influence purchase decisions is that each member may have a different set of evaluative criteria. Consider, for example, the purchase of a new computer system. The persons who will use the computer may be concerned with speed and reliability. The manager of the physical plant (an influencer) may be concerned about the space the ma-

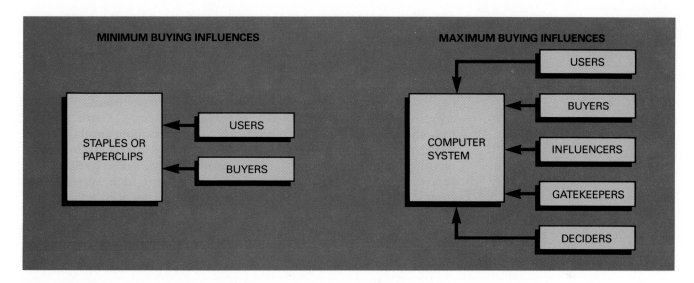

Figure 6.4
Buying Influences

chine will require and its tolerance for humidity and temperature variations. The purchasing agent (the buyer) may be concerned with the amount of discount given and whether the machine will have a guaranteed trade-in allowance if the company decides to trade up to a larger, more powerful model in the future. The Chief Executive Officer, or CEO (the decider), may be concerned with maintenance costs, the warranty, and the payment terms. Finally, the CEO's secretary (the gatekeeper) may be concerned about whether or not the computer will be purchased from a relative, who is a computer salesperson for a leading supplier.

There are several basic methods for reaching agreement among organizational members. One method is persuasion, which involves one member trying to convince others that the evaluative criteria and the importance it places on them are best for the organization as a whole. Persuasion is most effective when information can be portrayed in a way that is favorable to one's point of view. Another method is compromise, which involves a give-and-take posture: each party makes mutual concessions. In our computer example, the CEO may be convinced to decide in favor of a machine with higher maintenance costs in order to get the desired speed. However, the users may have been convinced to take a machine that only approximates the speed they want in order to get the CEO to make a favorable decision. In short, each party has compromised its original position.

Politics also may be used to resolve the conflict. For instance, the CEO may owe the secretary a favor and therefore decide to purchase from the secretary's relative, even though the CEO would prefer to purchase from a bigger and more well-known supplier.

Buyer Expectations

Organizational buyers develop beliefs and expectations about alternative products and suppliers based on information sources such as (1) salespeople, (2) exhibitions and trade shows, (3) direct mail, (4) press releases, (5) journal advertising, (6) professional and technical conferences, (7) trade newspapers, and (8) word of mouth (see Figure 6.2).[16] Expectations are also formed by experience because prior purchases have provided first-hand information on products and supplier performance. Many organizations keep files on all suppliers so that other members of the organization, such as purchasing agents, can benefit from the experience gained through prior transactions.

Making the Decision

How does an organizational buyer combine the evaluative criteria and buyer expectations to arrive at a decision?[17] Figure 6.5, which shows a supplier rating sheet developed by National Can Corporation, provides an example dealing with supplier selection. Note that National Can uses eight evaluative criteria: competitive pricing, on-time delivery, quality, emergency assistance, communication, technical service, cost-reduction suggestions, and inventory (stocking program). Importance weights are assigned to each of these, ranging from 0 to 1.0 (highest importance). These importance weights, which are constant for all suppliers, are multiplied by the supplier's performance rating. These performance ratings range from 0 (absolutely unacceptable) to 5 (excellent). The importance weight times performance rating are added to arrive at an overall supplier rating. In Figure 6.5, Alpha

Through trade shows and exhibitions, organizations provide buyers with information—and sometimes firsthand experience—on their products and services.

SUPPLIER RATING SHEET

SUPPLIER: _____ Alpha Manufacturing _____

LOCATION: _____ High Falls, Idaho _____

PLANTS SERVICED: _____ All Metal Container Division and Closure Plants _____

Rating Scale

5— Excellent— Top 10% of all suppliers
4— Good, but can be improved
3— Average
2— Below average
1— Poor
0— Absolutely unacceptable

Supplier Rating: Key Supplier Rating 21.0

	Rating	*Weight*	*Extended Rating*
1. Competitive pricing	2	0.8	1.6
2. On-time delivery	1	0.9	0.9
3. Quality	4	0.9	3.6
4. Emergency assistance	5	0.9	4.5
5. Communication	1	0.4	0.4
6. Technical service	4	0.4	1.6
7. Cost-reduction suggestions	3	0.5	1.5
8. Inventory (stocking) program	2	0.3	0.6
		Total	14.7

Supplier Rating: Key Supplier Rating 21.0

Maximum Points Possible: 25
18–25 Preferred supplier— does a good job for National Can Corporation
10–17 Acceptable— room for improvement
 5–9 Marginal— must improve to retain position. Specific programs required
 0–5 Unacceptable— replace at once

COMMENTS: Gives excellent assistance in emergencies; however, poor
communication and missed promise dates seem to create their
own emergencies. Pricing is noncompetitive. West coast service is
particularly poor. Quality has been very good.

__7/1/76__   Purchasing Manager
DATE   SIGNED

Figure 6.5

Supplier Rating Sheet

Source: Reprinted by permission of the publisher from D.W. Cravens and D.W. Finn. "Supplier Selection by Retailers: Research Progress and Needs," in William Darden and Robert Lusch (eds.), *Patronage Behavior and Retail Management* (New York: Elsevier North-Holland, 1983), p. 238. Copyright 1983 by Elsevier Science Publishing Co., Inc.

Manufacturing received a score of 14.7, which was below the 21.0 rating that National Can's key supplier received. Alpha Manufacturing is an acceptable, but not a preferred, supplier.

Before the decision is finalized, however, negotiation of price and terms of trade (i.e., credit and delivery) is common in organizational buying. Things other than price and terms of trade may also be negotiated, such as service contracts and free product installation. If a supplier fails to score well in the evaluation process, then some negotiation may occur. There is nothing unusual or improper about showing a supplier that he or she does not compare favorably to other suppliers, and it may help in negotiating a lower price or more attractive credit terms. Some words of caution should be sounded, however. Tough negotiations can result in a bad reputation. If buyers always try to squeeze the absolute best deal from suppliers, then in times of shortages, the organization will have trouble getting adequate supplies. It is wise to be fair in negotiations and to remember that suppliers also need to make a reasonable return on their investment. Also, as will be discussed in Chapters 16 and 17 on pricing, organizations may encounter legal problems in negotiating a price or terms that discriminate against competition.

Although one particular supplier may be superior to others, the organization should avoid purchasing all of its requirements from a single source and becoming too dependent on it.[18] If a shortage of goods does occur, the organization may be slow to find another supplier. In addition, by purchasing from several suppliers, you can keep your key supplier fighting for your business. If your key supplier realizes you are regularly considering new suppliers, then your key supplier will continue to try to please you. The relationship between single versus multiple sourcing and dependency is illustrated in Figure 6.6.

Figure 6.6
Single Versus Multiple Sources

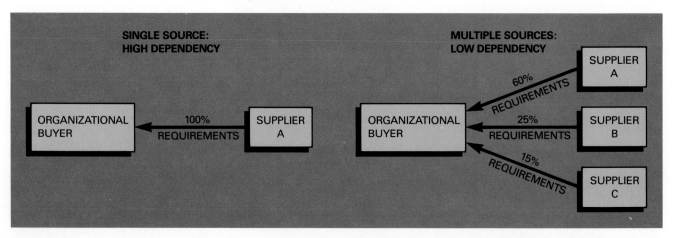

Wholesale and retail buyers, you will recall from the definitions given earlier in this chapter, are organizational buyers who make purchases for resale. They must look to the final consumer in order to help determine what items to stock in the store or warehouse. Retailers and wholesalers are primarily engaged in assortment building. The retailer attempts to assemble the assortment of merchandise that consumers will find useful in solving their purchasing problems. For instance, the grocery retailer attempts to build an assortment of merchandise that will help many different types of households solve their nutritional needs at a single retail location. Similarly, a food wholesaler builds assortments the retailer will need to stock. Thus, the grocery retailer can buy from a few wholesalers who warehouse a large assortment of food items (usually about 9,000 different items) rather than negotiating with a thousand or more producers.

WHOLESALE AND RETAIL BUYING BEHAVIOR

The Retailer's or Wholesaler's Open-to-Buy

The dollar amount that a retailer or wholesaler can spend on inventory at any given time is called **open-to-buy**. The following things are considered in this method: current inventory levels, planned end-of-month inventory, expected sales for the month, and merchandise that has been purchased but has not yet arrived at the store or warehouse (in-transit inventory).[19] A good analogy for this calculation is that of balancing your checkbook to determine how much money you have available to spend at any given time. If the retailers or wholesalers have no open-to-buy, then an attempt to sell to them would be futile. That is why most sellers regularly ask retail and wholesale buyers, "What is your open-to-buy?"

Forward Buying

Manufacturers are often uncertain about the level of demand that will materialize and want to be sure they have enough merchandise on hand to meet demand. Consequently, they sometimes overestimate demand and overproduce. Since manufacturers are not in the inventory and storage business, they will cut price on this excess merchandise to encourage wholesalers and retailers to forward buy. A **forward buy** occurs when *a retailer or wholesaler buys inventory more weeks in advance than it normally would.* For example, suppose that a food wholesaler typically buys a two-week supply of Scott toilet tissues, but because of a 15 percent price concession from Scott, the wholesaler decides to purchase a five-week supply. This wholesaler has bought three weeks forward.

Off-Premise Buying

Off-premise buying occurs *when wholesalers and retailers have buying offices geographically removed from the location of their headquarters.* Many department store chains have buying offices in New York City, Paris, and Hong Kong. These buying offices may be solely owned by a single wholesaler or retailer, they may be jointly owned by several organizations, or they may be independently owned by a separate organization that charges retailers and wholesalers a commission for performing part of their buying function.

ADDITIONAL CONCEPTS

Systems Selling

Systems selling is *a method of selling to organizations that recognizes the organization's total problem and attempts to sell a set of interrelated products and/or services that will solve this problem.*[20] Consequently, it is a tool that allows firms selling to other organizations to be customer oriented. IBM is a big proponent of systems selling. The IBM salesperson is concerned not only with selling a computer but with how the computer can solve the organization's problems. For example, if a law firm with twenty partners decides that it is getting bogged down in paperwork and legal research, then the IBM salesperson would attempt to design a computer system for the law firm that would solve this problem. Such a system could consist of the computer hardware as well as word processing software, accounting software, and terminals that would allow the legal staff to have computer access to all legal briefs from the fifty states. In addition, the salesperson would try to sell the law firm on the importance of a training program for its staff so that it could quickly and efficiently learn to work with this new office technology.

Value Analysis

Value analysis involves *dividing a product into its most basic components and then identifying parts that could be modified, substituted, or eliminated to reduce costs or increase product performance.*[21] Many companies trying to sell to organizations offer to perform a value analysis. Purchasing agents also perform a value analysis to determine which components of a product can be eliminated or replaced with cheaper components. For example, a manufacturer of fine furniture, such as Stanley, may decide to review all the components in their line of bedroom furniture in hopes of finding ways to shave costs. They might find that they could use plastic rather than metal rollers on drawers and pressed particle board rather than solid wood for the back of dressers. Substituting these lower cost materials would not reduce their product's durability or appearance, but it would help lower production costs.

Let's consider another example of value analysis. Between 1978 and 1982, sales at Philips Industries (a major supplier to the mobile home and recreational vehicle industries) declined 6 percent; however, profits rose 55 percent. Philips's value analysis program was one of the keys to the increasing profits during a period of declining sales. Their program's goal was to save at least as much as their supplier costs increased each year. The results were amazing. For example, Philips found that a redesign in smoke damper packaging could save $170,300 annually from the cost of lumber for crates and that $415,000 could be saved by substituting chemicals in plastic-molded plumbing fittings.[22]

Make or Buy Decisions

Manufacturers frequently face the **make or buy** decision—*the decision between making a product or component and purchasing it from an outside supplier.* Chrysler, for instance, must decide whether to produce or purchase axles, batteries, wheels, radios, and so on. The make or buy decision is not limited to manufacturers. A theatrical group must decide whether to make its own costumes and wardrobe or purchase the services of an outside supplier to do wardrobe design and creation.

Organizations may decide to make rather than buy a product for several reasons. They may (1) be unable to find an acceptable supplier; (2) be able to use excess capacity (i.e., space and resources not being fully used); (3) wish to protect the manufacturing process and product design; (4) have a product that is too specialized or needed in quantities too limited to attract a supplier; and (5) be able to produce the product on its own at a more favorable price.

SUMMARY

This chapter acquainted you with the scope of organizational markets (producer markets, government markets, and reseller markets) and organizational buyer behavior. Organizational markets consist of business units and organizations that purchase goods and services to be used, directly or indirectly, in the production of other goods and services or to be resold to governments, retailers, wholesalers, and producers. These organizations can be classified according to the standard industrial classification (SIC) system.

The producer market is a major part of the organizational market and consists of firms that purchase goods and services needed for the production of other goods and services. The types of products found in producer markets are raw materials, major equipment, accessory equipment, component parts, process materials, supplies, and industrial services.

The government market is also a major part of the organizational market. The government market consists of federal, state, and local agencies and the goods and services they purchase to conduct operations and serve the public. Government agencies purchase on a competitive basis through bid solicitations. Two types of bidding are popular: open bidding and negotiated contract bidding.

A final organizational market is the reseller market. The reseller market consists of business organizations that purchase products for resale to other business organizations and individuals. Two major types of resellers are wholesalers and retailers. When retailers and wholesalers purchase products for resale, they are primarily concerned with three things: gross margins, space productivity, and inventory productivity.

The second major function of this chapter was to discuss the behavior of the organizational buyer, the influences of evaluative criteria and buyer expectations on the buying decision, and the organizational buying process. Since organizational buyers are professional buyers, they are usually more rational and economically oriented than consumer buyers.

Evaluative criteria are used by organizational buyers to assess alternative products and alternative suppliers. Examples of evaluative criteria are cost, quality, speed, availability, and credit terms. These criteria are influenced by the decision situation—whether it is a straight rebuy, modified rebuy, or new task buy—by the type of good or service being purchased, and by members of the buying center who can be classified as users, influencers, buyers, deciders, and gatekeepers.

Organizational buyers develop beliefs and expectations about the alternative products and suppliers based on the information they receive through such sources as salespeople, trade shows, advertising, publicity and promotions, technical conferences, trade newspapers, and word of mouth. Buyers rate evaluative criteria in terms of their relative importance and the performance of each supplier or product on the criteria. These ratings can be used to construct an importance-performance grid and a supplier or product rating sheet.

We also discussed several unique aspects of wholesale and retail buying behavior and stressed the fact that retailers and wholesalers are assortment builders. The concepts of open-to-buy, forward buy, and off-premise buying were introduced.

The chapter concluded with a discussion of the concepts of systems selling, value analysis, and make-or-buy decision, which are important to a good understanding of organizational buying behavior.

KEY CONCEPTS

organizational markets (p. 149)
standard industrial classification (SIC) (p. 150)
producer markets (p. 151)
derived demand (p. 154)
joint demand (p. 154)
government market (p. 157)
open bid (p. 158)

negotiated contract bidding (p. 158)
reseller market (p. 160)
wholesalers (p. 160)
retailers (p. 160)
gross margin (p. 162)
space productivity (p. 162)
inventory productivity (pp. 162–163)
organizational buyer (p. 163)

buying center (p. 164)
importance-performance analysis
    (p. 164)
straight rebuy (p. 167)
modified rebuy (p. 167)
new task buying (p. 167)

open-to-buy (p. 173)
forward buy (p. 173)
off-premise buying (p. 174)
systems selling (p. 174)
value analysis (p. 174)
make or buy (p. 175)

REVIEW AND DISCUSSION QUESTIONS

1. What types of products are found in producer markets? Please give examples of each.

2. What are the special market characteristics of producer markets?

3. Name the two types of bidding that occur in government markets. Define and distinguish between these two types of bidding.

4. In purchasing products for resale, retailers and wholesalers are most concerned with what three things?

5. How is the organizational buyer different from the consumer buyer?

6. What are some of the common evaluative criteria used by organizational buyers to evaluate suppliers and products?

7. What is importance-performance analysis and how can a company that sells in the industrial market use it to develop more effective marketing programs?

8. What are the three major types of decision situations that organizational buyers confront? Give an example of each type.

9. Name the five types of organizational members who can influence an organization's buying decisions.

10. What are some of the basic methods for reaching agreement about a buying decision among organizational members?

11. How are buyer expectations developed?

12. Why is it safer for organizations to purchase from several suppliers rather than from just one?

13. What is open-to-buy and why does it exist?

14. What is forward buy and why does it occur?

15. Discuss the concept of systems selling and provide an example of this concept.

16. Define value analysis and discuss how it can be used as a tool in selling to industrial buyers.

17. Why would a company such as Whirlpool decide to make small motors for its washing machines rather than purchase them from a well-known motor manufacturer?

ACTION PROBLEMS

1. Locate several advertisements for manufacturers of industrial products. What evaluative criteria are being stressed in these advertisements?

2. You are a traveling salesperson for Eli Lilly company (a drug manufacturer) and travel approximately 1,400 miles weekly. Each salesperson has been asked to develop a list of five to seven evaluative criteria to be applied by the purchasing department in the acquisition of a new fleet of cars for the salesforce. Develop your list and state why each criterion is important to you.

3. You are director of marketing for a regional chain of hotels. The current occupancy rate is only 75 percent, and you wish to expand this rate significantly over the next six months. Write a memo to the company president suggesting how systems selling could be used to sell services to organizations and increase your occupancy rate.

4. Develop an importance-performance analysis grid for a hypothetical motor carrier or air freight carrier using criteria you believe would be appropriate.

5. Describe how a company such as Du Pont, which is trying to sell more plastic to the auto industry, might use the concept of value analysis.

6. You are a buyer for an office supply store. Examine Table 6.4 and decide how you would rank the evaluative criteria for the selection of a supplier (wholesaler).

NOTES

1. The following statistics were taken from U.S. Bureau of the Census, *Statistical Abstract of the United States: 1984*, 104th edition (Washington, DC, 1983).

2. "The Fortune Directory of the Largest U.S. Industrial Corporations," *Fortune* (April 29, 1985), p. 265; and "The Fortune Directory of the Largest U.S. Non-industrial Corporations," *Fortune* (June 10, 1985), p. 190.

3. *Standard Industrial Classification Manual* (Washington, DC: U.S. Government Printing Office, 1972).

4. Robert W. Haas, *Industrial Marketing Management* (New York: Petrocelli/Charter, 1976), pp. 21–26.

5. The characteristics of producer demand are further discussed in Richard M. Hill, Ralph S. Alexander, and James S. Cross, *Industrial Marketing* (Homewood, IL: Richard D. Irwin, 1975), pp. 46–47.

6. A good discussion of marketing to the federal government appears in John M. Rathmell, "Marketing by the Federal Government," *MSU Business Topics* (Summer 1973), pp. 21–28; Stanley E. Cohen, "Looking in the U.S. Government Market," *Industrial Marketing* (September 1964), pp. 129–138.

7. *Lawson Products, Inc. 1982 Annual Report*, p. 19.

8. David E. Gumpert and Jeffry A. Timmons, "Penetrating the Government Procurement Maze," *Harvard Business Review* (May–June 1982), pp. 14–24.

9. "Selling to the Government," *Sales and Marketing Management* (April 9, 1979), pp. 44–52.

10. *Lawson Products, Inc. 1982 Annual Report*, p. 19.

11. John Levin, "Programmed to Succeed," *Black Enterprise* (September 1985), pp. 56–60.

12. To obtain a better understanding of selling to resellers, see John S. Berens, "A Decision Matrix Approach to Supplier Selection," *Journal of Retailing* 47(Winter 1971–1972), pp. 47–53.

13. This concept is discussed further in John A. Martilla and John C. James, "Importance-Performance Analysis," *Journal of Marketing* 41(January 1977), pp. 77–79.

14. Patrick J. Robinson, Charles W. Faris, and Yoram Wind, *Industrial Buying and Creative Marketing* (Boston: Allyn & Bacon, 1967).

15. Frederick E. Webster, Jr., and Yoram Wind, *Organizational Buying Behavior* (Englewood Cliffs, NJ: Prentice-Hall, 1972), pp. 78–80.

16. Jagdish Sheth, "A Model of Industrial Buying Behavior," *Journal of Marketing* 37(October 1973), pp. 50–56.

17. For further discussion, see John S. Berens, "A Decision Matrix Approach to Supplier Selection," *Journal of Retailing* 47(Winter 1971–1972), pp. 47–53.

18. Robert A. Robicheaux and Adel I. El-Ansary, "A General Model for Understanding Channel Member Behavior," *Journal of Retailing* 52(Winter 1976–1977), pp. 13–30, 93–94.

19. John W. Wingate, Elmer D. Schaller, and F. Leonard Miller, *Retail Merchandise Management* (Englewood Cliffs, NJ: Prentice-Hall, 1972).

20. Philip Kotler, *Marketing Management* (Englewood Cliffs, NJ: Prentice-Hall, 1980), p. 353.

21. For more information on value analysis, see R.M. Hill, R.S. Alexander, and J.S. Cross, *Industrial Marketing* (Homewood, IL: Richard D. Irwin, 1975), Chapter 6; Donald Dobler, Lamar Lee, Jr., and David Burt, *Purchasing and Materials Management: Text and Cases* (New York: McGraw-Hill, 1984), Chapter 15.

22. "Philips Industries: Cutting Costs to Make the Best of Bad Times," *BusinessWeek* (January 10, 1983), p. 94.

CHAPTER **7**

MARKET SEGMENTATION AND TARGET MARKETING

MARKETER PROFILE

Joseph Unanue of Goya Foods

Joseph Unanue is chief executive officer of Goya Foods, one of the most successful Hispanic-owned businesses in the country. His father, Prudencio Unanue, started the company nearly fifty years ago by importing sardines from Morocco. Goya is still family owned: Joseph and his brother Frank each own 25 percent of the shares, and the rest is divided among eighteen additional family members.

The company, however, is at a crossroads. It must decide whether to expand within the Spanish-speaking population or seek the non-Hispanic market as well. Currently, its customers are located primarily on the East Coast, from Boston to Washington, and in

Miami and Puerto Rico. Thus, the firm must also decide whether to limit its operations to these areas or try to expand to California and the Southwest.

The case for further growth is strong, considering the demographics. The Hispanic population is the fastest growing minority in the United States; however, the fastest growing segment of the Hispanic market is Mexican, and Goya's customers are mostly Puerto Ricans, plus some Dominicans, Colombians, and Cubans. "If we can capture part of the Mexican-American market, we'll keep growing," says Unanue.

But Goya must also attract the non-Hispanic market or it will miss more than 90 percent of the domes-

tic population. Unanue has been taking a stab at the Yuppies, but his
only success with them so far has
been cream of coconut, an essential
ingredient for piña coladas.

Unanue wants to market Goya
products nationally but lacks the
sales and management personnel to
make the big push. "Too many companies grow too fast and then have
financial problems," says the conser-

vative Unanue. "We can do better
taking it easy."

As a family, the Unanues are more
than halfway toward the Forbes 400
status but will take no big risks to
get there in a hurry. Growth, yes,
but careful growth.

Source: Based on Jeffrey A. Trachtenberg.
"Latin Beat," *Forbes* (October 1, 1985), pp.
234, 236, 238.

INTRODUCTION

Trying to match the right marketing mix with the right customer is one of
the primary challenges of the marketing manager. Companies often will stay
for years in one market niche before they decide it is time to reach other
market segments. This was the case in the preceding Marketer Profile on
Joseph Unanue of Goya Foods. The time had come for him to decide which
market segments he should target.

This chapter explains some of the approaches used in segmenting consumer and organizational markets and discusses a six-step approach for
market segmentation and selecting a target market.

WHAT IS MARKET SEGMENTATION?

There are vast differences in the wants and needs of buyers in both consumer
and organizational markets. As a student, you do not have the same need
for an automobile as does a chief executive officer of a major corporation
earning $250,000 per year. A small liberal arts college, such as Ohio Wes-
leyan, does not have the same need for computer hardware and software
as does Harvard University. Because buyers' tastes, wants, needs, and preferences differ, marketers often segment the market. **Market segmentation**
is *the process of dividing a heterogeneous group of buyers or potential
buyers into more homogeneous groups with relatively similar product
needs.*[1] For example, the fragrance manufacturer Jovan has successfully
segmented the market by sex by producing Jovan Musk for Men and Jovan
Whisper of Musk for women.

Why do firms segment the market? Most organizations segment the
market to (1) better serve customers, (2) compete more effectively, and
(3) achieve organizational goals, such as profitability, more effectively. We
will explain each of these points.

When a firm segments a market, it can tailor a marketing mix to a well-
defined target market. It can design product attributes, set prices, and develop promotion and distribution policies to serve the needs of a target
market. Instead of having one product style or design, one price, one promotion program, and one distribution strategy for all customers, it can have
separate marketing mixes for each segment or one marketing mix for a

With Musk for Men and Whisper for Women, Jovan has successfully met one of a marketing manager's primary challenges—matching the right marketing mix with the right customer.

specific segment. Table 7.1 shows the marketing mix devised by the Cadillac and Chevrolet divisions of General Motors. Each division of GM focuses its marketing mix on a separate segment, and each marketing mix is unique in terms of product, price, promotion, and retail distribution.

By segmenting the market, firms can carve out a competitive niche in the marketplace.[2] For instance, the market for legal services is highly competitive largely because our nation's law schools have been graduating over 50,000 lawyers annually for the last decade. To be an effective competitor in this marketplace, many lawyers will focus their marketing efforts on households with specific needs, such as wills and trusts, divorce, bankruptcy, or personal injury. Note the variety of target markets for law firms in the advertising you encounter in the newspapers, magazines, television, radio, and outdoor signs.

Segmenting the market and focusing on well-defined target markets can help firms increase profits or better achieve some other organizational goal. This result is largely a direct outgrowth of the prior two reasons for market segmentation. If a firm can improve customer service through segmentation and target marketing, and if it can be a more effective competitor, then it should be able to achieve organizational objectives more effectively.

BASIC SEGMENTATION STRATEGIES

Firms can choose either to segment the market or not to segment it. Figure 7.1 shows the segmentation options open to firms. If they choose not to segment, they are pursuing undifferentiated marketing. **Undifferentiated marketing** occurs when *a firm ignores the heterogeneity of buyers in the market and instead focuses on what all or most buyers have in common.* An example of undifferentiated marketing is the lottery ticket sold by nu-

Table 7.1   General Marketing Mix and Target Market for Cadillac and Chevrolet Divisions of General Motors

	Cadillac Motor Division	Chevrolet Motor Division
Target market (market segment)	High socioeconomic status households	Low to middle socioeconomic status households
Product attributes	High quality Conservative styling Comfort	Value for the money Contemporary styling Durability
Price	$18,000–29,000	$7,000–16,000 (not including Corvette)
Promotion	Magazines such as *Fortune, Smithsonian, BusinessWeek*	National TV and radio; high circulation general magazines
Distribution	Cadillac dealerships	Chevrolet dealerships

merous states. Each ticket is the same within a state and is aimed to appeal to the risk taker in each of us. In the late 1970s, Black and Decker witnessed its worldwide market share in power tools drop from 20 percent to 15 percent because of low priced tools the Japanese began to market worldwide. As a result, Black and Decker stopped customizing products for every country and began to make a few products that could be sold everywhere with the same basic marketing approach. Thus, Black and Decker adopted an undifferentiated marketing strategy on a global basis and regained its 20 percent market share by the mid-1980s.[3]

The major advantage of undifferentiated marketing is its ability to create marked cost savings in production, promotion, and distribution because the firm is dealing with a standardized product. On the other hand, the name of the game is profit maximization, not cost minimization. In a highly competitive market, such as the United States, Europe, or Japan, it is becoming increasingly difficult to market a product designed for the masses. Consumers are demanding products tailored to their individual needs and wants. We will discuss two basic approaches to market segmentation: concentrated segmentation and multiple segmentation.

Concentrated Segmentation

A firm practicing **concentrated segmentation** *focuses its efforts on a single target market with a single marketing mix.* For example, the Steinway Piano Company concentrates on the concert and professional pianist. Although other people may purchase a Steinway, they are *not* Steinway's target market. The major advantage of concentrated segmentation is that the firm can control costs by advertising and distributing only to the market it wishes to attract. It does not have to advertise to the masses or make its

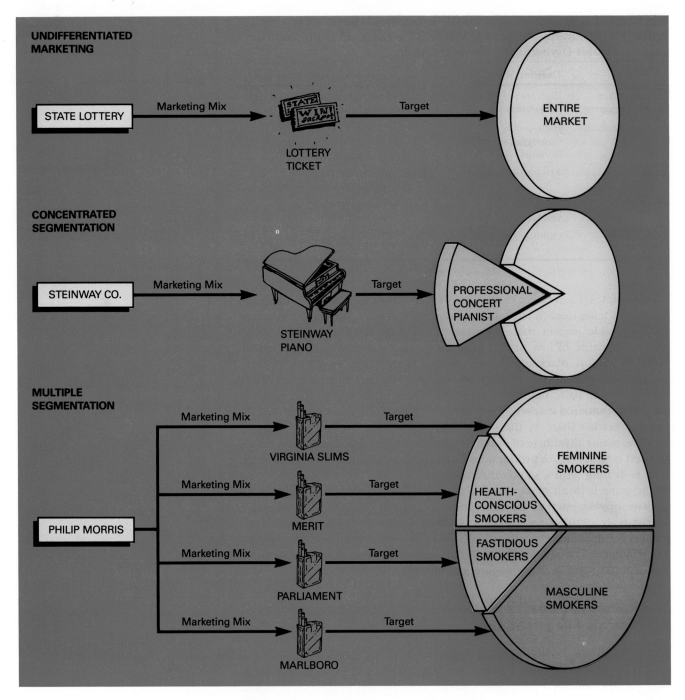

Figure 7.1
Segmentation Options

products available in numerous wholesale and retail outlets. The obvious disadvantage is that the firm may be concentrating on the wrong target and missing the real market for their product.

Multiple Segmentation

A firm using a **multiple segmentation** approach *focuses on several distinct segments* and *develops a separate marketing mix for each* of the market segments it wishes to reach. The advantage of multiple segmentation is that the organization can generate more sales by appealing to several segments. On the other hand, it must balance this higher level of sales with additional costs in the following areas:

1. *Production costs* would be higher because of higher production setup costs and shorter production runs to produce several products rather than one.
2. *Promotion costs* would be higher because different media vehicles would be needed to reach each segment.
3. *Inventory costs* would rise because the firm needs to stock more types of items and hold a higher inventory level for each item rather than a single item.
4. *Administrative costs* would increase, such as costs of separate product managers and expenses of a larger legal staff and more marketing research personnel.

Philip Morris uses a multiple segmentation strategy to market its cigarette brands. Philip Morris's Marlboro is targeted at the masculine smoker; Virginia Slims is targeted at the feminine smoker; Parliament, with its recessed filter, is targeted at the more fastidious smoker who doesn't want to come in direct contact with tobacco; and Merit is targeted at the smoker who is concerned with low tar and nicotine.[4] The Marketing in Action on page 186 illustrates how the Louisville Slugger manufacturer views each professional baseball player as a distinct segment.

Both organizational and consumer markets have four major requirements for an effective target market segmentation: measurability, accessibility, responsiveness, and substantiality. We will explain each of these requirements.

SUCCESSFUL TARGET MARKET SEGMENTATION

Measurability

If we are to segment a market by a variable or group of variables, these variables must be measurable. The advantage of objective variables, such as age, sex, income, education, geographic location, and race, is that they

MARKETING IN ACTION

How finely can a market be segmented? The ultimate in segmentation is viewing each individual as a unique and separate segment. Sound impossible? Not necessarily. Hillerich & Bradsby Company has been making baseball bats for over 100 years and still produces one million bats a year. Most of these bats are for amateurs, but H & B also produces its Louisville Slugger for professionals. A professional may use as many as six dozen bats a season—and some use as many as twelve dozen.

The bat-making process begins with the felling of highest grade white ash trees. These trees are a half century old and come from Pennsylvania and upstate New York. Because the wood for a professional bat needs to be heavier, it comes from 60- to 75-year-old trees that measure 12 to 14 inches in width. Thus, the process of creating a bat begins before the professional ball player is born.

The Louisville Slugger

Only one out of ten billets the bat makers cut is good enough for a professional bat. When a good billet is identified, the bat is built to the player's specifications. H & B has 20,000 bat specifications on file. "The professional bats are made on a hand lathe, with a model in front of the maker—for shape—and a small scale with which to constantly keep track of the bat's weight—for substance." The craftspeople who make the bats continuously pick up and put down a set of calipers, "comparing the embryonic bat with the model at each of fifteen critical diameters." When the bat is removed from the lathe, it is sanded and finished with a roasting over gas flames, which brings out the grain of the wood, branded with a trademark, autographed, and then dipped in a finish. H & B offers players seven different finishes.

Since the customer is a professional who knows precisely what he wants, he can easily detect an error. Ted Williams reportedly once returned a set of bats that had a 1/5,000 inch discrepancy. Of course, some players are never happy and further customize their bats themselves. Professional ball players have been known to put nails or lead in their bats to toughen them. One player reportedly put a tube of mercury in his bat to shift the weight when the bat was swung, giving him extra power, and in 1974, when Yankee player Craig Nettles broke a bat hitting a single, the head of the bat flew off to reveal a cork-plugged barrel. Use of an illegal bat has a relatively light penalty—the player is called out.

Source: Based on Phil Patton. "Wooden Bats Still Reign Supreme at the Old Ball Game," *Smithsonian* (October 1984), pp. 153–176. Used by permission of the author.

are easily ascertained and information and statistics on them are readily available through the U.S. Bureau of the Census. Conversely, a subjective variable such as personality is more difficult to determine. For example, how can a marketer reasonably or cost effectively measure the number of compulsive people in the United States?

Accessibility

Accessibility refers to the degree to which a firm can target its promotional and distribution efforts on a particular market segment and the ease of obtaining data about that segment. For example, Century-National Insurance, North Hollywood, decided to focus its auto insurance efforts on Hispanic consumers in Southern California. To do this, they had to find out

Pick a segment.
Radio can reach it.

Traditionally, magazines have been touted as the best way to reach many important market segments—such as college grads, professional and managerial types and high income earners.

But lately, more and more advertisers are discovering that radio is a better way to reach these segments. Yes radio, the sound alternative.

A recent study of national media habits by R.H. Bruskin Associates isolated almost 50 segments in which people spent four hundred percent more time with radio than they did with the so-called selective media of magazines. (In many target groups, radio even led television in "time spent.")

When you want to extend your budgets by "segmenting" your prospects, there's no better place for your message than the medium of radio. For more information, write or call Radio Advertising Bureau, 485 Lexington Ave., New York, NY 10017. Phone: (212) 599-6666.

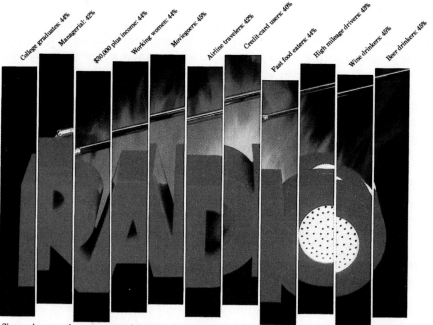

College graduates: 44%   Managerial: 42% $30,000 plus income: 44%   Working women: 44%   Moviegoers: 45%   Airline travelers: 42%   Credit-card users: 40%   Fast food eaters: 44%   High mileage drivers: 43%   Wine drinkers: 45%   Beer drinkers: 45%

Shown above are the percentages of time that these segments spend with radio, as compared to TV, magazines and newspapers, during an average media day. In all cases the time spent actually exceeds that of television.

Once demographic data has been collected, selecting the right media for the advertising message becomes simpler.

which magazines Hispanics read most often, what TV shows they prefer to watch, and which types of radio formats they listen to. Century National Insurance relied on media service companies, such as STARCH and Nielsen, for a wealth of readership, viewership, and listening data. With these demographic data in hand, Century-National spent $250,000 for print advertising in *La Opinion,* a Spanish-language daily, and five weeks of spot ads on KMEX-TV and two radio stations.[5]

Responsiveness

A firm should develop a unique marketing mix for a target market segment only if they believe that it will receive a favorable response. For example, the Morton Salt Company developed Morton Lite Salt because they believed that some consumers would react favorably to a table salt containing a low level of sodium. Del Monte has taken a similar approach with their line of "no salt added" vegetables.

Substantiality

Finally, successful segmentation requires a target market large enough to be a potential profit maker for the firm. General Motors could develop a line of cars with special seats and control features for very short people, but the number of potential customers is too limited to make this venture profitable. Firms should select those market segments that offer the most profit potential or that most help them achieve their nonprofit goals. For example, politicians try to develop political platforms and marketing programs that will appeal to voter segments of substantial size. Both major political parties pay attention to the United Auto Workers, the Teamsters, and the AFL/CIO because they represent large voting segments of the population.

SEGMENTING CONSUMER MARKETS

Many different variables can be used to segment consumer markets, and we will categorize them as demographic, geographic, psychographic, and behavioristic. Examples of these variables are presented in Table 7.2.

Demographic Segmentation

Demographic variables describe *the general characteristics of a population, such as age, sex, income, education, and family life cycle.* Levi Strauss segments the menswear market by age by producing jeans with distinct characteristics to appeal to middle-aged men, teens, or young men. The housing market is often segmented by income, because the amount individuals or families invest in housing is directly related to how much they earn. The credit card market also segments by income. American Express and Diners Club are for high income individuals, and Master Card and Visa appeal to moderate income individuals. Hand soaps is one market that is segmented by sex: Lava, Shield, and Safeguard are for men, while Ivory, Dove, and Caress are for women. Another sex-segmented market is disposable razors: Bic and Gillette Good News are for men, while Daisy and Bic

Table 7.2 Common Variables for Segmenting Consumer Markets

Segmentation Variable	Example
Demographic	
Age	Under 6, 6–11, 12–18, 19–24, 25–34, 35–49, 50–64, 65+ years
Sex	Male, female
Income	Under $7,500, $7,500–9,999, $10,000–14,999, $15,000–24,999, $25,000–34,999, $35,000–49,999, $50,000+
Education	Grade school or less, some high school, high school graduate, some college, college graduate
Family size	1–2, 3–4, 5–6, 6+
Family life cycle	Young: single, married without children, divorced without children, married with children, divorced with children Middle-aged: married without children, divorced without children, married with children, divorced with children, married without dependent children, divorced without dependent children Older: married, unmarried
Occupation	Professional; managers, officials, and sole proprietors; clerical and sales; craftspeople and foremen; operatives; farmers; retired; students; unemployed
Social class	Lower, middle, upper
Religion	Protestant, Catholic, Mormon, Jewish
Race	White, black, Oriental, Hispanic, Indian
Geographic	
Area of country	Northeast, Southeast, Midwest, Southwest, Central, Mountain, West, Northwest
City size	Under 5,000; 5,000–15,000; 15,000–25,000; 25,000–50,000; 50,000–100,000; 100,000–250,000; 250,000–500,000; 500,000–1,000,000; 1,000,000–2,000,000; over 2,000,000
Climate	Cold, moderate, tropical, arid
Density	Rural, suburban, urban
Psychographic	
Life-style	Outdoor oriented, indoor oriented, work oriented, culture/arts oriented
Personality	Compulsive, competitive, introverted, extroverted
Behavioristic	
Benefits sought	Quality, economy, service, status, convenience
Loyalty	None, low, moderate, strong, total
Usage Rate	Heavy user, moderate user, light user, nonuser

lady shaver are for women. The Marketing in Action on page 191 shows that babies, an age-related segment, are an attractive market segment.

Magazines often use education to segment markets. Magazines such as *National Geographic, Smithsonian, New Yorker,* and *Scientific American* appeal to highly educated individuals. Many bars segment by occupation—there are blue collar bars and white collar bars. Some retailers use social class to segment the market. For example, Neiman Marcus and Bergdorf Goodman appeal to the higher social classes. Religion can also be used as a segmentation variable (e.g., Kosher foods for Jewish people), as can race—witness the numerous beauty products made especially for blacks.

Family life cycle is an especially important demographic variable for segmenting consumer markets.[6] **Family life cycle** is *the stages and substages a person may go through from being young and single to being married to being old and unmarried.*[7] The stages and substages are used

To make sure your baby gets the right food at the right age, look for the right Gerber® label.

What's in a label?

Fifty years of innovation assure you that Gerber has the right system for feeding your baby.

Gerber has a most knowledgeable staff of nutritionists dedicated to feeding babies. The Gerber Nutritional Guidelines help you make sure your baby gets the right food at the right age.

As baby's nutritional and developmental needs change, all you have to do is look for the right color label.

Blue label means Strained Foods for Infants.

Some babies are ready to begin Strained Foods at 4-6 months. Many earlier. When you and your health advisor decide your baby is ready for single ingredient foods, Gerber has the largest variety. Of course, no single ingredient foods have added starch, salt, sugar, preservatives, or artificial flavors or colors. Offered along with breast milk or formula, Strained Foods provide nutrients essential for your baby's growth. Plus, spoonfeeding Strained Foods gives your baby new tastes, new textures and new stimulation. Once your baby has accepted single ingredient foods, strained combination foods can be included in the menu. For example, Gerber High Meat Dinners are an excellent source of protein and no one makes a strained dinner with more meat.

Red label means Textured Foods for Juniors.

When baby begins teething, add Gerber Junior Foods to the menu. The tiny bits in most Junior Foods give baby practice chewing. They're made without added salt, preservatives, artificial flavors or colors.

Brown label means Chunky Foods for Toddlers.

When your toddler is able to self-feed, it's time for Gerber Chunky Foods.

Your baby is as unique as you are. So let the Gerber Nutritional Guidelines help you and your health advisor make the right choices for your baby.

As Gerber shows, even the baby food market can be segmented by age.

MARKETING IN ACTION

The market for baby goods and services is one of the most attractive and rapidly growing markets in the United States. There were 3.6 million births in the United States in 1984, and a conservative estimate of the cost of raising a child until it enters kindergarten is $20,000. Disposable diapers alone will cost more than $750 for the two years it takes to toilet train a child.

Because many first-time parents are older and the wife typically returns to work within one year after the birth, they can afford to spend heavily on their babies. Many companies have recognized this growth market and have focused their marketing efforts on it. Consider the following examples:

- Johnson & Johnson has created a line of developmental toys that come with a sixteen-page booklet that explains how these toys enhance the

A Market Segment to Harvest

child's developmental process. Fisher-Price Toys is also using packaging and advertisements to show how their toys help a child develop.

- Toys "R" Us, the largest U.S. toy retailer, has started a chain of Kids "R" Us clothing stores that feature name-brand children's clothing at prices 30 percent lower than those of department stores.

- Kinder-Care Day Care Center has developed a chain of 1,025 facilities and, by 1985, had 250 more centers under construction or planned.

- My Child's Destiny, a children's specialty store in San Francisco, is laid out in a series of boutiques that sell everything from clothes and

haircuts to books and computers. The store has toddler-high counters, low handrails, and free diapers in the restrooms; it is definitely an upscale baby store.

- Aprica Kassai, Inc., a Japanese manufacturer of baby strollers, has captured 8 percent of the U.S. stroller market since 1980 by selling high quality, stylish strollers at the top end of the market—$100 to $300.

Source: "Bringing Up Baby: A New Kind of Marketing Boom," *BusinessWeek* (April 22, 1985), pp. 58, 59, 62, 65; "A Boutique Born To Be the Ultimate Baby Store," *Business-Week* (April 22, 1985), p. 65; "Aprica Kassai: A Fast Ride into the U.S. with Status-Symbol Strollers," *BusinessWeek* (January 21, 1985), p. 17; W. Stimson, "Bringing Up Baby," *Black Enterprise* (March 1984), pp. 67–69; and A. Ramirez, "Can Anyone Compete with Toys 'R' Us?" *Fortune* (October 28, 1985), pp. 71–72.

as a means of categorizing the population and do not necessarily mean that every person goes through every stage (see Table 7.2).

The product wants and needs of individuals change as their stage in the family life cycle changes. For example, young singles spend more money on recreation and vacations than do young marrieds with children. Middle-aged, divorced parents may be an especially good target market for life insurance since they have a strong need and financial obligation to provide for their children.

Geographic Segmentation

Geographic variables are *the areas where buyers reside, such as the east, west, north, or south, and the physical characteristics of these areas, such as population density, climate, and city size.* The needs and wants of consumers are often influenced by geographic variables. For example, a Texas home has a greater need for air conditioning than does a home in Maine, and wool sweaters are more in demand in Minnesota than in Florida.

Because these variations exist, it is sometimes wise to target the marketing mix to specific regions of the country. The advertisement for *INC.* magazine shows how they produce regional editions; this gives firms the ability to advertise in *INC.* and reach only particular geographic regions.

Most of the U.S. population resides in *standard metropolitan statistical areas (SMSAs),* which the U.S. Census Bureau defines as an urbanized area where at least one city has 50,000 or more inhabitants and a total SMSA population of at least 100,000 or 75,000 in the New England states. In June 1985, there were 323 SMSAs and approximately 75 percent of the U.S. population resided in these areas.[8] Because this is where the majority of the U.S. population resides and since incomes are higher in metropolitan areas than in rural areas, the bulk of U.S. marketing activity occurs in SMSAs (see Table 7.3).

ELEVEN REGIONS TO TARGET YOUR MARKET

When you need to reach specific geographic markets for your products, you need to reach us.

Inc. Regional Editions divide the country geographically into prime target markets. Perfect for pinpointing that particular group of 2 million Inc. readers you need. Or for testing new markets for compatibility.

Advertise in Inc. Regional Editions. Call (617) 227-4700.

California, Inc./Northern   Midwest, Inc.   Chicago, Inc.   New England, Inc.   New York, Inc.   Mid-Atlantic, Inc.   California, Inc.   California, Inc./Southern   Southeast, Inc.   Texas, Inc./Southwest   Full West, Inc.

Inc.

THE MAGAZINE FOR GROWING COMPANIES. 38 Commercial Wharf, Boston, MA 02110

Inc. magazine's regional editions give advertisers the ability to target the marketing mix to specific areas of the country.

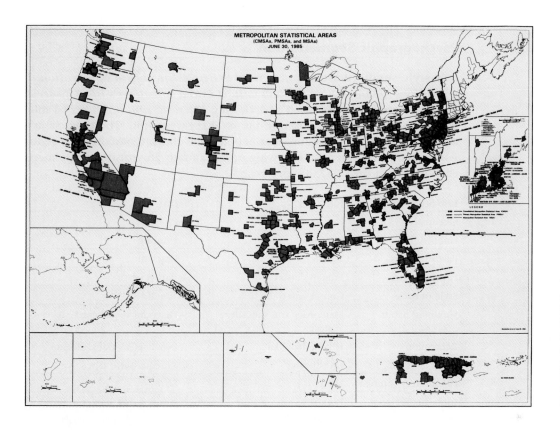

The bulk of marketing activity in the United States occurs in SMSAs—standard metropolitan statistical areas—where the majority of the U.S. population resides and where incomes are higher.

Table 7.3   Selected Characteristics of Eight SMSAs[a]

	New York City	Daytona Beach	Detroit	Louisville	Houston	Denver	Phoenix	San Francisco
Population	8,391,100	305,700	4,359,400	968,500	3,176,800	1,608,600	1,736,000	1,526,300
Households	3,312,100	127,800	1,576,700	353,200	1,141,600	638,300	669,100	638,100
Average household size	2.5	2.4	2.8	2.7	2.8	2.5	2.6	2.4
Median household income	$ 24,354	$ 20,617	$ 29,170	$ 25,648	$ 31,012	$ 29,984	$ 25,153	$ 31,439
Percent population over 50 years	29.2%	41.6%	24.8%	25.0%	17.5%	20.2%	25.7%	28.7%
Percent black population	21.3%	11.2%	20.5%	13.0%	18.2%	4.8%	3.2%	12.0%
Percent Spanish population	16.4%	1.6%	1.6%	0.6%	14.6%	10.7%	13.2%	10.8%
Average retail expenditure per household	$ 11,710	$ 14,283	$ 14,892	$ 15,074	$ 18,300	$ 17,137	$ 16,029	$ 18,827

[a]All numbers are 1984 estimates except percentage of black and Spanish populations, which are 1980 actual numbers.

Sources: Based on "1985 Survey of Buying Power," *Sales & Marketing Management* (July 22, 1985); U.S. Bureau of the Census. *State and Metropolitan Data Book 1982* (Washington, DC: U.S. Government Printing Office).

Psychographic Segmentation

Life-style segmentation is *often used to help refine a firm's promotional efforts by showing how a product will fit into a consumer's life. Life-style is usually measured in terms of activities, interests, and opinions.*[9] Table 7.4 shows items typically used in life-style segmentation. The types of activities, interests, and opinions that people have characterize their life-style. For example, consider the following profile of two 26-year-old single men, each of whom earn $32,000 per year.

Life-Style Item	John	Jim
Occupation	Lawyer	Plumber
Hobby	Stamp collecting	Hunting
Favorite sport	Tennis	Baseball
Favorite food	French cuisine	Barbecue
Style of dress	Conservative	Trendy
Shopping habits	Mail-order and specialty stores	Discount department stores
Recreation	Hiking, handball	Bowling, working on car
Entertainment	Live theater	Videocassette tapes
Community interest	High	Low
Club membership	Rotary, Lions	None
Major achievement	President of university debate club	Captain of high school baseball team

John and Jim, although they are the same age and earn equal incomes, definitely have different life-styles. John's life-style might be called "upscale,"

Table 7.4   Typical Items Used in Life-Style Segmentation

Activities	Interests	Opinions
Work	Family	Themselves
Hobbies	Home	Social issues
Social events	Job	Politics
Vacation	Community	Business
Entertainment	Recreation	Economics
Club membership	Fashion	Education
Community	Food	Products
Shopping	Media	Future
Sports	Achievements	Culture

Source: Joseph Plummer. "The Concept and Application of Life-Style Segmentation," *Journal of Marketing* (January 1974), p. 34.

whereas Jim's is "traditional middle America." You would not expect these two men to have the same likes and dislikes. This is essentially why life-style analysis can be used to segment the market.

Some marketers have tried to segment the market by *personality,* but the available evidence indicates that personality is a poor segmentation variable. This is not to say that personality does not have an impact on consumer needs and wants. The major problem appears to be the researchers' ability to devise reliable and valid measures of personality. Others argue that personality may be situation specific. For instance, aggressiveness may be a personality factor that comes into play when you purchase a sports car, but it may not be a factor when you purchase a family automobile.

This book club has identified its market's life-style characteristics and appeals to the active outdoors person.

Behavioristic Segmentation

A firm using **behavioristic segmentation** *segments a market based on how consumers behave or act toward particular products. The most common behavioristic variables are benefits sought, usage rage, and user loyalty.* (Look at Table 7.2 again for examples of behavioristic variables.)

Benefits Sought.   Different people seek different benefits in products.[10] For example, some automobile buyers may want a small car that is fuel efficient and durable and that has a good resale value, such as a Honda Civic. Another group of buyers may want a sporty looking auto that is fast, but comfortable and durable, such as a Pontiac Fiero. Later in this chapter we will discuss an approach to identifying market segments and selecting target markets that relies heavily on benefit segmentation.

Usage Rate.   When marketers segment the market by usage rate, they divide users into heavy, moderate, and light categories. The heavy user is a highly valuable segment,[11] often accounting for 80 percent of product usage. Heavy users are the top 20 to 25 percent of the users of a product in terms of consumption. This results in the 20-80 rule: 20 percent of the users often consume 80 percent of the product. For example, 20 percent of the aspirin users consume 80 percent of the aspirins, or 20 percent of the users of men's cologne purchase 80 percent of the cologne in the United States. To focus its efforts on heavy users, an organization must be able to identify their demographic or life-style characteristics.

It may also be advantageous to segment light users because they are usually less price-sensitive since they do not use the product often. For example, Lowenbrau and Heineken beers are targeted at light users who will pay premium prices once in a while.

Segmenting by usage is often important in certain nonprofit and service organizations. There are heavy users or patrons of symphonic orchestras, art museums, and zoos and heavy users of psychiatrists, dentists, lawyers, and dry cleaners. Knowing the usage patterns of these patrons can help the promoters target advertising toward the proper groups.

User Loyalty.   User loyalty is the continuing commitment a buyer has to a particular brand of product. Individuals can have loyalty to tangible goods, such as Campbell soup; to services, such as Sheraton Hotels; to organizations, such as the Democratic party; to places, such as Hawaii in December; or to causes, such as equal rights. Organizations must identify their loyal customers so that they can better serve them; however, this process often necessitates identifying the demographic characteristics of loyal customers. This has sometimes proved difficult because customers are not always willing to give out personal information.[12] One way to identify user loyalty is to give steady customers some type of reward or incentive. For example, Delta, Eastern, and American airlines have bonus programs: the more times you fly on their airline, the more points you earn toward free travel and prizes. Such programs not only give these airlines a list of names and addresses that can be used for direct mail advertising campaigns, but also encourage continued patronage.

Combining Variables

Marketers will often combine segmentation variables to create a more definable and action-oriented marketing mix. Consider the market for household furniture. The needs and wants of households for furniture vary by stage in family life cycle and household income. A furniture retailer may decide to focus on young single households with moderate incomes (demographic segmentation). The marketer might next identify the life-style and the benefits sought (behavioristic segmentation) by this group. Collectively, by using these several segmentation variables, the retailer should be able to design its marketing mix to be very attractive to its target market (see Figure 7.2).

Mallards, a specialty menswear store in Chicago, has used the approach of combining segmentation variables. Its demographic segment is 25- to 40-year-old men with limited discretionary income. Within this demographic segment they use benefit segmentation by catering to the man who wants moderately conservative apparel, high quality, and low prices. Mallards' segmentation strategy is extremely successful since the average customer spends $170 on merchandise per store visit.[13]

Major differences exist between consumer and organizational market segmentation, primarily because the organizational customer is not an individual but an organization or network of individuals in an organization.[14] The variables most often used to segment organizational markets are the characteristics of (1) the organization, (2) the buying center, and (3) the decision participants.

SEGMENTING ORGANIZATIONAL MARKETS

Organizational Characteristics

Organizational characteristics are similar to consumer demographics, except that the population is composed of organizations not individuals. The marketer must identify the industry affiliation, the size of the organization, and its geographic location.

Industry Affiliation. A major way to segment organizational markets is to identify the primary industry in which an organization operates. Industry affiliation can be segmented broadly (i.e., manufacturing, wholesaling, re-

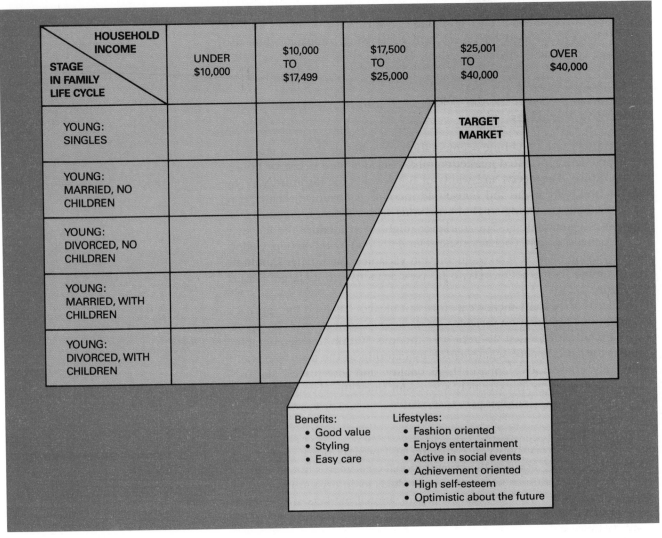

Figure 7.2

Combined Segmentation Variables

tailing, health care, education, or government). Segmentation can be narrower, such as tire manufacturing, hardware wholesaling, sporting goods retailing, drug companies, secondary education, and the U.S. Department of Defense. A firm that wants to market forklifts would probably focus efforts on organizations in industries such as hardware wholesaling and tire manufacturing.

Size of the Organization. The size of an organization is an important determinant of purchasing activity. Some of the size-related variables are annual sales volume, number of employees, and number of locations. For instance, the size of an organization is an important segmentation variable in the computer industry. As the organization grows, it needs computers with larger capacity. As the organization expands into more locations, it may need smaller computers at each location that can be linked to a large computer at corporate headquarters.

Geographic Location. An organization's demand for products is often concentrated in certain geographic areas based on the available natural resources and labor force and the regulations or incentives imposed on the industries by the individual states. For example, steel is produced in Pennsylvania and Indiana, publishing is concentrated in New York, furniture is made in Kentucky and North Carolina, computer chips come from California, oil well equipment producers are concentrated in Oklahoma and Texas, and autos are manufactured in the upper Midwest. Because of this concentration, firms that supply raw materials to or buy component parts from these industries often segment their market geographically.

Characteristics of the Buying Center

The organizational market can also be segmented by characteristics of the buying center. As you recall from Chapter 6, the buying center consists of all members of the organization who have an impact on the buying decision. Three characteristics of the buying center to consider when segmenting the market are (1) stage in the buying decision process,[15] (2) uncertainty perceived in the buying center, and (3) degree of buying responsibility decentralization. For example, a computer manufacturer could segment the market into those firms that have decided to purchase a new computer, those that are undecided, and those that currently do not recognize a need for a new computer. The firm could target its efforts on either firms that are uncertain about the specific features they want in a new computer or those that are fairly certain about what they want in terms of performance characteristics, price, and service. Finally, the computer market could be segmented by the degree of decentralization in buying responsibility. That is, some firms may have just one person who decides which computer to purchase; some may have representatives from several different areas in the firm (i.e., finance, production, research and development, and marketing) decide; and some may let a committee decide, with final approval accorded by the corporate controller and the president.

Characteristics of Decision Participants

A firm may also attempt to tailor its marketing mix to the characteristics of the participants in the decision-making process. This usually involves promotion and distribution more than the product or price, in which the sales approach is geared to the age, education, and industry experience of the decision maker. For example, a firm trying to sell ball bearings to a machinery manufacturer would benefit by knowing if the decision maker had a degree in engineering (in which case the facts about the product could be explained using engineering terms) or a degree in business administration (in which case the organization and style of presentation should be less technical and more broadly defined to relate to the firm as a whole).

The industrial market also may be segmented by the benefits sought by the decision participants, such as reliability, value, quality, and serviceability. Table 7.5 lists the common variables used to segment organizational markets.

Combining Variables in Organizational Market Segmentation

Because no single variable will allow the marketing manager to successfully segment an organizational market, a sequential approach is often recommended, which is similar to the way variables are combined when dealing with the consumer market.[16] In segmenting industrial markets, however, the variables used build on the prior ones. A manufacturer in the textile industry could first segment the market by end use and decide to focus on textiles used in building sofas. In stage 2 the manufacturer decides to focus only on sofa manufacturers with annual sales of over $10,000,000. In stage 3 the manufacturer focuses on those sofa manufacturers with annual sales over $10,000,000, who also desire high-quality, durable, synthetic, moderately priced textiles. Figure 7.3 depicts this sequential process as an inverted pyramid.

HOW TO SELECT A TARGET MARKET

We have briefly reviewed some basic segmentation strategies, the requirements for successful target market segmentation, and some bases or variables for segmenting consumer and organizational markets. All of this leads up to the most important aspect of market segmentation—how to select a target market. An extremely helpful tool in this regard is the **TARGET model**, which is *a six-step process used to select a target market:*

1. *Target a generic market.*
2. *Analyze benefits desired in the generic market.*
3. *Remove qualifying benefits.*
4. *Group remaining benefits into segments.*
5. *Enumerate customer characteristics of segments.*
6. *Target a market segment for cultivation.*

Note that the TARGET model begins and ends with a target. The first target is the broad **generic market**, which *consists of all products capable of satisfying the same basic needs.* We discussed this concept in Chapter 2 when we examined generic and industry competition. The second target

Table 7.5   Common Variables for Segmenting Organizational Markets

Segmentation Variable	Example
Organizational Characteristics	
Industry affiliation	Steel industry, machine tool industry, automobile industry, computer industry, rubber industry, health care industry
Size of organization	Less than 100 employees, 100–499 employees, 500–999 employees, 1,000–4,999 employees, over 5,000 employees
Geographic location	Northeast, Southeast, Midwest, Southwest, Central, Mountain, West, Northwest
Buying Center Characteristics	
Stage in buying decision	Need is unrecognized, undecided, interested in buying, intend to buy
Perceived uncertainty	High, moderate, low, or no uncertainty about what to buy
Buying responsibility decentralization	Single decider, several deciders, committee decision
Characteristics of Decision Participants	
Education	Engineering, business, law
Industry experience	High, moderate, low
Benefits sought	Reliability, quality, service, price, energy costs, or cost in use
Age	Under 30, 30–45, over 45 years

(actually the last step in the TARGET model) is the narrow segment of the broad generic market that a firm will attempt to attract by developing a marketing mix. This second target is analogous to the firm's target market. The TARGET model is essentially a systematic process for narrowing down a generic market into manageable segments worthy of separate market cultivation. To understand this further, we will examine the six steps in the TARGET model.

Target a Generic Market

The process of market segmentation and selecting a target market begins with identifying or targeting a generic market. A firm must decide what business it is in and thus the generic need it hopes to fill. By identifying a generic market, the firm will be focusing on a larger market than it can hope to reach. However, by beginning the search for a suitable target market

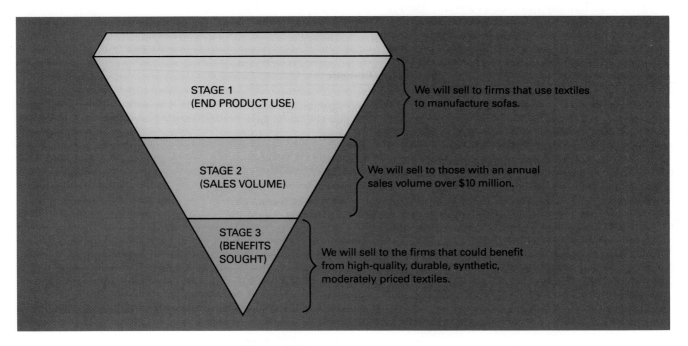

Figure 7.3

Possible Sequential Segmentation by a Textile Manufacturer

at this broad level, it will avoid the possibility of overlooking significant and attractive market segments that may be worth pursuing. In explaining the six steps of the TARGET model, we will use as an example a company that has defined its generic market as the market for storing perishable foodstuffs in the home.

Analyze Benefits Desired

The second step in the TARGET model is to analyze the benefits desired in the generic market. Many of the techniques and procedures of marketing research you learned about in Chapter 4 can be used to accomplish this task. This step identifies the benefits that people desire in a product to fill a need. Consider our example of the need to store perishable foodstuffs in the home. The benefits desired from the possible products that can meet this need may include:

1. A *safe* place to store perishables.
2. An *efficient* place to store perishables.
3. An *affordable* place to store perishables.

4. A *capacity* requirement (i.e., large or small storage area).

5. Some *type* of storage equipment (i.e., refrigerator versus freezer).

6. A desire for an *aesthetically appealing* place to store perishables.

Remove Qualifying Benefits

The third step in the TARGET model is to remove any qualifying benefits, which are benefits that *all* potential customers desire. Because everyone wants them, they are not useful for segmentation purposes. For example, in the U.S. market, all households would desire a safe, efficient, and affordable place to store perishables. Consequently, a marketer could not productively segment the market based on these desired benefits. Being able to design a marketing mix that offers these qualifying benefits is simply the price of admission to serve this broad generic market.

Group Benefits into Segments

After the qualifying benefits have been eliminated, the marketer must group the remaining benefits into segments or groups of potential customers who desire similar benefits. With our ongoing example, we reduced our six desired benefits to three by eliminating the qualifying benefits. The three remaining benefits are capacity, type of storage, and aesthetics. To segment the market using these benefits, they must be categorized into levels. For example, the desire for capacity could be split into small capacity (less than 6 cubic feet), moderate capacity (7–15 cubic feet), and large capacity (16 or more cubic feet). The type of storage could be broken into short term (primarily refrigeration), moderate mix of short and long term (moderate amount of refrigeration and freezer space), and long term (primarily freezer space). Finally, the desire for aesthetics could be dichotomous—desire or not desire aesthetics. Aesthetics would consist of both styling and color, but we will only use color in order to simplify this example. Figure 7.4 shows how the various levels of these three benefits (capacity, length of storage, aesthetics) can be used to create eighteen market segments.

Enumerate Customer Characteristics

The fifth step consists of enumerating the customer characteristics of the identifiable segments. These characteristics are usually the different demographic, geographic, and psychographic variables we discussed earlier in this chapter. These characteristics give the marketer a profile of the consumers or organizational customers in each segment.

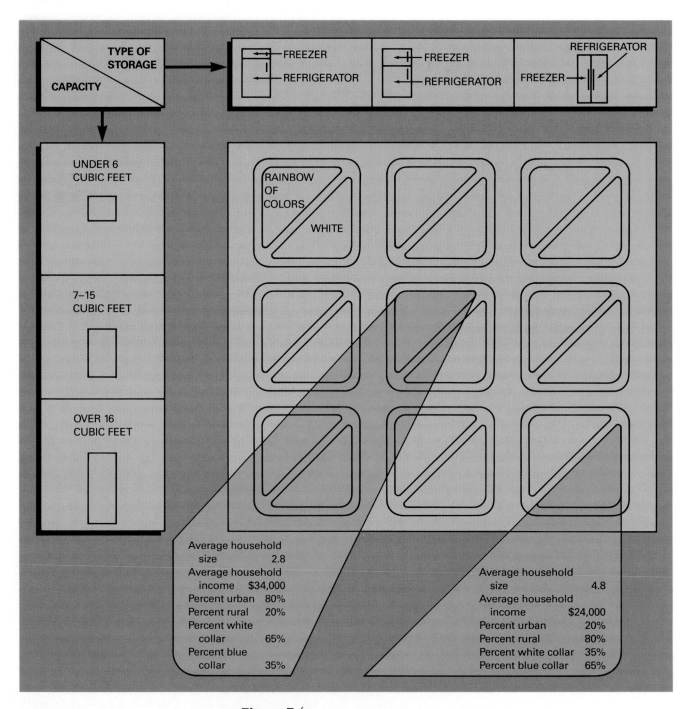

Figure 7.4
Benefit Segmentation of Market for Storing Perishable Foodstuffs in the Home

Figure 7.4 enumerates customer characteristics for two market segments. The first segment desires aesthetics, a 7- to 15-foot capacity, and a moderate mix of short-term and long-term storage. This segment is typically an urban household of 2.8 members with $34,000 in income and is most likely to be white collar. The second segment does not desire aesthetics, wants over 16 cubic feet of capacity, and primarily needs long-term storage. This segment is typically a rural household with close to five members with $24,000 in income and is predominantly blue collar.

Target a Market Segment

The last step in the TARGET model is to target a segment or segments for market cultivation. A market is cultivated by developing a marketing mix specifically tailored to the wants and needs of the target market. Chapters 8 through 17 of this book will be concerned with developing marketing mixes. Whether one or more segments will be targeted depends on whether the firm has a concentrated or multiple segmentation strategy, as discussed earlier in the chapter. Selecting the market segments to cultivate depends largely on the market potential in each segment and a firm's sales forecast in each segment. The goal is to select those segments to cultivate that offer the highest promise of helping the firm achieve its objectives.

As mentioned at the outset of this chapter, a successful target market selection requires substantiality. The market size must be substantial enough to be worth cultivating and segmenting. Substantiality can be assessed by examining market potential and forecasting sales.

MARKET POTENTIAL AND SALES FORECASTING

Market potential is *the maximum amount of a product that could be sold by all firms in a market during a given period with a maximum level of industry marketing activity under an assumed set of environmental conditions.* As industry marketing activity increases, sales level off because there is a maximum amount of a particular product that individuals or organizations will purchase in a given period. Typically, actual market sales will be less than the market potential because industry marketing activity rarely reaches its maximum level. A **market forecast** is *the expected sales for the market as a whole during a specified period under assumed environmental conditions with expected industry marketing effort.* Figure 7.5 shows the difference in sales levels between market potential and the market forecast. This is only a general diagram showing relationships; differences would vary given specific circumstances.

In forecasting sales, the environment must not be ignored. For instance, in estimating the market forecast for automobiles, certain assumptions must be made about gasoline prices, interest rates, and foreign competition. Any

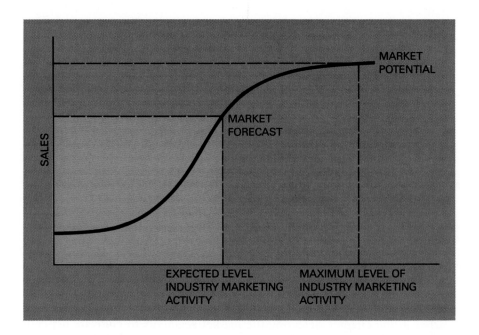

Figure 7.5
Market Potential and Market Forecast

change in these factors, however, would affect the market forecast, regardless of industry marketing activity. Although gasoline sells in the United States for less than $1.00 per gallon, if the price were to increase to $3.00 per gallon, the amount of driving would decrease and thus car sales would decline. Car sales are brisker when the interest rate on a car loan is 9 percent rather than 15 percent. Consumers are more apt to buy a Japanese car with the same qualities as a comparable American-made car if the import has a lower price tag.

A company's forecasted sales will be some share of the market forecast. A **sales forecast** is *the amount of the product that a firm expects to sell in a given period with a given level of marketing activity under an assumed set of environmental conditions.* The sales forecast is derived from the market forecast, which in turn is based on the market potential.

We will describe and analyze the advantages and disadvantages of several popular sales forecasting techniques: the jury of expert opinion, sales force composite, and buyer or user intention.[17] We will also touch briefly on regression analysis and time series analysis.

Jury of Expert Opinion

The **jury of expert opinion** is a simple and straightforward method of sales forecasting in which *the opinions of various experts in an area are collected in order to forecast company or industry sales for a given period, usually a year.* Usually, the forecasts of the various experts are averaged together. The jury can be composed of the firm's executives (e.g., the vice presidents of marketing, finance, and production and the president) or of experts outside the firm (e.g., a consulting economist, a retired executive, and a college business professor).

This method of sales forecasting has several advantages. First, it allows a firm to develop a new forecast very quickly. Second, it does not require the preparation of elaborate statistics—only addition and division are needed to compute an average forecast. Third, this method can be used when there is no past sales history.

A disadvantage of this method is that it usually cannot be broken down into forecasted sales by geographic area, product line, or month of the year. The experts are usually macro (broad) in orientation and do not have the specific knowledge or insight to forecast all of the refined breakdowns an organization might desire. Another disadvantage is that the method disperses responsibility for accurate forecasting. If actual sales are above or below the average forecast, it is hard to assign blame for poor forecasting since the average represented all of the views of the experts.

Sales Force Composite

The **sales force composite forecast** *enlists the members of the sales force to forecast sales.* For example, the salespeople of Alpha Office Furniture will be given a sales forecast form (see Table 7.6) and asked to complete it as accurately as possible. The form includes the salesperson's sales figures for the last period in that territory and thus provides a benchmark on which to base future estimates. Once these forms are completed, they can be totaled to obtain an aggregate forecast.

The sales force composite method of forecasting is popular and has several advantages. One of the major advantages is that it uses the people in the organization who are most familiar with buyers. Since the salespeople interact regularly with buyers, they should have a general feeling for sales trends. Another important advantage of the sales force composite forecast is that it can be used to forecast total sales as well as important breakdowns such as product lines and geographic territories. Finally, the sales force composite method is relatively inexpensive and quick.

The sales force composite forecast method is not without its shortcomings. A major problem is that salespeople often will not take the time to properly and thoughtfully complete the forms. Salespeople are rewarded for selling, not for filling out paperwork, and thus they may quickly fill out the forms in a cocktail lounge of a hotel or on an airplane on the way home from a long sales trip. Another problem is that, although the salespeople may be familiar with their customers' buying plans, they are often unaware of broader economic factors that could influence sales. They are not likely to be thinking about how changing interest rates, unemployment, and foreign exchange rates may affect next year's sales. Finally, the salespeople may be overly optimistic or pessimistic in their forecasts depending on how management plans to use the forecasts. For instance, if the forecast is used to set sales quotas, then salespeople will tend to be pessimistic in their forecasts.[18] On the other hand, if the forecast is used to allocate advertising expenditures to the salespeople's territory, that forecast may be overly optimistic—because this will get them a big advertising budget, which in turn will help them sell more.

The disadvantages of the sales force composite can be largely overcome by using three techniques to improve the salesperson's forecasting accuracy. When the organization prepares the forecasting form, it should show the salesperson's forecasting accuracy over the last few years. This will alert the salespeople about any tendencies they have to be overly optimistic or pessimistic. In addition, a brief macroeconomic forecast should accompany each forecasting form. This will ensure that all salespeople are making the same broad assumptions about the economic environment. Finally, for any overly optimistic or pessimistic forecast, the sales force manager should meet with the salesperson in question to discover the reasons underlying this projection. Most often, the salesperson has very good reasons to back up the forecast. Perhaps the salesperson heard from several key accounts that the company's leading competitor will be introducing a new product line next year that promises to be substantially superior to anything on the market. Management should be informed of this rumor and try to check its accuracy.[19]

Buyer Intentions

The **buyer-intention forecast** of sales forecasting *asks potential buyers about their purchasing plans.* This technique is most applicable for major consumer durables (i.e., autos, refrigerators, clothes dryers) or major industrial goods (i.e., factory machinery and computers). Regardless of whether the buyers are individual consumers or industrial purchasing agents, they are questioned about the likelihood or probability that they would purchase the item during a given period. After a sample of buyers has been surveyed, the results can be averaged and extrapolated to the total population to obtain an aggregate sales forecast.

The major advantage of this technique is that it goes directly to the potential buyer—if anyone knows what will be bought next year it should be the buyers themselves. Another advantage is that the marketer can obtain an understanding of what type of consumer is most likely to purchase the product by asking the respondents certain demographic questions. Also, the marketer can gain useful information by asking respondents to explain why they do or do not plan to purchase the product. Obviously, this information can help the marketing manager develop a more effective marketing mix.

Table 7.6 Worksheet for Sales Force Composite Forecasting: Alpha Office Furniture

	Salesperson	Mary Zinszer
	Territory	Nevada and Northern Arizona

Product Line	1985 Sales	1986 Forecast
Bookshelves	$ 58,000	_____
Chairs	71,000	_____
Conference tables	148,000	_____
Desks	329,000	_____
Filing cabinets	184,000	_____
Other	18,000	_____
TOTAL	$808,000	$_____

Buyer-intention forecasting can only be used successfully when the organization can identify its potential customers. This is necessary because a random sample must be selected from this population list. Another disadvantage is that buyers may change their plans because of unforeseen circumstances. For example, someone who plans to purchase a new dishwasher in six months may be laid off from work, become pregnant, or find that the roof on the house needs to be replaced, which means that money intended for the dishwasher will be spent elsewhere. Generally, for consumer goods, the buyer intention technique is only valid for forecasting sales three to six months into the future. Beyond that, consumer buying plans change rapidly. Industrial purchasing agents can also change their plans, but since most firms budget on a twelve-month basis, the buyer-intention method of forecasting is typically reliable for up to twelve months.

Regression Analysis

Regression analysis is a more statistically complex method of forecasting sales than the three previous methods we discussed.[20] **Regression analysis** is *the functional relationship between a dependent variable and an independent variable or set of independent variables.* The independent variable is one of the factors that can be used to predict sales, and the dependent variable is that thing we wish to predict or forecast (i.e., sales). To employ regression analysis, there must be past sales data on the product(s) for which we are forecasting sales, because we are looking for any regular pattern between prior sales and other factors that could be used to predict sales, such as population, household income, and advertising (see Figure 7.6).

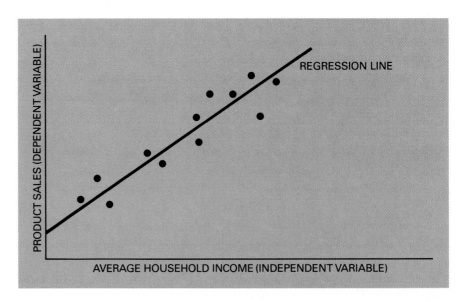

Figure 7.6

Regression Sales Forecast

Time Series Analysis

Time series analysis *examines the pattern of sales that has occurred over time.*[21] This technique, like regression analysis, can also get statistically complex. The pattern of sales over time is broken into four components (trend, cyclical, seasonal, and random) that are statistically isolated. See Figure 7.7.

1. *Trend* is the long-term general pattern of sales growth. Are sales trending upward or downward or remaining constant?
2. *Cyclical* is the up-and-down cyle that sales go through because of general economic conditions (prosperity, recession) and usually covers several years.
3. *Seasonal* is the short-term, recurring ups and downs in sales within cycles that are due to regularly occurring and predictable phenomena. Seasonal factors may be due to climate, traditions, or buying habits.
4. *Random* is the behavior in sales over time that is not explained by trend, cyclical, and seasonal factors. Factors such as labor strikes, war, and earthquakes are often treated as random factors that could influence sales.

SUMMARY

This chapter focused on market segmentation and target marketing. Market segmentation was defined as the process of dividing a heterogeneous group of buyers into more homogeneous groups with relatively similar product needs. We learned

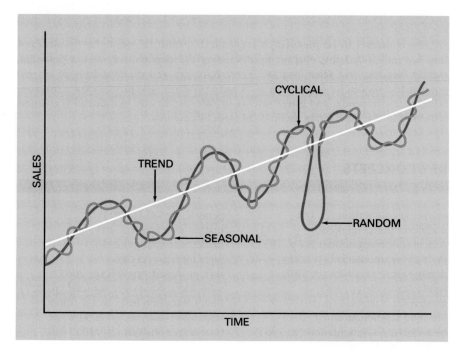

Figure 7.7
Time Series Forecast

that most U.S. firms segment markets because this allows them to (1) better serve customers, (2) compete more effectively, and (3) better achieve organizational goals.

Some firms practice undifferentiated marketing—essentially a nonsegmentation strategy. A firm using undifferentiated marketing ignores the heterogeneity of buyers in the market and focuses on what all or most buyers have in common. There are two basic segmentation strategies. A firm can practice concentrated segmentation, where it focuses on a single target market with a single marketing mix, or multiple segmentation, where it focuses on several distinct segments with several different marketing mixes. Multiple segmentation results in higher production, promotion, inventory, and administrative costs, and thus the firm must at least cover these higher costs with the higher level of sales this segmentation strategy will create.

There are four requirements for effective segmentation in both organizational and consumer markets: the segments must be measurable, they must be accessible, they must be differentially responsive to a unique marketing mix, and they must be substantial or worth separate market cultivation.

Some of the common variables used to segment consumer and organizational markets were reviewed. Consumer markets are most often segmented by demographic, geographic, psychographic, or behavioristic variables—or by some combination of these. On the other hand, organizational markets are most often segmented by organizational characteristics, buying center characteristics, and the characteristics of the decision participants. A sequential approach was recommended for segmenting organizational markets, in which the market is segmented by increasingly more specific characteristics.

In this chapter, we also presented and discussed the TARGET model, which shows how a marketer should select a target market. The six steps of the TARGET model are (1) target a generic market, (2) analyze the benefits desired in the generic market, (3) remove qualifying benefits, (4) group remaining benefits into segments,

(5) enumerate customer characteristics of segments, (6) target a market segment for market cultivation.

For a market to be pursued or segmented, it must be substantial in size, and thus we concluded this chapter by discussing the concepts of market potential, market forecast, and sales forecast. The advantages and disadvantages of several popular techniques for forecasting sales were reviewed: the jury of expert opinion, sales force composite, and buyer intentions. We also briefly introduced regression analysis and the time series methods of sales forecasting.

KEY CONCEPTS

market segmentation (p. 181)
undifferentiated marketing (p. 182)
concentrated segmentation (p. 183)
multiple segmentation (p. 185)
demographic variables (p. 188)
family life cycle (p. 190)
geographic variables (p. 191)
life-style segmentation (p. 194)
behavioristic segmentation (p. 196)
TARGET model (p. 200)

generic market (p. 200)
market potential (p. 205)
market forecast (p. 205)
sales forecast (p. 206)
jury of expert opinion (p. 206)
sales force composite forecast (p. 207)
buyer-intention forecast (p. 208)
regression analysis (p. 209)
time series analysis (p. 210)

REVIEW AND DISCUSSION QUESTIONS

1. Define *market segmentation* and explain why firms use it.
2. Name the two basic market segmentation strategies and describe their advantages.
3. Why do some firms choose not to segment the market?
4. Discuss the four major requirements for effective target market segmentation.
5. What are the four major categories of variables used to segment consumer markets? Provide examples of variables in each category.
6. Describe how your life-style differs from that of your parents and how this influences the products, brands, and stores you patronize.
7. Children can be viewed as durable goods that we pay rent on for eighteen to twenty-one years. How will the number of children you plan to have in your family influence your other purchasing decisions?
8. Explain why organizational markets are segmented differently than consumer markets.
9. What are the three major categories of variables used to segment organizational markets? Provide examples of variables in each category.
10. What are the six steps in the TARGET model?
11. Why is the third step in the TARGET model necessary?

12. Explain why there is usually a difference between market potential and market forecast.
13. Explain the difference between a market forecast and a sales forecast.

ACTION PROBLEMS

1. Recently, a friend opened a restaurant. In an effort to keep down costs, she decided to practice undifferentiated marketing. Explain how she might use undifferentiated marketing in the restaurant business. Do you think she made the right decision? Why or why not?
2. Identify several segmentation variables used in the United States to market each of the following: health insurance, shampoo, running shoes, airline travel.
3. Find an advertisement for a company that practices geographic segmentation and explain why you think this is the right (or wrong) segmentation variable for this company to use.
4. Visit two large department stores, such as a Sears store and a J.C. Penney store, or a K mart and a Target store. Carefully examine and study the store decor and merchandise. Decide if the stores are appealing to the same or different market segments and describe these segments.
5. Steve Austin belongs to a campus organization that annually sells Christmas trees to the community of 70,000 in which the college is located. He is in charge of ordering this year's inventory and has put together the following information:

Major Tree Lots in Town	Market Share
Boy Scouts	25.0%
Catholic church	21.7%
Baptist church	19.1%
Lion's club	16.8%
Steve's group	13.4%
All other	4.0%

If the market forecast for Christmas trees for this community is 9,800, calculate the sales forecast for each group. How many trees should Steve order if he expects to keep the same market share?

NOTES

1. Two excellent books on the topic of market segmentation are James F. Engel, Henry F. Fiorillo, and Murray A. Cayley, *Market Segmentation: Concepts and Applications* (New York: Holt, Rinehart & Winston, 1972); Ronald Frank, William Massy, and Yoram Wind, *Market Segmentation* (Englewood Cliffs, NJ: Prentice-Hall, 1972).
2. The strategic value of this maneuver for organizational markets is discussed in Joseph F. Barone, "Niche Marketing: What Industrial Marketers Can Learn from Consumer Package Goods," *Business Marketing* (November 1984), pp. 56–62.

3. "Fighting Back: It Can Work," *BusinessWeek* (August 26, 1985), pp. 62–68.

4. "Innovative Segmentation Distinguishes Philip Morris Firms," *Marketing News* (February 4, 1983), p. 11; "Jim Thompson Tells How Philip Morris Hit the Top," *Marketing and Media Decisions* (January 1984), pp. 62–63, 123.

5. Liz Murphy, "Hispanic Gets Manic," *Sales and Marketing Management* (November 14, 1983), pp. 39–42.

6. William D. Wells and George Gubar, "The Life Cycle Concept," *Journal of Marketing Research* (November 1966), pp. 355–363.

7. Patrick E. Murphy and William A. Staples, "A Modernized Family Life Cycle," *Journal of Consumer Research* (June 1979), p. 17.

8. These figures are somewhat fluid because the definition of a SMSA has changed several times. The definition cited is as of 1980 and supersedes the 1958, 1971, and 1975 definitions.

9. William Wells and Douglas Tigert, "Activities, Interests, and Opinions," *Journal of Advertising Research* (August 1971), pp. 27–35.

10. Russell I. Haley, "Benefit Segmentation: A Decision Oriented Research Tool," *Journal of Marketing* 32(July 1968), pp. 30–35; Paul E. Green, Yoram Wind, and Arun K. Jain, "Benefit Bundle Analysis," *Journal of Advertising Research* (April 1972), pp. 31–36.

11. For a further discussion of the heavy user, see Dik Warren Twedt, "How Important to Marketing Strategy Is the 'Heavy User'?" *Journal of Marketing* (January 1964), pp. 71–72.

12. Ronald E. Frank, "Is Brand Loyalty a Useful Basis for Market Segmentation?" *Journal of Advertising Research* (June 1967), pp. 27–33.

13. Ellen Wojahn, "The Price is Right," *INC.* (October 1985), p. 125.

14. For a detailed discussion of industrial market segmentation, see Frederick E. Webster, Jr., *Industrial Marketing Strategy* (New York: John Wiley & Sons, 1977), Chapter 4.

15. For a discussion of segmentation by stage in the buying decision process, see Charles W. Faris, "Market Segmentation and Industrial Buying Behavior," in M.S. Moyer and R.E. VosBurgh (eds.), *Marketing for Tomorrow . . . Today* (Chicago: American Marketing Association, 1967), pp. 108–110.

16. The multistage approach to industrial market segmentation is discussed in Yoram Wind and Richard Cardozo, "Industrial Market Segmentation," *Industrial Marketing Management* (April 1974), pp. 153–166.

17. How to select the proper forecasting technique is discussed in John C. Chambers, Sontinder K. Mullick, and Donald D. Smith, "How to Choose the Right Forecasting Technique," *Harvard Business Review* (July–August 1971), pp. 45–71.

18. For more details on using the sales force in forecasting and quota setting, see Thomas R. Wotruba and Michael L. Thurlaw, "Sales Force Participation in Quota Setting and Sales Forecasting," *Journal of Marketing* (April 1976), pp. 11–16.

19. In general, the sales force can be an important source of information; see R.A. Thietart and R. Vivas, "Strategic Intelligence Activity: The Management of the Sales Force as a Source of Strategic Information," *Strategic Management Journal* (January–March 1981), pp. 15–25.

20. The use of regression analysis in forecasting sales is discussed more completely in Douglas J. Dalrymple, *Sales Management: Concepts and Cases* (New York: John Wiley & Sons, 1982), pp. 137–139.

21. The use of time series in forecasting sales is discussed more thoroughly in Steven C. Wheelwright and Spyros Makridakis, *Forecasting Methods for Management* (New York: John Wiley & Sons, 1973), pp. 83–99.

8.

Quality Travel Agency (by Martin Meyers)

Quality Travel Agency has been in existence since 1982. It is owned and operated by Betty Sloan, a travel agent who had ten years of experience before starting her own business. Her travel agency is located in the downtown area of a midwestern city with a population of approximately 20,000.

Sloan provides a wide variety of services to her clients. She is well informed on the climate, currency exchange rate, shopping, theater, restaurants, festivals, sporting events, and so on of almost anywhere in the world. In addition to being a source of information to her clients, she is generally aware of the lowest priced air fares and can usually determine which hotel will best meet her clients' needs and budgets. She books reservations for planes, trains, hotels, tours, and cruises and arranges for car rentals.

Betty is compensated by the airlines, hotels, car rental agencies, tours, and cruise lines, but her clients pay the same price whether or not they use a travel agent. Betty has found, however, that many people believe that it is more expensive to use a travel agent than to make the arrangements themselves. Furthermore, some people are not aware of the information a travel agent can provide.

Betty decided to use the skills she learned in her college marketing courses to discover more about her target market so that she could better sell her services. She wrote a questionnaire to pinpoint the perceptions people held concerning travel agencies and, from a list of names and addresses of the people in the community, randomly selected 400 to receive the questionnaire. From the 400 questionnaires sent, 190 were completed and returned.

Questions

1. Analyze the questions Betty selected for her questionnaire. What changes would you suggest?
2. What do the research results tell her about people's perceptions of a travel agent's role? What decisions should Betty make based on these research results?

The Questionnaire and Results

1. How many airplane trips have you taken in the past three years? (If none proceed to question 5.)
   a. none __10__
   b. one __65__
   c. two __66__
   d. three __30__
   e. four or more __19__

2a. Did you *consult* a travel agent for the last airplane trip you took?
   1. no __75__ (Proceed to question 5.)
   2. yes __105__

2b. Did a travel agent book your last airline ticket?
   1. no __8__
   2. yes __97__

2c. Did you stay in a hotel when you took your last airplane flight?
   1. no __65__ (Proceed to question 2e.)
   2. yes __115__

2d. Did a travel agent make your hotel reservation?
   1. no __25__
   2. yes __90__

2e. Did you rent a car when you took your last airplane flight?
   1. no __80__ (Proceed to question 2g.)
   2. yes __25__

2f. Did a travel agent make your car rental reservation?
    1. no   15
    2. yes   10

2g. Did you travel with a tour when you took your last airplane flight?
    1. no   90   (Proceed to question 2i.)
    2. yes   15

2h. Did a travel agent make your tour reservation?
    1. no   15
    2. yes   0

2i. Did you take a cruise when you took your last airplane flight?
    1. no   95   (Proceed to question 3.)
    2. yes   10

2j. Did a travel agent make your cruise reservation?
    1. no   0
    2. yes   10

3. Check the appropriate line that indicates the commission you believe a travel agent charges you for the following services. (Results shown for those who have taken an airplane trip within past 3 years.)

Service	No Charge	Less Than 5%	5–10%	Over 10%
Booking domestic flight	95	8	2	0
Booking international flight	85	11	5	4
Arranging car rental	100	5	0	0
Booking domestic hotel	98	6	1	0
Booking international hotel	87	12	4	2
Booking domestic tour	101	4	0	0
Booking international tour	89	10	5	1
Booking cruise	92	7	5	1

4. How helpful do you believe a travel agent would be in answering your questions on the following topics for a trip you are considering to a foreign country? (Results shown for those who have taken an airplane trip within past 3 years.)

	Definitely Not Helpful	Probably Not Helpful	Might be Helpful	Probably Helpful	Definitely Be Helpful
Currency conversion	2	3	9	21	70
Climate	0	1	10	24	70
Shopping	2	3	15	20	65
Restaurants	1	5	9	23	67
Sporting events	6	6	20	19	54
Theater	11	9	14	20	51
Major attractions	0	1	0	19	85
Nightclubs	17	8	10	16	54

5. Check the appropriate line that indicates the commission you believe a travel agent charges you for the following services. (Results shown for those who have not taken an airplane trip within past 3 years.)

Service	No Charge	Less Than 5%	5–10%	Over 10%
Booking domestic flight	40	20	10	5
Booking international flight	30	25	14	6
Arranging car rental	45	21	9	0
Booking domestic hotel	44	20	10	1
Booking international hotel	33	28	11	3
Booking domestic tour	59	12	4	0
Booking international tour	48	19	6	2
Booking cruise	41	23	8	3

6. How helpful do you believe a travel agent would be in answering your questions on the following topics for a trip you are considering to a foreign country? (Results shown for those who have not taken an airplane trip within past 3 years.)

	Definitely Not Helpful	Probably Not Helpful	Might Be Helpful	Probably Helpful	Definitely Be Helpful
Currency conversion	25	15	15	11	0
Climate	18	25	20	10	7
Shopping	21	14	26	9	5
Restaurants	16	19	28	7	5
Sporting events	10	26	22	12	5
Theater	10	30	23	8	4
Major attractions	5	11	28	20	11
Nightclubs	21	21	24	6	3

9.

Tom's Meat Market

Tom's Meat Market, which was established in 1974 by Tom Hayes, is a 2,000 square foot butcher shop that specializes in quality meets. The shop is located in a community with a population of 48,000 and is open five days a week (Monday–Friday) from 10 A.M. to 6 P.M. Tom Hayes is the sole owner and worker except for a high school student who works part-time from 3:30 to 6:00 each afternoon and mainly performs janitorial chores. In 1985, the store had annual sales of $196,000 and net profits of $8,012. Tom pays himself a salary of $24,000.

No other meat market exists in the community; however, there are four supermarkets in the area with which Tom's must compete. One-half mile to the north is a Safeway that is 24,000 square feet. Another Safeway is three-quarters of a mile to the east and is 20,000 square feet. Approximately 1.5 miles to the north is a newly opened 41,000 square foot Alpha-Beta that is a combination food and drug store. Finally, an IGA supermarket of 18,000 square feet is 1.5 miles northwest of Tom's Meat Market. All four of these supermarkets have approximately 10 to 12 percent of their space devoted to meat products.

The Alpha-Beta was opened two months ago, and Tom has noticed that he is seeing fewer of his regular customers. He believes they are shopping at the new Alpha-Beta, which is located close to one of the highest income census tracts in town. The average household income in this census tract is $41,312, and most of the houses are in the $125,000 to $300,000 price range.

Tom decided to have a local management consultant conduct some marketing research to see if he could determine why his business was declining. The consultant conducted a telephone survey of a random sample of 300 households and obtained information on (1) shopping patterns for meat, (2) per capita annual consumption of meat, (3) most important attributes used in deciding where to purchase meat, and (4) eating habits away from home. All of the data were categorized and analyzed by socioeconomic status of the households surveyed. Eighteen percent of the respondents were placed in the lower socioeconomic status category. These households had an average income of $16,300, and the typical head of household had a high school education. Sixty-one percent of households were categorized as

middle class: average household income was $27,900, and the typical head of household had several years of college. Finally, 21 percent were upper class in terms of socioeconomic status. These households had an average income of $39,000 and were usually college graduates. The range of household income in the upper class was wide—varying from $32,000 to $140,000. Four percent of the households had incomes in excess of $60,000. The results of the market research study are presented in Tables 1 through 4.

Questions

1. What additional data might the consultant have collected for Tom's Meat Market? Give the purpose for collecting data.
2. What decisions or actions should Tom take given the research results?

Table 1 Shopping Patterns for Meat by Socioeconomic Status[a]

Store	Socioeconomic Status		
	Lower	Middle	Upper
Tom's Meat Market	4.8%	8.7%	13.1%
Safeway—north	15.3	20.3	8.7
Safeway—east	6.7	10.4	24.3
Alpha-Beta	3.8	20.4	29.1
IGA	44.9	22.6	18.3

[a]Numerical entries represent the proportion of people who purchase the majority of their meat at a particular store.

Table 2 Per Capita Annual Consumption of Meat by Socioeconomic Status

Meat	Socioeconomic Status		
	Lower	Middle	Upper
Beef (lb)	39.1	71.1	84.3
Pork (lb)	41.3	59.3	55.1
Poultry/fish (lb)	83.9	54.0	42.1

Table 3   Most Important Attributes in Deciding Where to Purchase Meat

| Attribute | Socioeconomic Status | | |
	Lower	Middle	Upper
Price/on sale	52.3%	31.4%	16.0%
Freshness	6.5	16.6	18.2
Service/cut to order	1.4	10.8	13.9
Selection	8.3	10.4	16.6
Convenient location	20.1	10.3	4.2
Neat, clean displays	7.1	8.1	8.0
Quality	4.3	12.4	23.1

Table 4   Average Number of Meals Eaten Away from Home Weekly (per capita)

| Place | Socioeconomic Status | | |
	Lower	Middle	Upper
Work/school cafeteria	4.1	4.5	4.8
Fast-food outlet	1.3	1.8	1.4
Full-service restaurant (medium priced)	0.6	1.1	1.1
Full-service restaurant (high priced)	0.04	0.2	1.2

10.

Firestone Masterminds the Auto Repair Market

Firestone Tire & Rubber Co. was faced with a dilemma when new auto sales declined in the late 1970s, since its primary business was selling tires to new car manufacturers. As the cost of owning and operating an automobile skyrocketed, people opted to hold onto their cars as long as possible, averaging seven years. At the same time, it became increasingly difficult to find a convenient and trustworthy auto repair shop. The neighborhood service station all but disappeared, replaced by self-service gas stations and convenience food stores selling gasoline.

Instead of throwing up their hands in despair, Firestone managers decided to concentrate on an expanding market opportunity, the auto repair market. Evidence of the strong demand for auto repair service was reflected in the nationwide 13.5 percent increase in service sales during 1982. At Firestone, service sales grew 50 percent to $300 million in the two-year period from 1981 to 1982. In 1982, they almost doubled capital spending and purchased 300 auto repair centers from J.C. Penney Co.

Firestone's most innovative idea was to develop the Master Care Program. At the heart of this program is the Master Mind computer—a $255,000 machine that will diagnose an engine's problems in eight to twelve minutes. If the Master Mind correctly diagnoses engine problems and the service personnel properly fix the engine, then customers will be satisfied and return. This is the central philosophy behind the Master Care concept.

When customers get their cars fixed at a Master Care Center, the work is performed by trained mechanics. Firestone is sending mechanics to five training centers to learn repair techniques. The work performed at Master Care Centers is guaranteed, and the guarantee is recognized at the other centers. For instance, if the work is done and guaranteed in Dallas and the car needs repair for the same problem in Phoenix, the Dallas guarantee is valid in Phoenix. The Master Care program is already in place at 300 outlets and should be in place at more than 1,500 outlets by 1986.

Questions

1. Use the psychological concepts of motivation, attitude, learning processes, and perceptual processes to suggest how Firestone could improve its marketing efforts.
2. How could Firestone maximize postpurchase satisfaction with its auto repair service?

Source: Corporate annual reports; "Firestone Tries The Service Business Again," *BusinessWeek* (June 20, 1983), pp. 70–71.

11.

Health Comfort Systems, Inc.

When Nancy Belford and Rita Hughes met six months ago in the cafeteria of Memorial Hospital, both found that they had something in common—they did not like working for someone else. Nancy had recently graduated from medical school and was working as an associate in a group practice with five other doctors. Rita had been a nurse for the past twenty-one years. One thing that Rita hated about being a nurse was having to take directions from doctors and hospital administrators. She had often thought of quitting, but with two children to raise as a single parent, she felt she had no choice but to continue with her nursing profession. Now, with both children in college, she was looking forward to possibly changing professions. Nancy, on the other hand, enjoyed practicing medicine but did not like working in a group practice, where she was the "junior person," and not a partner.

One evening when Rita was visiting Nancy at her apartment, they began to talk about their frustrations. In so doing, they hit on the idea of establishing their own health care company to provide in-home health services. Both were familiar with the phenomenal growth in home health care, a trend projected to more than triple in volume between 1984 and 1990.

Keeping in mind the increasing number of cancer patients in the United States, they decided to explore the possibility of establishing a firm that specialized in in-home chemotherapy treatment for cancer patients. Hospitals typically charge $750 per day for chemotherapy, and Nancy and Rita believed that they could halve this price with an in-home service.

Nancy and Rita spent all of their spare time over the next six months researching this business venture. They were convinced that there was sufficient demand. For their particular geographic region of the United States, they found that 14.8 people per 1,000 over the age of 65 years discovered each year that they had cancer. For other age groups, this statistic was:

- **25–44 years**   **1.8/1,000**
- **45–54 years**   **3.6/1,000**
- **55–64 years**   **8.5/1,000**

From 20 to 40 percent of these cancer patients were potential chemotherapy recipients. Nancy called together some of her fellow doctors and conducted a jury of expert opinion to estimate the market share their in-home chemotherapy service could hope to obtain. The estimates ranged from 2 to 10 percent with a mean of 7 percent. Nancy and Rita believed these estimates were very low; both thought they could generate a 15 to 20 percent market share within two years.

Although they were convinced of the potential demand, both Nancy and Rita were uncertain as to how to obtain the estimated $200,000 needed to start the business. This money was needed for office equipment, a microcomputer, software, laboratory instruments, and other medical machinery. Also, a close friend of Rita's, who owned a retail shoe store, told her that they should probably have approximately $50,000 in cash to allow the firm several months to reach its breakeven point. Between the two of them they could barely scrape together $10,000, so they had to devise a plan to raise the necessary capital.

The city where they lived had a population of approximately 400,000. Some of the demographic characteristics of ten major areas of the city are profiled in Tables 1 and 2. Both Nancy and Rita live in apartments in area C. Since the firm (Health Comfort Systems, Inc.) was to be staffed only by Nancy and Rita, they felt that they should locate relatively close to their target market. Consequently, they needed to decide in which of the ten geographic areas to locate. They wanted to design the firm so that it would be profitable initially by serving only one of the ten geographic areas.

Questions

1. Which sociological, psychological, and economic factors would influence a person's use of in-home chemotherapy?
2. Which geographic area should be the target market for Health Comfort Systems, Inc.? Give reasons.

Table 1 Population by Age Group (1980)

Area of City	Population by Age Group (years)				
	Under 25	25–44	45–54	55–64	65+
A	7,500	21,000	14,700	8,700	1,800
B	11,000	23,400	8,300	4,100	1,400
C	4,000	6,000	3,700	4,200	2,700
D	4,800	7,100	4,200	6,800	3,100
E	1,700	2,900	3,100	7,000	6,300
F	7,100	9,300	7,800	4,100	1,900
G	3,900	7,100	4,300	3,700	1,100
H	22,400	24,500	7,100	6,900	1,700
I	4,500	8,000	14,000	16,100	4,800
J	14,700	23,700	12,800	12,100	6,700

Table 2 Household Income

Area of City	Percent White	Household Income by Age of Household Head (years)				
		Under 25	25–44	45–54	55–64	65+
A	67.4	$13,100	$17,400	$21,300	$18,100	$11,300
B	71.0	13,700	17,500	21,100	17,900	12,000
C	91.0	23,000	29,000	37,000	32,000	19,000
D	88.9	20,700	27,100	34,300	29,400	16,900
E	93.4	23,100	31,000	39,700	40,100	26,100
F	78.3	17,400	21,000	24,700	30,700	15,000
G	61.4	11,100	13,700	17,700	16,900	9,800
H	59.4	11,000	13,700	16,900	15,800	9,500
I	84.5	16,300	17,800	24,100	23,900	16,200
J	76.7	15,400	18,300	26,900	25,000	17,300

12.

Consumer Research, Shopper Needs, and Market Segmentation

In the fall of 1980, Management Horizons undertook a major consumer research project in an attempt to identify shopper needs and store patronage habits. Management Horizons is an internationally known consulting firm headquartered in Columbus, Ohio.

Data in Table 1 describe customers based on their shopping needs, preferences, and expectations. These data reveal that 50 percent of consumers are price-sensitive in terms of their patronage behavior.

In Table 2, we see how two demographic factors—family life cycle stage and household income—can be combined to develop eight market segments. These segments are described in Table 3. The analysis of shopper needs and the life cycle stage–buying power segmentation can be combined to show the relationship between the two analyses, which is presented in Table 4.

The research by Management Horizons also revealed that the eight life cycle stage–buying power segments have a dramatic influence on where people shop. Figures 1, 2, and 3 show store preference by market segment for women's apparel, home entertainment, and sporting goods.

Questions

1. What is the logic behind combining family life cycle and household income to develop eight market segments? What effect do these market segments have on store choice for women's apparel, home entertainment, and sporting goods?
2. What is the implication of this research for Sears, J.C. Penney, and Montgomery Ward?

Source: Reprinted by permission of the publisher from William Haueisen, Jerome Scott, and Timothy Sweeney. "Market Positioning: A New Strategic Approach for Retailers," in William R. Darden and Robert F. Lusch (eds.), *Patronage Behavior and Retail Management* (New York: Elsevier Science Publishing Co., 1983), pp. 115–128. Copyright 1983 by Elsevier Science Publishing Co., Inc.

Table 1   Customers Based on Shopping Needs

Customer Group	Percentage of Market	Description
1. Quality shopper	20	These shoppers put quality and fashion before prices. They enjoy shopping and prefer a moderate degree of personal service in the store. They do not like mass merchandisers and are moderately loyal to a few stores. They are well educated and have high incomes and generally prestigious jobs.
2. Price-sensitive nonshoppers	30	These shoppers are primarily young and middle-aged families of moderate income with two or more children. They are price sensitive and rely on mass merchandisers and general mass merchandisers except for a few items such as men's and women's clothing. They dislike shopping around but are forced to do so because of limited incomes. In-store service is a low-priority item, time for shopping is not.
3. Sociable shopper	15	The sociable shopper wants in-store personal service and remains loyal to a few stores, especially the traditional department store, for most personal items and furniture. Since many sociable shoppers are older or retired, they have the time to shop. They avoid mass merchandisers except for toys for youngsters and domestics.
4. Price-sensitive shopper	20	These buyers are very price sensitive but, unlike segment 2, they like to shop and are heavy users of mass merchandisers for nearly all items. They require little in-store service and are not early adopters of new fashions, nor are they very store loyal. They are mainly younger families with downscale incomes, occupations, and educations.
5. Specialty shopper	15	Specialty shoppers are intensely store loyal and typically shop at specialty stores and traditional department stores. Price is far less important to them than quality, fashion, and in-store service. Unlike segment 1, they dislike shopping. They are mainly older, affluent couples with good incomes and jobs.

Table 2   Life Stage–Buying Power Segmentation

Life Stage	Household Income	
	Low	**High**
Bachelors and young couples	1. Modest young (7%)	2. Moneyed young (7%)
Young families	3. Budget-stretched young families (17%)	4. Prosperous young families (10%)
Older families and couples	5. Budget-strained older households (20%)	6. Affluent older households (16%)
Retired	7. Struggling retired (15%)	8. Comfortably retired (8%)
Total	59%	41%

Table 3 Description of Life Stage–Buying Power Segments

Segment	Percentage of Market	Description
1. Modest young	7	Bachelors and young couples under 30 with household income less than $20,000 per year; 70% rent their residences.
2. Moneyed young	7	These are different from segment 1 in that 70% own their homes and most have better jobs. They are typically professionals or managers.
3. Budget-stretched young families	17	This segment consists of families in which the men are craftsmen or operatives. Except for the retired segments they have the least amount of education. Most own their own homes, and family size ranges from 3 to 5. Income is less than $20,000.
4. Prosperous young families	10	This, the most educated segment, has incomes above $20,000. Age is less than 40, and most are professionals and managers; 90% own their homes.
5. Budget-strained older households	20	Income is less than $25,000 for this segment. Age ranges from 40–60 years. Most are craftsmen or operatives with high school educations. Family size is 2 or 3, reflecting the fact that some children have left home.
6. Affluent older households	16	This segment is the most prosperous, with incomes above $25,000. Many have college training, and most have excellent jobs; 96% own their own homes.
7. Struggling retired	15	These retired people have incomes of less than $10,000 per year, and only one half are high school graduates.
8. Comfortably retired	8	Income for the comfortably retired is above $10,000 per year, and 90% still own their own homes.

Table 4 Relationship Between Techniques

Life Stage–Buying Power Segment	Shoppers Need Groups
1. Modest young	60% are price-sensitive nonshoppers or price-sensitive shoppers.
2. Moneyed young	33% are quality shoppers, and 35% are price-sensitive nonshoppers.
3. Budget-stretched young families	70% are price-sensitive nonshoppers or price-sensitive shoppers.
4. Prosperous young families	30% are quality or specialty shoppers, 30% are price-sensitive nonshoppers.
5. Budget-strained older households	No pattern: almost all 5 shopper need segments are represented.
6. Affluent older households	50% are quality or specialty shoppers, 20% are sociable shoppers.
7. Struggling retired	All 5 shopper need segments are evenly represented.
8. Comfortably retired	35% are sociable shoppers, and 45% are quality or specialty shoppers.

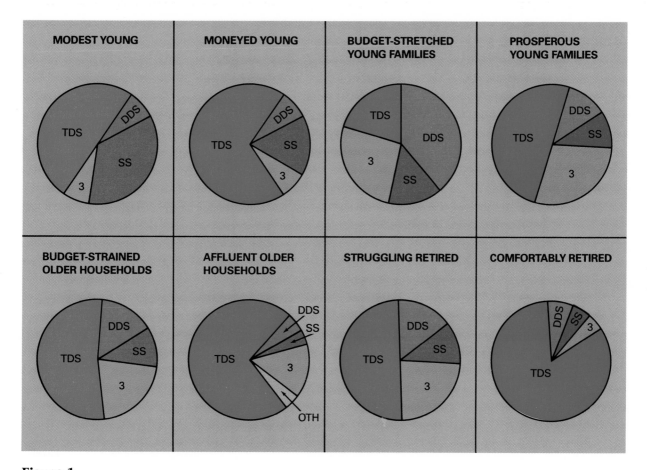

Figure 1

Intertype Competitive Assessment: Store Choice Preference by Market Segment for Women's Apparel[a]

[a]TDS, department stores; DDS, discount stores; SS, specialty stores; 3, Sears, Penneys, or Wards; OTH, other.

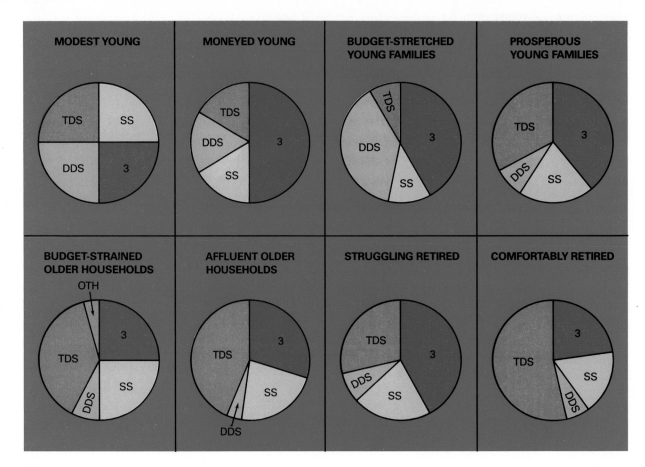

Figure 2

Store Choice Preference by Market Segment for Home Entertainment[a]

[a]The symbols are as defined in Figure 1.

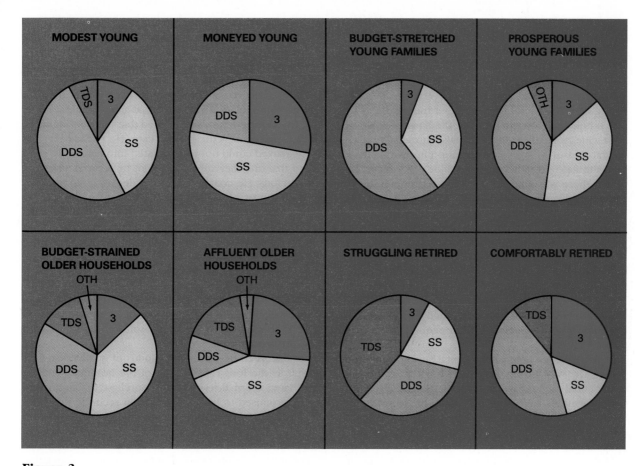

Figure 3

Store Choice Preference by Market Segment for Sporting Goods[a]

[a]The symbols are as defined in Figure 1.

13.

Trinity Memorial Hospital (by Gene R. Laczniak and Carolyn Streuly)

Trinity Memorial Hospital is located in a relatively small midwestern city and also serves several small, neighboring farm communities. Because of the large area for which it provides health services, the hospital must satisfy a wide range of health care needs. Through the years, several measures have been taken to improve the level of health care provided in each major department. Recently, there was a need for intensive care monitoring equipment.

Within the past sixteen months, the hospital witnessed the deaths of twelve heart attack victims. This prompted the intensive care unit (ICU) chairman and cardiologist, Dr. Frederick Weingarten, to present a purchase request to the hospital buying committee for the latest intensive care monitoring equipment that would be helpful in diagnosing and treating cardiac arrests. The head ICU nurse, Lee Englebough, also acknowledged the need for this equipment and sent a purchase request to the committee.

A month passed before the hospital buying committee invited Dr. Weingarten and Englebough to participate in the initial meeting to consider the purchase request. Other members of the buying committee were Robert Williams, the hospital administrator, Jack Dubrucz, the director of purchasing, and Dale Gabrys, an electronics technician.

At the meeting, Dr. Weingarten was given the opportunity to present his purchase proposal. To back up his request, Dr. Weingarten presented this description of the equipment to be purchased. Intensive care monitoring devices gather observations on as many as six to seven bodily functions, such as respiration, heart rate, and pulse. These variables are then projected on a monitoring screen at the patient's bedside or relayed to the nursing station. An electrocardiogram, an especially important physiological tool used by physicians and nurses in their diagnostic and therapeutic roles, also can be projected.

Administrator Williams questioned the necessity for the purchase at this time. Inflation had caused operating expenses to rise rapidly at a time when government regulators had imposed guidelines on rate increases. In addition, the federal government's austerity program resulted in unfavorably adjusted Medicare claims that further cut into profits. Thus, limited funding was available for the procurement of this equipment, especially since it was not included in the original annual budget plans.

Dr. Weingarten was astounded that this consideration was a factor in acute patient care. He replied that the lives saved could not be translated into economic costs and that one therefore should not be scrupulously cost conscious. He contended that under no circumstances would he or his colleagues continue to work with inadequate equipment and remain vulnerable to legal action. He reminded Williams that the majority of hospitals with intensive care facilities already had such monitoring equipment.

Lee Englebough added that the hospital was losing its ability to provide effective health care and, subsequently, its well-respected reputation. She cited the embarrassment caused when a prominent city official asked to be transferred to another hospital when he suffered a cardiac arrest.

Concerned by a possible exodus of qualified staff, as well as the long-run viability of the hospital, Williams initiated a formal resolution to purchase the equipment and promised to be instrumental in securing funds not included in the budget.

Dr. Weingarten was appointed chairperson of the buying committee at the next meeting. The consensus among committee members was that because of his association with colleagues at other hospitals, he would best be able to learn about the proposed equipment. As chairman of the ICU, his responsibility to the hospital included the procurement of medical equipment for the ICU.

Although he was familiar with the equipment, Dr. Weingarten admitted that he was not sure of all the characteristics that the equipment should have, because the equipment was changing rapidly as new features, options, and accessory equipment became available. He concluded, however, that the equipment ultimately selected should be of modular design to accommodate new developments in monitoring parameters. In addition, he thought a memory replay feature of deviant electrocardiographic wave patterns was especially important.

Although she often felt intimidated by Dr. Weingarten's authoritative manner, Lee Englebough decided to communicate her insights on the matter. She stated that as a nurse and primary user of the equipment, she felt that ease of use was essential. She further noted that simplicity was a virtue. Englebough was annoyed when Dr. Weingarten ignored her concerns and abruptly asked Dale Gabrys, the electronics technician, about his technical evaluation of the different equipment on the market. Gabrys slowly replied that because he had only limited information, a technical evaluation was not possible. He did say, however, that serviceability was very important.

The purchasing department had an explicit procedure for the evaluation of potential purchases, but it was not always followed. Jack Dubrucz's purchasing authority was limited to consumables and routine materials. For major capital expenditures, the purchasing department relied on the medical expertise of staff physicians. In this particular case, Mr. Dubrucz merely noted that a solid state monitoring unit of the latest technology was to be procured for each ICU bed.

The purchasing department was left with the task of identifying potential suppliers. According to established procedures, only financially stable suppliers with a well-known reputation were to be invited to meet with the members of the buying committee.

After five suppliers had visited the hospital, the buying committee met a final time. An argument soon ensued. Williams emphatically stated that the sales representatives had explained their equipment inadequately and that he was suspicious of the reliability of the information presented. Dr. Weingarten, on the other hand, thought that he was adequately informed of the strengths of each product. He cited as examples that the GE system had the best alarm system and the Electrodyne equipment had a nonfading scope. Overall, he was generally impressed with the presentations.

Englebough stated that she thought the presentation of the different product attributes was confusing and therefore thought Dr. Weingarten should accompany her to other hospitals to view the ease of use of the different equipment. In particular, she was concerned about the visibility of the display monitor. Dr. Weingarten then pointed out that this would be a waste of time because only one supplier had an essential feature and still met the other criteria he had established. The Space Labs monitoring equipment had an automatic memory device to freeze abnormal patient reactions on a screen. This feature ensured that the attending physician would take special notice of the abnormality.

Englebough protested that when the sales representative from Space Labs had demonstrated the equipment, the electrocardiographic image was not bright enough to be used comfortably in monitoring. In addition, the equipment lacked a swivel monitor, which she thought was very important. Englebough then asked Dale Gabrys whether another unit had the same memory-freeze device, which was not mentioned by the sales representative, or whether other equipment was adaptable to the device.

Gabrys was unable to answer both questions because he stated that he could not understand the technical jargon of the sales brochures. He was, however, concerned about the serviceability of the Space Labs equipment, in particular, the speed of parts and components delivery, since the firm was located on the East Coast. He also wondered whether he could service the more complex instrumentation without a course in basic repair. He added that there was no benefit from equipment that was not properly maintained and operational 24 hours a day.

Administrator Williams noted that the hospital's experience with GE equipment had been favorable in the past. Product quality and reliability were very high, and this was important when a malfunction could mean a loss of life. Ken Jensen, the GE sales representative, also personally guaranteed service. Englebough interjected that Jensen certainly was a fine person because he had conducted in-service training for the nursing staff.

Dr. Weingarten then proposed to adjourn the meeting. He still maintained that the purchase decision was clear. The Space Labs equipment had an important product attribute that the other equipment lacked. This statement was met by outrage from Dale Gabrys and Lee Englebough. Gabrys pointed out that the Space Labs equipment did not even have a service manual. Englebough maintained that since nurses were the primary users of the equipment, continuously monitoring patients, they should be the final decision makers.

Williams adjourned the meeting by stating that the final selection would rest on the price bids received from four suppliers. Because the fifth supplier had offered a bribe to Williams, it was eliminated from further consideration.

Dr. Weingarten believed that meaningful competitive bids were relatively unlikely when dealing with complex medical equipment. Thus, when he received a $227,000 price bid from Space Labs, he immediately sent a purchase order for ten intensive care monitoring units from Space Labs to the administrator for financial approval.

Administrator Williams noted that the price bid exceeded the $200,000 budget limit and subsequently called the supplier to investigate how the price could be brought within the budgeted amount. He found that a reduction in the recall capacity of the units would be necessary. When the Space Labs sales representative had written the specifications, she had included a four-hour memory storage capacity. This capacity was now reduced to two hours. The revised purchase order was then sent to the purchasing department, which acted as a collector of the paperwork from different departments.

Dale Gabrys was not aware of the final selection until the equipment arrived six months later and he was asked to evaluate the equipment's electrical hazards. In particular, there were several rigid safety standards that all hospital equipment had to meet.

Lee Englebough, likewise, was not aware of the selection until Gabrys installed the equipment in the ICU. She was aware, however, that acceptance of the equipment by the other nurses would be slow. She was also disturbed by her recently acquired knowledge that Dr. Weingarten was a part-time consultant for Space Labs.

Questions

1. Who were the members of the buying committee? Who played the role of buyer? User? Influencer? Decider? Gatekeeper?
2. What were the evaluative criteria? What factors influenced the evaluative criteria?

14.

Demographics of the Fast-Food Restaurant Business

Johnnies is a nine-unit fast-food hamburger chain operating in a southwestern metropolitan area with a population of 460,000. Freddie Gonzales opened his first restaurant in 1961, and when his son, Ray, graduated from college in 1976, they opened a second unit. In the following ten years, seven more outlets were opened.

Total sales for 1986 were slightly over $12 million, and net profits (before taxes) were $325,000. Johnnies sold 6.1 million burgers in 1986. In conducting a year-end financial analysis of each unit, Freddie and Ray Gonzales found that several units were experiencing a minor but continuing decline in unit sales, and on further investigation, they discovered that this trend had been occurring for several years. Dollar sales continued to increase, but this was due to rising prices and not to more burger sales. Both men speculated about the cause of this sales decline, but they could not identify any factors under their control. All nine restaurants had identical prices, promotion, store design, cleanliness standards, menus, and so on. Thus, they concluded it must be due to a change in consumer tastes or superior competitor offerings.

Fred and Ray shopped competing fast-food restaurants and were convinced this was not the cause of declining sales. One weekend afternoon when Fred was out in his yard cleaning up some debris, the answer suddenly hit him. When Fred moved into his neighborhood in 1964, there were lots of children and teenagers. But now the children were gone, and so was his biggest customer group.

Fred suggested this possible explanation to Ray, who thought it was logical. When they mentioned it to the managers of the restaurants experiencing declining sales, each manager reinforced their conjecture by observing that fewer children and teens were now eating at Johnnies.

Ray asked his close friend, a marketing professor at a nearby university, to do some market research on the changing population characteristics in the metropolitan area. The results are presented in Tables 1 and 2. The professor also reported that many affluent retirees were moving to the area because of its warm climate. The professor was also able to estimate, based on some prior research conducted on dining out, the number of fast-food hamburgers consumed annually by people in different age groups. These data are shown in Table 3.

Questions

1. What is Johnnies's estimated market share of the fast-food burger market in 1986?
2. What is the estimated total sales of burgers in this city in 1990 and in 2000?

Table 1   Population by Age Category

Age Group (years)	Actual (%)		Projected (%)	
	1980	1986	1990	2000
0–4	10	7	6	5
5–13	21	18	17	15
14–24	12	11	10	9
25–44	30	33	31	29
45–64	17	19	21	23
65+	10	12	15	19

Table 2   Population Projections (1986–2000)

Population Growth Forecast	1986–1990	1990–2000
Conservative	8%	10%
Most likely	13%	18%
Optimistic	16%	26%

Table 3   Annual Fast-Food Burger Consumption

Age Group (years)	Annual Consumption
0–4	20
5–13	40
14–24	65
25–44	30
45–64	15
65+	8

PRODUCT PLANNING AND DECISIONS

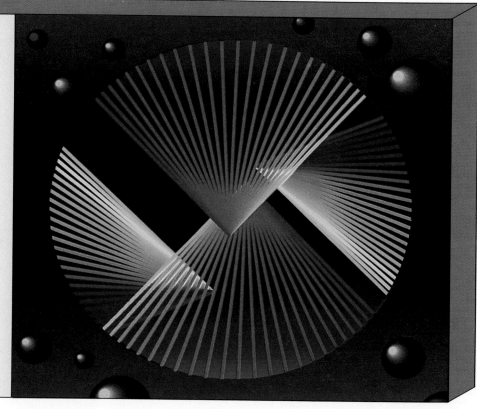

Part III focuses on the product component of the marketing mix. Chapter 8, "Product Concepts," introduces, defines, and explains numerous product concepts that relate to marketing, such as product positioning, product mix, product life cycle, product modification, branding, packaging, and product warranties. Chapter 9, "Product Planning and Development," illustrates how new products can be developed systematically, and how and when consumers adopt new products.

## CHAPTER 8

LEARNING OBJECTIVES

After you complete this chapter, you should be able to:

- **Define** the three dimensions of the product mix

- **List** the four stages of the product life cycle and explain how they affect the marketing mix and profits

- **Describe** the ways that existing products are modified

- **Outline** the six steps in conducting a product audit

- **Discuss** three different brand naming strategies

- **Explain** how packaging is related to market segmentation, product modification, and the marketing mix

- **Enumerate** and **discuss** the legal aspects of product safety and product warranties

PRODUCT CONCEPTS

MARKETER PROFILE

King Karpen of Aireloom

The Aireloom Bedding Co. in El Monte, California, is the Rolls Royce of the bedding industry. Its premium mattresses are constructed by master craftspeople who hand-stitch the sidewalls and hand-tie and knot each box spring coil.

King Karpen, who is now in his seventies, founded Aireloom in 1951 and still actively runs the company. When he was a boy, Karpen was diagnosed as having retinitis pigmentosa, which is a progressive eye disorder with no known cure. Karpen has never let his sight impairment hamper him, and he continues to supervise the selection of ticking fabrics by using his sense of touch.

Aireloom has been successful, in large part, because King Karpen has been dedicated to a single product attribute—*product quality.* He knows that the fine quality of Aireloom bedding is unique in an industry dominated by high volume mass marketers. Karpen also believes that all bedding manufacturers are Aireloom's competitors. "Every time a bed is sold, that's one more customer who is taken out of the market until such time as they feel the bed no longer fits their purposes. It's a mistake to consider yourself so exclusive. Whether or not we believe our beds are the best doesn't matter if the buying public doesn't perceive them that way." Incidentally, King believes that in a few years he may take Wednesdays off from work.

| Source: Based on Joel Engel. "Karpen of Aire-loom: At 70, A Tireless King," *Retailing* | *Home Furnishings* (October 3, 1983), pp. 16, 17. |

INTRODUCTION

King Karpen made Aireloom successful by dedicating himself to producing a superior product for a particular market niche. Because all of us desire products that meet our needs and wants, every product must be designed with a target market in mind. In this chapter, you will become familiar with product concepts that are important to marketing: product positioning, product classification, product mix, product life cycle, product modification, branding, packaging, and product warranties. In Chapter 9, you will learn about product planning and development.

WHAT IS A PRODUCT?

Our in-depth discussion of the marketing mix begins with the product variable, since firms usually make product decisions (i.e., what is offered to the market) before the distribution, promotion, and price decisions. As we discussed in Chapter 3, a product is a bundle of tangible and intangible attributes that a seller offers to the potential buyer and that satisfies the buyer's needs or wants.

Quite often when we talk about products, we refer to what a company produces, such as lawn mowers or food processors. These product conceptions, however, only deal with the tangible product attributes or physical dimensions of the product offering. Products also consist of intangible or unobservable product attributes, involving such things as safety, prestige, services offered with the product (e.g., delivery, credit, maintenance contracts), and the product warranty. These intangibles are important because the consumer may value them and seek them out in a product. In addition, they help to differentiate the seller's product offering in a highly competitive marketplace.

Theodore Levitt, a noted marketing scholar, believes that in the future, competition will occur not between what firms produce in the factory but between "what they add to their factory output in the form of packaging, services, advertising, customer advice, financing, delivery arrangements, warehousing, and other things that people value."[1] This total product concept is illustrated in Figure 8.1 and in the Kenmore appliance ad, which stresses the service component of the product.

The total product concept suggests that two firms selling the same tangible product may be satisfying different wants and needs because the intangible product attributes may differ. All Kraft strawberry jam is chemically equivalent; however, a consumer buying a 16-oz jar of Kraft strawberry jam at a 7-11, Circle K, or other convenience food store will pay more than if the jam is purchased at a Safeway, Food Giant, A&P, or other full-scale supermarket. Why? At the 7-11, the consumer is also purchasing more convenient parking, quicker checkout, and longer store hours.

Let us take this example a step further. What if Kraft also produces a

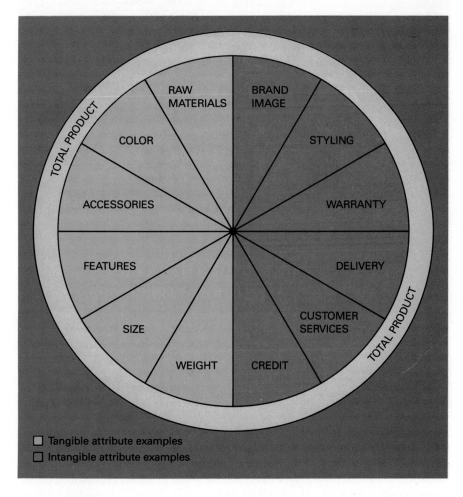

Figure 8.1
Total Product Concept

lower priced private brand jam that is chemically the same as its national brand but labeled with a store brand name such as "Safeway"? In other words, a Safeway customer could buy the same tangible jam at two different prices. Why? The Kraft brand name has more value to the consumer. The consumers buying the Kraft brand feel more assured that they are purchasing the highest quality strawberry jam available for their families, and this helps to satisfy some of their needs and wants.

Product position is *the place the product occupies in the consumer's mind with respect to a small number of key attributes, which can be tangible or intangible.* **Product positioning** is *the process marketers go through in manipulating the marketing mix to achieve a particular product position.* For example, hair shampoos can be positioned based on whether they are natural or unnatural. They can be geared to adults or children,

WHAT IS PRODUCT POSITIONING?

A few of the extras that come with every Kenmore appliance.

You're looking at just a small part of the Sears service organization.

All told, there are 15,000 technicians with 12,000 trucks standing by in hundreds of cities across the country.

As you may have guessed, it's the largest service network of its kind in America.

We're also proud to say, it's one of the fastest.

If something ever goes wrong, it isn't out of service for long.

In an emergency, we'll be out to your house the very same day.

If you bring your appliance to one of our 800 Sears Service Centers, often times we can fix it right on the spot.

Now, if all this sounds a little extraordinary, well, in fact it is.

But the way we see it, there's no reason why our service shouldn't be as dependable, as trouble-free as we try to make our Kenmore appliances.

There's more for your life at **SEARS**

Sears has taken into account an important intangible attribute of its products by stressing the service aspect of its Kenmore appliances.

males or females. In the past, Johnson and Johnson Baby Shampoo was positioned as a natural and gentle shampoo for babies and small children. As the birth rate declined, however, Johnson and Johnson repositioned this shampoo to appeal to all ages and both sexes. They accomplished this primarily through a series of advertisements with the slogan "If it's gentle enough for baby . . ." featuring people of both sexes and all ages—young mothers, senior citizens, teenagers, and even Fran Tarkenton, a successful business executive and former professional football player—using baby shampoo to wash their hair.

The marketer's objective is to create a unique position for its product in the consumer's mind. Johnson and Johnson Baby Shampoo is now positioned as the only shampoo that is gentle enough for the entire family to use. King Karpen of Aireloom Bedding has successfully positioned his product as the most durable and highest quality mattress on the market. A unique product position helps to protect a product from competitive onslaughts.

A **product positioning map** *shows how consumers perceive competing products that serve a particular need based on a set of key attributes.* Figure 8.2 shows a product positioning map for nightly lodging. The two key attributes are room atmosphere (ranging from no frills to luxury) and

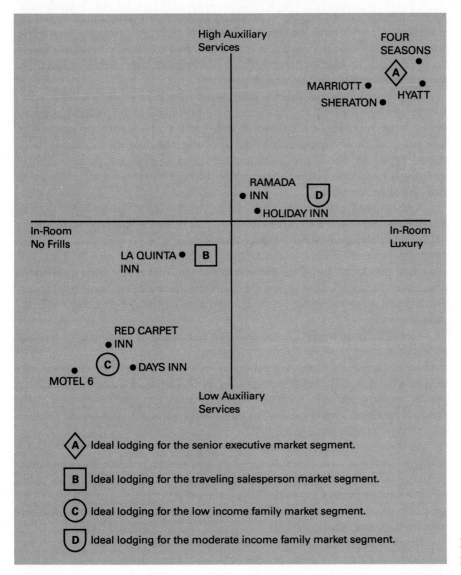

Figure 8.2
Product Position Map for Nightly Lodging

auxiliary services (low to high). Room atmosphere consists of such things as fixtures, carpet quality, television, stereo, bathroom, quality of bedding, and room size. Auxiliary services include such things as swimming pool, sauna, health club, gift shop, restaurant, bar, meeting rooms, hair salon, chauffeur service, and secretarial services. Figure 8.2 shows the ideal position for four market segments. For example, senior executives want a hotel that is high in auxiliary services and room atmosphere. Hotels that do a good job servicing this market are Four Seasons, Hyatt, Sheraton, and Marriott.

PRODUCT CLASSIFICATION

As we mentioned in Chapter 3, products that are primarily tangible can be classified as nondurable or durable. Products that are primarily intangible are referred to as services. But it is also possible to classify products based on the consumer search characteristics: this approach gives us convenience, shopping, specialty, and unsought products.

A **convenience product** is *purchased by the consumer with a minimum of time and effort.*[2] Consumer shopping effort is minimal because of the large number of retail stores that carry convenience products, the low price of these items, and because of the consumer's familiarity with them. Typically, these products are inexpensive and are purchased frequently; for example, chewing gum, cigarettes, a haircut, bread, milk, a taxi ride, gasoline, or beer.

A **shopping product** is *purchased after the consumer shops around to find the best deal based on comparisons of price, quality, style, durability, and other product attributes that are felt to be important.* Shopping products typically are more costly and purchased less frequently than convenience products, and thus the consumer can justify the increased shopping effort. Examples of shopping products are automobiles, home appliances, musical instruments, music lessons, and major clothing items, such as business suits.

A **specialty product** is *one that the consumer desires and is willing to make a special effort to find and purchase, sometimes traveling long distances.* Generally, these are products for which strong brand loyalty has developed, such as Hickey-Freeman suits, Rolls Royce automobiles, Steinway pianos, and Joy perfume. King Karpen made Aireloom mattresses a specialty product by emphasizing quality, so that people are willing to go out of their way to pay $1,200 for a mattress.

As the name implies, an **unsought product** is *one that the consumer does not yet want or know he or she can purchase.* Since the consumer naturally does not recognize a need for these products and therefore must be informed or persuaded to recognize a need, companies that sell unsought products face a formidable marketing challenge. Examples of unsought products include encyclopedias, life insurance, and preplanned funerals.

Keep in mind that the preceding classifications vary depending on the individual and that any given product can be either a convenience, shopping, specialty, or unsought product.[3] For example, a select few may view a new automobile as a convenience product. For most of us, however, it will be a shopping product. For those who have a strong brand loyalty, it may be a specialty product, and for someone who lives in New York City, where there is good public transportation, it may be an unsought product.

Marketers need to determine how their target market views their product because this will have implications for overall marketing mix development. For example, Motel 6 or Days Inn has targeted a market that views a motel as a shopping product and is looking for low-priced, clean facilities with few amenities. On the other hand, the target market for the Park Plaza in New York City or the Anatole in Dallas views these facilities as specialty products and will book reservations, not be very price sensitive, and expect luxury accommodations and special services.

The tangible/intangible characteristics classification of consumer products and the consumer search characteristics are independent of one another. Table 8.1 combines these characteristics to form a grid or matrix of consumer product types. Feel free to place some other products that you are familiar with into this matrix.

THE PRODUCT MIX

Most organizations have a product mix; it is unusual for an organization to offer only one product. *The total set of products a company sells* is called its **product mix,** which can be thought of in terms of its consistency, breadth, and depth.

Consistency of the Product Mix

The *consistency* of the product mix refers to the interrelatedness of the product lines represented. A **product line** consists of *a group of products that are closely related because they are intended for the same end use (all televisions), are sold to the same customer group (junior miss womenswear), or fall within a given price range (budget womenswear).* In conventional supermarkets, the product lines are typically closely interrelated—dry groceries, produce, meats, frozen foods, and beverages. However, some grocers are deviating from this conventional mode and decreasing the consistency of their product mix by stocking portable televisions, stereos, plants, casual clothing, and automotive supplies. A wholesaler of MRO (maintenance, repair, and operating) supplies may have a highly consistent

Table 8.1   Consumer Products Matrix

Consumer Search Characteristics	Primarily Tangible		Primarily Intangible
	Durable	**Nondurable**	**Services**
Convenience	Can opener	Groceries	Banking
Shopping	Automobile or major appliance	Major clothing items	Auto and home insurance
Specialty	Some autos (Rolls Royce) Steinway piano	Health foods or favorite brand of scotch	Preferred hair styling salon
Unsought	Encyclopedias	New brand of imported beer	Earthquake or life insurance

Whitehall Laboratories

E.J. Brach & Sons

American Home Foods

Boyle-Midway

These are some of American Home's products, an example of product mix.

product mix, such as twenty lines of industrial bearings, or a less consistent mix, such as seven lines of bearings, four lines of hydraulic hoses, five lines of fasteners, and four lines of pulley belts.

Breadth of the Product Mix

Breadth refers to the number of different product lines in the product mix, whether or not they are interrelated. For example, a retail bakery may be considered to have good breadth if it has pies, cakes, pastries, cookies, and breads. Or, a discount department store can be thought of as having good breadth if it stocks toys, women's apparel, men's apparel, garden equipment, household appliances, televisions and giftware. A bakery's product lines are broad and interrelated, while a discount department store's product lines are broad but not interrelated.

The concept of breadth in product mix can be applied to nonprofit and service institutions as well. For example, some large universities offer a broad mix of courses, while a small, four-year liberal arts college may offer majors in only a few areas.

Depth of the Product Mix

Depth refers to the number of items within each product line in the product mix. For example, if televisions are the line, the depth could be characterized by the number of black and white or color sets, the screen sizes and cabinet types carried, and the different brands offered. The ad on page 244 shows the depth of Canon's copier product line.

The **product life cycle (PLC)** represents *the stages a product moves through from its introduction to the market to its disappearance from the market.*[4] Our discussion of the product life cycle will deal with a new product innovation or product class. The product life cycle can also be applied, with some modification, to a firm's specific brands. *The product moves through four stages: introduction, growth, maturity, and decline.* It should be emphasized, however, that the product life cycle concept is an idealization and will not capture the behavior pattern of all products.[5] For example, products that are fads—Rubik's cube, the hula hoop, mood rings—may be introduced, grow rapidly and then quickly vanish from the market within twelve to eighteen months, never reaching the maturity stage. Other products, such as flashlights and automatic washing machines, have been on the market for decades and will not reach the decline stage in the foreseeable future.

THE PRODUCT LIFE CYCLE

The depth of Canon's copier product line is evident in this ad showing its many products' features.

Behavior of the Product Life Cycle

Figure 8.3 depicts the typical behavior of sales and profits over the four stages of the product life cycle for a product innovation (rather than a specific product brand).

In the *introduction stage,* sales grow slowly because customers are unfamiliar with the product and few people choose to be innovators. Throughout most of this stage, industry profits are negative because production and marketing costs are high relative to sales volume and no scale economies (i.e., declining unit costs as output increases) are being realized.

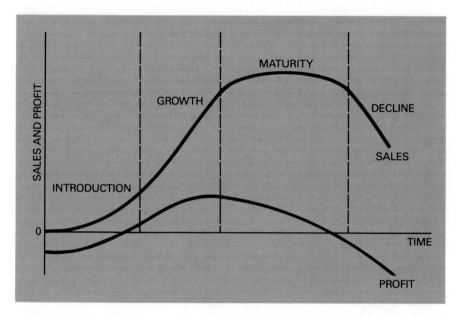

Figure 8.3
The Product Life Cycle

During the *growth stage,* sales grow rapidly because consumer trust and faith in the product rise dramatically and because the innovation begins to reach the masses. Profits climb rapidly because fixed production and marketing costs can be spread over a larger volume. Toward the end of the growth stage, however, profits begin to decline because of intensified competition as more companies enter this market. Most companies, like consumers, are not innovators and wait until the growth stage of a product before entering the market to compete for market share.

The *maturity stage* is the longest stage in the PLC. Industry sales level off in the maturity stage, and purchasing occurs for replacement demand and population increases. Profits continue to decline as competition further intensifies. Marketing expenditures, especially for promotion, are very high because many competitors are fighting for a share of a no-growth market.

Finally, in the *decline stage,* marketers cut back on brand promotion because industry sales have dropped and consumers have found more suitable replacements. For example, sales of black and white TVs declined because of the introduction of color TV, and wringer washer sales declined because of the invention of automatic washing machines. Although industry profits drop for obvious reasons in the decline stage, there may be a profit potential for a limited number of firms that continue to produce. For example, wooden wagon wheels reached the end of their product life cycle eighty years ago, but firms that continue to make them have a lucrative market niche because there is still a small but constant demand and little or no competition. For the same reason, even though there is little demand for wringer washers, Speed Queen continues to produce them.

Marketing Mix and the Product Life Cycle

The various product life cycle stages necessitate different marketing mixes because consumer and competitor behavior changes over the product life cycle.[6] Following are some of the general characteristics of marketing mixes during the various stages of the product life cycle, which is also summarized in Table 8.2.

Introduction Stage. At the outset there is only one product of this type—a true innovation. We are talking about those relatively few real innovations: radio, television, automobile, automatic transmission, microwave oven, videocassette recorder. Because we are dealing with an innovation, there is no direct competition in the introductory stage. Also, consumers are relatively unfamiliar with the unique attributes or advantages of this product and its proper use, so that the adoption rate is slow. This stage is risky for new products since many fail during introduction.

What type of marketing mix characterizes the introductory stage? Price is relatively high because there is no direct competition and because production and promotion costs are high. Since we are dealing with an innovation and the market is initially small and untested, the producer only makes a single model with little product variation (i.e., color combinations, optional accessories, styles). The product quality often leaves a lot to be desired until problems with the production process are ironed out.

One of the major problems in introducing a new product to the market is obtaining adequate wholesale and retail distribution. Because retailers

Table 8.2   The Marketing Mix over the Product Life Cycle

Marketing Mix	Product Life Cycle			
	Introduction	**Growth**	**Maturity**	**Decline**
Product	Minimal product variation	Increased product variation	Maximal product variation	Few product variations
	Poor product quality	Improved product quality	Excellent product quality	Drop in product quality
Distribution	Sparse coverage	Good coverage	Excellent coverage	Sparse coverage
Promotion	Develop primary demand	Develop selective demand	Heavy promotion spending focusing on minor product differences and intangibles	Minimal promotion
Price	Relatively high	Softening	High price competition	Rising prices

and wholesalers have limited space and capital to invest in inventory, they are unlikely to gamble on an unproven product.

Promotion expenditures tend to be high because consumers must be informed about the product innovation and retailers and wholesalers must be convinced to stock the product. Advertising is usually directed at developing primary demand for a product and is referred to as pioneer advertising or promotion. **Primary demand** is *demand for a product class rather than for a particular brand within that class.* Since the product innovation represents a different way of doing things, it is important to try to increase primary demand.

Growth Stage.   In the growth stage, the new product innovation begins to be widely recognized as an acceptable product for solving consumer problems and fulfilling their needs and wants. Sales begin to experience rapid growth, which invites competition. New competitors entering the market at this stage generally will introduce brands that have some degree of differentiation from the original innovation, so that the number of product variations on the market increases. This product variation allows consumers to find the brand that best fits their needs. In addition, product quality usually increases in the growth stage because problems with the production system have been remedied.

Price will begin to decrease because costs of production and promotion are usually lower and because the greater number of new sellers exerts downward pressure on prices. Because of this increase in competition, promotion begins to focus on developing selective demand rather than primary demand. **Selective demand** is *demand for a particular brand in a product class* (i.e., the demand for a Cuisinart food processor rather than a GE food processor). Promotion tends to stress the unique advantages or features of the seller's brand.

In the growth stage, distribution coverage increases as more wholesale and retail firms are willing to stock the product. Witness the number and types of retail outlets that now sell videocassette recorders. In fact, in this stage, wholesale and retail institutions seek out suppliers of this product rather than vice versa, as was the case in the introductory stage.

Maturity Stage.   As the name implies, the market stabilizes or becomes saturated in this stage because almost all potential buyers already have the product; thus, the repeat purchase or replacement market becomes more important. For example, the refrigerator is in its maturity stage because over 99 percent of households have at least one refrigerator. Furthermore, refrigerators can easily last fifteen to twenty years, and the growth in new household formations is modest.

During the maturity stage, product variation continues to increase and the market becomes highly segmented. For example, you can buy a refrigerator in at least fifteen different sizes, six colors, and with a variety of features such as ice makers, self-defroster, ice water dispensers, ice cream makers, and even stereo tape players. Product quality is at its highest level in the maturity stage because the technology of producing the product has been well developed.

Promotion activity, which is intense in the maturity stage of the PLC, typically focuses on minor differences among product brands and often deals with intangibles. A case in point is automobile advertising: it focuses on relatively minor differences in product attributes, such as trunk space, noise levels, fuel economy (38 MPG vs 41 MPG), and intangibles, such as style, sex appeal, and prestige.

During the maturity stage, a seller can only increase sales at a rate faster than the market in general by taking market share from competing sellers, because the overall market is not growing or is growing very slowly. Consequently, promotion expenditures are high and price competition is prevalent.

Distribution is at its peak in the maturity stage. The product is readily available at the retail level, and the wholesale distribution network is extensive.

Decline Stage.   In the decline stage, sales drop because another product innovation has been introduced that represents a better way of accomplishing a task or solving a problem or because the need for the product disappears. For example, the decline of reel-to-reel tape recorders was caused by the introduction of eight-track recorders and players—and these subsequently were replaced by cassette tape recorders. Technology influences both the introductory and decline stages of the product life cycle. The successful introduction of a new product innovation usually assists in the demise of an old product. For example, steel as a product class is in the decline stage because plastic technologies have replaced cast-metal parts in many products ranging from bicycles and autos to refrigerators. Recently, petrochemical technologies have had a similar effect. "Du Pont, for instance, has invented a new synthetic fiber called *Kevlar* that has the tensile strength of steel but is considerably lighter. Kevlar is now a substitute for steel in the belting for automobile tires and in the wrapping of wires for phone and electricity lines."[7]

During the decline stage, sales do not disappear overnight because some consumers hold on to old methods of doing things and continue to buy the product. For instance, some households still maintain non-interest-bearing checking accounts even though interest-bearing checking accounts have been available since 1980.

As industry sales decline, most sellers eventually decide to drop the product. Those sellers who remain raise prices and cut back on promotion.

As you might expect, during the decline stage, the number of variations of the product decreases and product quality usually slips because there is little incentive to keep the production facilities in top working order. Finally, distribution is sparse since most wholesalers and retailers cannot justify allocating space and inventory dollars to a product with a faltering demand. The few loyal customers who remain will seek out retailers that stock the product.

Product Life Cycle Extensions

We need to make a few qualifications about our prior discussion of the PLC, which detailed the PLC for a product innovation in terms of industry behavior. Obviously, companies can introduce their product brand at different stages in the PLC. Radio Shack introduced the personal computer to the U.S. market in 1976. In 1977, Apple also introduced a personal computer. In 1981, in the beginning of the growth stage, IBM introduced their version of the personal computer, the IBM Personal Computer, and in 1983 as growth really started to skyrocket, NCR introduced their Decision Mate V Personal Computer. Each of these brands can be thought of as experiencing its own life cycle.

Firms also can take actions to extend their product life cycles. This usually is attempted in the maturity or early decline stages of the product life cycle. There are basically three product life cycle extension strategies which extend the life cycle without modifying the product.

The first option is to try to get current customers to use the product more often and thus buy more of it. The orange juice industry is a good example of this strategy. Orange juice developed as a breakfast drink in the United States and was consumed in relatively small quantities. Lately, the orange juice industry, through groups such as the Florida Orange Growers, has begun to promote orange juice as a healthy, ideal, all-purpose beverage. The theme "orange you smart" compliments people for drinking orange juice at all times of the day and on all occasions.

A second option is to find new customers for the product, as Knox Gelatin did. The firm attempted to show that gelatin had a variety of often unthought of uses, as shown in their ads on page 250. Finding new uses for a mature product is further illustrated in the Marketing in Action on page 251.

A third option is to find new customers for the product. This is what many universities are doing as they face declining full-time student enrollment. They are trying to market education more to part-time adult evening students, and some are marketing courses to retired (over 65 years of age) consumers and high school students. Many times, the source of new customers is in expansion to foreign markets. For example, Kellogg's continues to achieve growth for many of its mature U.S. brands such as Rice Krispies by continuing to expand into foreign markets. It has found customers for its products in such diverse countries as Australia, West Germany, South Korea, Saudi Arabia, and Mexico.

Product Life Cycle and Product Modifications

A marketer also may decide to prolong the life of a product by modifying it to improve its performance. As with the other strategies to extend a product's life cycle, product modification is most effective during the ma-

THIS LITTLE FERN HAD KNOX.

THIS LITTLE FERN HAD NONE.

AFTER ONLY 3 APPLICATIONS.

Give your houseplants Knox® Unflavored Gelatine and watch them grow fuller and greener.

Knox Unflavored Gelatine has no artificial ingredients. But it does have lots of nitrogen, just what houseplants commonly need to flourish.

Just mix one envelope of Knox with one cup of very hot tap water to dissolve. Then slowly add three cups of cold water to make a quart of liquid. Prepare only as much of the mixture as you plan to use at one time. Once a month, use the

Knox mixture as part of your normal watering pattern and you'll see amazing results as we have shown above.

And here's another important fact to remember. To help your plants grow, they need to be periodically repotted into larger pots using a standard potting soil.

For fuller, greener plants, nourish them with Knox.

Knox Know-How on Houseplants 16-page booklet.
For your free copy, send name and address to: Knox Plant Booklet, P.O. Box 9515B, Clinton, IA 52732.
Include zip code to guarantee delivery. Offer good only in U.S.A. Allow 6-8 weeks for delivery. Offer expires December 31, 1983. An offer of Knox Gelatine, Inc., 800 Sylvan Ave., Englewood Cliffs, NJ 07632

Knox Blox. A great-tasting snack. Fun to eat. Easy to make.

Your youngsters will love Knox Blox, a fruity bite-sized snack that's fun to eat, easy to make. Wiggly. Wobbly. But firm enough to eat with your fingers, even at room temperature.

And Knox Blox are simple to make. Just combine Knox Unflavored Gelatine with fruit-flavored gelatine, chill, & serve!

Kids and moms love Knox Blox. A delicious, fun change of pace from ordinary snacks.

KNOX BLOX

4 envelopes Knox Unflavored Gelatine.
3 packages (3 oz. each) flavored gelatine.
4 cups boiling water.

In medium bowl, combine Knox Unflavored Gelatine and fruit-flavored gelatin, add boiling water and stir until gelatine is completely dissolved.
Pour into 8 or 9-inch baking pan. Chill until firm. To serve, cut into 1-inch squares.
Makes about 6 dozen blox.

For a FREE leaflet containing more wholesome and easy-to-prepare snack recipes, send your name and address to: Knox Good for You Snacks, P.O. Box 7151B, Clinton, IA 52736.

By finding new uses for its gelatin, Knox has extended the product's life cycle.

MARKETING IN ACTION

What does a company do with an established product for which sales have reached a plateau? This question confronted the Ventron Division of Morton Thiokol. Ventron had a mature product called *Vinyzene,* an antimicrobial agent used in plastics polyvinylchloride (PVC) processing. Antimicrobial agents impede the growth of microbes, especially bacteria and fungi. Bacterial growth in plastic products, such as shower curtains and wallcoverings, can cause a pink or black stain on the surface of the product, and this staining obviously can hurt the sales of these products.

By the late 1970s, Vinyzene had captured 90 percent of the PVC market and sales had stabilized. To refuel product growth, Ventron decided to search for new uses and markets for

Revitalized Growth for a Mature Product— Vinyzene

Vinyzene. Ventron found that since Vinyzene prevented the growth of bacteria, it also curbed the growth of odors, mold, and mildew associated with such bacteria. Since consumers were becoming more concerned about health, hygiene, and sanitation, this product attribute became marketable.

At about this time, Mobil Chemical, which produces and markets the Hefty line of trash bags, had completed some marketing research on trash bag buyers. The research showed that trash bag users were

concerned with odor and sanitation characteristics of trash bags. Ventron seized on the opportunity and showed Mobil how to use Vinyzene to create an odor-free trash bag. The result was Mobil's introduction of Hefty Odor Guard Trash Bags.

To further increase sales of Vinyzene (which is now trademarked as Bio-Pruf), Ventron continues to search for new uses. Recently, it showed General Foam how to use Bio-Pruf in its carpet cushioning made from urethane and it showed Harte & Co. how to use it to improve their antislip bathtub mats.

Source: Based on John A. Roberts. "From PVC to Trash Bags," *Business Marketing* (July 1983), pp. 89–92, used by permission; various advertisements.

turity or early decline stages of the product life cycle. Often, the sales performance of a product in the maturity or decline stages of the product life cycle can be recharged if the product is properly modified. Thus, before a company deletes products or spends too much effort on new product development, it should determine if existing products can be modified successfully. **Product modification** *can involve (1) changing product features, (2) changing product quality, and (3) restyling, or any combination of these.*

Feature Modification. By changing the features that the product possesses, the organization can make the product more valuable to the buyer in terms of safety, comfort, versatility, or convenience. In addition, feature modification (also sometimes called *functional modification*) allows the organization to develop a higher degree of product differentiation, which helps the firm create a more protected competitive market niche.

Automatic washing machines are one example of continual feature modification. Whirlpool has added more washing cycles, load capacity selectors, and water temperatures to their machines over the years. Their first automatic washers had only two cycles and no other options. Today, Whirlpool washers have many selections on each of these three variables.

Feature modification is relatively easy for a firm since it already has the basic product and is only making some engineering changes. This allows functional modification to be a good competitive tool because features can be added or dropped quickly and made optional at a relatively minor cost. In addition, feature modification can (1) help generate sales force and distributor enthusiasm, (2) result in publicity for the firm through news stories of the new features, (3) allow the firm to appeal to a new market or segment, and (4) help build the firm's image as being progressive and innovative.[8]

Quality Modification.   An organization may choose to increase or decrease product quality in order to increase profits. We usually think of increasing product quality to make the product more appealing, but reducing product quality can sometimes have the same result by reducing the price. For example, when Hartman Luggage Company changed their product mix to include several lines of vinyl-trimmed attache cases and luggage, they were making the product more appealing by lowering the cost without decreasing the luggage's durability. In this example, performance of the luggage would be only mildly affected, but the less expensive vinyl coverings would allow a fairly substantial price reduction, thus expanding the market.

Quality improvement has been a major part of Ford's strategy since the early 1980s. Often with a quality improvement program, it is necessary to increase advertising or offer exceptional warranties to let the consumer know that quality has been improved, as this is not always readily apparent to the consumer. For instance, how will consumers become aware that Chrysler has improved the reliability of the car's engine and transmission or Ford has improved its assembly line techniques? They must be communicated by the selling organization.

Before an organization decides to improve product quality, it should answer several questions. First, do buyers want improved quality? Second, will they pay for improved quality? Third, will buyers be able to perceive the improved quality? Fourth, will they believe the seller's claims of improved quality? A "no" answer to any of these questions suggests the seller probably should not improve quality at the present time.

Style Modification.   Style modification attempts to make the product more visually or aesthetically appealing to the consumer or buyer. Style changes in the product have nothing to do with the product's quality or functional features. Styling is especially important for products of high social risk, such as clothing, automobiles, and jewelry. A product of *high social risk* is one in which relevant others (i.e., reference groups) can observe you using the product.

Style modification occurs almost continuously in the apparel industry, but these are usually minor styling changes such as color combinations or sleeve shape. However, major style changes are undertaken every few years. Style modification allows a firm to differentiate its product. This is important because for many products, the different brands on the market have identical, or very similar, functional features. Can a pair of Calvin Klein jeans do anything that a pair of Levi jeans cannot do? Basically, no! Therefore, styling helps to differentiate these products that are functionally very similar.

A major risk associated with style modification is that consumer reaction to the new style is quite difficult to predict. If consumers do not like the new style, they probably will switch to a competitor's brand or they may decide to stick with the old style and not replace the product until absolutely necessary, causing the seller to heavily discount the products in order to get rid of them.

When a firm has a product mix that includes products in different stages of the product life cycle, it can have a balanced product portfolio in terms of risk and expected total company sales and profitability. It would be unwise for an organization to have all its products in a single stage of the PLC. For instance, if all products were in the introductory stage, there would be a high risk and a substantial drain on financial capital. Similarly, if all products were in the maturity stage, the firm's future would look dismal because future sales and profit growth would decline.[9] This is why a firm should use the BCG product portfolio matrix, which we discussed in Chapter 3, during strategic planning.

CONDUCTING A PRODUCT AUDIT

If the firm does not regularly add, modify, and drop products, the product mix will become lopsided, with a disproportionate number of old and decaying products. To prevent this situation from occurring, firms should conduct a product audit.[10] A **product audit** is *a regularly scheduled evaluation of all existing products in the product mix in terms of their strengths, weaknesses, and potential.* The frequency of the product audit depends on the industry within which the firm operates. The audit should be conducted yearly in a highly volatile industry, but once every three years would suffice in a more stable industry.

The product audit should include six components. First, the past and forecasted sales and expenses of the product should be assessed. Second, managers should consider excess production capacity within their firms. If there is none, then by dropping an unprofitable product, they can increase the emphasis on other products and thereby increase their sales and profits. Third, the level of competitive activity and any likely changes in it must be considered. For example, if a product's major competitor is exiting the market because of a decline in overall demand, there may be sufficient sales and profit potential for the remaining firms. On the other hand, if a product is in the growth stage, new competition, especially from foreign competitors, can change the strategies used to fight the competition. Procter & Gamble, for example, has recently had its market share in several product categories invaded by Lever Brothers, the U.S. branch of British-Dutch Unilever.[11] Fourth, changes in the technological environment must be considered. For example, if teleconferencing and video boardrooms expand and grow, they will adversely affect the demand for air travel. Alternatively, does technology offer ways to modify and improve products? Could the firm make use of aseptic packages, electronic components, artificial sweeteners, or new chemical compounds? Fifth, the availability and cost of raw materials used in the products must be examined. Changes in this aspect can have a major impact on product profitability. Sixth, and perhaps most difficult, the impact of this product on the sales of other products in the product mix must be considered. Retailers, for example, will often sell some products at a loss (called *loss leaders*) in order to create store traffic, which they hope will benefit the sale of other products in the store.

BRANDING

Branding is an important part of marketing decision making and the marketing mix because one of the major ways organizations identify their product(s) is by the brand. Think of all the different brands you know. To help you understand an organization's branding decisions, we will first define a series of related branding concepts:

❑ A **brand** is *a symbol, design, name, term, or combination of the preceding that uniquely identifies a seller's product and distinguishes it from the competition.*

❑ A **brand name** is *that part of a brand (including numbers, letters, and words) that can be voiced* (i.e., Crest or Geritol).

❑ A **brand mark** is *that part of a brand that can be seen but not voiced (usually a symbol or design;* i.e., the hood ornament on a Mercedes Benz automobile or McDonald's golden arches).

❑ A **trademark** is *the brand name and/or brand mark that the seller has an exclusive legal right to use.* For instance, Coca-Cola has trademarked its brand name and brand mark (its special way of writing Coca-Cola).

❑ A **trade name** is *the legal name of an organization rather than a specific product* (i.e., General Motors Company or Firestone Tire Company).

Companies can only protect their brands if they register their trademarks with the U.S. patent office. Even if a brand is trademarked, however, a company can only continue to have exclusive use of it if the trademark continues to be uniquely identified with the company's product. Many companies have lost their trademark rights because the trademark fell into the public domain and began to be used to identify a generic product class. The following brands were once trademarked: aspirin, nylon, kleenex, formica, and thermos.[12] The Marketing in Action on page 255 describes how the courts ruled that Parker Brothers Monopoly game had fallen into the public domain and become generic.

MARKETING IN ACTION

Does Parker Brothers Have a Monopoly on Monopoly?

Parker Brothers, which introduced the board game Monopoly, no longer has a monopoly on it because the Supreme Court, by refusing to review a federal circuit court ruling, has deprived Parker of one of its most valuable trademarks.

Parker Brothers sued the maker of a board game called Anti-Monopoly (essentially the same game as Monopoly). The federal circuit court in San Francisco ruled that *Monopoly* had now fallen into generic use and that any firm could use this trade-mark. In short, the trademark had fallen into the public domain.

The court was convinced that the trademark was not uniquely identified with Parker Brothers because of the results of marketing research that the makers of Anti-Monopoly had conducted. The research measured the motivation of consumers: Do people buy Monopoly because Parker Brothers makes it, or would they purchase the same game from any manufacturer? Sixty-five percent of the sample selected the latter response, and the court accepted this as evidence that Monopoly had become generic.

Source: Based in part on "No Monopoly on Monopoly," *BusinessWeek* (March 7, 1983), p. 36.

The Advantages of Branding

Branding is advantageous to both the buyer and the seller. To buyers, branding is important as an information source that tells them what to expect in a product. For example, if you stop at a Kentucky Fried Chicken restaurant and order some of the colonel's original recipe chicken, you know ahead of time what type of quality to expect. This is true whether you stop at a Kentucky Fried Chicken in Gary, Indiana, or Tokyo, Japan.

Some brands can also offer the buyer certain psychic rewards because of their image. A top of the line Oldsmobile and a Cadillac offer the consumer basically the same quality of transportation and riding comfort. However, even though the Oldsmobile may cost a few thousand dollars less, the Cadillac will be the better buy to a certain group of customers. Why is this so? To many, driving a Cadillac offers more than transportation—it also offers the owner a certain degree of status, since the Cadillac brand is a symbol to others that you have "arrived" in society.

The seller also benefits from branding. If a core segment of the market becomes brand loyal, then the seller has a firm base to rely on to cover fixed costs. A successful brand can also have a carryover effect on new products the seller introduces to the market. For instance, when Kraft introduced its Light n' Lively processed cheese, the Kraft name was a central theme of the advertisement, thus conveying the message that the new product had all the quality attributes associated with the Kraft name. Branding also can benefit the seller if the brand name is used on several products. In this situation, each time the seller advertises one of its products, the other products with the same brand name benefit.

Brand Sponsors

Brands can be developed or sponsored by manufacturers, wholesalers, or retailers. A **manufacturer's brand**, which is *owned by the manufacturer,* is the most common type of brand. Examples are Heinz catsup, Del Monte corn, Nestle Crunch candy bars, Sanyo stereos, General Electric refrigerators, and Levi jeans. If a manufacturer sponsors a brand, then it must design all the promotion, establish price levels, and provide for distribution channels for the product.

On the other hand, with a **reseller's brand**, which is *owned by a retailer or wholesaler, a retailer or wholesaler develops a brand and assumes major responsibility for the design of the marketing mix.* Usually reseller brands are produced by a leading manufacturer under a contract that requires the manufacturer to produce the product but leaves the marketing strategy up to the retailer or wholesaler. In fact, the design and technical specifications for the product are often set by the retailer or wholesaler. *Private label* is a term synonymous with reseller brands.

An example of a retailer brand is the Sears Kenmore line of home appliances, which are manufactured by Whirlpool (among others) to Sears' specifications. An example of a wholesaler brand is Fleming Company's Good Value line of dry groceries that are sold through independent grocery stores.

Competition among manufacturer, wholesaler, and retailer brands, often called the *battle of the brands,* is intense with some products. The battle of the brands is common in the tire industry, where four major manufacturers produce not only their own brands (Firestone, B.F. Goodrich, Goodyear, and U.S. Rubber's Uniroyal) but also reseller brands. Retailer tire brands are produced for such national chains as Sears, K mart, and Montgomery Ward, while wholesaler brands are produced for wholesale buying groups such as Delta and El Dorado.

Branding Strategies

In developing a branding policy, a firm must decide on an overall brand naming strategy.[13] One option—not to use a brand at all—is called **generic branding**. Generic branding *identifies a product only by its contents: soap, coffee, sugar, catsup, and so on.* Less than 2 percent of grocery product sales in the United States are generic brands.[14] Generic products are usually less expensive for the consumer than brand name items and require smaller expenditures for the manufacturer for packaging and promotion. They sometimes are not as high in quality as their brand name competitors, but this feature also helps to keep their cost lower. Generic branding is also popular with raw materials, such as copper, iron ore, coal, wheat, and corn, since these products are often undifferentiated.

If a company decides to brand its products, it has several options. One of these is **individual branding,** *the practice of giving each product in the product mix a distinct name.* Procter & Gamble uses individual branding (i.e., Cheer, Pringles, Tide, Pampers, and Crest). Individual branding allows each brand name to be tailored to a specific product. It also avoids any carryover effect from one brand to the next, which could be a problem if a brand develops a bad image. In addition, it avoids tying a company's reputation to that of a specific product.

A second option is the use of **family branding,** which is *the practice of using a single brand name (usually the organization's name) for all products in the product mix.*[15] General Electric and Heinz use this option, and most industrial products use only the corporate name and a model number. This alternative reduces the cost of introducing new products because brand name research can be eliminated. Also, since consumers are familiar with the brand name from other products the organization sells, the promotional efforts for the new product are more efficient. If an organization produces products that vary substantially in quality, target market, and nature, then it is unwise to use a family brand.

The third option is to use a *trade name in conjunction with a brand name,* as in Pillsbury Figurines or Pillsbury Fudge Jumbles. This strategy allows all brands to benefit from the overall company trade name but also have the advantage of a distinctive and descriptive name, such as *Kellogg's Pop Tarts,* which are breakfast pastries you can pop into your toaster.

Licensing Brands

The owner of a brand can allow others to use it by licensing it. **Licensing** is *the authorized use of a brand, brand name, brand mark, trademark, or trade name in conjunction with a good, service, or promotion in return for a royalty.*[16] Royalties usually run 5 to 15 percent of sales. This practice can take many forms, but the most common are character licensing, design licensing, and corporate brand licensing.[17] With *character licensing,* the creator of a character allows the use of that character for other purposes. Walt Disney was the first creator to extensively license his creations: Donald Duck and Mickey Mouse have appeared on thousands of children's products ranging from toys, drinking cups, and toothbrushes to sheets and clothing. Other popular characters that have been licensed include Pac-Man, Snoopy, Smurfs, Strawberry Shortcake, Care Bears, Raggedy Ann, and Cabbage Patch Kids.

Through character licensing, others are authorized to use the Smurfs on their products.

Design licensing occurs when a designer licenses his or her name to be used in conjunction with a product that they design, but that is manufactured by someone else. Ralph Lauren, Bill Blass, and Gloria Vanderbilt have successfully licensed their names. There are Ralph Lauren sheets, cologne, menswear, womenswear, luggage, and so on. Each of these products is made by a different manufacturer who pays Ralph Lauren a royalty for designing the product and use of his name.

Corporate brand licensing occurs when a company licenses its brand to be used on products that are typically produced by other firms. For example, Hershey has licensed its brand name to be used on t-shirts and coffee mugs. Coca-Cola recently licensed its trademark for use on a line of sportswear. Budweiser, Oreo cookies, and Life Savers have also been licensed. Not only does a company that has a popular brand name receive added revenues from the royalties, but it also gets a lot of publicity.

The package a product is placed in is often as important in determining its success as the product itself.[18] We will see that the package is more than a vehicle for protecting a product as we examine the important role packaging plays in many marketing decisions.

MARKETING THROUGH PACKAGING

Packaging and Market Segmentation

Packaging can be a vehicle for segmenting the market by offering the product in different sizes. This is especially common in the food industry. For example, people who live alone often like the convenience of single-serving packages, such as Campbell's Soup for One or Celeste's single-serving frozen pizzas. Another example of using package size in conjunction with market segmentation is the packaging of WD-40 (an all-purpose lubricant and rust inhibitor) in 6- to 12-ounce sizes for household use and in larger containers (up to 55-gallon barrels) for use in factories.

In international marketing, package size often needs to be varied because consumption habits and price factors differ from country to country. In the United States, Chiclets is packaged with eight to twelve pieces of gum in a light cardboard box. When this product was packaged in a similar manner in India, it failed because it was too expensive for the average Indian and because the individual pieces of gum would soften and melt together. A small change in packaging solved both of these problems. A package holding two separately wrapped pieces of gum resulted in an affordable price and prevented the merging of the separate pieces. Chiclets is now a popular gum in India.[19]

Package Modification

As we discussed earlier in this chapter, product modification can prolong a product's life. In some cases, products can be modified by merely changing the package. The package can be modified by any of the three methods we

The Hershey Company uses package restyling to increase the appeal of their Kisses at Christmas and Easter (left). Packages can be modified by changing features, as was done by Colgate on their new pump containers (right).

discussed for modifying products: changing the features, changing the quality, or restyling the package.

Examples of feature modification in packaging include Tubble Gum (bubble gum in a tube), margarine sold in reusable plastic tubs, Colgate and Check-up toothpaste in pump-type containers, Aziza nail polish in pen-like applicators, and the disposable needles and syringes used in hospitals that are packaged in individual sterile packages.[20] In the organizational market, you find computer paper packaged in boxes that become the paper-feed trays and cleaning fluids and lubricants in 55-gallon drums with viewing sections so that you can tell when the supply is getting low.

Egg cartons are an example of a change in package quality: styrofoam cartons result in less egg breakage than do cardboard containers. Asceptic juice boxes not only are more convenient, they also eliminate the plastic or metal flavor associated with canned juices.

Package restyling can be illustrated by Kleenex brand tissues, which have packages with designs that go with almost any decor, thus increasing their aesthetic appeal. And the Hershey Chocolate Company, which packages Hershey Kisses chocolates in silver foil, changes the foil color for distribution during the Christmas and Easter seasons to match the traditional colors of those holidays.

Packaging Creates Utility

Packaging can add to the product's utility.[21] For example, a package could add *functional* utility, such as a salad dressing packaged in a bottle with an easy pour spout, juices packaged in aseptic boxes complete with a straw, or TV dinners in microwaveable trays. The package can also add *psychic* utility by enhancing the consumer's favorable image of the product. An example would be deodorant packaged in a can with a nice floral pattern or wildlife scene. The concept of psychic utility also applies to services: a life insurance policy is merely a contract on a piece of paper, but its psychic value increases if it is packaged in a leather folder.

Packaging Influences Price

Packaging influences price because the presentation of the product in an attractive, useful manner to all the target market segments may require several different packages for the same product. The more variations of the package you have, the higher is the cost of each one, because it is more expensive to produce in small quantities than in large quantities. In addition, the type of packaging material used will influence price.

Packaging and Distribution

Packaging and distribution are interrelated because the package must protect the contents as products move through the distribution channel. As products go through the distribution channel, they are subject to handling damage and environmental damage (i.e., rain, snow, heat, dust). For example, when Yamaha pianos are in transit from Japan to the United States, they are placed in airtight containers to prevent the woods in the piano from warping from the wide variation in humidity conditions.

The package must also conform to the specifications of distribution. For example, manufacturers of food products must design their shipping boxes to fit standard-size wood pallets and shelf dimensions in food warehouses. Similarly, the manufacturer should consider the ease of stacking products on the retailer's shelves and in the household pantry. Peanut butter packaged in jars that look like peanuts may be clever, but sales of the product may be adversely affected if it creates stocking problems. Procter & Gamble has recognized the role of packaging in distribution and designed the packaging for its Always feminine maxipad to generate a 37¢ per case saving in storage and handling costs for food wholesalers and retailers.[22]

In many cases, the package must also be sterile or tamperproof.[23] This precaution became especially evident in the Tylenol scare, when someone spiked Tylenol with poison, resulting in several deaths. This case, however, showed that no package is completely tamperproof; thus, Tylenol switched to using caplets instead of capsules. With inherently dangerous products such as drugs and cleaning fluids, childproof seals are also important.

Packaging and Promotion

Packaging and promotion are also interrelated. An appealing and eye-catching package will attract the consumer's attention. In addition, the package can be used to communicate important product information, such as ingredients, product features, or instructions for proper use.

Packages can have labels that are informative, persuasive, or both. A *persuasive label* tries to convince the consumer that this product is unique and worthy of consideration. Often, the package is the last chance that a seller has to persuade the customer to purchase the product. Labels such as "new, improved Tide" and "advanced formula Crest toothpaste" are persuasive, although the consumer is given a message with no logic behind it—why is Tide new and improved, why is the formula for Crest advanced? On the other hand, *informative labeling* provides the consumer with concrete information that will be useful in evaluating the product and comparing it to competing brands. Sometimes this information is required, such as nutritional labeling required by the Food and Drug Administration. Often, it is optional, however. For example, Sears labels the back of its carpet with information such as weight in terms of ounces per yard and strands per square inch. Informative labels are found more frequently on industrial products, while persuasive labels are found most often on consumer products.

Packaging and Legislation

The major piece of federal legislation that deals with packaging and labeling is the Fair Packaging Label Act of 1966. The act states:

> Informed consumers are essential to the fair and efficient functioning of a free economy. Packages and their labels should enable consumers to obtain accurate information as to the quality of the contents and should facilitate value comparisons. Therefore, it is hereby declared to be the policy of the Congress to assist consumers and manufacturers in reaching these goals in the marketing of goods.

The Food and Drug Administration enforces the Fair Packaging and Labeling Act for food and drug products, while the Federal Trade Commission enforces the act for all other consumer products.

The last topic we will discuss in this chapter concerns product safety and product warranties. Marketers need to assure customers that the products they purchase will not be harmful to their well-being and will meet expected performance criteria.

PRODUCT SAFETY AND WARRANTIES

Product Safety

Businesses are responsible for the safety of the products they sell whether or not they manufactured the product. According to the Consumer Product Safety Act (1972), sellers have a specific responsibility to monitor the safety of consumer products.[24] Sellers are required by law to report to the Consumer Product Safety Commission any possible "substantial product hazard." Furthermore, *substantial hazard* is defined to include any failure to comply with an existing safety standard. These safety standards have often been developed under a set of industry-specific legislation such as the Child Protection Act (1966), which banned the sale of hazardous toys, or the National Traffic and Safety Act (1966), which created compulsory safety standards for automobiles and tires.

Product Liability

Product liability law has the *"foreseeability" doctrine,* which says that a seller of a product (especially a manufacturer) must attempt to foresee how a product may be misused and warn the consumer against the hazards of misuse. The courts have interpreted this doctrine to suggest that manufacturers should attempt to incorporate into their product design a protection against misuse. In one case, a consumer who had purchased a new vacuum cleaner decided to plug it into a 220-volt outlet and was subsequently injured. In the court trial, it was made clear that the product was marked "use only with 110-volt electrical outlet." However, the court found the manufacturer liable for the consumer's injury. The court argued that it was not sufficient to warn the consumer to use a 110-volt electrical outlet, the consumer should also have been warned of the consequences of using a 220-volt outlet. Furthermore, the manufacturer should have *foreseen* the misuse and should have designed some type of control device on the vacuum that prevented it from being used in a 220-volt electrical outlet.[25]

Warranties Are Express or Implied

Sellers are also responsible for product safety and performance under conventional warranty doctrines. If a consumer should bring suit against the manufacturer, this in no way relieves a retailer from responsibility for the

Even without using the words "warranty" or "guarantee," Polaroid offers an express warranty with its diskettes.

fitness and merchantability of the product. In fact, in many states, the consumer can sue both the retailer and the manufacturer in the same suit.

Firms can offer express or implied warranties. An **express warranty** is *the outcome of negotiations between the seller and the buyer and may be given either in writing or orally.* It can cover all characteristics or attributes of the merchandise or only one attribute. An important point for the marketer to recognize is that an express warranty can be created without the use of the words *warranty* or *guarantee.* For example, a salesperson might tell a buyer, "Everybody we've sold this model garage door opener to has used it at least five years with no problems whatsoever, and I see no reason why you can't expect the same. I wouldn't be surprised if you go ten years without any mechanical problems." This statement could create an express warranty. The court would have to determine whether this was just sales talk ("puffery") or was a statement of fact by the salesperson.

An **implied warranty** is *not verbalized by the seller but is based on custom, norms, or reasonable buyer expectations.* For example, if you purchase a swimsuit, you would expect that it would not lose its color and texture the first time you go swimming.

Magnuson-Moss Warranty Act

The Magnuson-Moss Warranty Act was passed in 1975 because consumer product warranties have frequently been confusing, misleading, and frustrating to consumers.[26] Under this act, anyone who sells a product costing more than $15 and gives a written warranty is required to provide the consumer with the following information:

1. To whom the warranty applies.
2. What products or parts of products are covered.
3. What the warrantor will do to remedy the problem.
4. When the warranty begins and ends.
5. What the consumer must do to remedy the problem.
6. What limitations or exclusions apply.
7. A statement that the consumer may have other rights in addition to those listed in the warranty.

SUMMARY

This chapter introduced you to some basic concepts related to managing marketing activities with respect to products. A product was defined as a bundle of tangible and intangible attributes that a seller offers to the potential buyer and that meets buyer's need or want satisfaction. A product's position is the place the product occupies in the consumer's mind on a small number of key attributes that can be tangible or intangible. Marketers should attempt to create unique positions so that the product can be protected from competitive forces.

You also learned that products can be classified according to consumer search characteristics, such as convenience, shopping, specialty, or unsought products, and that each of these types of products can be either durable or nondurable goods or services.

Organizations typically offer a product mix to the market. This product mix can be thought of in terms of the consistency, breadth, and depth of the product line. A firm's product mix should result in a balanced portfolio of products, which has a controlled level of risk and a good level of expected total firm sales and profit.

All products experience a product life cycle, which is the stages a product moves through from its introduction to the market to its removal from the market. The four stages of the product life cycle are introduction, growth, maturity, and decline. Different marketing mixes are called for during the various product life cycle stages because consumer and competitor behavior change over the product life cycle. Marketers can use several strategies to prolong a product's life cycle. They can try to get current customers to buy more of the product, they can find new uses for the product, or they can find new customers for the product. Product modification is another way to prolong a product's life. This process can involve changing product features, changing product quality, restyling the product, or some combination of these. A product audit can help the firm decide which products to add, drop, or modify.

We also discussed some concepts related to branding: brands, brand names, brand marks, trademarks, and trade names. Brands can be developed and sponsored by manufacturers, wholesalers, or retailers.

A sponsor has several options for selecting a brand name. The primary ones are individual branding, family branding, and using a trade name in conjunction with a brand name.

The role that packaging plays in marketing decisions was discussed. We saw that a package is more than a vehicle for protecting a product. Packaging can be used to segment a market or modify a product, and it is also related to a product's utility, pricing, distribution, and promotion decisions.

The next topic discussed in this chapter was product safety and warranties. Organizations are responsible for the safety of the products they sell, whether or not they produce the products. Product liability law deals with product safety. The doctrine of foreseeability that has evolved in product liability law basically suggests that a seller of a product must try to foresee how a product may be misused and warn the user against the hazards of misuse and/or design features into the product to prevent such misuse.

Sellers are also responsible for product safety under conventional warranty doctrine. Sellers can offer express or implied warranties, or both. The Magnuson-Moss Warranty Act attempts to clarify warranty terms and conditions and helps the consumer get good warranty service when needed.

KEY CONCEPTS

product position (p. 237)
product positioning (p. 237)
product positioning map (p. 238)
convenience product (p. 240)
shopping product (p. 240)
specialty product (p. 240)
unsought product (p. 240)
product mix (p. 241)
product line (p. 241)
product life cycle (PLC) (p. 243)
primary demand (p. 247)
selective demand (p. 247)
product modification (p. 251)
product audit (p. 253)

brand (p. 254)
brand name (p. 254)
brand mark (p. 254)
trademark (p. 254)
trade name (p. 254)
manufacturer's brand (p. 256)
reseller's brand (p. 256)
generic branding (p. 256)
individual branding (p. 257)
family branding (p. 257)
licensing (p. 257)
express warranty (p. 264)
implied warranty (p. 264)

REVIEW AND DISCUSSION QUESTIONS

1. What is product positioning? What is the advantage of a unique product position?

2. How can products be classified by consumer search characteristics? How does this classification relate to the classification of products such as nondurable, durable, and service?

3. List and give examples of the three major dimensions of a firm's product mix.

4. Why does product quality and the number of product variations change over the product life cycle?

5. How do promotion and distribution change over the product life cycle?

6. Describe what happens to price over the stages of the product life cycle.

7. What is the behavior of profits over the product life cycle? Explain why this behavior pattern occurs.

8. Why is it important for a firm to have a product mix that includes products in different stages of the product life cycle?

9. What are the advantages of feature modification?

10. What questions should a firm ask itself before it decides to improve product quality?

11. What is a product audit? What factors should be considered in a product audit?

12. What are the major brand naming strategies available to a company?

13. What are the benefits of branding to an organization?

14. Why can a company lose the exclusive right to use its own trademark?

15. How is packaging related to marketing decision making?

16. What are the three ways in which packages can be modified?

17. Explain and find examples of the different types of licensing.

18. What is licensing and what are its three most common forms?

19. What is the foreseeability doctrine?

20. Define and briefly discuss the legal aspects of product warranty.

ACTION PROBLEMS

1. What are the tangible and intangible attributes of the following products? Also, identify whether these products are most likely to be convenience, shopping, specialty, or unsought products.
   a. Texas Instruments calculator
   b. Schwinn bicycle
   c. Oscar Mayer bologna
   d. Dinner at a fine restaurant

2. You are the vice president of marketing for RCA and sales of your 19-inch color TV have flattened. Discuss how its life cycle could be extended.

3. As you learned in this chapter, products can be modified by changing product features, changing quality, and restyling. How would you recommend that your university administration modify your university (i.e., courses offered, dorms, social life, class scheduling)?

4. When you graduate and attempt to find a job, what skills and talents (i.e., product mix) can you offer prospective employers?

5. Explain which stage of the product life cycle the following products are in:
   a. pianos
   b. personal computers
   c. personal robots
   d. automobiles
   e. IRAs (individual retirement accounts)

6. Obtain the product warranties for several durable goods, such as a television, home computer, hair dryer, and radio. Is the warranty language clear and unambiguous? How could the language be improved?

NOTES

1. Theodore Levitt, *The Marketing Mode* (New York: McGraw-Hill, 1969), p. 2.

2. The original use of this classification was developed by Melvin T. Copeland, "Relation of Consumer's Buying Habits to Marketing Methods," *Harvard Business Review* (April 1923), pp. 282–299.

3. For a further discussion on classifying products by consumer search characteristics, see Richard H. Holton, "The Distinction Between Convenience Goods, Shopping Goods, and Specialty Goods," *Journal of Marketing* (July 1958), pp. 53–56; Louis P. Bucklin, "Retail Strategy and the Classification of Consumer Goods," *Journal of Marketing* (January 1963), pp. 50–55; Arno K. Kleinenhagen, "Shopping, Specialty, or Convenience Goods?" *Journal of Retailing* (Winter 1966–1967), pp. 32–39; J.B. Mason and M.L. Mayer, "Empirical Observations of Consumer Behavior as Related to Goods Classification and Retail Strategy," *Journal of Retailing* (Fall 1972), pp. 17–31.

4. For a thorough discussion of the product life cycle concept, see Chester R. Wasson, *Dynamic Competitive Strategy and Product Life Cycles* (St. Charles, IL: Challenge Books, 1974).

5. Some of the different patterns that the product life cycle can take besides the classical one are discussed in John E. Swan and David R. Rink, "Fitting Market Strategy to Varying Product Life Cycles," *Business Horizons* (January–February 1982), pp. 72–76; Susan Gurevitz, "Technology Will Shorten Product Life Cycles," *Business Marketing* (October 1983), pp. 12, 26.

6. For a review of product life cycle research, see David R. Rink and John E. Swan, "Product Life Cycle Research: A Literature Review," *Journal of Business Research* (September 1979), pp. 219–243.

7. Jagdish N. Sheth, *Winning Back Your Market* (New York: John Wiley & Sons, 1985), p. 119.

8. John B. Stewart, "Functional Features in Product Strategy," *Harvard Business Review* (March–April 1959), pp. 65–78.

9. Some of the organizational and service problems created by a lopsided product mix are discussed in Roger C. Bennett and Robert G. Cooper, "The Product Life Cycle Trap," *Business Horizons* (September–October 1984), pp. 7–16.

10. R.S. Alexander, "The Death and Burial of 'Sick' Products," *Journal of Marketing* (April 1964), pp. 1–7.

11. Faye Rice, "Trouble at Procter & Gamble," *Fortune* (March 5, 1984), p. 70.

12. For a discussion of trademark protection, see Louis E. Boone and James C. Johnson, "Trademark Protection: What's in a Name," *Business* (April–June 1982), pp. 12–17; Steven A. Meyerowitz, "Don't 'Xerox' This Article!" *Business Marketing* (December 1984), pp. 64–72.

13. For a good discussion of brand name development, see James U. McNeal and Linda Zeren, "Brand Name Selection for Consumer Products," *MSU Business Topics* (Spring 1981), pp. 35–39; Walter A. Woods, "Gravy Train Has it, Drive doesn't—How to Measure 'Impact' of Brand-name Candidates," *Marketing News* (September 16, 1983), pp. 10, 13.

14. The demographic and psychographic characteristics of purchasers of generic grocery brands are discussed in Martha R. McEnally and Jon M. Hawes, "The Market for Generic Brand Grocery Products: A Review and Extension," *Journal of Marketing* 48(Winter 1984), pp. 75–83.

15. Somewhat similar to family branding is the practice of extending an existing brand name to new product categories. This is discussed in Edward M. Tauber, "Brand Franchise

Extension: New Product Benefits from Existing Brand Names," *Business Horizons* (March–April 1981), pp. 36–41.

16. "Licensing Rap," *HFD* (January 23, 1984), p. 101; Teresa Carson and Amy Dunkin, "What's in a Name? Millions, If It's Licensed," *BusinessWeek* (April 8, 1985), pp. 97–98.

17. For more information on licensing, see "Corporate Licensing: It's a Serious Business Now," *HFD* (September 5, 1983), Section 3, pp. 1–8; "Inside Licensing: A Guide to the Industry," *HFD* (January 23, 1984), pp. 89–100.

18. William G. Nickles and Marvin A. Jolson, "Packaging—The Fifth 'P' in the Marketing Mix?" *SAM Advanced Management Journal* 41(Winter 1976), pp. 13–21.

19. Sheth, *Winning Back Your Market,* pp. 82–83.

20. "Bubble Gum in a Tube: Will it Stick?" *BusinessWeek* (August 29, 1983), p. 30; "Pride and Penmanship," *Working Woman* (March 1985), p. 72.

21. Dik Warren Twedt, "How Much Value Can Be Added Through Packaging?" *Journal of Marketing* 32(January 1968), pp. 58–61.

22. Procter & Gamble advertisement in *Progressive Grocer* (October 1984), p. 6.

23. For a discussion on this and other advances in packaging, see Lorna Opatow, "Packaging Is Most Effective When it Works in Harmony with the Positioning of a Brand," *Marketing News* (February 3, 1984), pp. 3–4; " 'Paper Bottles' Are Coming on Strong," *BusinessWeek* (January 16, 1984), pp. 56–57.

24. U.S. Public Law 92-573, Consumer Product Safety Act (1972).

25. For additional discussion of trends in product liability law, see "The Devils in the Product Liability Laws," *BusinessWeek* (February 12, 1979), pp. 72–78; Fred W. Morgan, "Marketing and Product Liability: A Review and Update," *Journal of Marketing* 46(Summer 1982), pp. 69–78; Senator Robert Kransten, Victor Schwartz, Joan Claybrook, and David Greenberg, "Product Liability: Should There Be a Federal Law?," *At Home with Consumers* (Washington, D.C.: The Direct Selling Education Foundation) 5(March 1984).

26. Magnuson-Moss Warranty Federal Trade Commission Act, U.S. Public Law 93-637, 93rd Congress, 1975; see also Janet Marr, "The Magnuson-Moss Warranty Act," *Family Economics Review* (Summer 1978), pp. 3–7.

PRODUCT PLANNING AND DEVELOPMENT

MARKETER PROFILE

Dick Stern and Pollenex

Successful new product ideas always fill some type of need in the marketplace. These unmet or unsatisfied needs, however, are not always uncovered through systematic marketing research efforts or new product planning. An excellent illustration of this involves Dick Stern and the birth of Pollenex.

Dick Stern is the founder and president of Associated Mills/Pollenex, a health product company. Dick got into the health product business because of his wife's health. When Dick's wife, Judy, gave birth to a son by cesarean section in 1948, she was given a gas anesthetic that damaged her respiratory system. As a result, Judy developed major hay fever and breathing problems and had to sleep sitting up. This unfortunate condition prompted Dick to begin developing an air purifier to help her breathe more easily. His first air purifier filtered 8 percent of the impurities from the air, but his current Pollenex room air purifiers are 99 percent efficient.

The privately owned Associated Mills/Pollenex Company now has many other health appliance products, including back massagers, heating pads, whirlpool baths, foot baths, hand massagers, water purifiers, humidifiers, massaging/steamy mist shower heads, smokeless ashtrays, blood pressure units, shower radios, and heater/fans. The company has estimated annual sales of $50 to $75 million. Dick Stern is understandably proud to be the owner of Associated Mills/Pollenex and to be able to do what he wants with the company— to expand the firm's line of health appliance products.

Source: Based on Dolph Zapfel. "Dick Stern: The Birth of Pollenex," *Retailing Home Furnishings* (June 27, 1983), p. 50.

INTRODUCTION

Dick Stern and his company, Associated Mills/Pollenex, have had a history of successful new product introductions, the most recent being the odorless ashtray, which inhales tobacco smoke and purifies the air. Although, in the case of the Pollenex room air purifier, Dick Stern did not precisely follow the new product development procedures we will discuss in this chapter, he developed a new product to satisfy unmet consumer needs and wants. As the marketer profile on Dick Stern also illustrated, it takes more than a single product success for a company to continue to grow over the years.

If an organization's product mix is to remain healthy, new products must be added, some existing products modified, and others deleted. This is an ongoing process at most companies. In Chapter 8, we discussed the concept of a product audit, which is a good vehicle for identifying products that should be dropped or modified. A product audit will also help to point out how severe the need is for new products. In this chapter, we will discuss product management, new product development, and product adoption decisions by consumers.

PRODUCT MANAGERS

A **product manager** is *the member of the organization responsible for the profitability of a single product or group of products. A product manager who is responsible for the profitability of a single product brand* is referred to as a **brand manager**. Product or brand managers attempt to work with other functional departments in the firm (promotion, distribution, finance, production, marketing research, research and development) to develop and coordinate the marketing mix for their product(s). For example, a product manager could work with a promotion manager on an advertising program for a product. This could include deciding on the type of advertising, the advertising budget, and the timing of advertising. Conversely, the product manager could consult with the marketing research manager in designing a research study to provide information on the best market segment for a particular product. Some of the more well-known firms that employ product managers are General Foods, Nabisco, General Mills, and Procter & Gamble.

The major disadvantage for product managers is that they are responsible for the profitability of their products, but they occupy staff positions in the organization and have no formal authority over the other personnel who control the resources and activities that can influence product profitability.

NEW PRODUCT DEVELOPMENT

In addition to planning and managing existing products, organizations should have a plan for developing new products.[1] Some successful new product developments over the last few years have been the Kodak Disc camera, the Jarvik artificial heart, electronic banking, the Sony Walkman, Jell-O Pudding Pops, and the national newspaper *USA Today.*

New product development is important for a variety of reasons. By developing and successfully introducing new products, an organization can help ensure that it will have a balanced product mix consisting of products at different stages in their life cycles. Also, a firm can be a more effective competitor because it can introduce something unique to the market that cannot be copied immediately by other firms. Finally, if an organization espouses the philosophy of the marketing concept, then new product development can be a vehicle for filling the needs and wants of consumers.[2] Goodyear, for example, developed a new tire with a better tread design and a higher percentage of natural rubber especially for the Peruvian market, where the roads are poor.

Although new product development is important, it is a high-risk endeavor.[3] Even large, well-established companies with excellent marketing personnel develop products that fail in the marketplace. Witness the IBM PC Jr. and Listerol disinfectant, which was introduced by Warner-Lambert, the producer of Listerine mouthwash. In fact, research has shown that approximately one out of every three new industrial and consumer products introduced fails.[4] Additional risks are incurred because companies sometimes decide not to introduce a product after considerable research has been undertaken. In fact, some research has shown that it takes fifty-eight new product ideas to produce one successfully commercialized product.[5] Stated alternatively, only about 2 percent of new product ideas reach the marketplace and are successful. A National Industrial Conference Board study suggested six reasons for new product failure: inadequate market analysis, product defects, higher costs than anticipated, poor timing, competitor reaction, and inadequate marketing effort.[6]

Since new product development involves high risk and a substantial commitment of resources, the firm must approach it systematically. This can be facilitated by having a proper organizational structure and a well-established process for new product development. We will explore each of these areas in more detail.

Organizational Structure

There are essentially three methods of organizing the new product development process in a firm: (1) the new product committee, (2) the new product department, and (3) the new product venture team. Note that product managers often are not responsible for developing new products because they are too preoccupied with attempting to achieve good profits for existing products.

New Product Committee. The **new product committee** consists of *personnel from all the departments in the organization who are responsible for developing a new product.* This committee typically includes representatives from production and engineering, procurement, finance and accounting, marketing, legal services, and administration. One of the main advantages of this structure is that it allows for a wide variety of inputs and pooling of expertise in the new product development process. In addition, the work and responsibility are spread among the members. Subcommittees are often created within this framework: several members can work on financial analysis, while others focus on marketing matters. These subcommittees can then report back to the main committee.

New product committees, however, do have their drawbacks. Since committees have no formal power in the organizational structure, the members may lack motivation to get involved. Also, executives have other, more important duties and thus may not devote the time necessary to do a good job when they are assigned to a committee. Because serving on the committee is not part of their job description, they often serve grudgingly and with a low level of involvement. In addition, the committee members may tend to view the new product from the perspective of how it would help or hurt their respective departments rather than how it would affect the overall company.[7]

New Product Departments. The primary *responsibility of a* **new product department** *is to evaluate new product ideas and develop these ideas into marketable products.* To accomplish this, the new product department must coordinate production, financing, and marketing research for the new product. This department has a full-time staff and manager.

The more formal structure of the new product department overcomes some of the problems of the new product committee. The new product department manager must have a substantial degree of authority since he or she coordinates activities across several departments. To help provide this authority, the new product manager often reports to the president of the firm. However, he or she may report to the marketing vice president or to the director of research and development.[8]

New Product Venture Team. A **new product venture team** is *an organizational unit that is established specifically to develop product innovations.*[9] One possible way of organizing the new product venture team or division is shown in Figure 9.1.

There are several things you should know about a new product venture team. First, the team is separated from the day-to-day operating organization. Second, the venture team is multidisciplinary, with members coming from manufacturing, marketing, engineering, and finance. Third, a spirit of entrepreneurship is fostered by allowing venture team members to share in the profits of the venture. Fourth, venture team managers usually report directly to a venture division head or to a chief administrative officer of the organization. Fifth, a team's mission is defined broadly and is typically market

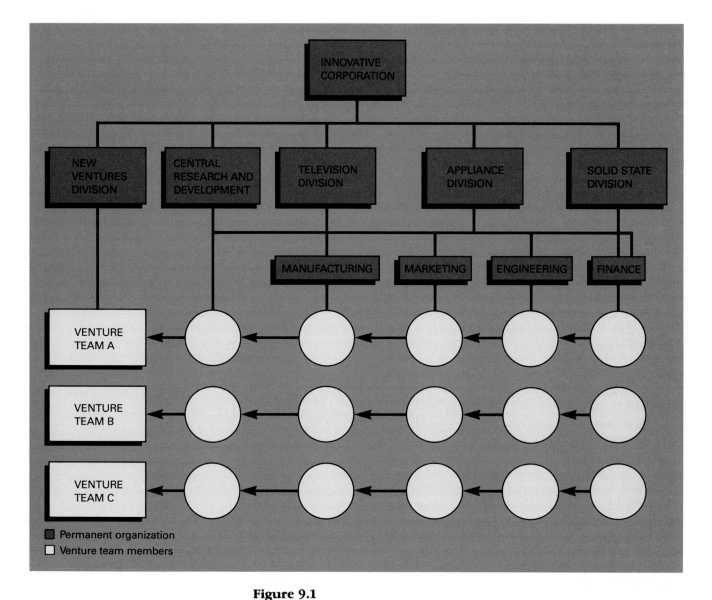

Figure 9.1

Organizational Structure for Venture Teams

Source: Richard M. Hill and James D. Hlavacek. "The Venture Team: A New Concept in Marketing Organization," *Journal of Marketing* 36 (July 1972), pp. 44–50. Used by permission.

oriented. Sixth, venture teams are often free of pressures imposed by strict deadlines, so that they can have sufficient freedom to be creative and innovative.

Experience has shown that new product venture teams are an effective way of organizing new product innovation.[10] They are better than new product committees because they eliminate the ineffectiveness of committee decision making. They are preferable to new product departments be-cause the venture team division or department has more authority and functional autonomy than the new product department. Finally, they are flexible and entrepreneurial, so that they can make a large organization behave like a small one—an important asset in today's bureaucratic world.

New Product Development Process

The **new product development process** *consists of six steps: exploration, screening, business analysis, development, test marketing, and commercialization.*[11] These steps are shown in Figure 9.2.

Exploration. The first step in new product development involves generating new product ideas with the objective of maximizing the number of ideas, regardless of their feasibility or potential. In later stages, the organization can concern itself with separating the good ideas from the bad.

One way to generate ideas for new products is by using some techniques that stimulate creative thinking.[12] One such popular technique is *brainstorming.* A brainstorming session involves assembling a group of executives, consumers, or industry experts/consultants who freely toss out new product ideas based on their personal experience and feelings as well as market research findings. These ideas are recorded but not discussed or criticized by the group as they are suggested. The purpose is to obtain the greatest number of ideas possible, even wild ones, for the greater the number of ideas, the greater the chance of obtaining one or more that are innovative. Other popular creative thinking techniques are also used but will not be discussed in this text.[13]

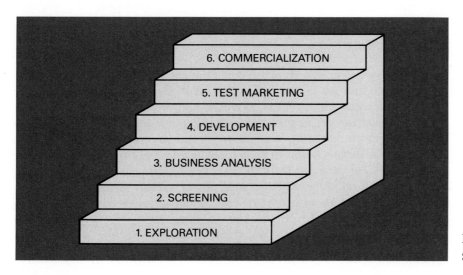

Figure 9.2
Steps in New Product Development

276

YELLOW IS A SIGN OF IMPORTANCE.

That's why people with important business messages use our Post-it™ Notes adhesive note pads. Bright notes that stick virtually anywhere. To make sure your messages get noticed. Call 1-800-328-1684 for a free sample. Then get more Post-it Notes from a nearby stationer or retail store. And start getting the recognition you deserve.

Commercial Office Supply Division/3M

3M

Today's hot-selling Post-it™ Notes were a new product idea that came from research scientists at 3M.

In attempting to generate new product ideas, an organization should rely on multiple sources. The firm should consider the input from consumer research studies and company executives as well as the ideas of salespeople, production workers, research and development employees, and other personnel. Since they are in frequent contact with buyers, salespeople may see opportunities that top-level executives would not notice. Production employees, since they are acquainted with the technology of production, also may see opportunities for new products that are not obvious to senior management. Research and development employees can also be a source of new ideas. For example, in 1970 Dr. Silver, a 3M scientist, was attempting to develop an adhesive with holding power greater than anything then available from 3M. However, he discovered an adhesive with the opposite effect: it would stick to objects but could be easily lifted off and then repositioned. Dr. Silver could not think of any uses for the adhesive, but when another 3M scientist, Dr. Fry, obtained a sample of it, he envisioned an application. Dr. Fry, who was a member of a church choir, was accustomed to using pieces of scratch paper to mark his place in hymnals, but these markers kept falling out. Dr. Fry coated pieces of paper with a thin layer of Dr. Silver's new adhesive, and the idea of 3M Post-it Notes became a reality. Today Post-it Notes are one of the hottest selling office supply items.

Individuals outside the organization, such as consumers, suppliers, and consultants, can also be sources of new product ideas. Finally, observing the new product introductions of competitors may help a firm generate new product ideas. Table 9.1 shows the major sources of new product ideas.

Screening. Once a company has generated a large number of new product ideas, it must attempt to screen them to find those that are worth pursuing. This early screening is a necessary step because a company has limited resources and cannot afford the financial expenditure or personnel commitment to thoroughly evaluate all new product ideas.

The purpose of screening is to allow ideas that are deemed consistent with the firm's objectives and mission and that are likely to become successful products to undergo further evaluation and development and to

Table 9.1   Sources of New Product Ideas

Source	Industrial Products (%)	Consumer Products (%)	Total (%)
Research and development	24.3[a]	13.9	20.8
Internal other than research and development	36.2	31.6	34.6
Suggestions/complaints from users	15.8	12.7	14.7
Formal research of user needs	10.5	17.7	13.0
Analysis of competitors' products	27.0	38.0	30.7
Analysis of published information	7.9	11.4	9.1
Suggestions from suppliers	12.5	3.8	9.5

[a]Read as follows: 24.3 percent of the industrial products studied had research and development as the source of the new idea. The percentages in each column sum to over 100 percent because more than one source was named for some products.

Source: Leigh Lawton and A. Parasuraman. "So You Want Your New Product Planning To Be Productive," *Business Horizons* (December 1980), p. 31. Used by permission.

discard those that are not. Decision errors can be made in this screening process, however. *A company may decide to go ahead with an idea that is not worth pursuing and, if developed into a product, would meet with failure in the marketplace.* This is often called a **go error**. The Concorde supersonic airplane is an example. On the other hand, *a company may decide to discard an idea that, if introduced to the marketplace, would have been a winning new product* that would have helped the firm meet its objectives and mission. This is often called a **drop error**. Drop errors are especially common in the publishing business, where even books like Edgar Rice Burroughs' *Tarzan* were rejected by various publishing houses.

To minimize decision errors in screening, a company should develop a formal device for systematically screening product ideas. This process could involve some type of checklist in which each idea was evaluated on factors such as the following:

1. Is it consistent with the firm's mission and objectives?
2. Can it use existing production knowledge?
3. Can it use the existing marketing organization?
4. Can it use existing production facilities and personnel?
5. Will it enhance the company's image?
6. Can it use raw materials that are plentiful?
7. Does it promise to have good sales in recession and prosperity?
8. Can it be developed in less than three years?

Other factors could be added or some of the preceding factors could be deleted at the company's discretion. The key is that all product ideas would be rated or screened by the same set of criteria. Point values could be assigned based on the extent to which a product idea meets a particular criterion, and then a total point value could be established as a cutoff point to determine which ideas should be evaluated further.[14]

Business Analysis. The products that have made it through the initial screening should next be given a business analysis. A *business analysis* is basically a dollars and cents analysis of the product idea in terms of expected sales, costs, and capital investment. This is a necessary step for all organizations. Even nonprofit organizations need to at least cover their costs and often generate a surplus to fund other projects or products.

Any type of business analysis that is conducted at this point will obviously be an estimate. Remember that the product is still an idea—engineering prototypes have not yet been developed. Nonetheless, some financial projection is necessary. The company proceeds by assessing whether the number of potential buyers is large enough to cover costs and generate a profit. Models have been developed for performing a business analysis on new products, and most of these models focus on estimating new product sales.[15] In estimating new product sales, firms should pay particular attention to **cannibalism**, *the extent to which a new product robs its sales from* *existing products the firm sells.*[16] For example, when Revlon develops a new nail polish, a portion of the new product's sales will come from customers who are buying the new Revlon product instead of an existing one, thus affecting the sales of the old product.

Standard financial analysis techniques can be used in the business analysis. For example, the estimated breakeven point could be determined. The breakeven point is the point at which total sales revenue equals total costs. This breakeven point should be compared to the estimated size of the market. The breakeven point would need to be substantially lower than the size of the market for the idea to look promising.

A company could also attempt to compute an estimated return on investment (ROI), which is the profit that an investment generates divided by the amount of investment. This figure could be compared with some target ROI for new projects. It is not unusual for firms to have a new product target ROI (after taxes) of 30 percent. This high target is due primarily to the high risks associated with new product development.

Finally, if the new product's sales and costs can be estimated for several years into the future, then a discounted cash flow could be conducted.[17] A discounted cash flow (or present value analysis) involves determining sales and costs for future periods and then estimating what these dollars would be worth today. The basic assumption is that a dollar received in the future will be worth less than a dollar today because of inflation and the prevailing interest rates. Therefore, these more sophisticated financial techniques involve some assessment of the expected length and nature of the product life cycle—not an easy task!

Development.   The next step in the new product development process is the development stage. Relatively few ideas reach this stage, because most of them have not survived the initial screening and business analysis.

The development stage consists of concept development, prototype development, and marketing strategy development. Initially, the basic concept of the new product idea must be refined by listing its attributes. Say, for example, that a manufacturer decides to develop a new automatic can opener. The product concept may involve the following attributes:

- Battery or electrically operated
- Automatically opens can by placing the can in a compartment that separates contents of the can from the can; can enters a built-in mini–trash compacter
- No larger than a small food processor
- Lightweight and portable
- Five-year warranty
- Priced below $100
- Handles cans up to 8 inches in diameter and 8 inches in height

With a technique called **concept testing,**[18] *a group of potential buyers are presented with a word description and/or drawing of the proposed product.* The concept test should seek answers to the following questions.

1. *Is the concept clear and easy to understand?* Often the concept test reveals that people are not really grasping the concept.
2. *Do you see some distinct benefits of this product over competing offerings?* The respondents must recognize the distinct benefits of this product over those of its near substitutes.
3. *Do you find the concept and claims believable?* The respondents may have strong doubts about the product claims, which the manufacturer will have to overcome.
4. *Do you like this product better than its major competitors?* The respondents report whether they really prefer this product.
5. *Would you buy this product?* The company must find out if there is a sufficient percentage of respondents with an actual intention to buy this product.
6. *Would you replace your current product with this new product?* The company must find out if the customer envisions not only trying this product, but also substituting it permanently for the current product.
7. *Would this product meet a real need of yours?* If consumers do not feel a real need for the product, they may buy it only once out of curiosity.
8. *What improvements can you suggest in various attributes of the product?* This question enables the company to bring about further improvements in form, features, pricing, quality, and so on.
9. *How frequently would you buy this product?* This question indicates whether the consumer sees it as an everyday product or as a specialty product.
10. *Who would use the product?* This question helps the marketer define the user target.
11. *What do you think the price of this product should be?* This question helps the marketer know the consumer's value perception of the product.[19]

Once the product concept is refined, it is turned over to the engineering and research and development departments for **prototype development**. Prototype development is *the building or producing of a model or sample of a new product.* Up until this point, the product has not physically existed; it has only been an idea, a drawing, or a crude facsimile of the proposed product. Now, the company must determine if the product can indeed be manufactured at a reasonable cost. This step often takes many years. Sometimes, the firm may confront certain technological hurdles—the idea may be great and consumers may be favorably inclined toward the product concept, but current technology may not allow the product to be produced, or produced economically within budgeted manufacturing costs. Major consideration also needs to be given to designing a safe product, especially in today's environment of product liability legislation (see Chapter 8). Finally, packaging must be developed for the product.

Some products may not survive prototype development, but if they do, the firm must develop a marketing strategy for them. In doing this, the company may go back to the marketplace with the product prototype and do additional marketing research. In principle, the research will be similar to concept testing, but the consumer can now be shown a tangible product. In fact, the product may be given to some consumers to allow them to use it and to gauge their reactions. Many companies give the product to some of their employees and then solicit feedback from them. By testing the product on employees, secrecy can be maintained so that competitors will be kept in the dark about the firm's new product development.

Once a prototype is developed by the research and development departments, it can be tested for manufacturing cost and safety. Technicians at Underwriters Laboratories Inc. test lamps and fixtures of all sizes (top left), run an impact test on the surface of a tanning bed (top right), and examine a television tube after an implosion test has been conducted (bottom).

Marketing research will be used to help the company define its target market, develop a brand name, and establish price, promotion, and distribution policies. Some of the product attributes or packaging may need to be changed before the company comes up with the right combination, but in any case, a total marketing program must be developed for the new product. The Marketing in Action on page 283 illustrates the use of market research and concept testing.

Test Marketing.   If the product survives the development process, it can then be tested in the marketplace. Note, however, that some firms decide to skip the testing stage and proceed directly to full-scale commercialization of the product.[20] This decision to bypass test marketing may occur for several reasons. Sometimes the company wants to get its product to market before competitors do. The firm may believe that if it were to test market, competitors would have the opportunity to improve on the product and beat the firm to full-scale commercialization. For example, Sara Lee introduced their line of frozen croissants in 1982 without performing the extensive test marketing the firm normally conducts because they were confident that their product was a winner and they were worried that a competitor would beat them to the punch.[21] There is also the possibility that testing may not be worth the cost. The company may feel confident enough about the product that it perceives low risk in full-scale commercialization, especially considering the additional financial and time costs involved in further testing.

A **test market** is *the introduction of a new product into a limited number of representative communities in order to assess potential product demand and the marketing mix.*[22] Table 9.2 shows a list of representative test market communities for consumer goods based on demographics, geographics, and media attributes.

Test marketing is used to find out how consumers will react to the new product offering in an authentic market environment. The firm can use actual sales in the test market to extrapolate and obtain a more accurate national sales forecast. In addition, the firm may try out alternative marketing mixes. For instance, if the company had four representative test markets, it

Table 9.2 Representative Test Market Communities	
Albuquerque, New Mexico	Oklahoma City, Oklahoma
Cedar Rapids, Iowa	Peoria, Illinois
Colorado Springs, Colorado	Portland, Oregon
Dayton, Ohio	Savannah, Georgia
Fargo, North Dakota	Spokane, Washington
Grand Rapids, Michigan	Tucson, Arizona
Knoxville, Tennessee	Wichita, Kansas
Lexington, Kentucky	

MARKETING IN ACTION

New Product Development at Kodak

Kodak faced a major challenge when it sought to design a new camera to restimulate the amateur photographic market. First of all, the majority of consumers were quite satisfied with existing cameras. In addition, 94 percent of U.S. households in 1980 owned at least one camera.

According to John J. Powers, vice president–director of marketing communications at Eastman Kodak in Rochester, New York, the firm's research began with a twofold objective, "First, to determine under what conditions consumers were and were not taking pictures; and second, once we determined where they *weren't* taking pictures, we set out to develop a photographic system which would function in those areas of photographic space."

Marketing research was instrumental in achieving the first objective, and product research and develop-

ment helped fulfill the second objective. The research and development team at Kodak devised a type of film that permitted enlargements from a negative about one-sixth the size of a postage stamp and that functioned at twice the speed of Kodacolor II film. Both of these innovations were important in allowing amateur photographers to take pictures in a wider variety of settings.

Once the development stage was complete, the new prototype was ready for a market test. For reasons of secrecy, Kodak decided to forego a massive market test and take the new disc camera prototype to 1,000 U.S. homes for demonstration and testing. From this home test re-

search, Kodak was able to decide (1) which of the sixty-four possible camera configurations developed by the research and development lab would be most acceptable to the marketplace, (2) which product attributes should be featured in its advertising, (3) the best introductory price, (4) how consumers compared the product to existing cameras, and (5) the intent to purchase among respondents.

Advertising campaigns were not test marketed either, again for reasons of secrecy; however, shortly after introducing the disc camera, Kodak conducted three consumer surveys to measure the effectiveness of the introductory advertising campaign and consumer reaction to the camera.

Source: Based on "Credit Success of Kodak Disc Camera to Research," *Marketing News* (January 21, 1983), pp. 8, 9.

could try out a combination of a low versus high price and a low versus high level of advertising. This can help the firm develop an optimal marketing mix.

Certain problems are involved in test marketing, however, including:

1. Obtaining a set of communities that is reasonably representative of the country as a whole.
2. Translating national media plans into local equivalents.
3. Estimating what is going to happen next year based on what has happened in this year's competitive environment.
4. Ascertaining competitor's knowledge of your test and deciding whether any local counteractivities are representative of what competition will do nationally at a later date.
5. Encountering extraneous and uncontrollable factors such as economic conditions and weather.[23]

Testing, if it occurs, is somewhat different for consumer goods than it is for industrial goods. A test market is usually conducted for most consumer goods; however, test marketing is rarely used for new industrial products because industrial buyers do not wish to try products whose future availability is uncertain. Also, building a few industrial machines or equipment for test marketing is unrealistic and too expensive. For example, Boeing would not build a few sample airplanes to test market.

Some of the ways of testing industrial goods are product-use tests, trade show displays or demonstrations, and displays in distributor or dealer showrooms. With **product-use testing,** *a few customers are selected to borrow or to be given the new product if they will use it under normal conditions and give the company feedback on its performance.* This is how Sensormatic Corp. tested the first antitheft tags and sensor systems that evolved into the antitheft devices now found in most retail stores.

During displays and demonstrations at major industry trade shows, the firm can distribute brochures and literature and salespeople can talk to potential buyers to try to gauge their level of interest in the product.

When a new industrial product is introduced in a distributor's or dealer's showroom, the product may be placed next to a competing product or the company's old model of the product. Promotional literature can be distributed in the showroom, and a tally maintained of inquiries about the product. The problem with this method is that some buyers may like the product so much that they insist on placing an order. This, of course, is not possible because the company has not yet entered into full-scale production of the product. This is also a problem with the trade show display/demonstration alternative.[24]

Commercialization. The last step in the new product development process is the most costly. A full-scale production line must be set up, a major media and promotional plan developed and budgeted, inventory built up, distributors lined up, and the sales force educated and motivated. The cost can be phenomenal: when Helene Curtis introduced the Finesse haircare line in 1982, the network TV advertising budget alone was $20 million.

Commercialization of the product is an exercise in time and resource management and scheduling. Assume that a manufacturer plans to introduce a new product ten months from today. If only one activity in the commercialization process fails to meet its target deadline, then the entire schedule can be jeopardized. For example, assume that the advertising for the product will begin to appear in magazines and on national TV thirty-eight weeks from today, but because of production and distribution problems the inventory buildup at wholesale and retail outlets is delayed several weeks. As a result, the consumer may begin to seek out the product on retail shelves before it is available. To help avoid such problems, some firms use a program evaluation and review technique (PERT) and the critical path method (CPM). These techniques were developed in the defense industry to keep major defense contracts on schedule. With PERT and CPM, a flowchart shows when major activities need to be accomplished in order to assign time allotments and priorities to each activity.[25]

The amount of time it takes to develop a new product varies considerably, from less than a year to over fifty years. Table 9.3 shows the time that elapsed between the initial development of several products and full-scale commercialization.

THE ADOPTION PROCESS

The adoption process begins where the product development process leaves off. The **adoption process** is *the series of steps a buyer goes through in deciding to try and then regularly use a new product: awareness, knowledge, evaluation, trial, and adoption.* If a sufficient number of buyers do not adopt the new product, its commercialization will fail. The Marketing in Action on page 286 illustrates the link between product development and product adoption.

Steps in Adoption

The steps in the adoption process are awareness, knowledge, evaluation, trial, and adoption (see Figure 9.3). As an example of this process, imagine that you would like to purchase a personal paper copier. First, you must be *aware* that personal or household paper copier machines exist. Next, you will probably search for more information to acquire more *knowledge*

Table 9.3   Elapsed Time Between Initial Development and Full-Scale Introduction

Product	Years Before Introduction
Strained baby food	1
Filtered cigarettes	2
Frozen orange juice	2
Dry dog food	4
Roll-on deodorant	6
Liquid shampoo	8
Fluoride toothpaste	10
Freeze-dried instant coffee	10
Penicillin	15
Xerox electrostatic copier	15
Transistors	16
Minute Rice	18
Instant coffee	22
Zippers	30
Television	55

Source: Adapted from Lee Adler. "Time Lag in New Product Development," *Journal of Marketing* (January 1966), pp. 17–21. Used by permission.

MARKETING IN ACTION

The Development and Adoption of a New Farm Product

For many years, southern Saskatchewan and Alberta wheat farmers have practiced fallowing. This is the process of leaving a field crop-free in alternate years. Since this region of Canada is extremely dry, fallowing significantly improves crop yields because the soil can store extra moisture during alternate years. However, leaving the field fallow allows weeds to grow and rob soil moisture. Consequently, farmers removed the weeds by mechanical cultivation, a process that causes further moisture loss.

Elanco Products Co., a division of Eli Lilly Canada, Inc., viewed this problem as an opportunity to develop a new product, which it called *HERITAGE Wheat Production System.* (The company used marketing research to identify the best name for this new product.) The company

developed a herbicide system to help the wheat farmer improve yields over each two-year cycle. The HERITAGE system helps to conserve moisture, reduce erosion, reduce cultivation, and boost wheat yields.

Elanco Products Co. recognized that the adoption process begins when the new product development process ends. "In the early days of its product launch, Elanco's sales reps sought out growers who would experimentally treat their land with HERITAGE. Elanco hoped these 'bell-cow' growers, leaders of the pack, would demonstrate the benefits of HERITAGE to neighbors.

One 'bell-cow' was Don Greschuk, 39, who farms 4,000 acres and declares: 'I like technology. I'll use anything that helps save money and works for me.'

Not everyone is as willing to take the risk. Wayne Clews . . . who tends 3,000 acres . . . acknowledged that when he first heard Elanco's pitch for HERITAGE, he stayed on the sidelines. 'I go by the book,' said the 45 year old, third-generation wheat farmer. 'I wait for a product to be licensed. But, this time it looks like they [the innovators] were right and I was wrong.' "

Source: Based on Jeff Leib. "Product Repositioning in the Face of Tradition, How Elanco Created A New Herbicide Market Niche," *Business Marketing* (November 1984), pp. 64–68. Used by permission.

of the product. Some things you would want to know are its capabilities, service requirements, operating cost, and price. This knowledge will help you *evaluate* the product innovation. If you evaluate the product favorably, and if you can afford it, you may be inclined to purchase it. Total adoption at this point may be too risky, however, as you still are not sure if it will do the job you want it to or that you will like the way it performs, and since the machine is relatively expensive, you want to be sure before you buy. Thus, *trial* may take place. Obviously, the paper copier manufacturer is not likely to give you a free machine to try out, but you may be able to lease one for a month from a local retailer. If you are satisfied with the product during the trial stage, you may decide to *adopt* it and purchase it outright.

Time of Adoption

The time of adoption depends not only on consumer characteristics, but also on the product itself.

Figure 9.3

Stages in the Adoption Process

Consumer Characteristics.   Continuing with our prior example, would you be one of the first to adopt a personal paper copier, would you wait until some of your acquaintances had done so, or would you wait until almost everyone else had decided to adopt and be one of the last people to do so?

Figure 9.4 depicts the adoption of innovation curve, which is based on over 500 research studies.[26] Research shows that the adoption of innovation is a bell-shaped curve. The adopters underlying this curve can be classified as (1) innovators, (2) early adopters, (3) the early majority, (4) the late majority, and (5) laggards. The typical characteristics of each of these are as follows:

❑ *Innovators* represent *the first 2.5 percent of the population who adopt a new product innovation.* They are almost obsessed with trying out new ideas and products. They have higher than average incomes, are well educated, are cosmopolitan, and are active outside their com-

Figure 9.4

Adoption of Innovation Curve

Source: Reprinted with permission of The Free Press, a division of Macmillan, Inc., from *Diffusion of Innovations* by Everett M. Rogers. Copyright © 1962 by The Free Press.

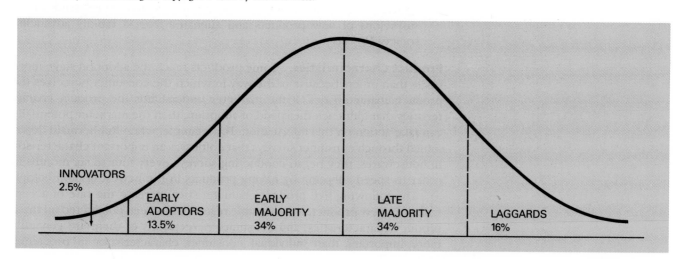

munities. They are self-confident and not very reliant on group norms. They are likely to obtain their information from scientific sources and experts.

❑ *Early adopters* represent *the next 13.5 percent to adopt the product.* This group is distinct from innovators since they are much more reliant on group norms and values. They are also more oriented to the local community in contrast to the innovator's cosmopolitan outlook. Early adopters are most likely to be opinion leaders because of their close affiliation to groups.

❑ The *early majority, the next 34 percent to adopt a new product,* are very deliberate. They are likely to collect more information and evaluate more brands than do either innovators or early adopters. Therefore, the process of adoption will take longer for them. They rely on the group for information but are likely to be the friends and neighbors of opinion leaders rather than opinion leaders. The early majority are an important link in the process of diffusing new ideas since they are positioned between earlier and later adopters.

❑ The *late majority, the next 34 percent to adopt a new product,* do so because most of their friends have adopted the product. Since they rely heavily on group norms, adoption is the result of pressure to conform. This group tends to be older and below average in income and education. They rely primarily on word-of-mouth communication rather than on mass media.

❑ *Laggards, the final 16 percent to adopt a new product,* are similar to innovators in not relying on the group norms. Decisions are made in terms of the past. By the time laggards adopt an innovation, it has probably been superseded by something else; for example, the first purchase of a black and white television set when color television is already widely owned. Laggards take the longest time to adopt and typically have the lowest socioeconomic status. They tend to be suspicious of new products and alienated from a rapidly advancing society.[27]

Product Characteristics. Some products reach the adoption stage more easily than others because of the way in which the consumer perceives the product characteristics. If the marketer understands the product characteristics that influence the speed of adoption, then the marketer potentially can take action on this information. For example, when Rubbermaid determined through consumer surveys that color was an important characteristic in housewares, they began conducting surveys every four to six months in order to speed adoption by having products in the newest fashion colors.

The following five product characteristics increase the rate of acceptance of a new product. Considerable research has been conducted on these product characteristics, and consumer perceptions of them are generally more important than individual consumer characteristics in predicting adoption.[28]

❏ *Relative advantage* is the degree to which consumers perceive the new product as superior to existing substitutes. For example, consumers perceive high relative advantage of a microwave oven in cooking time or of a food processor in versatility compared with conventional alternatives.

❏ *Compatibility* is the degree to which the product is consistent with the consumer's needs, attitudes, and past experiences. One study by a large appliance manufacturer found that consumers concerned with their appearance were more likely to buy personal care appliances. Another study observed that consumers who looked for time-saving products were more likely to buy new kitchen appliances such as food processors.

❏ *Observability* is the ease with which the product can be observed and/ or communicated to potential consumers. Products that are highly visible are more easily adopted. Fashion items and cars are good examples.

❏ *Simplicity* is the ease in understanding and using a new product. Products such as electric toothbrushes and prepared foods such as cook-in-the-bag vegetables are easy to understand and use and thus are easily adopted. More complex innovations that require an instruction booklet such as videocassette recording systems and computers may inhibit adoption.

❏ *Trialability* is the degree to which a product can be tried before adoption. Limited trial is possible through test runs or demonstrations in showrooms. Divisibility is related to trialability: if a product can be purchased in small quantities, then trial is relatively easy.[29] For example, manufacturers give trial-size packets of shampoo or cookies but do not give samples of tires or home exercise machines.

SUMMARY

In this chapter, we discussed the role of product managers, the new product development process, and the steps buyers go through in adopting a new product innovation. Product managers are responsible for the profitability of a single product or group of products and must coordinate activities with other departments in the firm to develop an effective marketing mix. The major obstacle confronting product managers is that, even though they are responsible for the profitability of their products, they do not have formal authority over personnel in other departments with whom they must work to develop an effective marketing program for their product(s).

In addition to managing existing products to increase sales, firms usually engage in new product development. We discussed the three methods of organizing the new product development process: the new product committee, the new product department, and the new product venture team.

The development of successful new products involves six steps. The first step is exploration for new product ideas. The second step involves screening the ideas to isolate those most worthy of further investigation and resource commitment. Next, the product ideas should receive a business analysis, which is an analysis of the product idea in terms of expected sales, costs, and capital investment. Those product ideas that meet the firm's standards in terms of expected financial performance will enter a development process, which is the fourth step. The development stage consists of concept development, prototype development, and marketing strategy development. Products that survive the development stage often will be tested in the marketplace or in a somewhat realistic market setting. This fifth step may involve test marketing, product-use testing, product display or demonstration at an industry trade show, or placing the product in the display or showroom of a few key distributors. Finally, if all seems well, the company will enter full-scale commercialization of the product, which is the last step in the new product development process.

The buyer adoption process begins where the product development process ends. The five steps in the adoption process are awareness, knowledge, evaluation, trial, and adoption. Individuals adopt new products with varying speed. A small proportion of the population are true innovators and quickly become aware of new products, learn about them, evaluate them, try them, and adopt them. At the other extreme are laggards, who only adopt after almost everyone else has adopted the innovation—in fact, when the laggard adopts, the product is really no longer an innovation. Others adopt somewhere in between the innovators and the laggards.

More important than consumer characteristics in the speed of adoption of new products are five product characteristics: the product's relative advantage over existing products, the degree to which the product is compatible with the consumer's past behavior patterns, the degree to which the product can be observed or communicated to potential consumers, the simplicity of the product in terms of its use and ease of understanding how it operates, and the ease of getting potential customers to sample the new product.

KEY CONCEPTS

product manager (p. 271)
brand manager (p. 271)
new product committee (p. 273)
new product department (p. 273)
new product venture team (p. 273)
new product development process
  (p. 275)
go error (p. 278)

drop error (p. 278)
cannibalism (pp. 278–279)
concept testing (p. 280)
prototype development (p. 280)
test market (p. 282)
product-use testing (p. 284)
adoption process (p. 285)

REVIEW AND DISCUSSION QUESTIONS

1. What is a product manager? What is the major obstacle that product managers face?

2. Why is it important for a firm to engage in new product development?

3. What are the advantages and disadvantages of using product committees to develop new products?

4. What are the advantages of using a new product venture team to develop new products? Do you see any problems?

5. What are the major sources of new product ideas?

6. In the new product development process, why is it important to have representatives from the major functional areas (e.g., finance, production, marketing, research and development)?

7. What is the difference between a go error and a drop error? How can these types of errors be minimized?

8. Why is a business analysis of a new product idea necessary?

9. Discuss the development stage: concept development, prototype development, and marketing strategy development.

10. What is concept testing? Give an example showing how it might be used to evaluate a new product idea in the food industry.

11. Why do companies test market new products? Why do some companies choose not to test market?

12. Name some ways that new industrial products can be tested.

13. Identify and discuss the five steps involved in the adoption process.

14. What are the five categories of adopters and their respective characteristics?

15. What product characteristics influence how quickly a new product innovation is adopted?

16. Identify several newly introduced products and discuss how the consumer adoption of these products could be hastened.

17. Based on the knowledge of the product life cycle that you gained in Chapter 8 and the knowledge you obtained in this chapter on the product development process, do you believe it is wise for firms to develop product innovations, or is product modification preferable?

ACTION PROBLEMS

1. The U.S. economy is increasingly moving toward a service rather than a tangible product economy. With three to five students in your class, brainstorm for thirty minutes about ideas for new services to develop and offer to the U.S. consumer or industrial market. Be sure to have someone in the group take notes or record the session.

2. Interview several families that have not yet purchased a home computer. Try to identify why they have not purchased this product innovation. See if there are any patterns to their responses.

3. Explain where and why you would place yourself in the adoption of innovation curve with respect to the following products:
   a. Personal computers
   b. Chicken nuggets
   c. Videocassette recording system

   d. Imitation bacon and low cholesterol or synthetic eggs

   e. Pay TV, cable TV

4. You are a new product manager for a new product that is being developed and you must devise a marketing strategy for it. Describe your new product and how you would market it.

NOTES

1. Roger Leigh Lawton and A. Parasuraman, "So You Want Your New Product Planning To Be Productive," *Business Horizons* (December 1980), pp. 29–34.

2. James L. Ginter and W. Wayne Talarzyk, "Applying the Marketing Concept to Design New Products," *Journal of Business Research* (January 1978), pp. 51–66.

3. Some important research is being conducted to help identify the success factors in new product introduction; for example, see Jean-Marie Choffray and Gary L. Lilien, "Strategies Behind the Successful Industrial Product Launch," *Business Marketing* (November 1984), pp. 82–94; Jeremy Main, "Help and Hype in the New-Products Game," *Fortune* (February 7, 1983), pp. 60–64.

4. David S. Hopkins, *New-Product Winners and Losers* (New York: The Conference Board, 1980).

5. *Management of New Products* (New York: Booz, Allen & Hamilton, 1968).

6. Betty Cochran and G. Thompson, "Why New Products Fail," *The National Industrial Conference Board Record* 1(October 1964), pp. 11–18.

7. For a major discussion of the committee structure for new product development, see Robert D. Hisrich and Michael P. Peters, *Marketing a New Product: Its Planning, Development and Control* (Menlo Park, CA: The Benjamin/Cummings Publishing Company, 1979).

8. For a more detailed discussion on how to organize the new product department, see Edgar A. Pessemier, *Product Management: Strategy and Organization* (New York: John Wiley & Sons, 1982); George Gruenwald, *New Product Development* (Chicago: Crain Books, 1985), pp. 87–99.

9. This section relies heavily on Richard M. Hill and James D. Hlavacek, "The Venture Team: A New Concept in Marketing Organization," *Journal of Marketing* 36(July 1972), pp. 44–50.

10. They do, however, have their problems; for instance, the failure of venture teams resulting from an imbalance of risk and incentive is discussed in Shelby H. McIntyre and Meir Statman, "Managing the Risk of New Product Development," *Business Horizons* (May–June 1982), pp. 51–55.

11. *Management of New Products.*

12. Harvey J. Brightman, *Problem Solving: Logical and Creative Approach* (Atlanta, GA: Business Publishing Division Georgia State University, 1980).

13. Creative thinking techniques are discussed in Edward M. Tauber, "HIT: Heuristic Ideation Technique—A Systematic Procedure for New Product Search," *Journal of Marketing* (January 1972), pp. 58–70; Charles L. Alford and Joseph Barry Mason, "Generating New Product Ideas," *Journal of Advertising Research* (December 1975), pp. 27–32; Hisrich and Peters, *Marketing a New Product,* pp. 57–61.

14. Barry M. Richman, "A Rating Scale for Product Innovation," *Business Horizons* (Summer 1962), pp. 37–44; E. Patrick McGuire, *Evaluating New Product Proposals* (New York: The Conference Board, 1973), pp. 5–25; Bob Donath, "Can Your New Product Pass this Test?" *Business Marketing* (July 1984), pp. 66–68.

15. Edward Tauber, "Forecasting Sales Prior to Test Market," *Journal of Marketing* (January 1977), pp. 80–84; Frank M. Bass, "A New Product Growth Model for Consumer Durables," *Management Science* (January 1969), pp. 215–217; Robert Blattberg and John Golanty, "Tracker: An Early Test Market Forecasting and Diagnostic Model for New Product Planning," *Journal of Marketing Research* (May 1978), pp. 192–202; Jerome E. Scott and Stephen K. Keiser, "Forecasting Acceptance of New Industrial Products with Judgment Modeling," *Journal of Marketing* 48(Spring 1984), pp. 54–67.

16. Roger A. Kerin, Michael G. Harvey, and James T. Rothe, "Cannibalism and New Product Development," *Business Horizons* (October 1978), pp. 25–31.

17. Tony Berridge, *Product Innovation and Development* (London: Business Books Ltd., 1977), pp. 81–83.

18. For a further discussion of concept testing, see Eugene J. Cafarelli, *Developing New Products and Repositioning Mature Brands* (New York: John Wiley & Sons, 1980), Chapter 6; Yoram J. Wind, *Product Policy: Concepts, Methods, and Strategy* (Reading, MA: Addison-Wesley, 1982), Chapter 10; David A. Schwartz, "Concept Testing Can Be Improved—And Here's How To Do It," *Marketing News* (January 6, 1984), Section 1, pp. 22–26. © 1980. Reprinted by permission of Prentice-Hall, Englewood Cliffs, NJ.

19. Taken directly from Philip Kotler, *Marketing Management: Analysis, Planning and Control* (Englewood Cliffs, NJ: Prentice-Hall, 1980), p. 323.

20. N.D. Cadbury, "When, Where and How to Test Market," *Harvard Business Review* (May–June 1975), pp. 96–105.

21. "A Leaner Consolidated Foods Rediscovers Marketing," *BusinessWeek* (August 29, 1983), pp. 58–59.

22. For a further discussion of test markets, see "Test Marketing for More Marketers, No New Product Without Its Test," *Sales & Marketing Management* (March 12, 1984), Special Section, pp. 81–114.

23. Alvin A. Achenbaum, "The Purpose of Test Marketing," in Robert M. Kaplan (ed.), *The Marketing Concept in Action* (Chicago: American Marketing Association, 1964), p. 582.

24. The discussion of industrial goods testing is based on Morgan B. MacDonald, Jr., *Appraising the Market for New Industrial Products* (New York: The Conference Board, 1967), Chapter 2; Kotler, *Marketing Management*, pp. 339–340.

25. Hisrich and Peters, *Marketing a New Product*, pp. 229–231; Bob Donath, "Threading Your Way Through Product Launch Details: A Critical Path Approach For Clarifying Potential Chaos," *Business Marketing* (June 1984), pp. 120–125.

26. Everett M. Rogers, *Diffusion of Innovations* (New York: The Free Press, 1962).

27. From Henry Assael, *Consumer Behavior and Marketing Action* (Boston: Kent Publishing Co., 1981), pp. 399–401. ©1981 by Wadsworth, Inc. Reprinted by permission of Kent Publishing Company, a division of Wadsworth, Inc.

28. Some of this research is reprinted in Laurence P. Feldman and Gary M. Armstrong, "Identifying Buyers of a Major Automotive Innovation," *Journal of Marketing* 39(January 1975), pp. 47–53; Lymond Ostlund, "Perceived Innovation Attributes as Predictors of Innovativeness," *Journal of Consumer Research* 1(September 1974), pp. 23–29.

29. Adapted from Assael, *Consumer Behavior,* p. 405; see also Everett M. Rogers and F. Floyd Shoemaker, *Communication of Innovations,* 2nd edition (New York: The Free Press, 1971).

15.

MCI Mail Expands Product Mix

Microwave Communications Inc. (MCI) began as a small company in the mid-1970s by creating a microwave radio link to send telephone messages between Chicago and St. Louis. After this bold move, MCI successfully challenged the courts and the Federal Communications Commission for the right to establish other microwave links. By fiscal year 1982, sales were over $1.1 billion and profits were $170 million. In 1982, MCI was AT&T's major long-distance competition and had approximately 3 percent of a $40 billion market.

Top management is not satisfied nor complacent with MCI's success. Management recognized that when AT&T divested itself of its twenty-two local phone companies on January 1, 1984, that price competition would intensify in the long distance phone service market. AT&T is expected initially to cut long-distance rates 10 to 15 percent, while at the same time, MCI will be required to pay higher fees to local phone companies for connection services so that local customers can be hooked up to MCI's long distance services. In short, MCI's traditional 50 percent price differential will begin to evaporate.

MCI believes that it must expand its product mix to remain competitive. One bold move is the spending of $100 million to enter the electronic mail market. MCI Mail will carry information between computers; however, customers who don't have computers can receive computer-generated letters on paper from fifteen MCI post offices. There will be no initial registration or sign-up fee for MCI Mail. A customer can send 7,500 characters, or about four pages of material, for $1.00 if both sender and receiver have a computer terminal and phone modem. If the receiver does not have a computer terminal, the messages can be sent to an MCI post office and delivered by carriers a day later at $2.00 for 7,500 characters. In addition, delivery of messages is available by Purolator, Inc. within four hours of being sent. A four page letter delivered in four hours will cost $25.00. MCI also has an agreement with Dow Jones & Co. in which the 55,000 customers of Dow Jones News Retrieval Service will be able to use MCI Mail by simply pressing a button on their computer terminals. In the first full year of operation, MCI expects to send 250 million messages.

Electronic mail service is being offered in a variety of forms by several companies (Tymnet, GTE, General Electric, and Western Union) and also by the U.S. Postal Service. The U.S. Post Office calls its service E-COM (*electronic computer originated mail*), and it is capable of turning computer messages into first-class mail. The U.S. postal service is carrying about 16 million messages annually with E-COM. Importantly, E-COM requires that 200 messages be sent at a single time and that they be delivered by regular first-class mail.

Questions

1. In what stage of the product life cycle is electronic mail service? What does this suggest for MCI's marketing mix?
2. Who are likely to be the innovators and early adopters of electronic mail service? Does this suggest any target markets for MCI Mail?

Source: Based in part on "MCI's Newest Strategy: Shooting for a Broader Spectrum," *BusinessWeek* (October 10, 1983), pp. 60–64; "MCI's Electronic Mail Service," *Fortune* (October 17, 1983), p. 7; advertisements for MCI Mail.

16.

Competition Encourages Product Modification in Soft Drink Industry

For the consumer of the 1950s, soft drink selection was relatively simple: you bought Coke or Pepsi if you wanted a cola, and 7-Up if you wanted a lemon-lime. They all came in bottles that held less than 16 ounces. Obviously, some local bottlers turned out grape, orange, and root beer, but they were minuscule in market dominance, a trend that continues.

Product proliferation began in the 1960s. We witnessed the arrival of diet beverages and the emergence of canned soft drinks. In the 1970s, package size variations became popular, such as 1- and 2-liter containers, as well as package type variation, such as the use of plastic bottles and nonreturnable glass bottles. The 1980s are witnessing product proliferation on product attributes. Bottlers are innovating with caffeine-free, sodium-free, and sugar-free soft drinks. For example, in 1982 and 1983 alone, the following products were introduced: Diet Coke, caffeine-free Coke, caffeine-free Diet Coke, sugar-free Tab; Diet Pepsi, Pepsi Free, Like, sodium (salt)-free, caffeine-free, sugar-free Diet Rite Cola. The big news of 1985 was Coke's decision to change the formula, which resulted in the introduction of New Coke, the reintroduction of the old formula now called Classic Coke, and Cherry Coke, which was followed closely by cherry-flavored Royal Crown Cola.

A major innovation in 1983 that rippled through the industry was the use of aspartame as a low-calorie sweetener in place of saccharin. The FDA approved aspartame in July 1983, and by late 1983, six major soft drink manufacturers had decided to use it. *NutraSweet* is the trade name for G.D. Searle's low-calorie aspartame sweetener. NutraSweet's major advantage is that it has none of the aftertaste that saccharin produces. Another advantage is its nutritive value, which is created because it is made of protein components. NutraSweet also can be used by diabetics, since it is metabolized as protein. Unfortunately, NutraSweet may have associated health risks (as does saccharin) and it costs twenty times more than saccharin. Consequently, manufacturers are using a blend of saccharin and NutraSweet, almost always with a higher proportion of saccharin than NutraSweet. Estimates are that only 25 to 50 percent of the blend is NutraSweet. Some manufacturers, however, are using 100 percent NutraSweet in their products and are promoting this feature as a product attribute.

Looking at the market share for all of the carbonated soft drinks is an interesting lesson in marketing. In 1982, carbonated diet soft drinks had a 17.7 percent share of all carbonated soft drinks. The two major diet flavors were cola (63.3% share) and lemon-lime (14%). Non-diet carbonated soft drinks had a 82.3 percent market share. In this category, colas had a 59.6 percent share, lemon-lime, 11.2 percent; pepper-types, 6.0 percent; orange, 5.1 percent; root beer, 2.8 percent; and all other flavors had a 15.3 percent share.

Another way to look at market share is by package type. Cans held a 36.5 percent share, refillable glass, 26.4 percent; plastics, 21.4 percent; and nonreturnable glass, 15.7 percent. To make the picture even more complex, there are at least five package sizes: 6 to 9 ounces, 10 to 12 ounces, 16 ounces, 24 to 32 ounces (1 liter), and 48 to 64 ounces (2 liters). The majority of all cans are in the 10- to 12-ounce category, but the other package alternatives come in all five size containers.

Questions

1. How much do you think the new caffeine-free, sodium-free, aspartame soft drinks will cannibalize existing carbonated soft drinks? How much will they affect the sales of other beverages such as fruit juices and milk?
2. As a product class, soft drinks are in the mature stage of their product life cycle. How has this influenced the marketing mix of soft drink manufacturers?

Source; Based in part on "The Soft Drink Market Bubbles Over," *Progressive Grocer* (November 1983), pp. 42–46; "Is Coke Fixing a Cola that Isn't Broken?" *BusinessWeek* (May 6, 1985), p. 47; Kenneth N. Gilpin. "Coca-Cola Resurrecting Old Taste," *New York Times,* as reported in the *Arizona Daily Star,* Tucson, AZ (July 11, 1985), p. 1C.

17.

Marriott Hotel Corporation Plans for Growth

Marriott Hotel Corp. is the ninth largest hotel chain in the United States, with over 51,000 rooms in 124 hotels. Between 1980 and 1983, the company doubled in size. In 1983, Marriott had annual sales of $2.54 billion and earnings of $94.3 million; its return on equity was close to 20 percent. Bill Marriott, Jr., the president of Marriott Hotel Corp., plans to add 9,000 new rooms a year for the next several years, and after that he believes the firm can still grow by 10 to 12 percent annually.

The original market niche that Marriott pursued in the late 1950s and early 1960s was hotels in suburban office complex locations with easy access to freeways into the city and airports. Other hotel firms were either concentrating on roadside motels or downtown city hotels. Seventy percent of Marriott's trade has been with business travelers and meetings, and Marriott's room occupancy has averaged 10 percent above the industry norm.

Marriott has developed two new hotel concepts to help it achieve its growth goals. One concept is to build large convention hotels in downtown locations in order to establish Marriott as a premier convention hotel chain. Two entries into this market are the $250 million, 1,674-room Marriott Marquis in Atlanta and the $350 million, 1,877-room Marriott Marquis in New York City on Times Square. The New York Marriott Marquis opened in spring 1985 and needs to charge $186 a night to be profitable. Comparable room rates in New York City are now running from $110 to $140. The rule of thumb for a convention hotel is that it must charge 1/1,000 of the construction cost of a room for a one-night stay. To be competitive, Marriott probably will not be able to initially charge $186 per night, but Bill Marriott believes they can charge a premium over competition because of the amenities of the New York Marriott Marquis. The Marquis is a major architectural marvel—with a forty-eight-story atrium, a 1,507-seat theatre, 1,400 lounge and restaurant seats, and a revolving sky-view restaurant.

Bill Marriott admits that profits may not be generated for four or five years. Nonetheless, he is encouraged that Marriott's marketing staff has already booked 225,000 room nights for conventions and business meetings over the next ten years and another 750,000 "tentative nights," of which about 50 percent probably will materialize into definite bookings.

Two of the major problems with Marriott's move into downtown convention center hotels are the high fixed costs of such an operation and the oversupply of hotel rooms in many major convention cities. A convention hotel requires one staff person for every room and one supervisor for every ten employees. Even more disquieting is the fact that cities such as Houston, Dallas, Miami, Atlanta, Chicago, Boston, and New York have too many hotel rooms.

A second hotel concept that Marriott is experimenting with is a modification of their old suburban hotel idea. The concept, named the *Courtyard,* consists of a 125-room hotel with minimal amenities. There will be a small restaurant and lounge next to the front lobby, a couple of meeting rooms, and a modest pool in the courtyard. Rooms will be grouped around the courtyard in a garden apartment format. Marriott plans to locate these hotels in cities that could support seven to twelve Courtyards. Collectively, these Courtyards will be operated as one big hotel. A general manager will be responsible for procurement, personnel, and marketing. A Marriott Courtyard Hotel can be built for $6 million, which is 50 percent less per room than a conventional Marriott suburban hotel, and can be priced in the moderate range ($25–55 a night). Each Courtyard can be operated with a resident manager and twenty-nine employees. Marriott is building two Courtyard Hotels in Atlanta as a pilot project.

Questions

1. Which of the new hotel concepts developed by Bill Marriott offers the highest return? Which offers the least risk? Into which concept should Marriott put most of their expansion capital? Give reasons.
2. Should the Courtyards use the Marriott brand name, or should the new product not be publicly identified with Marriott?

Source: Based in part on Thomas Moore. "Marriott Grabs For More Room," *Fortune* (October 31, 1983), pp. 107–122; "Bill Marriott's Grand Design for Growth: Upscale and Down in the Lodging Market," *BusinessWeek* (October 1, 1984), pp. 60–62.

18.

New Coke

Roberto C. Goizueta graduated from Yale University in 1955 with a degree in chemical engineering, and on graduation he returned to his native Cuba, where he went to work as a research chemist for Coca Cola. When Fidel Castro seized power in Cuba, Goizueta fled to the United States, joined Coca Cola, and eventually was named chief executive officer in March 1981.

Upon becoming CEO, Goizueta created an atmosphere of change and innovation at the traditionally conservative firm. Coca Cola had not borrowed any substantial sums of money since the Great Depression, had a 99 year old soft drink formula locked away in a bank vault, and refused to let its brand be associated with anything but its original product—Coca Cola. In 1981, Goizueta replaced many inefficient bottlers; and in 1982, he bought Columbia Pictures for $700 million, introduced Diet Coke (the first product to use the Coke brand other than original Coke), and initiated the "Coke is It" advertising campaign. In 1983 three new products were added: caffeine-free Coke, caffeine-free Tab, and caffeine-free Diet Coke. By 1984, Diet Coke had become the third most popular soft drink in the United States. But the most newsworthy event occurred in April 1985, when the company changed the 99 year old secret formula and introduced New Coke. The company introduced Cherry Coke in the same month.

New Coke was introduced largely because of Pepsi's consistent ability to win in blind taste tests. Consequently, Pepsi was using this fact in its advertising to gain increased market share. The new formula for Coke was sweeter, with eleven more calories in a twelve-ounce-size can.

The company spent $4 million to test New Coke with 191,000 consumers, and in tests in twenty-five markets, 55 percent of consumers chose the new product. Goizueta announced publicly when New Coke was introduced that it was the easiest decision the company had ever made.

In the first six weeks after the product was introduced, 110 million people had sampled New Coke and 80 million liked it enough to try it again. These numbers were bolstered by heavy promotion and price dealing. For example, at Von's Grocery Co. in Los Angeles, the price for two six-packs of 12-ounce cans was as low as 42¢ if the consumer redeemed three different coupons that were available in the market. The promotion budget for New Coke's introduction was around $10 million.

By late May and early June, enthusiasm for New Coke began to falter. Mr. Mullins of Seattle, Washington, founded "Old Cola Drinkers of America" to protest New Coke and attempt to get the company to bring back the old formula. Membership grew rapidly to 100,000 and the organization was planning a protest march for late July in Dallas and was attempting to organize a consumer boycott in Australia. The consumer "hot" line at Coca Cola Company began to ring constantly with angry customers complaining and urging the company to bring back the old formula. Also in June 1985, shipments in some important markets fell by as much as 15 percent.

Alarmed, Coca Cola Company began to conduct more research. In late June, Coke researchers surveyed 900 consumers and found that 60 percent liked old Coke better and only 30 percent liked New Coke. Leo J. Shap-iro & Associates of Chicago (an independent market research firm) conducted research showing that between 75 and 87 percent of people who tasted New Coke preferred old Coke or Pepsi. An internal Pepsi research study showed that 46 percent of New Coke tasters planned to switch to another brand or drink less Coke.

The evidence began to weigh in the favor of bringing back old Coke. Goizueta and his staff considered several possible names for old Coke, such as Original Coke, Coke 100, Coke 1886, Old Coke, and Coke 1, but finally decided on Classic Coke. On July 10, Goizueta held a press conference to announce the imminent reintroduction of Classic Coke. Mr. Mullins, founder of "Old Cola Drinkers of America," would receive the first case of Classic Coke. Incidentally, in two blind taste tests, Mullins picked New Coke as his preferred Coke.

Questions

1. What was the intangible item or mystique about Coca Cola that consumer taste research did not reveal?
2. Before the company introduced New Coke, it had considered making it a sister product to the original Coke and thus not eliminating the original formula from the market. What were the advantages and disadvantages of this approach?

Sources: Based on: "Is Coke Fixing a Cola That Isn't Broken?" *BusinessWeek* (May 6, 1985), p. 47; "New Coke Wins Round 1, But Can It Go the Distance?" *BusinessWeek* (June 24, 1985), p. 48; "Analyst Says Coca-Cola May Revert to Old Formula," *Arizona Daily Star* (July 6, 1985), p. 2 section A; "Coca-Cola to Bring Back Its Old Coke," *Wall Street Journal* (July 11, 1985), p. 2; "Marketing Experts Split in Appraisals of Move to Bring Back Old Coca-Cola," *Wall Street Journal* (July 11, 1985), p. 2; "Coke Fails Acid Test, Rivals Say," *Arizona Daily Star* (July 11, 1985), p. 1 section D; "Coca-Cola Resurrecting Old Taste," *Arizona Daily Star* (July 11, 1985), p. 1, section C; "Coca-Cola Faces Tough Marketing Task in Attempting to Sell Old and New Coke," *Wall Street Journal* (July 12, 1985), p. 2; "Intangible 'Something' Responsible for Old Coke's Return, Bosses Say," *Arizona Daily Star* (July 12, 1985), p. 5 section A; "How Coke's Decision To Offer 2 Colas Undid 4-1/2 Years of Planning," *Wall Street Journal* (July 15, 1985), pp. 1, 8; "Coke's Flip-Flop Underscored Risks of Consumer Taste Tests," *Wall Street Journal* (July 18, 1985), p. 25; "Coke's Man on the Spot," *BusinessWeek* (July 29, 1985), pp. 56–61.

DISTRIBUTION PLANNING AND DECISIONS

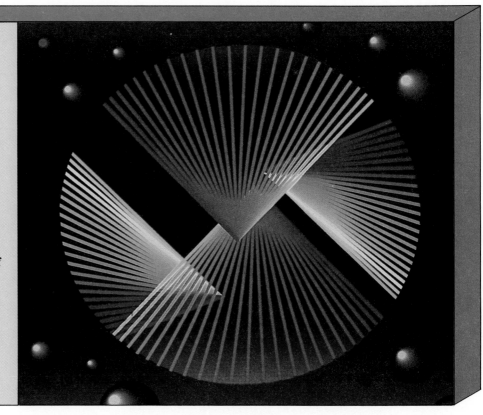

Part IV details the distribution, or "place," component of the marketing mix. Chapter 10, "Marketing Channels," reveals what marketing channels are, why they develop, their importance, their characteristics, and legal considerations involved with them. Chapter 11, "Physical Distribution," introduces the physical distribution system, its management, and its relation to the management of customer service activities. Chapter 12, "Retail and Wholesale Institutions," discusses the most popular types of retailing, retailer classifications, store atmosphere, the evolution of retail competition, the structure of wholesaling, and ways to market products more effectively through wholesalers.

MARKETING CHANNELS

MARKETER PROFILE

Dr. Louis P. Bucklin of the University of California, Berkeley

The Paul D. Converse National Award was given to Dr. Louis P. Bucklin on May 19, 1986, by the American Marketing Association. The Paul D. Converse awards, established in 1946, are granted to persons who have made outstanding contributions to the theory or science of marketing. Dr. Bucklin received the award for his book *A Theory of Distribution Channel Structure.* Bucklin's theory shows that the division of marketing tasks among a set of marketing institutions is undertaken to achieve cost savings or improve customer service. The division of these tasks, however, requires cooperation among the institutions in the marketing channel.

It is appropriate to honor a marketing educator in this Marketer Pro-file because a basic understanding of the marketing process requires the study and development of a theory of marketing channels. According to Professor Bucklin, "It is basic because it focuses upon the essential nature of marketing: the interactions among commercial institutions and between these institutions and the consumer. It is basic because it probes the mechanism through which the invisible hand of the private enterprise marketplace operates."

Source: Based on program brochure for the Twelfth Paul D. Converse Marketing Symposium, May 19–20, 1986, University of Illinois; direct quote is from the preface in Louis P. Bucklin, *A Theory of Distribution Channel Structure* (Berkeley: Institute of Business and Economic Research, University of California, Berkeley, 1966).

INTRODUCTION

In an advanced or developing economy, all individuals, households, businesses, and government agencies need goods and services to perform their daily functions. These goods and services are obtained from other individuals, households, business firms, or government agencies. However, this exchange process usually involves more than two parties. The household may buy goods from a retailer, but the retailer probably obtained those goods from a wholesaler, who obtained them from manufacturers. Also, the manufacturer had to obtain the goods and services in order to produce the final product.

What we have just described is a marketing channel. A **marketing channel** is *the set of institutions or people that participate in moving goods and services from point of initial source or production to point of final consumption or use.*[1] Dr. Bucklin received the Paul D. Converse National Award from the American Marketing Association for his development of a theory on the structure of marketing channels.

In this part of the text, you will be introduced to the second part of the marketing mix—distribution (or place, as it is sometimes called). This chapter will cover marketing channels—their definition, development, importance, and behavior, as well as legal considerations involved with them. Chapter 11 will discuss physical distribution, and Chapter 12 will cover retail and wholesale institutions.

WHY DO MARKETING CHANNELS DEVELOP?

Marketing channels developed because societies recognized them as a means of increasing the standard of living. Dr. Bucklin suggests that marketing channels result in cost savings and improved customer service, which increase the standard of living. Throughout recorded history, well-developed marketing channel systems have been a determinant of a society's economic growth. The following hypothetical example illustrates how marketing channels can increase the efficiency of the marketing process. The example deals with decentralized versus centralized exchange.[2]

In very primitive cultures, each family is self-sufficient: some family members hunt, some prepare housing or shelter, some make clothing and tools. Before too long, one family may become highly efficient at making pots while another may be very efficient at making knives. Both families have a surplus and therefore may enter into an exchange—pots for knives.

Let us assume that there are only five families in this primitive culture, that each specializes in a different product, and that each wants to exchange its surplus for some of the other products (hats, pots, baskets, hoes, knives). Figure 10.1 shows that ten exchanges would be necessary with decentralized exchange. Note that each decentralized exchange would occur at the household of one of the two families involved in the exchange. As you might expect, this exchange process would consume a lot of time and energy. Also, the more time and energy spent traveling to exchange, the less time the families could spend producing goods to exchange.

If a centralized market existed in this primitive culture, where all would

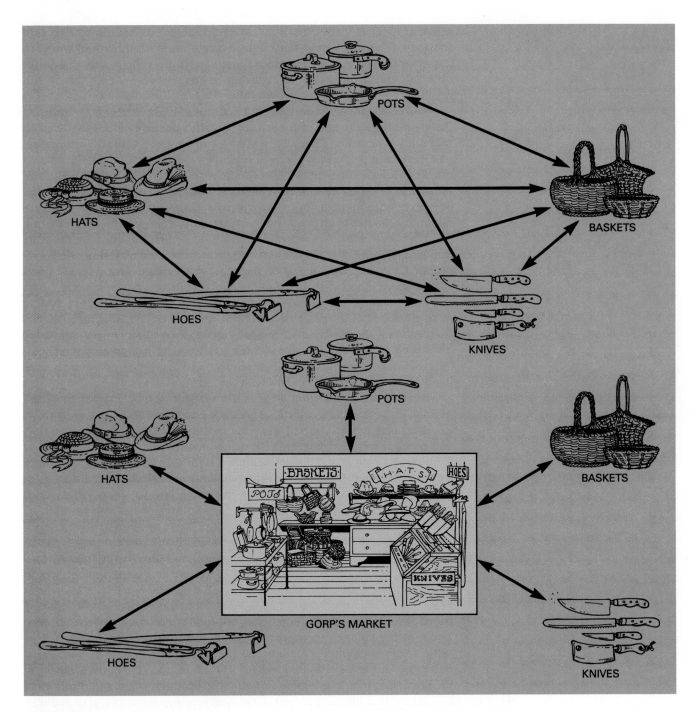

Figure 10.1

Decentralized and Centralized Exchange

Source: Adapted from Wroe Alderson. "Factors Governing the Development of Marketing Channels," in Richard M. Clewett (ed.), *Marketing Channels for Manufactured Products* (Homewood, IL: Richard D. Irwin, 1954), p. 7.

agree to meet at a specified time to exchange goods, then only five centralized exchanges would be required, since each family would travel to the central market. The centralized market would reduce the amount of time and travel necessary to exchange goods. However, each family still would have to negotiate with the other four families.

To reduce negotiation time and costs, we might envision an intermediary—perhaps the son of the hat maker, who decides he doesn't want to spend his time making hats. He would locate at some central location and take each family's surplus goods in return for credits that the families could use to purchase other goods. These merchandise credits would be a form of money. In this situation, each family only has to travel to negotiate with one party (the middleman). Consequently, time and negotiation costs are minimized, so that each family has more time and energy to spend producing goods to exchange for more merchandise credits and thus increase its standard of living. The middleman will support himself by selling the goods he purchased for a higher price than that paid. However, the system will still be more efficient than a totally decentralized exchange system.

Our example of a primitive culture also applies to the economic system of an advanced culture. In the United States, it is not unusual for manufacturers to sell their output to retailers through an independent wholesale institution. Manufacturers use wholesalers because it increases their marketing efficiency by reducing their contact and negotiation costs and, most likely, their transportation and inventory costs.

In fact, the distribution area of the marketing mix often is most important in determining a firm's success because a manufacturer with an excellent product will be helpless without the strong support of wholesalers and retailers in the marketing channel. Not surprisingly, one of the major problems of new start-up manufacturers, such as the many new computer software firms, is obtaining adequate wholesale and retail distribution. Most wholesalers and retailers do not wish to handle the products of unknown manufacturers. In addition, marketing channel intermediaries can often be key players in getting consumers to adopt new products. For example, imitation cheese made in part from vegetable oil and protein-rich soybeans is high in food value and low in cholesterol and also lower in cost. As a culture, however, the U.S. consumer has trouble accepting the concept of an artificial or nonnatural cheese. Since U.S. consumers will not knowingly accept dairy substitutes, the producers of imitation cheese have concentrated their selling efforts on schools, fast-food restaurants, and the military. These intermediaries incorporate the cheese into food that they sell or serve to their clientele. Already, 20 percent of the cheese people eat is imitation, and few know they eat it.[3] Therefore, the distribution aspect of the marketing mix is at least as important as product, price, and promotion.

Figure 10.2 illustrates how contact and negotiation costs can be reduced by using wholesalers. At the top of the figure, there are three manufacturers selling to eight retailers, which requires twenty-four contacts. At the bottom of the figure, the same three manufacturers sell through one wholesaler and only eleven contacts are required.

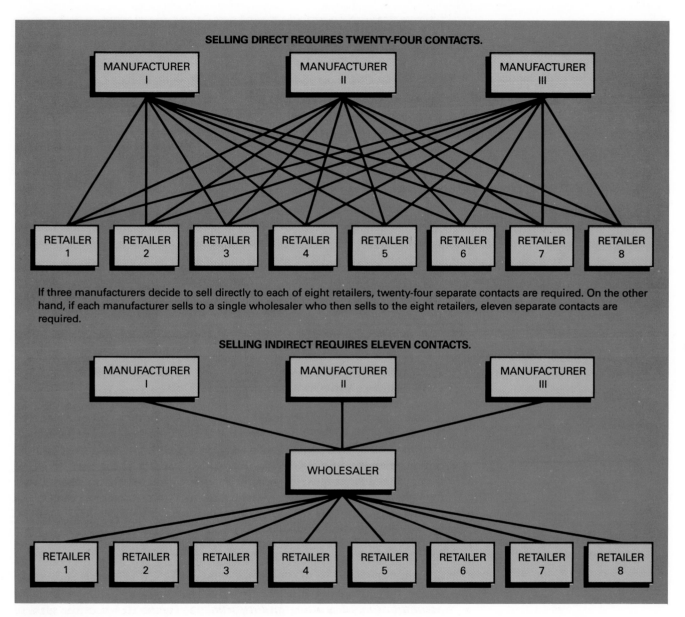

Figure 10.2
Contacts Required to Sell Direct Versus Indirect

Two categories of firms or individuals are involved in the marketing channel: (1) a **primary channel institution** *takes title to the products* and (2) a **facilitating channel institution** *does not take title but makes the marketing process easier by specializing in the performance of certain marketing activities.* Figure 10.3 presents a breakdown of these two categories.

WHO IS INVOLVED IN THE MARKETING CHANNEL?

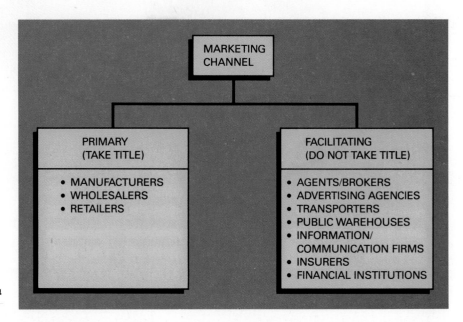

Figure 10.3

Classification of Major Participants in a Marketing Channel

Title Taking Institutions/Individuals

Manufacturers, wholesalers, and retailers take legal title to products as they flow through the marketing channel. Often, manufacturers are not considered marketing institutions, since they produce goods. But manufacturers cannot exist by only producing goods, they must also market the goods they produce. Since most manufacturers do not want to become distributors, they often need or desire the assistance of wholesalers, retailers, and certain facilitating institutions to market their products. The Marketing in Action on page 307 illustrates this point.

Wholesalers buy merchandise and resell it to retailers, wholesalers, and to commercial users. Retailers buy merchandise and resell it to the consumer or household market. Retailers and wholesalers are primarily engaged in the **sorting process**, which *involves* the following *four steps: sorting out, accumulation, allocation, and assortment.*[4] Figure 10.4 uses the glass of orange juice you drink in the morning as an example of the sorting process.

The first step in the sorting process is *sorting out,* which involves separating large, heterogeneous supplies into smaller, more homogeneous groups. For example, if you go to an orange grove, you will quickly realize that not all oranges are suitable for processing into orange juice. Some will be too ripe, some will be diseased, others may not be ripe enough or may be better suited to be sold as eating oranges. (The type of wholesaler that does this sorting out will be discussed in Chapter 12.) Sorting out occurs with eggs, wheat, and many other crops and raw materials.

MARKETING IN ACTION

Manufacturers Forced to Become Distributors

Most manufacturers would rather not be in the distribution business because they recognize that performing the warehousing and transportation functions can be costly and that profit margins are thin in the wholesaling sector of the economy. They prefer to concentrate their efforts on production and the development of national marketing programs. Sometimes, however, manufacturers are forced to take over the role of distributor. For example, when a distributor in a large metropolitan area goes bankrupt, even a short interruption of service and distribution in a major market can be disastrous for the manufacturer. In order to survive, the manufacturer is forced to take on this job.

Examples of manufacturers who purchased major distributors include:

- **RCA's purchase of Bruno Appliance Corp., its New York City distributor.**

- **Zenith's purchase of its Los Angeles distributor.**

- **Harnischfeger's (manufacturer of construction equipment) purchase of its Houston distributor.**

- **J.I. Case Co.'s acquisition of several of its troubled distributors.**

Manufacturers will often attempt to resell the distributorships they acquire as soon as possible, although they are not always able to do so until they find an appropriate and qualified buyer.

Source: Authors' background and experience; company annual reports; "Why Manufacturers Are Doubling as Distributors," *BusinessWeek* (January 17, 1983), p. 41.

The second step in the sorting process is *accumulation*. Accumulation consists of assembling groups of homogeneous supplies from many different sources in sufficient quantity for mass production or mass marketing. Sunkist, for example, must accumulate large quantities of high-quality oranges for its orange juice. There is a class of wholesalers who will buy in small quantities in order to accumulate the large quantities that food processors like Sunkist desire.

The third step in the sorting process is *allocation*, which consists of separating large amounts of goods into smaller quantities suitable for resale to retailers and wholesalers. Once again, the wholesaler enters the picture. A food wholesaler will buy Sunkist orange juice by the truckload (approximately 2,000 cases) and then sell it in smaller quantities to various supermarkets.

Assortment is the final step in the sorting process. *Assortment* occurs when someone, usually the retailer, assembles diverse supplies in a single place to meet customer demand. Surely, you do not want to go to separate stores for the bacon, eggs, bread, and butter you eat with your juice! All retailers are in the business of building assortments that match the demands of the consumers who patronize their stores.

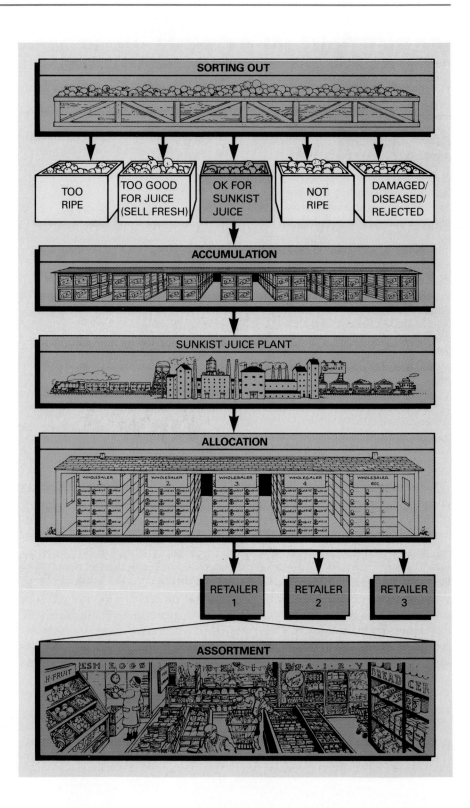

Figure 10.4
The Sorting Process

Facilitating Institutions/Individuals

Individuals and institutions that specialize in the performance of various marketing activities help to facilitate the flow of goods and services in the marketing channel (see Figure 10.3). None of these take title to the goods as they move through the marketing channel.

Agents and brokers are independent businesspeople who receive a commission when they are able to bring buyer and seller together to negotiate a transaction. Walters gives a concise description of the freelance broker, the manufacturer's agent, the sales agent, and the purchasing agent[5]:

1. The *freelance broker* has no permanent ties with any principal, and he may negotiate sales for a large number of principals over time. There is no limitation on the territory in which sales occur, but the agent is strictly bound by the principal for prices, terms, and conditions of sale.

2. The *manufacturer's agent,* like the freelance broker, negotiates for the sale of products for his or her principal. The manufacturer's agent has a rather loose arrangement with the principal that is seldom permanent beyond a year. This arrangement is usually renewed but can also be terminated on notice. The agent is strictly bound by the principal for the territory, prices, terms, and conditions of sale. Manufacturer's agents normally negotiate sales for several principals, but they have jurisdiction over only a part of the manufacturer's total output. A merchant using a manufacturer's agent does not need a sales force, but must have a sales department with a manager to coordinate the activities of the agents and to establish policy.[6]

3. The *sales agent* has long-term arrangements with from one to a very restricted number of principals. This agent sells the entire output for the principal and has no limitation on the territory in which he or she operates or on prices, terms, or conditions of sale. Sales agents also frequently finance their principals. When a merchant uses a sales agent, there is no need for any sales department because the agent handles all sales functions.

4. *Purchasing agents,* sometimes known as resident buyers, specialize in seeking out sources of supply for some merchant principal. They operate on a contractual basis for a limited number of customers and receive a commission just as sales agents do. Purchasing agents usually operate in the central market headquarters for a particular type of product. They are specialists on sources, prices, quality, shipping, fashion, and other considerations surrounding the purchase of merchandise. Chain stores make considerable use of resident buyers, as do department stores on occasion.

Advertising agencies also facilitate the selling process by designing effective advertisements and advising management on where and when to place these advertisements. Institutions that facilitate and help in the transportation function are motor, rail, and air carriers, pipelines, and shipping companies. These firms offer diverse advantages and disadvantages in terms of delivery, service, and cost, which will be discussed in Chapter 11. Generally, the quicker the delivery, the more costly it will be. Transporters can have a significant effect on how efficiently goods move through the marketing system and can be a major source of conflict when they fail to perform their jobs properly.[7]

The *public warehouse* is a facilitating institution that assists in performing the storage function. A public warehouse will store goods for a fee. Space charges or fees typically are based on cubic feet used per month, but some warehouses now charge daily fees. Frequently, wholesalers and retailers that take advantage of special buys have no space in their stores or warehouses and find it necessary to use a public warehouse.

The postal and telephone system are at the heart of the business communications system in the United States. Computers are playing an increasingly important role in information transmission. Retailers can now order many kinds of merchandise by using on-line computer ordering techniques. An order is typed into a computer console at the retail firm, such as Sears, and is fed directly into the wholesaler's or manufacturer's computer, which then prints out a purchase order and warehouse routing slip to show what items to ship to the retailer or end user. Market research firms also assist in the information function by providing problem-solving information in specialized areas.

Insurance firms can facilitate the marketing channel by assuming some of the risk-taking function. These firms insure inventories, buildings, trucks, equipment and fixtures, and other assets that are instrumental to performing marketing functions.

Finally, there are facilitating institutions that aid in financing, such as commercial banks, savings and loan associations, and stock exchanges. These institutions can provide or help the firm obtain funds to finance its marketing functions. For instance, companies may need capital to finance new warehouses, retail stores, inventory investments, and trucks.

MARKETING CHANNELS IN THE UNITED STATES

In the United States and in most countries, there are many different types of marketing channels. The major marketing channels for products in the United States can be categorized as follows: (1) marketing channels for consumer goods, (2) marketing channels for industrial goods, and (3) raw material supply channels for manufacturers. In addition to these, there are marketing channels for services and multiple channels.

Consumer Goods Channels

As shown in Figure 10.5, there are basically six alternative marketing channels for consumer goods, each of which will be discussed briefly.

Insurers assume the risk of most products being destroyed while in the marketing channel.

1. *Manufacturer–Consumer.* This marketing channel is *not* popular in the United States because it is a relatively inefficient and high cost method of marketing. Examples are a consumer whose clothes are custom made by a local tailor or a household that purchases a poured concrete swimming pool directly from the builder. Levi Strauss had 70 retail stores that allowed it to sell direct to the consumer, but it liquidated these stores in 1980 to concentrate on manufacturing.

2. *Manufacturer–Agent/Broker–Consumer.* This channel is used by Tupperware, Mary Kay Cosmetics, and Avon, to name a few. In this

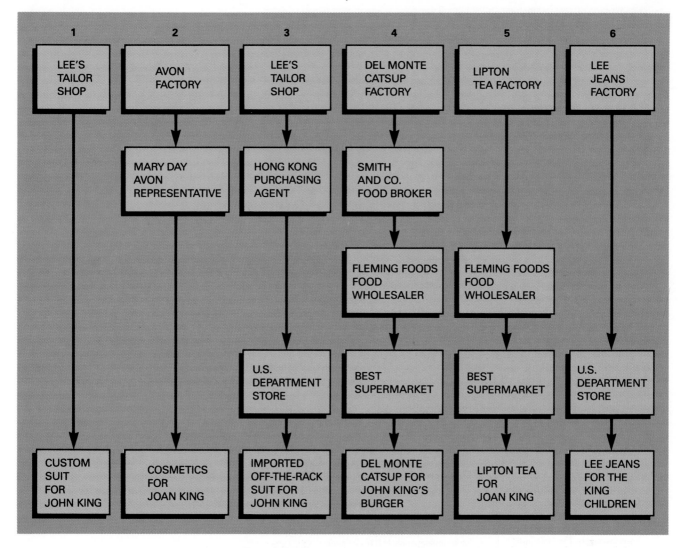

Figure 10.5
Alternative Marketing Channels for Consumer Goods

channel, Avon, for example, sells its products through individual sales agents to the consumer. In 1984, Porsche attempted to develop this type of channel in the United States to sell its $21,000 to $50,000 sports cars, but after substantial protest from auto dealers and the filing of $3 billion in lawsuits, Porsche dropped its plans to use this channel alternative.[8]

3. *Manufacturer–Agent/Broker–Retailer–Consumer.*   Sometimes, retailers use agents to acquire goods. For example, a department store may

use a broker or agent in New York, Paris, or Hong Kong to acquire apparel items from manufacturers, which they then sell directly to consumers. Apple Computer used this channel until October 1984, when it eliminated agents and developed its own sales force to sell to retailers of computers.[9]

4. *Manufacturer–Agent/Broker–Wholesaler–Retailer–Consumer.* This rather long channel is popular for distributing processed food. For instance, Del Monte may sell its catsup, through a food broker, to a food wholesaler. The food wholesaler then sells it to food retailers, who sell the catsup to the final consumer.

+ gasoline

5. *Manufacturer–Wholesaler–Retailer–Consumer.* This is probably the most common channel for consumer goods. Most consumer goods manufacturers sell much of their output to wholesalers, who in turn sell to retailers who are patronized by consumers.

mostly used in U.S.

6. *Manufacturer–Retailer–Consumer.* This marketing channel is used when retailers are large enough to purchase in large quantities directly from the manufacturer. Many large retail chains such as Safeway, Sears, J.C. Penney, and K mart buy the majority of their merchandise directly from manufacturers.

have products private labeled (vertical integration)

Industrial Goods Channels

There are basically four alternative marketing channels for industrial goods (see Figure 10.6), each of which will be briefly discussed.

1. *Manufacturer–User.* Many producers of expensive industrial equipment, such as steam generators, robots, and computers, will sell directly to the user.

– high priced items

2. *Manufacturer–Agent/Broker–User.* Often, a manufacturer of expensive industrial equipment would like to sell directly to the user, but the firm is not large enough to justify its own sales force. In this situation, the producer commonly engages an agent to sell its output to end users.

3. *Manufacturer–Agent/Broker–Wholesaler–User.* If a producer cannot afford its own sales force, and if the users tend to buy in small quantities, then the producer may use an agent who sells to wholesalers. The wholesalers then fill the relatively small and frequent orders of the users of industrial goods.

4. *Manufacturer–Wholesaler–User.* This channel typically is used when the manufacturer can justify the expense of its own sales force, but the users purchase the goods in small quantities. In this scenario, it is most profitable to sell to wholesalers and to let them handle the small orders of industrial goods users.

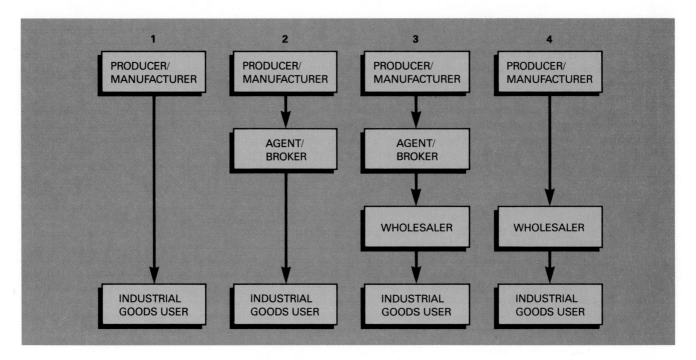

Figure 10.6

Alternative Marketing Channels for Industrial Goods

Computer manufacturers often sell directly to the user.

Raw Material Supply Channels

Up to this point, we have described marketing channels as beginning with the manufacturer. This description is somewhat inaccurate, however, because manufacturers typically need to purchase raw materials before they can produce anything. These raw materials are made available to manufacturers through a marketing channel that flows from the initial source of the raw material to the manufacturer. Table 10.1 shows the seven basic alternative supply channels for raw materials.

Service Channels

The marketing channel for services usually flows directly from the provider of the service to the user.[10] Consider such personal services as shoe repair, hairstyling, psychological counseling, and dry cleaning. This is also true for business services, such as consulting and accounting or auditing. Service channels can be longer, however, and may have several intermediaries. Service channels are detailed in Chapter 19.

Table 10.1 Raw Material Supply Channels

1. *Original Source–Manufacturer.* A timber forester may sell timber directly to a large manufacturer of wood furniture.

2. *Original Source–Agent/Broker–Manufacturer.* A farmer may sell corn through an agent or broker to manufacturers such as Kellogg.

3. *Original Source–Agent/Broker–Processor of Raw Materials–Manufacturer.* A timber forester may sell timber to a wood processor through a broker. The wood processor then sells some of the usable lumber to a furniture manufacturer.

4. *Original Source–Agent/Broker–Storers of Raw Materials–Processors of Raw Materials–Manufacturer.* A farmer sells corn through an agent to the owner of a grain elevator, who sells some of the corn to a processor, who makes corn syrup. Some of the corn syrup is then sold to a candy manufacturer.

5. *Original Source–Storer of Raw Materials–Processor of Raw Materials–Manufacturer.* Same as the prior channel, except no agent or broker is used.

6. *Original Source–Storer of Raw Materials–Manufacturer.* A farmer sells oats to the owner of a grain elevator, who then sells some of the oats to a dog food manufacturer.

7. *Original Source–Processor–Manufacturer.* A fishing fleet sells its catch to a fish processor, who then sells some of its output to a cat food manufacturer.

Multiple Channels

As the preceding discussions point out, many types of marketing channels exist in our economy. It should be stressed, however, that a manufacturer may use different channels to reach different target markets. We will use a paint manufacturer to illustrate the concept of multiple channels. The manufacturer produces household paints for interior and exterior use as well as a line of automotive paints. Household paints are sold through three different channels (channels 5 and 6 of the consumer goods channels, and industrial goods channel 1). In channel 5, the paint manufacturer sells its paint to a wholesaler who in turn sells it to hardware and home decorating stores, which sell it to the consumer. In channel 6, the paint manufacturer sells its paint directly to large chains, such as Sears, K mart, Target, and Wal-Mart. They also sell through channel 1 of the industrial goods channels because they sell paint directly to large home builders, such as U.S. Homes.

Automotive paints are also sold through several channels (industrial channels 1 and 4, and consumer channel 5). In industrial channel 1, the paint manufacturer sells directly to auto manufacturers. In industrial channel 4, it sells to wholesalers, who sell to auto body and auto paint shops, and in consumer channel 5, the paint manufacturer sells paint to a wholesaler, who sells it to auto supply stores, who sell it in small quantities to consumers who need touch-up paint for their cars.

HOW ARE CHANNELS ORGANIZED?

There are various ways of organizing marketing channels, but the two basic channel patterns are the conventional marketing channel and the vertical marketing channel, as shown in Figure 10.7.

The Conventional Marketing Channel

A **conventional marketing channel** is *one in which each member is loosely aligned with the others*. The major orientation is toward the next institution in the channel. Thus, the manufacturer interacts with and focuses efforts on the wholesaler, the wholesaler focuses efforts on the retailer, and in turn, the retailer focuses efforts on the final consumer. In the conventional marketing channel, there is no channel captain. A **channel captain** is *a member of the marketing channel who attempts to organize and lead the efforts of the institutions in the channel in order to obtain system-wide economies and maximum market impact.*

The conventional marketing channel, although historically predominant in the United States, has proven to be a sloppy and inefficient method of conducting business. It fosters intense negotiations at each stage in the channel, and the channel members do not see the possibility of shifting or dividing the marketing functions among *all* channel participants since no

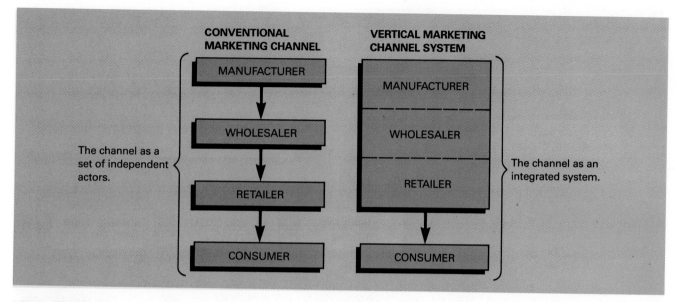

Figure 10.7

Conventional and Vertical Systems Compared

channel captain exists. Therefore, it is not surprising that its use has been declining in the United States since the early 1950s.

Vertical Marketing Systems

Vertical marketing systems have been described as "*professionally managed and centrally programmed networks that are preengineered to achieve significant operating economies and maximum market impact*. Stated alternatively, vertical marketing systems are rationalized and capital intensive networks that are programmed to realize technological, managerial and promotional economies."[11] There are three types of vertical marketing systems—corporate, contractual, and administered—each of which has grown explosively since the early 1950s.[12] The vertical marketing systems are shown in Figure 10.8. Each of the vertical marketing systems has a channel captain.

Corporate Systems. The **corporate vertical marketing system** *typically consists of either a manufacturer who has vertically integrated forward into the channel to reach the consumer or a retailer who has vertically integrated backward into the channel to create a self-supply network*. The first type includes manufacturers, such as Sherwin-Williams (paint), Hart/ Schaffner/Marx (men's apparel), Famolare (shoes), and Xerox (office equip-

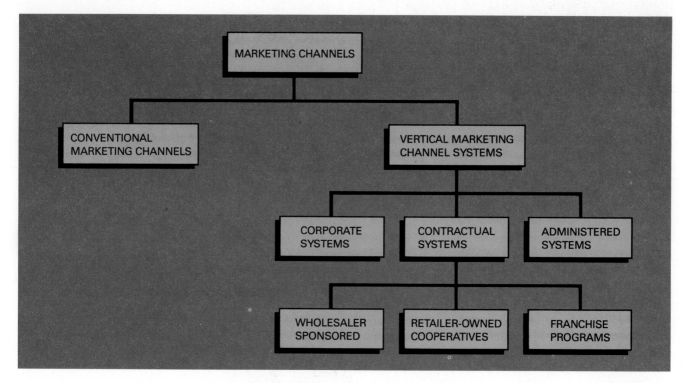

Figure 10.8
Alternative Marketing Channel Systems

ment), that have created their own warehousing and retail outlets and thus are channel captains. The second type includes retailers, such as Sears, which obtains over 50 percent of its merchandise from manufacturers in which it has an equity interest. For example, Sears obtains over 50 percent of its appliances from Whirlpool, over 50 percent of its apparel items from Kellwood, over 40 percent of its tires and tubes from Armstrong Rubber, and over 30 percent of its hand tools from EASCO, in which it has substantial equity.[13] Sears, therefore, performs the function of channel captain for these products.

Contractual Systems.   **A contractual vertical marketing system** *includes wholesaler-sponsored voluntary groups, retailer-owned cooperatives, and franchise organizations.* A *wholesaler-sponsored voluntary group* is created when a wholesaler offers a coordinated merchandising and buying program to a group of independently owned retailers, and the retailers agree to concentrate their purchases with the wholesaler. Since it is a voluntary relationship, there are no membership or franchise fees. The independent retailers may terminate this relationship whenever they desire, so it is to the wholesaler's advantage to build competitive merchandise assortments

Wholesaler-sponsored voluntary groups, such as Ace in the hardware field, provide a mutually beneficial relationship between the wholesaler and the independently-owned retailer.

and offer other services that will keep the voluntary group satisfied and allow it to be the channel captain.

The wholesaler commonly offers the retailers the following services: store design and layout, store site and location analysis, inventory management systems, accounting and bookkeeping systems, insurance plans, pension plans, trade area studies, advertising and promotion assistance, and employee training programs. Accordingly, the better the services and merchandising packages offered by the wholesaler, the more loyal the retailers will become and the more the wholesaler can direct and organize channel activities.

Wholesaler-sponsored voluntary groups have been a major trend in the structuring of marketing channels since the mid-1960s and are prevalent in many lines of trade. Consider, for example, Ace in the hardware field, Western Auto in the automotive accessories field, Ben Franklin in the notions and general merchandise field, and Economost in the drug field.

Another common form of contractual vertical marketing systems is the *retailer-owned cooperative.* These cooperatives are organized and owned by retailers and are most common in the grocery field (for example, Associated Grocers and Certified Grocers). They offer scale economies and service to member retailers, thus allowing them to compete with large chain-store organizations.

The third type of contractual vertical marketing system is the **franchise,** which can be defined as "*licensing of an entire business format* where one firm (the franchisor) licenses a number of outlets (franchisees) to market a product or service and engage in a business developed by the franchisor using the latter's trade names, trademarks, service marks, know-how, and methods of doing business."[14] Franchisors can come from different positions in the marketing channel. The franchisor could be a manufacturer, such as Chevrolet or Midas Muffler; a service specialist, such as Kelly Girl or Manpower; or a retailer franchising other retailers, such as McDonald's

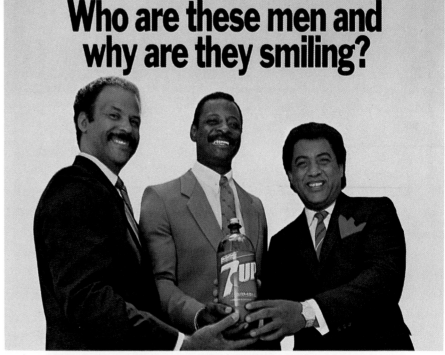

Who are these men and why are they smiling?

They are Chuck Wells, Mel Farr and Al Bennett, the owners of the first 100% Black-owned major soft drink franchise.

Chuck Wells, Mel Farr, and Al Bennett have made history.

They are the new owners of the first and only 100% Black-owned major soft drink franchise in America.

Not only is their purchase of the Flint, Michigan 7-UP Franchise a milestone in the soft drink industry, but it's also a purchase that will energize the economic life of the entire Flint/Saginaw region of Michigan.

The Seven-Up Company is proud to be associated with these outstanding businessmen. Al Bennett and Mel Farr have achieved national prominence through their respective auto dealerships, and both men are ranked in *Black Enterprise* Magazine's Top 100 Black Businesses. Chuck Wells is a leading tax consultant, financial planner, and attorney.

The Seven-Up Company has a simple philosophy: our business activities must make social sense, and our social activities must make good business sense. Nothing better exemplifies this philosophy than our association with the three newest members of the Seven-Up family.

"SEVEN-UP" AND "7UP" ARE TRADEMARKS IDENTIFYING PRODUCTS OF THE SEVEN-UP COMPANY © 1985

A 7UP soft drink franchise is a lucrative business to own because of the ability of The Seven-Up Company to be the channel captain.

or Kentucky Fried Chicken. In a franchise marketing channel, the franchisor is the channel captain.

Franchise systems are not a recent phenomenon. Major oil companies and auto manufacturers have used franchised retail outlets for more than fifty years. However, franchising in other lines of trade (such as convenience food stores, restaurants, motels, tax preparation services, and equipment rental stores) has experienced spectacular growth since the mid-1960s.[15] In 1983, there were 465,000 franchise businesses in the U.S. and their sales accounted for over 30 percent of all retail sales.[16]

Each of these channel types allows for a more coordinated and system-wide perspective than do conventional marketing channels. However, they are more difficult to manage than corporate vertical marketing systems because the authority and power structures are not as well defined. The principal requirement is that channel members give up some autonomy to gain system economies and greater market impact.

Administered Systems.   An **administered vertical marketing system** is, in principle, similar to a conventional marketing channel, but in this system, *one of the channel members uses the principles of interorganizational management to become the channel captain.* Interorganizational management is the management of relationships among organizational entities. In a marketing channel, it involves one member, such as a manufacturer, managing its relations with other organizations in the channel, such as wholesalers and retailers.

Although not a new concept, administered systems have greatly increased in number since the 1960s. Frequently, administered systems are initiated by manufacturers. As McCammon has observed[17]:

> Manufacturing organizations . . . have historically relied on administrative expertise to coordinate reseller marketing efforts. Suppliers with dominant brands have predictably experienced the least difficulty in securing strong trade support, but many manufacturers with "fringe" items have been able to elicit reseller cooperation through the use of liberal distribution policies that take the form of attractive discounts (or discount substitutes), financial assistance, and various types of concessions that protect resellers from one or more of the risks of doing business.

Some of the concessions manufacturers offer resellers are liberal return allowances, display materials for in-store use, advertising allowances, salesperson training programs, extended dating (i.e., extra days of free credit to pay for merchandise), and free goods (i.e., buy 10 cases, get 1 free).

INTENSITY OF DISTRIBUTION

In designing a marketing channel, careful thought must be given to the degree of distribution intensity desired. Distribution intensity refers to the number of middlemen (wholesalers and retailers) who handle a product in a given geographic area. There are essentially three levels of distribution intensity. **Intensive distribution** has *most of the available resellers in a geographic area sell the product.* **Selective distribution** is somewhere between intensive and exclusive distribution; *most suitable resellers sell the product, but selling through all available resellers is avoided.* **Exclusive distribution** has *only one reseller of a product in each geographic area.*

Intensive Distribution

Intensive distribution is used most often with convenience goods, such as cigarettes, milk, gasoline, and bread, and industrial goods such as office and janitorial supplies. These are products that buyers wish to purchase with little effort, and intensive distribution eases the buying task.

Since many resellers handle goods when intensive distribution is used, price competition and competitive activity are heavy. This results in low profit margins, so that resellers are unlikely to place much selling effort behind a particular manufacturer's products.

Selective Distribution

Selective distribution is used for most shopping products and industrial equipment. With selective distribution, the manufacturer is selective about who resells its products. The manufacturer feels that not all resellers have the proper reputation, the financial strength, or the experience or expertise to handle its products properly.

A manufacturer can more easily obtain resellers' support of its marketing program when selective distribution is used than when intensive distribution is used, because fewer resellers handle the product in each geographic region there will be less price competition, leading to more adequate profit margins. At the same time, selling costs are reduced because the manufacturer calls on fewer resellers.

The Marketing in Action on page 323 shows how some traditionally prestigious fragrance brands are no longer enjoying selective distribution.

Exclusive Distribution

Exclusive distribution is used for some highly prestigious specialty goods, such as Rolls Royce autos, and for some highly technical and specialized industrial equipment. Actually, exclusive distribution is an extreme case of selective distribution, where only one reseller is used in each geographic area. For this form of distribution to be successful, the buyer must be willing to go out of his or her way to buy the product.

With exclusive distribution, the manufacturer can exert considerable control over reseller efforts. Prices and services usually can be maintained at a specified level because each reseller essentially has a monopoly in its trade area—it is the only seller of the product.

CHANNEL BEHAVIOR: COOPERATION, CONFLICT, AND POWER

In a marketing channel, several firms are interacting with each other in order to move goods to the final user or buyer. Since each channel member must rely on others to perform certain tasks, cooperation is essential. For example, the manufacturer must rely on the retailer to put selling effort behind its products and to properly represent them to the consumer. On the other hand, the retailer must rely on the manufacturer to nationally

MARKETING IN ACTION

Traditionally, prestigious women's fragrances, such as those produced by Estee Lauder, Chanel, and Borghese have been distributed on a selective and almost exclusive basis. In the early 1980s, when Estee Lauder expanded its distribution in New York City to include Macy's and Lord & Taylor, critics proclaimed, "They'll be selling in supermarkets next!"

Several years ago, these fragrances began to receive much more intensive distribution because the market was experiencing faltering demand. High income consumers demanded more shopping convenience. They felt that if they could buy gourmet

More Intensive Distribution for Prestigious Fragrance Brands

foods in upscale supermarkets, then why not expensive perfume? There are only 10,000 department stores suitable for distributing prestigious fragrances, but there are over 100,000 drugstores/foodstores. If only 10 percent of these are in high income trade areas, the potential number of food/drug units would be

10,000, thereby doubling the number of resellers of prestige perfume brands.

Another factor that has encouraged more intensive distribution is the competition prestigious fragrances are receiving from store brands. Marshall Fields, Saks Fifth Avenue, and Bloomingdales have, for example, created their own brands of prestigious fragrances.

Source: Based in part on "Limited-Distribution Fragrance Brands Continue Expansion to 'Mass' Outlets," *Product Marketing* (June 1983), p. 56.

advertise the product and create a high level of consumer awareness for the product.

Because each channel member must rely on other channel members to perform certain tasks, they are dependent on each other. This interdependency is the basic cause of conflict in marketing channels.[18] Conflicts occur when a channel member does not do what is expected.[19] Consider, for example, a wholesaler who promises a 9 A.M. delivery to a local retailer. The retailer schedules two extra employees for the morning to help stock the new merchandise. When the wholesaler's truck doesn't arrive until 3 P.M., it is easy to imagine why the retailer is upset.

In a marketing channel, one member usually has more power or leadership ability than others. Power is the ability of one channel member to control the decisions of other channel members. A channel member can develop power or leadership ability by exercising certain bases of power over other channel members. There are five power bases, as listed in Table 10.2.[20]

Channel captains can be manufacturers, wholesalers, or retailers.[21] Large chain-store organizations, such as J.C. Penney and Sears, are examples of retail channel captains. Wholesale organizations that establish voluntary group programs, such as Fleming Companies and Super Valu, are examples of wholesale channel captains. Finally, many channels are led or captained by manufacturers. For example, Federal-Mogul, a manufacturer of automotive supplies, has recently moved into distribution and marketing of its products with the development of a new computerized inventory control/order system called SCAN. This system will allow Federal-Mogul to exercise

Table 10.2   Types of Power Bases

1. *Reward power* is based on the ability of A to mediate rewards for B. For example, Dole offers retailers advertising and promotional support if they handle Dole products.

2. *Expertise power* is based on B's perception that A has some special knowledge. For instance, Midas Muffler (a franchisor) has developed an excellent training program for store managers, and thus franchisees view the franchisor as an expert.

3. *Referent power* is based on the identification of B with A. B wants to be associated or identified with A. An example of this is an auto dealer who wishes to handle BMWs or Mercedes because of their status.

4. *Legitimate power* is based on A's right to influence B. A franchisor, McDonald's for example, has the right to cancel a franchisee's contract if it fails to maintain certain established standards concerning restaurant cleanliness, food, hours of operation, and employees.

5. *Coercive power* is based on B's belief that A has the capacity to punish or harm if B doesn't conform to A's desire. A manufacturer may, for example, threaten to cut off a retailer's supply if the retailer doesn't properly display the manufacturer's products.

expertise power and reward power over its warehouse distributors in the automotive, heavy-duty, and industrial channels.[22] Other examples of manufacturers as channel captains include Procter & Gamble, Pillsbury, Ethan Allan Furniture, and General Motors.

LEGAL CONSIDERATIONS

Organizations are restricted in the relationships and agreements that may develop with channel partners. These can be conveniently categorized into five areas: territorial restrictions, dual distribution, exclusive dealing, tying arrangements, and franchise distribution.

Territorial Restrictions

Territorial restrictions are *attempts by a supplier, usually a manufacturer, to limit the geographic area in which a reseller may resell its merchandise.* Courts sometimes view territorial restrictions as a violation of the Sherman Antitrust Act because they may potentially restrain intrabrand competition. Thus, even though both the manufacturer and the reseller may favor territorial restrictions, the courts often frown on such arrangements.[23] Intrabrand competition is competition between two firms selling the same brand, whereas interbrand competition is competition between firms selling different brands in the same product class. For example, one Chevrolet dealer engages in intrabrand competition with another Chevrolet dealer and in interbrand competition with a Ford dealer.

Because the courts have made conflicting rulings on territorial restrictions based on cases involving White Motor Company,[24] Schwinn Bicycles,[25] and GTE Sylvania,[26] it is difficult for a firm and its suppliers to know what is legal and what is not. The current message appears to be a rule of reason,[27] that is, assessing a case in a court of law on its individual merits and the particular situation. Stated alternatively, territorial restrictions are not automatic violations of the Sherman Act.

Dual Distribution

A manufacturer that resells to independent retailers and through its own retail or wholesale outlets is engaged in **dual distribution**. For example, occasionally Texaco or Exxon opens a corporate owned and managed gasoline station near an independently owned Texaco or Exxon gasoline station. Esprit, a leading clothes manufacturer, sells through independent department and specialty stores and is also developing a chain of its own retail stores; the initial stores are in Hong Kong, Los Angeles, and New Orleans.[28]

The courts have not viewed dual distribution arrangements as violations of the law. In fact, they have reasoned that dual distribution can actually foster, rather than reduce, competition. For example, the manufacturer may not be able to find a retailer to represent it in all trade areas, or the manufacturer may find it necessary to operate its own retail outlet to establish market share and remain competitive with other manufacturers. In these situations, the courts apply a rule-of-reason criterion. Therefore, a firm suing a manufacturer for dual distribution will have to convince the court that the manufacturer was unfair and damaged competition. For example, the independent firm may be able to show that the manufacturer-controlled firm was favored with excess advertising allowances or lower prices that harmed the independent's ability to compete.

Exclusive Dealing

Channel members sometimes enter into **exclusive dealing** arrangements, in which *the seller gives the reseller the exclusive right to sell a product in a particular geographic area.* In a *one-way exclusive dealing* arrangement, the supplier agrees to give the retailer or wholesaler the exclusive right to sell the supplier's product in a particular trade area. The retailer or wholesaler, however, does not agree to do anything for the supplier; hence the term *one-way*. A weak manufacturer may need to offer one-way exclusive dealing arrangements to get shelf space at the retail level. One-way arrangements are legal.

A *two-way exclusive dealing* arrangement occurs when the supplier offers a retailer or wholesaler the exclusive distribution of a merchandise line or product if the firm will agree to do something in return for the manufacturer—such as not handling certain competing brands. Two-way agreements violate Section 3 of the Clayton Act (1914) if their effect is to substantially lessen competition or to tend to create a monopoly. Specifically, the courts have been concerned with three potential negative consequences of two-way exclusive dealing agreements. First, if strong manufacturers attract strong resellers, the strength of each reinforcing the other could lessen competition from smaller manufacturers and resellers. Second, since there are many more national manufacturers than there are resellers represented in any given smaller city, there would not be enough outlets for all manufacturers to be represented. Third, price competition at the retail level would be less because intrabrand rivalry would be absent or severely restricted. The legality of two-way exclusive dealing arrangements is determined case by case on a rule-of-reason basis, usually by considering the three preceding points. For example, in 1983, the FTC modified a 1971 exclusive dealing ruling regarding Magnavox. The new ruling allows Magnavox to require dealers to carry only Magnavox products because the commission felt that Magnavox did not have sufficient market power to restrict a significant number of outlets or to restrict competitors from entering the market.[29]

Tying Arrangements

When a seller with a strong product forces a buyer to purchase a weak product as a condition for getting the strong product, a **tying arrangement** exists. For example, a large national manufacturer with several lines of merchandise that are in high demand may require the retailer to carry its entire merchandise assortment as a condition for being able to handle the most popular merchandise lines; this practice is called full-line forcing. Alternatively, a strong manufacturer may introduce a new product and, in order to get shelf space or display space at the retail level, may force retailers to handle some of the product before they can purchase more established merchandise lines.

Tying arrangements have been found to be in violation of Section 3 of the Clayton Act, Sections 1 and 3 of the Sherman Act, and Section 5 of the Federal Trade Commission Act. Tying is not viewed as an absolute violation of the law, but it will generally be viewed as illegal if a substantial share of commerce is affected.

Franchise Distribution

Franchise distribution has grown rapidly since the early 1960s, and substantial legal difficulties between franchisors and franchisees have been associated with this growth. In principle, a franchise is an arm's length relationship between two independent parties whose rights are determined by the contract existing between them. Because of the imbalance of power in this relationship (the franchisor has much more), however, the franchisee should know that certain requirements the franchisor may try to impose typically are viewed as illegal. Basically, the legal system has attempted to equalize the balance of power between the franchisor and franchisee. The franchisee should keep the following points in mind:

1. Although the franchisor may want the franchisee to set prices at a certain level, generally such agreements, if tested in a court of law, will be found in violation of the antitrust laws.
2. Requirements by the franchisor that the franchisee purchase materials and supplies from it when competitive goods of similar quality are available will be viewed as an illegal tying arrangement.
3. Geographic limitations may not be viewed as unlawful. A rule-of-reason approach must be considered, as we discussed earlier in the GTE Sylvania case.
4. Standards for operating procedures, quality control, and cleanliness are generally legal, since the franchisor has a legitimate interest in maintaining a consistent image in order to protect its name or reputation.

Thus, the franchisor should not take undue advantage of the franchisee (through tying or price fixing), but the franchisee should also not take advantage of the franchisor (for instance, by not following cleanliness standards).

One way that franchisors have taken advantage of franchisees is by unfair franchise termination. Traditionally, franchise contracts ran for a short period (typically a year), and the franchisor had maximum flexibility on canceling the franchisee. Currently, however, most franchise contracts specify the causes for cancellation (failure to make payments, bankruptcy of franchisee, failure to meet sales quotas). Also, many franchise contracts now contain an arbitration provision that allows a neutral third party to make a final and binding decision as to whether a breach of contract has occurred and whether it was sufficient to justify cancellation of the franchise. In fact, termination is now quite difficult because many states have statutes to protect franchisees from arbitrary termination.

Finally, fraud has occurred quite often in the sale of franchises to unsuspecting potential franchisees. Franchises have been sold to the small investor as "get-rich-quick" schemes and based on other misleading statements. Because of this practice, several states have enacted franchise investment laws. Under these laws, a franchisee who is deceived by misleading statements (typically in a prospectus) can sue for damages.[30]

SUMMARY

This chapter discussed marketing channels, which were identified as the set of institutions and individuals necessary to move goods and services from the point of initial source to the point of final consumption or use. Marketing channels have been developed to increase a society's standard of living. Marketing channels increase marketing efficiency by reducing contact and negotiation costs, as well as transportation and inventory costs. The institutions can be primary (take title) or facilitating (do not take title, but help move the products through the channel).

In the United States, there are different marketing channels for consumer goods, industrial goods, services, and raw materials. These channels can be organized as a conventional marketing channel or as a vertical marketing system. Over the last twenty-five years, vertical marketing systems have become dominant. They are preferable to conventional marketing channels because they are managed more professionally, centrally programmed, and preengineered to achieve marked operating economies and maximum market impact. In short, vertical marketing systems have channel captains.

Distribution intensity must be established when a marketing channel is designed. It is important to understand the concepts of exclusive, intensive, and selective distribution and the situation in which each is appropriate.

Cooperation and conflict are integral components of channel behavior. Since marketing channels are composed of several institutions and individuals interacting with each other to perform certain marketing activities, cooperation among these institutions will be needed. Conflict will develop if one channel institution does not do what another expects of it. Because of this underlying pattern of cooperation and conflict, one member of the channel needs to take a leadership or power position to resolve conflict. This channel leader can be a manufacturer, a wholesaler, or a retailer.

The U.S. legal system has developed a set of constraints on the design and operation of marketing channels in the areas of territorial restrictions, dual distribution, exclusive dealing, tying arrangements, and franchise distribution.

KEY CONCEPTS

marketing channel (p. 302)
primary channel institution (p. 305)
facilitating channel institution (p. 305)
sorting process (p. 306)
conventional marketing channel (p. 316)
channel captain (p. 316)
vertical marketing system (p. 317)
corporate vertical marketing system (p. 317)
contractual vertical marketing system (p. 318)

franchise (p. 319)
administered vertical marketing system (p. 321)
intensive distribution (p. 321)
selective distribution (p. 321)
exclusive distribution (p. 321)
territorial restrictions (p. 324)
dual distribution (p. 325)
exclusive dealing (p. 325)
tying arrangement (p. 326)

REVIEW AND DISCUSSION QUESTIONS

1. Define *marketing channels* and explain their role in economic development.

2. Why are facilitating institutions necessary to a marketing channel?

3. Define the *sorting process* and its four steps. Give an example of each step in the process.

4. The shorter the marketing channel (more direct), the more efficient it is. Agree or disagree with this statement and defend your position.

5. What are the existing U.S. marketing channels for consumer goods and industrial goods?

6. Why do some manufacturers use multiple channels?

7. Define and illustrate the different types of vertical marketing systems.

8. What distinguishes vertical marketing systems from conventional marketing channels?

9. For what types of products would intensive, selective, and exclusive distribution be most appropriate? Why?

10. Why are cooperation and conflict inevitable in marketing channels?

11. Explain why the concept of power and power bases is important for an understanding of the dynamics of marketing channels.

12. Why do you think large retailers such as J.C. Penney are able to be channel leaders? How might a wholesaler become a channel leader?

13. Define *exclusive dealing* and discuss its legality. Why do courts generally disfavor two-way exclusive dealing arrangements?

14. What is a tying contract? Comment on the legality of tying.

15. Why do you think the rule of reason is used to decide many court cases involving marketing channels?

ACTION PROBLEMS

1. You and your family operate a 4,000-acre cattle ranch in Montana and are disturbed that you receive only $0.30 to $0.35 of the dollar that consumers pay for beef in the grocery store. You would like to get a larger share of this dollar, perhaps up to 75 percent. Design a marketing channel to accomplish this goal. How realistic is the channel you designed?

2. Recently, you began work at Chevrolet Motor Company as a factory dealer representative, and your job is to call on Chevrolet dealers to take new car orders and explain new Chevrolet programs and products. You have encountered several dealers who like to disagree and argue about the number and mix of cars they should order. How might you get them to see your point of view more effectively?

3. As an employee of General Electric, you have been placed on a task force to study and assess the impact of new computer technology and its influence on the marketing channel for household durable goods, such as televisions, refrigerators, and stereos. Prepare a brief (1 page) report on the changes in distribution that may occur.

4. Your grandparents and parents have been in the junk car business for over forty years. Your parents own and actively manage one of the largest auto salvage yards in the United States, and they plan to sell it in five years unless you decide to become actively involved in the business after you graduate from college. Use the concept of sorting to discuss how you could expand your parents' salvage business to include junk household durable goods. In effect, develop a marketing channel to take junk products and funnel them back to raw material processors.

NOTES

1. A lot of misinformation about marketing channels exists, and one source that tries to clear up some of these myths is Michael M. Pearson, "Ten Distribution Myths," *Business Horizons* (May–June 1981), pp. 17–23.

2. Wroe Alderson, "Factors Governing the Development of Marketing Channels," in Richard M. Clewett (ed.), *Marketing Channels for Manufactured Products* (Homewood, IL: Richard D. Irwin, 1954), pp. 5–22.

3. Jagdish N. Sheth, *Winning Back Your Market* (New York: John Wiley & Sons, 1985), pp. 44–45.

4. The sorting function is discussed in detail in Wroe Alderson, *Marketing Behavior and Executive Action* (Homewood, IL: Richard D. Irwin, 1957).

5. Definitions are taken from C. Glenn Walters, *Marketing Channels* (Santa Monica, CA: Goodyear Publishing Co., 1977), p. 136. Used by permission of Scott, Foresman and Company.

6. How to select a good manufacturer's agent or rep is discussed in: Stewart A. Washburn. "How to Find the Manufacturers' Rep Who'll Really Work for You," *Business Marketing* (June 1983), pp. 82–89.

7. Frederick J. Beier, "The Role of the Common Carrier in the Channel of Distribution," *Transportation Journal* (Winter 1969), pp. 12–21.

8. David B. Tinnin, "Porsche's Civil War with its Dealers," *Fortune* (April 16, 1984), pp. 63–68.

9. "Apple-polishing the Dealer," *Sales and Marketing Management* (September 10, 1984), pp. 47–50.

10. For a more complete discussion of service channels, see James H. Donnelly, Jr., "Marketing Intermediaries in Channels of Distribution for Services," *Journal of Marketing* 40 (January 1976), pp. 55–57; William R. George, "The Retailing of Services—A Challenging Future," *Journal of Retailing* 53 (Fall 1977), pp. 85–98.

11. Bert C. McCammon, Jr., "The Emergence and Growth of Contractually Integrated Channels in the American Economy," in Peter D. Bennett (ed.), *Marketing and Economic Development* (Chicago: American Marketing Association, 1965), pp. 496–515.

12. Bert C. McCammon, Jr., Alton F. Doody, and William R. Davidson, "Emerging Patterns of Distribution," presented at the 1969 Annual Meeting of the National Association of Wholesalers, Las Vegas, Nevada, January 15, 1969. Reprinted in Bruce J. Walker and Joel B.

Haynes (eds.), *Marketing Channels and Institutions: Selected Readings,* 2nd edition (Columbus, OH: Grid, 1978), p. 195.

13. Carol J. Loomis, "The Leaning Tower of Sears," *Fortune* (July 2, 1979), pp. 78–85.

14. Louis W. Stern and Adel I. El-Ansary, *Marketing Channels* (Englewood Cliffs, NJ: Prentice-Hall, 1977), pp. 406–407.

15. Franchising is discussed in Phillip D. White and Albert D. Bates, "Franchising Will Remain Retailing Fixture, but Its Salad Days Have Long Since Gone," *Marketing News* (February 17, 1984), p. 14; Jacob Goodman, "Franchisor-Franchisee Relation Requires Delicate Balance," *Marketing News* (February 17, 1984), p. 4.

16. U.S. Bureau of the Census, *Statistical Abstract of the United States: 1984,* 104th edition (Washington, DC, 1983).

17. Bert C. McCammon, Jr., "Perspectives for Distribution Programming," in Louis P. Bucklin (ed.), *Vertical Marketing Systems* (Glenview, IL: Scott, Foresman, 1970), p. 45.

18. Channel conflict and cooperation are discussed in Louis W. Stern and Ronald H. Gorman, "Conflict in Distribution Channels: An Exploration," in Louis W. Stern (ed.), *Distribution Channels: Behavioral Dimensions* (Boston: Houghton Mifflin, 1969), p. 156; Jack Pangrazio, "How to Sell Through Independent Distributors . . . and Improve Channel Strategy," *Business Marketing* (September 1984), pp. 118, 120, 124, 126.

19. Methods for measuring channel conflict are empirically assessed and discussed in James R. Brown and Ralph L. Day, "Measures of Manifest Conflict in Distribution Channels," *Journal of Marketing Research* 18(August 1981), pp. 263–274; for an industry-specific example, see Martin R. Warshaw, C. Merle Crawford, and Robert M. Tank, "Resolving Channel Conflicts in the Office Furniture Industry," *Business Marketing* (March 1985), pp. 106–116.

20. J.R.P. French and Bertram Raven, "The Bases of Social Power," in Darwin Cartwright and Alvin Zander (eds.), *Group Dynamics: Research and Theory* (New York: Harper & Row, 1968).

21. Robert W. Little, "The Marketing Channel: Who Should Lead this Extracorporate Organization?" *Journal of Marketing* (January 1970), pp. 31–38.

22. Joseph Bohn, "Federal-Mogul Revamps Distributor Relationships," *Business Marketing* (January 1984), pp. 14–15, 32–33.

23. Legal considerations in developing a vertical marketing system are discussed in Saul Sands and Robert J. Posch, Jr., "A Checklist of Questions for Firms Considering a Vertical Territorial Distribution Plan," *Journal of Marketing* 36(Summer 1982), pp. 38–43.

24. *White Motor v. U.S.,* 372 U.S. 253.

25. *U.S. v. Arnold, Schwinn and Co.,* 388 U.S. 365.

26. *Continental T.V., Inc. v. GTE Sylvania, Inc.,* 97 U.S. 2549.

27. Rules of reason are further discussed in John F. Cady, "Reasonable Rules and Rules of Reason: Vertical Restrictions on Distributors," *Journal of Marketing* 46(Summer 1982), pp. 27–37.

28. Amy Dunkin, "Clothing Makers Go Straight to the Consumer," *BusinessWeek* (April 29, 1985), pp. 114–115.

29. Hal Taylor, "FTC Says Magnavox Can Restrict Dealers," *HFD Retail Home Furnishings* (July 18, 1983), p. 46.

30. Shelby D. Hunt and John R. Nevin, "Full Disclosure Laws in Franchising: An Empirical Investigation," *Journal of Marketing* 40(April 1976), pp. 53–62.

PHYSICAL DISTRIBUTION

MARKETER PROFILE

Marnette Perry Markets Flowers for Kroger

Selling flowers accounts for nearly $100 million in annual sales for Kroger, the Cincinnati-based supermarket chain, and Marnette Perry deserves a lot of credit for Kroger's success in the floral industry. Kroger's fresh-cut flower sales have tripled since Perry took over in 1984 as manager of floral merchandising, procurement, and distribution. Kroger sells flowers in 800 floral departments. Fresh flowers are procured from coast to coast, as well as in the Netherlands, New Zealand, South America, and literally the entire globe.

Perry realized early that "value for the consumer means freshness in floral products. When customers enjoy quality and value they continue to buy fresh flowers." So she designed a processing and distribution system that gives Kroger complete control—all the way from the greenhouse to the supermarket customer. Field inspectors and buyers select the flowers at the suppliers' greenhouses, refrigerate them at exact temperatures, and then deliver them to one of three central processing centers. There the flowers are inspected, cut, and arranged into bouquets. "Systems have been designed to handle each flower variety with the special care requirements that ensure its lasting quality." This tender loving care gives Perry the advantage over merchandisers who treat delicate flowers no differently than canned goods.

Perry's attention to detail and her marketing smarts have helped Kroger shift flowers from a special-occasion purchase to an everyday item. "People are now buying flowers the way they do in Europe," says Perry. She has also discovered a passion for

flowers. "I really enjoy flowers and I always have them in my house."

Source: Based on Debra Kent. "The Blossom Business is Blooming," *Working Woman* (May 1986), p. 68.

INTRODUCTION

The movement of goods is important in any economy. Consumers or users of products seldom live in the same geographic location where goods are produced. In the United States and other advanced economies, people consume goods from all over the world. We wear clothing made in Korea, drive cars made in Germany, heat our homes with oil from Saudi Arabia, drink wines from France, have kitchen floors covered with Italian tile, and listen to stereos made in Japan.

Manufacturers do not have all the materials they need to produce their intended output in their immediate geographic area. An auto assembly plant in Oklahoma City needs to obtain tires from Ohio, frames and axles from Michigan, paint from Pennsylvania, glass from Texas, textiles from South Carolina, and so on.

In our economy, on the average, over 20 percent of the final cost of a product is due to **logistical costs**,[1] which are *the costs of moving supplies to manufacturing and processing plants and subsequently moving the finished product to the final customers or buyers.* Figure 11.1 shows how

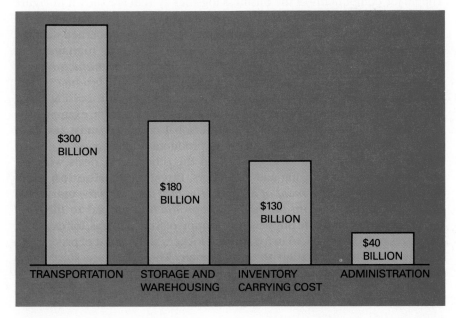

Figure 11.1

Estimated U.S. Logistics Expenditures (1982)

Source: A.T. Kearney, Inc. *Measuring and Improving Productivity in Physical Distribution* (Oak Brook, IL: National Council of Physical Distribution Management, 1984), p. 19.

A.T. Kearney, a major consulting firm, estimated logistics expenditures in the United States. The $650 billion estimate for logistics expenditures was 21 percent of U.S. gross national product in 1982.

Because the cost of logistics is so high, a firm's profitability can be heavily influenced by its ability to manage its logistical activities.[2] A country's ability to compete effectively in world markets is also based largely on the efficient performance of logistical activities. The Japanese are particularly good at worldwide sale of their products, not only because they produce quality goods, but also because they know how to market them effectively and manage logistical activities efficiently.

Logistical activities are important not only for marketers of tangible products but also for marketers of services because service marketers (such as hotels, hospitals, barber shops, and movie theaters) need supplies to operate their businesses. For example, a hospital needs linens, food, drugs, blood, toilet tissue, pens, detergent, and hundreds of other items on a daily basis in order to provide health care services.

This chapter introduces the physical distribution system and its management and then discusses the management of customer service activities as they relate to distribution. The Marketer Profile on Marnette Perry of Kroger illustrates how important physical distribution can be in getting fresh and attractive flowers to over 700 Kroger supermarkets. Perry emphasizes special handling and treatment from greenhouse to supermarket customers, and this attention to physical supply has helped to triple floral sales in two years.

WHAT IS BUSINESS LOGISTICS?

The major components of the business logistics system are shown in Figure 11.2. Business logistics is concerned with materials management and physical distribution management.[3] Materials management is concerned with the link between supply sources and manufacturing. **Materials management** is *the management of all activities that bring to the manufacturing or processing plant all the necessary supplies to produce a product.* Often, over 100 different kinds of items must be brought to a processing plant, which makes materials management a very complex task. For example, the plant that manufactures the Macintosh personal computer must regularly receive 300 different components for its production line.[4]

Physical distribution management, on the other hand, deals with the link between manufacturing and customers. **Physical distribution management** is *the management of all activities that deal with the movement of finished products from the end of the production process to the final consumer or buyer.* In the physical distribution of frozen pizzas, for example, the pizzas need to be stored in frozen food lockers at the point of production as they await transportation to a wholesaler. They are then stored in a refrigerated truck during transport; stored in a frozen food storage area at

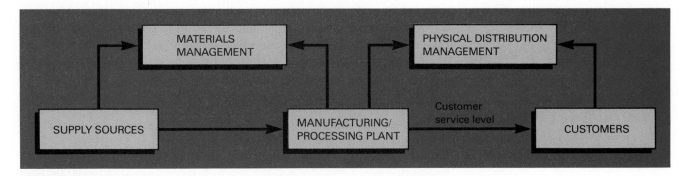

Figure 11.2
Scope of Business Logistics

the wholesaler's warehouse until they are needed for shipment to retail food stores such as Food Giant, Kroger, or Safeway; stored in a frozen food display case at these retail establishments; and finally, when the pizzas are purchased by consumers, they end up in the customer's freezer or oven.

The key decision areas in both materials management and in physical distribution management are (1) order processing, (2) materials handling, (3) warehousing, (4) inventory, and (5) transportation. Management must make these decisions to create **customer service**, which is *getting the right products to the right places at the right time.*

There are two important points about the business logistics system. First, both materials management and physical distribution management are primarily concerned with the same set of activities: order processing, materials handling, warehousing, inventory, and transportation. Materials management focuses on *input* coming into the manufacturing plant, whereas physical distribution focuses on *output* from the manufacturing plant. This process is shown in Figure 11.2. Second, marketing management is more concerned with physical distribution problems than it is with getting materials to the manufacturer because physical distribution decisions have a major impact on product demand and sales. Obviously, if a product arrives late, damaged, or in the wrong quantities or sizes, the present and future sales of the firm could be affected because of poor customer service. Predictably, customer service levels have a major impact on a firm's sales; thus, the customer service level is a key marketing decision.[5]

Because physical distribution activities influence customer service levels (and poor customer service levels will adversely impact sales), a firm must include customer service in the development of its marketing mixes. Often, an improvement in customer service caused by better performance of physical distribution activities can be as significant a factor as advertising or personal selling in stimulating demand and increasing customer loyalty.

WHAT IS THE PHYSICAL DISTRIBUTION SYSTEM?

Since marketing is our major concern in this book, we will concentrate on the physical distribution component of business logistics. We begin our discussion of physical distribution by viewing it as a system; that is, a set of interacting and interrelated elements that forms an entity. As we said before, the parts or components in physical distribution relate to transportation, materials handling, warehousing, order processing, and inventory. The collective performance of these activities will determine a firm's level of customer service. Also, a change in any of these activities will affect the others. This phenomenon is illustrated in Figure 11.3.

Key Components

Following are definitions of the five key components of the physical distribution system:

1. **Order processing** consists of *all activities performed to gather, check, and transmit sales orders.* Most of these activities are clerical.
2. **Materials handling** is *the actual physical handling of goods in a warehouse, retail store, or production facility.* Materials handling usually is facilitated with the aid of special materials handling equipment such as forklifts and mechanical conveyors.
3. **Warehousing** is *the placement of products in a storage facility to (1) store them, (2) consolidate them with other, similar products, (3) break them down into smaller quantities, or (4) build up assortments of products.*
4. **Inventory** consists of *the quantity of a product that is available to sell or use at any given time.*
5. **Transportation** is *the physical movement of goods by air, rail, water, truck, pipeline, or some combination of these from one geographic location to another.*

Key System Concepts

The physical distribution system rests on three premises.[6] First, *what is best for the entire company is more important than what is best for any subfunction or single activity.* In other words, **system objectives** are most important. Second, physical distribution activities have inherent **cost trade-offs;** that is, *things done to reduce the cost of one distribution activity may increase the cost of another distribution activity.* Third, one can have a **total cost orientation,** *minimizing total costs rather than the costs of a single distribution activity.* The manager knows that there are inherent cost tradeoffs, so he or she tries to balance the costs.[7] Let's examine each of these premises more closely.

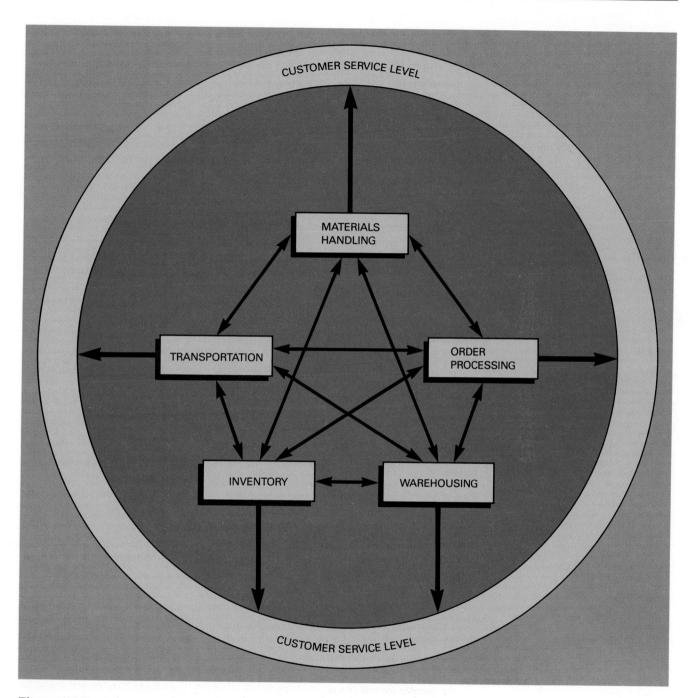

Figure 11.3

The Physical Distribution System

System Objectives. In a physical distribution system, the ideal system objective is to always get the right goods and services to the right places at the right times, at the lowest possible cost. However, as is the case with most things, the ideal is rarely achievable. It is possible to have 100 percent customer service accuracy, but the increased costs of transportation, warehousing, order processing, materials handling, and inventory would far outweigh the profitability of increased sales due to an increase in customer service. Therefore, the realistic system objective should be to increase customer service up to the point where marginal revenues generated from higher levels of customer service are equal to the marginal costs of providing them.

Cost Tradeoffs. Cost tradeoffs can best be explained with an illustration. Consider transportation costs for products such as typewriters, electronic calculators, and computer terminals. If the company shipping these products wants quick delivery to its customers, it can use air transportation, which will be quite expensive. On the other hand, if it can get by with slower delivery, it can use rail, which is cheaper. Next, consider the fact that the quicker a company can move its products to its customers, the less money it will need to invest in inventory, which will keep its inventory costs down. Figure 11.4 shows these conflicting cost curves. We can reduce inventory costs by increasing transportation costs or vice versa. These conflicting cost curves need to be balanced to arrive at the optimum lowest combined cost. In this hypothetical illustration, a mode of transportation with moderate speed, such as motor carrier, is suggested to achieve the lowest combined cost.

Total Cost Orientation. The preceding illustration leads up to the total cost concept by showing the interaction of transportation and inventory costs. However, the total cost concept is usually more complex because there are typically more than two conflicting cost curves. We saw that transportation costs rose as speed increased and inventory costs declined, but, in addition, materials handling and warehousing costs are affected. Materials handling costs for rail and motor are lower than those for air. Generally, because an airplane cannot land at a warehouse or plant, the products need to be put on a truck to be taken to the airport, removed from the truck and placed in some storage area at the airport, and finally, put in containers and placed on the airplane. This multiple handling is also necessary when the plane is unloaded and the product is delivered to the customer. On the other hand, warehousing costs would be lower with faster modes of transport because fewer warehouses would be needed. Often, managers want more warehouses so that the customer can be served more quickly. With air transport, however, the customer can be served quickly from long distances. These conflicting cost curves are shown in Figure 11.5. Figure 11.5 also shows that the lowest total cost is not where the low cost

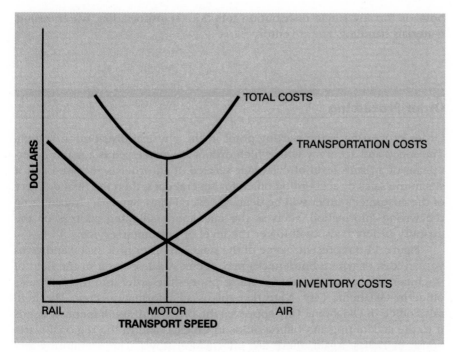

Figure 11.4
Cost Tradeoffs

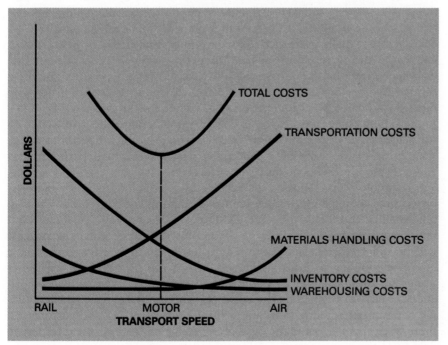

Figure 11.5
Total Cost Concept

point is for any single distribution function: transportation, warehousing, materials handling, and inventory.[8]

MANAGING PHYSICAL DISTRIBUTION ACTIVITIES

Order Processing

Order processing is the starting point in the physical distribution system. The speed and accuracy with which orders are processed is a major determinant of a firm's level of customer service. If an order is received and it sits in the sales or accounting office for several days, then the final delivery of the customer's order will be delayed several days. Similarly, transmitting the wrong information, such as the customer's shipping address or the quantity ordered, also will lower the level of customer service.

Figure 11.6 represents some of the stages in order processing and gives you an idea of where bottlenecks may occur. A salesperson in the field of Wichita makes a sale and, that evening, phones the order into the field sales office in Oklahoma City. Note that this is an information flow. The field sales office in Oklahoma City approves the order and simultaneously sends it to the accounting and billing office in Chicago and to the regional warehouse in Dallas. Again, these are information flows. The accounting and billing office checks the customer's credit, the prices, and the terms and keys into the computer to check if the merchandise is in the Dallas warehouse. When the go-ahead is given, the accounting and billing office notifies the warehouse to fill the order (another information flow). At this time, the Chicago office mails an invoice to the customer (another information flow), and when the warehouse finishes filling the order, it is shipped to the customer. Note that this is the only physical flow of the product and technically involves the transportation function and not the order processing function. A final step in order processing is when the customer sends money to the billing office in Chicago. Of course, not all companies go through all the stages in this example. Some have one or more of the facilities at the same location; the warehouse, field office, and accounting department may all be located in Dallas or some other large city.

Technology has a major impact on the speed and accuracy of order processing. For example, if a large central computer is located in the Chicago billing office and the salespeople, field sales office staff, and regional warehouse workers have terminals to access this computer, then the process will be quite efficient and rapid. The salesperson in Wichita could use a briefcase terminal to find out immediately if the products the customer wants are in stock in the warehouse. Furthermore, an immediate credit check could be obtained on the customer, and the warehouse and accounting department could be notified to fill the order and bill the customer. If there were any delays and the customer became concerned, the salesperson could use the computer to quickly locate the order in the system.

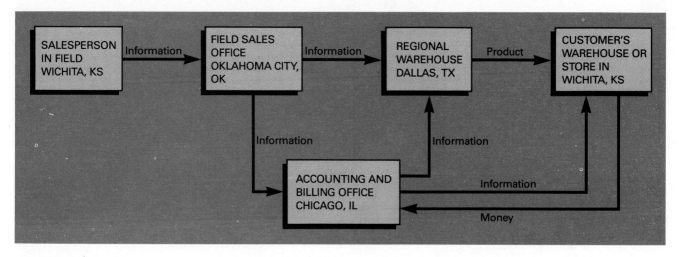

Figure 11.6
Order Processing Flows

Materials Handling

The type of equipment used is the major factor influencing time, effort, and money spent on materials handling. At one extreme, only manual labor is used to handle merchandise. For example, in a low technology warehouse, laborers pick up merchandise, carry it from the warehouse, and load it on a truck. With more advanced technology, the laborers could use electric forklifts to remove merchandise from the warehouse and load it into a truck trailer. At a high level of materials handling technology, a computer could be used to activate machines that select merchandise from racks, place it on conveyer belts, and automatically consolidate it into a shipment that is placed on a truck trailer.

Warehousing

Managers must make three major warehousing decisions: (1) how many warehouses to have, (2) where to locate them, and (3) whether the warehouse should be private or public.[9] When a firm has only one warehouse, all customers, regardless of their location, must be served from a single location. Therefore, on average, a firm with a single warehouse will take longer to get merchandise to customers than will a firm with several warehouses because customers will be located farther from the warehouse.

Materials handling can be as basic as a reliance on manual labor or as advanced as this highly automated system marketed by Rapistan.

Transportation costs from the manufacturer to the warehouse will tend to be lower, however, because bulk shipments can be made from the manufacturing plant to the single warehouse rather than smaller shipments being made to multiple warehouses. On the other hand, transportation costs from warehouse to customer will decline as the number of warehouses increases because customers, on average, will be located closer to a warehouse. Inventory costs will be lower because duplication will be avoided by having everything in a single warehouse. The optimum number of warehouses, of course, depends on these types of cost tradeoffs.

Once a firm's managers decide how many warehouses to have, they must choose the best location for them. In principle, the location of warehouses should be based on demand and cost considerations. Demand is important because the firm must consider where present and future customers are located geographically. The higher the density of demand in a given area, the closer a warehouse should be to that area. Cost is important because warehouse-related costs, such as labor, utilities, insurance, taxes, and building costs, vary by region of the country and size of the city. Computer software programs are available to help managers determine warehouse locations by analyzing these demand and cost factors.[10]

The decision about whether to use a private or public warehouse is important. A **private warehouse** is *a storage facility that a firm owns or leases and uses exclusively for its products.* The firm must incur an initial fixed investment to purchase the warehouse or sign a long-term lease (often 10 to 20 years). Also, the firm will have a relatively high level of fixed costs regardless of how much volume is put through the warehouse. It will need to pay rent or taxes on the facility and make insurance and maintenance payments even if the warehouse sits half empty. On the other hand, a private warehouse can be tailored to the firm's specific needs. For instance, racks and aisles can be designed to fit the dimensions the firm desires for ease of handling merchandise.

As stated in Chapter 10, a **public warehouse** *is an independently* *owned and operated storage facility that stores goods for a fee.* Thus, a firm using a public warehouse has no initial investment and can rent only the space it needs. If volume goes up or down, it can quickly and easily adjust its warehousing needs. Also, a firm using a public warehouse does not need to worry about the day-to-day problems of operating and managing a warehouse. On the negative side, the firm has no control over the design and layout of the facility and, if the firm is moving a large volume of merchandise, the cost may actually be higher than if it had a private warehouse.

Inventory

Inventory decisions are critical to the success of manufacturing, wholesaling, and retailing organizations, largely because inventory represents a significant portion of the firm's investment, typically between 30 and 50 percent of total assets. Therefore, any major error in inventory management will dramatically affect the firm's profitability because customer service and, thus, sales and costs will be affected.

Customer service is directly affected by inventory investment. As a firm invests more in inventory (thereby increasing the number of units in stock), the probability that an item will be out of stock decreases. For example, the Acme Sewing Machine Company wants to be able to fill 85 percent of its orders from existing stock. To do this, it will need an inventory investment of $200,000. Now, if Acme wants to increase the customer service level to 90 percent, inventory investment must rise to $250,000; a 95 percent customer service level requires an inventory investment of $350,000. What we see here is that inventory investment increases at an increasing rate as the customer service level approaches 100 percent (Figure 11.7). Obviously, maintaining a 100 percent service level would be unprofitable, in all likelihood because of the exponential growth required in inventory investment. The firm must establish some standard level of customer service, however, which requires a knowledge of the costs of maintaining different inventory levels and how sales (demand) respond to higher service levels.

Major inventory decisions involve the quantity to order and the frequency of the orders. A firm could decide to order only once a year, which would entail a large quantity and high average inventory investment. In this situation, inventory ordering costs would be low (only 1 order would need to be placed annually), but inventory carrying costs would be high. **Inventory carrying cost** is *the expense of holding inventory, including the costs of space, capital, insurance, and spoilage or obsolescence.* In U.S. firms, annual inventory carrying cost is estimated to be 20 to 25 percent of the value of the inventory. That is, if a firm has $1,000,000 in inventory, it costs $200,000 to $250,000 to carry or hold that inventory for a one-year period.[11]

At the other extreme, a firm could order daily. This policy would result in a relatively small order quantity and a low average inventory investment. With this alternative, inventory ordering costs would be high (365 orders

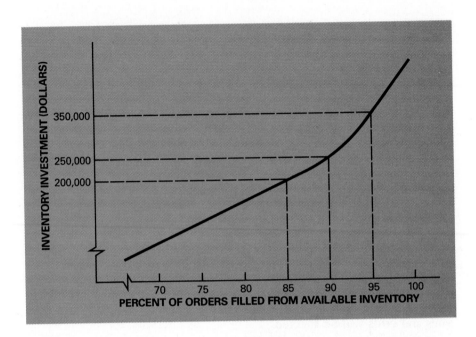

Figure 11.7
Customer Service and Inventory
Investment

would need to be placed annually), but inventory carrying costs would be low.

As you can see from the preceding discussion, inventory ordering costs and inventory carrying costs move in opposite directions as order quantity increases. These cost curves, illustrated in Figure 11.8, are the basis of an economic order quantity (EOQ) approach to inventory management. The **economic order quantity** is *the amount to order that will minimize the sum of inventory ordering costs and inventory carrying costs.* A numerical example is developed in Figure 11.9 to help illustrate this point. If you were this firm's manager, which alternative would you choose?

Transportation Modes

The five most popular modes of transportation are rail, truck, air, water, and pipeline. For any given product, not all of these alternatives will be available or capable of being used. Many firms and individuals are not located near waterways, and pipelines cannot be used to move many types of products.

Rail. Railroads usually are used for long hauls (over 500 miles) and travel at low average speeds (between 20–25 and 40–60 miles per hour). The U.S. rail network is extensive; most firms are within twenty-five miles of a major rail line. In fact, many companies locate their manufacturing plants and warehouses next to railroad tracks so that they can have a rail spur come right up to, or into, a building. For example, the Oldsmobile produc-

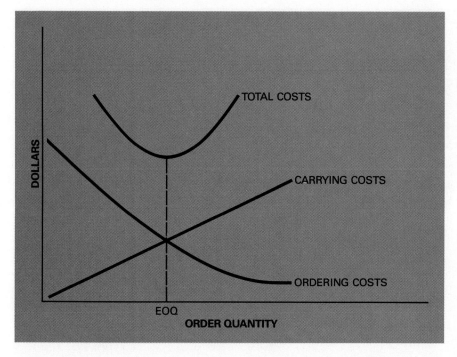

Figure 11.8
Economic Order Quantity (EOQ)

tion plant in Lansing, Michigan, moves new cars directly from the assembly line onto railcars of the Grand Trunk Western Railroad Co.[12]

Rail service is best suited for large shipments. Rates are either carload or less-than-carload. The carload rate is substantially lower than the less-than-carload rate because carload quantities require substantially less handling. High-value freight is moved increasingly by rail piggyback service—trailers or containers on flatcars. Overall, rail is a relatively moderately priced form of transportation. Products commonly shipped by rail include raw materials, such as iron, coal, and scrap steel; low valued manufactured products, such as canned food and laundry detergent; and an increasing number of automobiles. Thus, rail is capable of handling a wide variety of products.

Truck. Trucks can be used efficiently for either short or long hauls, but the average haul for trucks is shorter than that for trains. Trucks are a convenient and relatively rapid mode of transportation. They travel at a much higher average speed than do trains. Because of our extensive highway system, trucks are pervasive in the United States. In addition, they offer door-to-door service and frequent scheduling. Shipping by truck, however, is more expensive than shipping by rail. Products shipped by truck include finished and semifinished goods, such as clothing, books, automotive accessories, and fabricated metalwork. Trucks handle the widest variety of products.

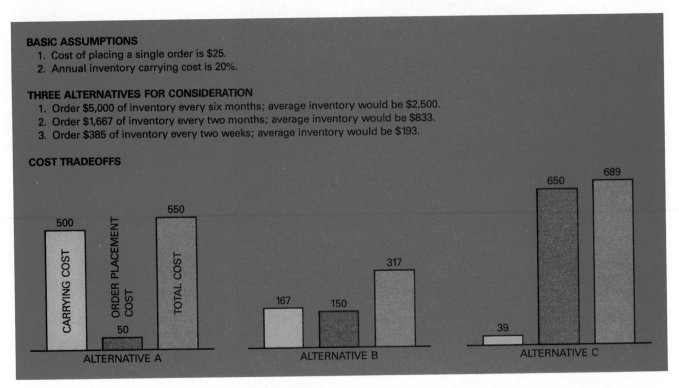

BASIC ASSUMPTIONS
1. Cost of placing a single order is $25.
2. Annual inventory carrying cost is 20%.

THREE ALTERNATIVES FOR CONSIDERATION
1. Order $5,000 of inventory every six months; average inventory would be $2,500.
2. Order $1,667 of inventory every two months; average inventory would be $833.
3. Order $385 of inventory every two weeks; average inventory would be $193.

COST TRADEOFFS

Figure 11.9
A Numerical Example of Inventory Cost Tradeoffs in Assessing Order Quantity

Air. Air transport is the fastest and most expensive mode of transportation. The average speed of an airplane is five to ten times that of a truck. When something is shipped by air, however, the shipment first needs to be placed on a truck and taken to the airport, since airports are widely scattered and thus are not as highly accessible as trucks and railroads. Once the plane reaches its destination, the product again must be transported by truck to the customer. Thus, although air transportation is quick, additional time and money are spent on this extra handling. A well-run trucking operation can sometimes beat the total time it takes for air transportation because delays caused by double handling of the product can be avoided. Products shipped by air are of highest value or highly perishable. Examples include highly technical scientific instruments, orchids, and lobsters.

Water. Water transportation is relatively cheap but extremely slow. Also, waterways are not widely accessible; a firm usually needs to use rail or truck first to move the product to the waterway.

The availability and dependability of water transportation are heavily influenced by weather conditions. The Great Lakes and St. Lawrence River can freeze in the winter months, and floods can make rivers hazardous.

Versatile, moderately priced, and well-suited for large shipments, freight railroads are a popular transportation mode.

Ocean-going vessels are also subject to severe weather fluctuations. Waterways are most often used for bulky raw materials of low unit value, such as crude oil, coal, and minerals.

Pipelines. Pipeline transportation is limited to products that are in a liquid or gaseous state. Movement of products by pipeline is relatively slow, but since the products can be moved around the clock, seven days a week, the transit time can be quicker than rail and water. Pipeline transportation also has the advantage of being relatively low in cost and extremely low in product damage and theft. Pipelines are not present everywhere, and thus their accessibility is low. They are best suited for moving petroleum products; however, there has been some experimentation with moving solid products, such as coal, in a liquid called "slurry" or in cylinders that move through a liquid.[13]

Comparison of Modes. Figure 11.10 compares the five transportation modes in terms of five performance attributes: cost, time, reliability (the

Yellow Freight stresses a teamwork approach to helping their customers distribute their products.

ability to deliver a shipment on time), accessibility (the nearness of the mode to the typical shipper), and potential for damage and theft. Note that no single transportation mode performs best *or* worst in all performance categories.

Intermodal Transportation. **Intermodal transportation**, *using two or more modes to transport a product,* is often used for international shipments. A shipment of General Electric household appliances destined for Saudi Arabia may move by rail, water, and truck on the long journey. During this process, the appliances would be loaded and unloaded and possibly repackaged several times as transport modes were changed. Predictably, this process is quite expensive.

Intermodal transportation has become more feasible since containers

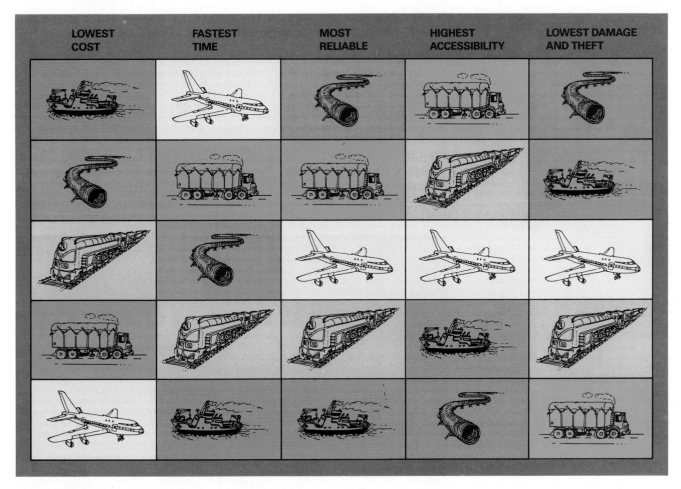

Figure 11.10

Transportation Modes Compared by Attribute Performance[a]

[a]Ranked best to worst (from top to bottom) by each attribute.

became popular in the 1960s. Containers are standard-size metal boxes in which products are placed and then sealed. These containers can then be transferred quickly and easily from one transportation mode to another. For example, a container can be lifted from a truck into the cargo bay of an airplane or placed on a ship or into a railcar. Not only does this method reduce labor and handling costs, but it also cuts down on thefts of merchandise in transit.

Intermodal transportation can also be made more efficient when truck trailers that contain merchandise are simply loaded onto rail flatcars, barges, or ships. For example, Alaska Hydro-Train is capable of transporting truck trailers and rail cars on their barges that travel from Seattle to Alaska.

The following terms are used most frequently to refer to the intermodal transport modes when the shipment remains in the same container:

1. *Piggyback*: a truck to rail transfer of containers.
2. *Fishyback*: a truck to ship transfer of containers.
3. *Birdyback*: a truck to airplane transfer of containers.

The Marketing in Action on page 351 shows how one transportation company has made intermodal transportation a major strategic orientation.

Freight Forwarders. A freight forwarder is not one of the five basic transport modes. Essentially, *freight forwarders* are wholesalers of transportation services. They make a profit by purchasing transportation services at low, large-shipment rates from companies in the rail, motor, water, pipe-

With the introduction of containers, intermodal transportation has become much more efficient.

MARKETING IN ACTION

CSX Moves into Supertransportation

For many years, when a company needed to move goods from one point to another, it had several distinct transportation choices: rail, truck, pipeline, air, or water. Today, there is another choice—supertransportation, an intermodal company that custom blends the means of transportation to fit the customer's needs. One such supertransportation company is CSX, a merger of two railroads, Seaboard Coast Line and the Chessie System.

Through its subsidiary companies, CSX can provide truck, piggyback (long-distance hauling of loaded truck trailers by rail), air, and water transport for its customers. Other rail and transport companies are moving into intermodal transportation, but not all of them to the extent or with the success of CSX.

No one knows whether the supertransportation companies are the wave of the future. As John Snow, senior vice president of CSX, stated in a recent interview, "The advantages of a supertransportation company are not overwhelming, but they're more than minimal."

Sources: Based on Peter Brimelow, "Where Those Hybrid Haulers Are Headed," *Fortune* (March 19, 1984), pp. 114–120; and CSX advertisements.

line, or air freight business and combining the shipments of many small shippers into a large shipment for which they charge a higher rate. Freight forwarders are advantageous to firms because they frequently can provide faster service, since large shipments move more quickly than small shipments. It is estimated that freight forwarders handle over 20 million shipments annually in the United States.[14] Some companies are heavy users of freight forwarders; for example, GTE Service Corp. spends approximately $9 million annually with air freight forwarders. Incidentally, GTE has a twelve-person transportation committee that regularly conducts evaluations of freight forwarders on two key factors—service quality and price.[15]

At several points in this chapter, we have discussed customer service, which we described as getting the right goods to the right places at the right time. To manage customer service effectively, a firm must be able to identify the types of things that satisfy customers.[16] Table 11.1 lists seven key components of customer service.

MANAGING CUSTOMER SERVICE ACTIVITIES

Customer Service Components

Product Availability. Having the product available when the customer desires it is an important component of customer service. When the product is not available, the customer may decide to buy elsewhere or buy something else. The major determinant of product availability is inventory investment:

Table 11.1   Customer Service Components

* Product availability	* Damaged goods
* Order cycle time	* Special handling
* Response time	* Consistency
* Error rate	

---

the bigger the investment in inventory, the greater the probability the product will be available and the higher the level of customer service. Firms should establish a specific target level of performance for product availability. For example, most grocery wholesalers have a target performance of filling 95 percent of orders from stock on hand.

In deciding to set standards on product availability, many manufacturers and wholesalers conduct an ABC inventory analysis. An **ABC inventory analysis** *divides the firm's products into three groups based on sales volume: A items are the most frequently sold and get the highest customer service; B items have a moderate sales rate and get moderate customer service; and C items sell slowly and get low customer service.* Figure 11.11 provides an example for Beta Bearings (a hypothetical wholesaler of industrial bearings). Twenty percent of the bearings are classified as A items, and they account for 80 percent of total sales. Management has established a goal of filling 99 percent of the A-item orders. Next, we see that 60 percent of the bearings are classified as B items, and they account for 15 percent of total sales. Management has established a goal of filling 95 percent of the orders for these bearings. Finally, the C items account for 20 percent of bearings but only generate 5 percent of total sales. The goal established for C items is an 80 percent order fill rate.

Order Cycle Time.   The time that elapses between when the customer places an order and the merchandise is received is called order cycle time. The shorter the order cycle time, the higher the level of customer service. Order cycle time will be influenced most heavily by the type of order processing system and the transport mode(s) used for shipping products to customers. Again, firms need to establish standards of performance for order cycle time. For example, many grocery wholesalers want an order cycle time of forty-eight hours or less for 98 percent of orders.

Response Time.   The time it takes the firm to answer a customer inquiry about the status of an order is called response time. Often, if an order is late in arriving, a customer will telephone to inquire about the nature of the problem. A firm should establish a response time standard, since a prompt response to these inquiries results in a higher level of customer service. A retailer gets extremely disturbed when a shipment does not arrive

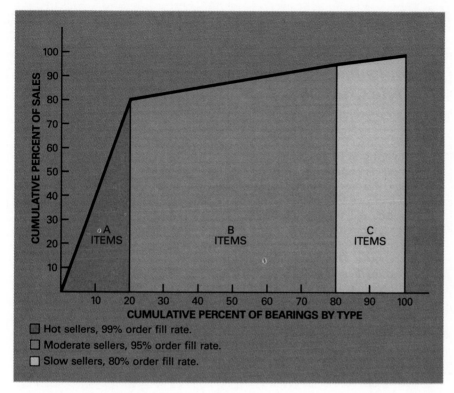

Hot sellers, 99% order fill rate.
Moderate sellers, 95% order fill rate.
Slow sellers, 80% order fill rate.

Figure 11.11

Beta Bearings, Inc.: ABC Inventory
Analysis

on time and when the manufacturer can provide no reasonable explanation
for the delay.

Error Rate.   Error rate is the number or percent of shipments that include
the wrong items or the wrong quantities or are shipped to the wrong
address. All of these errors contribute to poor customer service. Customers
are often more disturbed at receiving the wrong items or improper quantities than at not receiving the item at all. Error rates usually are due to
clerical mistakes or theft or to not having the right items in stock and
shipping a substitute without getting the customer's prior approval.

Damaged Goods.   When damaged merchandise is delivered to the customer, the customer is unhappy and the firm must make a price adjustment
on the goods or ship them back to the warehouse or factory to be repaired.
Damage can occur in transit if the items are not properly packed and handled, but damage can also occur in the firm's warehouse if materials handling
personnel are improperly trained. The Marketing in Action on page 354
illustrates how Nabisco is reducing damaged goods through their automated
warehouses.

MARKETING IN ACTION

That's the Way the Cookie Crumbles . . . Except at Nabisco

Delivering fresh, undamaged goods is imperative in the cookie and cracker business. In an effort to improve its customer service, Nabisco recently installed a computer-operated automated storage and retrieval system in its Chicago warehouse. The warehouse's old system involved moving the 250 different products handled at this distribution center by forklift. The forklifts damaged the goods, and the constant shifting of inventory from one place to another made inventory control difficult.

The new system, designed by Harnischferger Corporation's P&H Division, consists of conveyors, distribution spurs with high-rise storage areas, and aisle cranes to place and retrieve the merchandise. The entire operation (including the billing and inventory functions) is controlled by two computers that make sure that the cookies and crackers leave the warehouse in the right order (first in, first out) and with minimal damage.

Source: Based on Joanna Callas. "Automated Warehouse Systems: A System that Keeps the Cookies from Crumbling," *Traffic Management* (August 1984), p. 85. Used by permission.

Special Handling. If the company can provide any special handling services, then customer service will be increased. Some special handling services include (1) expedited shipments, (2) shipping one order to several locations, (3) last minute add-ons to the order, (4) special packaging of the product, and (5) premarking the price on the product at the warehouse or factory. For example, Converse's "at once" distribution system allows them to offer retailers expedited shipments, sometimes with an order cycle time of twenty-four to forty-eight hours.[17]

Consistency. Each of the six preceding components of customer service have an average performance level as well as variability in performance. The less variability there is, the greater the consistency of performance and the higher the level of customer service. As an example, consider a bicycle wholesaler whose average order cycle time is ten days: half the time it takes four days, and half the time it takes sixteen days to fill an order. With this low level of consistency, bicycle retailers are unable to plan their orders. They probably would be much happier with a consistent order cycle time of twelve days than an average time of ten days with a high degree of inconsistency or variability.

Setting Standards

There are no precise techniques to determine customer service standards, but most physical distribution and marketing executives suggest considering three things. First, the managers should consider customer needs and preferences, and thus they must know their target market. What do customers want, and what do they expect in terms of reasonable customer service? Next, consideration should be given to the level of customer service offered by competitors. If a firm wants to use customer service as a marketing tool to differentiate itself in the competitive marketplace, then standards should be set higher than those of competitors. Finally, managers must look carefully at the cost of customer service. No firm can always have the right product in the right place at the right time, because to do so would drive the company into bankruptcy. An increase in customer service can be quite costly, and the firm must weigh this cost against the expected increase in sales resulting from higher service levels.[18]

SUMMARY

This chapter introduced the business logistics system, which consists of materials management and physical distribution management. Materials management is concerned with the management of all activities that bring to the manufacturing or processing plant all the necessary supplies to produce a product. On the other hand, physical distribution management is the management of all activities that deal with the movement of finished products from the manufacturer to the final consumer or buyer. The system should have a customer service objective, and the system's management should adopt a total cost orientation that weighs the cost tradeoffs among the different physical distribution activities. Physical distribution consists of the following interrelated activities: (1) order processing, (2) materials handling, (3) warehousing, (4) inventory, (5) transportation.

Physical distribution activities have a major impact on customer service. Customer service is getting the right goods to the right places at the right time. The seven key components of customer service are product availability, order cycle time, response time, error rate, damaged goods, special handling services, and the consistency of performance on the prior six components. When setting standards of performance for customer service, a manager should consider customer needs and preferences, the level of customer service offered by competitors, and the costs of performing the services.

KEY CONCEPTS

logistical costs (p. 333)
materials management (p. 334)

physical distribution management (p. 334)

REVIEW AND DISCUSSION QUESTIONS

1. What is the difference between materials management and physical distribution management?
2. Why should physical distribution be viewed as a system?
3. What does physical distribution management have to do with marketing management?
4. Explain the total cost concept of physical distribution.
5. How can computers be used to speed up and make the order processing activity more accurate?
6. What are the cost tradeoffs in deciding the optimal number of warehouses?
7. Contrast the advantages and disadvantages of public and private warehouses.
8. What cost tradeoffs are involved in determining the economic order quantity?
9. What are the relative advantages and disadvantages of the five different transportation modes?
10. What are the key components of a firm's customer service?
11. How should managers determine a firm's customer service level?

ACTION PROBLEMS

1. Imagine that you are a physical distribution executive and you have been asked to address the annual convention of the American Medical Association on the topic of physical distribution considerations in the growing organ transplant (e.g., kidneys, livers, hearts) industry. Prepare a two- to three-page detailed outline of your planned presentation.
2. As director of distribution for Pillsbury, you are planning to add another warehouse location to your current distribution system, but you are not sure whether to use a private or public warehouse. Based on the discussion of warehousing in this chapter, choose one side or the other and try to construct a graph that will illustrate your point of view.
3. You are the sole owner of a small wholesale firm specializing in American Indian pottery, baskets, rugs, and other arts and crafts. The firm sells to 170 gift shops in twenty-four states—mostly in the Midwest and on the Eastern seaboard. Your average sale is for nine items with a wholesale price of $1,400, and your firm's

cost is $1,000. You have been shipping by United Parcel, and the typical order takes five to eight days for delivery. Your firm pays the freight on all orders over $1,000. The freight on a $1,400 order is usually $20 to $25. You are considering switching to air freight, which would speed up delivery to 24 hours for 95 percent of the orders but would triple your freight charges. Develop a list and explanation of other factors that should be examined in helping you decide whether or not to switch to air freight.

NOTES

1. Douglas M. Lambert and H.M. Armitage, "Managing Distribution Costs for Better Profit Performance," *Business* (September–October 1980), pp. 46–52.

2. David P. Herron, "Managing Physical Distribution for Profit," *Harvard Business Review* (May–June 1979), pp. 121–132.

3. A comprehensive guide to physical distribution is James F. Robeson and Robert G. House (eds.), *The Distribution Handbook* (New York: The Free Press, 1985).

4. "Getting the Case for These Apples Used to be the Pits," *Distribution* (January 1985), p. 20.

5. Bernard J. LaLonde and Paul H. Zinszer, *Customer Service: Meaning and Measurement* (Chicago: National Council of Physical Distribution Management, 1976).

6. Louis W. Stern and Adel I. El-Ansary, *Marketing Channels,* 2nd edition (Englewood Cliffs, NJ: Prentice Hall, 1982), pp. 156–160.

7. Surprisingly, most distribution managers don't have accurate cost data that allow them to make these tradeoffs, see Douglas M. Lambert and John T. Mentzer, "Is Integrated Physical Distribution Management a Reality?" *Journal of Business Logistics* 2(2, 1980), pp. 18–34.

8. When and how to use the total cost approach to distribution is discussed in Raymond Le Kashman and John F. Stolle, "The Total Cost Approach to Distribution," *Business Horizons* (Winter 1965), pp. 33–46.

9. There are also many decisions regarding the internal operation of a warehouse. For more information, see Kenneth B. Ackerman and Bernard J. La Londe, "Making Warehousing More Efficient," *Harvard Business Review* (March–April 1980), pp. 95–102.

10. William L. Berry and D. Clay Whybark, *Computer Augmented Cases in Operations and Logistics Management* (Cincinnati, OH: Southwestern Publishing Co., 1972); Ronald Ballou, "Dynamic Warehouse Location Analysis," *Journal of Marketing Research* 5(August 1968), pp. 271–276.

11. Inventory carrying costs are further discussed in Bernard J. La Londe and Douglas M. Lambert, "Inventory Carrying Costs: Significance, Components, Means, Functions," *International Journal of Physical Distribution* (Spring 1973), pp. 51–64.

12. "Place to 'Park' That's Cheap, Fast, and Safe!" *Distribution* (January 1985), pp. 16–17.

13. Ronald A. Ballou, *Basic Business Logistics* (Englewood Cliffs, NJ: Prentice-Hall, 1978), p. 143.

14. This section is based on Douglas M. Lambert and James R. Stock, *Strategic Physical Distribution Management* (Homewood, IL: Richard D. Irwin, 1982), p. 113.

15. "How GTE Selects its Airfreight Forwarders," *Traffic Management* (November 1984), pp. 62–63.

16. William D. Perreault and Frederick A. Russ, "Physical Distribution Service in Industrial Purchase Decisions," *Journal of Marketing* (April 1976), pp. 3–10; Douglas M. Lambert

and James R. Stock, "Physical Distribution and Consumer Demands," *MSU Business Topics* (Spring 1978), pp. 49–56; Harvey N. Shycon and Christopher R. Sprague, "Put a Price Tag on Your Customer Servicing Levels," *Harvard Business Review* (July–August 1979), pp. 71–78.

17. Al Urbanski, "Converse Breaks into a Run," *Sales & Marketing Management* (December 5, 1983), pp. 41–42.

18. A method for determining the optimal customer service levels using data on customer preferences and the cost of service levels is developed in Michael Levy, "Toward an Optimal Customer Service Package," *Journal of Business Logistics* 2(March 1981), pp. 87–109.

LEARNING OBJECTIVES

After you complete this chapter, you should be able to:

- **List** and **define** the common types of retailing and wholesaling

- **Discuss** how retailers can be categorized and explain how this influences marketing strategy

- **Identify** the factors that influence how a consumer perceives a retailer's in-store environment

- **Use** the wheel of retailing and retail life cycle theories to **explain** how retail competition evolves

- **Discuss** how manufacturers should select wholesalers

- **Explain** why manufacturers offer wholesalers assistances and the types of assistances offered

RETAIL AND WHOLESALE INSTITUTIONS

MARKETER PROFILE

Leslie H. Wexner of The Limited, Inc.

In 1963, Leslie H. Wexner founded The Limited Stores in Columbus, Ohio. His objective was to develop a retail store that appealed to the career-oriented upscale woman aged 18 to 35 years. The store he had in mind would offer quality fashion at a good value for the tastes and lifestyles of this target market. The stores would have about 5,000 square feet of selling area, and the fixtures and atmosphere would be designed to appeal to his target market. Wexner designed his store by applying basic marketing principles.

Almost from the start, the concept for The Limited proved successful. Four years after the firm's inception, there were four stores and sales exceeded $1 million. Ten years later, in 1978, sales were in excess of $200 million, with over 200 stores located throughout the United States, mostly in large regional shopping malls.

Leslie Wexner, an incipient workaholic, was still not satisfied. He dreamed of having sales of $1 billion. To help accomplish this, he steered The Limited, Inc., in the direction of acquiring other retail enterprises. In addition, Wexner began experimenting with some of his own new retail prototypes. These activities paid off: by the end of 1982, The Limited, Inc., had annual sales of $721 million and net profits (after taxes) of $34 million. By year-end 1985, the Wexner empire consisted of:

- 489 Limited stores in 125 major markets throughout the United States.

- 30 Limited Express stores; these stores offer a unique assortment of popular-priced sportswear and accessories designed to appeal primarily to fashion-forward women 15 to 25 years of age. These stores are located in regional shopping centers in the Midwest and California.

- 222 Lane Bryant stores in major markets throughout the United States. Lane Bryant is the nation's foremost retailer of women's special-size apparel. Lane Bryant stores specialize in the sale of medium-priced fashions designed to appeal to the special-size woman, with particular emphasis on those over 25 years of age.

- 78 Sizes Unlimited stores, which are mostly located in smaller shopping centers throughout the East and Midwest. Sizes Unlimited is an off-price retailer of women's special-size apparel focusing primarily on women 25 to 50 years of age. These stores offer nationally known brands and private label merchandise priced below similar grades in most department and specialty stores.

- 86 Victoria's Secret stores, most located in regional shopping centers. These stores specialize in the sale of European and American designer lingerie, and their target market is the fashionable contemporary woman, although gifts purchased by men account for a significant portion of the company's sales.

- Brylane Mail Order Division, which is the nation's largest catalog retailer of women's special-size apparel and shoes. Brylane is the third largest catalog retailer of all sizes of women's apparel and shoes.

- Mast Industries, which is a large, international supplier of moderately-priced apparel for fashion-conscious women. Mast employs a worldwide network of 150 contract production facilities, producing merchandise to special order principally for operating divisions of The Limited.

Source: Various annual reports of The Limited, Inc., from 1968 to 1985. Descriptions of lines of business are from the 1982 and 1985 annual reports.

INTRODUCTION

Managers of retail stores must develop marketing strategies, as the marketer profile of Leslie H. Wexner of The Limited, Inc. illustrates. Wexner had to identify a target market and develop an appropriate marketing mix for the Limited and the other retail enterprises in his empire, such as Sizes Unlimited and Victoria's Secret. In this chapter, we will present some concepts and principles of retail marketing, which is the type of marketing you observe most frequently in your daily activities. We will discuss the most popular types of retailing in the United States, how retailers make decisions based on the number of outlets, margins, turnover, store location, and store atmosphere. The evolution of retailing is discussed through the introduction of two opposing theories.

This chapter will also introduce wholesale marketing. Wholesaling is probably the marketing institution you are most unfamiliar with, although it is actually larger in magnitude than retailing. We will describe the structure of wholesaling in our economy and also discuss how manufacturers can market their products more effectively through wholesalers.

Any firm that *sells products to the final consumer* is engaged in **retailing**, regardless of whether the firm sells to the consumer in a store, through the mail, over the telephone, door to door, or through a vending machine. We can assess the magnitude of retailing by referring to the most recently published *Census of Retail Trade.* The U.S. Department of Commerce conducts the census of retailing every five years, in the years ending in two and seven (and releases the data about 2 years later). In 1982, there were 1.9 million retail establishments in the United States, or 230 retail establishments for every 10,000 households. These establishments typically were not mom and pop operated stores, as evidenced by their average annual sales volume of $554,000. These statistics are an average of all forms of retailing. To get a clearer perspective, look at Table 12.1, which provides statistics for some popular lines of retail trade. A careful study of this table shows that retailing is a major economic factor in the U.S. economy.

RETAILING IN THE U.S. ECONOMY

Some Popular Types of U.S. Retailing

Before we delve further into our discussion of retailing, you may want to refer back to the discussions of product mix, product line, and the breadth and depth of products in Chapter 8.

Department Stores. A **department store** is *a large-scale retail organization with a broad product mix consisting of many different product lines with above-average depth in each of them.*[1] Department stores are generally over 50,000 square feet, and some of the largest ones are over 500,000 square feet (for example, Marshall Field's store in downtown Chicago). Related product lines are merchandised in separate departments (menswear, womenswear, toys, sporting goods, home furnishings, furniture, and so on). Department stores have many customer services, such as knowledgeable and helpful sales clerks, delivery and wrapping services, liberal return policies, and store credit cards.

A *department store with a strong price emphasis* is called a **discount department store**. Because of their low prices, these stores tend to have few customer services and are usually self-service in nature. Examples include Target, Wal-Mart, and K mart. Discount department stores are usually 50,000 to 80,000 square feet. Most communities with a population over 10,000 have either a conventional department store or a discount department store.

Table 12.1   Size Characteristics of Selected Lines of Retail Trade

Retail Line of Trade	Number of Establishments with Payroll	Sales per Establishment	Establishments per 10,000 Households
Hardware stores	19,870	$ 419,481	2.4
Department stores	9,981	$10,736,684	1.2
Variety stores	10,989	$ 736,210	1.3
Grocery stores	128,494	$ 1,763,577	15.4
Auto dealers (new and used)	27,178	$ 5,693,079	3.3
Auto dealers (used)	11,421	$ 549,255	1.4
Gasoline stations	116,188	$ 815,219	14.0
Woman's ready-to-wear stores	44,163	$ 458,504	5.3
Shoe stores	36,277	$ 310,814	4.4
Furniture stores	29,609	$ 581,693	3.6

Source: *1982 Census of Retail Trade* and authors' computations.

Specialty Stores.   A **specialty store** is *a relatively small-scale retail establishment with a narrow assortment of merchandise but high depth in the lines carried.* Specialty stores are common in womenswear, menswear, jewelry, shoes, sporting goods, painting supplies, flowers, liquor, pets, bridalwear, and fabrics. Most specialty stores range from 3,000 to 7,500 square feet. Some popular specialty stores are Docktor Pet Center (pets and pet care supplies), County Seat (men's and women's leisure wear), Hickory

With over 800 stores and sales in excess of $30 billion, Sears is the largest retailer in the U.S. retail economy.

Farms (specialty cheeses and snacks), and Athlete's Foot (jogging and athletic shoes).

Most successful specialty stores pursue a strong store positioning strategy, in which all elements of a store appeal to a well-defined market segment based on demographic or life-style variables. For example, Standard Brands Paint Company is a specialty retailer with approximately 100 Standard Brands Paint and Home Decorating Centers in the western United States. These stores cater to the home decorating market segment; prices are 10 to 15 percent below competitor prices, which has great appeal to the do-it-yourself home remodeler. In addition, "employees at Standard Brands Paint and Home Decorating Centers are carefully trained to keep current on trends and new products and to provide assistance to the do-it-yourselfer."[2]

Supermarkets.   The supermarket concept of retailing was first developed in the 1930s, when the economic depression forced entrepreneurs to look for new ways to offer consumers lower prices. On August 30, 1932, Michael Cullen opened the first supermarket in Jamaica, New York, and by 1933, he had fifteen stores in the Long Island area.[3] Selling groceries through large-scale physical facilities with self-service and self-selection displays seemed like a good idea. These large-scale self-service food stores offered strong competition for the traditional mom and pop corner grocery. Today, most grocery retailing is done through supermarkets such as Food Giant, A & P, Safeway, and Kroger.

The **supermarket concept** *involves five basic principles* directed at improving retail productivity and reducing the cost of distribution[4]:

1. *Self-service and self-selection displays.*
2. *Centralization of customer services,* usually at the checkout counter.
3. *Large-scale, low-cost physical facilities.*
4. *A strong price emphasis.*
5. *A broad assortment of merchandise to facilitate multiple-item purchases.*

The supermarket retailing concept has been applied to many nonfood lines, such as toys (Toys "R" Us), sporting goods (Oshman's), and hardware (Scotty's Home Improvement Centers). Each of these stores has over 30,000 square feet and generates annual sales of over $4 million.

In addition to expanding the supermarket concept to include new types of stores, the traditional food supermarket is being expanded to market nonfood items such as clothing, small appliances, automotive supplies, nonprescription drugs, and cosmetics and fragrances, as is illustrated in the Marketing in Action on page 364. This phenomenon is referred to as scrambled merchandising. **Scrambled merchandising** is *the handling of merchandise lines based solely on the profitability criterion and without regard to the consistency of the product or merchandise mix. This results in unrelated lines of merchandise being carried by a single retailer (i.e.,*

MARKETING IN ACTION

Supermarkets Increase Market Share in Cosmetics

As women become more career oriented and time constrained, they are demanding more convenience in shopping. They don't want to make a special trip to a department store or specialty store to purchase cosmetics, and supermarkets are becoming a common outlet for cosmetics and fragrances. From 1978 to 1982, retail sales of cosmetics in supermarkets zoomed from $40.4 million to $137.3 million. Consider some examples of this broader distribution:

- **Tom Thumb supermarkets in Dallas stock such high-priced fragrances as Chloe and Opium.**

- **In selected markets in New York, Pathmark supermarkets distribute** fragrances such as Vanderbilt, Chaps, Halston, and Charlie and cosmetics such as Revlon's Touch and Glow, L'Oreal, Cover Girl, and Natural Wonder.

- **Safeway in Houston features Estee Lauder, Chloe, and other prestigious brands.**

One reason for strong sales of these brands in supermarkets is because each brand is heavily advertised nationally and in effect presold. Revlon spends $4.7 million on advertising for Charlie, Warner spends $6.5 million on Vanderbilt, and Coty spends $5.4 million on Sophia. In addition, cosmetics and fragrances have attractive gross margins of around 40 percent versus 18 percent for most food items. Although fragrances and cosmetics inventories do not turn over as quickly as food inventories do, they require only about one third of the space per $1,000 of inventory investment. These factors combine to make cosmetics and fragrances very profitable merchandise for supermarkets to stock.

Source: Arthur W. Weil. "Merchandising Savvy, Product Mix Bolster Supers' Share of Cosmetics $$," *Product Marketing Cosmetics & Fragrances* (October 1983), pp. 26, 29.

---

gas and milk). For example, some gasoline stations sell bread, milk, beer, cigarettes, and magazines.

Superstores.   A relatively new retail innovation in the United States is the **superstore**, which is *a large-scale* (usually over 50,000 square feet) *store using the concept of supermarket retailing but selling products that meet most of the consumer's needs.*[5] Superstores sell food, apparel, drugs, appliances, garden supplies, hardware, and services such as photo processing, banking, auto repair, and hairstyling. Kroger, Jewel, and Albertsons are experimenting with superstores. Superstores are not a uniquely U.S. retail innovation. Europe has had superstores (called *hypermarkets*) for over twenty years; for example, Carrefour in France and Wertkauf in Germany.

Convenience Stores.   A **convenience store** *stocks frequently purchased items such as bread, tobacco, and milk. These stores are generally small (2,000 to 4,000 square feet) and serve the surrounding neighborhood of about 0.5 to 1 mile from the store.* Because of the higher time and place utility these stores offer, they often charge higher prices on comparable items than do larger grocery stores. Convenience stores experienced considerable growth during the 1970s. The largest convenience store chain is operated by the Southland Corporation, which has over 7,000 conve-

From department stores to specialty stores to supermarkets, the many different retail organizations in the United States offer an almost infinite variety of products, prices, and services.

Convenience stores have expanded to neighborhoods throughout the United States and beyond, offering their customers frequently needed products at convenient times and places.

nience stores in forty-two states. Another leading chain is Circle K, which is expanding into Japan with its convenience stores.

Catalog Showrooms.   A **catalog showroom** has *a relatively large physical facility that is partitioned into a showroom and warehouse area.*[6] *The showroom* is usually only about 25 to 30 percent of the size of the entire store, and it *displays one item of each product the retailer sells.* This type of retailer usually creates store traffic by mailing catalogs to households. Catalog showrooms can offer lower prices than traditional department stores because they can operate with lower labor costs, maintain high rates of inventory turnover, and almost totally eliminate shoplifting. Catalog showroom retailers can be found in the furniture business (Sam Levitz Furniture), the jewelry business (Zales), and the appliance and housewares business (Service Merchandise Co.).

Classifying Retailers

Retailing is a diverse business activity taking on many different forms. By reviewing several ways of categorizing retailers, we can better appreciate the diversity in retailing and the need for various retail strategies.

Number of Outlets.   Generally, the more outlets a retailer has, the stronger the competitive edge because the firm can spread many fixed costs (such as advertising and top management salaries) over a larger volume of sales and can also frequently achieve economies in purchasing. However, single-unit retailers do have their advantages. Because they are generally owner-operated and family-operated, they tend to have harder working, more motivated employees. Also, they can focus all their efforts on one trade area and tailor their goods or services to that area. A trade area is the geographic area where the majority of a store's customers reside.

Table 12.2 profiles the changing role of single-unit and multiunit re-

Table 12.2   The Decline of Single-Unit Retailing

Number of Units	Sales As a Percentage of Total				
	1963	1967	1972	1977	1982
1	63.4	60.2	54.9	52.0	46.1
2–99	20.8	21.2	19.9	21.1	19.8
100+	15.8	18.6	25.2	26.9	34.1

Source: U.S. Bureau of the Census, *Census of Retail Trade* (Washington, DC: U.S. Government Printing Office, 1962, 1967, 1972, 1977, 1982).

tailers from 1963 to 1982. From these statistics, you can see that the proportion of sales for single-unit retailers has steadily declined while the proportion of sales attributable to 100 or more unit retailers has grown dramatically. At the same time, the share of sales accounted for by retailers with two to ninety-nine units has remained relatively constant. The Department of Commerce, in conjunction with the Bureau of the Census, classifies *any retailer with eleven or more units operating under the same name* as a **chain-store retailer**. Table 12.3 lists some of the largest retail chains in the United States.

Table 12.3   Examples of Large Retail Chains in the United States

Company	Annual Sales (millions)	Number of Stores
Food supermarkets		
Safeway Stores	$18,585	2,507
Kroger Co.	15,236	1,428
Lucky Stores	8,388	567
Drugstores		
Walgreen	$ 2,361	941
Jack Eckerd	2,325	1,319
Revco D.S.	1,793	1,661
Department stores		
May Co.	$ 4,229	144
R.H. Macy	3,827	93
Dillard's Dept. Stores	877	66
Womenswear specialty stores		
The Limited	$ 1,086	937
Brooks Fashion Stores	336	616
Paul Harris	101	171

Source: *Fairchild's Financial Manual of Retail Stores 1984,* 57th annual edition (New York: Fairchild Publications, 1984).

Margins Versus Turnover.   Retailers can be classified by their average gross margin and rate of inventory turnover.[7] The **gross margin** shows *how much gross profit (sales less cost of goods sold) the retailer makes as a percentage of sales.* A 40 percent gross margin indicates that on each dollar of sales, the retailer generates $0.40 in gross profit dollars. **Inventory turnover** refers to *the average number of times per year that a retailer sells its inventory.* Thus, an inventory turnover of twelve times indicates that, on average, the retailer turns over its inventory once a month. See Figure 12.1 for further classification in the areas of margin and turnover.

Typically a retailer with a low profit margin and low inventory turnover will not be able to generate sufficient profits to remain competitive and survive. When you notice a retailer in your community who has gone out of business, this is usually the reason. On the other hand, retailers with low margins and high turnovers, such as discount department stores and supermarkets, can be quite profitable. High-margin, low-turnover retailers, such as furniture stores, TV and appliance stores, jewelry stores, and hardware stores, are quite common in the United States. Finally, some retailers are able to operate profitably on both high margins and high turnover. The most popular example is the convenience food store.

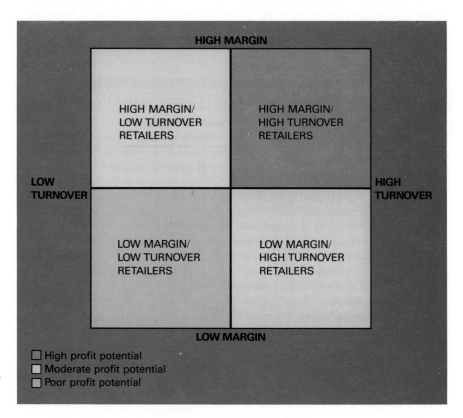

Figure 12.1

Retailers Classified by Margin and Turnover

Source: Based on Robert F. Lusch. *Management of Retail Enterprises* (Boston: Kent Publishing Co., 1982), p. 139.

Location.   Location can be a key element in a retailer's success because all retailers operating stores attract customers from a limited geographic area. For example, a convenience store attracts most customers from a 0.5 to 1 mile radius, a supermarket from a 1.5 to 3 mile radius, and a department store from a 5 to 10 mile radius. Retailers of services must also pay particular attention to location. For example, a movie theater, dry cleaner or barber shop will attract most of its customers from a 1 to 3 mile area. Retailers of convenience goods or services will have a smaller trade area than retailers of shopping or specialty goods and services. A physician specializing in cardiovascular diseases can attract patients from the entire community and beyond, as can the auto dealer selling Mercedes or Rolls Royce cars.

Locations range from the central business district to a shopping center to a free-standing unit. In the past, most retailers were located in the **central business district (CBD)**, *which is the geographic point where most cities originated and from which they grew.* This is also typically the point at which all public transportation systems converge. Many of the traditional department stores were located in the central business district along with a selection of specialty stores. Stores located in the CBD drew their clientele from the entire metropolitan area and even from nonresidents.

In the 1950s, CBDs in the United States started to decline because of the increase in shopping centers.[8] In the late 1970s and early 1980s, however, they experienced a rebirth due to such factors as the rehabilitation of many downtown areas and the migration of households back to the city from the suburbs because of rising transportation costs and an increasing disenchantment with suburban life.

Faneuil Hall Marketplace in Boston is an example of how downtown shopping areas have been revitalized to provide attractive locations for retailers.

There are three types of shopping centers, each with a distinctive function[9]:

1. A *neighborhood center* provides for the sale of convenience goods and personal services for the day-to-day living needs of the immediate neighborhood. It is built around a supermarket as the principal tenant and as a rule of thumb will have approximately 50,000 square feet in gross leasable space.

2. A *community center* provides the convenience and personal services of the neighborhood center as well as a wider range of facilities for the sale of soft lines (wearing apparel for men, women, and children) and hard lines (hardware and appliances). It makes greater depth of merchandise available—variety in sizes, styles, colors, and prices. In addition to a supermarket, it is built around a small department store, a variety store, or discount department store. It does not have a full-line department store, although it may have a strong specialty store. In theory, the typical size is 150,000 square feet of gross leasable area, but in practice this size may vary.

3. The *regional center* provides for general merchandise, apparel, furniture, and home furnishings in depth and variety as well as a range of services and recreational facilities. It is built around at least one full-line department store of generally not less than 100,000 square feet. The regional center is the largest type of shopping center in the United States. As such, the regional center provides services typical of a central business district. Sizes range from 400,000 to well over 1,000,000 square feet.

Freestanding Retailer. As the name implies, a freestanding retailer is not physically connected to other retailers, but instead has an individual building and parking area. Freestanding retailers generally locate along major traffic arteries. Most cities have strips of freestanding retailers on major traffic arteries. K marts built since 1961 have usually been freestanding stores, as have most fast-food restaurants and automobile dealerships.

Store Versus Nonstore. Retailers can be classified according to whether they are located in stores or conduct business from other facilities. Industry analysts forecast that between 1980 and 2000, nonstore retailers will become a major competitive force in the U.S. economy.[10] Nonstore retailing is not new, however; Sears and Roebuck began in the mail order business in the latter half of the 1800s, and Avon has concentrated its efforts on nonstore retailing since it started business in 1886. With accelerated communications technology and changing consumer life-styles, the growth potential of nonstore retailing is boundless. Consequently, marketing managers must continuously monitor developments in nonstore retailing.[11]

The U.S. Census of Retailing classifies nonstore retailers into three major types: mail order houses, automatic merchandising machine operators, and direct selling establishments. Table 12.4 explains the types of establishments that can be included in these broad categories.

Whether through mail-order houses, direct-selling establishments, or automated merchandising services such as CompuServe®'s Electronic Mail, nonstore retailing is gaining competitive force in the U.S. retail economy.

Table 12.4 Nonstore Retailing

Mail Order House. Mail order houses are primarily engaged in retail sale of products by catalog and mail order. Examples include book and record clubs, novelty merchandise firms, catalog divisions of general merchandise retailers, savings stamp order houses, sales incentive companies, and seasonal catalogs from conventional department stores without a catalog division.

Automatic Merchandising Machine Operator. This kind of retailer is primarily engaged in the retail sale of products by means of vending machines. Examples include candy and soft drink machines, cigarette machines, gumball dispensers, and newspaper boxes. It does not include coin-operated service machines such as pinball machines, lockers, or parking meters.

Direct Selling Establishment. This kind of retailer is primarily engaged in the retail sale of products by telephone or house-to-house canvass. Examples include magazine sales, home delivery of milk and baked goods, street vendors, party plan merchandisers, telephone sales of merchandise and services, and yard sales.

Store Atmosphere

Like all marketers, retail marketers must identify their target market and make marketing mix decisions. In addition, retail marketers must recognize that the store itself is a major part of their offering. All retailers project an image, and this image is dependent on the marketing mix—the store's location, prices, merchandise, advertising, and other promotions it uses. For example, compare the image that a Burger King projects with that of a traditional sit-down restaurant.

A store's image is also dependent on atmospherics. The term **atmospherics** means the *"conscious designing of space and its various dimensions to evoke certain effects in buyers."*[12] Marketers need to be concerned with how customers perceive the in-store environment and whether they are comfortable in it. Factors that influence customers' perceptions include the type and density of employees, merchandise, fixtures, sound, and odor.

The type of employee should reinforce the desired store image. For example, sporting goods stores often hire healthy looking people who look good in sportswear, just as fur salons often hire chic, well-groomed salespeople to fit their image. The fewer the employees, the more the store projects a self-service image (i.e., K mart employees are usually at the checkout counter, so you are on your own in the store).

The quality and style of the merchandise lines carried by a store reflect status. Furniture retailers that want to project a high-status image will include Pennsylvania House, Stanley, Henredon, and other upscale furniture lines. A high-status image would not be projected, however, if the furniture were displayed without adequate aisle and viewing space.

All store fixtures should be consistent with the overall image that the retailer wishes to project. If a retailer wants the store to look like an old English pub, fixtures should be made of dark wood and antique brass rather than chrome or Chinese lacquer. The density of the fixtures should also be consistent with the overall image the retailer is trying to project.

The sounds and odors of a store also affect customer perceptions. For example, laughing and yelling are desirable in a bowling alley but would be inconsistent with the desired image of, say, Neiman Marcus or a jewelry store. Some sounds will actually draw the customer's attention to the merchandise (i.e., wind chimes blowing in the breeze, music boxes playing, and of course, stereo equipment). If a retailer uses background music, the volume and music type must be appropriate for the in-store environment the retailer is trying to create. The same is true of smells. Some odors are helpful in stimulating the buying urge: the smell of flowers in a florist, perfume at a cosmetic counter, and cookies at a bakery. On the other hand, unpleasant odors, such as musty carpets and cigarette smoke can actually drive the customer away. Even when the odors are pleasant, the retailer should be sure they are subdued enough so that they do not distract or irritate the customer.

Evolution of Retail Competition

Scholars studying retailing have developed several theories to explain and describe the evolution of competition in retailing. We will review two of them briefly.[13]

Wheel of Retailing.   Professor Malcolm P. McNair developed the **wheel of retailing** hypothesis to describe patterns of competitive development in retailing.[14] This hypothesis states that new types of *retailers enter the market as low-status, low-margin, low-cost operators.* This modest strategy allows these retailers to compete effectively and take market share away from the more traditional retailers. *As they meet with success, they gradually upgrade their stores, resulting in higher prices, at which time new retailers enter the market with low margins and prices.*

As an example of the wheel of retailing consider the initial fast-food restaurants in the 1950s such as Burger Chef and McDonald's, which had a four- or five-item menu and sold one type of burger for 12 to 15 cents. These innovators operated low-cost, low-overhead facilities with no sit-down areas, minimal landscaping, and small buildings and made minimal use of atmospherics. Today most fast-food restaurants have plush interiors with comfortable eating areas, an elaborate menu (often with over 50 items), air conditioning, nicely decorated restrooms, and children's playgrounds—and higher costs. A typical meal at McDonald's is now over $3 and is thus not far away from the price of lunch or breakfast at Denneys or another full-service restaurant. Consequently, the fast-food industry is vulnerable to a low-status, low-margin, low-cost operator that would enter the market and serve one type of burger in a plain white wrapper and with limited ancillary services and atmospherics.

Retail Life Cycle.   A second theory argues that "*retailing institutions, like the products they distribute, pass through an identifiable cycle,*"[15] the **retail life cycle**, which *can be partitioned into four distinct stages* similar to the product life cycle: *(1) innovation, (2) accelerated development, (3) maturity, and (4) decline.*

In the first stage, innovation, retail operations typically are started by an aggressive entrepreneur who develops an approach to retailing that departs sharply from conventional approaches. Many times, the approach is oriented toward cost reduction: the supermarket in the early 1930s was able to operate on a gross margin of 12 percent, whereas conventional food outlets required 20 percent. At other times, however, the innovation centers on factors such as distinctive product assortment, shopping ease, advertising, or promotion. For example, the home improvement center, a retailing innovation of the late 1960s, offered a better product assortment and more information than the conventional hardware store.

If consumers perceive the new advantage to be significant, then sales will grow in the innovation stage. Profits in the innovation stage, however, will not be attractive, and in fact, they may be nonexistent because of high start-up costs, low initial sales, and operating problems that will need to be solved. At the end of the innovation stage, sales begin to grow more rapidly and operating problems are overcome, which stimulates profit levels.

During accelerated development, sales and profit growth increase dramatically. Many new entrants arrive to share in the expanding receptivity of this new form of retailing. The market share of the innovators rises, while that of conventional outlets declines, and the innovators now expand the number of their outlets. "However, toward the end of the period, these favorable factors tend to be counterbalanced by cost pressures that arise from the need for a larger staff, more complex internal systems, increased management controls, and other requirements of operating large, multi-unit organizations. Consequently, near the end of the accelerated development period, both market share and profitability tend to approach their maximum level."[16]

In the maturity stage, market share stabilizes and severe profit declines are experienced because of several problems. First, managers accustomed to managing small, simple firms in high-growth markets now must manage large, complex firms in a stable market. Second, the industry has typically overexpanded. Selecting markets and building new stores takes a long time (12–36 months). Therefore, many stores planned in the accelerated development stage will open in the maturity stage. Third, competitive assaults will be made on these firms by new forms of retailing (a bold entrepreneur starting a new retail life cycle).

Although decline is inevitable, retail managers will try to postpone it by repositioning, modifying, or adapting the firm. When successful, these attempts can postpone the decline stage, but a return to earlier attractive levels of operating performance is unlikely. Sooner or later, decline will occur, and "the consequences are traumatic. Major losses of market share occur, profits are marginal at best, and a fatal inability to compete in the market becomes apparent to investors and competitors."[17]

Three primary implications can be derived from the discussion of the retail life cycle:

1. Retailers should remain flexible so that they are able to adapt their strategies to various stages in the life cycle.
2. Since profits vary by stage in the retail life cycle, retail managers need to carefully analyze the risks and profits of entering the life cycle at various stages or expanding their outlets at various stages in the life cycle.
3. Retailers need to extend the maturity stage. Since they will have substantial investments in a particular form of retailing by the time the maturity stage arrives, they will have a strong interest in trying to work that investment as long as possible.

These three points are reinforced by the fact that the retail life cycle is growing shorter. The downtown department store took eighty years to reach maturity; the variety store, forty-five years; the supermarket, thirty-five years; the discount department store, twenty years; and the home improvement center, a short fifteen years.[18] Thus, retail managers must recognize that high-profit results can be achieved only over the long run by programming the firm to enter new lines of retail trade at appropriate points in time.

As we said earlier, wholesaling is a larger sector in the U.S. economy than retailing. In 1983, wholesale sales were $1,183.8 billion[19] and were actually greater than retail sales. How can wholesale sales be greater than retail sales? The answer lies in the fact that wholesalers sell not only to retailers, but also to manufacturers and other wholesalers. Consider an office supply wholesaler. This wholesaler may sell to retailers who sell office supplies, and it may also sell to manufacturers and wholesalers that need office supplies to conduct their day-to-day business. **Wholesaling** is concerned with the activities of *those persons or establishments that sell to retailers and other merchants, and/or to industrial, institutional, and commercial users, but do not sell in significant amounts to ultimate consumers.*

Wholesalers can be grouped into three broad categories:

WHOLESALING IN THE U.S. ECONOMY

1. **Merchant wholesalers** are firms that *purchase a product, take title to it, and resell it to another firm, but not to the ultimate consumer.*
2. **Manufacturer's sales branches** are *sales outlets of the manufacturer usually located in areas of high demand that serve as a base of operation for the manufacturer's sales staff* when calling on customers. *These outlets may or may not carry inventories.*
3. **Assemblers** are *wholesale institutions that primarily purchase farm products in small quantities to accumulate large quantities to sell to other firms.*

Table 12.5 shows the trends in the number of wholesale institutions between 1977 and 1982. Three major trends are apparent in these data: (1) a large increase in merchant wholesalers that are importers and exporters, (2) a major decline in manufacturer sales branches that carry inventory, and (3) a large drop in the number of assemblers.[20] A sizable increase also can be seen in merchant wholesalers that conduct business domestically. Most of our discussion of wholesaling will focus on these merchant wholesalers; however, we will first briefly discuss assemblers and manufacturer sales branches.

Assemblers

Most wholesalers perform the function of breaking bulk by buying in large quantities and selling in smaller quantities. This was called the allocation element of the sorting process in Chapter 10. Assemblers of farm products,

Table 12.5   Number of Wholesale Institutions

Wholesale Institutions	Establishments		Percent Change
	1977	1982	
Merchant wholesalers			
Domestic products	283,390	309,163	9
Importers	9,541	14,637	53
Exporters	3,762	5,518	47
Manufacturer's sales branches			
Branches with stock	26,892	22,121	−18
Branches without stock	13,629	16,113	18
Assemblers	10,571	8,625	−18

Source: *1982 Census of Wholesale Trade* and authors' computations.

on the other hand, are building bulk by buying from many relatively small producers or other sellers to accumulate large supplies to be able to sell and ship economically in large quantities. This was referred to in Chapter 10 as the accumulation element of the sorting process.

Farm products usually move from local markets to regional markets and then to terminal markets. At a terminal market, commodities are processed or packed for final shipment to wholesale or retail organizations. Assemblers buying locally know what the regional market price is and must buy below this price to be able to cover their costs (i.e., storage, transportation) and make a profit. Likewise, assemblers that buy at the regional level must buy below the terminal market price.

As noted in Table 12.5, the number of assemblers in the United States is declining due to the demise of the small farm. Agriculture and farming are becoming big business, and farms with several thousand acres do not need the services of an assembler to be able to sell to food processors.

Manufacturer Sales Branches

A manufacturer sales branch may or may not carry inventory. When inventory is carried, the manufacturer is essentially performing most, if not all, of the wholesaling function. Predictably, operating expenses of manufacturer sales branches increase when they have inventory. In 1982, the typical manufacturer sales branch without inventory had operating expenses of 4.5 percent, whereas the typical branch with inventory had operating expenses of 9.1 percent.[21]

Branches with inventory are declining, as shown in Table 12.5. Manufacturers are increasingly recognizing that distribution and warehousing can be performed more efficiently by merchant wholesalers. Manufacturers

have also learned that sales branches with inventories do not usually eliminate the need for wholesalers. In fact, they are often a form of double
wholesaling. Manufacturers ship to their distribution center and sales office,
which in turn sell to wholesalers who then sell to the ultimate user or
retailer.

Merchant Wholesalers

Many times, manufacturers find that it is more profitable to sell their output
to merchant wholesalers rather than directly to retailers or other business
firms that might use the purchased items in their business operations. Kraft,
for instance, sells its cheeses and dairy products to merchant wholesalers
who then sell to retail grocery stores.

The major reason a manufacturer uses merchant wholesalers is that it
may not be economical for the manufacturer's salespeople to call directly
on all accounts or to send separate shipments to all accounts. Basically,
using a merchant wholesaler is an exercise in applying the principle of
leverage. If each of the wholesalers have 200 accounts, then by selling to
ten wholesalers, the manufacturer can reach 2,000 customers, thereby reducing selling and distribution costs.

As shown in Figure 12.2, merchant wholesalers can be categorized as
consumer goods or industrial goods wholesalers. Although some wholesalers may sell both consumer and industrial goods, this is the exception

Figure 12.2

Types of Merchant Wholesalers

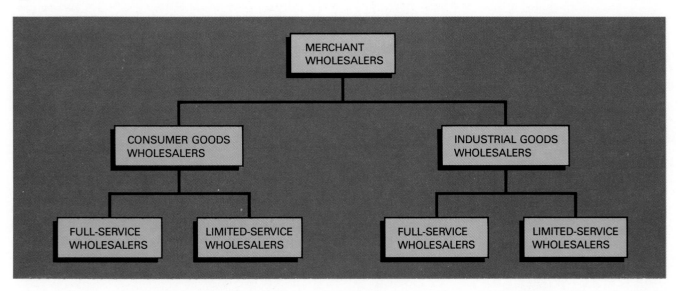

rather than the rule. Either consumer or industrial goods wholesalers can be categorized as full-service or limited-service wholesalers.

Full-Service Wholesaling. **Full-service wholesalers** are persons or establishments that sell to retailers or other merchants or institutions and *perform most of the marketing functions for either manufacturers or their customers.* For example, a full-service food wholesaler, such as Nash-Finch or Malone and Hyde, might perform the following marketing functions:

❑ *Buying* Purchases merchandise from hundreds of different food processors/manufacturers.

❑ *Selling* Employs a sales force to sell to retail food stores.

❑ *Storage* Operates a warehouse that allows for the storage of food and related merchandise.

❑ *Transporting* Operates a fleet of trucks to deliver food to retail grocery stores and occasionally picks up merchandise from food processors and transports it to the wholesaler's warehouse.

❑ *Sorting* Allocates (breaks down) large, homogeneous supplies into smaller lots (see Chapter 10). Sorting occurs because a variety of products are built up for use in association with each other so that the grocer and ultimately the consumer can buy from a minimum number of sources.

❑ *Financing* Helps to finance the marketing process (sells to retail accounts on credit and also must finance part of the investment in inventory, warehouses, and trucks).

❑ *Information* Monitors information on sources of supply and price movements and correlates this with changes in household demand patterns.

❑ *Risk-taking* Because the full-service food wholesaler performs all of the previous functions, he or she is placed in a risk-taking position. The warehouse could burn down, or the food could spoil.

Most full-service wholesalers, whether they are selling consumer or industrial goods, will perform most of the preceding eight marketing functions. The Marketing in Action on page 379 gives an example of a full-service industrial goods wholesaler, Anixter Brothers, and shows how they use quick delivery service as a marketing tool.

Limited-Service Wholesalers. A **limited-service wholesaler** *performs only a few of the marketing functions for manufacturers or their customers* or performs all of them on a more restricted basis than does a full-service wholesaler. They may avoid some functions by eliminating them entirely or passing them on to another marketing channel member or to the customer.[22] Some of the more popular types of limited-service wholesalers are described in Table 12.6 on page 381.

MARKETING IN ACTION

The motto at Anixter Bros. is "Service is our technology." The company is a merchant wholesaler distributor of wire and cable, buying it by the mile and selling it by the foot. Anixter has forty-one locations in the United States, ten in Canada, two in England, two in Scotland, one in Rotterdam, and one in Singapore and sells over a half billion dollars of wire and cable annually. The firm uniquely differentiates itself by providing a higher level of customer service than its competitors. Customer service is the firm's primary marketing tool.

Anixter tries to convince its customers that it is cheaper to use Anixter's inventory than their own. Factories or other users of wire need not tie up large dollar investments in inventory when Anixter can deliver within twenty-four hours any of 25,000 items it has in stock, all cut

Customer Service at Anixter Brothers

to specification. The firm uses a sophisticated computer system, with its own proprietary software (which took Anixter 10 years to develop), to help it manage its massive inventory that is spread over fifty warehouses throughout the world.

One memorable example of superior customer service occurred when Georgia Power and Light Co. blew a transformer. The downtime meant a loss of $50,000 to $75,000 per day. Georgia Power and Light needed several thousand feet of power cable, but most manufacturers wanted six weeks to deliver. Anixter was called, the company determined that the needed cable was in the New Orleans warehouse, and the cable was

shipped immediately. Another more dramatic example occurred when an electrical fire broke out at an Oregon International Paper plant, ruining hundreds of feet of special cable. International Paper put a call through to Anixter's twenty-four hour emergency number. The cable was located in the Montreal warehouse and delivered by chartered aircraft; it cost International Paper $80,000 for cable and $38,000 for the chartered aircraft. This was a bargain though, since the company was losing $170,000 every day the plant was shut down.

Source: "Wire Merchants Who Deal in Emergencies," *BusinessWeek* (October 13, 1975); Edwin Darby. "Anixter Wires the Country," *Commerce* (August 1980); John Mattes. "Buy by the Mile, Sell by the Foot," *Sales and Marketing Management* (July 7, 1980), pp. 30–33; *Anixter Bros., Inc. Annual Reports*, 1978 to 1983.

Industrial Versus Consumer Goods Wholesaling. Earlier in the chapter, we mentioned that a useful way to categorize merchant wholesalers is by using the industrial versus consumer goods dichotomy. These two broad types of wholesalers are confronted by substantially different conditions:

1. *Merchandise Mix.* Industrial goods wholesalers seldom handle competing lines. For example, a wholesaler of industrial hand tools for Ingersoll Rand would seldom handle a competing line from Cooper Industries. Consumer goods wholesalers, on the other hand, typically handle competing merchandise lines.

2. *Inventory Carrying Cost.* Inventory turns over much more slowly for industrial goods wholesalers and also is typically of a higher unit value than is that for consumer goods wholesalers. Predictably, therefore, industrial goods wholesalers require a larger profit as a percent of sales.

3. *Competition.* Industrial goods wholesalers usually face less competition than do consumer goods wholesalers because of the following factors: (a) exclusive dealing or selective distribution by industrial goods manufacturers is more popular, (b) personnel usually must have technical training or background, and (c) inventory investment is higher.

These major differences have resulted in more instability and higher turnover in consumer goods wholesaling than in industrial goods wholesaling. Although generalizations are dangerous, industrial goods wholesalers are generally more established, better organized, and more profitable than consumer goods wholesalers. Some of the most successful industrial goods wholesalers are Bearings, Inc. (industrial bearings), W.W. Grainger (electrical goods), Lawson (maintenance and repair parts and supplies), and National Steel Service Centers (steel products such as sheets, bars, or tubing). These companies are successful because of the high level of service they offer their customers. For example, National Steel Service Center provides "just-in-time" delivery by holding customers' inventory until they are ready to manufacture, and then sending only what they need. Once National unloads its trucks, they offer to reload them with their customers' products and transport them at a competitive rate. They also provide technical advice to customers; they helped one Wisconsin factory move to Florida and even helped another mediate a labor dispute.[23]

Marketing Through Wholesalers

Manufacturers who operate through wholesalers typically do so because they find it is more efficient and cheaper to sell through wholesalers than to sell directly to the customer. However, manufacturers can only use wholesalers successfully if they get the wholesalers' cooperation in marketing their products. To accomplish this, manufacturers must obtain some degree of control over wholesalers.

Selecting Wholesalers. The first and perhaps the most important step in getting good wholesaler cooperation is careful selection. To select the best wholesalers, manufacturers need a screening device that analyzes potential wholesalers on at least five broad dimensions: (1) management skills, (2) financial characteristics, (3) physical facilities, (4) objectives and policies, and (5) marketing skills/strengths.[24]

To help assess management skills needed to effectively manage the resources at their disposal and the manufacturers' products, wholesalers need to be screened on such points as their record and reputation, the planning and management systems and procedures used, cooperation and helpfulness, and receptiveness to constructive management suggestions. One such screen is shown in Table 12.7.

The wholesaler's financial strength, integrity, history, and future prospects must be considered. For example, wholesalers in a poor financial position may sabotage your product by not performing the necessary marketing functions and services. Therefore, it is important to assess financial characteristics such as whether the wholesaler is making a profit, if it is sufficiently capitalized, if credit is adequate, and whether it can afford to keep adequate stocks on hand.

The wholesaler's equipment and facilities should be assessed carefully, as considerable variation exists among wholesalers on this dimension. In this regard, it is necessary to know if the wholesaler has the needed facilities

---

Table 12.6   Limited-Service Wholesalers

1. *Drop-Shipper (Desk Jobber).*   Passes on customer orders with instructions to the manufacturer to ship directly to a location specified by the customer. Maintains no warehouse or inventory; *does not come in physical possession* of the goods. Usually contacts customers by telephone, so sales force may not be necessary and may be much less active in generating promotion. Particularly useful in bulky goods and where merchandise typically moves in carlot quantities. Sometimes called a "carlot wholesaler."

2. *Cash and Carry Wholesaler.*   Does not provide customers with credit or delivery. The customers must pick up the merchandise from the wholesaler and pay for it with cash or check. This type of wholesaler typically does not have an outside sales force. Customers are usually small retailers or small industrial accounts.

3. *Truck Jobber (Wagon Jobber).*   Their warehouse is their truck. Usually self-employed with little capital and generally does not extend credit to customers. May own their own goods, but usually gets merchandise on consignment from a larger full-service wholesaler. Travels to customers and sells directly from the back of the truck.

4. *Rack Jobber.*   Maintains racks stocked with merchandise at the retailer's location. Heavy assumption of risk since the jobber holds title and the retailer is billed only for goods sold from the rack. Retailer's only investment is in the space allotted to the rack.

Source: Adapted from Department of Marketing, University of Pennsylvania, Wharton School of Finance and Commerce, as reported in Louis W. Stern and Adel I. El-Ansary. *Marketing Channels* (Englewood Cliffs, NJ: Prentice-Hall, 1982), pp. 147–149.

Table 12.7   Wholesaler Selection Screens

Management Skills	Financial Characteristics	Physical Facilities	Objectives and Policies	Marketing Skills/ Strengths
1. Good reputation 2. Use appropriate systems and procedures 3. Cooperative and helpful 4. Accepts suggestions, participates in sales meetings	1. Making a profit; good record 2. Capitalized 3. Adequate credit 4. Can afford to carry sufficient inventory	1. Necessary facilities and equipment 2. Facilities and equipment in good shape 3. Have repair and maintenance facilities and training 4. Good service reputation 5. Adequate office facilities	1. Progressive management objectives and policies 2. Sound and stable 3. Integrity and reliability 4. Consistent with your policies 5. Minimum irreconcilable conflicts	1. Marketing and merchandising knowledge 2. Salespeople are reliable and credible 3. Large enough salesforce for adequate coverage

and equipment to handle your product, the age and condition of the facilities and equipment, the maintenance schedule, the wholesaler's reputation regarding service standards, and whether the office set up is adequate to handle your business.

Another important dimension for screening wholesalers is the extent to which their objectives and policies are compatible with the manufacturer's marketing channel. In evaluating this dimension, the wholesaler's management objectives and policies must be assessed in respect to growth, the stability and reliability of the organization, and the possibility of conflicts.

Wholesalers need to have the marketing expertise and stamina to successfully market and distribute the manufacturer's product line. Therefore, the wholesaler's marketing know-how and the size, reputation, credibility, and attitude of the sales force must be assessed.

By carefully assessing wholesalers on the five dimensions just discussed, the manufacturer should be able to maximize the chances of selecting the best wholesalers. Unfortunately, the best wholesalers may not always be willing to handle the manufacturer's product line. Consequently, it is important for the manufacturers to develop the proper mix of assistances to offer wholesalers, which will encourage them to handle the manufacturer's line.

Wholesaler Assistances. If manufacturers want the cooperation and commitment of wholesalers, they must offer them financial, promotional, training, and general management aids. Depending on the line of wholesale trade, some or all of these may be offered. The most important financial assistance that manufacturers can offer wholesalers is the spread between the price they sell to wholesalers and the price at which wholesalers must resell. This is referred to as the *planned gross margin*. The planned gross margin must be large enough so that wholesalers can still have adequate profit after properly performing the activities desired by the manufacturers. Other important financial assistances include inventory financing through liberal purchase terms, rebates, bonuses if quotas are achieved, seasonal dating to get wholesalers to stock up early in the season, and extra functional discounts for performing special services.

Frequently offered promotional assistances include national or regional advertising with the wholesaler's name mentioned; advertising allowances for local advertising; brochures, pamphlets, and other sales material to be distributed to potential customers; suggested advertising layouts or content for local advertising (i.e., prepared advertising mats); salespeople employed by manufacturers to generate new accounts for the wholesaler.

If the wholesaler has neither the human nor financial resources to properly train salespeople, the manufacturer may offer a sales training program. A good training program will help the wholesaler to service the manufacturer's merchandise line by informing sales representatives about the strengths and weaknesses of the manufacturer's products and those of competing products and by teaching them how to make effective sales presentations. Training of service personnel may also be advantageous, es-

Chevron's offer of monetary savings is an example of how manufacturers provide wholesalers with incentives and aids to ensure their cooperation and commitment.

pecially if the manufacturer's product line is technically complex and needs preinstallation or postinstallation service.

A major study found that wholesalers are becoming more concerned about internal operation problems,[25] including problems of credit and collection, inventory control, finance, planning, and personnel. Consequently, some manufacturers are designing executive development programs to help wholesalers solve their operating problems. By offering such programs, manufacturers are recognizing the fact that their marketing effort can only be successful if the wholesaler survives and prospers.

Once the wholesale distributors are selected and offered the proper mix of motivational assistances, they should be expected to become high performers. To assess their performance, an objective and regular evaluation needs to be conducted.

Evaluation.   All of the wholesale distributors should be given a sales goal based on the market potential and competitive intensity in the geographic territory the wholesaler serves. The manufacturer and wholesaler must discuss this goal and arrive at some agreement on its reasonableness.

Table 12.8   Questions for Annual Evaluation of Wholesalers

1. Has the target sales been reached? If not, why not?
2. Is the wholesaler stocking the level of inventory believed to be necessary for good customer service?
3. Is the wholesaler distributing promotional material that has been provided?
4. Is the wholesaler properly servicing the products?
5. Are the salespeople knowledgeable about the products' relative strengths and weaknesses?
6. Does the wholesaler pay on time?
7. Is the wholesaler properly handling merchandise in the warehouse and in shipment to the customer? For example, is the product damaged when it reaches the final customer? If so, why?
8. Is the wholesaler attempting to develop new accounts or merely relying on old established accounts for business?
9. Does the wholesaler have ethical business practices?

An annual evaluation is usually sufficient; however, this evaluation should include more than simply assessing whether the target sales were reached. For instance, a wholesale distributor may have achieved its target sales through unethical sales practices! Table 12.8 shows a sampling of things that are typically evaluated.

A word of caution needs to be sounded at this point. Any of the preceding problems identified in Table 12.8 could be largely due to the manufacturer's inadequacies. Manufacturers should not be too quick to criticize unless they are sure that their operations are in good shape. A recent study concluded[26]:

> Before a manufacturer can address the problems and needs of his distributors through a coordinated distributor marketing program, he must recognize his own problems. Certain weaknesses in a manufacturer's operations can affect the distributors. Until the manufacturer recognizes and addresses these problems, any program directed at solving the distributor's concerns will be jeopardized.

The importance of the preceding statement cannot be emphasized too strongly. For example, the wholesaler's salespeople may not be knowledgeable about the manufacturer's product line because the manufacturer did not take the time or resources to properly inform them.

SUMMARY

The primary purpose of this chapter was to acquaint you with the major types of retail and wholesale institutions. Although wholesalers come before retailers in marketing channels, we decided to discuss retailers first because they are more familiar to most students. A firm that sells products to the final consumer is performing the retailing function. Six of the more popular types of retailing were discussed: department stores, specialty stores, supermarkets, superstores, convenience stores, and catalog showrooms. We also discussed how retailers can be categorized on a variety of dimensions such as number of outlets, margins versus turnover, location, and store or nonstore formats.

To develop a successful retail marketing strategy, the retailer must identify the store's target market and develop a marketing mix. Retailers must also be able to provide the proper atmosphere in order to elicit the desired store image in the customers' minds. Atmospherics involves the designing of space and includes such things as the type of employees, merchandise, fixtures, sounds, and odors.

There are low entry barriers in retailing, and thus new retail institutions appear continuously. Several theories explain how retail institutions change over time as they develop. One of the more popular theories is the wheel of retailing, which states that new types of retailers enter the market as low-status, low-margin, low-cost operators. Over time, these retailers upgrade their facilities and thus raise margins and prices and become vulnerable to new types of low-margin retail competitors, who in turn go through the same pattern.

Another explanation is the retail life cycle theory. This framework suggests that retail institutions pass through four identifiable stages: (1) innovation, (2) accelerated development, (3) maturity, and (4) decline. Competitive intensity and management activities differ over the four stages.

Although three broad types of wholesalers were identified, most of our discussion focused on merchant wholesalers of consumer and industrial goods. A merchant wholesaler is a firm that purchases a product, takes title to it, and then resells it to another firm, but not to the ultimate consumer.

Both consumer goods or industrial goods wholesalers can be full-service or limited-service institutions by providing a varying number of the marketing functions. Some of the more popular limited-service wholesalers, such as drop shippers, cash and carry wholesalers, truck jobbers, and rack jobbers, perform only a few marketing functions and pass the remaining ones on to another institution or to the customer.

For manufacturers to operate successfully through merchant wholesalers, they must be able to get cooperation in marketing the manufacturer's products. Wholesalers should be selected on the basis of their management skills, financial characteristics, physical facilities, objectives and policies, and marketing skills/strengths. Once wholesalers have been selected, manufacturers should provide them with a package of assistances: financial, promotional, employee training, and general management guidance. In addition, manufacturers should evaluate wholesalers annually to assess their performance.

KEY CONCEPTS

retailing (p. 361)
department store (p. 361)
discount department store (p. 361)
specialty store (p. 362)
supermarket concept (p. 363)

scrambled merchandising
  (pp. 363–364)
superstore (p. 364)
convenience store (p. 364)
catalog showroom (p. 366)

chain-store retailer (p. 367)
gross margin (p. 368)
inventory turnover (p. 368)
central business district (CBD) (p. 369)
atmospherics (p. 372)
wheel of retailing (p. 373)
retail life cycle (p. 373)

wholesaling (p. 375)
merchant wholesalers (p. 375)
manufacturer's sales branches (p. 375)
assemblers (p. 375)
full-service wholesalers (p. 378)
limited-service wholesalers (p. 378)

REVIEW AND DISCUSSION QUESTIONS

1. In terms of product or merchandise mix, what is the major difference between department and specialty stores?

2. Define *supermarket retailing* and give several examples of it.

3. Why are convenience food stores able to charge higher prices than food supermarkets?

4. Why can catalog showrooms charge lower prices than conventional retailers?

5. Why are gross margins and inventory turnover important to retailers?

6. Why is location an important key to success in retailing?

7. What factors do you see contributing to the growth of nonstore retailers?

8. What are some of the more popular types of nonstore retailing?

9. What is atmospherics? What are the determinants of a store's atmosphere?

10. What is the wheel of retailing? Can you think of any current examples that support or discount the wheel of retailing hypothesis?

11. Discuss the retail life cycle. At what stage is the department store in its retail life cycle? What should department stores be doing given the stage they are in?

12. Explain why total wholesale sales are greater than total retail sales in the U.S. economy.

13. What is a manufacturer sales branch? Does it eliminate the need for wholesaling?

14. How do merchant wholesalers differ from assemblers?

15. Describe four popular types of limited-service wholesalers.

16. Contrast and compare industrial and consumer goods wholesalers.

17. What criteria should manufacturers use to select wholesalers to distribute their goods?

18. What types of assistances should manufacturers offer wholesalers to gain their cooperation and support?

ACTION PROBLEMS

1. Visit the shopping centers in your community or a nearby city of over 100,000 in population. Categorize these shopping centers into neighborhood, community, or regional centers.

2. Visit a discount department store and a conventional department store in your community. Compare and contrast these stores in terms of their atmospherics.

3. Assume you are vice president of marketing and distribution for a toy manufacturer. This toy manufacturer currently has twenty-one toys in its product mix, most of which are nonmechanical and targeted at children under 6 years of age. Sales are $4.1 million, and distribution is currently through five merchant wholesalers who are in Chicago, Pittsburgh, New York City, Atlanta, and Cincinnati. The president and founder of the company has asked you to explore the feasibility of expanding distribution west of the Mississippi River. You wish to seek out five toy wholesalers and plan to place an advertisement in several trade journals. Prepare a 100-word advertisement that clearly states the criteria you will use in selecting wholesalers to represent your product lines.

4. Based on library research or on a visit to several computer software stores, develop a description of several electronic in-home shopping services. What is the cost of using these services? Explain why you would or would not be interested in in-home electronic shopping services.

5. Use the yellow pages of your local telephone directory to develop a list of grocery or food wholesalers in your area. Do these wholesalers appear to be focusing on different market segments? If you can find a cash and carry grocery wholesaler, attempt to visit this wholesaler and observe how merchandise is handled and paid for by customers.

NOTES

1. For a discussion of competitive challenges in the department store industry, see Eleanor G. May and Malcolm P. McNair, "Department Stores Face Stiff Challenge in the Next Decade," *Journal of Retailing* (Fall 1977), pp. 47–58; Ronald W. Stampfl and Elizabeth Hirschman (eds.), *Competitive Structure in Retail Markets: The Department Store Perspective* (Chicago, IL: American Marketing Association, 1980).

2. *1982 Standard Brands Paint Company Annual Report,* p. 7.

3. Robert F. Hartley, *Marketing Successes Historical to Present Day: What We Can Learn* (New York: John Wiley & Sons, 1985), p. 53.

4. Albert D. Bates and Bert C. McCammon, Jr., "Reseller Strategies and the Financial Performance of the Firm," in Hans Thorelli (ed.), *Strategy + Structure = Performance: The Strategic Planning Imperative* (Bloomington, IN: Indiana University Press, 1977).

5. Walter J. Salmon, Robert D. Buzzell, and Stanton G. Cort, "Today the Shopping Center, Tomorrow the Superstore," *Harvard Business Review* (January–February 1974), pp. 89–98; Myron Gable and Ronald D. Michman, "Superstores—Revolutionizing Distribution," *Business* (March–April 1981), pp. 14–18.

6. Some of the problems confronting catalog showrooms are discussed in Kimberley Carpenter, "Catalog Showrooms Revamp To Keep Their Identity," *BusinessWeek* (June 10, 1985), pp. 117–120.

7. For a more complete discussion of classifying retailers by margin and turnover, see Ronald R. Gist, *Retailing: Concepts and Decisions* (New York: John Wiley & Sons, 1968), pp. 37–40.

8. For some interesting insights into the future of shopping centers as viable locations, see "Shopping Center Futures," *Stores* 62(April 1980), pp. 50–57.

9. The Urban Land Institute describes four types of shopping centers, but we collapsed their

regional and superregional centers into a single regional center category, see Urban Land Institute, *The Dollar and Cents of Shopping Centers* (Washington, DC: Urban Land Institute, 1978), p. 294.

10. Marcia Bielfield and Linda Nagel (eds.), *The Growth of Non-Store Retailing: Implications for Retailers, Manufacturers, and Public Policy Makers* (New York: Institute of Retail Management, New York University, 1978).

11. John A. Quelch and Hirotaka Takeuchi, "Nonstore Marketing: Fast Track or Slow?" *Harvard Business Review* (July–August 1981), pp. 75–84.

12. Philip Kotler, "Atmospherics As a Marketing Tool," *Journal of Retailing* 49(Winter 1973–74), p. 50.

13. Space will not allow discussion of the views of all scholars who have written on the evolution of retail trade. Some of the notable articles are A.C.R. Dressmann, "Patterns of Evolution in Retailing," *Journal of Retailing* 44(Spring 1968), pp. 64–81; Arieh Goldman, "The Role of Trading-up in the Development of the Retailing System," *Journal of Marketing* 39(January 1975), pp. 54–62; Delbert J. Duncan, "Responses of Selected Retail Institutions to Their Changing Environment," in Peter D. Bennett (ed.), *Marketing and Economic Development* (Chicago, IL: American Marketing Association, 1965), pp. 583–602; Thomas J. Maronick and Bruce J. Walker, "The Dialectic Evolution of Retailing," in Barnett Greenberg (ed.), *Proceedings: Southern Marketing Association* (Atlanta, GA: Georgia State University, 1975), pp. 147–151.

14. Malcolm P. McNair, "Significant Trends and Developments in the Postwar Period," in A.B. Smith (ed.), *Competitive Distribution in a Free High-Level Economy and Its Implications for the University* (Pittsburgh, PA: University of Pittsburgh Press, 1958).

15. William R. Davidson, Albert D. Bates, and Stephen J. Bass, "The Retail Life Cycle," *Harvard Business Review* 54(November–December 1976), p. 89.

16. Ibid., p. 92.

17. Ibid., p. 93.

18. Ibid., p. 94.

19. U.S. Bureau of the Census, *Statistical Abstract of the United States: 1985,* 105th edition (Washington, DC, 1984).

20. For a more complete discussion of the rise in merchant wholesaling, see James C. McKeon, "Conflicting Patterns of Structural Change in Wholesaling," *Economic and Business Bulletin* (Winter 1972), pp. 100–113.

21. *1982 Census of Wholesale Trade* and authors' computations.

22. Passing functions on to other channel members is discussed in Bruce Mallen, "Functional Spin-off: A Key to Anticipating Change in Distribution Structure," *Journal of Marketing* (July 1973), pp. 18–25.

23. Larry Riggs, "Service Centers Evade the Steel Trap," *Sales and Marketing Management* (September 9, 1985), pp. 46–49.

24. These concerns for evaluating wholesalers are based on John M. Brion, *Marketing Through the Wholesaler/Distributor Channel* (Chicago, IL: American Marketing Association, 1966), pp. 34–36.

25. Dennis A. Zalar, *Motivating the Distributor to Market Your Product* (New York: AMACOM, 1980).

26. Ibid., p. 20.

19. FORGET IT

Designing Marketing Channels for Microcomputers

In the early 1980s, there were over 150 microcomputer manufacturers in the United States, most of them quite new. With the start-up of so many small companies in the microcomputer industry, the toughest part of introducing a new microcomputer became the struggle over getting distribution.

Microcomputer manufacturers essentially have three basic marketing channels to select from, and some manufacturers have used more than one channel to distribute their computers. The first alternative is for a manufacturer to sell its product to an original equipment manufacturer (OEM). The OEM usually adds a printer, specialized software, or somehow adds value to the product but also puts its own name on the product. The design of the marketing channel and distribution system are then up to the OEM.

A second alternative is for the manufacturer to sell directly to the user, which means that the manufacturer needs a large sales force to call on potential users. A third option is for the manufacturer to sell to a group of distributors, who in turn sell to retailers or end users. Under this scenario, the manufacturer needs fewer salespeople because only distributors need to be called on.

Conflict can develop when the manufacturer uses more than one of these channels, because the discount structure varies; thus, a channel member with a bigger discount can resell the product and undercut the price of a competing channel. For instance, if a manufacturer is selling directly to a user at $5,000 and to distributors at $3,500, then the distributor could sell to the end user at $4,000 and be in direct competition with the manufacturer.

Another area that has caused conflict is the practice of microcomputer manufacturers offering attractive quantity discounts. If a distributor buys one to five computers, the price may be 25 percent off list price; a purchase of six to ten would result in a 30 percent discount; of ten to twenty, a 35 percent discount; of twenty-one to ninety-nine, a 40 percent discount; and a purchase of over 100 units would mean a 45 percent discount. Therefore, a distributor is tempted to order large quantities but then is sometimes forced to dump units at a modest profit or no profit at all in order to move inventory.

A final problem is that when the units are dumped at a low price, the distributor does not wish to provide any service support for the machines. In addition, the dealer who is buying the computers at a deeply discounted price usually is not an authorized dealer and wants to avoid providing service support to end users.

Questions

1. How might a microcomputer manufacturer structure its marketing channel to avoid unhealthy channel conflict?
2. How should a microcomputer manufacturer select from the three basic marketing channel patterns discussed? Can you think of a marketing channel pattern that might be more effective than the three patterns discussed?

20.

The Saguaro Barbecue Company

The Saguaro Barbecue Company is a small specialty manufacturer of gas barbecue grills located in the Southwestern U.S. Its volume is minuscule compared with the total industry volume. In 1983, Saguaro sold 6,618 gas grills for a gross sales dollar value of $592,769. In comparison with industry sales of close to $300 million, this amount is tiny (see Table 1). Saguaro does not produce or sell charcoal or electric barbecue grills, it concentrates on the gas grill market, which is the fastest growing product segment of the barbecue grill market.

Stephen Hogan started the Saguaro Barbecue Company in 1972 with $3,000 in savings. Steve had a college degree in engineering and was an artistic welder by hobby. One day, after pricing charcoal barbecue grills, he decided to attempt to make one on his own. The project went fast and smoothly, and soon he began to tinker with making gas grills. His friends began to ask him to make custom grills for them, and early in 1971, the owner of a local hardware store asked him to make a few grills for the store. The grills sold quickly, and thus Steve decided to enter business for himself. For three years, it was a one-man operation with Steve doing everything from making the grills in his two-car garage to selling and delivering them to several local hardware stores. The business finally outgrew the garage, and the company now occupies a 14,000 square foot facility in a low rent industrial area of the city. Steve is now married, and he and his wife, Nancy, both work in the business; she is office manager, and he is general manager. The firm's income statement for 1983 is shown in Table 2.

The product mix consists of three gas grills. The standard model has 400 square inches of cooking surface and a suggested retail price of $119. The deluxe model has 625 square inches of cooking surface, a 150 square inch wood serving board, and chrome trim and has a suggested retail price of $169. Finally, the custom deluxe model retails for $249 and is the top of the line with all the features of the deluxe model plus an electric motor for rotisserie cooking, heavy duty frame and wheels, a heavy duty vinyl cover, and brass plated fittings and trim instead of chrome. In 1983, the Saguaro Barbecue Company sold 1,852 standard, 4,117 deluxe, and 649 custom deluxe models.

Distribution is direct to retailers that are concentrated in seven cities in the Southwest: Phoenix, Tucson, Yuma, Las Cruces, Albuquerque, El Paso, and Las Vegas. All sales are made by one traveling salesperson, Melanie Mills, who calls on each account an average of six times per year. She is paid a salary of $18,000 and receives a commission of 3 percent of sales. The majority of customers are hardware stores, followed by appliance and TV stores, home improvement centers, and grocery stores (see Table 3). Melanie has been unsuccessful in trying to sell to large chain stores and mass merchandisers such as discount department stores. This is unfortunate because industry sources estimate that over 30 percent of sales are made through mass merchant outlets. In addition, catalog stores and showrooms (e.g., H.C. Wilson, Sears) have close to a 25 percent share of the market.

Retail accounts can either order through Melanie on one of her visits or call in mail orders directly to the company. In either case, the minimum order size is five grills or $500. Merchandise is shipped by motor carrier, and since the orders are small shipments, they take two to six days for delivery. The only exception is in the city where Saguaro is located, where merchandise is delivered within 24 hours in a pickup truck by a Saguaro employee. All accounts are billed at 2/10 net 30 terms

(2% discount if paid in ten days, net or full amount due in thirty days). Bad debt expense has been almost nonexistent due to a very conservative credit policy. Bad debt expense is covered in the miscellaneous expense category in the income statement. Sales tend to be seasonal, even though the firm is located in the Sunbelt (see Table 4).

Steve wants to see his business grow to over a million dollars in sales over the next few years but is in a quandary over what to do to bolster sales. Sales have been stagnating at the $500,000 level for several years. To assist him in deciding what alternatives he might pursue, Steve hired a local professor who specializes in marketing. The professor suggested that Steve consider two basic alternatives: changing the structure of the firm's marketing channel and adding salespeople.

The change in marketing channel alternatives consisted of using full-service wholesalers in Phoenix, Albuquerque, and El Paso to serve all seven cities. These wholesalers would be given a 15 percent margin on the price at which they would sell to retailers. Retailers would continue to receive the same price as before. The professor argues persuasively that Saguaro Barbecue could get a top wholesaler in each of these cities if it promised to turn over all existing accounts to the three wholesalers. With this incentive, and a 15 percent profit margin, the wholesalers could really get excited about the Saguaro line, and since three products compose the line, inventory could be managed conveniently and cost effectively. Because each of the wholesalers has an average of 300 accounts, the line would be exposed to an additional 900 potential accounts. The professor estimated that the immediate impact of this would be a 50 percent increase in sales, and with the right marketing effort, it could be 100 percent within two years.

The second alternative consists of hiring two additional salespeople. This would give Saguaro three salespeople. The professor suggests that one salesperson handle Phoenix, Tucson, Yuma, and Las Vegas; another handle Albuquerque, Amarillo (a new market), and Lubbock (a new market); and the third salesperson handle Las Cruces, El Paso, and San Antonio (a new market). Since it will take time to develop new accounts, the professor estimates that first-year sales would only increase 30 percent, but second-year sales should grow another 25 percent, and third-year sales, another 20 per-

Table 1   Size and Composition of the U.S. Barbecue Market

	Market Size (1982)			Market Size (1983)		
Product Category	Units	Retail Dollars	Average Retail Price	Units	Retail Dollars	Average Retail Price
Charcoal grills	10,788,969	$132,406,403	$ 12.27	10,588,906	$133,049,316	$ 12.56
Gas grills	2,043,508	216,493,348	105.94	2,432,456	299,999,174	$123.33
Electric grills	89,998	4,277,037	47.52	91,237	5,128,422	56.21

Source: Author's computations; "Barbecue Sales Set a Record in '83," *Retail Home Furnishings* (December 19, 1983), p. 39.

Table 2   The Saguaro Barbecue Company: 1983 Income Statement

Gross sales	
Standard model	$121,213
Deluxe model	382,675
Custom deluxe model	88,881
	$592,769
Less: Cash discounts	9,308
Allowances for damaged goods	11,412
Net sales	$572,049
Less: Direct manufacturing costs[a]	234,114
Gross profit	$337,935
Less: Transportation expense	52,019
Insurance	31,418
Rent[b]	37,400
Office utilities (including phone)	18,907
Auto and truck lease	7,309
Office supplies and machine rental	12,391
Salesperson salary, travel, and expense allowance	70,345
Office manager's salary	20,000
Owner's salary	40,000
Miscellaneous	7,218
Net profit (before taxes)	$ 40,928

[a]Direct manufacturing costs include direct labor, direct materials, and utilities in the manufacturing and warehousing facility.

[b]Rent is for a 14,000 square foot building; 8,000 is for manufacturing, 3,500 for warehousing, and 2,500 for office and employee kitchen and restroom facilities.

Table 3   The Saguaro Barbecue Company: Distribution of Sales by Retail Distribution Outlet (1983)

Retail Outlet	Number of Outlets	Total Sales Volume	Average Volume per Outlet
Appliance and TV stores	37	$181,097	$4,895
Hardware stores	48	$278,375	$5,799
Home improvement centers	11	$104,124	$9,466
Grocery stores	4	$ 29,173	$7,293

Table 4   The Saguaro Barbecue Company: Monthly Distribution of Sales (1983)

Month	Sales Distribution (%)
January	7.4
February	10.1
March	15.0
April	17.0
May	16.4
June	10.3
July	6.9
August	6.1
September–December	10.8

cent. The cumulative effect would be a 75 percent increase in sales over three years.

Questions

1. Should Saguaro Barbecue Company sell direct to retailers or use wholesalers? What other channel alternatives do you see?
2. If Saguaro used full-service wholesalers, what criteria should they use to evaluate and select wholesalers? How could a sales quota be developed for each wholesaler selected?

Source: Industry data are taken from "Barbecue Sales Set a Record in '83", *Retailing Home Furnishings* (Dec. 19, 1983), p. 39.

21.

Film Distribution

Over the last forty years, the external environment of marketing has had a profound and continuing impact on the distribution of films. In the early days of movies, the Hollywood film producers were vertically integrated: they produced, distributed, and retailed films by showing them in theaters they owned and operated. In 1948, however, the Justice Department declared illegal the ownership of theaters by the major film producers. As a result, the producers had to negotiate with independent theater owners to show their films. The norm that developed in the industry was for the theater owner and the film producer to split the box-office revenue 50/50. As a rule, film producers are comfortable with that arrangement.

In the 1970s, the industry was again shaken by the advent of cable TV and home videocassette recorders. The cable TV industry is a strong negotiator and will allow the film producers to keep only about 20 percent of revenues. If the film producers do not like this arrangement, then the cable firms simply will not run their films. In addition, with the growing popularity of home videocassette recorders, more people are staying home to watch movies rather than going to movie theaters. This is possible because videocassettes of a film are often available when the film is still in the first-run stage in theaters. The problem here is that videocassettes can be copied quite easily. Instead of paying $40 to $60 for a videocassette, people will rent one for $4 a day and make a copy of it. Obviously, this violates copyright law, but it is difficult, if not impossible, to police what people do in the privacy of their homes. Some of the videocassettes being sold in retail outlets also are illegally made copies. To compound the problem, pirated copies are making their way to Europe and other countries that show a great number of U.S. made films.

The growth of videocassettes and cable TV is cutting the film producers out of the distribution business, but the producers are not taking this development lying down. First, they are trying to buy pay TV and cable TV companies or start their own. Second, they are lobbying to have stiffer laws passed on sales of home videocassette recorders to compensate them for illegal recording of films.

Questions

1. How could the film industry have prevented the detrimental effects of its external environment in the last forty years?
2. What channel alternatives do you see for film producers?

Source: Based in part on "How TV Is Revolutionizing Hollywood," *BusinessWeek* (February 21, 1983), pp. 78–89; Kathryn Harris. "From Out of Nowhere, It's HBO," *Boston Sunday Globe* (July 17, 1983), pp. A33, A43.

22.

Ensuring Product Availability at Whirlpool

At Whirlpool, the Physical Distribution Division essentially is responsible for scheduling, costing, routing and otherwise facilitating the actual physical movement of products from company plants and warehouses to wholesale and retail outlets that service the ultimate consumer. Its goal? To balance the trade-offs required to reach the optimum mix of service and cost. That means maximizing product availability while minimizing levels of inventory at every stage of the manufacturing and distribution cycle.

To do its job effectively, the Division controls a variety of interrelated functions: order processing, inventory control, logistics planning, warehousing, transportation and more. Its actions guide manufacturing production schedules, ultimately influencing raw materials and components procurement as well.

Much time and effort in recent years has been directed toward improving order cycle times, or the speed of order processing and shipping. Dramatic gains have resulted, enabling dealers and distributors to substantially reduce their inventories while still offering quick delivery to customers.

TOPS, a sophisticated four-year-old Telephone Order Processing System, also is contributing to significantly improved service to retailers. It lets distributors dial directly from a dealer's showroom to Whirlpool computers for information about current stock, production and shipping dates. Orders usually can be placed immediately and are shipped straight to the retailer, thus bypassing the distributor's warehouse. This saves time, money and damage from excess handling.

Additional cost benefits are being derived from two "mixing warehouses," one in Findlay, Ohio for laundry products and one in Evansville, Indiana for refrigeration products. At these warehouses, small shipments to dealers from various company plants are consolidated into more cost-effective, full-trailerload shipments.

Along with its responsibility for product shipments, the Division also is accountable for damage control. It loads and braces products on trucks and boxcars, inspecting each and every vehicle for anything that might cause product damage. And it makes packaging recommendations to Manufacturing based on computer-analyzed experience.

The financial aspects of product movement from Whirlpool to dealer showroom floors and into consumers' homes are facilitated by Appliance Buyers Credit Corporation (ABCC), a wholly owned finance subsidiary of Whirlpool. As a credit merchandising service that helps market *Whirlpool* brand products, ABCC offers highly competitive consumer financing programs, finances dealer inventories and provides innovative floor-planning programs for dealer showrooms.

Questions

1. Discuss how Whirlpool's orientation toward physical distribution influences customer service.
2. Does Whirlpool's emphasis on physical distribution make it a strong competitor? Explain your answer.

Source: *Whirlpool Corporation Annual Report, 1983,* p. 11. Used by permission of Whirlpool Corporation.

23.

The Kroger Company

The Kroger Co. is the largest and most profitable supermarket chain in the United States. In 1982, it generated $144 million in profits on sales of $11.9 billion. Of the thirteen major food market territories it operates in, Kroger is number one or two in market share in eleven. In the late 1960s, however, the firm was fighting for survival, primarily because most of its stores were in no-growth or slow-growth cities such as Cleveland, Milwaukee, and Chicago. The company decided to pull out of cities where it had a low market share (usually less than 10 percent); resulting in the closing of 1,237 stores.

What have been some of the other keys to Kroger's success?

- **Kroger builds new stores that are over 40,000 square feet. In the 1970s, it built 260 of these superstores. These stores stock food, drug, and household products such as small appliances, kitchen utensils, and auto parts.**

- **Kroger interviews 250,000 consumers a year to find out what they want.**

- **If a trade area grows in population, Kroger will expand a store as necessary.**

- **The company plays hardball with unions. When the union in western Michigan made unreasonable demands and Kroger could not get them to negotiate, it sold twenty-one stores and left the market.**

- **When a warehouse food store enters one of Kroger's markets, Kroger will meet its prices in order to protect its market share. However, it will only do this with the two or three stores closest to the warehouse or no-frills store.**

- **In 1983, Kroger acquired Dillion, the eleventh largest food chain in the United States. It paid $600 million in Kroger stock for Dillion. In 1982, Dillion earned 24 percent on shareholder equity (after tax).**

Questions

1. What is the marketing advantage for Kroger to build 40,000 square foot superstores? Why does it build such large stores?
2. Is Kroger's concern for high market share justifiable? Why would a large market share lead to higher profits?

Sources: Bill Saporito. "Kroger, The New King of Supermarketing," *Fortune* (February 21, 1983), pp. 74–80; *The Kroger Co. Annual Report 1982.*

24.

Management of Software Inventory

The retail software business for home computers has grown explosively since 1982. Increasingly, general merchandise retailers such as K mart, Sears, and Penneys are evaluating whether they should stock software, and if so, how much they should stock, and which software titles. In addition, toy stores like Toys "R" Us and grocery stores such as Safeway are eyeing the retail software business. Since retail software is a new product category, no one really knows where and how it should be merchandised.

Most retail software is distributed through rack jobbers such as Lieberman Enterprises, Handleman Co., and Ingram Book Co., which are seasoned rack jobbers in records, tapes, books, and health and beauty aids. For example, Ingram Book Co. rack jobs 60 million books annually. In addition to the seasoned pros, there are many small new venture rack jobbers in the computer software distributor business, most of which operate in one or a few cities in a particular region of the United States.

A big problem and expense item for software rack jobbers has been excessive returns by retailers. In order to convince retailers to stock software, the rack jobbers have offered liberal return policies. Lieberman Enterprises and Handleman Co. both offer 100 percent returns, and Ingram offers 10 percent returns per quarter. The average return policy in the industry is probably 20 to 25 percent. Almost all of the rack jobbers are also willing to negotiate returns, which means that large retail accounts are able to negotiate a better return or exchange policy. Without a doubt, returns are a big source of conflict among retailers and rack jobbers. This conflict is heightened because most software producers are very conservative in the return privileges they grant distributors. In short, the distributor is caught in the middle and is being squeezed by the manufacturer and retailer.

Many retailers will stock $8,000 to $10,000 in software. A retailer could easily have close to 200 titles if it stocked software for the following home computers: Apple, Atari, Commodore 64, Commodore VIC, IBM, and Timex. However, it is not unusual for 20 percent of the titles to account for 80 percent of the retailer's software sales.

Questions

1. Why is there such a high return of software titles by retailers? How can software inventory management be improved at the retail level?
2. Should the manufacturer, distributor, or retailer assume primary responsibility for managing inventory in the marketing channel for software?

Source: Based in part on Lisa Braden. "Software Returns: A Growth Issue," *Retailing Home Furnishings* (October 10, 1983), Section 2, pp. 20, 21, 27, 31.

PART V

PROMOTION PLANNING AND DECISIONS

Part V concerns promotion, the third component of the marketing mix. Chapter 13, "Promotion," introduces promotion. An understanding of the marketing communication process is critical to developing successful promotion strategies. Chapter 14, "Advertising and Publicity," discusses advertising's role in our economy, different types of advertising, the advertising decision-making process, and publicity. Chapter 15, "Personal Selling and Sales Promotion," describes career opportunities in personal selling and the different types of salespeople, explains the selling process and sales force management, and discusses sales promotion.

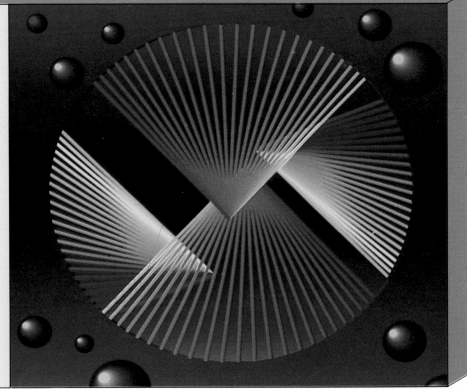

PROMOTION

MARKETER PROFILE

Brand Endorsements Mean Big Business

Hershel Walker, star running back for the USFL's New Jersey Generals, is able to nearly match his $1.3 million income as a football player by endorsing products. Walker endorses McDonald's hamburgers (under a multiyear $1 million contract), Adidas athletic shoes and outerwear (another $1 million deal), and many other products and brands.

Walker is not an isolated example of a star commanding high fees for endorsements. Professional basketball star Julius Erving of the Philadelphia 76ers has endorsed Crest toothpaste, and Michael Jackson and his family reportedly received close to $5 million to endorse Pepsi. Pepsi has also been endorsed by Lionel Richie, Tina Turner, and Geraldine Ferraro. Companies are willing to pay so much for endorsements because these celebrities are good vehicles for communicating to particular market segments.

Many athletes effectively endorse beer brands because athletes have an enormous appeal to beer drinkers. Similarly, teens are heavy cola drinkers, and Michael Jackson has a high appeal among this group. The celebrities also convey an image that many people want to emulate. Cannon Mills successfully used such stars as Bob Hope, Brooke Shields, Larry Hagman, and Joan Collins posing with sheets and towels to help increase total company sales to nearly $1 billion in 1984. Because

celebrities are idolized, they create high attention and awareness when they are featured in product advertisements.	Source: Based on "Super Deals for Superstars," *Black Enterprise* (July 1984), pp. 37, 39, 42, 57; "Sleeping with the Stars Pays Off for Cannon," *BusinessWeek* (September 24, 1984), pp. 67, 71; authors' experiences.

INTRODUCTION

Marketing communications is the way in which the seller gets the "need to buy" message to the customer and the way the customer responds to that message. This chapter will concentrate on one type of marketing communication—promotion—in which the seller tries to get the customer to respond in a certain way. For example, when you see brand endorsements, such as those discussed in the Marketer Profile, you should recognize that the company is trying to elicit the following response: "Wow, if I wear Adidas athletic shoes, I will be able to play football as well as Herschel Walker."

Promotion is *communication by marketers that attempts to inform, persuade, and influence potential buyers of a product in order to elicit a response.* The response may be covert, such as increased liking of the product, or it can be overt, such as purchase of the product. The marketers' job is to provide potential buyers with the information they need to make wise purchasing decisions. Since the marketplace is competitive, the marketer also must use promotion to persuade and influence potential buyers that the firm's offering is attractive. As such, the main function of promotional activity is not to tell both sides of a story or issue but to propagandize the firm's products.[1]

People often think of marketing as synonymous with advertising and personal selling, which are promotional activities. However, as you already know, promotion is only one aspect of marketing.

UNDERSTANDING THE COMMUNICATION PROCESS

Communication is an exchange process in which thoughts or ideas are exchanged.[2] This process is modeled in Figure 13.1.[3] **The communication process** *includes a sender who encodes a message, which is then transmitted through a message channel, and a receiver who decodes the message and provides feedback to the sender.* **Encoding** is the first step in the communication process—when *the sender puts a thought or idea into words, actions, or symbols.* Ideally, the sender's intended message is transmitted, although in reality this does not always occur. Have you ever tried unsuccessfully to express an idea? You knew what you wanted to say, but the words that came out of your mouth failed to reflect your thoughts.

The encoded thought is transmitted in the **message channel**, *the medium through which the message is carried.* Some message channels that marketers use for promotion are radio, television, newspapers, magazines, point-of-purchase displays, and the telephone.

Decoding is the next step in the communication process and consists

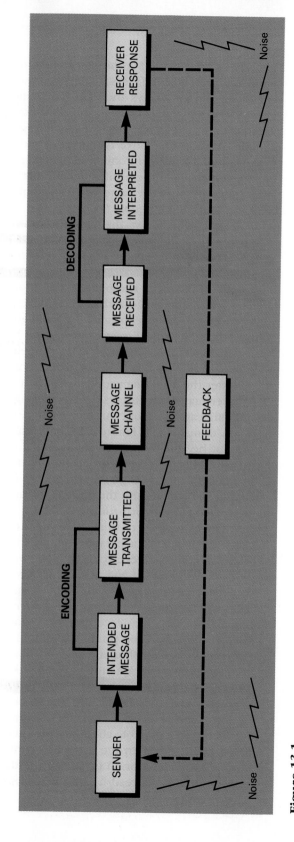

Figure 13.1
Communication Process

of *the receiver's receipt and interpretation of the message transmitted.* The sender hopes that the message received was identical to the one transmitted, but this is not always the case. For example, there might be technical problems, such as a poorly reproduced newspaper advertisement or a weak radio or TV signal that distorts a message so that the receiver hears the audio portion of a Coke commercial and while he or she sees the video portion of a Lite Beer commercial. Personal experience also can influence receivers, making them interpret the message differently than the sender intended because the same word, symbol, or action often means different things to different people.[4]

Figure 13.2 shows that only a portion of the sender's and receiver's experiences overlap, and this area of overlap is known as the **shared frame of reference**. The shared frame of reference is *where words, actions, and symbols will be understood in the same fashion by both sender and receiver.* This concept is especially important in international marketing because of the language and cultural differences. *Nova,* the name of a car produced by Chevrolet means "It doesn't go" in Spanish. When Pepsi changed the color of its cola dispenser from royal blue to ice blue in the late 1950s, its market share in Southeast Asia dropped considerably because light blue is associated with death in that part of the world.[5]

After the decoding process, the receiver responds to the message. The receiver may show interest in the message, may accept everything that is communicated without question, may react unfavorably to the communication, or may totally ignore it. From the marketer's perspective, the message will not be effective unless it elicits the desired response. Usually the response is *covert*—a favorable attitude change toward a product or increased awareness or knowledge of a product. Sometimes the response is *overt*—clipping a coupon from the newspaper and mailing it in to order a product or receive more information.

When the sender attempts to monitor the receiver's response, this is called *feedback.* In a personal selling situation where the sender is the salesperson and the receiver is the potential buyer, feedback can be obtained by carefully listening and observing how the potential buyer responds to the salesperson's suggestions and comments. With mass media, such as national magazine advertising, the sender may need to conduct marketing research to assess how receivers are responding, or the sender may monitor sales of the advertised product and infer from this data how receivers of the message are responding.

Noise appears frequently in Figure 13.1. **Noise** is *any interference that distorts a message in the communication process.* Noise is pervasive, occurring at each step of the communication process.[6] For example, a salesperson might be unable to clearly transmit her intended message because she feels uncomfortable about her boss accompanying her on the sales call. Noise could occur in the message channel (i.e., static over radio waves during a thunder storm) or during the decoding process because the receiver is trying to read a book while also watching television and thus advertisements.

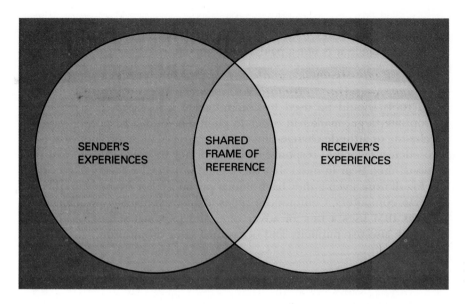

Figure 13.2
The Shared Frame of Reference

An organization can use a variety of different promotional tools to communicate with its potential customers. The major promotional tools are[7]:

ELEMENTS OF A
PROMOTION MIX

❑ **Advertising** is *any paid form of nonpersonal presentation of ideas, goods, or services by an identified sponsor.* Advertising is probably the most widespread form of promotion: each of us is exposed to over 2,000 ads and commercials every week through television, radio, magazines, newspapers, outdoor billboards and posters, catalogs, and even cabs and buses with advertisements on them.

❑ **Personal selling** is *an oral presentation in a conversation with one or more prospective purchasers for the purpose of making sales.* Personal selling includes such things as a salesperson explaining a product's features, a technician demonstrating a new phone system to office personnel, and even the person at the local supermarket who hands out free samples of pizza while telling about its ingredients.

❑ **Sales promotion** is *any marketing activity—other than personal selling, advertising, and publicity—that stimulates consumer purchasing and dealer effectiveness.* Sales promotion activities are usually short-term and fall into two categories: (1) special offers, such as coupons, refunds, cents-off offers, and contests, and (2) special methods, such as point-of-purchase displays, free samples (without personal selling), exhibits, and other nonroutine, nonpersonal selling efforts.

❑ **Publicity** is *nonpersonal stimulation of demand for goods, services, or business units by generating commercially significant news about them in the mass media. It is not paid for directly by a sponsor.* Publicity includes such things as news items about products and companies, and the mention of brands and companies in plays, books, and television shows. Publicity can be an inexpensive and effective promotional tool except that there is little control over its timing and content since it is not a paid advertisement.

The mix of advertising, personal selling, sales promotion, and publicity that composes a firm's promotional tools is its **promotion mix**. Promotional tools should be used to communicate a message to a person or appropriate target market in order to elicit a favorable response—such as purchasing or attitude change. Since the purpose of these promotional tools is to elicit a favorable response, it is important to create an optimal promotional mix. Bear in mind that there is no universally acceptable correct mix for all firms even if they have similar products. For example, in the sale of home computers, Commodore relies almost exclusively on advertising whereas IBM uses a mix of advertising and personal selling. Both firms obviously also use publicity and occasional sales promotions.

PLANNING PROMOTIONAL STRATEGIES

When planning promotional strategies, marketing managers must determine what emphasis to put on interpersonal versus mass communication, whether to select a push or a pull strategy, and how much importance to place on customer advertising. These are just some of the many decisions marketing managers have to make about promotional strategies.

Interpersonal or Mass Communication

Marketers use both interpersonal and mass communication for promotional purposes. **Interpersonal communication** occurs when *both sender and receiver can query each other directly.* Personal selling relies heavily on interpersonal communication. **Mass communication** involves *a sender communicating in an impersonal way with a large number of receivers, with no direct feedback from the receivers.* Advertising, publicity, and sales promotion rely primarily on mass communication, through television, radio, newspapers and magazines, sales brochures, packaging, circulars, and point-of-purchase displays.

Figure 13.3, which compares interpersonal and mass communication, shows that interpersonal communication has a high cost per individual reached coupled with a high ability to attract and hold attention because of its two-way message flow. On the other hand, mass communication is low in cost per individual reached but has a low ability to attract and hold attention because of its one-way message flow.

Firms vary considerably in their mix of interpersonal and mass communication. To illustrate this, Figure 13.4 shows the mix of interpersonal

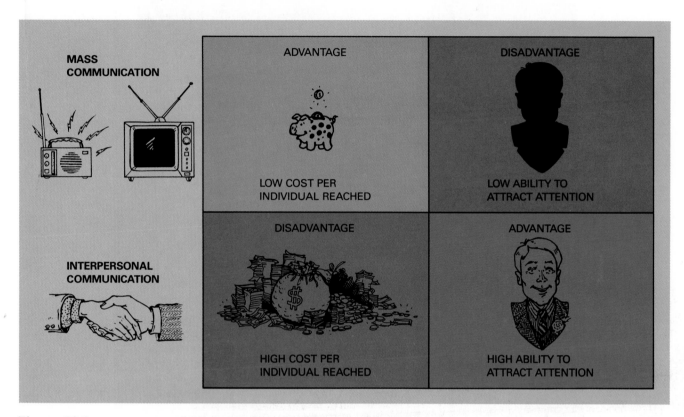

Figure 13.3
Interpersonal Versus Mass Communication

and mass communication used by Avon and Revlon, both of which are dominant firms in the cosmetics industry. Avon uses a large amount of interpersonal communication because of its national network of sales representatives who personally sell Avon products door to door. Avon doesn't totally ignore mass communication, however, since it does engage in some national advertising and distributes product brochures and catalogs. Revlon, on the other hand, uses considerably more mass communication. Revlon has national advertising directed to the consumer. It also advertises in trade magazines, which retail and wholesale buyers read, and has point-of-purchase displays, which retailers can set up in their stores to attract attention. Furthermore, retailers handling Revlon cosmetics will advertise Revlon's products in local newspapers. Nonetheless, Revlon still needs some interpersonal communication in its promotion mix. Revlon has salespeople who call on distributors, distributors have salespeople who call on retailers, and retail clerks personally sell Revlon cosmetics to customers shopping in the store. Also, Revlon sometimes places employees in large department stores to hand out free samples and demonstrate the Revlon line of cosmetics.

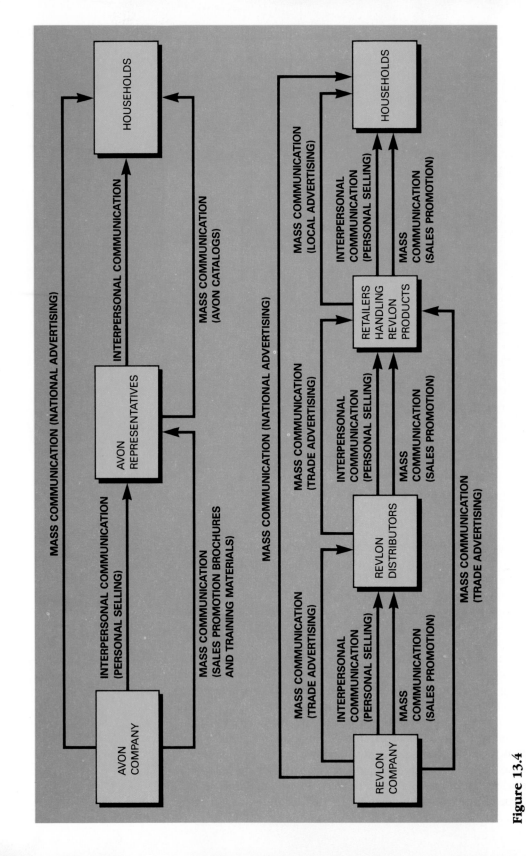

Figure 13.4

Interpersonal and Mass Communication in Two Companies

To Push or to Pull?

In the distribution section, we saw that promotional activities occur throughout the marketing channel from manufacturers to distributors and retailers. A marketing manager can use either a push or a pull strategy in designing a promotional program. For both of these strategies, the thing to remember is that no product will sell well unless it gets good wholesale and retail distribution.[8] Product availability is a necessary condition of sale.

In a **push strategy**, *the bulk of promotional effort is directed at the members of the marketing channel to get them to push the products forward in the marketing channel.* Personal selling, advertising, and sales promotions are directed at wholesalers and retailers to get them to handle the products. Middlemen are encouraged to promote the product to the next channel institution or, in the case of the retailer, to the final consumer. In principle, a push strategy involves pushing a product through the marketing channel.[9]

In a **pull strategy**, *the manufacturer directs the majority of its promotional effort toward the ultimate consumer in an attempt to get them to pull the products through the marketing channel.* This develops a high degree of consumer awareness, interest, and desire for the product. Consumers then go to retail stores to find a product, and if it is not there, they urge the retailer to stock it. The retailer then goes looking for the product and finds the wholesaler that carries it or, alternatively, asks a current wholesaler to carry the product. The wholesaler, in turn, seeks out the manufacturer. A pull strategy involves the development of a high level of customer demand in order to pull the product through the marketing channel. An example of a pull promotion strategy in the computer software industry is available in the Marketing in Action on page 409.

Figure 13.5 compares push and pull promotion strategies. In actuality, successful promotion programs have elements of both strategies because it is easier to push a product through a channel if the final consumer is pulling (requesting it from the retailer). For example, Kraft advertises heavily in *Progressive Grocer,* a magazine widely read by food wholesalers and retailers. It also has a sales force that calls on these marketing channel institutions. This promotion encourages the stocking of the Kraft line of cheeses and related products, thus fostering a push through the marketing channel. At the same time, Kraft advertises heavily to the final consumer in magazines such as *Good Housekeeping.* This helps to create consumer demand or a pulling of the Kraft line through the marketing channel.

Customer Word-of-Mouth Advertising

Word-of-mouth advertising can have a major impact on a product or firm's success or failure.[10] In fact, it is sometimes the most influential form of communication in the selection of a new product. *When consumers engage*

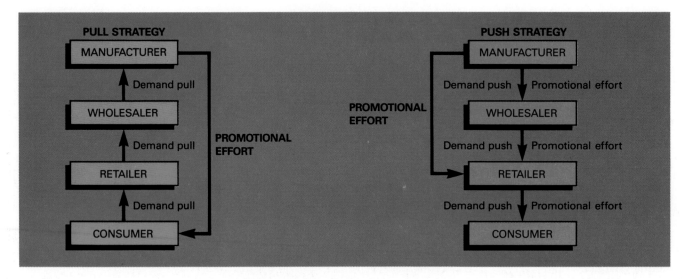

Figure 13.5
Pull Versus Push Promotional Strategies

in conversation about a marketer's products, this is referred to as **word-of-mouth advertising**. All of us have engaged in it at one time or another when we tell our friends about our good and bad experiences with products. Word-of-mouth advertising is especially important among teenagers, who tend to follow the suggestions of their peers.

Word-of-mouth advertising is also very important in the selection of a new product or innovation for which the consumer perceives high risk and therefore is likely to talk with friends about the product before trying it. For example, research has indicated that the recommendations of friends and relatives are the primary reason for selecting a physician.[11] This is especially noticeable of people relocating in a new town where they do not know any physicians. If you are attending a university that does not have its own student health center, you probably have asked the opinions of others when you needed the services of a dentist or physician. Clearly, the importance of word-of-mouth advertising cannot be overemphasized.

Word-of-mouth advertising is also important for products for which there are opinion leaders. An **opinion leader** is *someone who actively espouses his or her opinions about products or from whom others seek out the views and opinions of products.* Opinion leaders tend to be product-specific. If you are an avid amateur photographer, then your friends are likely to seek your opinion when they decide to purchase a camera. The existence of opinion leaders involves a two-step flow of communication: a flow from the organization to opinion leaders and then word-of-mouth advertising by opinion leaders to potential buyers. This two-step model is illustrated in Figure 13.6. The Marketing in Action on page 411 shows how Collagen Corp. uses opinion leaders to promote Zyderm Collagen Implant.

MARKETING IN ACTION

Consumers have pretty much ignored generations of computer software. The operating systems they acquired, and thus the software used, was whatever happened to come as part of the package when they purchased their computers. With an increasing number of firms writing software programs, the marketing effort is shifting toward a pull strategy. Software firms now advertise their wares mainly to end users or consumers. For example:

● **Digital Research Inc. instituted a "Procter & Gamble style" marketing program in which they increased their promotional budget to over $3 million and sponsored a convention**

The Software Industry Tries a Pull Strategy

for end users of its operating systems in an attempt to increase its direct sales market.

● **AT&T and Microsoft Inc. are advertising their software to consumers through media such as *BusinessWeek, Venture,* the *Wall Street Journal,* and television advertising.**

● **Lotus Development Corp. spent more than $1 million in a three-month period in 1983 for advertising its 1-2-3 software to end users.**

● **Computer Associates, Inc. installed a $250,000 television studio to make training videotapes for its software customers.**

Robert D. Baskerville of Computer Sciences Corp. sums up the shift by noting that today a software company has "to sell to end users, and you have to emphasize more than technical capability—you have to really sell the benefit."

Sources: "A Feverish Race in Operating Systems," *BusinessWeek* (February 21, 1983), pp. 96, 98; "Software: The New Driving Force," *BusinessWeek* (February 27, 1984), pp. 74–84; Microsoft and AT&T advertisements and the authors' background and experience.

Figure 13.6

Two-Step Flow of Communication for Downsak Sleeping Bags

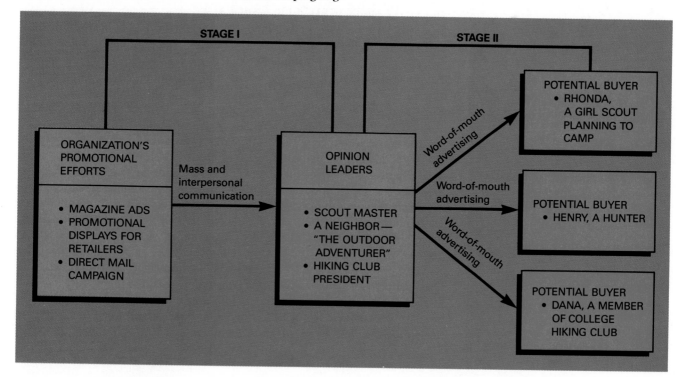

ELICITING THE DESIRED RESPONSE

AIDAS: A Response Hierarchy Model

We stressed earlier in the chapter that the purpose of all marketing communications was to elicit a response among potential buyers. Potential buyers go through a behavioral or psychological process before purchasing a product, and this process is usually referred to as a response hierarchy.[12] One of the most popular response hierarchies is called **AIDA**, which is *an acronym for the steps through which a buyer progresses on the way to purchasing a product.* The steps are a*wareness* (or attention), *interest, desire, and action.* The AIDA model simply suggests that buyers are unlikely to take action and purchase a product unless they first have an awareness of it, develop an interest in it, and desire the product. After a product has been purchased, consumers will find it to be rewarding, satisfactory, or punishing, creating dissatisfaction. Thus, to complete the AIDA model, *we can add a fifth step, satisfaction* **(AIDAS)**.

The AIDAS model incorporates psychological processes: awareness is a cognitive process, interest and desire are affective processes, action is a manifest behavior process, and satisfaction is a postpurchase evaluation process.[13]

Setting Promotional Objectives

The AIDAS model is helpful in setting promotion objectives. At the awareness stage, the promotion objective is to get the attention of those persons in the firm's target market.

The objective in the interest stage is to create and hold interest. For example, the Jenn-Air advertisement for grill ranges creates interest by offering a $75 to $100 rebate (most of us are interested in money), then holds interest by showing pictures of many tempting foods being cooked on Jenn-Air grills.

In the desire stage of the AIDAS model, a company tries to appeal to the target group's wish to fill some need (recall Maslow's hierarchy of needs from Chapter 5) by creating a desire for the product. The SAAB advertisement, for example, appeals to the upwardly mobile segment who want to fulfill esteem needs of prestige, success, and achievement without neglecting safety and physiological needs. By explaining how it is possible to achieve these aims, SAAB hopes to increase the number of target customers who desire the product.

The objective of the fourth stage, the action stage, is to motivate purchasing behavior. This is often done by making it easy for the target customer to take action, such as providing a toll-free phone number to call for immediate information and purchasing or an order blank to fill out and mail in. Notice the L.L. Bean advertisement includes an order blank and the

MARKETING IN ACTION

Collagen Corp. Recognizes Opinion Leaders

Collagen Corp. produces a product called *Zyderm Collagen Implant,* or ZCI, that is used as a treatment for repairing scars and wrinkles. Collagen has five target markets for ZCI: entertainers, status seekers (who want to appear wealthy whether or not they really are), people entering the work force at a later age, cosmetologists and other beauty specialists, and the estimated 12 million acne-scarred Americans.

Since ZCI is relatively new and expensive ($300–$600 per treatment), a potential user is likely to seek out opinions of others, especially the opinion of their physician, since the product must be injected by a physician. Recognizing the potential opinion leadership role of physicians, Collagen spent $3.5 million on promoting ZCI to 10,000 dermatologists, plastic surgeons, and head-and-neck specialists. The promotion was composed of direct mail, advertisements in medical journals, and special symposiums on the safety and value of ZCI. To further encourage use by the end user, Collagen is placing low-key ads in *Ladies Home Journal* and *Women's Day* (a pull strategy). These ads should result in more persons who have a potential need for the product seeking their physicians' opinions. To date, Collagen Corp. has been successful in getting 70 percent of its targeted physicians to use the product.

Source: Based in part on information in "The Smooth Selling of a Wrinkle Remover," *BusinessWeek* (March 5, 1984), p. 66; and advertisements for Zyderm Collagen treatments.

Following the AIDAS model, once awareness of the product is established, one sure way to create interest is by offering a monetary incentive, as Jenn-Air does in this ad (left). If prestige, success, and achievement are important to the target market, this ad for Saab (right) will create the desire for the product.

option of charging the purchase on a national credit card. The easier it is for customers to take action, the more likely they are to do so.

Finally, the objective of the satisfaction stage is to reinforce positive experiences with the product or positive aspects of the product. As the Etch A Sketch ad states, who wants to argue satisfaction with 50 million moms?

50 Million Moms Can't Be Wrong

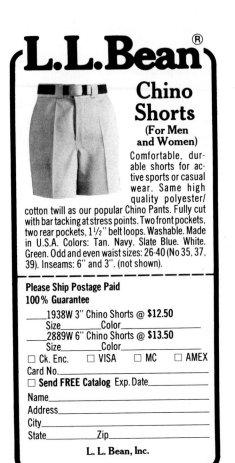

Moms know, nothing draws out creativity like the Etch A Sketch® Magic Screen. The power of imagination. To explore. To discover. To accomplish. To think. Remember? It's that one toy you would never use the same way twice, and it seemed to last forever. Open their world with the Etch A Sketch® Magic Screen. It's one of the nicest childhood memories anyone can have.

Once awareness, interest, and desire have been established, it is important to make it as easy as possible for the customer to take action—as L.L. Bean does by providing a simple form (above) to clip and mail. The final buyer response, satisfaction, is reinforced in this Etch A Sketch® ad (right).

AIDAS and the Promotion Mix

The promotion mix varies depending on the point in the response hierarchy where the organization wishes to direct its promotional efforts. This is illustrated in Table 13.1. If the firm's primary objective is to gain awareness, then advertising is the most effective promotional tool. Advertising is also generally most effective at creating and holding interest and for reinforcing positive aspects of the product to develop postpurchase satisfaction. Personal selling tends to be most effective at creating desire and motivating purchasing behavior.

Figure 13.7 illustrates the general effectiveness of promotion tools at different stages in the AIDAS model. You should be aware, however, that the figure is based on broad generalizations and there are exceptions.

AIDAS As a Diagnostic Tool

The AIDAS model is a useful tool for diagnosing the effectiveness of an organization's promotional program. With the tools of marketing research (See Chapter 4), an organization can collect information on the stages in the AIDAS model. Table 13.2 shows possible questions to measure each step in AIDAS for a hypothetical new breakfast cereal called Cheers. Responses to these types of questions can help point the organization to the stage in the hierarchy where more promotional effort is needed. For example, if 80 percent of the respondents were aware of Cheers (as reflected in their response to question 1), but only 40 percent of these people were interested in Cheers (as reflected in their responses to the three attributes in question 2), then a promotional campaign could be developed with the objective of increasing the level of interest to 70 percent.

Unfortunately, there is no precise or totally scientific approach to determining the optimal promotion mix, as the mix depends on the target market, type of product, competitive activity, profit margins, and a variety of other factors. Nonetheless, some general rules and guidelines can be given.[14]

HOW TO DEVELOP AN

OPTIMAL PROMOTION MIX

Table 13.1   The AIDAS Model

Stage	Response	Promotion Objective
Cognitive	*Awareness*	Gain attention
Affective	*Interest*	Create and hold interest
	Desire	Arouse desire
Manifest behavior	*Action*	Motivate purchasing behavior
Postpurchase evaluation	*Satisfaction*	Reinforce positive aspects of product

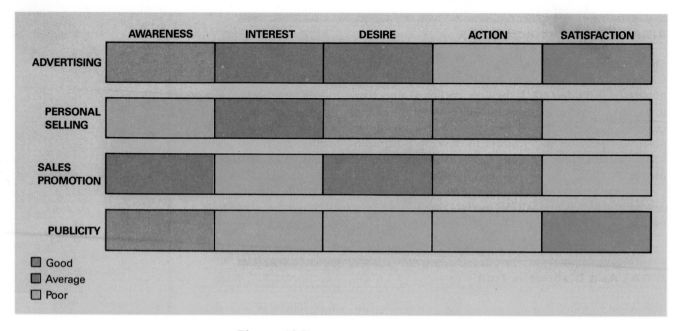

Figure 13.7
AIDAS and the Effectiveness of the Promotion Mix

Establish Your Promotion Objectives

A marketing manager must know the promotion objectives before the optimal mix decision can be intelligently approached, because the effectiveness of different promotion tools is related to their particular stages in the AIDAS model.[15] For promotion objectives to help establish an optimal promotion mix, they must be stated in measurable terms. Table 13.3 gives examples of measurable and immeasurable objectives.

One of the major advantages of stating promotion objectives in measurable terms is that it allows the organization to assess the effectiveness of its promotional mix. If the promotional mix is not effective, the manager can begin to alter certain aspects of the promotion mix and then monitor the change to see if promotional effectiveness was improved.

Aim for Your Target Market

In trying to develop an optimal promotion mix, the marketing manager must understand the size and characteristics of the target market as well as the buying decision process for the target market. (Target markets were discussed in Chapter 7.)

Table 13.2   Cheers Questionnaire

1. *Awareness:* Please name as many brands of breakfast cereal as you can.
Proceed to question 2 only if Cheers is mentioned; otherwise terminate interview.
2. *Interest:* Below are some attributes of Cheers. For each attribute, check your level
of interest in a breakfast cereal that has that attribute.

	no interest	moderate interest	high interest
a. low calorie	_____	_____	_____
b. low price	_____	_____	_____
c. high nutrition	_____	_____	_____

3. *Desire:* Please rank order your favorite (most preferred) breakfast cereals. Rank
from most (1) to least (7) preferred.

_____ Kellogg's Corn Flakes
_____ Raisin Bran
_____ Cheers
_____ Rice Krispies
_____ Shreaded Wheat
_____ Special K
_____ Cheerios

4. *Action:* Have you purchased or eaten Cheers in the last three months?

_____ yes
_____ no

Proceed to question 5 only if the answer yes is given; otherwise terminate interview.
5. *Satisfaction:* How satisfied are you with Cheers breakfast cereal?

_____ very satisfied
_____ somewhat satisfied
_____ don't know
_____ somewhat dissatisfied
_____ very dissatisfied

Table 13.3   Measurable Versus Immeasurable Promotion Objectives

Immeasurable	Measurable
Increase awareness	Increase awareness among 18- to 32-year-old men by 25% within 3 months
Arouse desire	Increase preference for the product by 15% among households with an income over $40,000 within 8 weeks
Motivate purchasing behavior	Increase our market share among first-time purchasers from 2% to 5% of the market within 1 year

As the size of the market increases, mass communication becomes more cost efficient than personal selling techniques. For example, the estimated per-person cost of one TV commercial that reaches 15 million households is only one half cent, whereas the average cost of one call by a salesperson would be considerably higher and, in many cases, even exceed $100. A paradox arises in this regard, however, because as the market gets larger, it is likely to become more heterogeneous. As a result, any single mass communication (for example, an advertisement) will become less effective. Thus, firms will often develop different advertisements for different market segments even though the same product is being offered.

Another factor to consider is the buying decision process. Are buyers likely to engage in habitual decision making, where they know the brand they want and the store where they can buy it, or is extended decision making predominant, where they do not know the brand or possibly the product class wanted and also have no strong store preference? With habitual decision making, the consumer will not actively seek information and thus in-store point-of-purchase displays and personal selling will be most effective. With extended decision making, however, the buyer will actively seek information, so that advertising and publicity will have a major impact.

Know Your Product

The product itself influences the choice of promotional tools. When products are relatively simple and easy for the consumer to understand (such as beer or breakfast cereals), then advertising can easily convey the basic information the consumer needs. On the other hand, personal selling and sales promotion tools, such as brochures and sophisticated point-of-purchase displays, are more effective and informative for complex products like computers, videorecorders, and industrial equipment.

The price of the product also has a bearing on the promotion mix. When the product is relatively inexpensive, the buyer assumes little risk and therefore an ad that provides little information is acceptable. With an expensive product, however, such as a new piano or house, for which the risk of making the wrong choice is high, the consumer will desire information from a variety of sources. In this case, personal selling, publicity, and word-of-mouth communication, in addition to advertising, can be very important.

Know the Economics of the Mix Elements

To develop an optimal promotion mix, you must know the cost of various promotional tools and relate this cost to the amount the organization plans to spend on promotion. Some promotional tools will simply be too expensive to use given the firm's budget, despite the fact that they may be the most effective tools. For example, if a small manufacturer has $250,000 to

READ

Baryshnikov
for America's
Libraries

American Library Association

The American Library Association aims at a target market in which extended decision making is predominant.

spend on promotion, then it could easily spend all of it on five, 60-second national television advertisements. For the same amount, it could hire and support five salespeople. It probably would be best to go with the five salespeople, since five advertisements spread over one year are unlikely to have as great an impact as five salespeople.

An organization wants to get the best return possible on their promotion dollars, or as they say in the trade, get the "biggest bang for the buck." The dilemma is that mass communication is lower in cost per person reached than interpersonal communication, but interpersonal communication is more effective in getting people to purchase a product. The marketing manager must try to balance this tradeoff to come up with the best mix of mass and interpersonal communication and subsequently the best mix of advertising, personal selling, sales promotion, and publicity.

Study Your Competition

Before you determine the best promotion mix for your product, you should consider your competitors' promotion mix. If Oscar Mayer increases its advertising budget by 50 percent, then Swift and Armour will also need to increase their advertising budgets if they want to hold onto their share of the luncheon meat market. Furthermore, if Oscar Mayer also increases its sales force, then competitors will be at a disadvantage if they do not follow suit.

There are alternatives to increasing promotional expenditures. One possibility that should always be considered is how to use existing resources more productively (i.e., can you make current advertising and sales force expenditures more effective?). You should assess the potential profit impact of responding to competitors' increased promotional spending. What is more profitable: increasing, decreasing, or keeping promotional expenditures the same? An additional possibility is to emphasize another element of the marketing mix (i.e., lower price, better customer service, or higher product quality).

Establish Proper Organization Structure

The optimal promotion mix can only be obtained if all promotional efforts are managed from a systems perspective.[16] Typically, different promotional tools have distinct managers who are responsible for selecting the proper methods, timing, training, and budget within their respective areas. For example, an advertising manager selects the right media, develops ads, and controls the advertising budget. The sales force manager is responsible for the firm's personal selling activities, including training and control of salespeople. The sales promotion manager handles the sales promotion efforts by developing brochures, point-of-purchase displays and catalogs and by controlling the sales promotion budget. The public relations director develops publicity for the firm by planting important items in the media that show the company in a favorable light.

The activities of all of these managers must be coordinated to reflect the best interest of the firm as a whole. As shown in Figure 13.8, these managers usually report to a senior marketing executive, who tries to get all the managers to work as a team even though they each have their separate jobs and responsibilities. One way this is often accomplished is to have them work together on committees to solve particular problems or make certain decisions. For example, as a committee they may develop the promotion plan for a new product introduction.

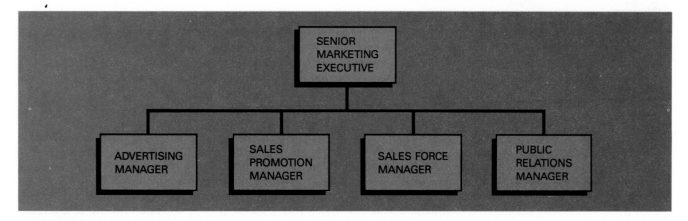

Figure 13.8
Organizing Promotion Managers

In the United States, promotion activities, especially advertising, are controlled or regulated by many groups.[17] State and federal laws regulate unfair and deceptive promotions. The major federal laws, the Federal Trade Commission (FTC) Act (1914) and the Wheeler-Lea Amendment (1938) to the FTC Act, outlaw unfair and deceptive practices in commerce, and deceptive advertising or promotion falls into this category.

The FTC has been granted considerable latitude and power to regulate advertising. The FTC can apply to a federal district court for a cease-and-desist order, which prevents a firm from running a particular advertisement. The cease-and-desist order automatically becomes final and binding sixty days after issuance. The FTC can also require a firm to substantiate its advertising claims.[18] In addition, the FTC can require a firm to run corrective advertising if prior advertising has misinformed or deceived a consumer.[19]

Promotion is also highly self-regulated by industry. Most firms that advertise, advertising agencies, local better business bureaus, trade associations, and the National Advertising Review Board (NARB) try to prevent unfair and deceptive advertising from occurring. The NARB is part of the nationwide council of better business bureaus and is composed of members from national advertisers, advertising agencies, and the general public. Its purpose is to serve as a self-regulatory vehicle for the advertising industry and to cut down the amount of deceptive and unfair advertising before the FTC has a chance to complain. The NARB has been quite successful in achieving this objective.[20]

Much of the self-regulation of advertising has been prompted by consumerism and consumer complaints about misleading advertisements. Most firms recognize that it is better to self-regulate than to allow government to step in and force regulation on them.[21]

WHO CONTROLS PROMOTION?

SUMMARY

This chapter introduced some basic concepts and models that will help you understand how promotion decisions in marketing are made. The most central model you should understand is that of the communication process, since promotion is a communication process.

Organizations have a variety of promotional tools they can use to communicate with potential customers. The major promotional tools are advertising, personal selling, sales promotion, and publicity. Personal selling is interpersonal communication, whereas advertising, sales promotion, and publicity are primarily mass communication. The firm can use its promotion mix to develop a push or a pull strategy. With a push strategy, the organization directs its promotional efforts at marketing channel institutions, which then push the product forward to the final buyer. On the other hand, with a pull strategy, the organization directs its promotional efforts at the final buyer in order to develop a strong demand that is used to pull a product through the marketing channel.

Word-of-mouth advertising is an important type of promotion over which firms have little or no control. Word-of-mouth advertising can have a big impact on customer response to new products. Opinion leaders play an important role in word-of-mouth advertising.

The purpose of all marketing communications is to elicit a response among potential buyers. One response model, called AIDAS, places the potential responses into a hierarchy of steps: awareness, interest, desire, action, and satisfaction. These five steps depict the steps a consumer goes through from initial product awareness to postpurchase evaluation. Each of the promotional tools has different degrees of effectiveness for eliciting these different responses.

There is no single optimal promotion mix and no well-accepted scientific approach to determining the optimal mix. Instead, the marketing manager needs to consider the following in developing a promotion mix: the objectives of the promotional effort, the size and characteristics of the target market and their buying decision process, the type of products being promoted, the economics of the mix elements, competitors' promotional efforts, and a proper organizational structure to implement these decisions.

This chapter also briefly discussed the control and regulation of promotion and, especially, advertising. On the national level, advertising is primarily policed by the Federal Trade Commission. Also, industry voluntarily self-regulates its advertising with the assistance of the National Advertising Review Board.

KEY CONCEPTS

promotion (p. 400)
communication process (p. 400)
encoding (p. 400)
message channel (p. 400)
decoding (pp. 400–402)
shared frame of reference (p. 402)
noise (p. 402)

advertising (p. 403)
personal selling (p. 403)
sales promotion (p. 403)
publicity (p. 403)
promotion mix (p. 404)
interpersonal communication (p. 404)
mass communication (p. 404)

push strategy (p. 407)
pull strategy (p. 407)
word-of-mouth advertising (pp. 407–408)

opinion leader (p. 408)
AIDA (p. 410)
AIDAS (p. 410)

REVIEW AND DISCUSSION QUESTIONS

1. List and explain the four steps in the communication process.

2. Identify some of the sources of noise in television advertising.

3. What are the four major elements of a promotion mix?

4. What are the advantages and disadvantages of mass communication and inter-personal communication?

5. Define *pull* and *push promotion strategies* and give examples of each.

6. What is the relationship between opinion leaders and word-of-mouth advertising?

7. What element of promotion is best for developing awareness? Interest? Desire? Action? Postpurchase satisfaction?

8. Explain the AIDAS model and discuss how it can be used to set promotion objectives.

9. Define *promotion mix* and then briefly discuss the factors to consider in developing an optimal promotion mix.

10. What is the problem with using "increasing sales" as a promotion objective?

11. How is promotion or advertising controlled or regulated in the United States?

ACTION PROBLEMS

1. What proportion of advertising and personal selling would you recommend for each of the following products? (Assume you have a large budget.)
   a. breakfast cereal
   b. farm tractor
   c. computer for a small business
   d. college
   e. cigarettes
   f. public accounting auditing services.

2. Identify a major durable good you recently purchased (auto, stereo, microwave oven, pair of skis, bicycle, and so on) and list all communications that you received. How did the AIDAS model fit into the communications you received?

3. Cut out several magazine ads and try to identify which step in the AIDAS model each advertisement represents.

4. Recently, you have been retained as a consultant to develop the promotion mix for a new brand of body deodorant. Write a memo to the vice president of marketing explaining how the communication process can be used as a model in designing the promotion program.

5. You are marketing manager for a large national brewery, and eight weeks ago your company introduced a new brand of low calorie, low alcohol beer. The introduction was accompanied by a $2 million promotional budget. Several days ago, a market research study was conducted among your target market group. The findings indicate that 70 percent of the target market are aware of the new brand, 60 percent of those who are aware have a high interest level, 80 percent of those who are highly interested have a high desire level, and 50 percent of those with a high desire level have bought or tried the brand. Of those that purchased it, 80 percent were satisfied.

(a) What percent of the target market tried or purchased the new brand?

(b) Analyze the research results and recommend where to concentrate your promotional efforts.

NOTES

1. Propaganda function in marketing communications is discussed in Edmund D. McGarry, "The Propaganda Function in Marketing," *Journal of Marketing* (October 1958), pp. 131–139.

2. This is discussed more thoroughly in Cassandra L. Book, *Human Communication: Principles, Concepts, and Skills* (New York: St. Martin's Press, 1980).

3. Several models of the communication process on which this model is based are presented in C. David Mortenson, *Communication: The Study of Human Interaction* (New York: McGraw-Hill, 1972); William J. Severin and James W. Tankard, Sr., *Communication Theories, Origins, Methods, Uses* (New York: Hastings House, 1979).

4. James F. Engel, Martin R. Warshaw, Thomas C. Kinnear, *Promotional Strategy,* 5th edition (Homewood, IL: Richard D. Irwin, 1983), pp. 20–22.

5. Max M. Lomont, " 'Ten Commandments' Guide Multinational Packaging," *Marketing News* (December 23, 1983), p. 3.

6. A more complete discussion of noise in the communication process is provided in John Parry, *The Psychology of Human Communication* (New York: Elsevier, 1968), pp. 83–126.

7. Adapted from Ralph S. Alexander, et al., *Marketing Definitions: A Glossary of Marketing Terms* (Chicago: American Marketing Association, 1960). Used by permission.

8. The importance of getting good retail and wholesale distribution is discussed in Peter R. Dickson, "Distributor Portfolio Analysis and the Channel Dependence Matrix: New Techniques for Understanding and Managing the Channel," *Journal of Marketing* (Summer 1983), pp. 35–44.

9. Obtaining resellers' support by developing a push strategy is discussed in Michael Levy, John Webster, and Roger A. Kerin, "Formulating Push Marketing Strategies: A Method and Application," *Journal of Marketing* 47(Winter 1983), pp. 25–34.

10. Johan Arndt, *Word of Mouth Advertising: A Review of the Literature* (Advertising Research Foundation, 1967).

11. Roger D. Blackwell and W. Wayne Talarzyk, *Common Attitudes Toward Health Care and Malpractice* (Columbus, OH: Grid Publishing, 1977).

12. A review of the research on response hierarchies is offered in Michael L. Ray, *Marketing Communications and the Hierarchy of Effects* (Cambridge, MA: Marketing Science Institute, 1973).

pothesis of a Hierarchy of Effects: A Partial Evaluation," *Journal of Marketing Research* (February 1966), pp. 13–24; Terence O'Brien. "Stages of Consumer Decision Making," *Journal of Marketing Research* (August 1971), pp. 283–289.

14. For further information on developing a promotion mix, see William Dommermuth, "Promoting Your Product: Managing the Mix," *Business* (July–August 1980), pp. 18–21.

15. Robert A. Kriegal, "Setting Tactical Communications Standards," *Business Marketing* (February 1984), pp. 66–68.

16. Dommermuth, "Promoting Your Product," pp. 18–21; William Dommermuth, *Promotion: Analysis, Creativity, and Strategy* (Boston: Kent Publishing Co., 1984), pp. 59–60.

17. An excellent discussion of regulatory policy in Europe and the United States can be found in John C. Driver and Gordon R. Foxall, *Advertising Policy and Practice* (New York: St. Martin's Press, 1984).

18. Dorothy Cohen, "The FTC's Advertising Substantiation Program," *Journal of Marketing* (Winter 1980), pp. 29–35.

19. Gary M. Armstrong, Martin N. Gurol, and Frederick A. Russ, "Detecting and Correcting Deceptive Advertising," *Journal of Consumer Research* (December 1979), pp. 237–246; David M. Gardner, "Deception in Advertising: A Conceptual Approach," *Journal of Marketing* (January 1975), pp. 40–46; Michael B. Mazis and Janice E. Adkinson, "An Experimental Evaluation of a Proposed Corrective Advertising Remedy," *Journal of Marketing Research* (May 1976), pp. 178–183.

20. Stanley E. Cohen, "Advertising Regulation: Changing, Growing Areas," *Advertising Age* (April 30, 1980), pp. 213–218.

21. Self-regulation of advertising is further discussed in Priscilla A. LaBarbera, "Analyzing and Advancing the State of the Art of Advertising Self-Regulation," *Journal of Advertising* 9(No. 4 1980), pp. 27–38; Priscilla A. LaBarbera, "Advertising Self-Regulation: An Evaluation," *MSU Business Topics* (Summer 1980), pp. 55–63.

LEARNING OBJECTIVES

After you complete this chapter, you should be able to:

- **Identify** what advertising can and cannot accomplish

- **Recognize** and **distinguish** between product and institutional advertising and informative, persuasive, and reminder advertising

- **Outline** the seven steps in the advertising decision process

- **Discuss** the five methods of budgeting for advertising

- **Describe** how to evaluate advertising effectiveness

- **Explain** why firms use advertising agencies

- **Identify** the purpose and uses of publicity

ADVERTISING AND PUBLICITY

MARKETER PROFILE

Barbara Proctor of Proctor & Gardner Advertising Inc.

Barbara Proctor, chief executive officer, founder, president, and creative director of Proctor & Gardner Advertising Inc. in Chicago—one of the nation's largest black-owned advertising agencies—never viewed her race and sex as handicaps. In fact, she owes her success to being born female and black. "Racism and sexism were only challenges to me, not obstacles," she says.

Born in Asheville, North Carolina, she won a scholarship to Talladega College in Alabama, where she earned two bachelor's degrees. After successful careers as a jazz writer and advertising copy writer, she founded Proctor & Gardner Advertising Inc. in 1970 with the help of an $80,000 Small Business Administration loan. Today the firm grosses over $8.5 million annually and has Jewel Food Stores, Kraft Inc., and Sears as its major clients. Much of the firm's success is based on Proctor's innovative ideas in marketing corporate concepts aimed at the black consumer market. And she still remains sole owner.

In 1984, she was cited by President Reagan in his State of the Union address as an example of one of "the heroes of the eighties." However, she cautions black agencies to consider how the social and political environments differ today from those of fifteen years ago, when most leading black agencies started. "This is not the 1970s where the administration and the corporate leadership of

America felt that affirmative action goals should have priority," she says. "When the decade closed, the cap went on and we got less business. This means that there are going to be fewer black agencies and fewer of us will survive, but those of us who do will survive big."

Source: Based on "I Made It Because I'm Black and a Woman," *Ebony* (August 1982), pp. 142–144; Ken Smikle. "The Image Makers," *Black Enterprise* (December 1985), p. 52.

INTRODUCTION

Advertising, as defined in Chapter 13, is *any paid form of nonpersonal presentation of ideas, goods, or services by an identified sponsor.* It plays a major role in the mass market economy because it is a method of communication for the purpose of eliciting a "buy" response from a large target group. Unless you live in the wilderness, it is difficult to avoid some type of advertising. You hear advertising on your favorite radio station, see it on television, in magazines and newspapers. When you travel to work or school, you see advertising on outdoor billboards. Most of the advertising you see and hear is designed and produced by advertising agencies like Barbara Proctor's, whom you read about in the Marketer Profile.

ADVERTISING'S ROLE IN THE ECONOMY

In the United States and Canada, over $200 per capita is spent annually on advertising. This is three times the rate one encounters in Europe and twenty-five times the rate experienced in Asia.[1] Because of its pervasiveness, there are approximately 250,000 jobs in advertising in the United States alone.

Some analysts have argued that advertising plays an important role in stimulating the growth of gross national product. One research study estimated that one dollar of advertising investment created an additional $16 in gross national product.[2] In fact, one of the reasons for the rapid growth of the U.S. economy after World War II may be that advertising expenditures were increasing rapidly as well. By 1986, advertising in the United States exceeded $100 billion.

Although advertising plays a key role in most U.S. industries, the amount spent on it varies from industry to industry. Table 14.1 presents some advertising-to-sales ratios for different industries. Note that marketers of consumer goods tend to spend more on advertising than marketers of industrial goods. Some of the largest U.S. advertisers are consumer goods manufacturers. For instance, in 1984, both Procter & Gamble and General Motors spent over $750 million each on advertising. Table 14.2 shows the amount spent on advertising by some leading U.S. firms.

Table 14.1   Selected Industry Advertising-to-Sales Ratios

Industry	Advertising As Percent of Sales	Advertising As Percent of Gross Margin
Bottled/canned soft drinks	6.5	12.5
Malt beverages	8.1	23.4
Office furniture	1.6	4.3
Drugs	8.9	14.6
Meat products	1.4	10.1
Construction machinery and equipment	1.4	5.6
Pollution control machinery	0.7	3.0
Retail department stores	3.3	13.5
Savings and loan associations	0.7	3.0
Electronic computing equipment	1.4	2.7
Equipment rental and leasing	3.6	5.9
Hospitals	3.2	11.5

Source: "1984 Advertising-to-Sales Ratios," *Business Marketing* (October 1985), pp. 99, 102. *Business Marketing* obtained this table from Schonfeld & Associates, Inc., 2550 Crawford Ave., Evanston, IL 60201. Used by permission.

What Advertising Cannot Accomplish

Although advertising represents a powerful force in our economy, it is not as powerful as some social critics believe. One critic has claimed that "there are large-scale efforts being made through advertising, often with impressive success, to channel our unthinking habits, our purchasing decisions, and our thought processes by the use of insights gleaned from psychiatry and social sciences."[3] Although marketers may wish that their understanding and use of advertising could create such powerful results, the simple truth is that advertising does not have the power that some claim it has. Advertising does not create consumer wants, it just reinforces them.[4] Consumers must be favorably predisposed toward a product class for advertising to be effective. No amount of advertising is going to convince American women to wear black veils in public as they do in Moslem countries such as Saudi Arabia. However, advertising could get American women to buy a new roll-on deodorant because they have been taught early in life that body odor is a negative personal trait.

Advertising is useless, however, without the backing of every other department in the organization. No amount of advertising will make the firm profitable if the production department manufactures a poorly made and unreliable product; if the physical distribution manager does not offer high levels of customer service; if the price of the product is simply too high; or if salespeople are poorly trained.

Advertising should be viewed as an investment that produces results

Table 14.2   Top Ten U.S. Advertisers[a]

Company	Advertising Expenditures
Procter & Gamble	$872.0
General Motors Corp.	763.8
Sears, Roebuck & Co.	746.0
Beatrice Cos.	680.0
R.J. Reynolds Industries	678.2
Philip Morris Inc.	570.4
American Telephone & Telegraph	563.2
Ford Motor Company	559.4
K mart Corp.	554.4
McDonald's Corp.	480.0

[a]Figures in millions.

Source: *Advertising Age* (September 26, 1985), p. 1. Reprinted with permission *Advertising Age* 9/26/85. Copyright Crain Communications Inc.

over time.[5] Advertising is like good exercise and physical fitness: for a person to stay in good shape, he or she must exercise regularly. It's the same for advertising: if a firm is to stay in good financial shape, it must advertise regularly to its target market.

What Advertising Can Accomplish

Although advertising is not a panacea, it can be a powerful marketing tool if properly used. The things advertising can accomplish are many and varied, such as:

❏ Increasing sales during slow periods.

❏ Moving old models or inventory at the end of the selling season.

❏ Explaining product attributes and features.

❏ Repositioning a brand within the minds of buyers.

❏ Making the sales force more productive by making their job easier.

❏ Increasing the awareness, interest, and desire for a brand.

These possible objectives suggest advertising's real power when properly managed.

One useful way to classify advertisements is product versus institutional advertising. Both product and institutional advertisements can be further categorized as informative, persuasive, and reminder.

TYPES OF ADVERTISING

Endless Vacation uses advertising to point out that advertising in their magazine will accomplish a powerful objective—results.

Product Advertising

Product advertising is concerned with *attempting to sell a good or service for a particular organization* and is the most prevalent type of advertising. Advertising that *attempts to provide customers with objective information about the product's attributes and does not try to persuade* is considered **informative advertising**. Informative product advertising is most often used in (1) marketing industrial goods, (2) in the early stages of the product life cycle when customers need information on the new product and when competition is sparse, and (3) when the product is technically complex (i.e., an advanced stereo system). A high proportion of informative product advertising is used to develop primary demand during the introductory stage of the product life cycle, when it is important for people to learn of the benefits of using the new product. As stated in Chapter 8, this type of advertising is also referred to as *pioneer advertising*.

Persuasive advertising *attempts to convince consumers that a particular product brand is the best one for them*. Persuasive product advertising is more characteristic of the growth and maturity stages of the product life cycle, where selective demand must be developed. *These advertisements incorporate a high proportion of subjective statements*. You will notice this if you look at a typical beer, cigarette, or automobile advertisement. Persuasive product advertising is also used more often for consumer rather than industrial products and for less technically complex products.

With **reminder advertising**, the firm's *objective is to keep its brand name(s) well entrenched in the customer's mind and to reinforce previous promotional efforts*. Ideally, the firm would like its brand to come to mind immediately when a person recognizes a need for a particular product.

Although product advertising can be neatly categorized into three types, overlap does exist. For example, all product advertising performs a reminder

Subjective statements such as "Living without boundaries" are prevalent in persuasive advertising.

Brush up on the evidence and you'll end up with Advanced Formula Crest on your brush.

		Advanced Formula Crest	Brand A	Brand B	Brand C
1.	The only toothpaste with Fluoristat,® the cavity-fighting system shown more effective than original Crest.	✓			
2.	The only fluoride toothpaste brand clinically proven to improve its cavity-fighting ability.	✓			
3.	The toothpaste proven effective in the largest clinical study ever for a toothpaste.	✓			
4.	The toothpaste with an effective fluoride.	✓	✓	✓	✓
5.	The toothpaste that freshens breath.	✓	✓	✓	✓
6.	The toothpaste that brightens teeth.	✓	✓	✓	✓
7.	The toothpaste more dentists' families use to fight cavities than any other.	✓			
8.	The cavity-fighting toothpaste that outsells any other.	✓			

"Crest has been shown to be an effective decay-preventive dentifrice that can be of significant value when used in a conscientiously applied program of oral hygiene and regular professional care." Council on Dental Therapeutics, American Dental Association.

© The Procter & Gamble Company 1982

Fight cavities with the best Crest yet.

Crest uses comparative advertising to be both informative, by listing the product's attributes, and persuasive in its statement, "Fight cavities with the best Crest yet."

function simply because the name of the brand is present. Similarly, some persuasive advertising can be informative. A good example is **comparative advertising** *in which a firm's brand is compared with competing brands on a set of product attributes.*[6] Comparative advertising is both informative and persuasive.

Institutional Advertising

Product advertising attempts to sell a particular product to the end user. **Institutional advertising** (often called *corporate advertising*), on the other hand, *is aimed at any of the organization's seven key publics* (customers, suppliers, employees, agents or intermediaries, stockholders and investors, or the general public) and *tries to enhance the image of the firm or organization rather than sell a specific product.* In this way, institutional advertising can be viewed as part of the firm's public relations effort.[7]

Institutional advertising can be informative, persuasive, or reminder. For example, General Electric uses informative advertising when it provides information to households on how to save energy, and Shell Oil did a series of booklets on topics of interest to drivers. Seagram Liquors uses persuasive advertising with ads that say that if you love your family and friends, you should not drink and drive, and R.J. Reynolds has advertised antismoking messages to teens. Examples of institutional reminder advertising include firms that regularly advertise their corporate logos or slogans in the *Wall Street Journal* in order to create awareness of their companies among the investing public.

Although product and institutional advertising are presented as distinct types, in reality, they overlap, and by promoting the institution, the products are also being promoted. In this regard, it is important to make certain that your product advertisements reflect the true image of your company and that your institutional advertisements have the ability to promote your products.

Sponsorship of Advertising

Although firms are often the sole sponsors of their advertising, there are other ways to pay for advertisements. If *a supplier (usually a manufacturer or wholesaler) picks up part or all of the cost of advertising,* this is called **vertical cooperative advertising**. If *several firms at the same level of distribution share the cost of advertising,* we have **horizontal cooperative advertising**. Most vertical cooperative and horizontal cooperative advertising involves retail institutions.[8]

With vertical cooperative advertising, a retailer usually shares advertising expenses with other marketing channel members. For example, Revlon might pay up to 40 percent of a drugstore's advertising costs of promoting Revlon products. There is usually a maximum reimbursement to the retailer, such as 4 percent of annual purchases of the manufacturer's products. Therefore, if the drugstore spent $10,000 to advertise Revlon's products, it could be reimbursed up to $4,000 (40%) as long as its annual purchase of Revlon products was at least $100,000. Note that 4 percent of $100,000 is $4,000. Retail vertical cooperative advertising is a significant form of advertising, representing between $8 to $10 billion in volume in 1983.[9]

The responsibilities of each party in a vertical cooperative advertising arrangement are generally specified in a contract that gives the supplier a good deal of control over the advertising content. For the supplier, this control helps ensure uniformity of company image, but it can act as a constraint for the retailer. As you flip through your local newspaper, this is one reason why you see similar ads for merchandise at competing stores.

Corporate logos serve as reminder advertising and create quick awareness of the company name.

An example of horizontal cooperative advertising at the retail level involves retailers in a shopping mall jointly sponsoring multipage advertising spreads in newspapers promoting special sales events such as "George Washington's Birthday Sale Days" or "Moonlight Madness Sales." These cooperative events are good traffic generators, as they pull larger crowds to the shopping center than could any individual merchant's advertising. Thus, all retailers benefit from the increased traffic in the shopping center or district.

THE ADVERTISING DECISION PROCESS

A marketing manager must make a number of decisions in planning a firm's advertising program. Figure 14.1 presents the seven steps to follow in developing an advertising program.

Identifying the Advertising Target

The **advertising target** is *that part of the target market that the firm wishes to attract.* It can be the entire target market or merely a small segment of that market. For example, the target market for income disability insurance by John Hancock Insurance Company may be 25- to 54-year-old professionals in households in which both husband and wife are employed. However, John Hancock might want to target a specific advertisement to a narrower segment, such as young, married professionals with one or more children. There is a bit of a "catch-22" here: advertising is mass commu-

Figure 14.1

Advertising Decision Process

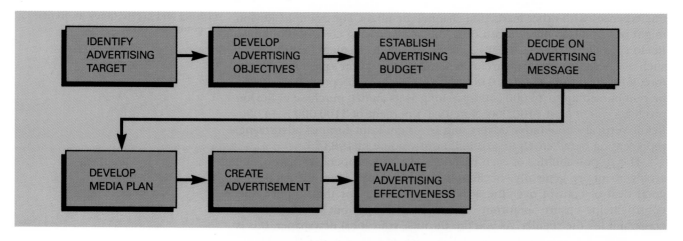

nication, and as such it is most cost effective when the advertising target is relatively large, although the smaller the target market, the more impact the advertising campaign can have.

Developing Advertising Objectives

A firm's advertising objectives should be based on its overall marketing strategy and objectives and thus should be stated in much the same terms. An ideal set of advertising objectives should be specific, measurable, and achievable.[10] To be specific, objectives need to focus on particular aspects of the communication process and include a time frame; for example, increasing the awareness level in the target market within the next six months. Objectives should also be measurable, and this is usually best accomplished by stating the objectives in quantitative terms. (See the discussion of establishing promotion objectives in Chapter 13). The preceding objective can be made measurable by stating that the objective is to increase the awareness level among those in the target market from 40 percent to 65 percent over the next six months. Although it is much easier to assess the effectiveness of advertising when objectives are stated in measurable terms, many firms choose to state objectives in general terms. Finally, to achieve objectives, they must be realistic given the economic and competitive environments.

Developing clear advertising objectives helps the marketer determine the most appropriate advertising budget. Also, a clear statement of objectives is helpful in controlling the creative people who design the advertising by giving them specific guidelines. This is critical because often their creativity gets in the way of designing practical and effective advertisements. They sometimes forget that they are not only artists, but more importantly, communicators.

Establishing the Advertising Budget

Determining how much to spend on advertising is theoretically straightforward, but in practice, extremely difficult.[11] Several popular methods are marginal analysis, affordability, competitive parity, percent of sales, and the objective and task approach, each of which will be briefly discussed.[12]

Marginal Analysis. The rule of marginal analysis is based on economic theory and suggests that a firm should continue to spend on advertising as long as revenues rise faster than costs. As with most theories, the rule of marginal analysis is difficult to put into practice because the relationship between advertising expenditures and sales is difficult to predict and measure.[13] One reason this relationship is difficult to assess is the constantly changing environments. Sales, for example, are influenced by many outside forces including interest rates, changing consumer tastes, weather patterns, employment levels, new competing products, and changes in competitors' advertising campaigns. Furthermore, advertising can be viewed as a capital expenditure since its benefits can be seen in the long run as well as the present.[14]

Marginal analysis is difficult, not impossible, to implement.[15] Coca Cola, which now owns Columbia Pictures, uses it to run tests, which increase advertising in one city and reduce it in another, to estimate the sales response function for a new movie.[16]

Affordability. A firm using the affordability method computes expected sales, costs, and profit goals and allocates the remaining funds to advertising. Although this method reverses the cause and effect relationship between advertising and sales performance, firms with limited funds usually are forced to use it since bankers are reluctant to lend money for advertising expenditures. Its major disadvantages are that it does not consider advertising objectives and that the firm risks spending too little on advertising.

Competitive Parity. A firm using the competitive parity method seeks to match its advertising with that of its competitors, either dollar-for-dollar or on a percent of sales basis. One disadvantage of this budgeting technique is that it assumes all competing firms have similar products, costs, and distribution patterns. Another disadvantage is that it is often difficult to obtain data on competitor sales and advertising expenditures. A form of competitive parity budgeting can be used in relation to market share goals by using the total industry advertising budget, say $500 million, and multiplying it by the percent of market share a firm wants.[17] In this example, if the firm desires a 20 percent market share, its advertising budget should be $100 million.

Percent of Sales. The percent of sales method figures advertising expenditures as X percent of either past or anticipated sales. The X percent value usually is decided based on past experience, conventional wisdom, or competitive parity. To figure an advertising budget using this method, let's assume the following:

Last year's sales	$ 90,000,000
Expected sales this year	$100,000,000
Percent of sales	3%

We will allocate $2.7 million to advertising if we base our budget on last year's sales, or $3 million if expected sales are used. This method is used extensively because it is fast and simple to compute. It does, however, have drawbacks. First, it indicates that a reverse relationship exists—that sales cause advertising rather than advertising causing sales. Second, it automatically allocates X percent to advertising without first assessing whether this amount is necessary for the proper promotion of the product or whether competitive conditions have changed to warrant more or less than X percent.

Objective and Task Approach.   The objective and task approach method begins by determining the tasks necessary to achieve the advertising objective(s) and then determining the advertising budget by summing the costs of those tasks. For example, assume a firm wants to increase product line awareness from 45 percent to 70 percent. It has determined that the following tasks are necessary: (1) twelve monthly ads in each of four leading national magazines, (2) fourteen 15-second radio advertisements per week for one year in the top 200 U.S. cities, and (3) two 30-second national television advertisements weekly for one year. The resulting advertising budget is the combined costs of these magazine, radio, and television advertisements. The major disadvantage of this technique is the difficulty in determining the exact set of tasks necessary to accomplish objectives.

Deciding the Advertising Message

The next step in the advertising decision process is for the firm to decide on the message it wants the advertisement to communicate. Remember from the section on types of advertisements, that informative, persuasive, and reminder ads can be used or combined to communicate a specific message. At this stage of development, a clear statement of the advertisement's goal is needed rather than actual copy. The following are some examples of advertising message goals:

❏ Communicate overall brand quality.

❏ Communicate the advantages of a new product feature.

❏ Communicate the value of product in terms of price.

❏ Communicate the proper use of the product.

❏ Communicate differences between the product and competitors' products.

Developing the Media Plan

The next step in the advertising decision process is to develop the media plan. The **media plan** consists of *establishing the media mix, selecting specific media vehicles, and developing the media schedule.*

Determining the Media Mix.   The **media mix** is *the combination of media types used to communicate a message.* The major media types available to marketers are radio, television, magazines, newspapers, direct mail, and outdoor displays. Billboards are the most common form of outdoor advertising, but this medium also includes ads printed on cars and trucks, skywriting, t-shirt and hat messages, signs on taxis and buses, and video displays at sports stadiums.[18]

Determining the proper media mix can be a complex task because there are so many variables to consider. It has been found, however, that "there is a direct relationship between the people to be reached, the message to be sent, and the media to use."[19] For example, local retailers of consumer goods usually find newspaper advertising preferable to television advertising because of the newspaper's more localized appeal, ability to promote both the store and the product, and relatively low cost. Marketers of industrial products, on the other hand, often advertise in trade journals or special interest magazines because of their ability to reach their advertising target.

When rating the available media, a marketer should consider six criteria:

1. **Intrusiveness**, or the ability of the media to reach a person who is not actively seeking information.
2. **Impact**, or the ability of the media to create an impression in the mind of the reader or viewer. Often related to how well the media can demonstrate a product and identify the product package.
3. **Permanence**, or the length of time an advertising message stays around.
4. **Selectivity** is the ability of a medium to focus on well-defined demographic or life-style segments.
5. **Cost-per-thousand** is the cost of one exposure unit in a media vehicle divided by the number of thousands of people reached.
6. **Economy** in production cost is the extent to which the advertising message can be prepared at a reasonable cost.

The media mix may include outdoor advertising in the form of billboards, which achieve low-cost-per-thousand exposure and get the message across with short, simple copy.

Table 14.3 evaluates the six major media on these criteria. Let's further discuss these media.

Newspapers are the most popular medium for advertising because they can segment markets according to geographic, demographic, and life-style characteristics; they can promote both stores and brands with a no-gimmick presentation; they are timely; and the costs of preparation and insertion are relatively low. The disadvantages of newspaper advertising are their poor print quality and limited use of color, the number of ads on each page competing for the reader's attention, lack of control over the ad's location (unless you pay extra), lack of creativity, and the relatively short life span of the advertisement.

Television is the second most widely used medium for advertising, and its popularity is gaining fast. Television's outstanding advantages are its ability to communicate a message both orally and visually; its ability to reach more households than all other media types; the fact that ads are presented one at a time, so they do not compete with each other for the viewer's attention; and its high intrusiveness. The disadvantages of using TV for advertising are its high production and insertion costs; the lack of permanence of the ads; its inability to concentrate on a select market segment; and the increasing use of videorecording devices, which allow viewers to tune out the commercial messages.

Direct mail advertisements include, among other things, mail, pamphlets, samples, catalogs, flyers, coupons, and newsletters that are mailed directly to the potential customer. Direct mail advertising has the following advantages: very low in cost for small, selected targets; ability to reach local markets easily; low cost of production and distribution; timeliness; and little simultaneous competition for reader's attention. The disadvantages of direct advertising are its high cost per thousand if used as a mass medium, the image of it as junk mail, the irritation caused by fake personalization of form letters, and the use of obsolete mailing lists.

Table 14.3   Major Media Evaluated on Six Criteria[a]

	Television	Radio	Magazine	Newspaper	Direct Mail	Outdoor
Intrusiveness	E	F	P	P	G	P
Impact	E	F	F	P	F	F
Permanence	P	P	G	P	P	E
Selectivity	F	E	E	G	E	F
Cost per Thousand	G	G	F	G	P	G
Economy in production cost	P	G	G	E	E	F

[a]E = Excellent; G = good; F = fair; P = poor.

Magazines can reach specific target markets because of the number of special interest magazines. Other advantages are the relatively low cost of preparation and insertion, the quality of print and color, a longer life span than some other media, ability to provide detailed information, and ability to add credibility to a product's image simply because the magazine has a favorable image. The three major disadvantages of magazine advertising are its lack of time flexibility since it takes several weeks for publication, the number of other things competing for the reader's attention (ads, stories, recipes, pictures, and so on), and its relatively poor intrusiveness.

The advantages of radio are its ability to segment the market geographically and by life-style or demographics, the low preparation cost, the ease of ad preparation, its timeliness, and its ability to stimulate word-of-mouth promotion. The major disadvantages are that people often use radio as a background noise without really listening to it, its use of sound as the only

TUMS.

:30 TV Commercial "3 REASONS"

WOMAN: Want a good reason why my antacid is Tums?

I'll give you three.

One. Tums is effective.

It neutralizes one third more stomach acid

than the other leading brand.

And that's what I take an antacid for.

Two. Sodium. I don't want any.

And Tums is sodium free.

Three. Tums is rich in calcium.

And to me, an extra source of calcium is extra good news.

SONG: TUM TA TUM TUM

TUMS!

While television ads can be expensive, fleeting, and less market-selective than newspaper ads, the media's many advantages have brought about its rapidly growing popularity with advertisers.

method of communicating the message, and the lack of permanence of the ads.

Outdoor advertising is probably the most permanent of advertising media types when billboards are used, can be selective geographically, and generally has a low cost per thousand exposures. This medium also has several disadvantages, including its lack of intrusiveness and a general non-selectivity by demographics or life-style. In addition, in response to recent beautification projects, many cities are banning billboards except along major roadways, and since outdoor advertising is usually viewed while in motion, the copy must be kept short and simple or it is missed. Outdoor advertising is very important in countries without commercial television, such as Belgium. However, even in the United States, where there are many competing media, outdoor is still popular. For example, there are approximately 275,000 billboards in the United States.[20] Miller Brewing has used outdoor billboards extensively to advertise its Miller Lite Beer.

Advertisers need to evaluate the different media types based on their advertising objectives and budgets.[21] Typically, companies decide on a mix of several different media types. Table 14.4 presents the media mixes for several firms competing in the U.S. auto market. Note that direct mail is excluded because the data were not part of the study.

The Marketing in Action on page 440 relates how VISA's media mix was consistent with the firm's advertising goals, target market, and budget.

Selecting Specific Media Vehicles.   An example of selecting a specific **media vehicle**, which is *a specific device for carrying advertising messages,* is deciding whether to advertise in *Working Woman* or *Ms* after first deciding to advertise in the magazine media. In selecting a specific vehicle within a medium, the advertiser first selects those that most likely appeal to the product's target market, then narrows down the selection based on cost, consistency of the vehicle's image to that of the product, and the

Table 14.4   Advertising Mixes: Selected Auto Companies in the 1982 U.S. Market

Auto Manufacturer	Advertising Mix (%)				
	Magazine[a]	Television	Radio	Newspaper	Outdoor
American Motors	43.2	52.6	0.4	3.7	0.1
Ford	18.2	50.1	18.7	12.3	0.7
Cadillac	30.8	56.9	4.1	4.9	3.3
Chevrolet	21.7	58.9	14.1	2.2	3.1
Honda	33.1	51.3	10.7	4.2	0.7
Volkswagen	38.0	56.7	3.1	2.1	0.1

[a]Also includes supplements.

Source: "Auto Sales Green—So Are Ads," *Marketing & Media Decisions* (October 1983), p. 156.

MARKETING IN ACTION

## VISA's Advertising Plan	### Media Used
### Overall Goal Enhance and increase the VISA presence in the consumer market.	● *29% of budget for prime time network television.* **It was used for its broad reach within the target market.** ● *23% of budget for network television news.* **It was used because it permits greater frequency of exposure per dollar than other time periods.**
### Target Market Adults, aged 25 to 65 years, who have a household income of over $20,000.	● *13% of budget for network television sports programs.* **They reach the higher income man who may not watch prime time television and news programs.** ● *25% of budget for national and regional magazines.* **They are effective for reaching the higher income households who are light television viewers and thus not as frequently reached by network schedules.**
### Media Selection Guideline Place ads where the greatest number of VISA customers will see and/or hear the advertising the most number of times per dollar expended.	● *10% of budget for radio.* **This helps to bridge hiatus periods between television exposures, thereby sustaining the memorability of the VISA music.**
### 1982 Budget $20.3 million.	Source: "How They Made the Top 200," *Marketing & Media Decisions* (September 1983), pp. 14–143. Used by permission.

number of advertisements in the vehicle. To compute the vehicle cost, the **cost per thousand method** is often used. Cost per thousand equals *the cost of one exposure unit divided by (the number of people reached divided by 1,000):*

$$\text{Cost per thousand} = \frac{\text{Cost of one exposure unit}}{\text{Number of people reached}/1,000}$$

As an example, let's assume you wish to place a four-color, full-page advertisement in *Field & Stream,* which costs $39,550, and your target market is men aged 25 to 49 years. *Field & Stream* has an audience of 4,007,000 men in this age group. The cost per thousand for reaching this group is $9.87. On the other hand, the same advertisement placed in *Newsweek* would cost $73,695 and reach 4,685,000 in your target market at a cost of $15.73 per thousand.

Even these numbers can be misleading, because this calculation is based on circulation (how many people purchase the magazine) rather than exposure (how many people read the magazine). Don't you and your friends read each other's magazines? What about newspapers? In some countries, hundreds of people read one copy of a newspaper, and even in New York City, there are 2.89 readers per newspaper copy.[22]

To make the vehicle selection process a little easier, several national research firms have specialized in providing media data. Arbitron measures radio audiences, Starch concentrates on magazines, and Nielsen does ratings for television.[23] In addition, Standard Rate and Data, Inc. publishes monthly directories on rates, mechanical requirements, circulation figures, and other information about key media.

Developing the Media Schedule. The **media schedule** *consists of how often to advertise and when to advertise.* Two important factors should be considered in deciding how often the advertisement should run: reach and frequency. **Reach** is *the percentage of the advertising target that is exposed to at least one of your advertisements within a given period.* **Frequency** is *the average number of exposures to a firm's advertising by those who were reached within a given period.* The relationship between reach and frequency is called **gross rating points (GRP)** and is *obtained by multiplying reach by frequency.* A media schedule usually has a gross rating points objective. To illustrate, suppose you want to reach 75 percent of your target market over the next four weeks. With a frequency of three, your GRP objective would be 75 times 3, or 225.

The second part of media scheduling is the timing of advertising. A firm has three basic options: (1) spread advertising expenditures evenly over the year, (2) concentrate advertising at critical seasons or selling times, (3) space advertising in an intermittent pattern. These timing patterns are illustrated in Figure 14.2. Some products, such as convenience goods, are

Figure 14.2

Timing of Advertising Exposures

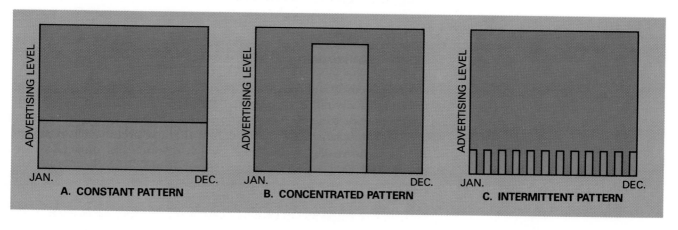

purchased at approximately the same rate throughout the year. Therefore, they usually are advertised at a constant level (graph A) throughout the year, and the advertising budget for them will remain at a constant level from month to month. A concentrated pattern is often used for products with a seasonal appeal, such as Christmas cards, air conditioners, school supplies, and lawn furniture. Graph B shows how advertising expenditures and frequency are concentrated between the months of March and July for some hypothetical product. An intermittent advertising pattern is usually a function of the medium used. For example, if the product is advertised in a magazine that is published monthly, the advertising pattern will look similar to that shown in graph C.

Creating the Advertisement

It is only after the media plan has been developed that the advertisement is created. The creative dimension is very important to the success of an advertisement. It must be kept in mind, though, that the objective is not only to create ads that are pleasant to look at or listen to, but also to accomplish the advertising objectives. There are several things to remember when creating the advertisement:

1. Keep the advertisement consistent with the other marketing mix elements.
2. Stick to the basic message and be sure it communicates what it is supposed to.
3. Use the best medium for the effect wanted.
4. Do not forget the budget.
5. Keep the advertisement consistent with the overall flavor and image of the chosen media vehicle.
6. Keep the advertisement ethical—don't mislead or be deceptive.
7. Be familiar with competitive advertising so that your ad will be distinctive rather than a carbon copy of a competitor's.

Evaluating Advertising Effectiveness

Advertising is costly and requires many subjective decisions based on judgment and creativity rather than on hard facts. Therefore, it is often difficult, but still important, to assess the advertising's effectiveness in communicating its message. Most large advertisers such as IBM use pretests and posttests to measure advertising effectiveness, which research has shown to vary substantially.[24]

The purpose of a pretest is to determine whether the advertisement communicates the right message to the right advertising target before the firm commits to large-scale production and placement of the ad. One method of pretesting is to use a dummy media vehicle, which is a hypothetical media vehicle such as a magazine with a full complement of editorial material and advertising. These dummy magazines are read by a representative group of people who are then questioned about the magazine's content. From their responses, it can be ascertained which ads were memorable without aid, which were remembered after more specific reference, and which were not remembered at all.

Another pretesting technique is the focus group, which is a group of six to twelve carefully selected consumers who are shown advertisements and then questioned by a moderator, who attempts to obtain their reactions and feelings toward the ads. The ads are not shown in the context of a medium. Given the small size of the group, these research findings cannot be viewed as conclusive. However, a good moderator can use the group to help identify the ads' major strengths and weaknesses, and this can be done quickly and with a limited budget.[25]

Some of the more popular posttests are readership tests, recall tests, and attitude change tests. In a readership test, the respondents are shown an advertisement and asked if they read, saw, or heard it before. A recall test is similar to a readership test, but in this case the respondents are not shown any advertisement but are asked if they previously read, saw, or heard advertising for a firm's product(s). For example, Burke Marketing Research Corporation conducts "day-after recall" tests for television. The day after a commercial is aired, Burke surveys a sample of television viewers to determine how many people can recall an advertisement and the selling points it communicated.

An attitude change measure gives a firm an idea of the impact an advertisement has had on attitudes toward the product. The firm first conducts a study to measure attitudes before the advertisement has been placed, and then, after the ad has run for some time, another test is conducted to measure attitudes toward the product. Any change in attitudes can be used to assess the effectiveness of the ad.

THE ROLE OF THE ADVERTISING AGENCY

Our discussion of the advertising decision process has revealed that advertising is a complex and multifaceted area of managerial decision making. Often, managers feel that they do not have the expertise to wisely and efficiently make these kinds of decisions. Consequently, most firms with large advertising budgets use the services of an advertising agency.[26] An **advertising agency** is *a firm that specializes in developing advertising programs or plans for a fee or commission for client firms.* An advertising agency may perform some of the following services for a client[27]:

1. Determining a product's advantages and disadvantages as compared with those of competitors.
2. Verifying target markets for product.
3. Deciding on the best distribution and sales techniques.

4. Suggesting the best media types and specific media vehicles for your message.
5. Formulating a complete advertising plan.
6. Preparing advertisements.
7. Purchasing media space and time and verifying insertions.
8. Handling billing between vehicles and client.

An advertising agency can only create effective advertising if the firm works closely with it and clearly tells the agency who the target audience is, what the advertising objectives are, how much money they have to spend, and what message needs to be communicated.

The fee or commission an agent charges is usually 15 percent of the value of the advertising placed. However, fees vary depending on the level of service provided. For example, some large firms that have an in-house advertising department generally pay an advertising agency less than the usual 15 percent since their own departments are taking care of a portion of the work. Table 14.5 lists the ten largest advertising agencies in the world in conjunction with their gross billings. The Marketing in Action about Du

Table 14.5   Top Ten Advertising Agencies in World Income[a]

Agency	1984 Gross Income	Some Major Clients Gained in 1984
Young & Rubican	$480.1	AT&T Intl. long distance, Ajax dishwashing liquid, Tupperware home parties
Ted Bates Worldwide	424.4	Anheuser-Busch Michelob, Uncle Ben's of Mars Inc.
Ogilvy & Mather Intl.	421.0	Hallmark, Hardee's, Gates Rubber
J. Walter Thompson, Co.	405.8	Baskin-Robbins, Emery Worldwide, Miller Brewery
BBDO International	340.0	Coldwell-Banker, Anderson Clayton, Bally Corp's Six Flags Great America
Saatchi & Saatchi Compton	337.5	Procter & Gamble, Nabisco Brands in Spain, Carnation in Germany and France
McCann-Erickson Worldwide	325.2	Flakey Jake's Hamburgers, Blue Cross, Sony audio products
Foote Cone & Belding	268.5	Colgate-Palmolive, Long John Silver, ComputerLand
Leo Burnett Co.	253.5	Kraft Inc., Hewlett-Packard personal computers
Grey Advertising	224.2	Toys "R" Us, Waldenbooks, Old El Paso

[a]Gross income in millions.

Source: *Advertising Age* (March 28, 1985). Reprinted with permission *Advertising Age* 3/28/85. Copyright Crain Communications Inc.

MARKETING IN ACTION

With over 600 products, Du Pont is the eighth largest industrial advertiser in the United States and works closely with six advertising agencies: BBDO, Rumrill-Hoyt, Sudler & Hennessey, Barnum Communications, Kelly Advertising, and N.W. Ayer, Inc. Harry E. Davis of Du Pont has said, "I hate to sound trite and talk about the old 'partnership' bit, but because of the way we do it, we and our agencies are really pulling the oars together."

Du Pont does not abide by the standard 15 percent commission structure for advertising agencies. Rather, it has a time-based fee compensation program that it negotiates annually with each agency. The compensation is determined by time rates and direct personnel costs, indirect agency cost allocations, profit margins, and an inflation adjustment. Other expenses such as production are billed at net cost.

Du Pont's cooperative attitude toward its agencies is also facilitated by a two-way performance auditing program. Du Pont annually rates each agency account group on a scale of 1 to 5 according to:

- **Background knowledge of markets and products**
- **Administration of account**
- **Initiative in developing facts and ideas**
- **Responsiveness**

Du Pont's Partnership with Six Advertising Agencies

- **Cost consciousness**
- **Evaluation and recommendation of media**
- **Quality of art**
- **Understanding advertising fundamentals**
- **Quality of copy**
- **Quality and efficiency of production**
- **Budget control**
- **Maintenance of schedules and paperwork**
- **Attention to detail**
- **Maintenance of contact**
- **Use of ad research.**

To get the other side of the equation, agency people rate Du Pont's performance on:

- **Background knowledge of markets and products**
- **Annual budget preparation**
- **Determination of marketing and advertising objectives**
- **Development of facts and ideas**

- **Stimulation and encouragement of agency personnel**
- **Constructiveness of criticism**
- **Scheduling of assignments**
- **Validity of media requests**
- **Responsiveness of requests**
- **Overall administration of work load**
- **Cost consciousness**
- **Budget control**
- **Clarity and completeness of instructions**
- **Attention to detail**
- **Maintenance of schedules and paperwork**
- **Use of ad research**
- **Maintenance of contact**

The responses to both of these questionnaires are studied by senior management at the agencies and in Du Pont's marketing communications department. These senior managers then meet to determine which procedural changes need to be made or which personnel may need new assignments.

Source: Based on Bob Donath. "Managing the Partnership: How Du Pont Works with its Six Advertising Agencies," *Business Marketing* (September 1983), pp. 70, 72, 74, 76. Used by permission.

Pont and its six advertising agencies on this page stresses the need for cooperation between the ad agency and the client firm.

Publicity is *nonpersonal stimulation of demand for goods, services, or business units by generating commercially significant news about them in the mass media* or obtaining favorable presentation of them on radio,

MANAGING PUBLICITY

television, or stage. Unlike advertising, this form of promotion is not paid for by the sponsor. Publicity is not free, however. To be effective, publicity must be a planned part of the marketing program, and this requires personnel and dollars.[28] The **public relations director** *is the head of a firm's public relations department and is responsible for planning publicity.*[29]

It is often difficult for organizations to integrate publicity into the marketing program and promotion mix because the public relations director typically is not part of the marketing department. Consequently, the public relations director and marketing vice president, marketing manager or advertising director act independently of each other. This is unfortunate because any type of publicity about a company's products or practices will influence the company's image and thus indirectly influence sales. In short, public relations is too powerful a sales tool not to be integrated into the promotion mix and be part of the marketing department.

The public relations department is charged with the responsibility for developing favorable publicity that comes to the attention of not only consuming publics, but also its other publics—suppliers, employees, agents or intermediaries, stockholders and investors, creditors, and the general public. (These publics were discussed in Chapter 2.) A major task of public relations departments is to obtain favorable publicity in the news for the firm. As shown in Table 14.6, four techniques for getting in the news are the press release, the exclusive feature, the press conference, and the press kit.

Publicity can be generated from five major areas: management activities, product promotions, sales activities, manufacturing and engineering, and personnel activities.[30] Management activities that are good sources for pub-

---

Table 14.6   Getting Publicity in the News

Press Release.   An announcement to the news media of significant changes in a firm or product or to introduce a new product. It is the most popular technique for obtaining publicity.

Exclusive Feature.   An in-depth article or broadcast message about something of interest to a particular public. An exclusive feature could focus on a new concept, an industry trend, a special new technique, and so on. The feature usually does not focus solely on a company's products but will use them as examples to illustrate certain points. An exclusive feature usually requires extensive coordination between public relations personnel and editors or broadcast managers.

Press Conference.   A meeting for the media sponsored by the firm. Press conferences can be overdone and used too often. They should be used to announce major news items such as a new product introduction or the appointment of a new president.

Press Kits.   Sometimes used in connection with a press conference and may include press releases, pictures, tapes and films, product samples, and complimentary passes.

Source: Based on Michael Ray. *Advertising and Communication Management* (Englewood Cliffs, NJ: Prentice-Hall, 1982), pp. 347–348; David P. McClure. "Publicity Should Be Integrated in Marketing Plan," *Marketing News* (Dec. 10, 1982), p. 6.

licity include personnel changes and promotions, speeches and special ap-
pearances at banquets, graduations, and parties, and stories about the
company's history and future. The private lives and interesting activities of
the management personnel are also a publicity source. Stories about their
hobbies and charitable and volunteer activities are especially helpful in
tearing down the "uncaring corporate giant" image by playing on the human
side of the company.

Many sources of publicity come from product promotions. Perhaps the
most common source of publicity is the new product announcement. Within
this aspect, however, there can be many topics of interest that lend themselves to publicity. For example, a new product could have three or four
industrial uses, each with its own story, or the product may have a unique
design or feature that merits a news story. There are also stories to be found
concerning old products. Maybe the engineering department has come up
with a new use or a new way of combining several products for a new use.
Are there sales trends that indicate that the consumers have discovered a
new use for an old product? Check with them and your distributors to find
out.

Sales activities are a little harder to publicize, but not altogether impossible. Sources for publicity in this area are national and regional sales
conferences and trade shows, sales training programs, and recognition of
key sales personnel. In this area, the publicity can also be used as a means
of raising and maintaining the morale of your sales employees.

Publicity about manufacturing and engineering aspects of the product
or company helps to build confidence in the minds of the customers; for
example, a better or unusual method of manufacturing, storing, or transporting the product; perfect safety records; technical employees recognized
for their abilities; and personnel appointments and promotions.

Other public relations activities connected with personnel include winners of safety, waste reduction, and cost-cutting awards, retirements, and
stories about employees' leisure-time activities.

Firms may also get publicity in nonprint media. Examples are use of
the product in a television program or a movie; sponsorship of special events,
such as Macy's Thanksgiving Day Parade; having executives appear as guest
speakers for civic or educational organizations; or developing educational
films and sponsoring educational exhibits that show the company in a favorable light. For example, Philip Morris sponsored the U.S. tour of "The
Vatican Collections: The Papacy and Art," which was shown at art museums
in New York, Chicago, and San Francisco in 1983 and 1984.

One particularly interesting public relations program is the Chevrolet
Motor Company's annual sponsorship of a competition in which college
students majoring in marketing or advertising design a promotion campaign
for a new Chevrolet car. Winning teams fly to Dearborn, Michigan, to present
their promotional program to top management at Chevrolet. This public
relations program helps Chevrolet recruit outstanding college graduates.

All of our illustrations and examples have thus far dealt with favorable
publicity. This is obviously the type of publicity a company desires. Firms

inevitably make errors, and thus negative publicity is likely to occur. To minimize bad publicity, firms should produce safe products, treat employees fairly, honor product warranties, create safe work environments, and so on. If a negative event does occur (i.e., a defective product is recalled, an explosion occurs in an office building or factory, the company is convicted of price fixing), however, a company must be prepared to help expedite news coverage. Resistance often will create more negative publicity than will openness and truthfulness in dealings with news reporters and the general public. In addition, resistance often creates rumors that make an unfavorable event look worse than would a truthful reporting of the facts.

SUMMARY

This chapter discussed the major role that advertising plays in the U.S. economy and within many U.S. businesses. Over $200 per capita is spent annually on advertising in the United States, and roughly 250,000 people work in advertising in this country.

Although advertising is a powerful force in our economy, it cannot make people purchase goods and services they do not want to buy. For advertising to be effective, consumers must be favorably predisposed toward a product. Advertising can be a powerful marketing tool if properly used. For example, advertising may help increase sales during slow periods, explain product attributes and contribute to the productiveness of the sales force by making their jobs easier.

One useful way to classify advertising is product versus institutional advertising. Product advertising is primarily concerned with selling the goods or services of a particular organization. On the other hand, institutional advertising primarily tries to enhance the image of the institution or organization by attempting to change the attitudes of various publics toward the institution. Both product and institutional advertising can be informative, persuasive, or reminder—or any combination of these.

Advertising involves a series of decisions that must be made by the firm or its advertising agency, or both. Seven major decision areas are (1) identifying the advertising target, (2) developing advertising objectives, (3) establishing the advertising budget, (4) deciding on the advertising message, (5) developing media plan, (6) creating the advertisement, and (7) evaluating the advertising effectiveness through pretesting and posttesting.

Because many firms believe that they cannot make all of these decisions wisely and efficiently, they use the services of an advertising agency. If advertising agencies are to do a good job on behalf of their clients, the agency and client must develop a cooperative relationship.

This chapter ended with a discussion of publicity. Publicity is often managed by the firm's public relations department, which is responsible for developing favorable publicity that comes to the attention of not only consuming publics, but also its other publics—suppliers, employees, agents or intermediaries, stockholders and investors, creditors, and the general public.

KEY CONCEPTS

advertising (p. 425)
product advertising (p. 428)
informative advertising (p. 428)
persuasive advertising (p. 429)
reminder advertising (p. 429)
comparative advertising (p. 430)
institutional advertising (pp. 430–431)
vertical cooperative advertising (p. 431)
horizontal cooperative advertising
  (p. 431)
advertising target (p. 432)
media plan (p. 435)

media mix (p. 435)
media vehicle (p. 439)
cost per thousand method (p. 440)
media schedule (p. 441)
reach (p. 441)
frequency (p. 441)
gross rating points (GRP) (p. 441)
advertising agency (p. 443)
publicity (p. 445)
public relations director (p. 446)

REVIEW AND DISCUSSION QUESTIONS

1. Why do consumer goods marketers spend more on advertising than do industrial goods marketers?

2. What are some of the things advertising can and cannot accomplish?

3. What is the difference between product and institutional advertising? Discuss any interactions between these two types of advertising.

4. What is the difference between vertical and horizontal cooperative advertising?

5. Why should retailers carefully evaluate the desirability of participating in vertical cooperative advertising?

6. Explain why the advertising target may be only a small part of your target market.

7. Outline and briefly discuss the seven steps in the advertising decision process.

8. Why should advertising objectives be specific, measurable, and achievable?

9. Name the five popular methods for establishing an advertising budget and the disadvantages or problems of each method.

10. What are the components of a media plan?

11. List and define the six criteria for evaluating and comparing the six major types of media.

12. Define *reach* and *frequency*. Why can't reach and frequency both be maximized with a fixed advertising budget?

13. Explain cost per thousand and name the problems associated with using it to select media to advertise in.

14. What are advertising pretests and posttests? What are some methods of pretesting and posttesting?

15. What are the possible advantages of using an advertising agency?

16. What is publicity? Give several examples of publicity.

17. What are the five major areas from which publicity can be generated, and how can they be helpful to the overall company image?

ACTION PROBLEMS

1. Get copies of several recent newspapers and magazines and cut out examples of product and institutional advertisements. Try to include informative, persuasive, and reminder advertisements and also try to include examples of advertisements for consumer products and industrial products.

2. Your company is in the process of forecasting next year's sales as well as developing budgets for the different departments and divisions in the firm. The firm only sells one product line, which is hard disk storage for personal computers. This line has 40 percent gross margin on the prices at which your firm sells to dealers. Sales last year were $3.8 million. You have told the vice president of finance that with a 50 percent increase in advertising, you can increase sales by 20 percent. The advertising budget last year was $200,000. The finance vice president has asked you to show the profit impact you expect from your proposed increase in advertising.

3. The local Rotary Club has invited two college students to their monthly luncheon meeting. One student has been asked to make a five-minute speech on the social and economic benefits of advertising, and the second student has been asked to address, also in five minutes, the social costs and economic disadvantages of advertising. Assume that you are one of these students and write a speech on either of these topics.

4. Develop a media plan for a product of your choice.

5. You are employed in the public relations department of Zorbo Corp., a new firm that manufactures vitamins. Develop a press release or exclusive feature news stories for one of the following:
   a. development of Zorbo Hi-Pro, a superpotency vitamin.
   b. civic accomplishments of Zorbo's vice president of finance, who was recently voted "volunteer of the year" by the mayor and city council.
   c. Zorbo's contribution to City Hospital's Research Fund.
   d. a recent Food and Drug Administration ban on the sale of one of Zorbo's new superpotency vitamin drugs.

NOTES

1. *World Advertising Expenditures* 1980 edition (New York: STARCH INRA Hooper, 1981).

2. Charles Y. Yang, "$1 in Ads Generates $16 in Income," *Advertising Age* (December 29, 1965), pp. 1, 39; Robert Jacobson and Franco M. Nicosia, "Advertising and Public Policy: The Macroeconomic Effects of Advertising," *Journal of Marketing Research* (February 1981), pp. 29–38.

3. Vance Packard, *The Hidden Persuaders* (New York: McKay, 1957).

4. Michael Schudson, *Advertising, The Uneasy Persuasion* (New York: Basic Books, 1984).

5. Joel Dean, "Does Advertising Belong in the Capital Budget?" *Journal of Marketing* (October 1966), pp. 15–21.

6. For more information on comparative advertising, see William L. Wilkie and Paul W. Farris, "Comparison Advertising: Problems and Potential," *Journal of Marketing* (October 1975), pp. 7–15; Linda Golden, "Consumer Reactions to Explicit Brand Comparisons in Advertisements," *Journal of Marketing Research* (November 1979), pp. 517–532; Linda Swayne and Jack M. Starling, "What Ever Happened to Brand X?" *Business* (July–August 1982), pp. 22–28; Stephen Goodwin and Michael Etgar, "An Experimental Investigation of Comparative Advertising: Impact of Message Appeal, Information Load, and Utility of Product Class," *Journal of Marketing Research* (May 1980), pp. 187–202; William R. Swinyard, "Interaction Between Comparative Advertising and Copy Claim Variation," *Journal of Marketing Research* (May 1981), pp. 175–186; Steven A. Meyerowitz, "The Developing Law of Comparative Advertising," *Business Marketing* (August 1985), pp. 81–86.

7,. S. Watson Dunn and Arnold M. Barban, *Advertising: Its Role in Modern Marketing,* 5th edition (New York: College Publishing, 1982), p. 12.

8. A good discussion of how to manage vertical retail cooperative advertising is in Stephen A. Greyser and Robert F. Young, "Follow 11 guidelines to strategically manage co-op advertising program," *Marketing News* (September 16, 1983), Section 1, p. 5; see also "Pulling Together," *Sales and Marketing Management* (May 13, 1985), pp. 81–88.

9. Laura Jereski, "Co-op's Quiet Revolution," *Marketing & Media Decisions* (November 1983), p. 139.

10. William P. Dommermuth, *Promotion: Analysis, Creativity, and Strategy* (Boston: Kent Publishing Company, 1984), p. 409.

11. Careful budgeting of advertising is especially important because of the rapid escalation in media costs, see Carol Swain, "Media Cost in 1984 Will Jump Another 9.4%," *Marketing & Media Decisions* (September 1983), pp. 120, 121, 191.

12. Andre J. San Augustine and William F. Foley, "How Large Advertisers Set Budgets," *Journal of Advertising Research* (October 1975), pp. 11–16.

13. Advertising elasticity and response curves are discussed in Malcolm A. McNiven, "Plan for More Productive Advertising," *Harvard Business Review* (March–April 1980), pp. 130–136; Julian L. Simon and Johan Arndt, "The Shape of the Advertising Response Function," *Journal of Advertising Research* (August 1980), pp. 11–28.

14. D.G. Clarke, "Econometric Measurement of the Duration of Advertising Effect on Sales," *Journal of Marketing Research* (November 1976), pp. 345–357; D.H. Mann, "Optimal Theoretic Advertising Stock Models: A Generalization Incorporating the Effects of Delayed Response from Promotional Expenditures," *Management Science* (March 1975), pp. 823–832; Ronald W. Ward, "Measuring Advertising Decay," *Journal of Advertising Research* (August 1976), pp. 37–41; David A. Aaker, James M. Carman, and Robert Jacobson, "Modeling Advertising-Sales Relationships Involving Feedback: A Time Series Analysis of Six Cereal Brands," *Journal of Marketing Research* (February 1982), pp. 116–125.

15. It should be noted, however, that it is not impossible to assess the profit impact of advertising, see Roger W. Brucker, "How to Estimate Your Advertising Profit Payoff," *Business Marketing* (January 1984), pp. 60–66.

16. Myron Magnet, "Coke Tries Selling Movies Like Soda Pop," *Fortune* (December 26, 1983), p. 122.

17. David E. Bell, Ralph L. Keeney, and John C. Little, "A Market Share Theorem," *Journal of Marketing Research* (May 1975), pp. 136–141; Masao Nakanishi and Lee G. Cooper, "Parameter Estimation for a Multiplicative Competitive Interaction Model—Least Squares Approach," *Journal of Marketing Research* (August 1974), pp. 303–311; Philip Maher, "New PIMS Data Ties Ad Outlay to Market Share," *Business Marketing* (June 1984), pp. 10, 27.

18. Kevin Higgins, "Often Overlooked Outdoor Advertising Offers More Impact and Exposures than Most Media," *Marketing News* (July 22, 1983), pp. 1, 10, 11; Christine Dugas, " 'Ad Space' Now Has a Whole New Meaning," *BusinessWeek* (July 29, 1985), p. 52.

19. William G. Nickels, *Marketing Communications and Promotion,* 3rd edition (Columbus, OH: Grid Publishing, 1984), p. 165.

20. Kevin Higgins, "Often Overlooked Outdoor Advertising Offers More Impact and Exposure than Most Media," *Marketing News* (July 22, 1983), p. 10.

21. The economics of different media is in a state of change due to changing technology, see Joseph Dunn, "Cable Costs all Over the Lot," *Marketing & Media Decisions* (Fall 1983 Special), pp. 55–60; Fred Gardner, "MTV Rocks Cable," *Marketing & Media Decisions* (August 1983), pp. 66–68, 113; Melissande Block, "What Price Videotex," *Marketing & Media Decisions* (Fall 1983 Special), pp. 49–53; Rebecca Fannin, "Newspapers Pause at the Crossroads," *Marketing & Media Decisions* (September 1983), pp. 163–170.

22. Lionel Kaufman, "How Many People Will Read Her Newspaper?" *Marketing & Media Decisions* (September 1983), pp. 70, 71, 172, 174.

23. Daniel Starch, *Measuring Advertising Readership and Results* (New York: McGraw-Hill, 1966), pp. 167–176.

24. Byron G. Quam, "How IBM Assesses its Business-to-Business Advertising," *Business Marketing* (January 1985), pp. 106–112; Dik W. Twedt, *1983 Survey of Marketing Research* (Chicago: American Marketing Association, 1983), p. 41; S. Watson Dunn and Arnold M. Barban, *Advertising: Its Role in Modern Marketing* (Hinsdale, IL: The Dryden Press, 1981), p. 273.

25. Don Ailloni-Charos, *Promotion: A Guide to Effective Promotional Planning, Strategies, and Executives* (New York: John Wiley & Sons, 1984), p. 249.

26. The decision to use or not use an advertising agency is important, see Bob Donath, "Should Your Agency Be In-House or Independent?" *Business Marketing* (September 1984), pp. 90, 98.

27. *Advertising Agencies—What They Are, What They Do, and How They Do It* (New York: American Association of Advertising Agencies, 1976), pp. 10–18.

28. David P. McClure, "Publicity Should Be Integrated in Marketing Plan," *Marketing News* (December 10, 1982), pp. 6, 7.

29. Robert S. Mason, "What's a PR Director for, Anyway?" *Harvard Business Review* (September–October 1974), pp. 120–126.

30. Bernard E. Ury, "A Basic Guide for Developing Publicity," in James U. McNeal (ed.), *Readings in Promotion Management* (New York: Appleton-Century-Crofts, 1966), pp. 197–201.

CHAPTER 15

LEARNING OBJECTIVES

After you complete this chapter, you should be able to:

- **Identify** the roles of different types of salespeople

- **Explain** the six steps in the selling process

- **Describe** the seven elements in sales force management

- **Distinguish** between trade and consumer sales promotion tools and list the types of each

- **Discuss** the five steps in sales promotion management

PERSONAL SELLING AND SALES PROMOTION

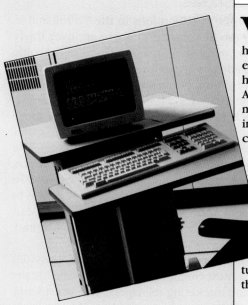

MARKETER PROFILE

Supersalesman Nicholas M. DiBari

When Nicholas M. DiBari was a student at Dayton University, he was a star baseball pitcher and easily major league material. During his senior year, however, the U.S. Army drafted him for two years of military service, effectively destroying any hopes he may have had for a career in baseball.

At age 23, DiBari went to work in the underwriting department of Sears' Allstate Insurance. There, Nick met many salespeople when they turned in their contracts for processing. One day, he totaled the commissions on contracts that one of the salespeople had turned in and quickly concluded that the money was in sales.

DiBari went to his boss and asked for a transfer into sales. When his boss turned down the request, he quit. Shortly thereafter, he went to work at Computer Trading Corp., a computer leasing company. DiBari credits this company with teaching him that selling is a process of gathering information to help people solve problems. In 1971, he left Computer Trading Corp. to become a sales representative for Storage Technology, a maker of computer storage systems. From 1971 to 1976, when sales grew from $50 million to over $500 million, he was the top salesperson.

In 1976, DiBari left Storage Technology to become marketing vice president for Comdisco, Inc., a lessor of computer equipment, where he was the primary force in boosting Comdisco's sales from less than $50 million to over $600 million by 1983. From 1976 to 1983, he earned over $7 million in commissions. In 1983 alone, his commissions totaled $1.5 million.

In November 1983, at the age of 38, Nick DiBari called it quits and retired to Florida, where he lives with his wife and two children. He lounges around the Florida water-front in a t-shirt with the caption "There Is No Finish Line." It is difficult to predict what DiBari's next move will be, but if one takes the motto on his shirt literally, he is unlikely to stay retired.

Source: Based in part on James D. Snyder. "What Made Supersalesman Nick DiBari Call It Quits?" *Sales and Marketing Management* (April 2, 1984), pp. 43–49. Used by permission of *Sales and Marketing Management.* Copyright (April 2, 1984).

INTRODUCTION

In Chapter 13, *personal selling* was defined as an oral presentation with one or more prospective purchasers for the purpose of making sales. Nicholas DiBari and other "supersalespeople" are only a small portion of the over 8 million people who earn their living selling to organizations and consumers in the United States. Almost all organizations employ personal salespeople, and most firms spend more money on personal selling than on any other element of the promotion mix. This chapter explores the field of personal selling, the different types of salespeople, the selling process, and the management of the sales force. The chapter ends with a discussion of sales promotion and its role in the promotion mix.

A CAREER IN SELLING

Personal selling, which represents over 8 million jobs in the United States, is a major career option. For every job in advertising, there are over thirty jobs in selling; selling is the lifeblood of most companies. Good salespeople earn excellent incomes. College graduates typically start in a sales trainee program at $20,000 to $22,000 and should be making $30,000 within two years. Most experienced salespeople earn over $40,000 annually, and some, such as Nicholas DiBari, earn much more. Successful salespeople can be men or women and can sell products to the ultimate consumer or to other organizations (business-to-business selling). For example, in 1984 Jessie Thatcher sold 480 Buicks worth $5.3 million for Tatone Buick in Fairborn, Ohio. Kathy Monthei sold $9 million of group dental insurance from 1976 to 1984 for California Dental Service. There is nothing like experience to polish a salesperson's skills, as Markita Andrews clearly demonstrated. Markita sold 648 boxes of Girl Scout cookies when she was 6 years old and, by the age of 13, Markita's sales had skyrocketed to 8,012 boxes.[1]

A career in sales, especially for the recent college graduate, provides an excellent stepping stone for advancement in an organization. Many salespeople have gone on to become marketing managers, vice presidents, and presidents of organizations. A sales position provides valuable background and training because it supplies an excellent knowledge of a firm's products and customers and allows one to demonstrate initiative, creativity, time management, and communication skills, which are all prerequisites of a good manager. This is why business firms often look to successful salespeople as candidates for management positions. A talented salesperson should be able to move up to a management position within three to five years.

Why Do We Need Personal Selling?

As discussed in Chapter 14, advertising helps to make potential customers aware of a firm's product offerings as well as builds interest and desire for the product. Although advertising "warms up" the potential customer, to get the customer to act, there is no substitute for face-to-face communication—this is where personal selling comes into play. Firms need a mix of advertising and personal selling, for salespeople will have an easier job if advertising has been effective. Firms that sell to organizational markets have a mix weighted more toward personal selling, while firms that sell to consumer markets are more heavily weighted toward advertising. There are some exceptions, however. For example, Tupperware and Rubbermaid sell similar products to consumer markets. Tupperware relies more on party plan personal selling than on advertising, while Rubbermaid relies more heavily on advertising than on personal selling.

Personal Selling Is a Two-Way Communication Process

Personal selling is a two-way communication process, where both the salesperson and the potential customer can respond immediately to questions. If the potential customer voices doubts or reservations about the product, the salesperson can adapt his or her message to try to overcome the potential buyer's objections. When detailed explanations or demonstrations of the product are necessary, personal selling is an especially effective way of communicating. Since personal selling is a communication process, the salesperson should realize that words as well as dress, mannerisms, and personality send messages.

Personal Selling Should Be Professional

Although you may have a tendency to view salespeople with suspicion and distrust because you have been exposed to unethical salespeople, the majority of the salespeople are honest and conduct themselves in a professional manner.[2] Many have acquired advanced training or education, which helps increase their effectiveness. Many abide by a strong code of professional

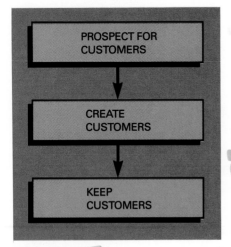

Figure 15.1

Tasks of Personal Selling

ethics.[3] Today's highly educated consumer and organizational purchasing agent demand professionalism in selling, which is why the sales field is an excellent career choice for today's college graduates.

The Tasks of Personal Selling

As shown in Figure 15.1, the specific tasks of personal selling fall into three categories: (1) prospecting for customers, (2) creating customers, and (3) keeping customers. Because customers usually will not beat a path to your door, the salesperson first must identify the characteristics of potential buyers and then try to locate and contact these potential buyers. Other promotional tools, such as advertising, may help bring potential buyers and the salesperson closer together; however, the salesperson must do some amount of prospecting so that potential buyers who do not visit or contact the firm directly can be identified. Even in the funeral business, salespeople must prospect!

The second task of personal selling, creating customers, is accomplished by providing prospects with the information and persuasive arguments needed to convince them to buy. This suggests that salespeople need to be thoroughly familiar with their products and with competing products—they should know how different products can help potential buyers fulfill and satisfy their needs.

The third task of personal selling is to hold onto customers. Any customer is a potential repeat customer and thus represents a potential stream of revenue to the firm. Most established and successful new car salespersons do a considerable amount of their business with repeat customers. In fact, some have customers that have bought more than ten cars over the course of twenty years. Any firm that wishes to survive and prosper over the long run needs repeat sales.

To generate repeat business, the customer must remain satisfied after the sale. The salesperson is in an excellent position to maintain postsale contact with the customer to ensure that he or she is satisfied and receiving the appropriate aftersale service. A customer's dissatisfaction must be transmitted to the appropriate manager, who can try to correct the situation. Satisfied customers are also important because they engage in a lot of word-of-mouth advertising. An extremely satisfied and dissatisfied customer lets their acquaintances and friends know, and this will also impact the firm's sales volume.

The three different tasks of personal selling can be performed by each salesperson, or the sales force can be specialized to perform these tasks. Part of the sales force may concentrate on locating potential customers. These leads can be turned over to another group of salespeople who specialize in creating customers and closing the sale. A third group of people may be responsible for maintaining customer satisfaction by providing good postsale service and handling complaints.

Sales personnel can be classified into three broad categories according to the functions they perform: order takers, order getters, and support personnel. A salesperson may perform all of these functions or specialize in one or two.

DIFFERENT TYPES OF SALESPEOPLE

Order Takers

An **order taker** *writes up the sale and is not actively involved in persuading customers to purchase.* Order taking is common in many lines of retail trade, especially in discount stores, like K mart and Toys "R" Us, and catalog showrooms, such as United Jewelers. Here, the salesperson may help the customer locate an item in the store, write up the sales ticket, and collect the money. Order taking is also common in business-to-business sales, where industrial supplies and maintenance and repair items are regular purchases. In this situation, the customer may phone in an order and the order taker records this information.

Although order takers do not actively attempt to generate demand, their actions and behavior affect sales. A polite, courteous order taker creates more repeat business than an unfriendly, rude order taker. All of us have encountered both kinds in stores and know the positive value of the former and how the latter can deter us from future visits.

Order Getters

An **order getter** *finds or creates new customers and also tries to get present customers to buy more.* This type of salesperson must recognize and understand customer needs and know how to present the firm's products in an appealing way so as to influence customers to buy.[4]

Most firms need order getters, but this is especially true in highly competitive industries that sell high-priced items. More expensive items require more selling effort to convert a prospect into a customer. Also, competitors are "beating the bushes," so that it is more difficult to locate good prospects.

Support Personnel

As the term implies, **support personnel** *support the work of order getters and order takers to help ensure the viability of selling efforts.* Support personnel do not make actual sales and are usually found in industrial sales. Two popular types of support personnel are missionary salespeople and technical advisors.

The **missionary salesperson** *attempts to create goodwill in the marketing channel by providing potential or existing customers with product information, advice, or assistance on product use. This type of salesperson does not obtain or take orders.* For example, pharmaceutical companies employ missionary salespeople who provide doctors with free samples and information on new drugs. Missionary salespeople who visit retailers are called *detailers.* These detailers may help the retailer set up displays and arrange merchandise on shelves. They may also advise retailers on optimum inventory levels, handle complaints, or return damaged merchandise. Missionary salespeople facilitate the jobs of order getters and order takers.

When a product is highly technical, the firm will often employ technical advisors to call on current or potential customers. These technicians usually do not talk with the person in the organization who makes the purchasing decision but will converse with the technicians about the technical aspects of the product that the salesperson is selling. This is helpful because the technical advisor and the technician speak the same language. If the technicians who will be using or servicing the product are convinced that it is technologically superior, the order getter's job will be less demanding. Technical advisors are employed most often by sellers of highly complex industrial equipment and machinery, such as industrial robots, computers, nuclear power plant equipment, and automated warehouse equipment.

Retail Versus Business-to-Business Selling

Up to this point, our discussion of selling has concentrated on business-to-business selling in the field—the salesperson travels to the customer's place of business. In retail selling, however, the customer typically travels to the retailer's place of business, although there are some door-to-door retail salespeople, such as encyclopedia salespeople and the familiar "Avon lady."

Since most retailers must attract customers to the store before salespeople can do their jobs, advertising and a convenient location are important. Personal selling seldom occurs in a large, limited-service discount store, since customers have been sold by advertising, catalogs, or in-store, self-service displays. In full-service stores, however, personal selling is very important. Two popular types of selling in full-service stores are suggestion selling and selling up. In *suggestion selling,* the salesperson suggests that the customer purchase related items or special items that may be on sale. For example, a man purchasing a suit would be advised to buy a shirt, belt, tie, or other accessories. In *selling up,* the salesperson attempts to move the customer up to a higher-priced item. For example, an appliance salesperson may try to move the customer up from a $589 standard 15 cubic foot refrigerator to a 19 cubic foot model with an ice maker and frost-free freezer priced at $819.

YOU AND KRAFT— WINNING THE BATTLE OF THE AISLES

No matter how tough the economy is, your Kraft Sales Representative has what it takes to help you win bigger sales.

After all, Kraft reps are the best trained in the grocery business. They learn all about your market and your sales trends, and then they use that expertise. They'll give you mouthwatering recipe ideas, exciting P.O.P. and aggressive storewide merchandising ideas to help you sell more.

Your Kraft rep is a carefully trained expert who can help you win a victory.

You & Kraft

THE MERCHANDISERS

Kraft advertises their sales representatives as missionary salespeople (specifically detailers because they call on retailers), who offer assistance to their store customers.

To sell effectively, a salesperson must understand the **selling process**, which is *the six-step process used by salespeople* in selling[5]: *(1) prospect for customers, (2) plan the approach, (3) make the presentation and/or demonstration, (4) handle objections, (5) close the sale, and (6) follow up*. Follow-up is important because satisfied customers are a good source of repeat business. These six steps are illustrated in Figure 15.2 and will be discussed in more detail.

THE SELLING PROCESS

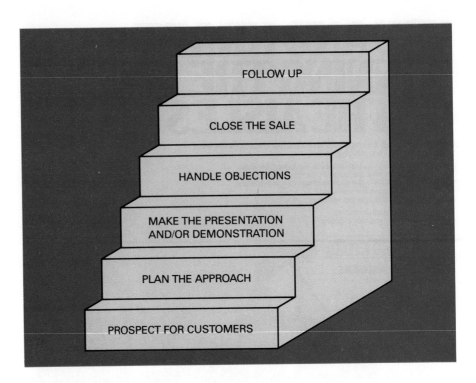

Figure 15.2

The Selling Process

Prospect for New Customers

A good salesperson should set aside a certain amount of time each week to prospect, or look for new customers.[6] Even a successful salesperson with a long list of regular clients should devote time to prospecting because there will always be some customer attrition.

There are several ways for salespeople to obtain customer prospects. Many firms will include cutout coupons in ads that customers can mail in for further information. Another source of prospects are unsolicited phone calls from people seeking information about the firm's products.[7] Other sources of prospects are directories and referrals. For example, *Thomas Register of American Manufacturers* provides a wealth of information on manufacturers: it lists their products, asset size, and other information that can be used to identify and rank order potential customers. Referrals are names of potential customers supplied to the salesperson by past customers. Many salespeople make it a practice to ask current and past customers for the names and addresses of others who might be interested in their products. In addition to these methods, there is also cold canvassing, which is what most people think of as door-to-door selling. The cold canvasser has no prior knowledge of the prospect's buying habits but calls with the hope of making a sale.

All customer prospects need to be qualified as to their ability and authority to make a purchase decision. The salesperson doesn't want to waste time trying to sell to a customer who is a poor credit risk or who has no authority to make a purchase decision.

Plan the Approach

The next step in the selling process is approaching the prospect or existing customer. The approach step is easy with an existing customer because the salesperson is known and conversations can begin by referring to old business. With new customers, however, it is often difficult to see anyone with purchase authority. This is especially true in business-to-business sales, where the salesperson first has to deal with a secretary or receptionist. In this situation, it is wise to set up an appointment in advance.

Once in the buyer's office or home, the salesperson must be able to initiate a conversation. This is a good time to hand the prospect a business card and a token gift embossed with the company's name (e.g., pens, pencils, calendars, or product samples). It is also helpful to know something about the organization or person being visited (i.e., a product they recently introduced, a new warehouse, their alma mater, and so on). Although small talk can initiate the conversation and promote rapport, the purpose of the visit should be introduced quickly, since time is valuable to both the salesperson and the customer.

Make the Presentation/Demonstration

The purpose of the presentation or demonstration is to inform or show customer prospects how the product will fill their needs. To accomplish this, salespeople must know their product(s) and something about their potential customer's needs. The presentation should also be interesting enough to hold the potential customer's attention and interest. Finally, the presentation must be persuasive in order to convince the prospect to make a buying commitment. We will discuss three types of widely used sales presentations: the canned presentation, the methodical presentation, and the free-form presentation.

There are actually several types of *canned presentations,* ranging from showing slides or pictures and reading flip charts to memorizing a complete sales presentation that covers all the points that the firm believes are necessary to sell a product. The canned presentation helps young and inexperienced salespeople make a coherent sales presentation and is usually used for low-cost items sold door-to-door, such as magazines and "miracle all-purpose cleaners," and for telephone sales for products like photographs, cemetery plots, aluminum house siding, and health club memberships. The disadvantages of the canned approach are its lack of ability to adapt to the needs of the buyer and its cold, mechanical presentation.[8]

A salesperson using the *methodical presentation,* also called the *formula approach,* has an established method or formula for selling. For example, if the salesperson used the AIDA model (see Chapter 13), he or she would first secure the prospect's attention or awareness, next work at building interest and creating desire, and then take the necessary steps to get action or close the sale.

With the methodical approach, the salesperson maintains flexibility in the sales presentation, while still covering certain established bases. This approach requires the salesperson to be alert and responsive to customer feedback so that he or she knows when to move on to the next step or to go back to an earlier step to reinforce the customer. An effective methodical presentation takes a lot of training and experience to make, but once refined, it can have considerably more impact than a canned presentation.

A salesperson using the *free-form presentation* has no set approach or method of presentation. The salesperson tries to ascertain indirectly the buyer's product preferences and what product attributes are most important to the buyer. Training people to make a free-form presentation is difficult, since it is really more of an art form than a science. Only the most experienced salespeople can handle an unstructured or free-form presentation. Also, since the presentation is unstructured, the salesperson may pursue areas where questions or objections are raised that cannot be adequately answered.

With any of these three types of sales presentations, a salesperson may include a demonstration of how the product works to get customers more interested in the product. For example, letting a potential customer test drive a new car is an excellent method of stimulating buyer interest.

Increasingly, salespeople are using audiovisual equipment to demonstrate products. Videotape recorders, film and slide projectors, and desktop computers are becoming part of the salesperson's tools of selling. The Marketing in Action on page 464 shows how one firm's salespeople are using the computer as a sales tool.

Handle Objections

It is unusual to give a sales presentation and not hear some objections raised by the potential buyers. The salesperson needs to anticipate likely objections and have a set of well-thought-out responses to these objections. When customers raise objections, they are asking for more information, and as such, objections offer opportunities for expanded discussion and for getting the potential buyers more involved in the selling process.

Prospective customers are likely to raise one or more of the following types of objections. *Source objections* ("I never buy GE products"), are directed against the supplier or sales representative and can often be countered by hearing the grievance. When prospects deny having a need for the product, *need objection,* it could mean that they do not know about the product. *Product objections* ("Ajax forklifts are too large"), are grievances against the product itself and can sometimes be handled by listening to the complaint and then explaining how the product has been improved to remedy that problem ("We have a smaller model now that is just as strong"). *Timing objections* ("I really don't need one right now") are difficult to counter, but a good salesperson can create a feeling of urgency that makes the prospect want to act now. Finally, prospects may have *price objections* ("The price is too high"), which can often be worked out by stressing quality, value, or quantity discounts.

A salesperson should handle objections politely and professionally and should not get defensive about them since many objections are only convenient excuses not to buy. In addition, most potential buyers feel compelled to raise objections because they view it as part of their role as good consumers.

Close the Sale

Surprisingly, many salespeople hesitate or are reluctant to *close a sale.* Few buyers ask to buy the product, however, so it is up to the salesperson to ask for the sale. There is nothing wrong with asking for it several times. If the salesperson asks too early and the buyer is not ready to commit, then the salesperson should offer more information and inducements and come back again and ask for the sale. Some common techniques of closing are presented in Table 15.1.

Follow Up

Regardless of whether the sale is closed, there should be some *follow-up* activity to bring the product's name to the prospect's mind once more. If the sale is not closed, the salesperson should jot down a few notes on the buyer's major objections and consult these notes before the next sales call. Also, it is a good idea after a sales call to write or phone the person and thank them for their time.

If the call was successful, the salesperson should also check with the buyer after the product has been received to see if everything is satisfactory. In addition, it is helpful to keep a file on each buyer that contains such information as complaints, inquiries, special needs of the buyer, and personal background data. This information will serve as a quick refresher before the next call on this customer.

MARKETING IN ACTION

After the motor carrier industry was deregulated, Transus Inc. (formerly Georgia Highway Express) developed a new pricing policy. Transus implemented a cost-based pricing policy based on a rate per hundredweight that declined steadily as total weight rose. The price system charges from zip code to zip code, which results in a single-rate structure regardless of point of origin or destination.

When Transus salespeople called on prospects, they found it hard to convince prospects that the new price policy could save them money. The salespeople needed a tool to help them demonstrate the potential cost savings. After visiting a trade show in Atlanta, top management became impresssed with the potential

Using the Computer As a Sales Tool

of using a desktop color graphics computer as a sales tool.

Transus devised a novel scheme for making sales presentations. They use a Winnebago motor home equipped with wood paneling, office furniture, carpeting, and a microcomputer with color graphics capability. Now, a salesperson can call on a prospective shipper, ask about their class of freight, weight, and average shipment, and within three minutes, present a color graph showing how Transus rates can save the shipper money. Salespeople can also offer shippers software that they can use

to determine costs on their own microcomputers. Customers now think that the new price policy is fantastic. Billie Ray Rummage, traffic and distribution manager at General Electric's Distribution Transformer department in Hickory, North Carolina, says, "We use that software in our computer to determine costs on any Transus shipment ahead of time. We can take full advantage of tariff benefits that way, and it cuts our auditor time dramatically."

Source: Adapted from Blanton Winship. "Overcoming Sales Resistance with a Computer on Wheels," *Business Marketing* (December 1983), pp. 54, 56. Reprinted with permission from *Business Marketing;* copyright Crain Communications Inc.

HOW TO MANAGE THE SALES FORCE

The sales force is a valuable resource for a firm, and the effectiveness of its management will have a big impact on the firm's profitability.[9] As shown in Figure 15.3, we will discuss seven steps in developing a sales force management strategy: establishing sales force objectives, determining sales force size, recruitment, screening, training, motivating, evaluation and control of salespeople.

Establish Sales Force Objectives

One of a sales manager's first jobs is to determine the objectives the sales force needs to accomplish. The objectives are usually stated for both the total sales force and each salesperson. Each salesperson usually has a variety of objectives to accomplish, such as:

❑ Increase average number of calls per week from twenty to twenty-five over the next ninety days.

❑ Increase average order size from $380 to $420 for next quarter.

❑ Open seven new accounts in the next four weeks.

Table 15.1   Techniques for Closing Sales

Closing Technique	Description
Direct close	In this technique, the salesperson asks directly for the order. It is used when the presentation has gone smoothly and objections that have been raised have been handled to the prospect's satisfaction.
Recapitulation close	In this approach, major benefits are summarized just before the closing attempt. This approach is especially pertinent when several previous sales calls have been made and a variety of benefits have been given; it is wise to bring the benefits to the prospect's attention again.
Assumptive close	In the assumptive close, the salesperson makes a statement that essentially obligates the prospect to purchase if he or she responds affirmatively. When a salesperson asks for a decision about writing up the order, installation, warranties, deliveries, or emergency shipments, a favorable reply essentially implies a purchase because the arrangement agreed to normally occurs after a purchase has been made.
Dual-choice close	In this closing approach, the prospect is offered two choices. Choosing one of them is tantamount to accepting the salesperson's proposal. For example, "Would you prefer the leatherbound or clothbound book?"
Minor-decision close	This closing effort seeks to get the prospect to agree on a small decision. The theory is that it is easier to get a decision to buy (the big decision) if the prospect has made a minor decision (or a series of minor decisions) first. A potential new car buyer is more likely to purchase if he or she has decided on upholstery and accessories.
Last-chance close	The last-chance close might also be called the "penalty you pay if you don't purchase now" close. In using it, the salesperson reveals some kind of penalty that can be avoided by purchasing or one that will result if the purchase is not made. Price is frequently the leverage employed during a last-chance close. A price increase can be avoided by purchasing now; if the prospect waits until later to buy, he or she will have to pay a higher price.
Benefit-in-reserve close	This closing technique generally is used at the end of a presentation when the prospect has not yet purchased. The salesperson offers a benefit not previously mentioned in an effort to capture the sale.

Source: Adapted from *Effective Salesmanship* by Richard T. Hise. Copyright © 1980 by the Dryden Press, a division of Holt, Rinehart & Winston, Publishers. Reprinted by permission of CBS College Publishing.

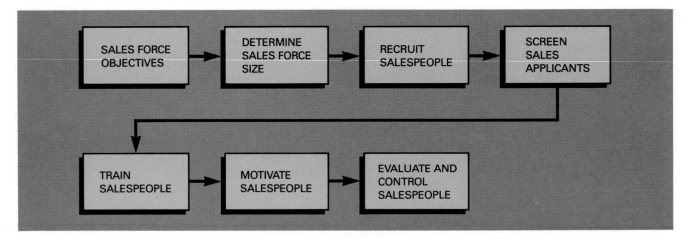

Figure 15.3
Sales Force Management

❏ Increase by 10 percent your sales of the premium product lines in the next year.

Note that since these objectives are quantitative and are associated with a specific time frame, they can also be used to evaluate salespeople at the end of a predetermined period. Like the objectives for advertising (see Chapter 14), the objectives set for the sales force should help the firm achieve its overall objectives.

Determine the Size of the Sales Force

A firm must decide how many salespeople to employ. A sales force that is too large can be bad for employee morale, while a sales force that is too small can represent lost profit opportunities. The two methods for determining optimum sales force size are the workload approach and the incremental approach.[10]

With the **workload approach** *to establishing the size of the sales force, the sales manager estimates how many hours each salesperson works per year and the total number of hours required to serve the customers.* This is shown in the following basic formula:

$$\frac{\left(\begin{array}{c}\text{number of}\\\text{customers}\end{array}\right) \times \left(\begin{array}{c}\text{number of}\\\text{calls per year}\end{array}\right) \times \left(\begin{array}{c}\text{average call}\\\text{length}\end{array}\right)}{\text{Time each salesperson works}} \quad /\!/ \quad \begin{array}{c}\text{number of}\\\text{salespeople}\end{array}$$

For example, consider a manufacturer who has 4,050 existing or potential customers who each normally receive four calls annually. If an average call requires two hours, and each salesperson works 1,800 hours per year, eighteen salespeople are needed.

With the **incremental approach** *to determining the size of the sales force, the expected gross profit an additional salesperson would generate is computed and compared with the cost of supporting the salesperson.* As long as the salesperson's incremental gross profit is above the incremental costs, the added salesperson should be employed. In principle, this type of analysis is a marginal cost and marginal revenue approach to determining sales force size.

Recruit Salespeople

Every business firm eventually needs to acquire new salespeople, and since good salespeople seldom come seeking employment, organizations must aggressively seek out and recruit them.[11] Experienced salespeople will cost the firm significantly more in terms of wages, but they will generate immediate profits for the company. For this reason, many small new electronics and high technology firms in Silicon Valley (Santa Clara, California, and surrounding areas) have hired experienced salespeople from Xerox and IBM. One disadvantage of hiring experienced salespeople is that they tend to be set in their ways and resistant to changes in their selling techniques, whereas inexperienced sales personnel can be obtained at relatively low wages and trained to follow prescribed company procedures for selling (balanced against this is the expense of training them and their attrition rate).

Several sources are used to recruit salespeople. Walk-ins are one source. During periods of high unemployment, organizations will have many applicants walk in off the street seeking employment. Using the services of public or private employment agencies is another source. Many firms recruit on college campuses. Other sources are competitors, former employees, friends and acquaintances of current employees, and people who answer classified ads.

Screen Sales Applicants

All applicants for sales jobs should be subject to a formal screening process. Screening errors, however, are inevitable. A sales force manager may classify an applicant as a potential loser when, in reality, he or she would be excellent for the job. On the other hand, the applicant may be classified as a potential winner and be hired, but turn out to be a real loser. Nonetheless, fewer of these errors should occur with screening than with no screening at all. Screening methods include application blanks, personal interviews, psychological and skills tests, references, and a physical examination, as shown in Figure 15.4. Note that the total applicant pool for the sales job opening is progressively reduced as the applicants are subjected to each screen.

Train Salespeople

New and inexperienced sales recruits should receive some form of training and development if the firm is to get a good return on its investment in the sales force. Until recently, most organizations gave new sales recruits one of two types of training, both of which were on-the-job and informal in their approach—the sink-or-swim approach and the sponsorship approach. With **sink-or-swim training** *new sales recruits are thrust into the field and have to learn in any way possible or quit or get fired.* **Sponsorship training** involves *assigning the new sales recruit to one of the more successful salespersons in the firm, who directs, guides, advises, and watches over the new recruit until the tasks and techniques associated with selling are learned.*

Recently, many firms have adopted more formal training programs, in which all new sales recruits are exposed to a standardized set of learning material. The material generally covers four areas: product knowledge, market-industry orientation or background, company orientation and policies, and selling techniques. The length of these formal training programs varies from several hours to several months. For example, the office products division of Xerox has a ten to twelve week formal sales training program for recent college graduates hired for their sales force.

Motivate Salespeople

A good reward system will not only help motivate the sales force but will also attract top salespeople to the firm and foster company loyalty. A good reward system, comprised of extrinsic and intrinsic rewards, is critical to the success of the sales force.[12] **Extrinsic rewards,** which are *external to the individual, consist of wages, bonuses, fringe benefits, job promotions, and so on.* **Intrinsic rewards** are *internal to the individual and consist of personal feelings such as job satisfaction, sense of worth, and freedom.* Wise sales managers will create a job environment that promotes job satisfaction.[13] Such things as giving the salesperson the freedom to make important decisions, providing challenging opportunities, and opening the lines of communication to top management can be very important in motivating salespeople.

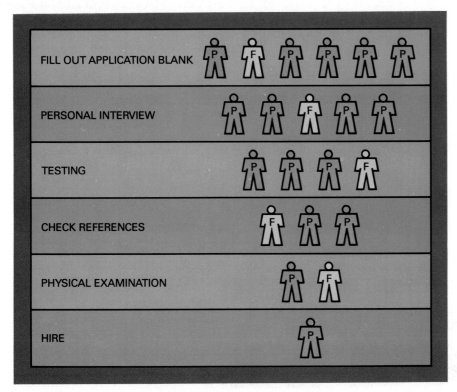

FILL OUT APPLICATION BLANK

PERSONAL INTERVIEW

TESTING

CHECK REFERENCES

PHYSICAL EXAMINATION

HIRE

Figure 15.4

The Sales Applicant Screening Process[a]

[a]P = candidates that pass screen; F = candidates that do not pass screen.

Source: Robert F. Lusch. *Management of Retail Enterprises* (Boston: Kent Publishing Company, 1982), p. 314.

Evaluate and Control Salespeople

One of the sales manager's most difficult jobs is to evaluate the performance of salespeople and, when appropriate, take corrective action to control their selling activities. Evaluation of performance is usually tied to objectives set for the salespeople. The most important objective is usually the total dollar sales the salesperson generates, which can be stated as the total days he or she works multiplied by the average number of calls per day, which in turn is multiplied by the proportion of calls that result in orders, and this is then multiplied by the average dollar sales per order.[14] This relationship is shown in the following equation:

$$\text{Sales} = \text{days worked} \times \text{average sales calls per day} \\ \times \text{proportion of calls resulting in order} \\ \times \text{average dollar sales per order}$$

A salesperson who does not generate the expected sales can be directed to improve one or more of the key variables that affect the sales performance. This can be illustrated by examining the data in Table 15.2 on four sales-

The Love Boat.
A whole boatload
of incentives.

A Love Boat cruise is something your people will really work for. Because nothing can compare to this magnificent resort. Whether it's a Princess Cruise to the sunny Caribbean, the festive Mexican Riviera, or breathtaking Alaska, top-selling travel agents rate Princess as the best cruise line overall.

And nothing can compare to our many extra incentives, such as discounts of up to 20% on groups of fifteen or more.

But, here's the most glorious difference: The Love Boat gives your people all the things they dream about in a cruise vacation. They'll be pampered from the moment they step aboard.

Call Rick James, Director, Group Sales at (213) 553-1770. Join the incentive planners who've discovered the Love Boat makes all the difference in the world.

Sumptuous dining served by charming Italians.

Big, bright, beautiful entertainment! Every night!

More of the most popular ports.

More things to do than hours in the day!

The exclusive Princess Discovery Program®— enriching insights into each new port of call.

Ships designed expressly for luxury cruising.

Superb service from British officers and crew.

Delightful new friends.

MEXICO · CARIBBEAN · ALASKA

PRINCESS CRUISES
All the difference in the world.

A cruise vacation is a popular extrinsic reward used by some firms to motivate their salespeople.

people. For example, Tim Reynolds has the lowest sales volume of the four because he only gets orders from 40 percent of the calls he makes, he worked fewer days than the other salespeople, and he makes the fewest average calls per day. Tim should work on improving his performance in each of these three control areas.

Table 15.2 Evaluating the Performance of Four Salespeople

Performance Variables	Fred Garcia	Tim Reynolds	Sue Cohen	Beth Currin
Sales	$714,000	$523,222	$1,031,098	$570,375
Average orders per call	50%	40%	60%	45%
Average days worked	200	190	204	195
Average sales per order	$1400	$1405	$1560	$1300
Average calls per day	5.1	4.9	5.4	5.0

In evaluating salesperson performance, the sales manager should also look at monetary measures other than sales, such as gross profit generated and selling expenses. Each salesperson could be viewed as a profit center, and an income statement for each could be developed.

Another factor to consider when evaluating a salesperson's performance is the sales territory.[15] Not all territories have equal potential and competitive activity, so that some salespeople may do better than others because their territories are more lucrative. The size of the territory and the density of customers are factors to consider.[16] If the salesperson needs to travel great distances because of a sparsely populated territory, fewer calls per day will be made and a lower sales volume will be generated.

SALES PROMOTION ACTIVITIES

In Chapter 13, we defined *sales promotion* as any marketing activity—other than personal selling, advertising, and publicity—that stimulates consumer purchasing and dealer effectiveness. **Trade sales promotions** *get dealers to push the products* more, while **consumer sales promotions**

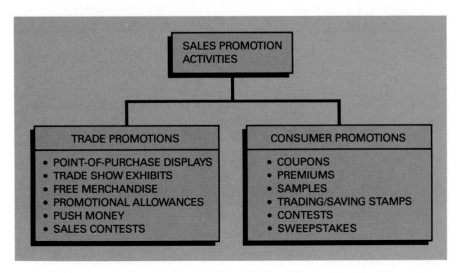

Figure 15.5
Sales Promotions

are *intended to motivate customers to pull the product through the marketing channel.* Figure 15.5 on page 471 identifies the major types of consumer sales promotions and trade sales promotions.

Trade Promotions

A major type of trade promotion is the **point-of-purchase display,** which is *a special presentation of merchandise or signing in a store that communicates a message, which is usually "buy me."* A point-of-purchase (POP) display is not directed at one person, as is personal selling, but it

Point-of-purchase displays, such as this one by Eastman Kodak Company, are designed to stimulate additional sales of products—for both the manufacturer and the retailer.

Reprinted courtesy of Eastman Kodak Company.

Have you got what it takes to turn 10 sq. ft. into 16,000 sales?

Capitalize on impulse sales in your supermarket with this high-visibility, self-service merchandiser. It holds about 1000 rolls of Kodak film when fully stocked. According to national research, Kodak film, when promoted, turns from 16 to 24 times a year. That means you could sell from 16,000 to 24,000 rolls from this one attractive display unit alone. Not a bad return from 10 square feet of floor space, is it?

That's just the beginning. This versatile sales tool allows you to remove pegs and insert a showcase to spur sales of Kodak cameras—like the popular, low-priced Kodak disc 3100 camera and the Kodak Trimprint™ 920 instant camera—and profit from even bigger sales.

If profitable impulse sales of favorite Kodak films are important to your supermarket, contact your regular supplier soon. And get what it takes to move 16,000 rolls of Kodak film.

© Eastman Kodak Company, 1984

MARKETING IN ACTION

Toyota Motors and all auto manufacturers faced a problem: independent auto parts manufacturers took a large share of the aftermarket repair business. Toyota also had another problem: because of import quotas, the dealerships often sold their entire allocation of Toyotas before year-end, which left Toyota salespeople sitting in showrooms with nothing to sell. Toyota decided to use these idle dealerships and salespeople to help solve its problem in penetrating the aftermarket.

Toyota developed an incentive program called *STAR,* which stands for *s*upport *t*o *a*ftermarket *r*epairs. A Toyota dealership became a STAR dealer by selling genuine Toyota parts to independent garages. The STAR incentive program was three tiered because it was directed at independent garage owners, at sales representatives selling to them, and at the dealership parts manager. The incentive program worked differently

Toyota Uses Incentive Program to Solve Aftermarket Problem

at each tier. A sweepstakes was developed for garage owners, who received a calendar covered with pictures of merchandise for different days of the year and three-day weekend vacations. The visiting sales representative gave the garage owner a sweepstakes ticket to be used to enter a drawing for any of the merchandise or free trips.

The sales representatives participated in the "field goal" part of the incentive program, in which the prizes were the same as those given to garage owners. Sales representatives qualified by achieving sales gains or by accumulating points that they earned by holding Toyota training seminars at independent garages, by selling metal tool cabinets

stocked with Toyota parts, or by placing metal signs at garages that read "genuine Toyota parts."

The parts managers at the dealership could qualify for free merchandise and trips by achieving a 10 percent increase in sales of wholesale parts over the previous year. The entire incentive program, called *Super STAR,* awarded a grand prize for each of the three tiers—a weekend trip to the Super Bowl. Overall, the Super STAR program was very successful. Toyota increased the number of independent garages buying Toyota parts by 70 percent, and wholesale parts sales at Toyota increased by 114 percent.

Source: Adapted from Philip Maher. "Incentive Programs Boost Sales . . . and Then Some," *Business Marketing* (December 1983), pp. 58–59. Reprinted with permission from *Business Marketing;* copyright Crain Communications Inc.

does reach individuals at a location where buying decisions are made. In 1982, close to $6 billion was spent on point-of-purchase displays.[17] The POP display can demonstrate products, elicit an immediate response, has a relatively long life span, and can give out free samples. On the other hand, it faces competition for floor space in retail stores and for attention with other POPs as well as regular merchandise.

A **trade show** is *an industry convention where manufacturers, resellers, and sometimes consumers meet to discuss, study, and observe industry trends.* Many manufacturers will set up merchandise displays and have company representatives available to discuss and demonstrate their products. Manufacturers may also have hospitality suites at trade shows where they entertain resellers.

Another *form of trade promotion* is the offer of **free merchandise,** *which is usually tied to some unit purchase volume.* For example, if the retailer purchases 100 cases of car wax, he receives a free AM/FM car stereo.

The merchandise could also be a free service. For instance, with every 500 shock absorbers the retailer purchases, she gets a free round trip to Hawaii.

A **promotional allowance** can be either *some form of vertical co-operative advertising* (as discussed in Chapter 14) *or some other monetary incentive given to the reseller to promote the manufacturer's products.* For example, retailers commonly are given a promotional allowance if a manufacturer's salesperson is allowed to set up a POP display in the retailer's store.

Push money, *also called "spiff,"* is *a direct payment by a manufacturer to the reseller's salespeople to get them to push a particular product or group of products.* A wholesale beer salesperson, for instance, may be paid $25 for every $1,000 of beer sold. This push money is paid by the brewer and is on top of what the wholesaler pays the salesperson. Push money is also sometimes paid at the retail level. One of the disadvantages of spiffs is that salespeople may be tempted to sell a customer a product or brand that is unsuitable.

Manufacturers often sponsor sales contests, in which wholesale or retail salespeople are offered the chance to win a prize if they reach a certain sales level or if they outperform other salespeople. For instance, Lincoln-Mercury may offer their top three car salespersons free European vacations for two, or the top salesperson may win a Lincoln Mark VII. The Marketing in Action on page 473 highlights a unique sales contest developed by Toyota.

Consumer Promotions

Probably the most popular form of consumer promotion is the **coupon,** which *almost always offers "cents-off" on the next purchase of an item. Coupons are distributed in the package of the product, by direct mail, or in newspapers and magazines.* An interesting example of the use of coupons was a joint effort by Britain's Barclays Bank and Kellogg's in a three-month promotion directed at getting 10- to 16-year-olds to open savings accounts. Coupons were printed on cereal boxes, and up to ten of these could be redeemed for 50 pence each (approximately $0.60) for a deposit in a special account in the child's name at Barclays Bank.[18]

Premiums *offer free or lower priced merchandise if the customer makes a certain purchase or a store visit.* For example, a store's first 100 customers on Saturday morning may be given a free coffee mug, or McDonald's may offer free Coca-Cola glassware with the purchase of a large Coke. The premium can also be packaged with the product; for example, laundry detergent has been sold with free hand towels included in the box.

Giving away **samples** of the product is another method of sales promotion. Often *nondurable consumer goods are introduced with the aid of free samples,* which are either handed out or mailed to millions of households. For example, approximately 10 million pounds of Ralston-Purina "Mainstay" (a dog food) were given as samples to dog owners throughout the United States. The samples were handed out at grocery stores as shoppers departed. Samples of Yoplait, a European brand of yogurt, have been distributed at many state fairs, where thousands of consumers were exposed to the product for the first time.[19]

Trading stamps are *a form of coupon that is distributed by retailers in proportion to the amount of the consumer's purchase. The trading stamps can then be traded at redemption centers for free merchandise.* Trading stamps were used heavily in the 1950s and 1960s but have since lost popularity. However, a version of the trading stamp sales promotion that has found success in recent years in grocery stores is the use of savings stamps given in proportion to the consumer's purchase that can be used to purchase special merchandise such as dishes, flatware, cookware, and books at reduced prices. These merchandise offers usually run for several months, then stop for several months before another one starts.

Contests consist of *customers competing for prizes based on skill.* For example, the child who draws the best picture of dad on father's day wins a free recliner for dad. In a **sweepstakes,** the *winners are selected solely by chance.* In some sweepstakes, such as the Publisher's Clearing House annual sweepstakes, prizes include new homes, new cars, thousands of dollars, and expensive jewelry. Consumers submit their names, and the winner, selected at random, receives the prize. Consumer sweepstakes are illegal in some states.

SALES PROMOTION MANAGEMENT

Figure 15.6 illustrates the process of sales promotion management. A sales promotion manager must first develop the sales promotion strategy. Sales promotion strategies can be categorized as push, pull, or push-pull strategies. A push strategy attempts to get additional cooperation in selling a firm's products from marketing channel members and uses trade promotions. A pull strategy is directed at stimulating consumer or final buyer demand and uses consumer promotions. A push-pull strategy tries to develop reseller cooperation as well as stimulate consumer or final buyer demand so that a coordinated mix of trade and consumer promotions is used.

Figure 15.6
Sales Promotion Management

A sales promotion strategy should have an objective(s). As in advertising, these objectives should be specific, measurable, and achievable. The following are possible objectives for a push sales promotion strategy:

❑ Increase wholesaler average inventory of our products by 25 percent in the next ninety days.

❑ Increase retail shelf space devoted to our products by 10 percent over the next forty-five days.

❑ Increase average order size by wholesalers to 600 cases within thirty days.

❑ Increase retailer advertising of our products by 50 percent during the next year.

Note that each of these objectives is specific, that is they relate to a specific activity, such as inventory, order size, shelf space, or advertising, and to a specific time period. The objectives are also measurable, since they are quantitative. Whether they are achievable naturally depends on the particular company and the competitive environment it faces. One important determinant of the achievability of a sales promotion objective is the time allowed to achieve the objective. Sales promotion managers should be realistic in setting the time required to achieve an objective.

Once sales promotion objectives have been identified, a sales promotion budget should be developed. A well-developed sales promotion program is not inexpensive, and a realistic budget should be established if the objectives are reasonably expected to be achieved. The objective and task method of budgeting, which was discussed in Chapter 14, is especially helpful in establishing realistic sales promotion budgets.

The sales promotion program must next be developed. First, the content of the program must be designed and to do this, the sales promotion manager must select from the consumer and trade promotion activities listed in Figure 15.5. Second, the sales promotion manager must coordinate the planned sales promotion activities with the advertising manager and sales force manager because the promotions usually need to be communicated to the trade or consumers, or both, with advertising and the help of the sales force. Predictably therefore a high level of coordination is necessary to create a successful sales promotion. Third, the sales promotion program must be implemented. This involves such things as shipping point-of-purchase displays to retailers, placing advertisements in media, and having enough inventory on hand for the expected increase in demand.

Because sales promotions are expensive, one last activity in sales promotion management is evaluating the success of the sales promotion. Various methods are used, such as before-after analysis of sales, inventory, and shelf space or, with a coupon redemption promotion, counting the number of coupons redeemed.

SUMMARY

This chapter focused on three main topics: the personal selling process, management of the sales force, and sales promotion activities. This chapter began by emphasizing the many excellent career opportunities in personal selling and its value as a stepping stone to numerous management positions. We described personal selling as a communication process in which the salesperson provides the prospect with information and reasons to purchase the product. The basic tasks of personal selling fall into three categories: (1) prospecting for customers, (2) creating customers, and (3) keeping customers. The basic tasks of personal selling can be expanded into a six-step selling process. The salesperson must *prospect* or locate potential customers, *approach* the prospects to gain their attention and develop rapport with them, and then *present and/or demonstrate* the product. Next, since most potential buyers will raise questions or criticisms, the salesperson must be prepared to *handle objections* and then try to *close* the sale by asking the prospect to purchase. Finally, salespeople should *follow up* with customers to make sure they are satisfied and, if not, to remedy their dissatisfaction.

The sales force is a valuable resource and must be well managed. Sales force management should begin with a clear statement of the objectives that the sales force needs to accomplish. Next, the size of the sales force must be determined, and we discussed two methods for determining this: the workload approach and the incremental approach.

Another activity of sales force management is recruitment. The firm must decide if it should hire experienced salespeople or sales trainees. Once the best people are hired, most firms will expose the new employees to some type of training program.

A good reward system helps motivate existing salespeople and attract new ones to the firm. It has the right balance of extrinsic and intrinsic rewards and is based on performance in terms of dollars of sales generated and the salesperson's profit contribution. A final element of sales management is evaluating the performance of salespeople and, if necessary, taking corrective action to improve their performance.

The chapter ended with a discussion of sales promotion activities and sales promotion management. The two major types of sales promotion are trade promotions and consumer promotions. Trade promotion tools include trade show exhibits, promotional allowances, sales force contests, push money, free merchandise, and point-of-purchase displays. Popular consumer promotions are coupons, samples, trading stamps, contests, sweepstakes, and premiums. Trade promotions are push promotional tools since they are intended to get dealers to put more push behind a product. On the other hand, consumer promotions are intended to motivate customers to pull the product through the marketing channel, and so they are referred to as pull promotional tools. The process of sales promotion management consists of (1) developing either a push, pull, or push-pull sales promotion strategy, (2) establishing sales promotion objectives, (3) developing a sales promotion budget, (4) creating the sales promotion program, and (5) evaluating sales promotion success.

KEY CONCEPTS

order taker (p. 457)   support personnel (p. 457)
order getter (p. 457)   missionary salesperson (p. 458)

selling process (p. 459)
workload approach (p. 466)
incremental approach (p. 467)
sink-or-swim training (p. 468)
sponsorship training (p. 468)
extrinsic rewards (p. 468)
intrinsic rewards (p. 468)
trade sales promotions (p. 471)
consumer sales promotions
  (pp. 471–472)
point-of-purchase display (p. 472)

trade show (p. 473)
free merchandise (p. 473)
promotional allowance (p. 474)
push money (p. 474)
coupon (p. 474)
premiums (p. 474)
samples (p. 474)
trading stamps (p. 475)
contests (p. 475)
sweepstakes (p. 475)

REVIEW AND DISCUSSION QUESTIONS

1. Explain how personal selling is a two-way communication process.

2. List and explain the three major tasks of personal selling.

3. Compare and contrast order takers, order getters, and sales support personnel.

4. How is retail selling different from business-to-business selling?

5. What are the six steps in the selling process? Define or briefly explain each step.

6. For each of the following products, explain which type of presentation—canned, methodical, or free-form—is preferable.
   a. Life insurance
   b. Floorcoverings for an office building
   c. Microwave oven
   d. Lawn mower
   e. Storm windows
   f. Acre cabin site in the mountains
   g. Encyclopedias
   h. One-year membership in health club

7. What are the five types of objections that potential buyers may raise during the selling process? How can each be handled?

8. Define the various techniques for closing a sale. Which technique is a real estate salesperson most likely to use?

9. Name some of the ways that a salesperson can follow up on a sale.

10. What are the seven steps a manager should follow when planning sales force strategy?

11. How should a firm determine the size of its sales force?

12. Should a firm recruit experienced or inexperienced salespeople?

13. How should applicants for a sales position be screened?

14. Define and briefly discuss the three methods for training salespeople.

15. How could most salespeople be motivated with extrinsic and intrinsic rewards?

16. How can the performance of salespeople be evaluated and causes of weak performance be identified?

17. In your opinion, is personal selling a science or an art? Give reasons.

18. List and define or give examples of the major types of trade sales promotions.

19. List and define or give examples of the major types of consumer sales promotions.

20. What are the five major activities in sales promotion management?

ACTION PROBLEMS

1. Go through a magazine or newspaper and cut out examples of several types of trade and consumer sales promotions. Use them as guides and develop several original sales promotions for a hospital that is attempting to increase its baby delivery business.

2. a) You are vice president of marketing for a manufacturer of electric forklifts. Your 3,940 customers can be classified as wholesalers, public warehouses, and transportation companies. The national sales manager has told you that ideally each customer should be called twice annually and that a typical sales call (including travel time) requires three hours. Each of the firm's fifteen salespeople works five days a week, fifty weeks a year and is required to work eight-hour days. Does the firm have a sufficient number of salespeople?

b) The president of the company recently informed you that sales must increase 20 percent next year. You believe that sales will grow 5 percent with the existing customer base. To accomplish the additional growth, you estimate that the company must expand its customer base by 425 customers. How many additional salespeople are needed to accomplish the sales growth objective?

3. a) You are regional sales manager for a manufacturer of executive office furniture. Ten salespeople are under your direction and control. Performance data for these salespeople are listed in the following table. Which salesperson is the best performer? What guidance and advice can you provide the two salespeople who sell the least?

SALES PERFORMANCE

Salesperson	Orders per Call (%)	Days Worked	Sales per Order	Calls per Day
Sandra Adams	32	231	2,200	2.8
Jim Barnes	31	225	2,405	2.4
Bill Bentz	38	230	2,304	2.9
Harold Cox	21	248	2,187	2.7
Phil Egert	40	219	2,624	3.0
Jessica French	34	249	2,412	2.7
Heather Lemon	40	242	2,709	2.8
Tom Moore	33	239	2,537	2.9
Susan Yu	36	247	2,489	2.6
Jerry Zelby	38	209	2,319	3.0

b) Assume that each salesperson receives a $20,000 salary and a sales commission of 5 percent on sales. Compute each salesperson's compensation.

4. You are a salesperson at Computerland and spend five days a week, eight hours a day selling personal computers to walk-in customers. Most customers are only browsing and seeking information. How would you handle the following objections:

   a. "I'm not ready to buy a computer."
   b. "Your prices seem high."
   c. "I really can't afford to buy a computer."
   d. "I really don't need a computer, but I just wanted to stop in and look around."
   e. "A friend of mine purchased a computer at Computerland and wasn't pleased with your aftersale service."

NOTES

1. "Best Sellers," *Ambassador* (June 1985), pp. 36–38. For other examples of women in sales, see Rayna Skolnik, "A Woman's Place Is on the Sales Force," *Sales and Marketing Management* (April 1, 1985), pp. 34–42; "Saleswomen Speak Out," *Sales and Marketing Management* (June 4, 1984), pp. 76–82.

2. Conway Rucks, "It's Time for Salespeople's Lib," *Sales & Marketing Management* (March 1978), pp. 51–52, 54, 58.

3. For a discussion of ethics in personal selling, see Alan J. Dubinsky, Eric N. Berkowitz, and William Rudelius, "Ethical Problems of Field Sales Personnel," *MSU Business Topics* (Summer 1980), pp. 11–16.

4. Order getters are involved in an interpersonal influence process; for a further discussion, see John O'Shaughnessy, "Selling as an Interpersonal Influence Process," *Journal of Retailing* 47(Winter 1971–72), pp. 32–46.

5. There are many excellent books on personal selling; for example, James F. Robeson, H. Lee Mathews, and Carl G. Stevens, *Selling* (Homewood, IL: Richard D. Irwin, 1978); David L. Kurtz, H. Robert Dodge, Jay E. Klompmaker, *Professional Selling* (Dallas, TX: Business Publications, 1976); Carlton A. Pederson, Milburn D. Wright, and Barton A. Weitz, *Selling Principles and Methods,* 8th edition (Homewood, IL: Richard D. Irwin, 1984).

6. One popular method of prospecting is networking, which occurs when businesspeople meet after hours with other professionals; see Al Urenski, "Not Working for Sales," *Sales and Marketing Management* (May 16, 1983), pp. 41–42.

7. A method for maximizing the potential of sales leads or inquiries is discussed in "An Inquiry-based MIS," *Business Marketing* (August 1983), pp. 54–68.

8. One researcher argues that the canned presentation can be made more effective; see Marvin A. Jolson, "The Underestimated Potential of the Canned Sales Presentation," *Journal of Marketing* (January 1975), pp. 75–78.

9. Two excellent books on sales management are Charles Futrell, *Sales Management: Behavior, Practice and Cases* (Hinsdale, IL: The Dryden Press, 1981); Gilbert A. Churchill, Jr., Neil M. Ford, and Orville C. Walker, Jr., *Sales Force Management: Planning, Implementation, and Control* (Homewood, IL: Richard D. Irwin, 1981).

10. An additional model is discussed in Leonard M. Lodish, "A User-Oriented Model for Sales Force Size, Product, and Market Allocation Decisions," *Journal of Marketing* (Summer 1980), pp. 70–78.

11. A good discussion of recruitment and selection is in Chapter 7, "Recruiting and Selecting Salespeople," in Joe L. Welch and Charles L. Lapp, *Sales Force Management* (Cincinnati: South-Western Publishing Co., 1983), pp. 151–170.

12. Orville C. Walker, Jr., Gilbert A. Churchill, Jr., and Neil M. Ford, "Motivation and Performance in Industrial Selling: Present Knowledge and Needed Research," *Journal of Marketing Research* (May 1977), pp. 156–168.

13. A discussion of the role of different rewards and the structure of the selling job is available in Stephen X. Doyle and Benson P. Shapiro, "What Counts Most in Motivating Your Sales Force?" *Harvard Business Review* (May–June 1980), pp. 133–140.

14. Douglas J. Dalrymple, *Sales Management: Concepts and Cases* (New York: John Wiley & Sons, 1982), p. 422.

15. David W. Cravens, Robert B. Woodruff, and Joe C. Stamper, "An Analytical Approach for Evaluating Sales Territory Performance," *Journal of Marketing* (January 1972), pp. 31–37.

16. Adrian B. Ryans and Charles B. Weinberg, "Territory Sales Response," *Journal of Marketing Research* (November 1979), pp. 453–465.

17. Additional information and statistics on point-of-purchase displays are available from the Point-of-Purchase Advertising Institute, Two Executive Drive, Fort Lee, NJ 07624.

18. Christopher H. Lovelock and John A. Quelch, "Consumer Promotions in Service Marketing," *Business Horizons* (May–June 1983), p. 66.

19. Examples are from Don Ailloni-Charas, *Promotion: A Guide to Effective Promotional Planning, Strategies and Executions* (New York: John Wiley & Sons, 1984), pp. 56, 57, 66.

25.

Vital Toy Company

Vital Toy Company boasted sales of approximately $25 million in 1985. Unfortunately, this level of sales was 8 percent less than the prior year and represents Vital Toy's first annual sales decline since it was established in 1953. Top management at Vital believes that company sales have been hurt by the rapid growth of computer/TV screen games since 1980.

Vital does not produce any computer games, but instead concentrates on conventional board and action games. It has fifteen product items in its product mix, and detailed information on these items is presented in Table 1.

Andy Felty, marketing vice president at Vital Toy, is in the process of establishing a final advertising budget for the June 1, 1986, to May 31, 1987, period. During this period, Vital will be introducing two board games for children and one family board game. The two games for children will each have suggested retail prices of $6.89, and the family board game will retail for $9.95. These games will be sold to retailers at $4.47 and $5.98, respectively. The variable cost per unit for each child's game is $1.55 and for the family board game, $2.25. Mr. Felty has estimated that each of these games could have sales of 250,000 units over the twelve-month planning horizon. Importantly, the bulk of games are sold during the Christmas season (an estimated 62%); therefore, Mr. Felty must also decide on a final sales estimate soon. Pam Jones, vice president of production, wants a final sales forecast on each of these new products by February 1, 1986.

Most board and action games are sold through mass merchandisers. The data in Table 2 further illustrate the retail distribution of board and action games. There is heavy retail price competition on games: it is not unusual for a retailer to discount a game 10 to 25 percent of the suggested retail price. This is especially true if retailers find themselves sitting on too much dead inventory. Table 3 provides a consumer profile of buyers of Vital Toy board and action games. These data were obtained from a marketing research study that Mr. Felty recently commissioned.

Questions

1. Which elements should Vital Toy include in its promotion mix? Which elements should receive the most emphasis?
2. Should Vital Toy increase its advertising budget? Why or why not? If you answered yes, explain how much should it be increased and on what types of games should the increased advertising dollars be spent.

Table 1   Vital Toy Company Product Line Data (1985)

Game Type	Total Product Items	New Product Items	Unit Sales	Unit Production	Variable Cost per Unit	Price per Unit[a]	Advertising Expenditures	Assignable Fixed Costs
Child's action	4	1	1,489,190	1,618,350	$1.68	$4.98	$1,304,000	$841,094
Child's board	6	0	1,479,010	1,591,104	1.27	4.79	698,714	629,347
Family action	2	0	214,011	218,987	4.19	7.12	141,340	161,989
Family board	3	1	1,268,748	1,270,340	2.13	7.06	312,224	714,198

[a]Price that Vital Toy receives from its retail accounts, not price consumer pays.

Table 2   Retail Distribution of Board and Action Games (1985)

Game Type	Discount Department Store (%)	Conventional Department Store (%)	Sears, Penneys, Wards (%)	National Toy Chain (%)	Local Toy and Hobby Store (%)	Variety Store (%)	Other (%)
Child's action	48	3	7	18	4	8	12
Child's board	45	4	6	14	3	11	17
Family action	36	8	14	6	4	10	22
Family board	38	6	12	8	4	12	20

Table 3   Consumer Profile Board and Action Games (1985)

Profile Characteristic	Child's Action Game	Child's Board Game	Family Action Game	Family Board Game
Age of recipient				
6–23 months	2%	—	3%	—
2–5 years	40%	34%	21%	6%
6–9 years	40%	41%	43%	30%
10–12 years	9%	15%	23%	35%
13–17 years	6%	8%	7%	16%
18+ years	3%	2%	3%	13%
Average purchase price	$6.10	$5.78	$8.49	$8.19
Percentage of planned purchases	34%	38%	36%	64%

26.

Fred's IGA

Fred Hopkins owns and operates a 20,000 square foot IGA Supermarket in a small midwestern city with a population of 24,900. The town also has a 16,000 square foot A&P store.

Fred reads *Progressive Grocer* and other trade magazines and has noted a lot of discussion on the growth in the wine market. Industry analysts suggest that wine is becoming an everyday pleasure, the wine market is growing three times faster than all other beverage markets combined, and the premium price wine market is growing the fastest.

Fred does have a liquor department in his store and has sold wine since 1972. However, Fred only stocked the lower-priced, more popular wines that sold in the $2 to $3 price range (per quart). Fred sold approximately fifty quart bottles of wine weekly at an average price of $2.89 with a 32 percent markup on retail price.

Recently, a sales representative of a large national wine maker visited Fred. The sales representative tried to persuade Fred to handle premium wines, which sell in the $4 to $8 range and offer a 35 percent markup on retail. The representative argued that many of Fred's regular customers would be encouraged to trade up if Fred properly merchandised the premium wines.

On the way home that evening, Fred visited the local A&P's liquor department. He noticed that they stocked premium wines by Inglenook and Gallo. Fred also knows that the two local liquor stores carry premium wines because his wife purchased a premium wine from them for special occasions.

About a week later, Fred called the wine representative. After considerable discussion, the representative offered to set up a 30 square foot end-of-aisle display in Fred's liquor department. This display would feature eighty-eight quart bottles of a premium wine. The wine would be priced at $6.79, which would allow a 35 percent markup on retail. The wine being featured was scheduled to receive a lot of exposure in magazine advertising. The display would run for two weeks.

Fred was very surprised at the results. Fred sold seventy-two bottles of the premium wine in the first week, and eighty-one bottles in the second week. Sales of his lower priced wines fell to about thirty bottles weekly.

Recently, the sales representative phoned Fred to tell him about a new cooperative advertising program. This program would pay the retailer for 60 percent of the cost of its newspaper wine advertising. There were two conditions: (1) the wine company would supply the newspaper advertising mats and (2) the total advertising allowance could not amount to more than 20 percent of the retailer's monthly wine purchases. Fred is seriously considering participating in this cooperative program. Fred regularly advertises in the local newspapers, and the cost per day for a one-page advertisement is $1,500; a half-page ad is $1,000; and a quarter-page ad is $500.

Questions

1. Should Fred regularly display premium wines?
2. Should Fred participate in the proposed cooperative advertising program?

27.

Negative Publicity for the Alcohol Industry

In a recent book entitled *The Booze Merchants*, the Center for Science in the Public Interest (CSPI) challenges the alcohol industry with unethical marketing practices. The CSPI wants to see a ban on alcohol ads in broadcast media and the elimination of ads directed at heavy drinkers and young people. In addition, CSPI advocates:

● **Presentation of ads that stress health problems related to drinking.**

● **Health warnings in print ads similar to those found in cigarette ads.**

● **Guidelines on what information may be contained in the ads (price, taste, and so on) and a ban on imagery and "puffery."**

● **No use of celebrities in ads.**

● **Restrictions on the channels of distribution for beer, wine, and distilled spirits.**

Most people, whether inside or outside the alcoholic beverage industry, admit that alcohol is related to major social and health problems—drunk driving and alcoholism. The CSPI is not attacking these problems but the practice of marketing and how marketing intensifies these problems. Two central questions are:

● **In spending more than $1 billion a year to sell their products, are beer, wine, and spirits advertisers merely shifting sales from one brand or category to another or are they expanding the market?**

● **In trying to sell their products, are marketers aggravating alcohol-related problems or are they only catering to social behavior that would occur anyway?**

Generally, the alcoholic beverage industry, through their trade association called the Distilled Spirits Council of the United States (DISCUS), recognizes that alcohol advertising must be controlled. However, DISCUS believes that it is doing a good job in self-regulating alcoholic beverage advertising. DISCUS believes that current alcohol ads are in good taste and not offensive.

However, CSPI likes to cite examples of ads in bad taste. For example, they cite a Riunite ad showing a cartoon in which construction workers on a steel beam of a skyscraper were offered a bottle of wine and a Budweiser advertisement that showed a crew of lumberjacks leaning on their chainsaws while "a superimposed hand seemed to be offering the resting workers a drink." On the other hand, CSPI believes that a few firms, such as Paul Masson, which associates drinking with eating, and Seagram, which emphasizes taste but advises consumers to drink in moderation, show a greater degree of responsibility. Regardless, the CSPI is working to get alcohol advertising severely restricted.

Questions

1. How should an alcoholic beverage company counteract the bad publicity that CSPI generates about the alcohol industry?
2. How can the alcoholic beverage industry better regulate itself?

Source: Based on Kevin Higgins. "Debate Rages Over Marketing and Alcohol Problems," *Marketing News* (September 30, 1983), pp. 1–4.

28.

SOFPAC

Robert E. Greenwood is president and founder of SOFPAC, a firm specializing in custom computer software development. SOFPAC was founded in 1982 shortly after Greenwood earned his undergraduate college degree in accounting and information systems. While in college, he became an avid computer enthusiast and was president of the campus computer club during his senior year. Although he had many attractive job offers, he decided to start his own venture.

During college, Greenwood, an only child, lived at home with his parents. Both his parents were employed outside the home. Robert enjoyed a quiet place to study and to work on computer programs he was writing for clients. He often had two or three clients for whom he was developing software programs, and this became very lucrative. By the time he was a senior, Greenwood had

paid cash for a new Firebird and had accumulated another $8,000 in savings. He had also acquired over $10,000 in personal computer hardware.

When he was a student, one of Greenwood's regular clients was a local hospital where his mother worked as a nurse. His mother had often complained about the increasing amount of paper work that nurses had to complete. Greenwood immediately saw the opportunity to computerize this recordkeeping. After several visits with Mr. Henson, the hospital administrator, Greenwood convinced Henson to retain him to develop custom software for the nursing function. The initial project had a budget of $10,000, for which Greenwood had to purchase a personal computer for a single nursing station and develop software to handle all of the recordkeeping for patients. Over a two-year period, this project became quite large, and ultimately all nursing stations had a personal computer that was linked to the hospital's main computer in the accounting department. The software ultimately was able to handle data on patient care (such as services provided, data on bodily vital functions, and dietary requirements), nurse scheduling, and cleaning and janitorial activities in the area.

In a somewhat similar but smaller project, Greenwood developed software for ten departments in a liberal arts college. This software allowed each department chairperson to schedule courses, arrange secretarial support, control the expenses of supplies and communications, and have readily available data on all students majoring and taking courses in the department.

SOFPAC was a one-person operation during 1982 and 1983. The firm was operated from Greenwood's two bedroom apartment. Sales were $52,000 in 1982 and $56,000 in 1983. Greenwood concentrated on writing custom software for clients. During slow periods, of which there were few, he worked on making the nursing software and college department software more generic. He finally completed this undertaking in November 1983. During that month, SOFPAC also moved into a 500 square foot office suite and Greenwood hired a half-time secretary. From December 1983 through February 1984, Greenwood spent four half-days a week making sales calls on hospitals and colleges trying to sell his two software products. In total, he worked forty-one half-days and called an average of 2.5 times on thirteen hospitals and three colleges in Santa Clara County in California. He sold his nursing software to three hospitals for a one-time licensing fee of $7,500; in addition, there was a $200 annual charge for software updates. His sales calls also resulted in one custom software project for an emergency room in a large hospital. This hospital also purchased the nursing software, and SOFPAC sold this institution a total of $17,200 in services. The licensing fee on the college department software was $5,000 plus $200 annually.

Greenwood believes that he could expand SOFPAC's business by hiring a sales force. Some secondary data that were collected (as shown in Table 1) indicate that four other counties in California besides Santa Clara have a sizeable number of hospitals and colleges. Salespeople could call on these institutions to sell the two generic software programs SOFPAC has developed; custom software development services also could be sold. Almost all of the selling price of the generic nursing and college department software is profit, since all the costs are previous research and development costs. Variable costs are minimal. On the other hand, custom software is priced at twice the direct labor costs of writing the software.

Table 1   Size of Firm Statistics

County and SIC[a]	Number of Establishments		Shipments/Receipts[c] (millions)	Percentage in Large Establishments[d]
	Total	**Large[b]**		
Alameda				
8062	21	20	$ 729.6	99
8221	6	4	293.1	98
Los Angeles				
8062	176	149	5,160.6	98
8221	40	19	726.0	95
Orange				
8062	39	35	867.8	98
8221	6	3	69.5	96
San Francisco				
8062	25	21	917.8	99
8221	10	3	56.6	66
Santa Clara				
8062	13	13	687.2	100
8221	5	3	96.7	97

[a]SIC 8062 is General Medical and Surgical Hospitals; SIC 8221 is Colleges and Universities.

[b]A large establishment is one with 100 or more employees.

[c]Shipments/receipts is the total dollar value of goods produced or distributed or of services rendered.

[d]Percent in large establishments is the share of shipments/receipts accounted for by establishments with 100 or more employees.

Source: "1984 Survey of U.S. Industrial & Commercial Buying Power," *Sales & Marketing Management* (April 23, 1984), pp. 58–60.

The costs of hiring a salesperson on a yearly salary would be $21,000. Fringe benefits would add another 20 percent, and travel and entertainment are estimated at $6,000 annually. SOFPAC pays Greenwood a salary of $30,000 and in 1982 and 1983 had net profit (after taxes) of $8,204 and $9,120, respectively. As of March 1, 1984, SOFPAC had cash on hand or in checking accounts of $11,714.

Questions

1. Should SOFPAC hire a sales force? If you answered yes, how many salespeople should be hired?
2. Should the sales force be compensated on a salary or commission basis? Explain your reasoning.

29.

Improving Sales Force Productivity at Avis

The car leasing business is very competitive because new car dealers and fleet leasing firms such as Avis battle aggressively for customers. In order to enable its salespeople to do a better job in this highly competitive market, Avis decided to target its marketing efforts on the small to medium auto fleet market—on those firms using ten to forty automobiles per year.

Lawrence D. Mazur, vice president of marketing and sales services at Avis Car Leasing, wanted to develop a selling program that would:

● **Lower cost per sale.**

● **Offer direction and sales call appointments for the sales force.**

● **Motivate the sales force and improve morale by giving the salespeople more quality sales leads.**

● **Generate more contracts and new orders.**

The company began with its list of current customers, and with the aid of a statistical procedure called *multiple regression analysis,* it isolated the factors common to its most desirable customers. Four factors were identified: (1) the firm's SIC code, (2) the county the company was located in, (3) the number of employees the firm had, and (4) the firm's financial strength—its cash flow and profit margins. The resulting regression equation told Avis some very interesting and useful things. For example, it was found that manufacturing firms will lease one car for every ten employees, whereas firms in the service industries will lease one car for every six employees. This is important because service industries are growing more rapidly than manufacturing industries and more than one-half of gross national product is due to the service sector. The equation also allowed Avis to estimate the lease potential in different territories which allowed it to create sales territories of approximately equal potential by balancing off the distance salespeople would need to travel with the number of prospects to be covered.

Next, Avis developed a telemarketing program, for which a telephone sales script was written, tested, and refined. It was then stored in the computer, and phone operators could access the script and read it over the phone, immediately entering the data on a cathode-ray terminal. The following technique was used. The operator asked to speak with the chief financial officer or chief executive and then obtained information on seven key questions, such as the number of cars the firm owns or leases and whether or not they would see a sales representative without obligation. Eighty-seven percent of the chief financial officers or executives were reached and answered the questions, and 20 percent of those reached asked to see a sales representative from Avis.

Avis's new selling program has provided salespeople with more selling time and eliminated confusion about which person the salesperson should call on next.

Questions

1. When the salespeople visit a prospect that has been contacted through the Avis telemarketing program, what type of sales presentation should be made: canned, methodical, or free-form?
2. Develop a sales promotion program to further improve the effectiveness of the Avis telemarketing program.

Source: Based on Lawrence D. Mazur. "How Avis Tries Harder (and Succeeds) with Targeted Telemarketing," *Business Marketing* (October 1983), pp. 114, 116. Reprinted with permission from *Business Marketing*; copyright Crain Communications Inc.

PART VI

PRICE PLANNING AND DECISIONS

Part VI of *Principles of Marketing* concerns the importance of price and its relationship to other marketing mix elements: product, distribution, and promotion. Chapter 16, "Price Concepts," discusses how price is influenced by the firm's external environments and how managers develop pricing objectives and policies. Chapter 17, "Price Determination," discusses the price strategies a firm can establish and explores the economic approach to price setting, how prices are set, and different pricing tactics.

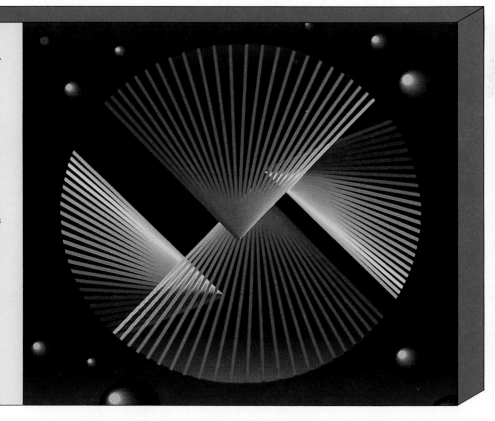

LEARNING OBJECTIVES

After you complete this chapter, you should be able to:

- **Explain** the role of price in society

- **Discuss** how pricing decisions relate to other marketing mix decisions

- **Describe** how the competitive and legal environments affect pricing decisions

- **Compare** and **discuss** four different price objectives firms can set

- **Enumerate** and **explain** the six different price policies available to a firm

PRICE CONCEPTS

MARKETER PROFILE

*Lenny Mattioli—Champ of Negotiated Prices
for American TV*

Lenny Mattioli grew up in Chicago but moved to Rochester, New York, in the 1960s, where he worked as a mechanical engineer for Eastman Kodak Co. He became disillusioned with Kodak's compensation plan because he thought that their "one size fits all" salary policy didn't encourage hard work. He would often speculate that things would be different if he ever ran a business.

Mattioli returned to the Midwest in 1969, when his brother died, leaving the struggling TV sales and service shop he had owned in Madison, Wisconsin. Mattioli had no intention of running the business but soon found that he enjoyed hustling TV sets and was able to get the shop back onto the road to success in a very short time.

The secret to Mattioli's success with American TV is a unique marketing strategy based on negotiated pricing and compensating salespeople based on their performance. The salespeople know the absolute lowest price and will negotiate right down to it. American TV has no fixed prices, except on sale items, and the company advertising invites people to "come in and negotiate your own price."

According to Mattioli, "The rule of thumb [in the electronics industry] is to tie your prices to your costs. But, we try to tie ours as close as we can to just how much the customers are willing to pop." His system seems to be working: his stores in Madison, Appleton, and Milwaukee are each the size of several football fields, the company employs around 850 people, and annual sales have topped $160 million.

Source: Based on Ralph Whitehead, Jr. "Name Your Price," *Inc.* (December 1984) pp. 214–216; authors' personal experience and purchases at American TV.

INTRODUCTION

All organizations must decide the price at which they are willing to sell their goods and services. All buyers, whether they are consumers or organizational buyers, must decide the price they are willing to pay for those goods and services. Frequently, sellers have what buyers want, but no exchange occurs because the price is too high. You may want a new car when you start your first job, but you will probably not be able to afford most of the cars that you want (e.g., Porsche 928 or BMW 320i).

Price can be defined as *something of value that is exchanged for something else.* In the U.S. economy, most products usually are priced in terms of dollars; money is the medium of exchange most often used. Price does not have to involve dollar values; an exchange made without money is called *bartering.* Bartering is used worldwide as a means of dealing with markets that would otherwise be unreachable. For example, Ford of Britain has bartered cars for coffee (Colombia), cranes (Norway), toilet seats (Finland), potatoes (Spain), and cotton (Sudan).[1] Services are also bartered between persons who exchange such skills as home repair for legal counsel.

As was shown in the Marketer Profile on Lenny Mattioli, price decisions are vitally important to the overall success of an organization. This chapter and the following chapter deal with various aspects of the price decision. We start with an overview of the importance of price and its relationship to the other elements of the marketing mix: product, distribution, and promotion. We then move on to the relationship of price to the firm's external environments. We discuss how managers develop pricing objectives and plan pricing policies. Chapter 17 covers how managers establish a firm's pricing strategies and pricing tactics.

ROLE OF PRICE IN SOCIETY

Consumers

Price is obviously important to us as consumers because we have limited or fixed incomes that affect our purchasing power. The higher the price of goods and services, the lower the total quantity or quality of goods and services we can purchase. As prices rise, the dollar shrinks in terms of purchasing power because it can buy fewer items or items of lesser quality. In 1960, a Hershey chocolate bar cost 5¢ (you could buy 20 for $1.00); today it is about 35¢ (thus, you can't even buy 3 for $1.00).

As long as income rises at the same rate as prices, the consumer is no worse off. When prices rise faster than income, however, the consumer is harmed and price becomes a more important determinant of consumer purchasing decisions. Price is also important to consumers because price is anything of value that is given up to acquire a product. Buying a product costs money and also involves travel, time, and psychic costs. There is no admission to a house of worship (your contribution is voluntary), but to attend you must incur travel costs and give up several hours of time that you could use otherwise. Some psychic costs also may be involved if, for instance, the services are scheduled at a time that is inconvenient to you (i.e., when you normally sleep). Marketers that do not recognize that price involves more than money will have difficulty developing an effective marketing strategy.

Organizations

Organizations must be concerned with the price they pay for goods and services, as they also have limited budgets. If an organization pays too high a price for goods and services needed to operate its business, it must in turn raise prices to its customers—which will predictably result in the loss of some customers. Although the price of products is an important factor to organizational buyers, research has revealed that other factors, such as product quality, product servicing, and reputation of the supplier, are generally more important.

Naturally, the price they receive from the sale of goods and services is very important to organizations. Most manufacturers, wholesalers, and retailers operate on a very thin net profit margin—usually 1 to 5 percent. (A firm's net profit margin is the profit after all expenses are paid divided by total sales revenue.) In other words, on each dollar of sales, a typical firm has a net profit of 1 to 5 cents. These very thin profit margins help to dramatize how important it is to receive the appropriate price for goods and services. Table 16.1 shows average net profit margins for manufacturers, wholesalers, and retailers for 1984.

Table 16.1   Average Net Profit Margins for U.S. Corporations[a]

Manufacturers	4.6%
Wholesalers	1.1%
Retailers	2.6%

[a]Net profit margin = net profit (after taxes)/net sales.

Source: Authors' computations and U.S. Bureau of the Census. *Quarterly Financial Report for Manufacturing, Mining, and Trade Corporations.* (Washington, DC: U.S. Government Printing Office), 1st quarter 1985.

The Economy

Price is important to the overall economy because it serves the role of a resource allocator. If demand rises for a particular product, then firms can charge a higher price and thus increase profits. This higher profitability will attract competition, which will increase the total supply of the product (resource) and in turn help to soften prices. A prime example of this resource allocation process has been the supply and price of oil over the last ten to fifteen years. As worldwide demand for oil increased due to more rapid industrialization in the 1960s and early 1970s, the oil-producing countries decided to raise prices substantially from about $2 a barrel in 1972 to over $30 a barrel in 1982. No doubt the rapid rise in price dramatically increased the profit potential of oil exploration, drilling, and refining. Consequently, a worldwide search for oil began, and new oil was found in Alaska, the North Sea, and Mexico, as well as in other areas. The net result was a major increase in supply and a softening of prices beginning in the summer of 1982.[2]

CONSIDER THE MARKETING MIX

Price setting does not occur in a vacuum. When making pricing decisions, marketers must carefully consider the other marketing mix variables: product, distribution, and promotion. As we have seen in our discussions of these other mix variables, a change in one often affects the others.

Product

In setting price, executives must take into account the attributes of the product being sold. How distinctive are these attributes, and what value does the buyer place on them? For example, a standard model, 16 cubic foot, white refrigerator may sell for $598, but if it is painted almond and has an ice maker, it may sell for $749. The cost of these changes to the manufacturer may be only $45, but the added price to the consumer is $152. The most important thing in setting price is not what these product attributes cost the seller to create or manufacture, but how valuable they are to the consumer.[3]

Because the purchaser is buying more than the tangible product, the seller should also consider the value of its brand name to the buyer. A brand with a good reputation can demand a higher price.

Other product attributes to consider when setting price are warranty, styling, durability, performance ratings, and quality of workmanship. It is useful to compare the firm's product with its strongest competitor on each of these attributes. If the attributes generally are better and more valued by the consumer, a higher price than that of competitors may be warranted.

Distribution

The distribution component of the marketing mix needs to be carefully considered when setting price so that these costs are covered without sacrificing profitability. The distribution decision involves the structuring of a marketing channel composed of one or several middlemen who are compensated for their efforts. Thus, in setting price, managers need to determine not only what the final buyer is willing to pay, but how large a margin the reseller needs to profitably handle the product.

Manufacturers often suggest what they consider to be the best prices for the products they produce (manufacturer's suggested retail price). Assume that a manufacturer decides that the best retail price for a product is $20. If the marketing channel used is composed of a wholesaler and a retailer, the manufacturer must consider their margin requirements. If the retailer wants to make 30 percent on the sale of that product, then the most he or she can pay for it is $14 ($20 $\times$ (1 $-$ 0.30)). For the wholesaler also to make money on the product, say 10 percent, he or she needs to buy it from the manufacturer for $12.60 [$14 $\times$ (1 $-$ 0.10)]. The key question is "Can the manufacturer afford to sell it at $12.60?" If not, the manufacturer needs to find a less expensive marketing channel; although a lower cost channel may not be the one that can generate the largest sales or profit for the manufacturer.

Promotion

Promotional expenditures, especially advertising, can be used to reinforce in the buyers' minds the value of certain product attributes. Also, intangible attributes, such as the status or prestige of the product, can be promoted, thus increasing its value in the eyes of the buyer. Consequently, if a company plans to have a big promotional budget for a product and spends this budget efficiently and effectively, it should be able to (1) sell more of a product at a given price or (2) get a higher price for the product without sacrificing much in terms of volume sold.

The Competitive Environment

CONSIDER EXTERNAL ENVIRONMENTS

The actions of competitors should be addressed in setting prices: what will competitors do if the company sets the price lower than that of competitors? Will they quickly meet the low price, beat it and offer an even lower one, or raise prices and put the additional money into advertising? Similarly, how will the competition react to a higher price? Will they raise their prices

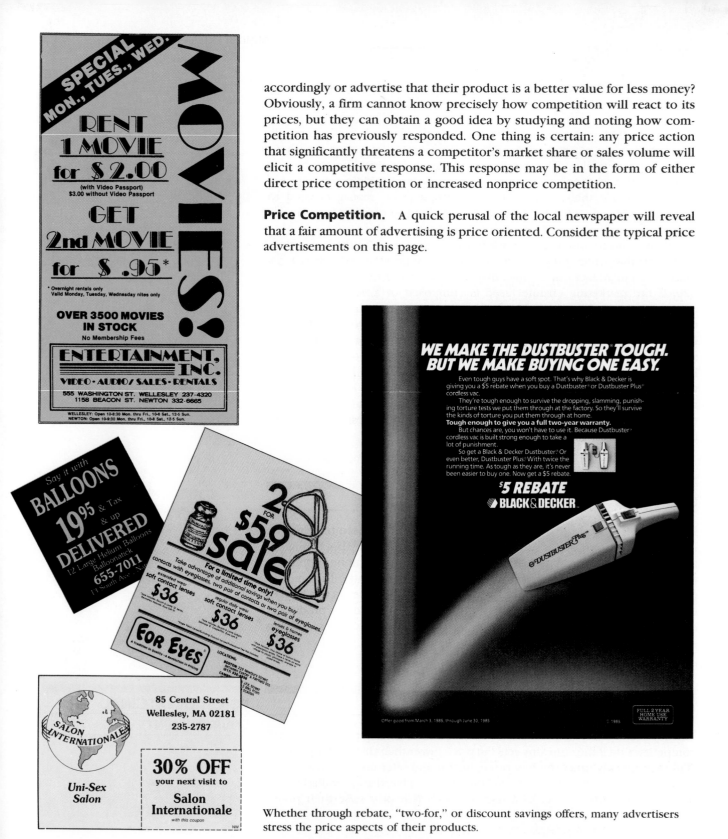

accordingly or advertise that their product is a better value for less money? Obviously, a firm cannot know precisely how competition will react to its prices, but they can obtain a good idea by studying and noting how competition has previously responded. One thing is certain: any price action that significantly threatens a competitor's market share or sales volume will elicit a competitive response. This response may be in the form of either direct price competition or increased nonprice competition.

Price Competition.   A quick perusal of the local newspaper will reveal that a fair amount of advertising is price oriented. Consider the typical price advertisements on this page.

Whether through rebate, "two-for," or discount savings offers, many advertisers stress the price aspects of their products.

Nonprice Competition.   Although price is an important competitive tool, most U.S. firms try to compete primarily on nonprice variables[4] for the following reasons. First, if a firm decides to compete primarily on price, its price cuts typically can be matched or even beaten by a competitor. For instance, in early 1985 when American Airlines offered ultimate supersaver air fares (70% off regular prices), all the other major airlines immediately followed suit with almost identical plans. When one gasoline station in your neighborhood markedly lowers its prices, other area stations do the same in a few days, if not hours.

Second, many U.S. firms try to compete on nonprice variables, such as prestige, convenience, and taste, because buyers are looking for more than the lowest price. For example, one bottle of Chevas Regal scotch is the same as another. Yet a drink of Chevas at home costs about $0.50 per glass, while a drink of Chevas at a local bar may cost $1.75, and at a dinner club, $3.00. Obviously, the person willing to pay $3.00 rather than $0.50 is shopping for something other than the lowest price. In this case, it is probably atmosphere, prestige, or companionship. This is not an isolated example. Why, for instance, are some consumers willing to pay $500 for a Whirlpool washer from a local appliance dealer when they can buy the same washer at K mart or some other discount store for $430?

Third, firms compete on a nonprice basis because it allows them to change the position of their demand curve. A *demand curve* shows the quantity that will be purchased at different prices. Figure 16.1A shows a demand curve. If a firm emphasizes nonprice factors such as product quality, brand image through advertising, or good customer service, then it could increase demand and shift its demand curve to the right. This is shown in Figure 16.1B.

Shifting of the demand curve is especially important when the firm is selling an undifferentiated product in a perfectly competitive market, as is true for farm products. In this situation the seller has no control over price and must sell at the market price unless the shape of the demand curve can be changed. Frank Perdue, president of Perdue Farms, recognized this fundamental truth and transformed his chicken broilers into a highly differentiated product by improving broiler quality, branding his broilers, and heavily advertising Perdue chickens on radio, on television, and in newspapers.[5] Frank Perdue was able to get higher prices for his birds because of his nonprice marketing strategy, and sales grew from $50 million in 1970 to over $500 million in the early 1980s. The Marketing in Action on page 499 illustrates how a nonprice marketing strategy can give the marketer more control over price.

The Legal Environment

Marketers do not have total flexibility in their pricing decisions because of a variety of state and federal laws that regulate price decisions for businesses. We will focus our discussion primarily on federal legislation.

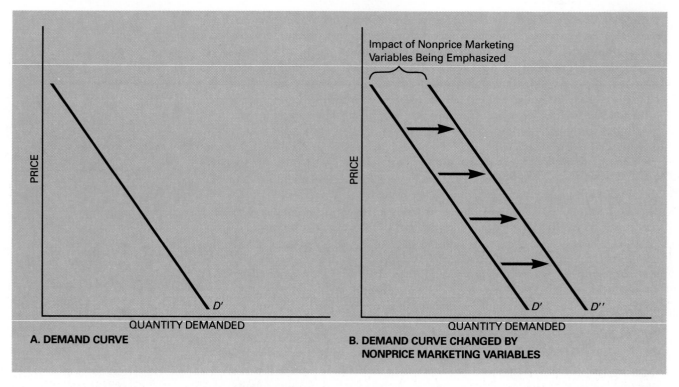

Figure 16.1
Demand Curves

Horizontal Price Fixing. *When a group of competing sellers establish a fixed price at which to sell their products,* they are engaged in **horizontal price fixing.** For example, all retail grocers in a particular trade area may agree to sell large grade AA eggs at $0.89 per dozen. Regardless of its actual or potential impact on competition or the consumer, horizontal price fixing violates Section 1 of the Sherman Antitrust Act (1890), which states, "Every contract, combination in the form of trust or otherwise, or conspiracy, in restraint of trade or commerce among the several states, or with foreign nations is declared to be illegal."[6]

The Marketing in Action on page 500 deals with an attempt to monopolize and fix prices in a part of the airline industry. Do you believe American Airlines was doing something illegal or unethical?

Vertical Price Fixing. **Vertical price fixing** occurs *when a retailer or wholesaler agrees with a manufacturer or other supplier to resell a product at an agreed-on price.* This is *also often referred to as "resale price maintenance."* These agreements are illegal and have been viewed as a violation of Section 1 of the Sherman Act. This does not mean that manufacturers cannot recommend to retailers or wholesalers a price at which they would

MARKETING IN ACTION

Produce commodities, such as peaches, apples, pears, and oranges, are relatively undifferentiated. Increasingly, producers of such commodities are recognizing the need to use nonprice strategies to influence demand and thus be able to charge higher prices. Since growers number in the thousands for any given produce commodity, it is unlikely that a single grower could develop an effective strategy. Hence, industry trade associations such as the International Apple Institute are beginning to develop demand expansion programs.

Shelagh Thomee, a vice president for Ketchum Public Relations, has helped the International Apple Institute develop such a program. This program has helped per capita consumption of apples rise from 17 pounds to 21 pounds in three years. The following are some tenets of the program she developed:

● **The variety of apples available to the public should be increased. One research study found that increasing**

Shifting the Demand for Apples

the variety of apples from three to five yielded a sales increase of 36 percent. When consumers have more choice, they are more likely to find the apple that best suits their needs and thus increase their purchases of apples.

● **There is an opportunity to create an image for apples as a snack food, since the snack food business is large and growing. She helped to develop a promotion campaign with the theme "Crunch an apple instead."**

● **Since consumers often rely on recipes in magazines for meal ideas, Shelagh Thomee invited food editors of national magazines to a series of apple tastings. As a consequence, major features appeared in *Family Circle, Food & Wine, Weight Watchers, Cuisine, Gourmet, Women's Day*, and six other publications.**

● **Since the average American consumer eats 3.5 meals away from home each week, a promotion campaign was developed to be directed at the food service industry. The campaign consisted of distributing 30,000 kits that illustrated uses for apples, cost-effective recipes, and case studies, which resulted in dramatic sales increases for food service operators following apple promotions.**

Ms. Thomee is now suggesting to the apple industry that they must begin to think internationally to more profitably dispose of larger crops. "There is only so much that can be consumed in the domestic market. The export market is critical," Thomee suggests. "Unfortunately," she adds, "America has been slow in realizing that we're part of a worldwide economy, and we're already shut out of a lot of markets."

Source: Based on Kevin Higgins. "Marketing Becoming Essential for Commodity Producer Groups," *Marketing News* (April 29, 1983), pp. 1, 16.

---

like to see an item sold, but they cannot establish a price for resale, nor can they legally threaten them with supply cutoffs if they do not sell at the recommended price.[7]

Price Discrimination.   **Price discrimination** occurs *when two business firms buy identical merchandise and/or services from the same supplier but pay different prices.* Not all forms of price discrimination are illegal, however. Federal legislation addressed the legality of price discrimination in Section 2 of the Clayton Act, which made certain forms of price discrimination illegal.[8] Section 2 was amended and strengthened by the passage of the Robinson-Patman Act in 1936. This act had two primary objectives: (1) to prevent suppliers from attempting to gain an unfair advantage over their competitors by discrimination among buyers either in price or in providing allowances or services and (2) to prevent buyers from using their

MARKETING IN ACTION

In early 1983, a civil suit was filed in federal district court in Dallas on behalf of the Justice Department that charged American Airlines President Robert L. Crandall with violating the antitrust laws. The suit claimed that Crandall attempted to get Braniff Airlines president Howard Putnam to raise certain fares by 20 percent during February 1982. Several months later, Braniff Airlines ceased operations and filed for bankruptcy.

The Justice Department's case was based in part on a February 1982 telephone conversation between Crandall and Putnam. The following is a transcript of that conversation.

Mr. Crandall: I think it's dumb [expletive], all right, to sit here and pound the [expletive] out of each other and neither one of us making a [expletive] dime.

Mr. Putnam: Well . . .

Mr. Crandall: I mean, you know [ex-

Was American Airlines Trying to Monopolize the Industry and Fix Prices?

pletive], what the [expletive] is the point of it?

Mr. Putnam: Nobody asked American to serve Harlingen, nobody asked American to serve Kansas City, and there were low fares in there, you know, before. So . . .

Mr. Crandall: You better believe it, Howard. But, you . . . you . . . you know, the complex is here—ain't gonna change a [expletive] thing, all right. We can . . . we can both live here and there ain't no room for Delta. But there's, ah, no reason that I can see, all right, to put both companies out of business.

Mr. Putnam: But if you're going to overlay every route of American's on

top of, over, on top of every route that Braniff has—I can't just sit here and allow you to bury us without giving our best effort.

Mr. Crandall: Oh sure, but Eastern and Delta do the same thing in Atlanta and have for years.

Mr. Putnam: Do you have a suggestion for me?

Mr. Crandall: Yes, I have a suggestion for you. Raise your [expletive] fares 20 percent. I'll raise mine the next morning.

Mr. Putnam: Robert, we . . .

Mr. Crandall: You'll make more money and I will, too.

Mr. Putnam: We can't talk about pricing.

Mr. Crandall: Oh [expletive], Howard. We can talk about any [expletive] thing we want to talk about.

economic power to gain discriminatory prices from suppliers so as to gain an advantage over their own competitors.

In order for price discrimination to be considered illegal it must fit one of the following criteria according to Section 2a of the amended Clayton Act. First, the transaction must occur in interstate commerce. Trade among the states—called interstate commerce—encompasses most companies, because the products they produce or market typically originate in another state. Second, the actual competition does not have to be lessened, but the potential of a substantial lessening of competition must exist. Third, the buyer who knowingly receives the benefit of discrimination is just as guilty as the supplier granting the discrimination.

Considerable attention has been given to the phrase "commodities of like grade and quality" contained in the Robinson-Patman Act. What does this phrase mean? To begin with, commodities are goods, not services. This implies that discriminatory pricing in the sale of services, such as advertising space or the leasing of real estate, is not prohibited by the act. For example, shopping center developers frequently charge varying rates for equal square footage depending on the tenant and the type of merchandise sold. In a case brought by Plum Tree, Inc. (a franchisor of a nationwide chain of retail shops) against N.K. Winston Corporation (a shopping center developer), Plum Tree charged the developers with price discrimination under the Robinson-Patman Act for charging different rents for equal space.[9] "Plum Tree contended that the commodities under the act are equivalent to lease-holds in shopping centers and that a landlord must charge equal rent for equal space. The court held that a lease for real property is not 'selling goods, wares or merchandise' " and Plum Tree lost the case.[10]

"Like grade and quality" has been interpreted by the courts to mean "of identical physical and chemical properties."[11] This meaning implies that different prices cannot be justified merely because the labels on the product are different. However, if the seller can establish that an actual physical difference in grade and quality exists, then a differential in price can be justified.

Discrimination in Providing Promotional Services. Sellers are not only prohibited from discrimination in price, they are also banned from discrimination when providing promotional services and payments, such as advertising allowances, displays and banners to promote the goods, in-store demonstrations, and distribution of samples or premiums. Sections 2(d) and 2(e) of the Robinson-Patman Act deal specifically with these practices and state that such promotional services and payments must be made available on *proportionately equal terms* to all competing customers.

Deceptive Pricing. Companies should avoid using a misleading price to lure customers into the store. **Bait and switch** pricing is *advertising or promoting an item at an unrealistically low price to serve as "bait" and then attempting to steer the customers away from the low-priced item to a higher priced model.* Also included within this category of deceptive pricing is advertising goods or services at a price below what the seller would be willing to take and then adding on hidden charges. The Wheeler-Lea Amendment (1938) of the Federal Trade Commission Act (1914) made illegal all "unfair or deceptive acts in commerce." Not only is a firm's customer being unfairly treated when the firm uses deceptive pricing, but the firm's competitors potentially are being harmed because some of their patrons may be diverted unfairly to the deceitful firm.

Below-Cost Pricing. Many states have sales-below-cost legislation that applies to the retail and wholesale distribution of merchandise. The specific content of these laws varies from state to state, but generally they forbid the firm from selling merchandise below cost plus some fixed percentage markup (6% at retail and 2% at wholesale are typical). Most of these state laws are unclear as to whether the firm can offer other forms of price reduction, such as giving merchandise away or offering prizes, premiums, or services.

Predatory Pricing. If a business charges different prices in different geo-graphic areas in order to eliminate competition in selected areas, it is in violation of Section 3 of the Robinson-Patman Act. This law forbids the sale of goods at lower prices in one area for the purpose of destroying competition or sales of goods at unreasonably low prices for such purpose. The Federal Trade Commission's Bureau of Competition generally investigates complaints about predatory pricing.

ESTABLISH PRICE OBJECTIVES

After considering the other elements of the marketing mix and the external environments, the marketer needs to determine the organization's pricing objectives. **Price objectives** are *the firm's pricing goals,* and like the objectives of the other elements of the marketing mix, they must be consistent with the mission and objectives of the firm. Price objectives are usually financially based or market based.

Financial-Based Objectives

Two types of financial-based objectives are profit maximization and target return. **Profit maximization** is *when prices are set as high as possible to get "all the traffic will bear."* It should be stressed, however, that high prices do not necessarily bring the highest possible profits for the firm as a whole. Obviously, a high price will yield a high profit per unit sold, but a price that is too high and results in a smaller quantity being sold may actually have lower profits. The marketing manager needs to reach a careful balance between price and estimated units sold when setting prices. The Ford Motor Company made enormous profits from 1910 to 1920 by pricing its Model T at well below the prices of competitive auto manufacturers. In the early 1980s, Commodore Computers made good profits by pricing its home computers at low prices. The economic approach to price setting to maximize profits will be discussed in Chapter 17.

When establishing a **target return** objective, *a firm sets a specific profit goal for a particular period, which is usually stated as a target return on investment (profit divided by investment), commonly called "ROI."*[12] In the United States, the target return on investment is usually in the 15 to 40 percent range. To illustrate, assume your firm expects a profit of $100,000 and has $400,000 investment. Your target return would be 25 percent ($100,000/$400,000). Note that this is a target return before taxes; U.S. corporate taxes usually run from 25 to 45 percent of total profits.

Frequently, the marketing manager determines the desired target return on investment percentage by using a build-up approach. The manager looks at the items for which the company needs funds, such as (1) cost of capital (i.e., the cost of borrowing or using money), (2) future growth needs of the firm, and (3) reward for taking risks (i.e., otherwise, the money could merely be put in the bank). A U.S. firm might arrive at a desired percentage as follows:

15%	cost of capital
5%	Future growth needs
7%	Reward for risk taking
27%	Target return on investment

In the following chapter, we will discuss how to set prices to achieve a target return on investment.

Many nonprofit organizations set prices to achieve some target return on revenues or sales. For instance, a labor union may set member dues at a certain percent over the cost of operating the union. This is necessary because, even though an organization like a labor union is nonprofit, it must have more revenue than expenses to be able to set monies aside for emergencies and for growth and expansion.

Market-Based Objectives

Two types of market-based price objectives are sales growth and status quo. Firms that have a sales growth objective use price as a vehicle to obtain a certain sales level or market share. **Market share** is *the percentage arrived at by dividing the firm's sales in a particular market by total market sales.* Managers who pursue this objective usually believe that rapid sales growth or gains in market share will lead to competitive dominance and ultimately to higher profitability. In addition, many corporate executives have their bonuses more closely tied to sales than to profits.[13]

A considerable amount of research conducted during the 1970s suggested that market share is a key to profitability.[14] As firms gain market share, they end up accumulating more experience in production and marketing, which lowers their costs. This lower cost can lead to greater profits. Thus, pricing goals directed at increasing market share may have a strong economic rationale.

Some companies will make pricing decisions based on what the competition charges: they wait to see what other firms charge and then follow suit. Often, marketing managers who follow a status quo objective regarding price will use a nonprice variable—product, distribution, and promotion—as a major competitive vehicle because nonprice strategies are more difficult to copy or duplicate. For example, Ivory Soap concentrates on the purity and gentleness of the product as a nonprice promotional variable rather than using price as the product's major attribute.

After a firm has decided on its overall pricing objectives as previously discussed, it can more readily establish price policies. **Price policies** are *guiding principles for price setting. These guiding principles deal with price lining, geographic pricing, negotiation policies, leasing, credit policies, and discounts.*

ESTABLISH PRICE POLICIES

Price Lining

Price lining occurs *when a firm has multiple products in a particular product line and each product is given a different price.* For instance, Cuisinart has a line of food processors that range in price from $135 to $400 depending on their size and other features.[15]

Marketing managers must try to develop significant functional, quality, or styling differences among items in a product line to support the price differentials because the products will have an *interrelated demand*—that is, one product can be substituted for another. In the case of Cuisinart food processors, the $135 model can substitute for a $195 model and vice versa. Consumers are quick to recognize this and will ask themselves, "What will the next higher priced model provide me that the lower priced one doesn't? A larger capacity? A more powerful motor? More accessories?" Obviously, the greater the price difference among items in a product line, the more difficult it will be for consumers to decide to go with the higher priced model unless they can recognize substantial differences in the quality or features.

Products in the same product line also typically have **joint costs,** which are *costs that cannot be uniquely identified with a particular product, but are common to two or more products.* For example, when a manufacturer sets up a production assembly line to produce a line of seven different models of food processors, then the fixed cost of that production assembly line is common or joint to all output. Because of this phenomenon, the only actual difference in cost of producing the different models are direct costs. **Direct costs** *can be traced specifically to a particular product.* The $135 model has a six-cup capacity and a 0.85 horsepower motor, whereas the $195 model had a ten cup capacity and a 1.0 horsepower motor. The cost of the larger workbowl and motor represents a direct cost of producing the higher priced model. The cost may be an added $10, and as long as the price differential is greater than the added direct cost, the higher priced model will be more profitable for the firm. Of course, the overall profitability of this situation will depend on how many people are willing to trade up to the $195 model from the $135 model.[16]

Geographic Policies

Many organizations sell their products to customers over a wide geographic area—sometimes an entire country or even the world. The cost of distributing this product can be a significant part of the total price paid by the customer. Thus, the marketing manager must establish policies on how to charge for transportation to various geographic areas.

Both joint costs and direct costs play roles in establishing the price lines for products.

FOB Origin. A policy of **FOB origin** states that *the product is placed free on board (FOB) at a certain geographic point,* which is usually the seller's place of business. *The buyer pays for the transportation costs from the point of origin.* Also, when the seller turns over the goods to the carrier, title passes to the buyer. Therefore, if the goods are damaged in transit, the buyer must file a claim against the carrier.

   With a policy of FOB origin, there is no geographic price discrimination. All buyers pay the same price at point of origin. The farther they are located from the point of origin, the higher the transportation costs because these costs generally increase with distance. If all sellers in an industry used FOB origin, then natural monopolies would be created because those buyers located close to a seller could purchase at a lower total cost (price at origin plus transportation costs) than those farther away. Consequently, one way a more distant competing seller could capture the buyer as a customer would be to lower its price at origin to help offset higher transportation costs.

Uniform Delivered Pricing. With **uniform delivered pricing,** *all buyers pay an identical price regardless of where they are located.* Uniform delivered pricing is *also referred to as "postage stamp pricing."* With this type of pricing, all buyers pay a uniform or fleet freight charge. Consequently, buyers located far away receive a favorable price discrimination since they pay the same freight charge as someone located very close to the seller.

   Although uniform delivered pricing is discriminatory, it is not illegal according to the Federal Trade Commission. Often it is merely a convenient way of administering prices over wide geographic areas. Also, if the firm wishes to advertise prices nationally, this method allows a uniform price to be stated and thus helps to avoid consumer confusion.

Zone Pricing. **Zone pricing** falls somewhere between FOB origin and uniform delivered pricing. With zone pricing, *a seller's territory is divided into two or more zones, and within each zone, all buyers pay an identical freight charge regardless of where they are located in that zone.* Thus, the seller is averaging the total freight costs across a zone and charging each buyer an average rate. As zones are farther removed from the seller, the average freight charge rises, so that these zones are charged a higher rate.

Figure 16.2 shows a map of the United States that is divided into four zones. The manufacturer is located in Pittsburgh and produces industrial machinery. For a typical machine, any buyer located in zone 1 pays a freight charge of $40 per machine; in zone 2 the charge is $55; in zone 3 it is $65; and in zone 4 it is $80.

Zone pricing is discriminatory in that all buyers in a zone pay the same freight charge regardless of how close they are to a seller. For instance, a customer in Pittsburgh, the city where the manufacturer is located, pays a

Figure 16.2
Zone Pricing Freight Charge

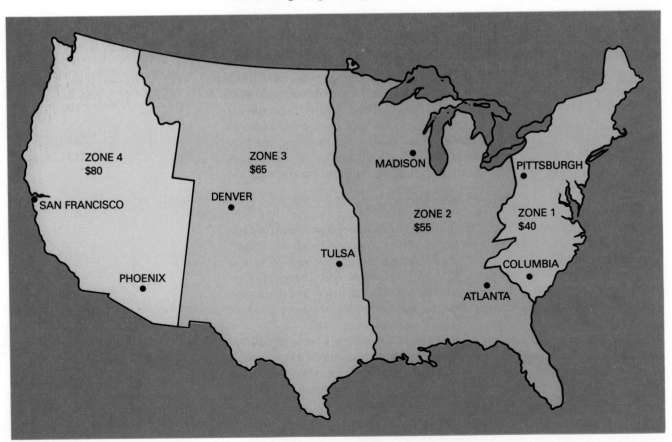

$40 freight charge—as does a customer located in Columbia, South Carolina (600 miles from Pittsburgh).

Zone pricing substantially reduces the clerical and paperwork required in shipping to thousands of customers. In the prior example, the buyer can be charged one of four freight charges depending on location rather than calculating a precise freight charge for each customer.

Freight Absorption Pricing.   With **freight absorption pricing** *a supplier who is located far from buyers who are located near competing suppliers will charge a reduced freight rate to those buyers. The distant seller can thus compete with the nearby seller.* Referring to Figure 16.3, note that the selling organization is located in Atlanta, Georgia, and the potential customer is in Portland, Oregon. The actual freight charge for the merchandise that is being sold would be $1140; however, the buyer in Portland could purchase the identical merchandise from a supplier in Los

Figure 16.3
Freight Absorption Pricing

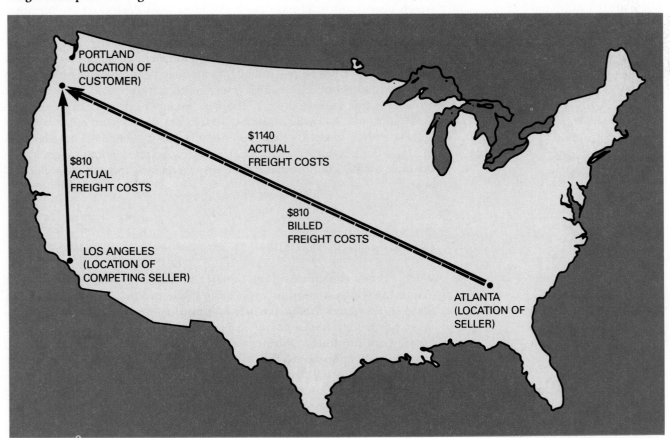

Angeles and pay only $810 in freight charges, a savings of $330. Therefore, the seller in Atlanta may offer to absorb $330 of the $1140 freight charge in order to compete with the supplier in Los Angeles.

A policy of freight absorption is used to compete more effectively in geographic areas that are far from the seller. In these distant locations, there will likely be competing sellers who can sell to buyers in this area at a much lower price because transportation costs will be lower.

Negotiated Prices

Marketing managers also need to establish a policy regarding whether to charge a single price or to negotiate price with each customer. Although a single price policy is now more common in the United States, negotiated prices were prevalent in the past. Today, most manufacturers, wholesalers, and retailers offer a product at a preestablished price, and the buyer can either take it at that price or leave it.[17] Could you imagine yourself going into a food store and offering the checkout clerk $2.10 a pound for a steak that is marked $2.98 a pound? There are some lines of trade, however, in which negotiated prices are common: most auto dealers, many furniture stores, and TV and appliance stores, such as American TV highlighted in the Marketer Profile, will negotiate the price with each buyer.

Negotiated prices are not widely used for many reasons. One problem is that the buyers who pay a higher price may become disgruntled when they learn someone else paid a lower price for the same item. Another problem is that salespeople may too willingly lower price because this can be a quick way to make a sale. Also, if every supplier or seller were to negotiate price, excessive price competition might occur as each seller tries to beat a competitor's "best price." Finally, negotiated pricing takes a considerable amount of time and can be very frustrating to both the seller and buyer.

Leasing Policies

When a buyer cannot afford the outright purchase of a product, the seller may still have an opportunity for a sale if the product can be leased.[18] A **lease** is *a contract that grants use of a product during a specified period in exchange for a rental payment.* Both consumer and industrial goods are leased. Cars, furniture, appliances, and houses are consumer goods that are often leased. Industrial goods that are often leased are buildings, office equipment, industrial machinery, and transportation equipment.

In addition to allowing buyers to use products they cannot afford to buy outright, leasing offers several other advantages. The buyers can use their limited capital for other purchases. This is especially true for young and growing organizations and families. Another advantage is that the product can be easily disposed of at the end of the lease period by returning it to the seller, thus avoiding the problem of selling a used product. Alternatively, if the leasor decides to buy the product at a later date, the seller may allow a portion of the lease payment to be applied toward the purchase.

Leasing offers another advantage when dealing with technologically complex equipment like computers. Since computer technology is changing rapidly, a lease enables the seller to get state-of-the-art equipment as often as needed.

Credit Policies

The U.S. economy is based largely on credit.[19] When consumers and organizations purchase goods and services, few pay cash. Attractive credit terms can be a way of stimulating sales without cutting price. For example, in March 1984, in an effort to boost sales of its Adam Computer System, Coleco increased the number of days retailers had to pay for purchases from thirty days to ninety days.[20]

The price of credit can drastically increase the final price the customer pays. For example, if a customer purchases a room of furniture from a local furniture store for $1400, and the retailer finances the purchase for thirty-six months at 21 percent interest, then the final price the consumer pays is $1899. On the other hand, if another local retailer would sell the merchandise at $1500 but would finance the purchase for thirty-six months at 12 percent, the customer would end up paying $1674, a lower total cost.

Both the Consumer Credit Protection Act (CCPA) and Regulation Z adopted by the Federal Reserve Board of Governors attempt to "assure a meaningful disclosure of credit terms so that the consumer will be able to compare more readily the various credit terms available to him and avoid uninformed use of credit."

To ensure that the consumer can make more informed purchases when using credit, the CCPA and Regulation Z require that the customer receive information on the total cash price; the required down payment; the number, amounts, and due dates of payments; and the annual percentage rate of the credit charges.

The marketing manager, usually in conjunction with the firm's senior financial executive, must decide on the interest rate charged on credit purchases and also establish policies on credit granting and credit collections. Figure 16.4 illustrates four distinct credit philosophies: tight credit, liberal granting/strict collection, conservative granting/lenient collection, and loose credit. Each will be described briefly.

A tight credit policy involves strict collection procedures and careful screening to determine which customers are creditworthy. Although this conservative policy ensures a high percentage of good credit customers, it is costly in terms of lost goodwill. As a result, few organizations use it.

While buying on credit offers some attractive advantages, consumers and organizations pay more in the end for the products purchased.

In today's marketing environment, a liberal granting of credit combined with a strict collection procedure is commonly used. With this type of policy, the organization maintains goodwill in the credit granting stage by giving most applicants credit, thus allowing them to prove their credit worthiness, but, the firm uses a strict collection policy to minimize its bad debt losses.

The conservative granting and lenient collection philosophy is also used frequently. This policy minimizes bad debt by using strict screening to choose creditworthy customers, which may upset some applicants. By issuing credit to a select group, however, the firm increases the probability of payment and is able to be more lenient when it comes to reminding customers to pay.

A loose credit philosophy consists of a lenient screening of credit applicants and a lenient collection policy that does not push customers to pay promptly. This policy may build goodwill, but it can be expensive in terms of bad debts, since many of the customers will be unable to pay, and it also will be expensive because many customers will be late payers. Therefore, the loose credit policy is used infrequently.

Discount Policies

The regular price at which a firm expects to sell its products may be lowered by the use of discounts. Four of the most widely used types of discounts are quantity discounts, functional discounts, seasonal discounts, and promotional discounts.

Quantity Discounts.   With a **quantity discount,** *a firm offers to sell products at a lower cost per unit if the buyer purchases a given quantity.* For instance, a manufacturer of personal computers may offer wholesalers a price of $875 if one to five units are purchased; a price of $840 if six to twenty units are purchased; a price of $790 if twenty to fifty units are purchased; and a price of $750 if more than fifty units are purchased. Quantity discounts are more commonly offered by manufacturers and wholesalers than by retailers.

Quantity discounts can be either cumulative or noncumulative. A **cumulative quantity discount** is *given for accumulating a certain quantity of purchases over a stated period.* For example, a wholesaler that purchases $100,000 of goods from a manufacturer over a 12-month period receives a 5 percent rebate, for purchasing between $100,000 and $250,000 it gets a 6 percent rebate, and for purchasing over $250,000 it gets a 7 percent rebate. A **noncumulative quantity discount** is *a one-time discount based on the number of units purchased or dollar volume purchased,* as we illustrated with the personal computer example.

Quantity discounts accomplish two things for the seller. First, they encourage buyers to purchase in larger quantities, which result in lower

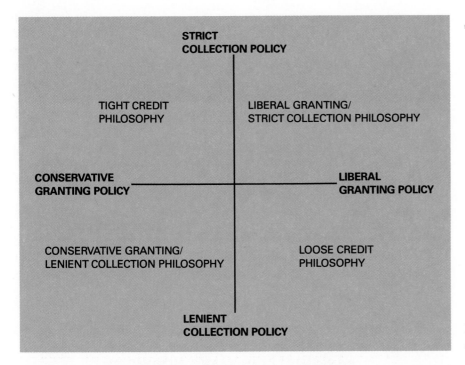

Figure 16.4
Credit Philosophies

freight and/or servicing costs. Second, by encouraging buyers to purchase in larger quantities, the seller can get a larger share of the buyer's business, eliminating the immediate need to purchase from another supplier.[21]

Functional Discounts. A **functional discount** is *a price break given to one who performs certain marketing activities for other channel members.* For example, a manufacturer produces a tire that has a retail price of $85. The functional discount offered to retailers for performing the storage and selling tasks is 35 percent and the discount to wholesalers for performing the storage, selling, and transportation tasks is 20 percent. Thus, the price the retailer pays is $85(1 − 35%), or $55.25, and the price the wholesaler pays is $55.25(1 − 20%), or $44.20.

Note that functional discounts are applied in a chain fashion. Thus, in the preceding example, the total channel discount was not 55 percent, but 48 percent, because the second discount was taken on the amount remaining after the first discount was taken or {35% + [(1 − 35%) × 20%]}.

Retailers also may offer functional discounts to consumers. For example, the Sam Levitz Furniture Warehouse offers a piece of furniture at three prices: the regular price of $319; the discounted price of $299 if the customer transports the item from the store but has Levitz finance the purchase; and a cash and carry price of $275. This latter price includes functional discounts for the customer performing the transportation and financing activities.

Cash discounts are also common. Gas stations around the country offer

By offering end-of-season sales, retailers hope to deplete their stock of items so they can stock only new or fresh merchandise for the coming season.

the customer a discount, usually 4¢ or 5¢ per gallon, for a cash purchase.[22] The wholesaler or retailer offering a cash discount is being relieved of part of the finance function.

Seasonal Discounts.   Because demand is concentrated during certain periods of the year for many types of goods and services, such as snowblowers, lawn services, pool accessories, and formal dress, sellers often offer *a special discount in the off-season,* known as a **seasonal discount,** in order to spread their sales activities more evenly over the year. Manufacturers offer before-season discounts, whereas retailers and wholesalers prefer end-of-season discounts to dispose of unsold items and make room for the next season's stock.

Promotional Allowances.   Promotional allowances are payments made by the manufacturer to the retailer or wholesaler in return for promoting the manufacturer's product. They were covered earlier in this chapter and in Chapter 15. Since promotional allowances lower the overall costs of selling a product, they are considered a form of discount. The cost of the actual products is not lowered, but total costs are lowered because the manufacturer absorbs some of the promotional costs. Promotional allowances may also be given in terms of free goods. For example, if a retailer agrees to set up an end-of-aisle display featuring the manufacturer's products, then the manufacturer may give the retailer two free cases of merchandise.

SUMMARY

The major purpose of this chapter was to introduce some fundamental price concepts. Price is an important marketing mix component and as such is a major determinant of the firm's profitability. Although price is an important aspect of economic competition, many firms also compete on nonprice dimensions because price changes are so easy to copy.

The marketing manager must make price decisions in the context of the other marketing mix decisions and the external environments. For example, product attributes should be consistent with recommended price, the promotional program should reinforce the price, and the price must allow sufficient margins for wholesalers and retailers to perform their marketing functions. The price decision should reflect the expected reactions of competitors: if the company sets prices significantly lower or higher than competitors, how will they react? Generally, competitors will react to any price decisions that significantly threaten market share. The price decision must also take legal constraints into account. The laws we discussed dealt with horizontal and vertical price fixing, price and promotional service discrimination, deceptive pricing, below-cost pricing, and predatory pricing.

Pricing objectives can be financially based or market based. The two major financially based objectives are profit maximization and target return. We noted that the profit maximizing price is not necessarily the highest price; a low price may maximize profits. The target return objective establishes price to achieve a specific return on investment. The mechanics of setting prices for both of these financially based objectives will be discussed in Chapter 17.

The two market-based objectives are sales growth and status quo. A sales growth objective involves a shift in price away from competitors' prices in order to attract attention and gain more sales, while the status quo objective follows whatever prices leading competitors establish.

The firm must next establish policies that serve as guiding principles for price setting. Price policies need to deal with pricing multiple products in a given product line; setting price for customers in different geographic areas; deciding between a rigid price or negotiable prices with individual buyers; using lease arrangements as an alternative to outright selling; and deciding what types of credit terms should accompany established prices. Finally, a firm may establish discount policies for quantity discounts, functional discounts, seasonal discounts, and promotional allowances.

KEY CONCEPTS

price (p. 492)
horizontal price fixing (p. 498)
vertical price fixing (p. 498)

price discrimination (p. 499)
bait and switch (p. 501)
price objectives (p. 502)

profit maximization (p. 502)

target return (p. 502)

market share (p. 503)

price policies (p. 503)

price lining (p. 504)

joint costs (p. 504)

direct costs (p. 504)

FOB origin (p. 505)

uniform delivered pricing (p. 505)

zone pricing (p. 506)

freight absorption pricing (p. 507)

lease (p. 508)

quantity discount (p. 510)

cumulative quantity discount (p. 510)

noncumulative quantity discount
   (p. 510)

functional discount (p. 511)

seasonal discount (p. 512)

REVIEW AND DISCUSSION QUESTIONS

1. Define *price*. What would be the price for the following:
   a. Voting for a senator
   b. Going to church weekly
   c. Being a girl scout or boy scout leader for your child's troop

2. Give your reasons why bartering is not more popular in the United States.

3. Why do many U.S. firms compete primarily on nonprice as opposed to price variables?

4. How is the price decision related to other marketing mix decisions?

5. Explain why charging the highest price possible does not always result in the highest possible profits.

6. Identify the two major forms of price fixing and discuss their legality.

7. What is price discrimination? What key federal legislation regulates price discrimination?

8. Is all price discrimination illegal? Explain.

9. Define and briefly discuss the legality of *deceptive pricing, below-cost pricing,* and *predatory pricing.*

10. Discuss the possible price objectives a firm can establish.

11. Discuss some of the difficulties or problems in price lining.

12. Explain how monopolies can occur in an industry in which all firms use FOB pricing.

13. Does uniform delivered pricing result in price discrimination? Explain why or why not.

14. How can freight absorption pricing be used as a competitive tool?

15. Why do many U.S. firms have a single price policy rather than a negotiated price policy?

16. What is a lease? Why do some people or organizations prefer to lease rather than buy?

17. Why is credit a pricing decision?

18. What types of credit policies or philosophies are most popular in the United States? Why?

19. Distinguish between a cumulative and noncumulative quantity discount.

20. Why do manufacturers and retailers offer seasonal discounts?

ACTION PROBLEMS

1. As marketing manager for ABC Industries, a wholesaler of industrial valves and fittings in Pittsburgh, you are increasingly concerned about meeting competitors' prices in Cleveland and Boston. You see no problem in charging identical prices, but freight costs typically result in ABC's prices being 5 to 8 percent higher when ABC sells to a customer in Boston or Cleveland. In addition, delivery time is longer. Discuss several alternative courses of action to overcome these disadvantages.

2. As assistant store manager for a local furniture store, you are considering recommending that owner Brenda Cox implement a single price policy. Currently, all merchandise is marked up 100 percent; thus, a sofa that costs $350 is retail priced at $700. The salesperson then can negotiate with the customer down to 25 percent over cost, which for the sofa would be $350 plus 25 percent of $350 ($87.50), or a price of $437.50. The salesperson gets a 10 percent commission on the price over this $437.50; that is, 10 percent commission is earned on all sales dollars over cost plus 25 percent.

   The year-end financial statements reveal that storewide the firm realized cost plus 40 percent. You have recommended to Ms. Cox that the firm implement a low everyday price strategy of cost plus 40 percent and eliminate negotiated prices. This policy would allow the firm to advertise, say, a $2,000 dining room suite that costs $1,000 for $1,400. Also, salespeople could be paid a flat 1 percent commission of the sale price since their selling role would be substantially reduced. What are the advantages and disadvantages of your recommendation?

3. Find ads about credit from two different firms. Try to find ones with different credit philosophies. Compare and contrast the philosophies and try to pinpoint the firm's target market for credit.

4. a) Fred Gooch, a minister at a local church, recently has been urged by his board of advisors to implement a standardized contribution program. Any household or single church member would be asked to contribute 1 percent of gross income to the church. Members would be invoiced monthly, and a nonpaying member would be removed from the church's mailing list. Four of the five advisors support this type of program. Karen Omann is the one dissenting voice and believes churches should not set prices or fees but should be free to all— the objective should be to maximize the share of the population that regularly attends church. The others believe that churches are too expensive to operate without running them like a business. Fred is undecided but is leaning toward Karen's view. What should Fred Gooch do?

   b) Tom Hayes, one of the board members, has suggested that the church pledges or donations be collected by electronic funds transfer. Each church member would sign a pledge card that would authorize the bank to withdraw the monthly donation from the member's bank account and place it in the church's bank account. Tom is vice president at a local bank and argues that this is how many mortgages and auto loans are now being paid. What are the advantages and disadvantages of this suggestion? How would you believe the church members would react to this proposal?

NOTES

1. Vern Terpstra, *International Marketing*, 3rd edition (Chicago: The Dryden Press, 1983), p. 514.

2. Peter Nulty, "Playing the New Oil Game," *Fortune* (June 13, 1983), pp. 58–64; "The Problems OPEC Can't Solve," *BusinessWeek* (March 21, 1983), pp. 22–23.

3. Daniel A. Nimer, "Pricing the Profitable Sale Has a Lot to Do with Perception," *Sales Management* (May 19, 1975), pp. 13–14.

4. This finding has been supported in research conducted by Jon G. Udell, "How Important Is Pricing in Competitive Strategy?" *Journal of Marketing* (January 1964), pp. 44–48. Research suggesting the opposite conclusion—that price is the most important element in the marketing mix—is presented in a report by Louis E. Boone and David L. Kurtz, *Pricing Objectives and Practices in American Industry: A Research Report* (1979); Robert A. Robicheaux, "How Important Is Pricing in Competitive Strategy?" in Henry W. Nash and Donald P. Robin (eds.), *Proceedings: Southern Marketing Association* (Mississippi State University: Southern Marketing Association, 1976), pp. 55–57.

5. Robert F. Hartley, *Marketing Successes* (New York: John Wiley & Sons, 1985), pp. 167–176.

6. Sherman Act, 26 Stat. 209(1890), as amended, 15 U.S.C., Articles 1–7.

7. Mary Jane Sheffet and Debra L. Scammon, "Resale Price Maintenance: Is It Safe to Suggest Retail Prices?" *Journal of Marketing* (Fall 1985), pp. 82–91; Louise L. Luchsinger and Patrick M. Dunne, "Fair Trade Laws—How Fair?" *Journal of Marketing* (January 1978), pp. 50–53.

8. Clayton Act, 38 Stat. 730(1914), as amended, 15 U.S.C., Articles 12–27.

9. *Plum Tree, Inc. v. N.K. Winston Corp. et al.,* Trade Cases 74, 245(1972).

10. Joseph Barry Mason, "Power and Channel Conflicts in Shopping Center Development," *Journal of Marketing* 39(April 1975), p. 33.

11. Morris L. Mayer, Joseph B. Mason, and E.A. Orbeck, "The Borden Case—A Legal Basis for Private Brand Price Discrimination," *MSU Business Topics* (Winter 1970), pp. 56–63; Jacky Knopp, Jr., "What Are 'Commodities of Like Grade and Quality'?" *Journal of Marketing* (July 1963), pp. 63–66.

12. For a further discussion of target rate of return pricing, see Douglas G. Brooks, "Cost-oriented Pricing: A Realistic Solution to a Complicated Problem," *Journal of Marketing* (April 1975), pp. 72–74.

13. Joseph W. McGuire, John S.Y. Ghin, and Alvan O. Elving, "Executive Incomes, Sales and Profits," *American Economic Review* (September 1962), pp. 753–761; "For the Chief, Sales Sets the Pay," *BusinessWeek* (September 30, 1967), p. 174; Alfred Rappaport, "Executive Incentives Versus Corporate Growth," *Harvard Business Review* (July–August 1978), pp. 81–88.

14. Bradley T. Gale, "Market Share and Rate of Return," *Review of Economics and Statistics* (November 1972), pp. 412–423; Robert D. Buzzell, Bradley T. Gale, and Ralph G.M. Sultan, "Market Share—A Key to Profitability," *Harvard Business Review* (January–February 1975), pp. 97–106.

15. Cuisinart is used only as an example. Prices and features were taken from the pamphlet, "Which Cuisinart Food Processor Is for You?"

16. For additional information on price lining, see Alfred Oxenfeldt, "Product Line Pricing," *Harvard Business Review* (July–August 1966), pp. 137–144.

17. Variations from the one-price policy in retailing are discussed in Stanley C. Hollander, "The 'One-Price' System—Fact or Fiction?" *Journal of Retailing* (Fall 1955), pp. 127–

144. Research is being conducted on price negotiation; see Wesley J. Johnston and Thomas V. Bonoma, "The Effect of Power Differences on the Outcome of Consumer Bargaining Situations," in Thomas Kinnear (ed.), *Advances in Consumer Research,* vol. 11 (Ann Arbor, MI: Association for Consumer Research), pp. 170–174.

18. For a discussion of how leasing can be an effective marketing tool, see Paul F. Anderson and William Lazer, "Industrial Lease Marketing," *Journal of Marketing* (January 1978), pp. 71–79.

19. Robert H. Cole, *Consumer and Commercial Credit Management,* 5th edition (Homewood, IL: Richard D. Irwin, 1976).

20. Martin Brochstein, "Coleco Gives Adam 90-day Dating," *HFD* (April 9, 1984), Section 1, p. 71.

21. Quantity discounts are further discussed in Asho K. Rao, "Quantity Discounts in Today's Market," *Journal of Marketing* (Fall 1980), pp. 44–51.

22. Determining the proper cash discount is discussed in Charles A. Ingene and Michael Levy, "Cash Discounts to Retail Customers: An Alternative to Credit Card Sales," *Journal of Marketing* (Spring 1982), pp. 92–103; R.M. Grant, "On Cash Discounts to Retail Customers: Further Evidence," *Journal of Marketing* (Winter 1985), pp. 145–146; Charles A. Ingene and Michael Levy, "Further Reflections on Cash Discounts," *Journal of Marketing* (Winter 1985), pp. 147–148.

LEARNING OBJECTIVES

After you complete this chapter, you should be able to:

- **List** and **explain** three price strategies for existing products and two strategies for new products

- **Explain** how a knowledge of demand and cost curves can be used to establish a profit maximizing price

- **Define** and give examples of target return pricing, markup pricing, and breakeven pricing

- **Compute** a bid price using the price bidding model

PRICE DETERMINATION

MARKETER PROFILE

Sol Price of the Price Company

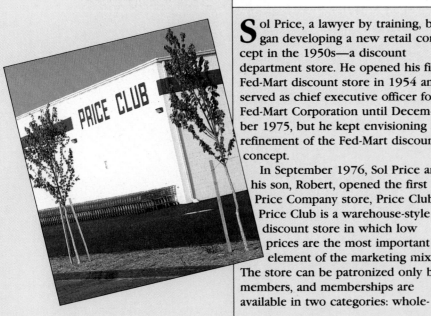

Sol Price, a lawyer by training, began developing a new retail concept in the 1950s—a discount department store. He opened his first Fed-Mart discount store in 1954 and served as chief executive officer for Fed-Mart Corporation until December 1975, but he kept envisioning a refinement of the Fed-Mart discount concept.

In September 1976, Sol Price and his son, Robert, opened the first Price Company store, Price Club. Price Club is a warehouse-style discount store in which low prices are the most important element of the marketing mix. The store can be patronized only by members, and memberships are available in two categories: whole-sale members, who are businesses or individuals who hold business licenses, and group members, who are retail households that belong to member groups such as credit unions, employee groups, and labor unions. Wholesale members are charged an annual fee of $25, and group members, although they are not charged a fee, pay 5 percent more than wholesale members on all purchases except liquor.

To keep prices at below-market levels, the investment devoted to the other marketing mix elements is low. The Price Club selects merchandise based primarily on its ability to turn over rapidly, to sell itself, and to need little or no special handling. Most merchandise is shipped directly

to Price Club stores, thus eliminating the need for a central distribution center. Promotion is almost non-existent because the merchandise is self-service, the members do not need to be enticed into the stores, and word-of-mouth advertising draws new customers most effectively. The company uses media advertising only when they open a new store.	Sol Price's concept of below-market pricing of rapid turnover merchandise achieved through a lower cost of doing business is the Price Company's secret of success.
	Sources: Based on information in the *Price Company Annual Report Fiscal 1982* and the Price Company Securities and Exchange Commission Form 10-K, August 13, 1982.

Chapter 16 dealt with general price concepts and how price interacts with the firm's marketing mix components and the firm's external environments. These factors, in turn, affect how the firm determines price objectives and price policies. In this chapter, after discussing different pricing strategies a firm can implement, we will explore the economic theory of price setting, how prices are set in practice, and different pricing tactics. The marketer profile on Sol Price showed how a firm can establish a pricing strategy, then gear the rest of the elements of the marketing mix to accomplish that strategy.

INTRODUCTION

Pricing strategies reflect *where a firm wants to position its product's price with respect to the prices of competing products. There are three basic pricing strategies* that all organizations can pursue for existing products: *pricing above the market, pricing below the market, and pricing at the market.*

PRICING STRATEGIES

Pricing Above the Market

A firm pricing above the market is pricing its products higher than similar products sold by competitors. When a firm follows this strategy, its products must be distinct in the eyes of the customer. For example, IBM prices all of its products above the market because its products are perceived as durable, high quality, state-of-the-art, and having excellent serviceability by well-trained IBM personnel.

World Courier Inc., an international small package delivery firm, uses an above-market pricing strategy. The company charges $99 for a New York to London delivery, whereas Emery and Federal Express charge around $30. World Courier differentiates its product by providing 10 A.M. next-day delivery anywhere in the world. In Europe, the company will pick up as late as 8 P.M. and guarantee delivery in New York by 9 A.M.[1] Other companies that price above the market include New Balance athletic shoes, Rolls Royce autos, Curtis-Mathes televisions, Hilton Hotels, Sony Electronics, Neiman-Marcus retail stores, and Hickey-Freeman men's suits.

Pricing Below the Market

Firms price below the market by adding a lower profit per unit or keeping costs per unit lower than their competitors, as Sol Price of the Price Company was able to do. When the profit per unit is small, the firm hopes to make it up in a higher volume of business. When a firm keeps costs per unit low, it also is usually lowering quality or providing fewer services. In this situation, the distinguishing attribute of the product becomes its low price. Examples of pricing below the market are BIC ballpoint pens, Southwest Airlines, Wal-Mart Discount Stores, Kuppenheimer men's suits, and King Cola.

Pricing at the Market

Firms pricing at the market establish prices that reflect the prevailing market price for a particular type of product. Most firms price relatively close to the market because their products are not so outstanding that they can price above the market, nor are their costs so low that they can price below the market. Organizations that tend to price their products at the market are Levi Strauss, J.C. Penney, Tandy computers, Procter & Gamble, and Sanyo.

New Product Pricing

The preceding pricing strategies can be applied to existing products or new products. When a company introduces a new product to the market, it can price above, below, or at the market. If the product is an innovation (as discussed in the product life cycle in Chapter 8), then the initial price is usually set quite high. However, if the company introduces the product after the introductory stage of the product life cycle, the company generally will price at the market or below the market. Many companies introducing products in the latter stages of the product life cycle will set a price below the market because this gives them a wedge to enter and gain market share. In the introductory stage of the product life cycle, there are two basic strategic pricing alternatives: (1) skimming and (2) penetration. There are certain market situations in which each is warranted, as will be discussed.[2]

Skimming. A **skimming price strategy** *sets prices high at the introduction stage of the product life cycle and then lowers prices in later stages.* The firm is essentially deciding to skim the cream of demand by making those people that strongly desire the product pay a premium price when the product is first put on the market. Then, when the price is lowered later in the product life cycle, the more price-sensitive consumers will purchase the product. When a high price can generate more sales dollars than a low price in early stages of market development, this greater revenue can be used to finance later stages of market development.

Two requirements are vital to the success of a skimming price strategy. First there should be few, if any, close substitutes for the product, because if there were people would not pay a premium price. Second, there must be a sufficient number of people willing to pay a premium price for the product. The Polaroid Company uses a skimming strategy when it introduces a new camera to the market; however, within six months Polaroid begins to lower its price and to introduce new models at lower prices to appeal to the mass market.

Penetration. The **penetration price strategy,** which is the opposite of the skimming strategy, *sets price low at the outset of the product life cycle and uses it as a wedge to enter the market.* The penetration strategy can be successful under the following conditions. First, it is useful when all segments of the market are sensitive to price, even in the early stages of the product life cycle. Second, when production, distribution, and promotion costs decrease rapidly per unit as output increases, penetration pricing may be used to increase volume as rapidly as possible so as to drive down unit costs. Third, it is used to grab as much market share as possible when competitors are likely to enter the market quickly.

Once managers establish a firm's pricing strategy, they need to determine what approach to take in actually setting prices. If a firm is to use economic theory to set price, demand and cost curves must be determined.[3]

THE ECONOMIC APPROACH TO PRICE SETTING

Demand

Most firms in the United States are confronted by a negatively sloping demand curve. A negatively sloping demand curve suggests that as prices are raised, the quantity demanded falls. Most personal care items, such as toothpaste and shampoo, have negatively sloping demand curves (see Figure 17.1A).

Not all firms are faced with a negatively sloped demand curve, however. Some firms have a nearly horizontal demand curve. In this situation, a rise in price will eliminate demand completely. For example, Farmer Newell

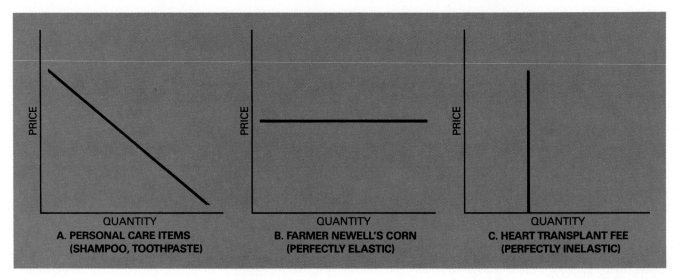

Figure 17.1

Typical Demand Curves

produces a tiny fraction of all the corn grown in the United States, so that he must take the market price for his corn. An above-market price would result in an inability to sell any of his corn. A below-market price would be ridiculous because he can sell all of his corn at the market price. Figure 17.1B shows the demand curve for Farmer Newell's corn.

At the other extreme, some products have a nearly vertical demand curve. In this case, almost regardless of the price charged (within reason), the quantity demanded will not be altered. An example is the demand curve for heart transplant surgery. Whether the fee for a heart transplant is $50,000 or $100,000, the quantity demanded will not change significantly because lowering the price will not encourage a person to purchase an unneeded operation. Conversely, if a person needs a heart transplant, most would pay whatever is asked. Furthermore, because there is relatively little competition among qualified physicians to perform heart transplants, the demand curve is vertical (see Figure 17.1C).

Price Elasticity.   Clearly, the preceding examples suggest that the change in quantity demanded as a result of a price change varies considerably depending on the product. For example, in Figure 17.1A we saw that raising the price of toothpaste or shampoo greatly reduces the quantity demanded. In Figure 17.1B, even a small rise in the price of corn by Farmer Newell reduced the demand for his corn to zero. In Figure 17.1C, a rise in the price of heart transplants did not reduce demand for them.

Price elasticity of demand is *the percentage change in quantity demanded divided by the percentage change in the price of a product and is stated as an absolute value.* For example, if the percent increase in price is 10 percent and the percent decline in quantity demanded is 20 percent, then the price elasticity is 2.0:

$$\frac{20\% \text{ Change in quantity demanded}}{10\% \text{ Change in price}} = \text{price elasticity of 2}$$

When the price elasticity is greater than 1.0, we say that the demand is *price elastic,* which means that *a given percentage of change in price produces a more than proportionate change in quantity demanded.* When the price elasticity is less than 1.0, we say that the demand is price inelastic. When demand is price inelastic, a given percentage change in price produces a less than proportionate change in quantity demanded. If you refer to Figure 17.1, you will see that the demand for Farmer Newell's corn is perfectly elastic and that the demand curve for heart transplants is perfectly inelastic.

Price and Sales Revenue. The **total sales revenue** for a product can be viewed as *the price per unit multiplied by the total units sold during a specified time period.* For example, suppose K mart is selling the Sony Walkman for $139 (*P*) and, in a specified period, sold 200 of them (*Q*). The total sales revenue (*TR*) equals $27,800.

We can also define two other important revenue concepts. *Average revenue* can be defined as total sales revenue divided by quantity sold. **Marginal revenue** can be defined as *the change in total sales revenue divided by the change in one unit of quantity.* Table 17.1 presents some data to help illustrate these concepts; in this example, the demand for the product is represented as a negatively sloping curve.

Table 17.1   Basic Price and Revenue Concepts

Price (P)	Quantity (Q)	Total Revenue (TR)	Average Revenue (AR)	Marginal Revenue (MR)	Price Elasticity
$50	1	$ 50	$50	NA[a]	Elastic
$45	2	90	45	$40	Elastic
$40	3	120	40	30	Elastic
$35	4	140	35	20	Elastic
$30	5	150	30	10	Elastic
$25	6	150	25	0	Unitary
$20	7	140	20	−10	Inelastic
$15	8	120	15	−20	Inelastic
$10	9	90	10	−30	Inelastic
$ 5	10	50	5	−40	Inelastic
Formula	—	(P × Q)	(TR/Q)	(ΔTR/ΔQ)	(% ΔQ/% ΔP)

[a]NA = not applicable.

Several things should be noted about the data in Table 17.1. First, the marginal revenue is always less than the average revenue, because, to sell additional units, the firm must lower the price of the product on the entire quantity sold—even those that could have been sold at a higher price. Second, marginal revenue becomes negative when the total revenue lost by lowering the price on the units that could have been sold at a higher price exceeds the revenue from the incremental unit sold at the lower price. As an example, consider that Table 17.1 deals with clock radios and the price of a clock radio is lowered from $25 to $20. In this situation, the firm sacrifices $5 a unit on the six radios that could have been sold at $25— a total sacrifice of $30. In turn, they receive only an additional $20 for selling the seventh unit. In this case, the marginal revenue is − $10. Third, when marginal revenue is negative, total sales revenue declines. This suggests that price cuts after a certain point will decrease total sales revenue. Fourth, the price elasticity of demand varies in different parts of the demand curve. Demand is elastic at high prices, but it becomes inelastic at lower prices. This is true of all negatively sloped demand curves that are linear or approximately linear.

There is an important relationship between price elasticity of demand and the behavior of total revenue. When demand is inelastic, a change in price results in a change in total revenue in the same direction as the price change (i.e., if price is cut, then total revenue declines and vice versa). On the other hand, if demand is elastic, then a change in price produces an opposite movement in total revenue (i.e., if price is cut, then total revenue rises and vice versa). Finally, if price elasticity of demand is *unitary* (yellow area), then a change in price produces no change in total revenue. Go back to Table 17.1 and note that when price was cut from $30 to $25, there was no change in total revenue. At this point, the price elasticity of demand is unitary. Figure 17.2 summarizes the relationship between price elasticity and total revenue.

Costs

Analyzing demand provides only part of the information the marketing manager needs to set price. He or she also needs information on the behavior of the firm's costs.[4] In short, demand curves tell the firm what the consumer is willing to pay for a product and consequently what the firm's total revenues may be at different prices, while cost curves illustrate the price the firm can afford to charge for the product. If a firm's costs are significantly higher than competitors, its prices will also need to be higher, and thus it will risk losing market share. This is precisely what happened in the 1970s and early 1980s to U.S. bicycle producers, such as Schwinn, Huffy, and Murray, as their costs became significantly higher than Japanese and Taiwanese bike manufacturers. To counteract this cost disadvantage, Schwinn

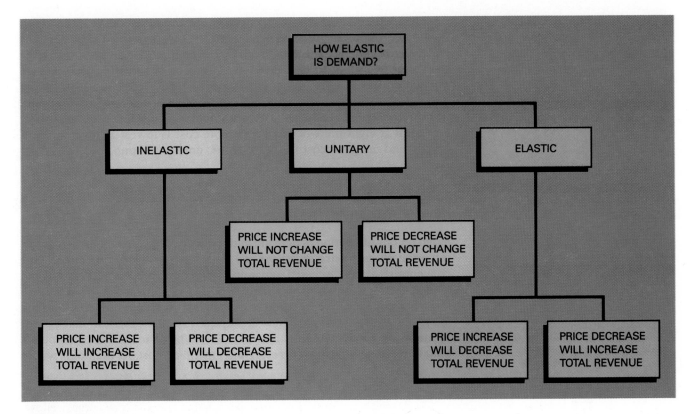

Figure 17.2

Price Elasticity and Total Revenue Behavior

now has 75 percent of its bicycles produced by Asian companies and Huffy has its upscale Raleigh bike made in Taiwan and Japan.[5]

Several key terms are essential to an understanding of the cost approach:

1. **Total fixed cost** is equal to *the sum of all costs for a particular period that will not change as output volume rises or falls.*
2. *Average fixed cost* is equal to total fixed cost divided by the quantity of output.
3. **Variable cost** is equal to *any costs that rise or fall in direct relation to changes in output level.* Variable cost should be viewed as variable cost per unit of output.
4. *Total variable cost* is equal to variable cost multiplied by the quantity of output.
5. *Total cost* is equal to total fixed cost plus total variable cost at a given output level.
6. *Average total cost* is equal to total cost divided by the quantity of output.
7. **Marginal cost** is equal to *the change in total costs as a result of a change in one unit of output.*

All of these basic cost concepts are illustrated in Table 17.2, which shows two important relationships. First, the average fixed cost declines rapidly as volume is expanded, because the fixed costs can be spread over an increasing output level. Second, the behavior of variable costs, average total costs, and marginal costs are U-shaped. These costs are high at low output levels, and they decrease as output increases, but only up to a point, when they begin to rise again. For example, average total cost reaches a low point at eight units of output, variable cost is lowest at seven units of output, and marginal cost is lowest at five units of output.

How to Maximize Profit

Based on our discussion of demand and cost concepts, how might a manager set price so as to maximize profits, if this is the firm's objective? Two concepts that we discussed—marginal cost and marginal revenue—will help answer this question.

If marginal revenue is greater than marginal cost, then the firm is making money on the last additional unit of output. Obviously, the firm that desires to maximize profits would continue to lower price to sell more output as long as marginal revenue is greater than marginal cost. At the point where

Table 17.2   Basic Cost Concepts

Quantity (A)	Total Fixed Cost (B)	Average Fixed Cost (C)	Variable Cost (D)	Total Variable Cost (E)	Total Cost (F)	Average Total Cost (G)	Marginal Cost (H)
1	$100	$100.00	$12.00	$ 12.00	$112.00	$112.00	NA[a]
2	100	50.00	10.50	21.00	121.00	60.50	$ 9.00
3	100	33.33	8.50	25.50	125.50	41.83	4.50
4	100	25.00	7.00	28.00	128.00	32.00	2.50
5	100	20.00	5.25	28.75	128.75	25.75	**0.75**
6	100	16.67	5.00	30.00	130.00	21.67	1.25
7	100	14.29	**4.75**	33.25	133.25	19.04	3.25
8	100	12.50	6.00	48.00	148.00	**18.50**	14.75
9	100	11.11	8.00	72.00	172.00	19.11	24.00
10	100	10.00	10.25	102.50	202.50	20.25	30.50
Formulas	—	(B/A)	—	(D × A)	(B + E)	(F/A)	(ΔF/ΔA)

[a]NA = not applicable; quantity that minimizes marginal cost (5); quantity that minimizes variable cost per unit (7); quantity that minimizes average total cost (8).

marginal cost is equal to marginal revenue, the firm would no longer be able to increase profits.

Table 17.3, which combines the data from Tables 17.1 and 17.2, shows how the behavior of revenue and costs helps a firm to set a price that maximizes profits. Examination of the data in this table reveals that the best price is $30. At this price, marginal revenue is $10, marginal cost is $0.75, and profit is $21.25. If the price is lowered to $25 to sell another unit, the marginal revenue is $0, but marginal cost is $1.25, and profit is $20.00. The firm would do best to stay with the $30 price.

What would happen in the prior example if the firm's objective was to minimize average total costs? Average total costs would be minimized at eight units of output at a price of $15 per unit, but this would result in a loss of $28. As you can see, minimizing average costs is not necessarily consistent with maximizing profits. Figure 17.3 illustrates some of the important revenue and cost concepts we have discussed. Note the intersection of marginal revenue and marginal cost in Figure 17.3C—this yields the price at which profit is maximized.

Demand and Cost Curves

Estimating a firm's demand and cost curves will undoubtedly help the executive to make informed pricing decisions. Although it is not possible to know exactly what a product's demand and cost curves look like because

Table 17.3 Setting a Price to Maximize Profits

Price	Quantity	Total Revenue	Marginal Revenue	Total Costs	Average Total Costs	Marginal Costs	Profit
$50	1	$ 50	NA[a]	$112.00	$112.00	NA	− $62.00
45	2	90	$40	121.00	60.50	$ 9.00	− 31.00
40	3	120	30	125.50	41.83	4.50	− 5.50
35	4	140	20	128.00	32.00	2.50	12.00
30	5	150	10	128.75	25.75	0.75	**21.25**
25	6	150	0	130.00	21.67	1.25	20.00
20	7	140	− 10	133.25	19.04	3.25	6.75
15	8	120	− 20	148.00	**18.50**	14.75	− 28.00
10	9	90	− 30	172.00	19.11	24.00	− 81.99
5	10	50	− 40	202.50	20.25	30.50	− 152.50

[a]NA = not applicable; setting price to maximize profits ($30), setting price to minimize average total costs ($15).

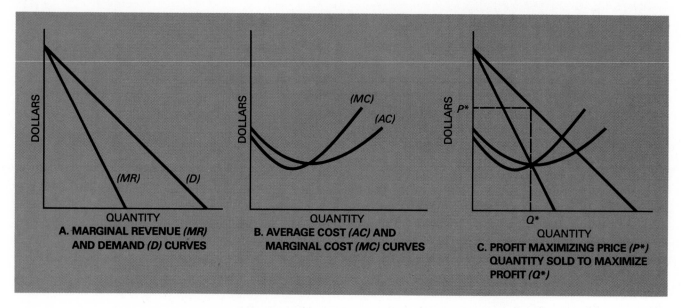

Figure 17.3
Revenue and Cost Concepts

of our inability to see into the future, there are techniques available to estimate them. It is usually easier to estimate cost curves than demand curves, because demand curves involve an analysis or understanding of buyer behavior, which is always somewhat unpredictable.

Cost Curve Estimation.   Generally, it is not too difficult for a company to estimate what its cost will be at a certain level of activity (i.e., production output or sales volume) as long as the firm has previously operated close to that level of activity. Problems occur, however, with new products or when the company wishes to estimate demand at an output level considerably below or above what it has been in the past. In the latter case, the firm may not be able to accurately estimate its **scale economies,** which is *the change in output per unit of resource input (such as labor and materials). Constant scale economies* represent a situation of no increase in productivity as output rises. *Diseconomies of scale* represent a decrease in productivity as output rises. *Increasing economies of scale* represent an increase in productivity as output expands.

Most manufactured products have increasing scale economies because as output rises, labor becomes more efficient and unit labor costs of the product fall. This only happens up to a certain point; for instance, if too many workers are put into a factory of a given size at a given time, the area may get congested and labor efficiency could actually decline, resulting in diseconomies of scale.

Demand Curve Estimation.   Three methods are commonly used to estimate demand curves: (1) statistical analysis of historical data, (2) survey research, and (3) experimentation. With *statistical analysis* of historical data, the analyst needs information on past sales to obtain a demand curve estimate. A major problem with this approach is that, because the data are collected at different times, the results are not necessarily comparable because other variables affecting demand are not constant. For instance, income levels, interest rates, and population itself probably changed, which may have influenced demand.

With the *survey research method,* potential buyers are questioned directly about their purchasing patterns under different prices. A key problem with this method is that buyers do not actually know how they would react in the marketplace to different price levels. In addition, even if they thought they would still buy the same quantity at a higher price, most people would not say so. Another problem with the survey method is that it is difficult to use with new products. Unless buyers have had some experience with a product, they do not know how much they would be willing to pay for it.

The *price experiment* method can be a powerful tool when properly used. With this method, the marketer systematically varies the price of a product while attempting to control extraneous factors and then observes the resulting change in quantity demanded. Price experiments are often conducted in retail stores. For example, in a set of forty stores, one of four different prices would be randomly assigned to each store, so that each price would be tried in ten stores. After several weeks, the marketer could tabulate the volume sold at each of the four prices to obtain an estimate of the demand curve. In the Marketing in Action on page 530, a price experiment shows the demand schedule for Quaker State Motor Oil.

PRICING TOOLS: PRICE SETTING IN PRACTICE

The setting of prices in the day-to-day practice of business is often quite different from that suggested by economic theory, although a thorough understanding of demand and cost curves provides an important basis on which to build. Marketing managers use a variety of practical pricing tools to help them set prices. A **pricing tool** is *a mechanical method, often a mathematical formula, that is used to help set prices in day-to-day business.*

Profit-Oriented Pricing

If a firm's objectives include a profit motive, the use of target return pricing may be helpful. A **target return pricing** formula calculates *the price re-*

MARKETING IN ACTION

Using Quaker State Motor Oil as one of their subjects, Sidney Bennett and J.B. Wilkinson set out to study short-term price-quantity relationships by systematically lowering price to determine the sales response and the effect of these price changes on the sales of competing brands.

The price experiment was conducted at a discount department store with about 34,000 square feet of selling space and an average weekly sales volume of $20,000. In the study, Quaker State's price was lowered by 15 percent each week for six weeks, from a high of $0.73 to a low of $0.32. These prices were advertised each week. The prices, shelf space, and advertising of competing brands remained unchanged during the experiment, and no new competing products were advertised or introduced during that period. No promotions for Quaker State or com-

Price Experiment for Quaker State

peting brands were noted at any of the retailer's competitors during the test period.

Results of the experiment are shown in the accompanying graph.

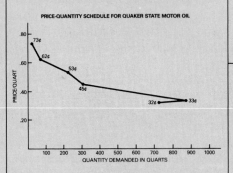

PRICE-QUANTITY SCHEDULE FOR QUAKER STATE MOTOR OIL

Note that as price for Quaker State decreased, quantity increased, fol-

lowing the typical demand curve. At the lowest price, however, the demand curve took a backward bend characteristic of the prestige price demand curve (discussed later in the chapter). This backward bend could be due to stockpiling at the previous price, or it could indicate that the consumer is beginning to associate the lower price with a lower quality product and is thus purchasing less.

Source: Based on Sidney Bennett and J.B. Wilkinson. "Price-Quantity Relationships and Price Elasticity Under In-store Experimentation," *Journal of Business Research* (January 1974), pp. 27–38. Graph is reproduced by permission of the publisher, from Sidney Bennett and J.B. Wilkinson, "Price-Quantity Relationships and Price Elasticity under In-Store Experimentation," *Journal of Business Research* (January 1974). Copyright 1974 by Elsevier Science Publishing Co., Inc.

quired for the firm to make a specified profit or rate of return on investment. One such formula is:

$$P = F/Q + V + (r \times I)/Q$$
where

P = price to be charged
F = total fixed costs
Q = quantity to be produced and sold
V = variable cost per unit
r = desired rate of return on investment
I = investment needed to produce and market product

Careful examination and study of this formula will reveal that price is set to equal the sum of three components: average fixed cost per unit (F/Q), variable cost per unit (V), and profit per unit (($r \times I)/Q$).

Assume that total fixed costs were $100,000, variable costs were $10 per unit, investment was $200,000, and the desired return on investment was 20%. The company believes it can produce and sell 10,000 units annually. What should price be? Using the formula:

$$P = (100,000/10,000) + 10 + [(20\%)(200,000)]/10,000$$
$$P = 10 + 10 + 4$$
$$P = \$24$$

There are two primary problems with a target return pricing formula. First, the managers must estimate quantity to be sold before price is established. This is counterintuitive to economic theory, which argues that quantity demanded is a function of price and not vice versa. Second, the formula is sensitive to errors in estimating quantity, and the errors will cause profits to rise or fall by more than the planned profit per unit. This occurs because essentially no fixed costs exist for sales greater than those estimated, since all fixed costs were paid for by the initial volume planned. On the other hand, for sales that are less than planned, profits fall by the profit per unit planned plus the average fixed cost per unit, because all fixed costs have not yet been absorbed or paid for.

Cost-Oriented Pricing

Cost-oriented pricing is an easy-to-use pricing tool in which the price is determined by adding a dollar amount or percentage on to the cost of the product. Cost-oriented pricing is often used because of its simplicity. Two popular cost-oriented pricing formulas are cost-plus pricing and markup pricing.

Cost-plus pricing is used most often by business-to-business marketers to price custom products, such as the construction of a hotel, dam, warehouse or nuclear power plant. *Cost-plus pricing* involves keeping track of the costs of producing a product, then adding an additional dollar amount or percentage of costs to arrive at the final price. For example, cost-plus pricing is common in the construction business where a contractor is paid all expenses of building the project plus 15 percent of the costs. Cost-plus pricing is used most often when it is difficult to estimate the costs of producing a product. This occurs for custom-made products and when the rate of inflation is high and unpredictable. For instance, the 1985 inflation rate in Brazil was over 100%, and thus almost all building contractors used cost-plus pricing.

Markup pricing is used extensively by wholesalers and retailers and consists of *taking the dollar cost of merchandise and adding to it a dollar markup, which is intended to cover the wholesaler's or retailer's cost of doing business and allow for a profit.* A basic markup equation is:

$$P = C + M$$
where C = dollar cost of merchandise per unit
M = dollar markup per unit
P = selling price per unit

If a retail or wholesale firm has a cost per unit of $10 and a dollar markup of $5, then the selling price per unit is $15.

In the retail and wholesale trades, markup typically is not discussed in terms of dollars, but in terms of percent. Two methods exist for computing markup percentages, and they differ in terms of the base on which markup is computed. They are the cost-based markup method and the price-based markup method. The **cost-based markup** method uses the following formula:

Percent markup on cost $= (P-C)/C.$

Using the previous example with P equal to $15 and C equal to $10, the markup on cost would be 50 percent. The formula for the **price-based markup** is:

Percent markup on price $= (P-C)/P.$

If P equals $15 and C equals $10, the markup on price would be 33.3 percent. Since price is always higher than cost, the percentage markup on cost will always be greater than the percentage markup on price. In actual practice, most retailers and wholesalers use a price-based markup.

Breakeven Analysis

Another useful pricing tool is **breakeven analysis,** *a method of determining the number of units that must be sold at a given price to recover costs.* The breakeven point for a product occurs when total sales revenue equals total costs. This is the point at which neither profit nor loss is being made on the product. The breakeven quantity is:

$$Q = F/(P-V)$$

where these terms are as previously defined. For example, with a fixed cost of $100,000 and a variable cost of $10, the breakeven quantity can be determined if a certain price is set. At a price of $20, the breakeven quantity would be $F/(P-V) = [100,000/(20-10)] = 10,000$; if the firm sells 10,000 units it will break even.

The breakeven formula can be especially helpful to nonprofit organizations. Assume that a high school band has been invited to march in the Rose Bowl parade on New Year's Day. There are fifty band members (this is the quantity), the variable travel and lodging costs are $380 per person, and the fixed costs are $2000, which will pay for transporting the instruments and the expenses of the bandleader and an assistant. Using the breakeven formula, the school could determine that a price of $420 per band member would allow it to break even on the trip. Figure 17.4 graphs a product's total sales revenue curve, fixed costs, variable costs, and total costs. In this graph, the breakeven point is where total costs intersect with total revenue.

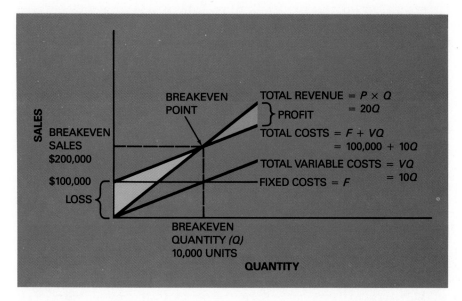

Figure 17.4
Breakeven Graph

It is especially important to understand that in the breakeven chart in Figure 17.4, we are assuming constant scale economies and a constant price. Therefore, we are showing the variable cost curve and the total revenue curve as linear. This suggests that there is an entire family of breakeven points, each corresponding to a particular price.

Figure 17.5 shows how different prices affect the breakeven point for our previous example. Recall that a $20 price results in a breakeven quantity of 10,000 units. As price is lowered to $15, the breakeven quantity rises to 20,000. Conversely, with a price of $30, breakeven can be reached at only 5,000 units. Whether the lower or higher price will be more profitable will depend on demand conditions.

The Marketing in Action on page 535 illustrates how fixed and variable costs influence the pricing of automobiles. Notice the high fixed costs necessary to produce an automobile.

Learning Curves

Learning curves are another useful pricing tool because they recognize that workers learn to perform certain operations more efficiently the longer they do them. This learning or experience effect is common in industries with a large labor component in the assembly of the product; for example, airplanes and computers.

A **learning curve,** *or experience curve, shows the percentage reduction in average costs per unit as cumulative output doubles.* In the airplane industry, this percent reduction is usually 20 percent. If the first jet airplane

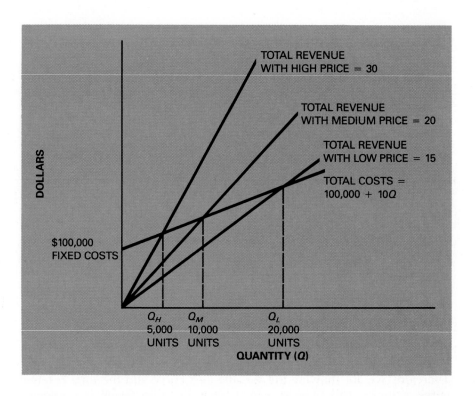

Figure 17.5
Breakeven Point with Different Prices

costs $50 million, the average cost after two units will be $40 million (20% less) and after four planes, $32 million (another 20% less).

The central thing you should note about the learning curve is that it provides strong logic for setting price low—even below the firm's initial average unit costs. For example, Boeing will price the first few units of a new model of jet aircraft substantially below its initial unit costs, but as Boeing gains experience, its unit costs begin to drop dramatically, allowing the firm to profit on later units it sells. Because price is set low, it allows the firm to increase its cumulative output and thus market share, and drive costs significantly downward. In the long run, then, the lower price would be quite profitable.[6]

Price Bidding Model

In business-to-business and government markets, prices are often established by a bidding process.[7] **Bidding** occurs when *multiple sellers submit proposals to a buyer and the lowest price is accepted.* Bidding is common in the construction of large buildings, highways, bridges, or other physical structures. Also, bidding often occurs in the provision of large quantities of equipment or supplies. For instance, the U.S. Department of Defense may solicit bids for the purchase of 100,000 truck tires.

MARKETING IN ACTION

Automobile manufacturers have a difficult time establishing prices for their cars. It takes four to five years to develop a new car model, during which time hundreds of millions of dollars can be spent on research and development and tooling. Before this process begins, the company must have an idea of the price segment to which they will be targeting the finished product—Are they going after the $10,000 price segment, the $25,000 segment, or some other segment? As the five-year development process unfolds, inflation takes its share of final costs and unexpected design problems can increase costs. Also, the intensity of foreign and domestic competition is in a constant state of flux. The prices of competitive offerings cannot be ignored. For instance, in 1986 Malcolm Bricklin began to market a Yugoslavian-built car in the United States for under $4,000.

The U.S. auto industry typically employs some type of target return pricing. The target profit is 10 percent of variable costs and fixed corporate headquarters costs. Let's look at how the price of a typical 1986 small car might be determined.

The research and development

Automobile Pricing

costs for a new small car are assumed to be $1 billion, and the manufacturer elects to amortize these over the first four years of production. Thus, the fixed charge per year for research and development and special tooling will be $250 million. The charge for fixed corporate overhead would be $238.5 million annually. The variable manufacturing and assembly costs per unit would be as follows:

Engine	$374
Body	662
Transmission	108
Chassis	602
Vehicle assembly	640
Total variable costs	$2,386

If the company expects to sell 250,000 cars per year, then the average fixed cost for corporate overhead is $954—$238.5 million/250,000 units—the average cost for research and development and special tooling is $1000—$250 million/250,000 units. The profit goal per car is 15 percent of variable cost and

corporate overhead, or 15 percent of $3340, or $501.

Also note that the dealer will be allowed an 18 percent markup on cost (before transportation) to arrive at a retail selling price. In addition, freight and final destination charges will average $425. Based on the preceding, we can compute the price charged the dealer and the suggested retail selling price:

Variable production and assembly costs	$2,386
Fixed corporate overhead	954
Research and development and special tooling	1,000
Profit goal	501
Price charged dealer	$4,841
Dealer markup	871
Retail price before freight	$5,712
Freight and final destination charge	425
Retail price including freight	$6,137

Source: Authors' computations and selected information in "Why Detroit Can't Cut Prices," *BusinessWeek* (March 1, 1982), pp. 110–111.

Bidding is like a game, and the prize is winning the bid. The higher a firm's bid is above its costs, the more the firm will profit if it wins the bid but the lower will be the probability of winning it because as the bid price rises, there is an increasing chance that the bid is above the lowest competitor's bid. On the other hand, it would be suicidal to bid below costs.

Because bidding involves uncertainty, the bidding firm can use an expected return model. An *expected return model* multiplies the profit the firm would obtain if a bid were accepted times the probability of the bid being accepted. This type of analysis is illustrated in Table 17.4. In this example, a firm has known costs of $50,000 on a particular project it is bidding on. If it bids $100,000, it will have a profit of $50,000 if the bid is

Table 17.4   Competitive Bidding and Expected Returns

Bid (A)	Cost (B)	Profit (C)	Probability of Acceptance (D)	Expected Profitability (E)
$100,000	$50,000	$50,000	0.05	$ 2,500
90,000	50,000	40,000	0.15	6,000
80,000	50,000	30,000	0.30	9,000
70,000	50,000	20,000	0.50	10,000
60,000	50,000	10,000	0.75	7,500
55,000	50,000	5,000	0.95	4,750
Formula	—	(A − B)	—	(C × D)

accepted. However, the probability of winning the bid is only 5 percent. Thus, the expected profit from a $100,000 bid is $2,500, or ($50,000 × 5%). The data in Table 17.4 show that the bid price of $70,000 has the highest expected profit—$10,000. The expected return model of bidding suggests that the firm should go with the $70,000 bid.

PRICING TACTICS

To assist in using the preceding pricing tools, a variety of pricing tactics have evolved in the U.S. economy. Price tactics involve the decisions concerning the actual numbers used as the price of a product. As such, price tactics are the final step in the price setting chain of decisions that range from the broadest setting of price objectives through calculating approximate price figures, all the way to setting the actual prices. Two widely used price tactics are psychological pricing and unit pricing.

Psychological Pricing

Psychological pricing *pertains to customers' perception of price rather than the actual price.* The concept of psychological pricing suggests that a change in price must reach a certain magnitude before it is perceived. For example, if the price of a satellite TV receiver is cut from $1,995 to $1,975, there will probably be no change in quantity demanded because the change in price in relation to the original price was too small to be noticeable. In this situation, the demand curve is assumed to look like that shown in Figure 17.6. Note that vertical drops in the demand curve represent prices that consumers perceived as the same. When price is initially high, it takes more of a drop in price to increase quantity demanded than when price is initially low. Obviously, a $75 price cut on a $10,000 item means less to the consumer than a $75 price cut on a $500 item.

One form of psychological pricing is **odd-even pricing,** which *uses a*

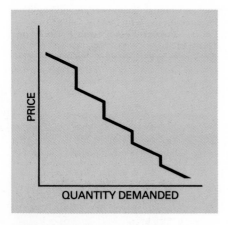

Figure 17.6

Psychological Pricing Demand Curve

Instead of listing their price at an even $6,800, Mazda uses a variation of odd-even pricing for its psychological impact on the buyer.

numbering system that gives the impression of a lower price. In the United States, marketing managers believe that buyers react more favorably to prices that end with a 3, 5, 7, or 9 when products are priced under $50 (i.e., $4.95, $12.99, or $39.97). With products priced over $50, the price is typically set at $1 below an even dollar figure (i.e., $99, $199, or $349).[8]

Prestige pricing is used for *a product whose image of quality is directly associated with its price.* For these products, *if price is set too low, the sales may be lower than with a higher price because of the poor quality inferences associated with a low price.*[9] Prestige pricing reflects the demand curve shown in Figure 17.7. The curve has a back-bending shape. At first, the curve looks like a normal demand curve with a negative slope, but then it bends back to result in a positive slope.

With a positive sloped demand curve, the lower the price, the less that is demanded. This type of demand curve would be found for custom goods and services, jewelry, and fine restaurants. For instance, if a world-class restaurant lowered its menu prices from an average of $40 per entree to $20, the initial demand for its food might drop significantly.

Unit Pricing

Consumers find it difficult to compare prices on products that come in different size packages. How does one conveniently compare the price of one brand of catsup in a 16-ounce bottle for $0.89 with another in a 30-ounce bottle for $1.49? A solution to this problem is unit pricing. With **unit**

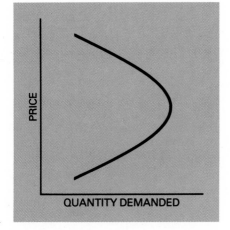

Figure 17.7
Prestige Pricing Demand Curve

Unit pricing allows the consumer to compare the values of different brands and make informed buying choices.

pricing, *the price is stated in some common unit of measurement, such as the price per ounce or price per pound.*[10] Unit pricing of grocery items is mandatory in some states; however, many grocery retailers in other states have voluntarily adopted it as a pricing tactic.

SUMMARY

The purpose of this chapter was to build on the pricing concepts you learned in Chapter 16 so that you could proceed step-by-step to actual price setting. Before setting prices (but after establishing price objectives and policies), a firm must decide on its general price strategy. The three main price strategies are pricing above, below, or at the market level. New product pricing poses special problems, so that a firm may have a skimming or penetration strategy in this situation. A skimming strategy involves setting prices high at the introduction stage of the product life cycle and then lowering prices in later stages. Conversely, a penetration strategy involves setting price low at the outset of the product life cycle in order to use it as a wedge to enter the market and obtain a dominant market share.

With an understanding of the economic approach to price determination, managers can make carefully considered pricing decisions. With knowledge of demand and cost curves, they can equate a firm's marginal revenue and marginal costs and thus pick a price at which a firm can maximize its profits. In most actual price setting situations, however, managers rely on practical tools, not just economic theory.

Practical price setting tools include target return pricing, cost-oriented tools such as cost-plus and markup, breakeven analysis, learning or experience curves, and bidding.

Once a firm has determined how to set prices, it can employ additional price tactics such as unit pricing techniques and psychological pricing tactics, including odd-even pricing and prestige pricing.

KEY CONCEPTS

pricing strategies (p. 519)
skimming price strategy (p. 521)
penetration price strategy (p. 521)
price elasticity of demand (p. 522)
total sales revenue (p. 523)
marginal revenue (p. 523)
total fixed cost (p. 525)
variable cost (p. 525)
marginal cost (p. 525)
scale economies (p. 528)
pricing tool (p. 529)

target return pricing (pp. 529–530)
markup pricing (p. 531)
cost-based markup (p. 532)
price-based markup (p. 532)
breakeven analysis (p. 532)
learning curves (p. 533)
bidding (p. 535)
psychological pricing (p. 536)
odd-even pricing (pp. 536–537)
prestige pricing (p. 537)
unit pricing (pp. 537–538)

REVIEW AND DISCUSSION QUESTIONS

1. Why might a company choose to price above the market rather than at or below the market?

2. When a firm introduces a new product, how should it decide between a skimming or penetration price strategy?

3. Almost all of the costs of operating an airplane between two cities are fixed: that is, the costs are virtually unchanged whether the plane is 90 percent full or only 20 percent full. Given this situation, when an airline lowers price in an attempt to raise profits, what is it assuming about the price elasticity of demand for air travel?

4. What is the relationship between price elasticity of demand, price changes, and the behavior of total sales revenue?

5. Can the degree of competition influence the price elasticity of demand? Explain.

6. Can the demand for a product be both elastic and inelastic? Explain.

7. How should a marketing manager set price if the objective is to maximize profits? What are the problems or obstacles with this approach?

8. How could a firm estimate the demand curve for one of its products?

9. How is price set to achieve a target return? Identify the problems with this approach to pricing.

10. Explain the difference between markup on cost and markup on price.

11. In pricing a new product, how can a manager determine the breakeven point?

12. If a firm reduces its fixed costs, what happens to its breakeven point? Illustrate with an example.

13. What is the expected return model of competitive bidding? Describe some of

the difficulties that might occur in using the expected return model of competitive bidding.

14. Are the principles or procedures for setting price for a nonprofit organization any different than those for a profit-oriented organization?

15. For each of the following products, identify if odd-even, psychological, prestige, or unit pricing could be used.

a. Canned peas   f. Potato chips
b. Television   g. Wine
c. Aspirin   h. Swimwear
d. Designer dress   i. Crystal vase
e. Legal services   j. Child day care services

ACTION PROBLEMS

1. Your firm produces a portable tape recorder that has fixed costs of $500,000 and variable cost per unit of $20. At a price of $40, what is its breakeven quantity? What would happen to breakeven if price was cut to $30? What if the price was raised to $50?

2. Your family corporation has an investment of $1,000,000 to produce and market a new type of motorcycle helmet and desires a 30 percent return on this investment. The variable cost of producing and selling the product is $20, and the fixed costs are $300,000. If you believe you can sell 100,000 helmets, how much should the helmet cost? Use the target return formula to compute this price. What will the profits be if you actually sell 100,000 units? 99,999 units? 100,001 units?

3. A pharmaceutical manufacturer has spent $2 million to develop a nasal decongestant in capsule form. The variable unit production cost (including packaging) is $0.20 per twelve pack. Variable unit marketing and distribution costs are $0.25 per twelve pack. The fixed production cost is $800,000 annually, and fixed distribution and marketing costs are $750,000. The market research firm has estimated the demand curve as: $Q = 5,000,000 - 1,500,000 P$, where Q equals quantity demanded (in 12 packs) and P equals price per twelve pack.

a. If the firm wanted to receive a 20 percent return on its investment and if it estimated it could sell 1,000,000 twelve packs per year, what price should be established?

b. Provide the breakeven point in units if the following prices were charged: $1.75, $2.00, $2.25, $2.50.

c. What price would maximize profits?

4. Your father operates a large construction firm, and you have worked for him during the summers for the last three years. Recently, he decided to bid on building a 100,000 square foot, three-story addition to a hospital in your community. He asked your help in preparing a bid. Both of you carefully went over the required specifications and estimated costs at $4.1 million. Your father is sure that a bid of $4 million or below would win the contract, because he is bidding against two other contractors and knows their cost structure and their past bidding behavior. For every $200,000 above $4 million, he estimates the probability of winning the bid would drop by 10 percent. Recommend a bid on the hospital project.

NOTES

1. Marie D'Amico, "World Courier Skims the Cream," *Venture* (April 1985), pp. 100, 102.

2. For a more complete discussion of new product pricing, see Joel Dean, "Pricing Policies for New Products," *Harvard Business Review* (November–December 1976), pp. 141–153.

3. For a good discussion of the economic theory of price setting, see Richard H. Leftwich, *The Price System and Resource Allocation* (New York: Holt, Rinehart and Winston, 1966).

4. Arthur Corr, "The Role of Cost in Pricing," *Management Accounting* (November 1974), pp. 15–18.

5. Ellyn E. Spragins, "U.S. Bikemakers Gear Up to Beat Back Imports," *BusinessWeek* (April 1, 1985), p. 97.

6. For more information on learning curves, see William J. Abernathy and Kenneth Wayne, "Limits of the Learning Curve," *Harvard Business Review* (September–October 1974), pp. 109–119; "Selling Business a Theory of Economics," *BusinessWeek* (September 8, 1973), pp. 86–88.

7. Franz Edelman, "Art and Science of Competitive Bidding," *Harvard Business Review* 43 (July–August 1965), pp. 53–66; Douglas G. Brooks, "Bidding for the Sake of Follow-on Contracts," *Journal of Marketing* 42 (January 1978), pp. 35–38; Murphy Sewall, "A Decision Calculus Model for Contract Bidding," *Journal of Marketing* 40 (October 1976), pp. 92–98.

8. Dik W. Twedt, "Does the '9' Fixation in Retailing Really Promote Sales?" *Journal of Marketing* (October 1965), pp. 54–55; H.J. Rudolph, "Pricing and Today's Market," *Printers' Ink* (May 29, 1954), pp. 22–24; "Strategic Mix of Odd, Even Prices Can Lead to Increased Retail Profits," *Marketing News* (March 7, 1980), p. 24.

9. Research on the price-quality relationship appears in Arthur G. Bedian, "Consumer Perception of Price as an Indicator of Product Quality," *MSU Business Topics* (Summer 1971), pp. 59–65; David M. Gardner, "An Experimental Investigation of the Price/Quality Relationship," *Journal of Retailing* (Fall 1970), pp. 25–41; Kent B. Monroe, "Buyers' Subjective Perceptions of Price," *Journal of Marketing Research* (February 1973), pp. 70–80; N.D. French, J.J. Williams, and W.A. Chance, "A Shopping Experiment on Price-Quality Relationships," *Journal of Retailing* (Fall 1972), pp. 3–16; Peter C. Riesz, "Major Price–Perceived Quality Study Reexamined," *Journal of Marketing Research* (May 1980), pp. 259–262; J. Douglas McDonnell, "Comment on 'A Major Price–Perceived Quality Study Reexamined,' " *Journal of Marketing Research* (May 1980), pp. 263–264.

10. A discussion of the usefulness and benefits of unit pricing can be found in Kent B. Monroe and Peter J. LaPlaca, "What Are the Benefits of Unit Pricing?" *Journal of Marketing* (July 1972), pp. 16–22; Michael J. Houston, "The Effect of Unit Pricing on Choices of Brand and Size in Economic Shopping," *Journal of Marketing* (July 1972), pp. 51–54; J. Edward Russo, "The Value of Unit Price Information," *Journal of Marketing Research* (May 1977), pp. 193–201.

CASES FOR PART VI

30.

Price Competition in the Rental Car Business

The four leading firms in the rental car business are Hertz, Avis, National, and Budget. Hertz, the leader, has a market share of approximately 35 percent. In 1979, the top four companies made $250 million before taxes; in 1982, they made less than $50 million. Avis had an operating loss of $35 million.

Since the mid-1970s, price and nonprice competition in the rental car business have intensified. This was about the time that Budget began to expand its locations by moving heavily into airports and offering a discount price with no charge for mileage. Budget further increased its marketing effort in 1978 by offering free gifts with the rental of a car. Typical gifts were a calculator or pen and pencil set. In 1976, Budget had a market share of 7 percent, but by 1982, it had increased to 16 percent.

Because of Budget's success, the other three major car rental firms began offering discount prices with no mileage charge and free gifts such as luggage, portable stereos, clocks, watches, and calculators. One major problem with this approach is that it does not expand the total market for rental cars. People will not rent more cars because they get free gifts. Instead, they will shift their business to the firm that offers the best combination of low price and free gifts. As a result, the industry is giving away its profits.

Questions

1. How or why did this industry get into a situation of cutthroat price competition?
2. What types of price policies should a car rental firm such as Hertz develop?

Source: Corporate annual reports; Carol J. Loomis. "The Rumble in Rental Cars," *Fortune* (March 7 1983), pp. 92–94.

31.

Longchamp Stemware

One of the most popular and best selling lead crystal stemware patterns in the United States is Longchamp from J.G. Durand International. In fact, in many department stores Longchamp outsells Waterford's Lismore.

Because the pattern has become so popular, many discount department stores (which seldom handle leaded crystal stemware) have attempted to get supplies of Longchamp and sell it at a deeply discounted price. Since J.G. Durand International prefers to sell to conventional department stores rather than to discounters, discounters have purchased bootlegged merchandise. This bootlegged crystal comes from conventional department stores that purchase large quantities of Longchamp only to immediately resell it to discounters at a minimal markup.

Not unexpectedly, this has created considerable conflict and tension among J.G. Durand International and the stores it chooses to sell to. The source of this conflict is the discounter's practice of selling Longchamp at $2.99 to $3.33 per stem, while the conventional department stores are pricing at $4.99 or more. Some retailers have threatened to stop stocking Longchamp if it continues to show up in discount stores. Other retailers are beginning to put more shelf space and promotional effort behind other brands of crystal stemware. Still others are trying to locate supplies of lower priced stemware that they can use as promotional items to create more store traffic. However, all the conventional U.S. department stores that sell a large proportion of crystal stemware are disturbed by the heavy discounting of Longchamp stemware.

Questions

1. Do J.G. Durand and the discount department stores have different pricing objectives? If so, what are they?
2. What can J.G. Durand do to halt retail price discounting?

Source: Based in part on Denise Gallagher. "Longchamp Off Price Creates Dilemma," *Retailing Home Furnishings* (June 27, 1983), p. 29.

32.

Jefferson Cinema (by Martin Meyers)

Jefferson Cinema has been in existence since the end of the Civil War. It was owned and operated by the Jefferson family for several decades. In the Spring of 1983, it was sold to Nan Lynch.

Jefferson Cinema is the only movie theater in a small

New England town. The theater shows only first-run movies that are generally changed the first Thursday of every month. Each movie is shown fifteen times a week. The theater seats 300 people comfortably, although a typical showing is half-filled.

Jefferson Cinema serves popcorn, candy, and soft drinks, but Ms. Lynch is considering the addition of ice cream bars. She plans to order the bars weekly, and her cost would be $0.20 each for quantities less than 75, $0.18 each if she purchases between seventy-five and 250, and $0.16 each if she purchases in quantities over 250. Table 1 provides an estimate for the demand of ice cream bars at different price levels.

Questions

1. Is the demand for ice cream bars elastic or inelastic?
2. At which price level is the revenue highest? At which price level is profit highest?

Source: Used by permission of Martin Meyers, University of Wisconsin — Stevens Point.

Table 1 Weekly Quantity Demanded of Ice Cream Bars at Different Prices

Price	Quantity Demanded
$1.00	60
0.90	154
0.80	248
0.70	342
0.60	436
0.50	530
0.40	624
0.30	718
0.20	812
0.10	906

33.

Vera's Orange Juice Palace (by Martin Meyers)

Vera's Orange Juice Palace, which has been in existence since 1968, is a sole proprietorship, owned and operated by Vera Burke. Vera's is located on a main thoroughfare between two large hotels on the east coast of Florida in a town of about 150,000 people. Approximately 30 percent of the permanent-resident population consists of senior citizens who have retired from northern states, while the rest is mainly young married couples with children. During the tourist season (November to April), the tourists outnumber the permanent residents.

The Orange Juice Palace is 400 square feet and seats thirty-five people. Burke takes tremendous pride in the tropical plants, which occupy approximately one-third of the available floor space.

Vera's offers freshly squeezed orange juice in three sizes. Customers have the option of enjoying the juice inside or taking it outside. The only other product offered is oranges, which can be purchased individually or by the bag. The majority of Vera's sales are walk-ins from the surrounding hotels. Few people drive to the Orange Juice Palace, even though there is parking for fifteen cars behind the building. Sales remain constant over the year because more orange juice is consumed during the warmer months, even though there are fewer tourists then. Vera attracts very few of the town's permanent residents.

The restaurants in the surrounding hotels do not offer much competition since the customers who are attracted to Vera's prefer her relaxed atmosphere over the formality of hotel restaurants. Vera has very little competition from the numerous fruit shippers' outlets, as the nearest one is two miles away.

Burke has been able to charge high prices because the tourists are willing to pay for the convenience and freshness of her product. Table 1 outlines the cost, selling price, and profitability for her orange juice.

During 1983, sales fell sharply as the number of tourists dropped. Two reasons for declining tourism were an abnormally cold and wet winter and a weak economy. Table 2 outlines profitability for the years 1978–1983.

Questions

1. What are the mark-ups based on cost and on selling price of orange juice?
2. Identify target markets Vera could attract. Should Vera maintain her present target market or attract a different target? For the target market you selected, what pricing changes would you recommend?

Table 1 Profitability for the Different Drink Sizes

Size	Selling Price	Cost[a]	Profit
Small	$0.50	$0.20	$0.30
Medium	0.90	0.30	0.60
Large	1.20	0.40	0.80

[a]Cost = fruit, cup, and napkin.

Table 2 Vera's Profitability

Year	Revenue	Expenditures	Net Income
1978	$200,000	$174,000	$26,000
1979	215,000	184,900	30,100
1980	260,000	213,200	46,800
1981	245,000	205,800	39,200
1982	250,000	210,000	40,000
1983	120,000	106,800	13,200

Source: Used by permission of Martin Meyers, University of Wisconsin — Stevens Point.

34.

Red Rock Drug

Herb Swartz graduated from college with a degree in pharmacy in 1971, and after working as a pharmacist for Walgreens for three years, he decided to open his own drugstore. In March 1974, he opened Red Rock Drug, a 7,000 square foot drugstore in a neighborhood shopping center. Swartz negotiated a favorable ten-year lease because the shopping center was newly constructed and on the outskirts of town and the developer was having difficulty renting all of the vacant store space.

When the store was opened, there were only 2,500 households within the three-mile radius where Red Rock drew 90 percent of its customers. For the first five years, Red Rock Drug had little direct competition, but as the population grew, more retailers chose to locate in the area. By 1980, the population within the three-mile radius had reached 10,000 households. Red Rock Drug's pharmacy business was little affected by the competition because Swartz had developed a loyal clientele and because most of his business came from patients visiting two clinics that were located within a half mile of his store. Unfortunately, only 25 percent of Red Rock's sales were pharmaceutical goods. Greeting cards, stationery, school supplies, beauty aids, small appliances, film supplies, and small gift items made up the remaining 75 percent of his sales. In these merchandise lines, Red Rock Drug was increasingly confronted by competition from discount department stores, superstores, and large chain drugstores.

As of the fall of 1986, there were two Kroger Superstores, a Target Discount Department Store, and a Jack Eckerd Drug in Red Rock's trade area. The two Krogers were each 40,000 square feet, the Target was 50,000 square feet, and the Jack Eckerd was 18,000 square feet. Table 1 shows how Red Rock priced nine different film items and also how Kroger, Target, and Jack Eckerd priced the same items. Swartz was especially concerned about Red Rock's film sales because net sales had dropped 50 percent since 1980. Red Rock Drug carries thirty-six different film items, but the nine in Table 1 represent 80 percent of sales. Red Rock has maintained a 40 percent markup on price on the other twenty-seven items.

Swartz is concerned about the increased competition not only from Kroger, Target, and Eckerds, but also from one-hour photo stands and from mail order film services, which give a free roll of film with each roll developed. Swartz is wondering if there is sufficient profit potential in film to continue to carry it. One of his major concerns in this regard is the fact that his ten-year lease will expire shortly and he expects his rent to triple from $1,000 monthly to $3,000 monthly. Consequently, every merchandise line must pay its way.

Questions

1. What markup on price would be necessary for Red Rock Drug to be price competitive with Target on the nine merchandise items in Table 1? For each of these items, how

Table 1   Price Comparison Statistics

	Red Rock Drug			Competitor Prices		
Merchandise Item	Price	Markup	Monthly Sales	Target	Kroger	Eckerd
Kodak Color-24 ASA 100	$ 2.79	28%	38	$2.19	$2.49	$2.49
Kodak Color-24 ASA 400	3.47	26	24	2.99	3.59	3.29
Kodak Instant single pak	9.37	30	12	7.99	7.39	7.99
Kodak Instant twin pak	18.37	34	7	13.99	—	—
Polaroid 640 film	9.57	30	18	9.49	7.99	9.69
Polaroid time-zero single pak	8.88	28	22	6.99	7.19	7.99
Polaroid time-zero twin pak	16.67	32	11	13.49	13.48	15.95
GTE Sylvania flip flash	1.63	22	33	1.49	1.88	1.99
GTE Sylvania flash bar	1.97	20	23	1.99	1.99	2.69

much would unit sales need to rise to justify meeting Target's price?

2. Should Red Rock Drug drop film from its product mix?

35.

Queen of Hearts (by Martin Meyers)

The Queen of Hearts, a neighborhood pub in a large midwestern city, is owned and operated by Maureen Drennan. Since it opened in 1978, annual sales have grown from approximately $40,000 to $130,000.

The atmosphere in the Queen of Hearts is informal. There is a long bar, which seats twenty people, and there are thirty tables, which hold four people each. Often, patrons push several tables together.

Drennan carries a wide selection of domestic and imported beer. She estimates that 55 percent of her sales volume is derived from beer, 30 percent from mixed drinks, and the remainder from menu items: french fries, potato chips, and sandwiches prepared on her grill.

The majority of Drennan's customers live within a few miles of the pub, and she knows many of them personally. They are mostly blue collar skilled laborers in their thirties and forties, and the men usually outnumber the women two to one.

Prices are considered reasonable by most of her customers: a domestic draught beer costs $0.75, and imported beers range from $1.00 to $2.25. Mixed drink prices range from $1.25 to $2.50. Most of the sandwiches cost approximately $2.00, and french fries are an additional $0.50. It is not unusual for the establishments in the downtown and suburban areas to charge twice the prices charged at the Queen of Hearts.

Many customers have asked to have pizza added to the menu. Drennan estimated that if she were to make pizzas, she would have to spend $5,000 for an oven and $1,000 for dishes and appliances. She estimated that the ingredients in a typical pizza would cost $2.25 and the additional labor expense per pizza would be $0.20. She could expect the utilities involved in preparing each pizza to be $0.05.

Questions

1. Assume that Drennan will sell a pizza for $5.00. What is her breakeven point in units and in dollars? Assume that she sells twenty-five pizzas a day. How many days will it take her to break even?
2. Should Drennan add pizza to her product line? Explain your answer.

Source: Used by permission of Martin Meyers, University of Wisconsin — Stevens Point.

SPECIAL GROWTH OPPORTUNITIES

Part VII describes the rapid growth of international, services, and nonprofit marketing practices. Chapter 18, "International Marketing," discusses the different orientations a firm can have toward international marketing, the importance of understanding foreign environments, and foreign market entry strategies. Chapter 19, "Services Marketing," explains how services differ from goods, the competitive forces service marketers confront, and how to understand the service customer. Chapter 20, "Nonprofit Marketing," describes the differences between nonprofit and conventional marketing, how to develop a marketing plan for a nonprofit firm, and the ethics of nonprofit marketing.

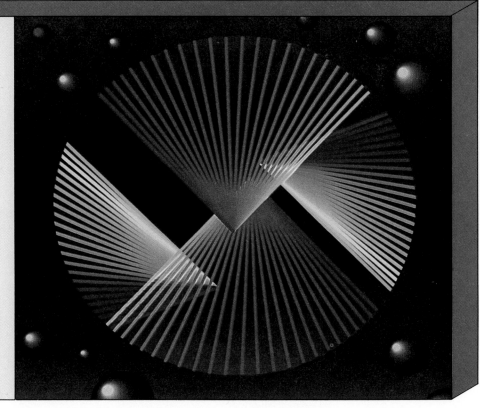

CHAPTER 18

LEARNING OBJECTIVES

After you complete this chapter, you should be able to:

- **Explain** why the balance of merchandise trade is unfavorable in the United States

- **Discuss** and give examples of why understanding foreign environments is a prerequisite to successful international marketing

- **Describe** the four types of foreign market entry strategies

- **Outline** the steps or considerations in developing an international marketing program

INTERNATIONAL MARKETING

MARKETER PROFILE

Masatoshi Ito of Ito-Yokado

Masatoshi Ito is president and founder of Ito-Yokado, Japan's second largest retailer, with over 3,000 units. When Masatoshi Ito began his retailing career, the economy was dominated by mom-and-pop operations and chain stores were nonexistent.

Ito's concept of retailing was strongly influenced by a visit to the United States in 1961. He attended an NCR seminar, where he was introduced to self-service retailing, and traveled throughout the country, observing how chain store retailing was applied and seeing implications for its usefulness in Japan. On his return to Japan, he opened two 30,000-square foot superstores. Ito used these prototypes to fine-tune his new concept of retailing and then began to expand operations. By 1985, he had 126 superstores.

Ito also adapted other U.S. retailing techniques to Japan. In 1974, he introduced Japan's first Denny's-style coffee shop. A licensing agreement was signed with Denny's of California, and by 1985, Ito had 253 Denny's restaurants in operation in Japan. In 1975, Masatoshi Ito signed another licensing agreement—this time with the Southland Corporation. That year witnessed Japan's first 7-11 convenience store. By 1985, Ito had 2,715 such stores operating in Japan.

Source: Based on Michael Friedman, "Masatoshi Ito: Defying Japanese Retailing Tradition," *Chain Store Age Executive* (October 1981), pp. 33–37. Reprinted by permission. Copyright Lebhar/Friedman, 425 Park Avenue, New York, NY 10022.

INTRODUCTION

The preceding Marketer Profile demonstrates that a marketing success in one country is often successful in a foreign country. This is true regardless of whether the success is a manufactured good or a service concept, such as the 7-11 convenience store concept that Ito-Yokado successfully introduced to the Japanese consumer. Many U.S. products have been successfully introduced abroad and vice versa: Levi jeans, Kentucky Fried Chicken, and Coca Cola are popular outside the United States, while Sony televisions (Japan), Waterford Crystal (Ireland), Sinclair computers (Britain), and BMWs (Germany) are popular in the United States.

In this chapter, we will discuss **international marketing,** which is *the marketing of goods and services between countries.*[1] When Daimler-Benz builds Mercedes Benz autos in West Germany and ships them to the United States to sell to American customers, it is engaging in international marketing. Similarly, when IBM builds personal computers in the United States and ships them to Australia, it is engaging in international marketing. If you examine the products you own or use, you will see that international marketing is a major force in your daily life. For example, before you arrived at today's class, you may have splashed on Zizanie cologne, tied your Adidas running shoes, strapped on your Seiko watch, slipped your Yves Saint Laurent sweater over your head, and picked up your Canon calculator.

Many of the principles of marketing that we discussed in earlier chapters can be applied to international marketing, but the keys to marketing success vary from country to country because of diverse external environments. In short, it is often necessary to modify the marketing mix in international marketing because different countries have different external environments.

In West Germany, Campbell's reportedly lost over $10 million trying to change the wet soup habits of the German consumer from dehydrated soup to a canned soup concentrate. In the United States, CPC International faced the same problem in reverse in trying unsuccessfully to significantly penetrate the U.S. soup market (90% canned) with Knorr dehydrated soups. Knorr was a Swiss company acquired by CPC that had a major share of the European prepared soup market where bouillon and dehydrated soups account for 80 percent of commercial soup sales.[2]

GROWTH IN INTERNATIONAL MARKETING

Post–World War II Economy

Following the rapid growth of the U.S. economy after World War II and the simultaneous reindustrialization of Japan and Europe and improved worldwide communications, many Japanese and European firms began to aggressively market their products in the United States. In the 1950s, most U.S. citizens wouldn't think of buying Japanese-made products because of a negative attitude stemming from the Japanese attack on Pearl Harbor during the war and because of the poor quality of Japanese products in the 1950s. By 1975, however, products such as Honda automobiles and motorcycles, Yamaha pianos, Sony televisions, and Canon cameras were in demand by the U.S. public because they offered high quality at a fair price. The Japanese success is not limited to U.S. markets: the biggest threat to the European auto market is Japanese-produced cars. By the mid-1980s Japan was producing three-fourths of the world's videocassette recorders, single-lens cameras, and motorcycles; one-half of the world's ships; two-fifths of its televisions; and one-third of its semiconductors and cars.[3]

While Japanese and European products flooded the U.S. marketplace in the 1960s, most U.S. firms continued to operate mainly on the domestic front, generally ignoring foreign market opportunities. Since domestic markets were growing rapidly because of population increases and regular increases in real consumer income, they did not feel the need for foreign business. In the mid-1970s, however, this favorable growth pattern began to slow: birth rates declined and increases in consumer incomes adjusted for inflation stagnated. Meanwhile, foreign firms continued their assault on U.S. products, resulting in intensified competition because domestic firms were struggling to maintain or increase their market shares. During the late 1970s and the early 1980s, U.S. firms began to realize that they could only continue to achieve adequate growth if they began to pursue foreign market opportunities. For example, Allen-Edmonds, a manufacturer of high quality men's shoes, saw sales fall as foreign shoe manufacturers bombarded the United States during the 1960s and 1970s. In 1981, the company decided to fight back and now sells its shoes in Italy, South Africa, and Singapore. By 1983, Allen-Edmonds's international sales were approximately 10 percent of total sales.[4]

The present time is favorable for U.S. firms to pursue foreign markets because countries in Europe, Latin America, and the Far and Near East have grown considerably since the 1950s and now have a high level of demand for many types of U.S. industrial and consumer products. However, U.S. firms must be prepared to enter these markets with appropriate products and marketing strategies because companies from around the globe are beginning to achieve critical mass in the area of international marketing. *Critical mass* occurs when a firm concentrates enough resources in pursuing a foreign market to upset the competitive equilibrium. For example, in 1984, NEC (formerly Nippon Electric Corporation) began to apply the concept of critical mass to its efforts in the U.S. computer market and was successful in gaining market share and thus creating a competitive disequilibrium. Competitive intensity increased as firms fought back for market share. Similarly, if U.S. firms decide to achieve critical mass in foreign markets, the resulting competitive disequilibrium is bound to intensify competition.[5]

U.S. Export/Import Record

Exporting occurs *when a firm, government, or individual from one country sells a product to a firm, government, or individual in another country.* When Saudi Arabia sells its oil to U.S. oil companies, it is exporting a product. On the other hand, *when a firm, government, or individual in one country purchases a product from a firm, government, or individual in another country,* this is called **importing.** The U.S. oil companies are importing Saudi Arabian oil. All governments are concerned with *the balance of their exports and imports,* which is called **balance of trade.** All countries would like to have *more exports than imports, or a surplus or a favorable balance of trade. If imports are greater than exports, the balance of trade is in deficit or unfavorable.* The balance of trade only considers the trading of products between countries; it does not include foreign aid, funding of military bases overseas, and money spent by tourists traveling abroad. These items, as well as others, are considered in determining the balance of payments for a country. The **balance of payments** reflects *the total outflow of currency (or its equivalent) contrasted to inflow of foreign currency (or its equivalent). A favorable balance of payments occurs when inflows exceed outflows, and an unfavorable balance of payments occurs when outflows exceed inflows.*

Our discussion of exports and imports will focus on merchandise. In 1985, the United States had exports totaling $219.1 billion and imports totaling $339.1 billion, resulting in an unfavorable balance of trade of $120 billion. Figure 18.1 shows the U.S. record for merchandise exports and imports from 1960 to 1985. The data in Figure 18.1 reveal that the United States began to experience a deficit in the balance of merchandise trade in the mid-1970s. Figure 18.2 shows the U.S. export-import record in 1984 divided into six broad product categories. These data show that the United States has a trade surplus in (1) foods, feeds, beverages, and live animals and (2) industrial supplies and raw materials, and a trade deficit in (1) automobile vehicles and parts and transportation equipment, (2) fuels and lubricants, (3) capital goods (except transportation equipment), and (4) consumer goods (nonfood).

In Table 18.1, the top 25 U.S. firms in terms of dollar exports are profiled in terms of volume of exports, products exported, and exports as a percent of total company sales. Although these firms have a substantial dollar volume of exports, the percentage of sales accounted for by exports tends to be less than 25 percent. In fact, General Motors, which exports over $4.6 billion annually, derives less than 8 percent of its sales from exports.

The U.S. balance of trade deficit is slowing domestic economic growth by eliminating jobs. When a country is importing more merchandise than it exports, it is using foreign labor. As this trend continues, more jobs are lost to foreign countries. In 1983, the trade deficit cost the U.S. economy an estimated 1.5 million jobs.[6]

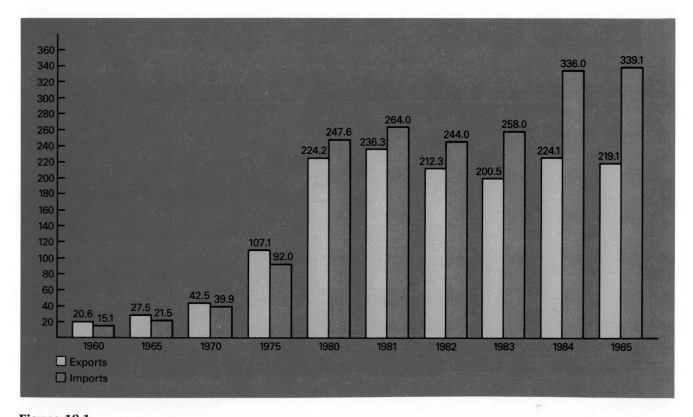

Figure 18.1

U.S. Exports and Imports of Merchandise: 1960–1985[a]

[a]Figures in billions of dollars.

Source: U.S. Bureau of the Census. *Statistical Abstract of the United States,* 1983 and 1985 editions (Washington, DC); Department of Commerce. *Survey of Current Business* (Washington, DC, February 1986); authors' computations.

Some economic analysts contend that the biggest single factor preventing the United States from obtaining a favorable trade balance is the lack of a national export policy.[7] For example, many governments, such as Japan's, try to encourage exports by providing favorable tax treatment for exporters and giving them below-market financing. The U.S. government provides relatively few of these special incentives. Another export growth problem facing U.S. firms is that more countries are becoming protectionist and are enacting laws that limit imports.[8] Finally, the United States excels in the production of high technology products, but many of these are vital to national security interests and exports are highly restricted. Examples are nuclear weapons, technical data, and sophisticated communications and surveillance devices. This puts America at a disadvantage compared with countries like France, which also produces high technology products and more liberally sells weapon systems and similar products. Despite these

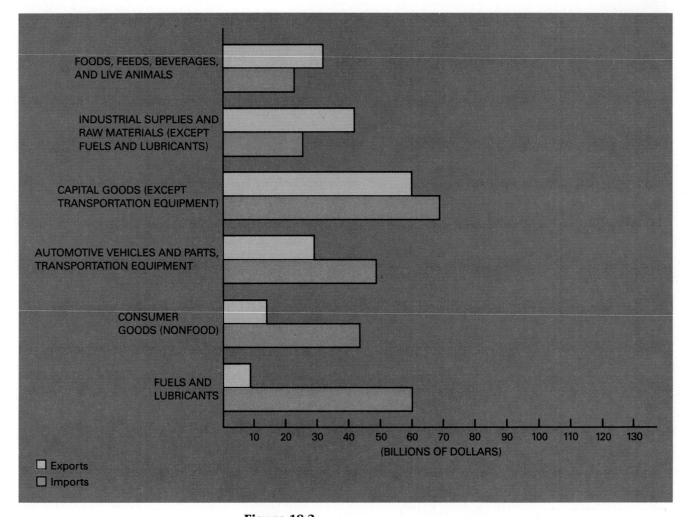

Figure 18.2

Selected U.S. Exports and Imports: Value by Broad Category (1984)

Source: Department of Commerce. *Survey of Current Business* (Washington, DC, September 1985); authors' computations.

obstacles, the major reason for poor export performance is a lack of knowledge among many U.S. businesspeople of overseas markets, lack of foreign trade expertise, and general disinterest in expanding abroad, especially for small and medium-sized firms.

Multinational Enterprise

A large proportion of international marketing is being accomplished by multinational corporations, which have grown rapidly since the early 1960s.[9]

Table 18.1   Top 25 U.S. Multinational Firms in Terms of Exports

Firm	Export Volume ($000)	Products Exported	Exports As % of Total Sales
General Motors	7,276,500	Motor vehicles and parts, locomotives, diesel engines	8.67
Ford Motor	6,041,000	Motor vehicles and parts	11.54
General Electric	3,935,000	Aircraft engines, generating equipment, locomotives	14.08
Boeing	3,621,000	Commercial aircraft	34.97
International Business Machines	3,074,000	Information-handling equipment	6.69
Chrysler	2,707,900	Motor vehicles and parts	13.83
E.I. Du Pont de Nemours	2,650,000	Chemicals, fibers, polymers, petroleum products	7.38
United Technologies	2,387,810	Aircraft engines, helicopters, air-conditioning equipment	14.62
McDonnell Douglas	2,133,700	Aircraft, missiles, space systems	22.08
Eastman Kodak	1,949,000	Photographic equipment and supplies	18.39
Caterpillar Tractor	1,768,000	Construction equipment, diesel engines and turbines	26.89
Hewlett-Packard	1,420,000	Computers, electronic equipment	23.49
Digital Equipment	1,136,030	Computers and related peripheral equipment	20.34
Westinghouse Electric	1,129,095	Generating equipment, defense systems	11.00
Union Carbide	1,115,000	Chemicals, industrial and high technology products	11.73
Motorola	1,062,000	Semiconductors, radio communications equipment	19.19
Philip Morris	1,053,000	Tobacco products, soft drink ingredients, beer	10.39
Exxon	1,013,000	Petroleum, chemicals	1.11
Monsanto	950,000	Herbicides, chemicals, polymer products, fibers	14.20
Signal Cos.	890,000	Engines, chemicals, audiovideo systems	14.82
Archer Daniels Midland	883,253	Soybean oil, flour, corn by-products	18.00
Occidental Petroleum	882,000	Agricultural chemical products	5.74
General Dynamics	876,900	Tanks, aircraft, missiles, gun systems	11.19
Weyerhaeuser	871,000	Logs, pulp, paperboard, newsprint, lumber	15.69
Dow Chemical	851,000	Chemicals, plastics, magnesium metal	7.45

Source: "The 50 Leading Exporters," *Fortune* (August 5, 1985), p. 61. Used by permission.

A **multinational corporation (MNC)** is *an enterprise with direct invest-ment in manufacturing and/or marketing facilities in multiple countries (usually 4 or more), whose parent company is located in a single country that serves as its base for coordinating worldwide operations and activ-ities.* The MNCs view the world as their marketplace. Some of the MNCs you may be familiar with are ITT (telecommunications), Shell (oil), Abbott Laboratories (pharmaceuticals), and Nestle (processed foods).

The phenomenon of multinational corporations has been both praised and criticized. Those who praise MNCs argue that they can be excellent vehicles for fueling the growth of technology, production, and marketing capabilities in developing economies because of the large investments of capital made in these countries.[10] Critics of MNCs believe that they have too much power and can use it to influence government policy, labor practices, and the social fabric of a society.[11] The critics argue that the

aerospatiale
this is who we are:

one of the world's largest aerospace manufacturers

Not the first in the world, but already the first in Europe in terms of turnover (above 16,5 billion french francs in 1981) and diversity of products. We were incorporated in 1970 under the name of Société Nationale Industrielle Aérospatiale, as a result of the merger of Nord-Aviation, Sud-Aviation and Sereb. Some have been inclined to shorten our name, retaining only the initials S.N.I.A.S.; with the same object in mind we prefer to be called commonly **aerospatiale**. It is our signature.

top manpower

Men whose imagination and creativity have made our achievements possible. Close to 40,000 employees, specialists, engineers, chosen for their skill in particular fields.

ways and means

The most modern research, development and production facilities, where data processing plays a leading part: Computer Aided Design (CAD), Computer Aided Manufacturing (CAM). Behind these means, a policy: to come up with the best product at minimum cost.

products

The most diversified range of aerospace products: airplanes, helicopters, tactical missiles, space and ballistic systems, combining top performance and low cost of operation in order to satisfy market requirements.

We are the largest manufacturer of helicopters and tactical missiles in Europe, and the French Nuclear Defence Forces are equipped with our strategic ballistic missiles.

Finally, in the framework of multinational industrial programs, we are responsible for the success of a number of famous products that are not signed only with our name: AIRBUS A 300/A 310 · ARIANE · CONCORDE · HOT · MILAN · ROLAND · INTELSAT V · METEOSAT...

exports

We are exporting 80 % of our helicopter production, 70 % of our missiles, 90 % of our airplanes, as a mark of quality of our products - tailored to market requirements, and of our competitive sales policy.

aerospatiale
37, bd de Montmorency 75781 Paris Cedex 16, France

In some countries such as France, manufacturers of high-tech products and weapon systems are able to export their products and thereby help the country's balance of trade.

Multinational corporations are responsible for a substantial amount of international marketing.

MNCs are relatively free to exercise their power to make as much money as possible without any concern for the consequences of their actions on society. Obviously, MNCs must be controlled, just as any domestic enterprise needs to be controlled.[12] Nations are working together to obtain greater harmony of policies in areas such as company law, patent law, company taxation in relation to overseas earnings, merger and monopoly regulation, and the movement of financial capital between countries.[13]

When firms decide to practice international marketing, they may follow some general orientations such as ethnocentrism, polycentrism, and geocentrism, as shown in Figure 18.3[14] Most firms initially practice **ethnocentrism** (i.e., *home country orientation*). In an ethnocentric orientation, *an operation in a foreign country is viewed as secondary or as a child of the domestic operation.* Typically, the foreign market is viewed as a convenient place to dispose of excess domestic production. All planning for the foreign market is conducted at the home office by home country nationals. Little, if any, research is conducted on the foreign market, and the complete marketing mix is as similar, if not identical, to the home country mix.

> **Polycentrism** (i.e., *host country oriented*) occurs when *a firm establishes an autonomous subsidiary in each foreign country where it markets products.* For example, the foreign subsidiary has its own marketing plans and objectives. It designs a marketing mix based on local marketing research in its country of operation. If necessary, product lines are developed in each country, or home product lines may be modified to meet local needs. Local nationals compose the sales force, and that country's traditional distribution channels are used. Pricing and promotion policies are established by each foreign subsidiary.

> **Geocentrism** (i.e., *world orientation*) *views the world as a single market.* In a geocentric orientation, the firm attempts to develop global marketing strategies. Obviously, this is difficult from a practical perspective because laws, customs, geography, and economic climate vary across the globe.[15] Nonetheless, some firms, such as Ford and Nissan, are trying to develop a global automobile and companion global marketing strategy. Coca-Cola and McDonald's probably come close to practicing a global orientation.

ORIENTATIONS TOWARD INTERNATIONAL MARKETING

International marketing managers must understand the external environments in which they operate. Gaining an understanding of foreign environments can be quite difficult, however, because the marketing managers are not necessarily familiar with the foreign cultures and languages. Consequently, high priority and funding must be given to marketing research and intelligence gathering.

> Chapter 2 discussed the external environments of a domestic firm, and these environments are the same ones with which international marketers must be concerned: social, technological, competitive, legal/political, economic, physical, and ethical.

UNDERSTANDING FOREIGN ENVIRONMENTS

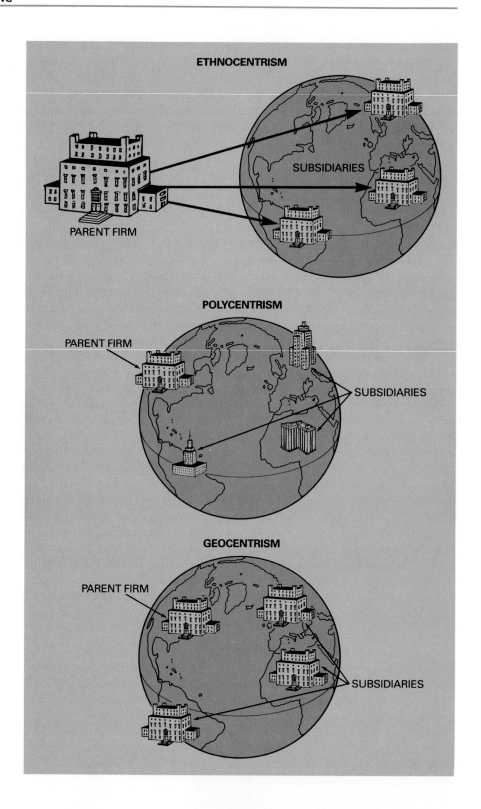

Figure 18.3

Ethnocentrism, Polycentrism, and Geocentrism

Social Environment

Different cultures possess different values, rules, family structures, symbols, and languages. Individual cultures also behave differently because of the attitudes and beliefs they hold about time, the future, right and wrong, authority figures, family obligations, tolerance for personal differences, and mobility between social classes.[16] The way a society relates to each of these dimensions clearly will affect the design of marketing strategies and, especially, promotional campaigns. The following are several examples of cultural differences[17]:

❑ Death is symbolized by different colors. It is purple in Brazil, white in Hong Kong, yellow (flowers) in Mexico, and black in the United States.

❑ Roles are quite rigid in Portugal. In middle-class families, housewives are reluctant to purchase cleaning supplies because maids are supposed to do the physical labor in the home.

❑ In many parts of Southeast Asia, betel-nut chewing is an elite habit and results in black teeth, which are a status symbol. Consequently, a sales pitch for a toothpaste that promises white teeth would not have much success.

❑ In Italy, home cooking is central to the family structure, so that frozen TV dinners have little appeal.

❑ In many countries, clothes are washed by hand in streams using bar soap, thus powdered laundry detergent is a poor seller.

The Marketing in Action on page 560 shows that Apple Computer's failure in Japan was due largely to its lack of understanding of Japanese culture.

Economic Environment

The international marketing manager also must be familiar with the economic environment of the foreign country. As we discussed in Chapter 2, the purchasing power of a particular population must be considered, not just the size of the market. Purchasing power is a function of gross national product and total population. *Gross national product (GNP)* is the total value of all goods and services produced in an economy, and it is usually stated on an annual basis. One useful way to combine these two factors is to compute the GNP per capita, which is defined as GNP divided by total population. Table 18.2 shows total population, GNP, and per capita GNP for 20 countries. These data show that two countries of similar population size, such as Greece and Belgium, can have substantially different levels of purchasing power because of dramatic differences in GNP per capita. Greece

MARKETING IN ACTION

Failure of Apple Computer in Japan

When Apple Computer entered the Japanese market in 1977, it was the first personal computer on the market in a country that is fascinated by new gadgets and computers. Unfortunately, Apple failed to make a significant dent in the Japanese market. Why?

The marketing managers of Apple Computer committed the classic marketing mistake—they did not understand the foreign consumer and culture. For example, the Japanese are very particular and aftersale service is even more important in Japan than it is in the United States. Because Apple tried to manage its overseas business from the United States, it could not respond quickly to con-

sumer complaints. Apple failed to recognize that software must relate to a user's culture and so failed to modify software sufficiently to fit Japanese users. Japanese computer firms such as Nippon Electric Company (NEC) made a similar mistake when they initially brought their computers to the United States. An even bigger obstacle for Apple to overcome was the configuration of the keyboard. Since Japanese executives speak and work in Japanese, a standard American keyboard is inap-

propriate and a keyboard that incorporates the over 3,000 commonly used characters would be unworkable. Finally, it is considered a symbolic lack of commitment to Japan for top executives to conduct business in a language other than Japanese, so that Apple's executives, as well as any others who want to be competitive, needed to become a part of the culture to have a chance of surviving there.

Source: Based on information in Sharon Noguchi. "In Japan, Software and Distribution Are Key to Success," *Business Marketing* (November 1983), pp. 74, 76. Reprinted with permission from *Business Marketing*; copyright Crain Communications Inc.

has a GNP per capita of $4,646 versus $12,469 for Belgium. The data also reveal that many countries have a large population, such as India with 685 million individuals, but are low in purchasing power, with a GNP per capita of $233.

Per capita GNP can be misleading because the distribution of wealth and income in a country may not be equal. Consequently, the market analyst should also pay particular attention to the distribution of income in a society. For example, a country with a per capita income of $5,000 could have (1) a large number of very poor families with an income of below $1,000, a small number of wealthy families with incomes above $100,000, and no middle income families; (2) few poor families, few rich families, and many middle income families; or (3) an equal number of poor, middle income, and high income families. Each of these scenarios represents a different potential market. For example, Honda may find a lucrative market in the society with a large middle class, whereas Rolls Royce would find more opportunity in a society that has a substantial upper class. If you refer back to Table 18.2, you will note that Mexico is a poor country; however, 10 percent of the population accounts for close to 50 percent of the income,[18] and thus there is a market in Mexico for Christian Dior suits, Mercedes autos, Lenox china, and Rolex watches.

A country's economy reflects its industrial base (i.e., where its people

Table 18.2   Per Capita GNP for Selected Countries (1980)

Country	GNP (in billions)	Population (in millions)	GNP per capita
United States	$2,370.0	227.7	$10,408
Algeria	35.5	18.8	1,888
Argentina	118.3	28.2	4,195
Bangladesh	11.0	88.1	125
Belgium	122.2	9.8	12,469
Canada	243.3	24.1	10,095
Egypt	22.6	42.1	537
Ethiopia	4.4	29.8	148
France	634.3	53.8	11,790
Greece	44.6	9.6	4,646
India	159.4	685.1	233
Iran	72.7	38.8	1,874
Italy	368.1	56.2	6,550
Japan	1,152.6	116.8	9,868
Kenya	6.6	16.4	402
Mexico	142.4	70.1	2,031
Poland	175.5	35.6	4,930
Switzerland	114.4	6.4	17,875
Turkey	78.5	46.0	1,707
Yugoslavia	73.2	22.3	3,283

Source: U.S. Bureau of the Census. *Statistical Abstract of the United States: 1984,*
104th edition (Washington, DC, 1983), pp. 857–859, 865; authors' computations
for GNP per capita.

derive employment and income). Kotler identifies four different types of
economic structures[19]:

1. *Subsistence economies.* In a subsistence economy, the vast majority of
   people engage in simple agriculture. They consume most of their output
   and barter the rest for simple goods and services. They offer few opportunities for exporters.
2. *Raw material exporting economies.* These economies are rich in one
   or more natural resources but poor in other respects. Much of their
   revenue comes from exporting these resources. Examples are Chile (tin
   and copper), Congo (rubber), and Saudi Arabia (oil). These countries
   are good markets for extractive equipment, tools and supplies, materials
   handling equipment, and trucks. Depending on the number of foreign
   residents and wealthy native rulers and land holders, they are also a
   market for Western-style commodities and luxury goods.
3. *Industrializing economies.* In an industrializing economy, manufacturing is beginning to account for between 10 and 20 percent of the

Subsistence economies rely primarily on agriculture for their employment and income bases.

country's gross national product. Examples include Egypt, the Philippines, and Brazil. As manufacturing increases, the country relies more on imports of textile raw materials, steel, and heavy machinery and less on imports of finished textiles, paper products, and automobiles. The industrialization creates a new rich class and a small, but growing, middle class, both demanding new types of goods, some of which can be satisfied only by imports.

4. *Industrial economies.* Industrial economies are major exporters of manufactured goods and investment funds. They trade manufactured goods among themselves and also export them to other types of economies in exchange for raw materials and semifinished goods. The large and varied manufacturing activities of these industrial nations and their sizable middle class make them rich markets for all sorts of goods.

There are other types of economic structures besides these four.[20] Furthermore, any given economy can have elements of each structure; for example, the United States is an industrial economy, but it exports raw materials such as grain and other agricultural commodities.

Legal and Political Environments

All countries have laws that regulate business activities, although foreign governments will often apply a different set of laws or regulations to foreign firms than to their own enterprises. Generally, a product manufactured by an international firm that is central to a nation's economy is considered politically vulnerable and subject to special political attention. Table 18.3 lists some clues that can be used to identify a product's political vulnerability.

There are several ways in which a foreign government can intervene in a firm's marketing program. A government can levy taxes and tariffs on certain restricted goods and set numerical quotas, such as those placed on Japanese automobiles for import into the United States. Governments can also boycott other countries and prohibit the importation of their goods. The United States has often boycotted goods from Communist countries, and Saudi Arabia forbids imports from Israel as well as from firms that sell to Israel.

Numerous regional trade groups have been established to regulate trade, such as the European Economic Community (EEC) and the Latin American

---

Table 18.3   Is a Product Politically Vulnerable?

1. Is the product ever the subject of important political debates in respect to adequacy of supply? (Sugar, salt, kerosene, gasoline, foodstuffs, transport facilities, public utilities, tires, medicines, etc.)

2. Is the production one on which other industries rest? (Cement, steel, power, machine tools, construction machinery, etc.)

3. Is the product one in which effective competition is difficult in small national markets?

4. Is the product held to be essential, either economically or socially? (Key drugs and medicines, laboratory equipment.)

5. Is the product important to agriculture? (Farm tools and machinery, pumps, fertilizers, seed, etc.)

6. Is the product of national defense significance? (Communications equipment, transport equipment, etc.)

7. Does the product include important components that would be available from local sources? (Labor, skills, materials.)

8. Is the product one for which competition from local manufacture may be reasonably expected in the foreseeable future?

9. Does the product relate to channels of mass communication media? (Newsprint, radio equipment, etc.)

10. Is the product primarily a service?

11. Does the use of the product, or its design, rest upon some legal requirement?

12. Is the product potentially dangerous to the user? (Explosives, drugs.)

13. Does the product induce a net drain on scarce foreign exchange?

Source: Reprinted from Richard D. Robinson. "The Challenge of the Underdeveloped National Market," *Journal of Marketing* (October 1961), pp. 24–25. Used by permission.

Free Trade Association (LAFTA). Another method governments use to restrict trade is to place administrative barriers based on health, packaging, labeling, or nationalistic norms. For example, Germany's strict packaging and labeling requirements keep out most foreign foods; France forbids the importation of walnuts before September 25 in order to exclude Italy's crop; and Italy seeks bids for government projects only from national firms.[21]

The home country government as well as a foreign government may intervene in a firm's marketing activities. For instance, the U.S. government regulates and constrains U.S. firms in their foreign market pursuits. The U.S. antitrust laws apply to international marketing activities as well as to domestic business.[22] Section 1 of the Sherman Act (1890) states that "every contract, combination . . . or conspiracy in restraint of trade or commerce among the several states or with foreign nations is hereby declared illegal." Section 2 makes it a violation to "monopolize, or attempt to monopolize, or combine or conspire with any person or persons, to monopolize any part of the trade or commerce among the several states, or with foreign nations." The application of U.S. antitrust laws to foreign ventures has harmed many U.S. firms. For example, Gillette Co. (a U.S. manufacturer of razors, among other things) acquired Braun A.G. (a German company that has a successful electric shaver), but the U.S. Justice Department forced Gillette to divest itself of Braun A.G. in 1977 because they claimed the acquisition lessened competition.[23]

The U.S. government has also intervened with legislation prohibiting bribery payments. The Foreign Corrupt Practices Act (FCPA) states that a U.S. firm is prohibited from making or authorizing payments, offers, promises, or gifts for the purpose of corruptly influencing action by governments or their officials in order to obtain or retain business for a company. If the law is violated, the firm is subject to a million dollar fine, and any officer, director or stockholder who willfully violates the law is subject to a $10,000 fine or five-year imprisonment, or both.[24] The FCPA places U.S. firms at a competitive disadvantage because payoffs or bribes are a commonly accepted way of conducting business in many countries, such as Nigeria, Zaire, and Korea. For example, Gulf Oil Company paid $4 million to help finance the reelection of President Chung Hee Park in South Korea; Gulf Oil viewed this as a necessary payment in order to protect its $350 million investment in South Korea.

One of the biggest risks of investing in foreign countries is the possibility that the firm's operations may be confiscated or expropriated. **Confiscation** occurs *when a foreign investment is taken over by a government without any payment.* **Expropriation** occurs *when a foreign investment is taken over by a government, but some form of payment is made.*[25] Obviously, expropriation is preferable to confiscation, but both are risks that need to be carefully weighed before a firm decides to invest in a foreign country.[26] The risk is highlighted by the fact that between 1970 and 1974, thirty-four countries in Latin America, Africa, and Asia expropriated $1.2 billion of U.S. overseas investments.[27]

Other Environmental Forces

The international marketer must also carefully research and analyze the foreign country's technological, physical, competitive, and ethical environments. Some important questions to be answered are:

1. How will the country's altitude, humidity, and temperature extremes affect the functioning of products?
2. How will the geography of the country influence the type of transportation used?
3. What is a country's availability of raw materials and energy resources?
4. What is the population density and urban versus rural character of the population?
5. Are domestic competitors given favorable tax treatment?
6. Are competitors large or small? What is their financial strength?
7. What are the dominant technologies being used in production methods?
8. What are the standards of marketing and business ethics in this country?[28]

In general, the more research that is conducted on foreign environments, the more able a firm will be to select the most attractive markets. Naturally, there is a limit to the amount of research that a firm can afford to conduct, but generally speaking most firms conduct too little research before they enter foreign markets.

Selecting Markets to Enter

Given its capital constraints, a firm must limit the number of foreign markets it chooses to enter, selecting only the most attractive ones.[29] Some attributes of an attractive foreign market are (1) low political risk, (2) few restrictions on business, and (3) high purchasing power, which translates into a good market potential for the firm's product(s).[30] These factors may be assessed by analyzing the relevant environments in foreign countries. For example, political risk usually is assessed by such indicators as frequency of changes in the ruling party and incidences of violence, disruptions, and demonstrations. Restrictions on business can only be assessed by a detailed investigation of the laws and regulations of business in each country. Finally, market potential or purchasing power can be assessed by demographic factors, such as per capita income, the distribution of income, education levels, and family size.

Table 18.4 shows the degree of political risk and purchasing power of several countries. Note that any countries that fall into the lower right corner should be given high priority because they have low political risk and high purchasing power. Ideally, a firm will select markets in this area as long as there are not too many restrictions on business. For example, Saudi Arabia has many restrictions on business, and thus many firms are hesitant to enter this lucrative foreign market. Countries that are in the upper right corner should be entered with caution. These countries have high/moderate political risk and high purchasing power. A firm also needs to assess the restrictions on business. For example, China and Singapore are both in the lower left corner of Table 18.4; however, Singapore has low restrictions on business while China has high restrictions. Finally, countries in the upper left corner should be avoided unless the expected returns far outweigh the risks.[31] These countries are characterized by high/moderate political risk and low/moderate purchasing power. Also, many of these countries, such as Portugal, Turkey, and Pakistan, have many restrictions on business.

FOREIGN MARKET ENTRY STRATEGIES

Once a firm decides to engage in international marketing, and assesses the foreign environments, it must decide the best way to enter foreign markets. Four possible market entry strategies are exporting, licensing, joint ventures, and direct ownership. Each of these four possibilities involves an increasing amount of commitment or involvement on the firm's behalf and thus allows the firm to have more control over its marketing efforts in foreign countries but at the same time involves higher investment risks (see Table 18.5).

Exporting

To minimize risk and investment, a firm may simply export its products to foreign markets by using the services of an export-import agent. An **export-import agent** *brings buyers and sellers from different countries together and collects a commission on all sales transacted.* This method involves a low investment because no permanent facilities need to be developed in a foreign country. In fact, all that may be necessary to prepare the product for sale in another country is some additional packaging to protect the product from damage in shipment and, perhaps, some relabeling of the product using a different language. The risk is also low because the export-import agent is only paid a commission if a sale is transacted. In addition, the company can terminate the relationship with the agent on relatively short notice. The biggest problem with using an export-import agent is that the company has no control over the pricing, promotion, distribution, or use of the product after it is sold. A firm in Dallas that is selling its products through an export-import agent to a firm in Nigeria has no idea how its products are being marketed or used in Nigeria, and even if it did know, it could not do anything to alter these marketing practices.

To gain more control over its export business, a company may establish a *company sales branch* in a foreign country. This sales branch would be

Table 18.4   Assessing Foreign Market Attractiveness

Political Risk	Purchasing Power			
	Low/Moderate		High	
High/moderate	Argentina	Peru	Poland	
	Turkey	Greece	Israel	
	Egypt	India	South Africa	
	Panama	Pakistan	Ireland	
	Portugal	Philippines	Italy	
	Yugoslavia	Burma	Libya	
	Mexico			
Low	Taiwan		Australia	Sweden
	South Korea		Canada	United Kingdom
	Chile		Finland	West Germany
	China		France	Belgium
	Singapore		Japan	New Zealand
	Brazil		Kuwait	Saudi Arabia
	Thailand		Norway	

Table 18.5   Risk and Control for Strategies of Foreign Market Entry

Foreign Market Entry Strategy	Investment Risk	Control of Marketing Efforts
Exporting	Low	Low
Licensing	Low	Moderate
Joint venture	Moderate	Moderate/high
Direct ownership	High	High

responsible for developing the foreign market by aggressively selling the firm's products and controlling the selling effort so that the products are sold to well-defined target markets using a uniform marketing program.

Licensing

Another strategy for market entry is **licensing.** Licensing to foreign countries is similar to domestic licensing discussed in Chapter 8 and involves *granting a firm in another country the right to produce and/or market your products for a fee.* It also may give the foreign firm the right to use certain patents, trademarks, or other technology. To secure these rights, the foreign firm typically pays a one-time fixed fee, such as $1 million, and a royalty fee, such as 2 percent of all sales.

Licensing is a low-investment form of market entry that also gives the firm some degree of control over the production and/or marketing of its product because the licensing agreement can stipulate that the foreign firm must follow certain production and marketing methods. Coca Cola uses licensing to market its products worldwide. Unfortunately, it is difficult to police production and marketing methods from thousands of miles away, and the foreign firm will not appreciate a licensor that stations someone in the foreign country to police the agreement. Another problem is that the licensee eventually acquires a certain degree of expertise and may decide it can do without the licensor. Westinghouse experienced this problem when it signed a licensing agreement with Framatome, a French company. Framatome grew from a minor atomic power producer in 1972, when the agreement was signed, to a major producer second only to Westinghouse in 1980, when the agreement was terminated.[32]

Joint Venture

A joint venture is a third way of entering a foreign market.[33] In a **joint venture,** the *firm becomes partners with a foreign firm and they share in financing, management, and decision-making responsibilities.* For example, Apple Computer entered into a joint venture with a group of Mexican industrialists to assemble personal computers in Mexico. The company, called *Apple de Mexico,* is 49 percent owned by Apple Computer and 51 percent owned by the Mexican industrialists.[34] One of the major advantages of a joint venture is that risk is shared between firms. The Mexican government told Apple Computer that it could own 100 percent of the computer assembly operations in Mexico, but Apple preferred to only own 49 percent. As E. Floyd Kramme, executive vice president for marketing and sales, explained, "We prefer 49 percent of something viable right out of the chute rather than 100 percent of something more risky."[35]

Joint ventures may be pursued for reasons other than their risk reduction potential, however. For example, some third world countries use joint ventures as a method of obtaining foreign capital. Other reasons to form a joint venture include gaining access to the foreign partner's distribution system and other specialized skills and knowledge of the local cultural and economic system. Fijitsu, Japan's largest computer manufacturer, needed the marketing knowledge and distribution to enter the highly competitive U.S. market and thus entered into a joint venture with TRW.[36]

Perhaps the biggest problem with a joint venture is one of cooperation. Cooperation is essential, but when tough decisions must be made, someone must have the final say or majority vote. Predictably, this can create conflict that may be difficult to resolve.

Direct Ownership

The most risky form of foreign market entry and the one involving the biggest commitment is **direct ownership,** *in which the firm establishes a wholly owned subsidiary in a foreign country.* Few firms will take this approach until they have tested the demand potential in a foreign country with another of the market entry strategies.

Direct ownership certainly allows the firm to have maximum control over its production and marketing activities. However, the firm runs the risk that its wholly owned subsidiary may be expropriated or confiscated by the host government. Also, the company may be required to invest the profits it earns in that same country.

Joint ventures and wholly owned subsidiaries are both forms of direct investment that vary in magnitude. A major reason for pursuing these two strategies is that many countries have high tariffs on imported goods. The way around the tariff is to build a production plant in the foreign country, which is precisely why Honda has a plant in Marysville, Ohio.

Market Research

Once an international marketing manager gets the green light to enter a foreign market, he or she must develop a marketing program for that market. An international marketing program, like a domestic marketing program, involves the selection of a target market and the marketing mix. One lesson that has been demonstrated repeatedly is that an international marketing program implemented without marketing research is a program for disaster. Money expended on international marketing research is usually money well spent. Unfortunately, conducting reliable and valid marketing research in foreign countries is often a difficult and frustrating experience. For example, high illiteracy may prevent people from responding to mail surveys; telephone surveys may be limited by the availability of phones; and long questionnaires may be discarded because of the time required to complete them. Sometimes questionnaires are not completed for surprising reasons. One firm found that questionnaires were not returned in parts of Africa because paper was a scarce commodity and the recipients wanted to keep the paper the questionnaires were printed on.

Many foreign countries in earlier stages of economic development in relation to the United States have less secondary data available. For example, demographic information, such as average household size, age distribution, educational levels, and retail sales by different lines of trade can be difficult to obtain in Chad and Algeria. Since the U.S. government is attempting to encourage more international marketing by U.S. firms, the U.S. Department of Commerce offers several international information sources, which are profiled in Table 18.6. An example of one of these sources, the export statistics profile, is given in Table 18.7.

PLANNING THE INTERNATIONAL MARKETING PROGRAM

Table 18.6   Export Information Services

Export Statistics Profile—A *new product* that provides a variety of export statistics by product and that arrays data in ways that make market analysis easy. Specific features of the profile include multiyear coverage, percentage market shares already calculated, and top markets for products rank-ordered. Profiles are available for select industries at three levels of depth and specification. The price for Level One is $30. It offers three tables showing aggregate export figures for products, countries, and regional areas. The price for Level Two is $70. It offers five tables (including those in Level One) showing individual export figures for specific products and countries. Additional information regarding the composition and price of Level Three Profiles is available on request.

Trade Opportunities Program (TOP) Notice Service—Trade opportunity notices are individual messages sent directly to Notice Service subscribers based on the subscriber's computerized interest profile. Each interest profile describes the industries, activities, and countries about which the subscriber desires information. Each message contains detailed information regarding a current foreign trade lead, typically including the specifications, quantities, end-use, delivery, and bid deadlines for the product or service desired by the foreign customer. These leads, developed by U.S. commercial officers at more than 200 American embassies and consulates worldwide, are telexed to the department's computer center in Washington, where they are matched by computer with the pertinent subscriber and transmitted via "speedmailer."

The TOP Notice Service is sold for $25.00 to set up the subscriber's interest profile, and $37.50, prepaid, for each block of fifty leads up to five blocks.

TOP Bulletin—A weekly publication of all trade leads at the computer center received during the prior week. Included are direct sales opportunities, overseas representation opportunities, and foreign government tenders. A year's subscription to the TOP Bulletin cost $175.

Trade Lists—Published lists of all foreign companies in a given industry or country included in the Commerce Department's automated Foreign Traders Index (FTI). The FTI encompasses over 145,000 firms worldwide in nearly all industry categories. The information provided on each firm includes name, address, key contact, telephone, cable, kind of business, and age of information. Trade Lists are useful in identifying a wide range of buyers, agents, distributors, manufacturers, and other potential business contacts abroad in a particular country or industry of interest. Trade Lists are priced from $12.00 to $40.00 each depending on the age of the publication.

Customized Export Mailing Lists (EMLs)—Custom-tailored lists of foreign companies in the particular industries, countries, or types of business requested by a client. EMLs, also drawn from the Foreign Traders Index, contain the same "profile" information on each firm as Trade Lists. Since they are more selective, however, they enable the client to specify only his/her most relevant potential contacts. EMLs are also available as gummed mailing labels to permit convenient, direct mailings to each listed firm. The charge for EMLs is $35 and up depending on country selection.

International Market Research (IMR) Surveys—In-depth analyses of the market for a given product category in a given country, ranging up to 400 pages in length. Each survey contains statistics and their interpretation, and also analyzes the market for select products, end-users, and their purchasing plans, marketing practices, and trade restrictions. IMRs also list key potential buyers, government purchasing agencies, and similar relevant organizations. IMRs are priced from $50 to $200.

Table 18.6 continued

Country Market Surveys (CMS)—The more detailed information in IMR surveys is abstracted into convenient, 10- to 15-page reports on a single industry in a single country. The CMS price is $10.00 per copy or $9.00 per copy for orders of six or more.

Global Market Surveys (GMS)—Compilation of individual Country Market Surveys for a given product category. GMS prices vary depending on the number of CMS contained in each.

Export Trading Company (ETC) Contact Facilitation Service—A computerized matching service to help ETC and other export support organizations, such as banks, find clients needing their services, and vice versa. Participants register in a central data base for matching by product interest. The names and addresses of the matched firms are provided to both the potential customers and service organizations for follow-up. There is no fee to register. To retrieve, the cost is $50 plus $5 per name.

World Traders Data Reports (WTDRs)—Background reports on individual foreign firms, containing information about each firm's business activities, its standing in the local business community, its credit-worthiness, and its overall reliability and suitability as a trade contact for U.S. exporters. WTDRs are prepared by U.S. commercial officers abroad. They are designed to help U.S. firms locate and evaluate potential foreign customers before making a business commitment. A typical WTDR includes:

- Name, address, and key contact
- Year established
- Number of Employees
- Sales territory
- Type of business
- Products handled
- General reputation in trade and financial circles
- An assessment of the firm's suitability as a trade contact

WTDRs cost $75 per report.

Agent Distributor Service (ADS)—A custom overseas "search" for interested and qualified foreign representatives on behalf of a U.S. client. U.S. commercial officers abroad conduct the search and prepare a report identifying up to six foreign prospects that have personally examined the U.S. firm's product literature and have expressed interest in representing the firm. The ADS charge is $90 per market or specific area.

Source: U.S. Department of Commerce, Office of Trade Information Services, P.O. Box 14207, Washington, DC 20044.

Target Market

Simply because a product sells well to a particular domestic market segment does not mean that a similar target market can be reached outside the United States. Buick and Pontiac are considered middle-income cars in the United States, but in Nigeria, they are definitely for the wealthy. A firm must study carefully the foreign environments to determine the best target market(s). McDonald's has successfully identified families with young children as their primary target market in all countries they have entered; Ronald

Table 18.7 Export Statistics Profiles[a]

Level 1
Total Sales of Medical Instrument Subgroup to Major World Trade Areas

	1978	1979	1980	1981	1982
European Community	312	390	439	511	583
Asia	194	256	277	343	349
North America	154	176	215	260	258
Total for industry	1,352	1,666	2,006	2,341	2,402

Total Sales of Medical Equipment to Top 75 Countries

	1978	1979	1980	1981	1982
Canada	213	238	291	333	344
Japan	158	236	260	280	264
Germany, West	124	163	197	192	197
Total for top 75	1,342	1,652	1,989	2,322	2,390
Total, all countries	1,352	1,666	2,006	2,341	2,402

Exports of Individual Medical Equipment Products to World

	1978	1979	1980	1981	1982
7091605					
Pacemakers	46	46	51	56	54
7095000					
Hearing aids	10	12	14	15	17
4385500					
Opacifying preps.	7	9	12	14	12
Total, all products	1,352	1,666	2,006	2,341	2,402

Level 2
Total Sales of Zener Diodes to Top 75 Countries

	1978	1979	1980	1981	1982
Germany, West	6.0	6.7	9.5	6.4	5.8
Canada	1.6	9.2	2.1	2.4	2.1
Hong Kong	2.1	2.9	2.3	1.8	1.8
Total for top 75	15.8	17.1	23.7	21.0	15.1
Total, all countries	15.9	17.2	23.8	21.1	15.2

Level 3
Exports of Individual Electronic Components to the United Kingdom

	1978	1979	1980	1981	1982
6876087					
Chips, dice, wafers	7.5	7.9	12.7	10.7	9.9
6876062					
Thyristors	0.5	0.8	0.6	0.4	0.5
6876059					
Zener diodes	0.5	0.7	0.7	0.5	0.5
Total, all products to U.K.	188.4	233.8	275.7	259.8	331.8

[a]Figures in millions of dollars. Rank order as of 1982.

Source: Brochure by Richard L. Barovick. *Commerce Department Expands Its Export Information Services* (Washington, DC: U.S. Department of Commerce).

Sometimes the target market is the same both within and outside the United States, as McDonalds has successfully learned.

McDonald speaks many languages, including Japanese. Sometimes, however, the target market the firm has in the United States may be totally different from that in a foreign country. For example, in the United States, most records are sold to 12- to 18-year-olds, but in countries such as Pakistan and India, this age group does not have such purchasing power or access to a stereo.

Marketing Mix

When entering a foreign market, a firm could pursue three basic marketing mix options: (1) the marketing mix could remain unchanged, (2) certain elements could be modified, or (3) a totally new mix could be developed. If the marketing mix is unchanged, it is called a *standardized marketing mix*. In this situation, product, price, promotion, and place elements are essentially identical on both domestic and international markets. Price could obviously be slightly different depending on cost considerations, but the same basic pricing strategy would be used, such as penetration or skimming (see Chapter 17). Marlboro and Coca-Cola have been successful with their standardized marketing mixes since their products have universal appeal. The Marlboro cowboy image and the youthful Coke image have been well received in many countries.

The more similar environments are, the more successful standardization will be (i.e., the United States and Canada), which suggests that firms initially might wish to enter the foreign markets that are most similar to their own because the marketing program could be easily transplanted without modification, thus minimizing costs. A second rationale for a standardized marketing mix is the existence of some cross-cultural appeal. This could account for Coca-Cola's and Marlboro's successes.

A modification of the mix can occur in one or any combination of the mix elements. Although our discussion will treat each element separately, a change in one element obviously will affect the marketing mix as a whole.

Product. A firm often finds it necessary to *modify* its product(s) to meet local tastes and conditions. Food companies, such as Nestle and Pillsbury, alter their products' ingredients to meet local tastes. Firms may also modify their products' features. For example, NCR (National Cash Register) eliminates the electronics from cash registers in parts of Asia and sells hand-cranked models. Table 18.8 lists some of the key factors that determine the need to modify a product for a foreign market.

Sometimes product modification may not be feasible, and a totally new product must be developed. For example, General Motors developed a low cost jeeplike vehicle that could withstand rough dirt roads in many developing countries such as Kenya. The low cost also was necessary because of the low per capita income in these countries. Another example is Colgate-Palmolive's development of a low price, all plastic, manual washing machine that could be used in homes without electricity. Since an estimated 600 million people still scrub their clothes by hand, the market potential for this product is phenomenal. Obviously, the development of a new product is more costly than product modification. The profitability may be higher, however, if the new product can generate a sufficiently greater demand.

Distribution. International distribution channels can only be identical to the domestic ones if similar distribution institutions exist and buyers patronize similar institutions.[37] For example, Procter & Gamble cannot sell soap worldwide through the same distribution channels as in the United States because supermarkets are not a universal form of retailing. Thus, in some countries, P & G sells soap door-to-door, in drugstores, and in small food markets, depending on what retail institutions are available and on where customers are used to buying soap.

To get wholesale and retail distribution in foreign countries, the international marketing manager often needs to "grease" the channel by paying bribes.[38] Even though this violates the Foreign Corrupt Practices Act, there is often no way around these payments. Developing a corporate marketing channel may be too expensive or impossible if the families that control distribution also control the banks and politicians. The choice is sometimes between paying the bribe and not marketing products in that country.

One of the biggest problems in dealing with foreign middlemen is in controlling how they handle the product.[39] It is very difficult to tell a foreign businessperson how to handle and promote a product—after all, once they purchase the product, they own it and can do with it as they see fit. Although this problem also occurs in domestic channels, it is intensified in foreign channels because of cultural and language differences.

Logistics problems often occur if the product is manufactured domestically and shipped to a foreign market.[40] Because distribution costs can be a major part of the marketing costs, the best mode of transportation must be carefully determined. For example, if the total costs of distribution are considered, it may be cheaper to use air transportation than water transportation, as is illustrated in Table 18.9.

Careful attention to customer service levels must be maintained. If a product is being shipped over great distances, across many foreign borders, it is easy to lose track of the shipment and difficult to keep it on schedule.

Table 18.8 Product Characteristics for Foreign Markets

Key Factor	Design Change
Level of technical skills	Product simplification
Level of labor costs	Automation or manualization of product
Level of literacy	Remaking and simplification of product
Level of income	Quality and price change
Level of interest rates	Quality and price change (investment in high quality might not be financially desirable)
Level of maintenance	Change in tolerances
Climatic differences	Product adaptation
Isolation (heavy repair, difficult and expensive)	Product simplification and reliability improvement
Differences in standards	Recalibration of product and resizing
Availability of other products	Greater or lesser product integration
Availability of materials	Change in product structure and fuel
Power availability	Resizing of product
Special conditions	Product redesign or invention

Source: Dr. Richard Robinson. Used by permission.

If you promise a foreign customer a product in four weeks and it takes eight weeks or even six months to get there, then repeat business will be difficult to obtain. In addition, since the product may be transported by several different modes, it may receive a lot of rough handling. Imagine a product that is shipped by rail from a U.S. manufacturing plant in Toledo to Los Angeles, where it is loaded on a ship going to Chile. In Chile, it is loaded onto a truck that takes it to a wholesaler; this wholesaler stores the product and then ships it by truck to another wholesaler, who, after storing it for several weeks, transports it by truck to a retail store. It is no wonder that many products get damaged in this process and arrive weeks, if not months, late. The firm that best protects its products from damage in international transit and delivers them on time will be able to offer better customer service and thus have an attractive marketing tool at its disposal.

Promotion. Many firms standardize their international promotion efforts.[41] For example, Esso's "tiger in the tank" campaign was translated into different languages: "Pack'den Tiger in den Tank" (West Germany), "Stop 'n Tijger in uw Tank" (Netherlands), "Mettez un tigre dans votre moteur" (France), and "Netti un tigre nel motore" (Italy).[42] However, numerous unfortunate language bloopers have been made by firms that didn't realize the connotations of certain words. For example, Chrysler used the slogan "Dart is power," which, when translated into Spanish, implied that customers lacked (but were seeking) sexual vigor. American Motors found that their brand "Matador" meant "killer" in Puerto Rico, and Ford learned that their brand "Fiera" meant "ugly old woman" in Spanish.[43]

Table 18.9 Cost Comparison of International Surface Transportation with Air Distribution: A Case History

Product: Scroll Cutting Line Used in Can-Producing Firm
Weight: 56 tons
Origin: Chicago, Illinois, USA
Destination: Denmark
Cost of Machine Down Time: $2,000 per day

Comparative Shipping and Handling Costs

Surface		Air	
$14,000	Crating for export (5 men, 3 weeks, 5,000 ft of lumber)	$ 300	Cost of applying thin coat of oil, wrapping units in vinyl film
2,000	Land transportation to port		
782	Dock charges (truck to pier charge, heavy lift charge)	200	Pallets
		500	Truck to airport
8,000	Ocean freight	28,195	Air freight
600	Overseas dock charge	500	Truck to factory
700	Land transportation to factory	500	Take units off pallets, unwrap vinyl film, wipe
2,500	Uncrating, getting rid of 5,000 ft of broken lumber, wiping off cosmolene		
$28,582		**$30,195**	

Loss in Production Time

Surface		Air	
24	Days to crate for export	1½	Days to apply thin coat of oil, wrap in vinyl film, and palletise
7	Days to truck to port	½	Day to truck to airport
14	Days on the ocean	3	Days to load and fly two planeloads overseas
14	Days in customs storage		
3	Days from port to factory	3	Days to truck to factory
12	Days to uncrate	2	Days to unload, unwrap, wipe off
4	Days to wipe off the cosmolene		
78	Days × $2,000 = $156,000	**10**	Days × $2,000 = $20,000

Total Cost for Surface and Air Distribution

Surface		Air	
$ 28,582	Shipping and handling	$30,195	Shipping and handling
156,000	Loss in production time	20,000	Loss in production time
$184,582	Total cost	**$50,195**	Total cost

Source: Adapted from advertisement entitled "They Exploded the Myth that Heavy Equipment Was too Damned Expensive to Ship by Air," in the *Wall Street Journal,* February 23, 1971, p. 10; James R. Stock and Douglas M. Lambert. "International Physical Distribution—A Marketing Perspective," *International Journal of Physical Distribution and Materials Management* 12 (November 2, 1982), p. 11. Used by permission.

Because of these sorts of translation problems, it sometimes may be best to develop new promotional themes in foreign countries.[44] Also, all advertising should be related to buyer motivation. For example, sexual themes may motivate buyers to purchase jeans in the United States, but this is not true in all cultures; in fact, sexual themes are taboo in many cultures.

It is very difficult to standardize a firm's advertising program worldwide. Even if the theme is standardized, frequently the media plan must be altered because of various technical, economic, and legal factors.[45] Consider, for example, the following[46]:

❑ Austria taxes the advertising media, and the tax can vary by state, municipality, and media type.

❑ Comparative advertising is against the law in Germany.

❑ A string of ten to fifty commercials is shown during one station break in Brazil.

❑ Lebanon, with a population of less than 2 million, has 210 newspapers, and only four have a circulation of over 10,000.

❑ One research study revealed that the cost of reaching 1,000 magazine readers in eleven different European countries ranged from $1.58 in Belgium to $5.91 in Italy.

❑ Television advertising directed at children is banned in Quebec, Canada, as are commercials that urge people to borrow money.

In addition to making advertising decisions, the international marketing manager must also determine sales force management and personal selling techniques. Since people in different cultures respond differently to salespeople, standardizing personal selling techniques is difficult. For example, in some countries, door-to-door selling is in bad taste, or negotiation with the salesperson is expected in order to arrive at the final price and terms of trade (such as credit and delivery). If the company uses salespeople in its promotion efforts, it must also decide how to recruit, train, and motivate these salespeople. Again, standardization may not be possible. In the United States, it may be possible to recruit college graduates for many sales positions, but in some foreign countries, college graduates may be too scarce to employ as salespeople. Also, formal training programs are popular in the United States, but in some countries, the sales force (at least initially) may be too small to justify a formal training program. The methods of motivating salespeople also may be culturally determined. For example, the mix of salary, commission, and fringe benefits may vary depending on the needs of salespeople in different countries.

Price.   The price charged in the foreign market is seldom identical to that charged domestically because of differences in costs of many things, such as transportation, advertising, selling, and middlemen markups. Special tariffs and taxes on foreign products also cause price variances. One major cost factor that affects foreign prices is the allocation of overhead and fixed costs, such as research and development. When *a firm ignores these fixed costs and merely assesses marginal or variable costs, the price arrived at can be lower than it charges domestically.* This practice is called **dumping.** The Japanese have been accused of dumping such products as autos and televisions in the United States because the U.S. price is often lower than that charged in Japan for the same product.

Because of the differences in costs experienced in different countries, most firms use some form of cost-plus pricing to set foreign prices. Demand factors do need to be analyzed, although most firms concentrate on covering their costs first. Importantly, however, there is no effective way of controlling the price the final buyer pays, unless the firm operates its own retail outlets in the foreign country or sells directly to the buyer. If the product is sold to a foreign wholesaler or retailer, they will set the price on the product that the market will bear. This price may not be the price the manufacturer would have chosen.

Foreign prices are also a function of foreign currency exchange rates. A **foreign currency exchange rate** is *the price of one country's money in terms of another country's money (i.e., 1 U.S. dollar equals 5 French francs, or a franc costs 20¢).* The foreign currency exchange rates fluctuate just as do the prices of most objects. For example, in 1983, the British pound was worth approximately $1.52, but by early 1985, it was only worth $1.10. This represented a drop in value of the pound versus the dollar or a rise in the value of the dollar versus the pound.

When the U.S. dollar rises in value against foreign currencies, U.S. products sold in foreign markets become more expensive and foreign products sold in U.S. markets become less expensive. Consider the rise in value of the U.S. dollar versus the British pound and how this might affect the price of an IBM personal computer sold in England. If the price of an IBM PC was $3,000 in 1983, this would translate into 2,000 pounds ($3,000/1.50 exchange rate = 2,000). Recall that a single pound was worth $1.50. Now, assuming the $3,000 price remains unchanged and that the exchange rate drops to $1.10 (as it did in early 1985), then the price in pounds is $3,000 divided by $1.10, or 2,727 pounds. Thus, the price of the IBM PC in London increased from 2,000 to 2,727 pounds. Obviously, this increase makes it more difficult for IBM to export its products. At the same time, British firms will be better able to penetrate the U.S. market. For example, assume that in 1983, British Caledonia prices its round-trip airfare from London to New York City at 500 pounds, which would be equal to $750 (500 × 1.50 = 750). If the price is held at 500 pounds, then in early 1985, the price in dollars would be $550 (500 × 1.10 = 550).

Table 18.10 illustrates how the U.S. dollar has gained in value against several foreign currencies. The trend of a strong U.S. dollar since 1980 has been a major cause of the U.S. balance of trade deficit since it has caused U.S. products to be priced less competitively in foreign markets and thus has hurt U.S. exports. At the same time, foreign products have been priced more competitively in U.S. markets, which increases U.S. imports.

In international trade, the price is often nonmonetary and involves the

Table 18.10   Fluctuating Foreign Exchange Rates[a]

Country	Currency	1965	1970	1975	1980	1985
Australia	Dollar	$2.23	$1.11	$1.31	$1.14	.71
Canada	Dollar	0.93	0.96	0.98	0.86	.73
France	Franc	0.20	0.18	0.23	0.24	.10
West Germany	Deutsche mark	0.25	0.27	0.41	0.55	.32
Italy[b]	Lira	0.16	0.16	0.15	0.12	.05
Japan[b]	Yen	0.28	0.28	0.34	0.44	.39
South Africa	Rand	1.39	1.39	1.36	1.29	.50
United Kingdom	Pound	2.80	2.40	2.22	2.33	1.19

[a]U.S. dollars per unit of foreign currency.

[b]U.S. cents per unit of foreign currency.

Source: Board of Governors of the Federal Reserve System. *Federal Reserve Bulletin* (monthly).

bartering or exchange of one commodity or service for another. For example, one country will trade machinery for another country's copper. *An international trade that is not transacted totally in cash* is referred to as **countertrade**—barter is the most popular type of countertrade.[47]

Over the last 5 to 10 years, countertrade has grown rapidly. An estimated 50 percent of the Fortune 500 companies regularly engage in countertrade.[48] and as much as 20 percent of the $2 trillion in world trade is countertrade.[49] One notable example of the growth of countertrade is Motors Trading Corp., which was established as a subsidiary of General Motors in late 1979. By 1983, it was estimated that Motors Trading Corp. was transacting hundreds of millions of dollars in annual countertrade volume.[50]

Countertrade has grown because many countries with huge trade deficits are trying to protect or conserve hard currency. In addition, countertrade helps to protect weak domestic industries. In fact, to stimulate countertrade, some countries such as Brazil, Mexico, Korea, and Indonesia have required it by law. Almost all centrally planned Soviet bloc nations require countertrade in dealings with the West.

The major disadvantage of countertrade is that it prevents other firms that are not part of the countertrade agreement from competing, thus locking them out of sometimes lucrative markets even if they have better prices or better quality products. Consider, for example, an agreement by Canada to purchase $2.4 billion in F-18 jet fighters from McDonnell Douglas Corp. McDonnell Douglas Corp. had to agree to provide over $2 billion worth of benefits to Canada over fifteen years. This deal included an agreement that McDonnell Douglas would subcontract $349 million worth of parts to Canadian firms, which excludes some other parts makers from McDonnell Douglas' business.[51] The Marketing in Action on page 580 provides another example of countertrade.

MARKETING IN ACTION

How to Sell Chrysler Trucks to Jamaica via Countertrade

Jamaica is short on currency and credit. In order for Chrysler to sell trucks to Jamaica, it had to enter into a complex countertrade agreement. First, American and Canadian mining companies that mine bauxite in Jamaica and refine it into alumina must give 50,000 tons of alumina to a trading company owned by the Jamaican government. The Jamaican trading company then gives the alumina to Metallgesellschaft, a German metal company. In turn, Metallgesellschaft sells the alumina to a German-based refiner, who converts it to aluminum. Most of the money Metallgesellschaft receives from the refi-ner is deposited with the European American Bank, which is Chrysler's adviser in Europe. Next, the bank transfers part of the money to a Jamaican trading company, which in turn, pays the American and Canadian mining companies. The remainder of the money goes to finance a letter of credit made out to Chrysler. When Chrysler receives the letter of credit, it ships its trucks to Jamaica. At this point, another government-owned Jamaican trading company (different from the one referred to earlier) takes title to the trucks. The trading company sells the trucks to a local Chrysler dealer, and the dealer then sells the trucks to the public.

Source: John W. Dizard. "The Explosion of International Barter," *Fortune* (February 7, 1983), pp. 88–95. Used by permission.

SUMMARY

This chapter discussed the importance of international marketing and how firms engage in and practice international marketing. We discussed the growth of international marketing since World War II and the recent unfavorable merchandise balance of trade in the United States. The growth of multinational corporations and the praise and criticism surrounding them were also highlighted.

Firms that engage in international marketing adopt one of three orientations—ethnocentrism, polycentrism, and geocentrism. In an ethnocentric orientation, a foreign country operation is viewed as secondary or as a child of the domestic operation. A polycentric orientation occurs when the firm establishes an autonomous subsidiary in each foreign country. A geocentric orientation views the world as a single market.

Before entering a foreign market, the firm must attempt to understand foreign market environments. Especially important are the social, legal/political, and economic environments, but the physical, technological, competitive, and ethical environments must be considered as well. After researching these environments, the firm should identify the most attractive markets to enter. A foreign market is attractive if it has (1) high political stability, (2) few restrictions on business, and (3) a high demand or market potential for the firm's product(s).

Some possible strategies for entering foreign markets are exporting, licensing, joint ventures, and direct ownership. Exporting is the least risky strategy but provides little control of the firm's marketing efforts, whereas direct ownership provides a good means for controlling marketing efforts but is the most risky strategy.

Once the firm decides how to enter a foreign market, it must develop a marketing program. The international marketing program, like a domestic marketing program, involves the selection of a target market and development of the marketing mix. The marketing mix could remain unchanged from the domestic marketing mix, certain elements could be modified, or a totally new mix could be developed. Usually, some aspect of the mix is modified, such as product attributes, distribution channels, advertising media, or price. Product attributes could be modified because technical skills, consumer incomes, climate, or a variety of other factors in the foreign environment are different. Distribution channels could be different because some types of middlemen (especially retailers) may not exist in foreign countries. Media types may be different because of literacy and technology, and language translation problems naturally create additional advertising obstacles. Finally, price may differ because of tariffs, foreign exchange rate differentials, and differing margin requirements for middlemen.

KEY CONCEPTS

international marketing (p. 550)
exporting (p. 552)
importing (p. 552)
balance of trade (p. 552)
balance of payments (p. 552)
multinational corporation (MNC)
  (pp. 554–555)
ethnocentrism (p. 557)
polycentrism (p. 557)
geocentrism (p. 557)

confiscation (p. 564)
expropriation (p. 564)
export-import agent (p. 566)
licensing (pp. 567–568)
joint venture (p. 568)
direct ownership (p. 569)
dumping (p. 578)
foreign currency exchange rate (p. 578)
countertrade (p. 579)

REVIEW AND DISCUSSION QUESTIONS

1. What differences and similarities do you see between domestic marketing and international marketing?

2. What does the term *balance of trade* mean and what is its relation to imports and exports?

3. What is a multinational corporation and why have they been both praised and criticized?

4. Contrast and compare the ethnocentric, polycentric, and geocentric approaches toward international marketing.

5. Why are culturally based marketing errors so common in international marketing?

6. Which is a better indicator of the market potential for automobiles in a country,

aggregate GNP or per capita GNP? What other information would be useful in assessing the market potential for automobiles in foreign markets?

7. Why are some products more politically vulnerable or risky than others?

8. Explain confiscation and expropriation as they relate to international marketing. Why should these factors be considered in deciding which markets to enter?

9. How should a firm decide which foreign markets to enter?

10. Define four basic foreign market entry strategies. How do these strategies vary on investment risk and the ability to control marketing efforts?

11. What are the advantages and disadvantages of entering a foreign market through a licensing agreement?

12. In developing an international marketing program, how should a firm decide if its target market needs to be changed?

13. When can a firm enter a foreign market without changing its marketing mix?

14. List at least five factors in a foreign environment that would cause a firm to modify its products before marketing them in a foreign country.

15. What are some of the distribution problems in international marketing?

16. Explain why use of air transportation in shipping products to foreign countries can be cheaper than use of water transportation.

17. Why is it difficult to standardize international advertising?

18. Name some factors beyond a firm's control that can influence the price it charges for its products in foreign markets.

19. Explain the consequences on the U.S. auto industry of a 50 percent decline in the U.S. dollar value in relation to the Japanese yen.

20. Describe and give an example of countertrade.

ACTION PROBLEMS

1. Assume there is a major breakthrough in a series of trade negotiations between the United States and the USSR and that both countries agree to lift all restrictions on trade for 180 days. At the end of this period, the results will be judged and trade policies renegotiated. Write a 500-word essay on what you believe would be the consequences of free trade between the superpowers.

2. You are selling earth-moving equipment to a foreign government where it is customary to provide gifts to the key decision makers in the purchasing process in order to win business. You receive an 8 percent commission on all sales, and the government you are negotiating with is embarking on a major road-building project and will need twelve large earth movers, at a cost of $500,000 each. The customary gift for a sale of this size is $100,000, to be given to two key government decision makers. Explain what you would do in this situation.

3. Locate a foreign student from Saudi Arabia, Nigeria, Pakistan, India, Turkey, Korea, or Japan on your campus and show him or her three or four magazine advertisements for cologne, cigarettes, alcoholic beverages, jeans, or swimwear. Ask the student to identify aspects of the advertisement that are favorable or

unfavorable and to explain his or her reasoning. Note: If you are a student from one of these countries, then you may respond to this action problem without interviewing another student.

NOTES

1. This definition is similar to the one presented in Philip R. Cateora and John M. Hess, *International Marketing* (Homewood, IL: Richard D. Irwin, 1979), p. 4.

2. Warren J. Keegan, *Multinational Marketing Management,* 3rd edition (Englewood Cliffs, NJ: Prentice-Hall, 1984), p. 115.

3. "Fighting Back: It Can Work," *BusinessWeek* (August 26, 1985), pp. 62–68. Japan's success has also been due to the refined development of *sogo shoshas* (international trading companies); see Kuang-Ming Lin and W.R. Hosking, "Understanding Japan's International Trading Companies," *Business* (September–October 1981), pp. 20–31.

4. "A Shoemaker Kicks Back at Imports," *BusinessWeek* (September 19, 1983), pp. 37–38.

5. Robert S. Attiyeh and David L. Wenner, "Critical Mass: Key to Export Profits," *Business Horizons* (December 1979), pp. 28–38.

6. "America's Hidden Problem," *BusinessWeek* (August 29, 1983), pp. 66–71.

7. H. Ralph Jones, "Clearing the Way for Exporters," *Business Horizons* (October 1980), pp. 26–32.

8. "The Riding Winds of Trade War," *BusinessWeek* (September 19, 1983), pp. 37–38.

9. James Livingstone, *The International Enterprise* (New York: John Wiley & Sons, 1975).

10. David A. Heenan and Warren J. Keegan, "The Rise of Third World Multinationals," *Harvard Business Review* (January–February 1979), pp. 101–109.

11. John Kenneth Galbraith, "The Defense of the Multinational Company," *Harvard Business Review* (March–April 1978), pp. 83–93.

12. Peter P. Gabriel, "Management of Public Interest by Multinational Corporations," *Journal of World Trade* 11(No. 1, 1977), pp. 15–36.

13. V.H. Kirpalani, *International Marketing* (New York: Random House, 1985), p. 73.

14. The following discussion is based on Yoram Wind, Susan P. Douglas, and Howard V. Perlmutter, "Guidelines for Developing International Marketing Strategies," *Journal of Marketing* (April 1973), pp. 14–23.

15. Because of differences in environments, market information is very important; see "Global Marketing Success Is Contingent on a Solid Bank of Foreign Market Intelligence," *Marketing News* (December 23, 1983), pp. 1, 12.

16. Avind Phatak, *Managing Multinational Corporations* (New York: Praeger, 1974), p. 139.

17. Some of these examples are adapted from David Ricks et al., *International Business Blunders* (Columbus, OH: Grid, 1974); Charles S. Mayer, "The Lessons of Multinational Marketing Research," *Business Horizons* (December 1978), pp. 7–13; Vern Terpstra, *International Marketing,* 3rd edition (Chicago: The Dryden Press, 1983), p. 284.

18. Keegan, *Multinational Marketing Management,* p. 62.

19. This is a direct quote from Philip Kotler, *Marketing Management: Analysis, Planning and Control* (Englewood Cliffs, NJ: Prentice-Hall, 1984), pp. 447, © 1984. Reprinted by permission of Prentice-Hall, Englewood Cliffs, New Jersey.

20. Note also that different categorizations exist, see W.W. Rostow, *The Stages of Economic Growth* (Oxford: Cambridge University Press, 1961).

21. Thomas C. Kinnear and Kenneth L. Bernhardt, *Principles of Marketing* (Glenview, IL: Scott, Foresman and Company 1983), p. 734; Cateora and Hess, *International Marketing*, p. 64; Vern Terpstra, *The Cultural Environment of International Business* (Cincinnati, OH: South-Western Publishing Co., 1978), pp. 268–269.

22. Interestingly, U.S. principles of antitrust have been adopted and similar laws enacted in many European countries; see Robert T. Jones, "Executive's Guide to Antitrust in Europe," *Harvard Business Review* (May–June 1976), pp. 106–118.

23. "Marginal Competition Enough to Knock Out Gillette Acquisition," *Business International* (July 25, 1975), pp. 234–235; "The Antitruster Aim Overseas," *BusinessWeek* (March 14, 1977), p. 100.

24. Jack G. Kaikati and Wayne A. Label, "American Bribery Legislation: An Obstacle to International Marketing," *Journal of Marketing* (Fall 1980), pp. 38–43.

25. Cateora and Hess, *International Marketing*, p. 157.

26. Measurement of political risk is discussed in Lars H. Thunell, *Political Risks in International Business: Investment Behavior of Multinational Corporations* (New York: Praeger, 1977); F.T. Haner, "Rating Investment Risks Abroad," *Business Horizons* (April 1979), pp. 18–23.

27. Peter Nehemkis, "Expropriation Has a Silver Lining," *California Management Review* (Fall 1974), p. 15.

28. Gene R. Laczniak and Jacob Naor, "Global Ethics: Wrestling with the Corporate Conscience," *Business* (July–August–September 1985), pp. 3–10.

29. The rate of entering foreign markets and the allocation of resources to these markets are discussed in Igal Ayal and Jehiel Zif, "Market Expansion Strategies in Multinational Marketing," *Journal of Marketing* (Spring 1979), pp. 84–94.

30. Using political instability and restrictions on business as factors to assess foreign markets is discussed in Bob Donath, "Handicapping and Hedging the Foreign Investment," *Industrial Marketing* (February 1981), pp. 56–58, 60–61.

31. This could be due to the foreign government offering incentives to induce the firm to enter the market; see Robert Weigand, "International Investments: Weighing the Incentives," *Harvard Business Review* (July–August 1983), pp. 146–152.

32. Terpstra, *International Marketing*, p. 346.

33. How to successfully structure a joint venture is discussed in J. Peter Killing, *Strategies for Joint Venture Success* (New York: Praeger, 1983).

34. "What Made Apple Seek Safety in Numbers," *BusinessWeek* (March 21, 1984), p. 42.

35. Ibid., p. 42.

36. Cateora and Hess, *International Marketing*, p. 15; Terpstra, *International Marketing*, p. 350.

37. Innovations in retailing occur in different countries at different times; see Johan Arndt, "Temporal Lags in Comparative Retailing," *Journal of Marketing* (October 1972), pp. 40–45.

38. Stan Reid and James McGoldrick, "Greasing the Foreign Channel Mechanism," in Bruce J. Walker et al., *An Assessment of Marketing Thought and Practice* (Chicago, IL: American Marketing Association, 1982), pp. 318–321.

39. One of the keys is selecting the best and most cooperative middleman; see S. Tamer Cavusgil, "Exporters Wrestle with Market and Distributor Selection Problems in Penetrating New Markets," *Marketing News* (December 23, 1983), p. 10.

40. For a thorough discussion of international logistics, see James R. Stock and Douglas M. Lambert, "International Physical Distribution: A Marketing Perspective," *International Journal of Physical Distribution and Materials Management* 12(No. 2 1982), pp. 3–39.

41. Ralph Z. Sorenson and Ulrich E. Wiechmann, "How Multinationals View Marketing Standardization," *Harvard Business Review* (May–June 1975), pp. 38–55, 167.

42. Cateora and Hess, *International Marketing,* p. 423.

43. Ibid., p. 426.

44. Europe is discussed in S. Watson Dunn, "Effect of National Identity on Multinational Promotional Strategy in Europe," *Journal of Marketing* 40 (October 1976), pp. 50–57.

45. For example, advertising is regulated in many countries; see J.J. Boddewyn, "The Global Spread of Advertising Regulation," *MSU Business Topics* (Spring 1981), pp. 5–13.

46. Cateora and Hess, *International Marketing,* pp. 422–436.

47. For a more complete discussion of countertrade, see Robert E. Weigand, "International Trade Without Money," *Harvard Business Review* (November–December 1977), pp. 28–30, 34, 38, 42, 166.

48. Philip Maher, "The Countertrade Boom," *Business Marketing* (January 1984), p. 50.

49. John W. Dizard, "The Explosion of International Barter," *Fortune* (February 7, 1983), p. 89.

50. Ibid.

51. Maher, "The Countertrade Boom," p. 52.

## CHAPTER 19

SERVICES MARKETING

LEARNING OBJECTIVES

After you complete this chapter, you should be able to:

- **List** and **discuss** the five major characteristics that distinguish services from tangible products

- **Discuss** the competitive environment surrounding service products

- **Explain** the six aspects of consumer behavior that differ between service products and tangible products

- **Explain** how to develop a marketing program for service products

- **Discuss** and **provide examples** of the three major strategies for improving productivity in services marketing

MARKETER PROFILE

Jo-Ann Friedman of Health Marketing Systems, Inc.

Founder and president of Health Marketing Systems, Inc., Jo-Ann Friedman parlayed a six-month bout with a poliolike paralysis into a decision to market home health care services and goods. Speaking of her disease, which forced her to spend five months convalescing at home, she says, "It sure was a nice reintroduction to what had happened in home health care." She found that rising health care costs were forcing patients to leave the hospital sooner and recuperate at home longer. She also discovered that the consumer market for health care services and goods was practically virgin territory.

Friedman was no stranger to the fields of health and marketing when she founded Health Marketing Systems, Inc. Her early training was in speech therapy, and she eventually rose to chief of the speech pathology department at Albert Einstein College Hospital. In 1971, she left the hospital to work at Medcom, a pharmaceuticals marketing firm. Then came an opportunity to work as a consultant for Best Foods of Englewood Cliffs, New Jersey, where she helped mainstream nutritional marketing with her "ask your doctor" campaign.

When she founded Health Marketing Systems in 1976, she hoped to do for the home health care market what she had done for nutritional marketing. To this end, she has written a book entitled *Home Health*

Care: A Complete Guide for Patients and Their Families. In her book, Friedman intends to make consumers aware of home health care options just as in her office she makes health care marketers aware of the consumers at home.

Source: Based on Lenore Skenazy. "Friedman's Homecare Diagnosis," *Advertising Age* (October 3, 1985), p. 62.

INTRODUCTION

In 1985, U.S. consumers spent approximately 1.8 trillion dollars on services, including such things as air travel, life insurance, medical care, electricity, college tuition, and landscaping. In addition, business organizations spent an enormous amount on such services as legal advice, accounting, advertising, maintenance, insurance, car rentals, and hotel and motel rooms. The U.S. government is also a large purchaser of services. For example, in 1983, the Department of Defense paid RCA $49.5 million for the operation and maintenance of thirteen Alaskan Air Command Stations.[1]

The growth of Health Marketing Systems is only one example of the explosive growth in the service sector of the U.S. economy. Witness the growth of firms such as Kelly Girl (temporary help services), Federal Express (overnight parcel delivery), MCI (phone service), Avis (car rental), Mary Moppets (child care), and Service Master Industries. What is Service Master? Service Master is essentially a handyman for educational institutions, hospitals, and other organizations. For example, hospitals employ Service Master to do laundry, housekeeping, equipment maintenance, and food preparation and order medical supplies.[2] Service Master is unique because, from 1974 to 1983, it was the most profitable of the 1,000 largest corporations in the United States in terms of average return on stockholder's equity. During this period, it averaged 30.1 percent return of equity (after taxes). In 1983, it had annual sales of approximately $700 million.

The United States, West Germany, and France are often thought of as industrial countries because of their records for producing manufactured products in highly automated factories. The truth is, however, that these countries, as well as many others, have stronger and more dominant service sectors than manufacturing sectors. The data in Table 19.1 clearly reveal this surprising fact. Because of the large role services play in the world economy, this chapter will acquaint you with some of the unique phenomena confronting service marketers.

HOW SERVICES DIFFER FROM GOODS

In Chapter 3, we defined services as largely intangible tasks that satisfy buyer or user needs. In this chapter, we will explain why these intangible tasks require different marketing approaches than those required for goods, which are tangible products. Although services are indeed different from goods, most of the principles needed to develop a marketing plan for goods (i.e., market segmentation, product, price, promotion, and place) can also be applied to services. However, the application of these previously learned principles requires an understanding of how services differ from tangible products.[3] To this end, we will discuss the problems caused by intangibility, inseparability of production and consumption, heterogeneity, and perishability.

Intangibility

The major problem that intangibility creates is the difficulty the customer has in judging the value of the service before it is actually purchased. For example, Energy Consultants sells brain power to public utilities. Unfortunately, a utility can only decide whether the service is valuable after they have used it. Knowledge is one of the most difficult products to market. Diet Center offers instruction on how to lose weight permanently. Their advertisements show thin, healthy people who have lost weight with the assistance of Diet Center; however, potential overweight customers cannot judge how much weight they will lose or how they will look after weight loss. Thus, Diet Center's promise or offer of weight reduction is intangible.

Inseparability of Production and Consumption

Production and consumption of services are inseparable, and selling comes before both. Goods, however, are first produced, then sold, and finally consumed. For example, a customer must first be sold on the idea of getting a haircut, then the haircut is produced and consumed simultaneously. In renting an automobile for a family vacation, the customer is first sold on whether to rent from Hertz, Avis, or some other car rental agency and then rents the car. While the car is being driven, the service of transportation is being both produced and consumed. Inseparability of production from consumption usually results in distribution being rather direct to the customer, as is displayed in Figure 19.1.

Heterogeneity

Since services are produced and consumed simultaneously, the consumer actually becomes part of the production process. Consequently, it is difficult to standardize services, which results in output that can vary widely in quality. Take psychiatric counseling as an example. All counseling sessions provided by the counselor are not equal because the clients interact differently with the counselor, and this determines the benefits received and

Table 19.1   The Service Sector in Industrialized Countries (1980)

Country	Service As a Percentage of	
	Gross Domestic Product	**Total Civilian Employment**
Canada	63	66
USA	63	66
Japan	53	54
Belgium	61	62
Sweden	65	62
France	61	55
West Germany	49	49
Italy	50	48
Netherlands	59	62
United Kingdom	62	59

Source: Organization for Economic Cooperation and Development (OECD), as reported in Eric Langeard. "Services Marketing in Europe and the USA," in Leonard L. Berry, G. Lynn Shostack, and Gregory D. Upah (eds.), *Emerging Perspectives on Services Marketing* (Chicago: American Marketing Association, 1983), p. 5. Used by permission.

the quality of the service. Education is an example with which you may have firsthand experience. Have you taken a college course that you thought was first rate but one of your classmates thought was terrible? Can each opinion be correct if you were both taking the class and received the same educational service? The answer is yes, because you both did not receive a homogeneous service—you, as the customer, help to produce the service. The major problem created by heterogeneity is quality control. The producer can control the production of the service, but not the consumption.

Perishability

Services cannot be stored or inventoried because they are intangible. If a cabin on an ocean liner is not occupied, the potential revenue from that cabin at that time is lost forever. "In essence, the service manager is without an important 'shock absorber' available to most of his counterparts in the manufacturing sector to absorb fluctuations in demand."[4]

Because services can not be inventoried, the demand for them must be forecast accurately. The service marketer needs to have the proper number of employees and other resources available to meet the demand for services. If there are too many employees, labor productivity will fall. On the other hand, if there are too few employees, customers will leave dissatisfied. For example, have you ever been kept waiting an hour or two at your dentist's office even though you had an appointment?

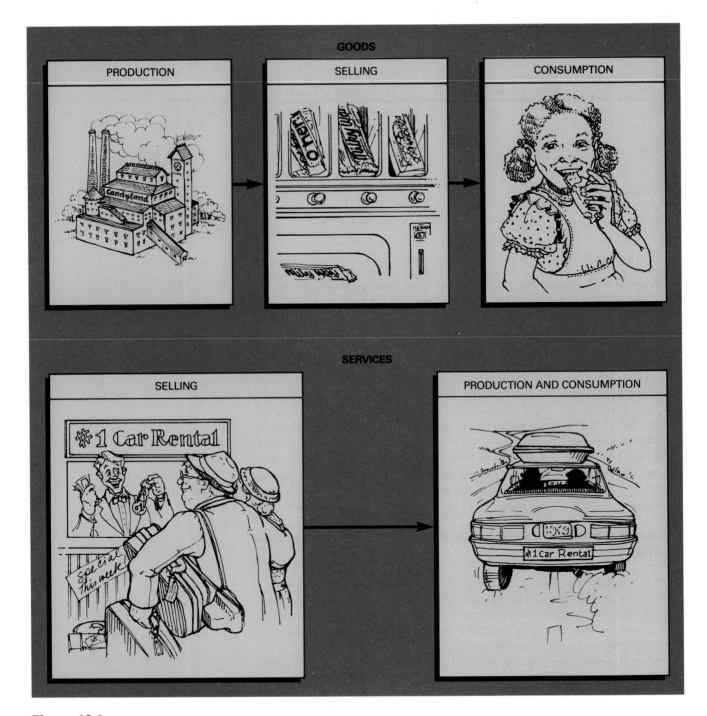

Figure 19.1
Production, Consumption, and Selling Process for Goods Versus Services

Influence on the Marketing Mix

In the last ten years, substantial deregulation has occurred in the transportation, telecommunications, and banking industries. During this same time, lawyers and doctors won the right to advertise and accountants, architects, and other professionals discovered that marketing can be a key to growth and profitability.

This deregulation and discovery of marketing have influenced service enterprises in all areas of the marketing mix. First of all, there is more pricing flexibility. For example, in 1985, Humana Hospital advertised price specials on complete face lifts for $675, down from $941, and a tubal ligation for $345, reduced from $441.[5] Service industries are also experiencing more product innovation. Witness all of the new financial products that banks and savings and loan institutions offer, such as money market checking accounts, check guarantee cards, credit and debit cards, and individual retirement and Keough accounts. Innovation in promotion has also skyrocketed. Promotional messages for many lawyers appear in newspapers, on television, and on the radio, and they are also plastered on billboards, buses, and trains. One lawyer in Tucson, Arizona, boldly suggests in his advertisements that the first two things to do if you are in an automobile accident are to get a good doctor and then to call his law firm. Distribution innovations have also proliferated. Dentists, lawyers, and optometrists now have offices in shopping malls. Banking from electronic terminals in various locations is common in the urban environment. Many hospitals now offer expectant parents the option of having their baby delivered in a special birthing room with a homelike setting rather than in an austere delivery room.

This increased innovation in product, distribution, promotion, and pricing in the service industries has intensified competition, and the natural response to increased competitive intensity is a higher degree of market segmentation. For example, Christ Hospital in Oak Lawn, Illinois, has created a VIP service for high income patients. For a premium of about 20 percent, a patient "can recover in rooms decorated with 18th century–style furniture while dining on specially prepared meals served on fine china. In the evening, they'll find a Godiva chocolate on their turned-down beds."[6]

International Competition

Services marketers are battling for foreign as well as domestic markets. For example, Price Waterhouse (accounting), Hertz (car rental), J. Walter Thompson (advertising), Donovan, Newton, and Leisure (legal), and Bechtel (construction engineering) have had a history of aggressively competing for customers worldwide. Today, many other U.S. service firms are expanding their international operations. Holiday Inn has identified 140 sites in western Europe where, between 1985 and 1995, it will build hotels, most of which will have 250 to 300 rooms. Ramada Inn and Marriott each plan to add twenty more hotels in Europe by 1990, and Sheraton will double its holdings to fifty hotels in Europe by 1990.[7]

In Chapter 18, we discussed the fact that the United States is experiencing a large international trade deficit. These data are deceiving, however, because they attribute the deficit only to merchandise or tangible products. As shown in Table 19.2, the United States exports more services than it imports. In 1983, for instance, the United States had a $27,628 million surplus in the international trade of services. Future growth in the services area can help offset the large merchandise deficits the United States has been experiencing.

Understanding Competition

A service marketer faces competition from other firms selling the same services; for example, MCI, Sprint, and AT&T all compete with each other to provide households with long distance telephone service. Competition also can occur among service firms whose services provide different benefits. For example, a young successful, professional couple (i.e., a physician and a lawyer) might be considering rewarding themselves for their hard work with a $15,000, thirty-day luxury ocean cruise. On the other hand, they may be considering taking out a ten-year, $1,000,000 life insurance policy on both their lives for a one-time premium of $15,000. Their children, aged 2 and 4 years, would be the beneficiaries. Thus, spending $15,000 for a long-awaited vacation is competing with their parental duties.

Table 19.2   U.S. International Transactions[a]

Year	Service Exports	Service Imports	Surplus (Deficit)
1960	$ 8,877	$ 5,883	$ 2,994
1965	13,796	8,340	5,456
1970	21,704	15,331	6,373
1975	44,593	30,000	14,593
1980	109,562	73,448	36,114
1983	119,208	91,580	27,628

[a]Figures in billions.

Source: 1960 to 1980 data from U.S. Bureau of the Census. *Statistical Abstract of the United States: 1982–1983,* 103rd edition (Washington, DC, 1982); 1983 data from same source, 105th edition.

A service firm can also compete with a goods producing firm that offers the same benefit. For example, a young single could either lease a new Chevrolet Corvette for thirty-six months at $439/month with a $1,000 non-refundable deposit or purchase the identical car with a $3,000 down payment and forty-eight monthly installments of $549 each.

Finally, a service firm can compete with a goods producing enterprise that offers different benefits. For example, the young couple who was trying to decide between a luxury cruise and life insurance alternatively may consider spending the $15,000 on a new Saab automobile. One innovative California savings and loan association recognized that it competed with tangible products and offered a free new Cadillac with each $100,000 three-year certificate of deposit. Even though the new car was in lieu of interest on the account, the savings and loan association was able to sell the notion of thrifty savings as well as the tangible aspects of the new car.

Often, the do-it-yourself consumer competes with the service firm. Consumers can prepare their own tax returns, be their own legal advisors, repair their homes and cars, cut their own grass, and so on. This may not be a feasible alternative for the time-pressured household, but for many lower income households, and for some high income households with lots of free time, do-it-yourself services are quite common. Actually, since a large number of households need or prefer to perform their own services, a market niche exists for teaching do-it-yourself projects. Many home improvement center chains, such as Scotty's and Hechinger, offer short courses that teach customers how to do certain household projects, such as building a deck, paperhanging, or making simple household repairs. Other companies, such as Heath Kits, have developed and marketed in-home self-study courses in electronics for several decades. The do-it-yourself alternative appears to be limitless; for example, psychological counseling and brain trauma rehabilitation are now available on computer disks for in-home use.[8]

Based on our discussion of the inherent differences between goods and services (intangibility, inseparability, heterogeneity, and perishability), we can expect consumers to behave somewhat differently toward services than they do toward goods. We will discuss these differences in behavior and give examples of them.[9]

UNDERSTANDING THE SERVICES CUSTOMER

Personal Sources of Information

The usefulness or enjoyment of a service is directly related to the service provider's performance. Since it is difficult to communicate customer satisfaction through the mass media, the consumer of services is likely to rely on personal sources of information, especially word-of-mouth advertising. For example, in selecting a physician or lawyer, most consumers ask friends and relatives for referrals. Because a person considering a foreign vacation frequently will ask the travel agent's opinion, many airlines, hotels, cruise ships, and tour groups offer travel agents free vacations. Consumers of services also tend to rely on personal sources of information because many service firms are small, local establishments that cannot afford large promotion budgets.

Evaluating Quality

Because it is difficult to sample services and because services are intangible, the consumer is often forced to use price and physical appearance to evaluate quality when making a purchase decision. A lawyer in a nicely decorated office located in a first-class office building, who charges $150 per hour for consultations, is perceived as high quality. A doctor with dirty fingernails and a hair dresser whose hair looks as though it was cut with a lawn mower are poor marketers. Some service marketers have found a way of allowing their customers to sample their services through free introductory lessons or sessions.

Adoption of Innovation

Service innovations take longer to capture a widespread market than do innovations involving tangible products for several reasons. First, many services cannot be sampled, which reduces their exposure to the marketplace. Second, since services are intangible, it is difficult to communicate their benefits. Third, a new service innovation may be inconsistent with existing values and behavior. This is especially true when people are accustomed to providing the service for themselves. Fourth, service innovations often involve complex concepts that consist of a bundle of attributes, and the same bundle of attributes may not be offered to all buyers on each purchase.

We will use a banking example to illustrate the slowness in the adoption of service innovations. Many banks have offered financial planning and counseling services to their clients, but the adoption of this service innovation has been slow because of the reasons we just discussed:

1. Financial planning cannot be sampled effectively since a good financial plan requires planning total income and expenses over several years.
2. It is difficult for banks to use the mass media to effectively communicate the benefits of financial planning.
3. Financial planning using a person outside the home is inconsistent with traditional norms that consider financial matters "private" family matters.

Service professionals such as chiropractors and psychologists often offer a free, introductory visit to give the consumer a way to evaluate the quality of their services.

4. The attributes of financial planning are complex, involving such things as tax-deferred savings, present value of money, portfolio management, and liquidity, and the application of these concepts will vary with each customer.

Perceived Risk

The purchase of any type of product involves some degree of perceived risk on the part of the buyer, but because of their intangibility, the perceived risk when purchasing services is higher than that when purchasing goods. This is especially true of high-priced services such as cosmetic surgery, major home improvements, auto repairs, and luxury vacations.

Since the quality of services is heterogeneous, the customer is never sure what to expect. For example, even though you may have stayed at the Park Plaza in New York City several times and have had good service each time, there is always the risk that hotel service will not be up to standard on your next visit.

Traditionally, services were sold without guarantees or warranties. If you did not like your stay at the hotel or the weekly therapy session with your counselor, it was difficult (if not impossible) to get a refund. In an attempt to cushion the high risk feeling associated with services, more and more firms are beginning to offer special guarantees. For example, Super Cuts offers to recut your hair if you are not satisfied, H & R Block offers to accompany you to tax audits to explain their procedures, and Holiday Inn offers a no-excuses guarantee that promises to correct any problems that arise or provide the service at no charge.

Loyalty

Consumers tend to develop a high level of loyalty to service providers. Once you find an acceptable bank, physician, insurance agent, and so on, you tend not to switch to an alternative provider, largely because of the high risks involved in services and the lack of information about substitutes. Because of the high degree of customer loyalty, many young professionals, such as lawyers, physicians, and dentists, have trouble building a practice.

DEVELOPING THE MARKETING PROGRAM

When developing a marketing plan for services, the marketers must take into account the differences between services and goods, the nature of competition surrounding services, and the behavior of consumers of services. As with goods, the marketing program should consist of segmenting the market, identifying the target market, and developing a marketing mix to attract that target market. The marketing mix for services includes product, place (or distribution), promotion, and price discussed in Chapters 8 through 17, as well as an additional element—people.

Market Segmentation

Although service marketers can use the general concepts and principles of market segmentation discussed in Chapter 7, they need to be especially aware of problems that might arise from sharing service facilities with different market segments. This is a problem when the customer is in direct contact with the service provider and other customers. For example, if a hotel has as its target market the business traveler who desires a quiet and peaceful night's rest, it would be unwise to rent out thirty of the 150 rooms to a traveling high school band. It may be possible to do this on Saturday night when there are few business travelers, but to do it on a weekday could undermine the hotel's strategy to cater to the businessperson.

Many times, the utility or pleasure received from a service is highly influenced by the other customers present. In 1985, when the exchange rate was quite favorable to the American tourist, high class French restaurants were inundated by Americans. In an effort to retain their French aura and appeal, many restaurants put quotas on the number of foreigners allowed per night. Quite often customers feel more comfortable interacting with others of similar stature and background. If you have $100,000 on deposit in a bank, you might not want to wait in line in the lobby with those who have only limited funds deposited. Therefore, some banks have established separate windows or areas of the bank for their prestige accounts. Airlines also recognize this problem and have established lounges where their frequent flyers can wait in comfort. American Airlines has its Admiral's Club and TWA its Ambassador Club, where a business traveler who belongs to the club can relax in leather chairs, be served cocktails, and watch television.

In periods of off-season demand, some service marketers might cater to a totally different market segment. For example, the Sheraton El Conquistador in Tucson, Arizona, is a first-class resort hotel that attracts visitors from the Midwest, Northeast, and Canada from November 1 to April 1. The target market is high income couples, and rates begin at $135 per night. During the summer season, however, Northerners do not want to vacation in 100+ degree weather, so the resort offers special room rates that it promotes to Phoenix families who are used to hot weather, consider 100 miles far enough to travel for a short vacation, and view Tucson as cooler and dryer than Phoenix.

Product

In addition to considering the product concepts and principles discussed in Chapters 8 and 9, a service marketer confronts other challenges in making a good product offering to the market. These challenges relate to the four unique characteristics of services that we discussed earlier in the chapter: intangibility, inseparability, heterogeneity, and perishability.

To counteract the problems associated with intangibility, the service marketer should attempt to create some concrete evidence of the service. Consider the following examples: life insurance companies often package their policies in fancy leather folders; real estate agents give away packets of information on home buying, household budgeting, and community information; hotels provide their guests with fancy soaps, shoe shine towels, shower caps, and bubble bath; and health clubs give their members T-shirts.

An integral part of the service marketer's product is its physical facility, especially when customers regularly come in contact with the facility. The physical facility can be the storehouse of tangibility and thus be extremely important in creating an image of the service marketer in the customer's mind. The style of the building, the type of building materials, the signs, the neighborhood, the parking facilities, and the general accessibility of the site all influence customers' perception of the service. Interior design factors are important too. Wall and floor coverings, fixtures, ceiling height, plants and artwork, employee uniforms, and color combinations must be pleasing and convey a predetermined image.

The design of the physical facility can also be a major factor in determining the effectiveness and consistency of service performance. Good design can improve the quality of the service and make it more homogeneous. McDonald's is perhaps the best example of this, with its standardization of restaurants to provide quality, service, convenience, and value to the consumer.

Producer and consumer cannot be separated completely in service products, nor is this separation desirable. The usefulness of the service can often be increased, however, by creating some separability in the service. For example, marital counseling can be more valuable if outside reading of selected materials is assigned and done between sessions. Similarly, before going to a financial planning session, a client may be asked to fill out a detailed questionnaire, thus making the service encounter more productive. Stanley H. Kaplan Educational Centers, which specialize in preparing students to take LSAT and other college entrance tests, have found that their course is more beneficial if the student studies between training sessions.

Even though the actual content of the service may need to be varied, such as hairstyling or legal service, the service marketer should always strive for consistent quality. The more homogeneous the quality of the service is, the lower is the risk the customer will associate with the service. Homogeneity of service quality can be provided by developing standardized procedures. For example, American Airlines frequently has attendants with clipboards and stopwatches positioned at the ticket counters to monitor how long it takes a customer to be waited on. If the time is greater than the firm's standard, corrective action will be taken. They also have standards for baggage pickup and flight arrival times. Other procedures deal with airplane cleanup and food service.

Perishability is probably the most difficult service characteristic to alter, but clever marketers can find ways to do so. For example, many dental hygienists give their patients special instructions on brushing and flossing their teeth, which helps the professional cleaning last longer. Some cruise lines provide pictures of guests enjoying their vacation in an attempt to preserve the moment. These cruise lines may also send follow-up letters six to nine months later with pictures included to remind their guests of the great time they had and to encourage them to take another cruise. In general, some type of tangible evidence of a service can make the experience of the service less perishable.

Distribution

The distribution or place decisions for the services marketer are different from those of the marketer of goods because of the intangibility factor. The service marketer has four primary distribution decisions: (1) location of service facilities, (2) pickup and delivery service, (3) design of the marketing channel, and (4) determination of the supply channel.

The importance of the location of service facilities varies directly with the amount of contact that will occur between the customers and employees of the service firm. A convenient location is not important for equipment-based services, such as electricity or telephone, where the customer seldom needs to visit the business office. Conversely, a convenient location is critical when the service provider and customer must meet face-to-face. For this reason, many service firms are moving from freestanding locations into shopping centers, where customers can combine shopping for goods with shopping for services. Shoe repair shops, dentists, banks, travel agents, movie theaters, and restaurants are some of the services that are locating in shopping malls across the country. A dental service located in a Sears store provides customers with a beeper so that they can shop while waiting for their appointment.

The service marketer must also decide whether to provide pickup and delivery services for the customers at their homes or places of business. Not all services firms need to offer this benefit; some repair shops, child care facilities, animal grooming services, copying services, and car and

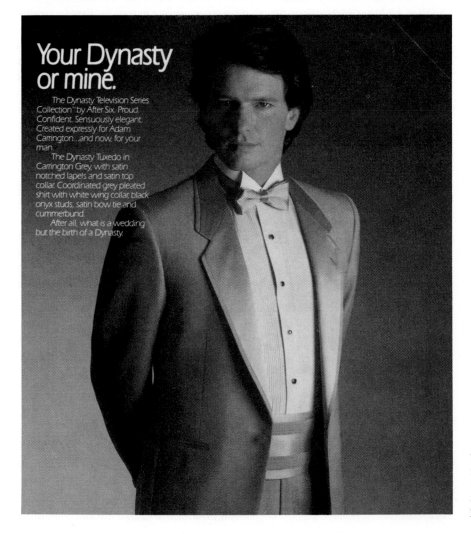

Tuxedo rental services that offer evening wear similar to what is shown in this ad often find shopping centers and malls popular locations because they provide convenience for the consumer.

equipment rental agencies offer pickup and delivery. Some management consultants prefer to go to the client's office, whereas others require the client to travel to theirs. Very often, these pickup and delivery decisions are based on personal preferences or habit, although financial or profitability criteria should be a major determining factor.

Most marketing channels for services are direct because the service provider and customer usually interact directly. Service channels can be longer, however, as illustrated in Figure 19.2. Notice that insurance can be sold directly through either the mail or a company sales staff or indirectly through insurance agents. In fact, as is shown in Figure 19.2, the marketing channel may go from the insurance company to an agent who sells it to a user's employer, who shares the cost with the employee or provides it as a fringe benefit.

A final distribution decision concerns the logistics of obtaining the supplies and materials necessary to operate a service business. Ocean liners need to have food and drink available for passengers and fuel and supplies to operate the ship at sea; janitorial service firms need cleaning fluids and

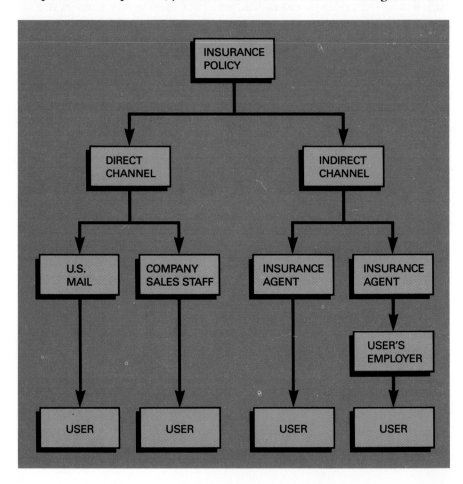

Figure 19.2
Marketing Channels for Insurance

supplies; advertising agencies need office and art supplies; and radio stations need transmitters and programming supplies. If a service enterprise does not have the supplies it needs to perform its services, then no amount of promotion or other marketing activity will overcome this problem.

When purchasing supplies and materials needed to carry on business, the service marketer will have to decide whether to buy directly from a manufacturer or from a wholesaler. The marketer must order large quantities to justify purchasing directly from a manufacturer. Hotel chains such as Ramada Inn and Holiday Inn are large enough to purchase bedding directly from manufacturers; however, most service firms are relatively small and will purchase supplies from a wholesaler, where they can get quick delivery on small orders.

Promotion

When developing an effective promotion program as part of its marketing mix, a service marketer should follow the guidelines established in Chapters 13, 14, and 15. In addition, service marketers should take certain other factors into account when planning promotion.[10]

Employees.   Many services heavily rely on employees who directly affect a firm's promotional efforts. These employees need to promote the service philosophy and standards of the service marketer. Promotion by the service marketer should be designed to communicate not only with the target market, but also with employees, especially those employees who have contact with customers.[11]

Word-of-Mouth Advertising.   When we discussed consumer behavior in relation to selecting and evaluating services, we noted that consumers are highly prone to rely on personal sources of information, especially word-of-mouth advertising. The services marketer's promotion program should recognize this fact and capitalize on this type of advertising.

> Making a conscious effort in advertising to leverage word-of-mouth might involve persuading satisfied customers to let others know of their experience, developing communication material for customers to make available to non-customers, targeting advertising to opinion leaders, or guiding prospective customers in soliciting word-of-mouth information. Yet another approach involves featuring the comments of satisfied customers in the advertising itself, a strategy which in effect merges conventional and word-of-mouth advertising.[12]

Tangible Symbols.   When we discussed the product element of the marketing mix, we suggested that a service marketer should design its service product to help create tangibility. Similarly, the promotion plan, especially the advertising program, should develop tangible symbols that help to position the service and the product correctly in the consumers' mind.[13]

There are many examples of service marketers' use of tangible symbols. Merrill Lynch prominently displays a bull in its print advertisements and a charging herd of bulls in its television advertising. This is intended to reinforce the idea that Merrill Lynch is bullish on America and a breed apart from other stock brokerage firms. For many years Prudential Insurance Company used the rock of Gibraltar in all its advertising to convey the idea of stability and invited its customers to "own a piece of the rock." In the advertisement for the Williamsburg (a Four Seasons nursing center), a pineapple is used as a tangible symbol of the service concept of welcome and hospitality that the Williamsburg offers.

Continuity.   Since it is impossible to obtain a patent on a service, unique service attributes are often copied by competitive service providers. For example, if a local equipment rental firm that caters to the small contractor/builder offers free delivery and pickup of its backhoes and tractors, a competing firm can quickly copy this added service. To remain competitive in services marketing, a firm must constantly modify its service offering. Consequently, a firm's specific advertising and promotional campaigns change regularly. Therefore, a continuous use of the same symbols or themes is needed to create a desired image even though the specific service offering may change over time. When you see an advertisement for a tax-sheltered annuity that features a bull standing on a cliff, you know Merrill Lynch is the advertiser. Similarly, McDonald's comes to mind when you see an advertisement for a fast-food restaurant with two golden arches—that's what advertising continuity is all about.

Kept Promises.   As we discussed earlier, it is difficult to provide—and control—the same level and quality of service to all customers. Therefore, a service marketer should not make false promises. For example, a pizza restaurant that wants to increase its lunch business may begin to advertise a "no more than ten minute wait between 11 A.M. and 1 P.M." However, since the actual wait may be from five to fifteen minutes and 10 percent of the customers wait more than ten minutes, the restaurant would be unwise to promote what it cannot deliver.

People

Since employees play such a key role in services marketing, we have added a fifth element to the marketing mix—people. Service employees can be categorized into four types, all of whom can have a positive or negative effect on the performance of the service. These employees may be either visible or invisible to the customers, and they may or may not have contact

Growing older should be just as delightful as growing up.

Laughter, friendship, sharing – these are some of the finer things in life.

And at The Williamsburg, we don't think people should stop enjoying them just because they need nursing care.

That's why we make sure everything is perfect, from the fresh flowers to the gourmet cuisine served in the private dining room. We provide our residents with the highest quality nursing care, 24 hours a day. And we surround

them with all the things they so richly deserve. Like elegance, dignity and warmth.

Call 1-800-637-1400 for a free pamphlet that details our special care and services. Or visit The Williamsburg soon.

And in everything from the gleaming brass to the professional staff, you'll see a reflection of our philosophy. No matter how good the past has been, the best years should always be the ones ahead.

The Williamsburg
at Four Seasons

North, 7703 Briaridge, San Antonio, TX 78230, (512) 341-6121

A Member of the Manor HealthCare℠ Community. ©1985 Manor HealthCare℠ Corp.

Service marketers often use tangible symbols to bring their message across, as this ad for a nursing home does.

with customers. We will use the airline industry to give examples of the four types of service employees (see Table 19.3):

1. *Visible/contact.* A flight attendant is visible and has contact with passengers. If the flight attendant is rude or panics during an emergency, the passengers will feel angry or frightened.

2. *Visible/no contact.* Baggage handlers are visible to customers but do not have direct contact with them, although they do have direct contact with their luggage. If passengers waiting in an air terminal look out the window and see a baggage handler drop several pieces of luggage off an overloaded cart, they will wonder what's happening to their own suitcase.

3. *Invisible/contact.* A telephone reservation clerk has voice contact with customers but is not visible. Obviously, the clerk's physical appearance does not affect the service performance, but his or her telephone eti-

Table 19.3   Airline Personnel

	Contact with Passenger	No Contact with Passenger
Visible to passenger	Airport ticket agent Check-in agent Flight attendants	Baggage handler Pilot/copilot
Not visible to passenger	Telephone reservation clerk	Maintenance crew

quette and knowledge are quite important. In fact, since this employee cannot be seen, the passenger will form an evaluation solely on the basis of what is said and how it is said. If the clerk is rude or mistakenly books the customer in first class, the overall image of the airline will be damaged.

4. *Invisible/no contact.* The members of the ground maintenance crew are invisible to passengers and have no contact with them. If they do not perform their jobs competently, the consequences could be written up in *Newsweek* and make the nightly news.

To help ensure that a service firm's personnel reinforces the desired standards, at least four things should be emphasized.[14] First, high priority should be placed on the careful selection, training, and proper compensation of service personnel. Investments in these areas are time and money well spent. It is disquieting that many service firms attempt to cut costs in these areas, a mistake that actually results in low service performance and profitability, which serves as further justification for additional cost cutting. This cycle is illustrated in Figure 19.3.

Second, a firm should emphasize internal marketing, or as we suggested in our earlier discussion of promotion, employees as well as customers should be the target of promotional efforts. Third, practices should be developed to obtain consistency of job performance. For example, telephone personnel should follow set procedures in greeting callers and thanking them for calling. Also, personnel should be monitored by superiors to make certain these procedures are being followed. Finally, all employees who are visible to the customer should have a consistent appearance. For example, desk clerks and bellhops at fine hotels wear uniforms that distinguish them as hotel personnel with particular tasks and duties.

Price

When referring to *price,* service marketers often prefer to use different terms, such as *tuition* (the price of schooling), *premium* (the price of insurance), *commission* (the price charged by a stockbroker or real estate

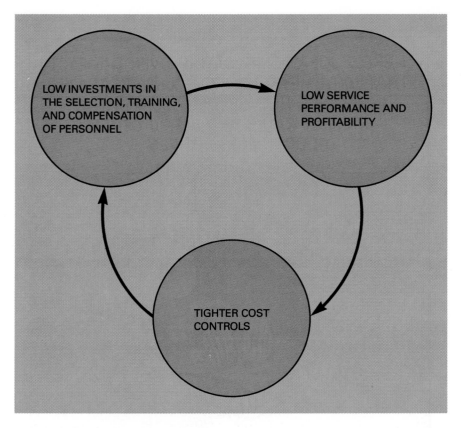

Figure 19.3
The Low Productivity Trap in
Service Firms

agent), *fee* (the price charged by a lawyer and consultant), *rent* (the price
for the use of property or equipment), *admission* or *cover charge* (the
price of entering), and *interest* (the price of borrowing money), but a price
by any other name still costs the same! Recall our definition in Chapter 16,
"price is something of value that is exchanged for something else."

The price concepts and methods of price determination discussed in
Chapters 16 and 17 are applicable to services as well as to tangible goods.
However, three concepts that we discussed earlier need more elaboration
with regard to services: negotiated prices, discount policies, and prestige
pricing.

Negotiated Prices. We mentioned in Chapter 16 that negotiated prices
for tangible goods were unusual in the United States. Many service marketers, however, are willing to negotiate price. After being informed of the
psychiatrist's $100 per hour counseling fee, a potential patient may decide
this is too much money. This may open the way for a negotiated price. The
psychiatrist could begin by suggesting a lower rate, or the patient could
start negotiations by asking about other alternatives. Negotiated prices are
also common for the services that organizations purchase. For example, a
sales manager planning the firm's annual sales meeting may need 180 hotel

Service marketers must deal with the same price issues as other marketers, but they often choose to refer to their prices in different terms.

rooms in Chicago for three days in the second week in June. The sales manager and the hotel manager would negotiate on the price per room as well as certain complimentary perks, such as a free cocktail hour for all the salespeople. Price negotiations are also common among small service businesses such as home repair, lawn and garden care, child care, construction, and tailoring.

Perishability is the major reason that price negotiation is popular with services. If the psychiatrist in the prior example does not fill her calendar

MARKETING IN ACTION

Frequent Flier Programs: A Form of Quantity Discount

Many major airlines have frequent flier programs that reward passengers with free travel and other prizes. Essentially, these programs are a type of quantity discount for business travelers who fly often and are not able to take advantage of many of the special, early purchase discount fares.

There are an estimated 10 million members in frequent flier programs in the United States, and American Airlines leads the pack with close to 2 million members. An American Airlines frequent flier can receive two free coach class tickets for 50,000 miles of accumulated travel.

Some marketers wonder whether these frequent flier programs actually boost airline revenue and profitability. Pan American World Airways believes that its frequent flier program

helped to attract customers from other air carriers and boosted its revenue by $500 million, but other airline executives are more suspicious of the benefits of such programs. They reason that if all the major airlines offer frequent flier programs, each program cannot be boosting revenue without somehow taking business away from the others. In addition, these programs are expensive to administer: the direct costs (including promotion) can range from $2 million to $12 million annually.

Another disadvantage to the airlines is that many frequent fliers

don't wish to have free travel awards since they are already traveling as much as 100,000 to 500,000 miles annually. Thus, these travelers often sell their mileage credits to coupon brokers, who then resell them to other people. For example, a frequent flier can get $1,000 for 50,000 miles of travel on TWA. The net result of this activity is that many of these free travel awards end up being sold by coupon brokers to people who normally would purchase tickets from airlines.

Source: Based on authors' personal experience and knowledge; "Does the Frequent Flier Game Pay Off for Airlines?" *BusinessWeek* (August 27, 1984), pp. 74, 75; "Subtle Variations Guide the Savvy in Choice of Frequent Flier Plans," *Wall Street Journal* (March 22, 1985), p. 23, Section 2.

---

with patient appointments and spends that time nonproductively, the income potential from those idle hours is lost forever. If the hotel in Chicago has 180 rooms that sit empty as opposed to being booked at a reasonable rate, the income potential from the empty rooms has also vanished. Organizations tend to negotiate prices for services more than households do, mainly because many consumers do not realize they have the right to negotiate the fee with a lawyer, the interest rate on a new home loan from a bank, the commission of a real estate agent, the charge for a hotel room, or the rent on a piece of property.

Discount Policies.   Quantity discounts, seasonal discounts, and early purchase discounts are quite popular with service marketers. Life insurance firms offer quantity discounts by substantially lowering the premiums on additional $100,000 increments of insurance. Child care facilities may offer quantity discounts to families with two or more children enrolled at the same time. Sports, arts, theatrical organizations, and amusement parks also often offer quantity discounts. For example, a large amusement park may sell tickets for rides at $1.25 each, six for $5.95, and twelve for $9.95. (Note the use of odd-even pricing in this illustration.) A host of other services also use quantity discounts. The Marketing in Action on this page shows how the airline frequent flier programs are a type of quantity discount.

A seasonal discount refers to any discount that is time related, such as time of day, day of week, or season. A seasonal discount can also be used as a form of market segmentation, as we discussed earlier in this chapter. Lodging in Aspen, Colorado, is less expensive in the summer than during the ski season; movie theaters have afternoon matinees at discount prices; bowling alleys and tennis clubs charge lower prices at midmorning and midafternoon; and weekend rates for car rental are lower than weekday rental rates. Seasonal discounts reflect the changing shape of the demand curve over different time periods, allowing service marketers to more fully use their capacities. This is crucial because of the perishable nature of services.

Another type of discount commonly used with services (and one that was not mentioned when we discussed pricing of goods) is the early purchase discount. An early purchase discount is given to the buyer who agrees to purchase a service well in advance of when the service will actually be performed. Sports and arts groups frequently offer early purchase discounts. For example, a six-ticket book for six theatrical events spread over four months may be purchased for $59.95, whereas the single ticket price may be $15. Similarly, an outdoor pool club may offer lower fees if you pay your summer membership in January. Once again, this discount policy is influenced by the perishability of services. The earlier that capacity can be sold by a service marketer, the lower the probability that a firm will be caught with surplus supply. Early purchase discounts are also a good way to guard against the problems caused by the external environments, such as changes in the economy, the weather, and the competition. People usually are willing to brave a storm to attend a function to which they already have tickets, and they tend to be loyal to the service they have already purchased when faced with price cuts from that service firm's competitors. From the service marketer's point of view, it is better to have the service presold at a discount than to risk not selling it at all.

Prestige Pricing.   Because the quality of services is difficult to assess, consumers frequently use price as an indicator of quality. Therefore, prestige pricing is common among service marketers. When prestige pricing is used, however, the marketer must ensure that all other tangible elements of the marketing mix reinforce this prestige image. A health club that charges a $1,500 annual fee should have the physical facilities, staff, and programs to reinforce this image.

SERVICE PRODUCTIVITY

Productivity in the service sector of the U.S. economy has lagged behind productivity growth in the manufacturing sector.[15] The high labor intensity in service businesses is largely responsible for this state of affairs. Productivity in service industries can be improved using three different types of strategies: labor-related strategies, demand-shifting strategies, and function-shifting strategies.

Labor-Related Strategies

There are several possible labor-related strategies for improving productivity of service businesses. The firm can have a few full-time employees who provide a base level of labor to meet a constant level of demand and then hire part-time employees for periods of peak demand. For example, a 300-room hotel may rent anywhere from 140 to 300 rooms per night, so that it should have enough full-time employees to service 140 rooms and schedule part-time help at other times as demand fluctuates. Essentially, the goal is to have the supply of employees fluctuate in relation to demand fluctuations.

A second strategy is to train employees to perform multiple job functions. This gives employees something productive to do during periods of slack demand. For example, auto mechanics may be trained to operate the company's word processing equipment. During slow periods, they may send personalized letters to regular customers reminding them of the need to bring their auto in for servicing. One enterprising pizza restaurant entrepreneur trained his telephone order takers to call previous customers and local business establishments to see if they would like to order a pizza and have it delivered. Instead of sitting around waiting for business, they used the phone to solicit orders. Incidentally, approximately every third or fourth call resulted in an order.

A third strategy is to use paraprofessionals for routine repetitive types of tasks so that the professional can concentrate on areas that require more expertise. A paralegal aid can do routine legal research, which allows the lawyer to concentrate on developing a strategy to win a court case. Graduate students can grade tests and look up references, so that professors can concentrate on teaching and research. A master mechanic may have several aids who dismantle parts from a malfunctioning auto, while the master mechanic assists and gives advice when needed.

A fourth strategic alternative is to substitute capital for labor. This has occurred with such businesses as automated car washes; computerized college instruction; bowling alleys with automatic pin setters and ball return machines; and landscaping services, where employees are equipped with power mowers, edge trimmers, vacuums, and other equipment to speed up the time it takes to do a job. Recently, professional house painters have switched to power spray painting, which not only saves time, but also improves the quality of the paint job.

Demand-Shifting Strategies

Productivity can be harmed when supply and demand for services are unequal. To avoid this, the service marketer may attempt to align the timing of demand with supply capabilities. Market segmentation and the discount

MARKETING IN ACTION

Public utilities do not face a constant demand for energy because changing seasonal weather patterns influence the residential demand for electricity and natural gas. Summer peak demand for electricity is very high in the Oklahoma City area, where temperatures often reach 100+ degrees and air conditioning becomes a way of life. Unfortunately, this summer peak demand requires capacity that is only used for a limited time per year.

Oklahoma Gas & Electric Co. recognized that by controlling electrical consumption during peak periods, it

The PEAKS Program at Oklahoma Gas & Electric

could reduce the need for future construction and thus hold down the costs of providing electric service. In addition, such a strategy would also improve company financial performance. Consequently, the company developed the PEAKS (*p*lanned *eco*nomy *and* *k*ilowatt *saver*) program. The PEAKS program enabled the company to control residential air

conditioners during the hot summer months. It works this way: every half hour, a radio-controlled device switches off, for a short time, the air conditioner compressors of homes participating in the PEAKS program, thereby controlling some of the demand. Customers participate voluntarily and are rewarded by a monetary credit on their summer electric bills.

Source: *Oklahoma Gas and Electric Company 1981 Annual Report*, p. 6; authors' firsthand experience and participation in the PEAKS program.

pricing policies that we discussed are all attempts to modify demand. Promotion can be used to modify demand as well. For example, an income tax preparation service may urge people to make an appointment in early January or February to avoid the onslaught of people requesting tax advice in late March and early April. Ski resorts may advertise midweek bargains to encourage people to avoid the long lift lines on weekends. The U.S. Postal Service advertises in late October and early November to urge people to mail early to avoid the Christmas rush. The Marketing in Action on this page shows how a large public utility devised a program to reduce summertime peak demand for electricity.

Function-Shifting Strategies

The service marketer may attempt to shift certain functions to the consumer or to other firms in order to improve productivity. For example, a house painter may require that all furniture be removed from the rooms to be painted, an athletic club may require members to replace weights in their proper location after use, and many fast-food restaurants require customers to pick up their orders at a self-service counter and urge them to clean their own tables after they are finished eating.

Functions can also be shifted to other organizations. A phone answering firm may be hired to take reservations, a cleaning service may be more cost effective than a janitorial staff, and an auto repair firm may subcontract brake and suspension work to a specialist in that line of work rather than purchase the necessary equipment to do the job themselves.

SUMMARY

This chapter acquainted you with some of the unique problems confronting service marketers and suggested possible strategies to deal with these problems. To understand these problems, you must recognize that services are different from goods because they are intangible, heterogeneous, and perishable and because production and consumption of services are inseparable.

Competitive intensity in U.S. service industries has increased over the last decade because of the deregulation of many service industries (especially transportation, banking, and telecommunications) and because of the increased use of marketing by many professionals (such as doctors, lawyers, and dentists). International competition in services is also increasing. Service marketers face competition not only from other service firms selling services that provide the same or different benefits, but also from firms that offer tangible products that fulfill the same or different benefits. In addition, the customer is a competitor in many situations in which do-it-yourself service is possible.

The marketer needs to understand several facets of consumer behavior toward services: (1) the consumer of services is likely to rely on personal sources of information, especially word-of-mouth advertising, (2) the service customer often uses price and physical facilities to evaluate quality, (3) service innovations are adopted less rapidly than innovations involving tangible products, (4) consumers perceive a high risk in purchasing services, and (5) consumers tend to develop a high level of loyalty to service providers.

As with marketers of tangible products, service marketers must develop a marketing program that segments the market, identifies the target market, and develops a marketing mix. Importantly, however, the marketing mix includes not only the four elements that were used to market tangible products (product, place, promotion, and price), but also an additional element—people.

Productivity in the service sector has lagged behind productivity in manufacturing and in agriculture, because it is so labor intensive. Programs to improve productivity in services involve strategies directed at reducing labor, shifting demand, and shifting functions. Labor-related strategies include (1) more use of part-time employees to meet fluctuations in demand, (2) training employees to perform multiple job functions, (3) using paraprofessionals for routine repetitive tasks so that professionals can concentrate on areas that require more expertise, and (4) substituting capital (machines) for labor. Demand-shifting strategies involve synchronizing demand with supply capabilities and are usually accomplished with advertising or pricing strategies that encourage people to shift the timing of demand. A final strategy for improved labor productivity is functional shifting, in which the service marketer attempts to shift certain functions to the consumer or to other firms.

REVIEW AND DISCUSSION QUESTIONS

1. What are the marketing problems created by the intangibility of services?

2. Give examples of how services can be produced and consumed at the same time.

3. What marketing problems are created by the heterogeneity of services?

4. How does the perishability of services influence price policies for services?

5. Explain and give an example of how a tangible product can compete with a service.

6. Why does the buyer of services rely heavily on personal sources of information when evaluating providers of services?

7. Why and how does the consumer often use price to evaluate providers of services?

8. Why do consumers adopt service innovations less rapidly than innovations involving goods?

9. Why do consumers perceive the purchase of many services as highly risky?

10. How does the marketing mix for services differ from that for goods?

11. Give some examples of what a marketer can do with a service product to help overcome the problems caused by its intangibility, inseparability, heterogeneity, and perishability.

12. What impact do physical facilities have on a consumer's perception of a service product?

13. Summarize the five guidelines service marketers should follow in developing a promotional program.

14. What are the types of "people" that a service marketer should include in the marketing mix? Why is each important?

15. Because services are intangible, a service marketer can ignore distribution decisions in the marketing mix. Agree or disagree with this statement, and explain your position.

16. Why is price negotiation common with services?

17. Name some common types of discounts offered by service marketers. Find advertisements to illustrate each.

18. What are four labor-related strategies for improving productivity in service firms? Give an example of each.

19. Why is demand forecasting especially important for services?

20. How can functional shifting be used to improve productivity in service organizations? Provide examples.

ACTION PROBLEMS

1. You are a manager of a health club with four indoor and four outdoor tennis courts. The club is open seven days a week from 6 A.M. to 10 P.M. Your peak season for indoor courts is from November 1 to April 30, and the indoor courts

are occupied 75 percent of the time during this season. However, from 7 to 9 A.M. and from 4 to 6 P.M., the indoor courts are in use 99 percent of the time. An indoor court during the peak season rents for $15 per hour. A local tennis club has recently had two of its three courts destroyed by a fire and would like to reserve one court for exclusive use by its members from February 1 to April 30. They have offered to pay $3,000 per month for the use of the court. What would you do?

2. Your uncle in Milwaukee has been in the car wash business since 1955, and you worked for him every summer while you were in high school. Recently, he saw you at a family gathering and the following conversation took place:

"Sarah, how are you doing? I hear you are attending college now. What are you studying?"

"Oh, you know, the usual stuff you take when you're a business major."

"Like what?"

"Accounting, business law, communications, marketing, you know."

"Marketing? That sounds interesting. Maybe you can help me with a problem."

"What's that, Uncle Sam?"

"Well, Sarah, business is slow, especially during the winter months and between 1 and 3 P.M. on weekdays throughout the year. Can you think of any ideas that would help me?"

"Let me think about that for a few days. I'll write you next week, OK?"

"Great! You always were a good kid."

Write Uncle Sam a letter suggesting three or four things he might consider doing to improve his business.

3. On graduation, you take a job as assistant director of marketing for an 800-bed hospital in a city of 890,000 people. Your boss, the director of marketing, was recently promoted to this position. He was the assistant purchasing agent before his promotion and holds a degree in accounting. He is unfamiliar with marketing and wants your help in developing a marketing program for the hospital, which currently does not have a marketing program. Write a two-page memo to your boss outlining the steps he should follow in developing a marketing program.

NOTES

1. *RCA Annual Report, 1983,* p. 27.

2. Carol J. Loomis, "How the Service Stars Managed to Sparkle," *Fortune* (June 11, 1984), p. 158.

3. This section relies on Donald W. Cowell, *The Marketing of Services* (London: William Heinemann, Ltd., 1984), pp. 19–28; Christopher H. Lovelock, *Services Marketing* (Englewood Cliffs, NJ: Prentice-Hall, 1984), pp. 4–5.

4. W. Earl Sasser, R. Paul Olsen, and D. Daryl Wyckoff, *Management of Service Operations: Text, Cases, and Readings* (Boston: Allyn & Bacon, 1978), p. 16.

5. "A High-powered Pitch to Cure Hospitals' Ills," *BusinessWeek* (September 2, 1985), p. 60; "Doctors Are Entering a Brave New World of Competition," *BusinessWeek* (July 6, 1984), pp. 56–61.

6. Ibid.

7. "U.S. Hotel Chains Are Following the Tourists to Europe," *BusinessWeek* (June 3, 1985), p. 58.

8. "Therapy on a Disk: The Computerized Road to Mental Health," *BusinessWeek* (August 19, 1985), pp. 75–77.

9. The following discussion relies heavily on Valarie A. Zeithaml, "How Consumer Evaluation Processes Differ Between Goods and Services," in James H. Donnelly and William R. George (eds.), *Marketing of Services* (Chicago: American Marketing Association, 1981).

10. The following guidelines are largely drawn from William R. George and Leonard L. Berry, "Guidelines for the Advertising of Services," *Business Horizons* (July–August 1981), pp. 52–56.

11. Franklin Acito and Jeffrey D. Ford, "How Advertising Affects Employees," *Business Horizons* (February 1980), pp. 58–59.

12. George and Berry, "Guidelines," p. 53.

13. G. Lynn Shostack, "Breaking Free from Product Marketing," *Journal of Marketing* (April 1977), p. 77.

14. Cowell, *The Marketing of Services,* p. 207.

15. Victor R. Fuchs (ed.), *Production and Productivity in the Service Industries* (New York: National Bureau of Economic Research, 1969); John W. Kendrick, *Postwar Productivity Trends in the United States* (New York: National Bureau of Economic Research, 1973).

## CHAPTER 20

NONPROFIT MARKETING

LEARNING OBJECTIVES

After you complete this chapter, you should be able to:

- **Explain** the four important ways in which nonprofit organizations differ from profit-oriented firms

- **Discuss** the scope of nonprofit marketing by identifying the four types of things a nonprofit organization can market

- **Identify** the two types of target markets that nonprofit organizations have

- **Describe** the development of a marketing plan for a nonprofit organization and identify any special situations that these organizations face

- **Comment** on the ethical nature of nonprofit marketing, especially the marketing of social causes

MARKETER PROFILE

Richard Wirthlin of Decision/Making/Information

Richard Wirthlin is president of Decision/Making/Information, a marketing research firm headquartered in McLean, Virginia. His specialty is the marketing of political candidates, where the goal is getting a majority of votes cast, not financial (profit or dollar sales). In political marketing, the customers exchange their votes for promises from a political candidate (the seller). Wirthlin has convincingly demonstrated that sophisticated marketing techniques and marketing research can be used successfully in the nonprofit sector of the economy. D/M/I, which handles over 100 campaigns in a typical election year, has an enviable track record for developing successful campaigns for political candidates. For example, in one Canadian election, twenty-one of twenty-two candidates it backed for Canada's Constitutional Convention were victorious.

Repeated experience over fourteen years has shown Wirthlin that well-designed market research can be the basis of successful campaigns. The firm has found that 10 to 16 percent of voters wait until the last weekend before an election to decide how to vote. Knowing this, D/M/I decided to test several alternative campaign strategies for the last weekend of the Carter-Reagan 1980 presidential election when its client was the National Republican Party. One campaign had Reagan attacking or criticizing Carter, and the other, in a positive vein, was directed at providing undecided voters with more information for decision making. In a process similar to the way in which a company might test market a new product, the firm selected two comparable cities to test these advertising approaches prior to the last weekend of the campaign. Results clearly indicated that with the attack mode, the hard-core Reagan supporter was reinforced, but the swing voter was turned off. Consequently, the final weekend of campaigning by Reagan used the positive campaign almost exclusively. Richard Wirthlin believes that, while political polling and advertising will always be arts, the research that his firm conducts helps to make these art forms more successful in marketing political candidates.

Source: Based on material in "Research's Expanding Role Is Helping Elect Candidates, Improve Political Parties' Images," *Marketing News* (December 9, 1983), pp. 1, 14.

INTRODUCTION

As the preceding profile of Richard Wirthlin indicates, marketing tools can be applied to organizations other than firms that sell goods and services for profit. Art museums, colleges, political parties, police departments, and other nonprofit groups all develop exchanges with certain groups and can benefit from applying marketing principles to their particular problems. **Nonprofit marketing** is *all marketing effort that is conducted by firms or individuals to accomplish nonfinancial goals.* Some nonprofit organizations have realized that they face marketing problems and have added marketing managers. However, many top executives in nonprofit organizations think that marketing only applies to profit-oriented firms. Furthermore, many of them view marketing as costly and unethical because of its manipulative or propaganda role.

Although many executives in nonprofit organizations view marketing with suspicion, the growth in the popularity of marketing in nonprofit organizations has been phenomenal since 1970.[1] Before 1970, it was difficult to find nonprofit firms actively engaged in marketing. The turning point came in 1969, when two noted marketing scholars, Philip Kotler and Sidney Levy, published a classic article, "Broadening the Concept of Marketing." This article argued that marketing is not an activity that is unique to business (i.e., profit-making) firms.[2] Two years later, an entire issue of the *Journal of Marketing* was devoted to nonprofit marketing, and topics discussed included fund raising, population control, health services, and solid waste recycling.[3] Although some marketing scholars argued against the spread of marketing into these areas, their recommendations were largely ignored.[4]

HOW NONPROFIT MARKETING DIFFERS

Some of the most common types of organizations involved in nonprofit marketing are religious, educational, government, health, social cause (such as civil rights), political, and cultural. These organizations or institutions may be involved in the marketing of people, places, and causes, as well as goods and services. Much of what you have learned about marketing in the preceding nineteen chapters can be applied to nonprofit organizations; however, these firms face some unique problems that require special marketing tools and procedures.[5]

Nature of Objectives

Nonprofit organizations, by their very nature, do not seek to make a profit but often find it necessary to generate a surplus of sales revenues over expenses. This surplus may be necessary to help finance new ventures, purchase new equipment, or retire a debt. For example, the Daughters of the American Revolution may generate surpluses to help cushion deficits that might occur unexpectedly in the future.

It is quite difficult to gauge the performance of nonprofit firms because their objectives are always nonfinancial. For example, a public transit system's objective may be to provide safe and efficient public urban transportation, or a state university may seek to provide education for the masses. Although these organizations can be viewed as creating some form of "social" profit, it is next to impossible to measure. Obviously, this creates problems for managers because it is difficult to allocate resources when the performance of your allocation decisions is intangible. How does a university president gauge the correctness of a decision to cut faculty in history and philosophy and add engineering and business school faculty?

Objectives are most difficult to assess when no price is charged for the services rendered or products provided. While the university president could use the change in total student tuitions as the basis of an evaluation, if we are talking about changing the mix of courses in a public second grade class, where no tuition is charged directly to the students and where they have no choice in course selection, then gauging performance is extremely difficult.

Resource Attraction

Because nonprofit organizations seldom can generate internally sufficient revenues to cover all of their expenses, they must develop programs to attract outside resources. They often seek volunteer labor, tax concessions, and donations of money or supplies in order to continue operations. Therefore, nonprofit organizations have the dual marketing task of attracting resource contributions and of allocating these resources to achieve objectives. This dual marketing task often creates conflicts in the organization—for example, a volunteer employee or a financial donor may want to have a direct say in how donations of the organization are allocated.

Applicability of the Marketing Concept

An organization that practices the marketing concept is customer oriented and tries to meet the customers' wants and needs. This orientation may be inconsistent with the missions of nonprofit firms. Antidrug, antitobacco, and antialcohol organizations need to convince people that their wants are not good for them. Universities cannot offer students only the courses they want but must consider what is needed for a well-rounded education.

Nonmarket Pressures

Profit-oriented enterprises usually are guided by market conditions in deciding which segments to serve, what products to produce, how to price and distribute them, and what promotion strategies to employ. Decision making in nonprofit organizations, on the other hand, often is pressured by major nonmarket groups, including political parties that might control government and thus various government agencies, such as the Federal Trade Commission, the Justice Department, or the Department of Transportation. Another group might be industry associations, such as the American Association of Collegiate Schools of Business (AACSB), which influences course offerings of business colleges. Professional associations such as the American Medical Association influence the marketing decisions of health care institutions.

SCOPE OF NONPROFIT MARKETING

Nonprofit marketing involves institutions that market people, places, causes, and goods and services for nonfinancial goals. We will examine each of these areas to get a better idea of the scope of nonprofit marketing.

Marketing of People

Marketing practices are often applied to political candidates and celebrities, such as actors and sports figures. Consider a person who has decided to enter politics and run for an elective office. The office seeker begins as a relatively unknown product and must go through the following steps. He or she must "develop a personality (brand image), get the approval of an organization (company image), enter a primary election (market test), carry out a vigorous campaign (advertising and distribution), get elected (market share), and stay in office (repeat sales)."[6]

Marketing of Places

Marketing activities can also focus on places, such as cities, states, or nations. For example, Australia and Canada both have attempted to attract new residents through ads. Other places may wish to attract tourists. Consider the advertisement that promotes the Bahamas as a place to vacation. Some places may wish to attract investment capital in the form of real estate investment or construction of manufacturing plants, warehouses, and office buildings. This is usually done through chambers of commerce or economic development boards.

Institutions are often involved in non-profit marketing of places for various reasons, such as the promotion of tourism and thereby the attraction of investment capital.

Marketing of Causes and Ideas

Social marketing can be defined as the *"design, implementation, and control of programs seeking to increase the acceptability of a social idea or cause in a target group."*[7] Examples include marketing programs that encourage family planning,[8] reduction of alcohol and tobacco consumption, and prevention of child abuse. The Joan B. Kroc Foundation (named for the widow of McDonald's founder) is involved in social marketing. The foundation was formed in 1984 with the objective of encouraging people to take an active role in critical social issues. One of its first large-scale marketing efforts occurred on July 17, 1985, when it ran an advertisement in ninety-four daily newspapers urging citizens to speak against nuclear weapons. To assist them in speaking out, the advertisement included two mail-in coupons: one for President Reagan and the other for Soviet General Secretary Mikhail Gorbachev. The coupons urged these leaders to "stop all nuclear weapons testing immediately."[9]

One of the most difficult tasks that a marketer can face is changing a target group's ideas, attitudes, values, and resulting behavior.[10] Consequently, social change is often accomplished indirectly. Consider the oil shortage problem that developed in the early 1970s. The American public needed to conserve energy; however, advertising and a pure informational approach were not enough to convince them to do so. Thus, laws were passed (a legal approach) requiring that motor vehicles consume less fuel and that consumers conserve fuel by driving at slower speeds. Auto manufacturers invested in research and development to create innovations (a technological approach) that resulted in cars with better gas mileage. Finally, petroleum products were taxed more heavily (an economic approach), which increased the cost of energy and thus lowered demand.

If social marketing is to be effective, its efforts must be directed at three levels. First, cognitive change needs to be fostered. Assume that you are trying to market the idea that high school dropouts should return to school. The first challenge is to communicate effectively to the high school dropout the benefits of a high school education. Second, value change needs to be fostered. You must get your target audience to value the benefits of a high school education. Simply because they know the benefits does not mean they will value these benefits. Third, you must stimulate action or behavior; that is, a marketing strategy must be designed to get them to actually re-enroll in high school and complete the required course of study.

The Group Against Smoking and Pollution (GASP) is involved in social marketing, and some of its activities are highlighted in the Marketing in Action on page 621.[11] Also note the advertisement by the U.S. Committee for Energy Awareness, which is promoting the cause of "energy independence."

MARKETING IN ACTION

GASP: Group Against Smoking and Pollution

Group Against Smoking and Pollution (GASP) promotes the rights of nonsmokers to live and work in an environment free of tobacco smoke. Active in several countries, it is organized into regional chapters whose efforts include filing legislation at all levels of government; initiating and pursuing lawsuits to protect nonsmokers: picketing promotional programs by tobacco companies, and presenting medical, environmental, and economic evidence of the problems caused by

smoking to smokers and nonsmokers alike. In addition, some GASP chapters are now working to develop fee-based consulting services for large employers to assist them in planning and implementing no-smoking policies, especially as these relate to the creation of smoke-free areas in the

workplace. GASP leaders hope that these efforts will assist nonsmokers and also generate additional income to supplement the funds obtained from individual contributions.

Source: Christopher H. Lovelock and Charles B. Weinberg. *Marketing for Public and Nonprofit Managers* (New York: John Wiley & Sons, 1984), p. 289. Copyright © 1984 by John Wiley & Sons. Reprinted by permission of John Wiley & Sons, Inc.

Changing consumers' ideas, attitudes, values, and in turn their buying behavior can be a difficult and challenging task for marketers.

By marketing the idea of "energy independence," the U.S. Committee for Energy Awareness tries to gain acceptance of their social cause.

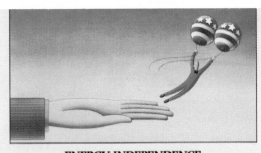

ENERGY INDEPENDENCE
Can nuclear energy and coal free America from foreign dependence?

Marketing Goods and Services

Nonprofit organizations can also market traditional economic goods and services. The Lincoln Park Zoo Shop is an upscale gift shop on Chicago's North Michigan Avenue that sells lifelike stuffed animals and other gift items. During the Christmas season, the store does $10,000 weekly in sales and profits are used to support Chicago's Lincoln Park Zoo.[12] Other examples of nonprofit organizations selling traditional economic goods and services are hospital gift shops and cafeterias, college-owned bookstores, art museum courses in art appreciation or art history, Unicef gift stores, Salvation Army thrift stores, and local fund-raising carnivals organized by civic organizations, such as the Lions Club.

The techniques for marketing goods and services by nonprofit versus profit-oriented firms are essentially identical; the major difference is in the organization's objectives. The same set of marketing decisions must be made: target market and marketing mix decisions.[13]

DEVELOPING THE MARKETING PLAN

Many nonprofit organizations are myopic and self-centered and find it difficult to assess the needs, wants, and desires of their target markets. Universities and colleges are notorious for overlooking the needs of their target market—the students. Increasingly, students have full-time and part-time jobs and thus must take early morning or evening courses, but few colleges adjust course offerings to reflect this situation. As nonprofit organizations face increasing competition, they will be forced to do a better job of identifying and analyzing target markets and implementing a successful marketing mix.

Target Markets

One major problem all nonprofit organizations must face is identifying at least two target markets. First, donor target markets, which we will call **target donor publics,** are *those people who give time, money, or other resources to a nonprofit organization.* Second, client target markets, which we will call **target client publics,** are *those people who will receive the output or benefits of the nonprofit institution.* Sometimes these two targets are identical, such as when church members both donate money and receive church services; the two targets can differ in other situations, such as in a nonprofit blood bank where the blood donors and blood receivers differ.

There are many bases for segmenting markets, and all of the methods discussed in Chapter 7 are applicable to nonprofit firms.

Target Donor Publics. The nonprofit organization must recognize that there are various reasons why different segments of the public do or do not donate to the cause. These reasons can serve as a useful way of categorizing or segmenting donors. Table 20.1 lists some of the most common reasons people have for giving to nonprofit organizations. With these reasons for giving in mind, the marketing manager can develop a marketing plan based on the motivations of the various target groups.

Target Client Publics.   Using the common variables for segmenting markets discussed in Chapter 7, target client publics can be segmented by (1) demographic variables, such as age, income, education, and occupation; (2) geographic variables, such as region of country or city size; (3) psychographic variables, such as life-style or personality; and (4) behavioristic variables, such as benefits sought or loyalty.[14] Consider the marketing of a presidential political candidate.[15] Some possible ways of segmenting eligible voters (client publics) are by:

1. *Age.*   People of different ages will have vested interests in different political issues. For example, voters over 50 years of age will be more concerned about the candidate's stand on social security and medicare. Those under 30 years of age may be more concerned with the control of interest rates, since they are likely to be first-time home buyers. Middle-aged people may be more concerned with national educational policies (because they are more likely to have school-aged children) or with national defense (because their children may have to fight in wars).

2. *Geography.*   People in the older industrial regions of the United States, such as the Northeast and Midwest may be concerned with the candidate's stand on industrial policy (a policy to give federal aid to old and decaying industries to help modernize them and make them competitive on a worldwide basis). On the other hand, people in the Sunbelt

Table 20.1   Motivations for Giving

1. A personal interest or involvement in the institution or a project of the institution.
2. Gratitude for past help or benefit from the nonprofit organization.
3. Habit.
4. A desire to help others.
5. Giving money is easier than volunteering time.
6. To gain a sense of power over the organization and how the funds are spent.
7. To be polite or to get rid of the solicitor.
8. Because everybody else gave.
9. The need for a tax deduction.
10. Public recognition for a large donation.
11. To receive a special "donor's gift" or chance to win a prize.
12. The solicitor is a friend, relative, or respected public figure.

Source: Based on Christopher H. Lovelock and Charles B. Weinberg. *Marketing for Public and Nonprofit Managers* (New York: John Wiley & Sons, 1984), p. 505. Copyright © 1984 by John Wiley & Sons. Reprinted by permission of John Wiley & Sons, Inc.

may be concerned with federal grants to build highways and other infrastructures required by rapidly growing cities.

3. *Life-style.* Individuals with liberal and open life-styles may be interested on the candidate's stand on the legalization of marijuana. On the other hand, those with a conservative or religious life-style may be interested in the issue of prayer time in public schools.

4. *Loyalty.* Loyalty to a particular political party may be another way of segmenting the market. Some people will always vote a Republican or Democratic ticket regardless of the candidate's stand on particular issues.

Special Problems. Nonprofit marketing managers confront at least two special problems when attempting to analyze and segment target client publics and target donor publics.[16] First, there is not much useful past research (secondary data) available for segmenting nonprofit client and donor publics. Firms like A.C. Nielsen and Burke Marketing Research conduct relatively little research for nonprofit organizations because research involving primary data collection involves a monetary expenditure that most nonprofit firms find difficult to justify. It is difficult to convince a volunteer board of directors to vote in favor of spending hard cash on intangible research. However, market research can provide useful information. For example, a study of the psychographic and demographic characteristics of blood donors found that donors tend to have low self-esteem and rare blood types and to be male, married with children, low risk takers, very concerned with health, well educated, religious, and quite conservative.[17]

Another special problem nonprofit marketing managers face is the difficulty in getting the donor and client publics to express views or feelings on many of the nonprofit firm's offerings. Trying to find out why someone doesn't donate to the March of Dimes, won't attend religious services, or opposes Planned Parenthood is indeed a difficult task. Consumers can more easily state what they expect from a breakfast cereal or a motorcycle than from some of the items mentioned.

Marketing Mix

Once the nonprofit organization has done its best to identify its target clients and donor publics, it must establish a marketing mix consisting of product, distribution, promotion, and price components. Most nonprofit organizations rely heavily on managerial judgment rather than research in designing marketing mixes, although preliminary research has been conducted on the use of quantitative techniques for developing optimum marketing mixes.[18]

Product. The heart of most marketing programs, for profit or nonprofit organizations, is the product offering. Product decisions must always begin with a careful and detailed assessment of competition. The competitive environment, however, consists of more than just similar types of organizations offering similar goods or services. In trying to serve its target market, a nonprofit organization, such as the Girl Scouts, can face up to four major types of competitors.[19]

1. **Desire competitors** are the *other immediate desires that the consumer might want to satisfy*. Desire competitors for the Girl Scouts include competing desires girls might have such as learning, recreation, friendship, and service to others.
2. **Generic competitors** are the *other basic ways to satisfy a desire*. For example, to learn more, a girl could read books, watch educational television, and join clubs.
3. **Service form competitors** are *the different types of organizations that can help fulfill a particular desire*. For example, if a girl wants to join a club, she could join a religious group, school club, community club, social/fraternal club, or sports group.
4. **Enterprise competitors** *are similar organizations competing for the consumer's business*. For instance, if the girl wants to join a social/fraternal club, she could join the YWCA, 4-H, Campfire Girls, or Girl Scouts.

Note that we mention service form competitors rather than goods form competitors since most nonprofit firms market services or ideas rather than tangible goods. Figure 20.1 illustrates the competitors that confront the Girl Scouts.

The various product concepts that were discussed in Chapters 8 and 9, such as product mix, product life cycle, product deletion, are also applicable to nonprofit firms. For example, Figure 20.2 shows an art museum's product mix.

For all product decisions, the nonprofit organization needs valid information to make sound decisions. Marketing research can supply useful information, although it is often too expensive for most nonprofit organizations. Consider Table 20.2, which shows how marketing research techniques can be used to develop church sermon product lines.

Distribution. The nonprofit organization must design a distribution system that facilitates convenient exchanges with target client and target donor publics. For example, to be more convenient to target client publics, a university could develop branch campuses or offer courses in factories, in office buildings, or even on commuter trains. The same goal of convenience also applies to target donor publics. For example, Jerry Lewis sponsors the yearly Muscular Dystrophy telethon held during the Labor Day weekend. This telethon has thousands of telephone banks in shopping centers and other public places in all fifty states where people can easily call in their pledges or visit the local telethon location and donate. In addition, in some years, the telethon has used thousands of 7-11 stores as depositories where people can conveniently donate.

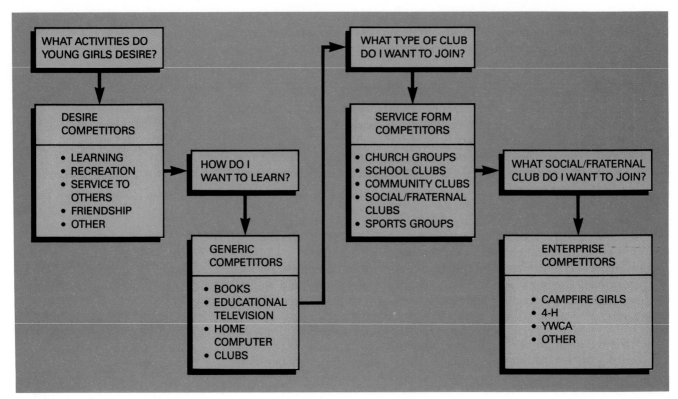

Figure 20.1

Competitors Facing the Girl Scouts

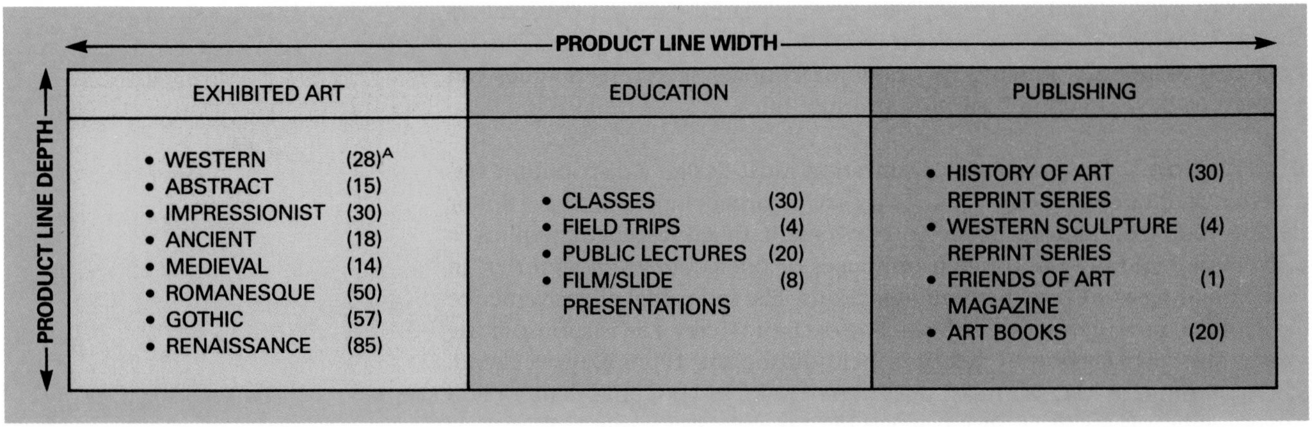

Figure 20.2

Product Mix for an Art Museum

[a]Numbers within parentheses indicate the number of items of each type in the museum's collection/offerings.

Table 20.2   Using Marketing Techniques to Develop Church Sermon Product Lines

Topic Area	Mean Rating[a]	Topic Area	Mean Rating[a]
Following God's direction for my life	1.9	How to deal with social unrest in my community	2.6
Understanding other people's ideas and feelings	2.0	How to deal with crime in my community	2.6
Interpreting the meaning of the Bible for my life	2.0	Improving my ability to speak in public	2.7
Making prayer more meaningful	2.0	Ecology and pollution	2.7
Improving communication among family members	2.0	Developing my ability to lead small groups	2.7
Dealing with drug abuse	2.1	Improving community health care	2.7
Finding what is most important in my life	2.1	Improving participation in an organization	2.7
How to make decisions about right and wrong	2.1	Famous and ordinary people talking about their lives and faith	2.7
Sharing my faith with others	2.1	Issues of war and peace	2.7
Facing personal crises	2.2	How to plan for my old age	2.8
Helping people without "putting them down"	2.2	The prison system	2.8
How to find the best in people	2.2	Improving my ability to use arts and news media in working with others	2.8
Giving and receiving affection	2.2	How to build and use a family budget	2.9
Dealing with conflicts	2.2	Great religious leaders of the past	3.0
Strengthening my ability to counsel with people	2.2	Equal employment opportunity	3.0
Improving services of worship	2.3	The meaning of sex	3.0
Spiritual rebirth and conversion	2.3	Population problems	3.0
How to solve problems	2.3	The religions of the world	3.0
Meeting the needs of people in a community	2.4	Integrating a community	3.2
Expressing my ideas and feelings	2.4	The history of minority groups	3.3
Poverty and what can be done about it	2.5	Becoming involved in political action	3.4
Improving my skills as a teacher	2.5	Women's rights and liberation	3.6
Developing my own leadership ability	2.5		
Helping others to plan and set goals	2.5		
Facing death	2.5		

[a]Mean rating for each topic area is simply the mean importance given that topic area by all respondents; 1.0 = of highest importance; 5.0 = of little importance.

Source: Reprinted by permission of the publisher from James L. Ginter and Wayne Talarzyk. "Applying the Marketing Concept to Design New Products," *Journal of Business Research* (January 1978), pp. 51–66. Copyright 1978 by Elsevier Science Publishing Co., Inc.

Often, it is difficult to be conveniently located because the organization may be burdened by a large physical plant in a poor location. A museum or theater may be located in an undesirable downtown area because the location was ideal when the site was chosen fifty years ago. If the building has been paid for, changing locations may be economically infeasible.

Since most nonprofit organizations offer services (intangibles) rather than goods (tangibles), they usually have short or direct distribution channels with no intermediaries. When intermediaries exist, they are usually agents. For example, a community symphony may have ticket agents in shopping centers in various locations in the city, which makes it convenient for target client publics to purchase tickets.

The Marketing in Action on page 628 shows how one nonprofit firm

MARKETING IN ACTION

The International Small Enterprise Development Center (ISEDC) is a nonprofit corporation established in 1979 through a grant from the United States Agency for International Development to the New Trans-Century Foundation in Washington, DC. The ISEDC has identified its role as that of a catalyst for bringing together marketing and related entrepreneurial resources of the developed world to the producers of the less developed world.

The ISEDC has several marketing channel programs that helps it achieve its mission. It has launched one of these programs with American Field Service (AFS), which is a New York–based organization that promotes international cooperation and understanding through exchange of high school students. Members of the 2,700 U.S. chapters of AFS work actively each year to raise funds (minimum of $925 per chapter) to

The International Small Enterprise Development Center: Developing Alternative Marketing Channels

support the national organization and its efforts and to sponsor an international student in their local community. The ISEDC has recognized this need and has responded with a marketing channels program that consists of in-home parties called *global exchange parties*. These parties allow the ISEDC to market Third World products (typically arts and crafts) through AFS chapters (the middleman), which allow the local AFS chapters to raise money. These in-home parties also allow the ISEDC and AFS to increase awareness of international issues.

The in-home party functions in a manner similar to Tupperware's well-known direct selling program. A typical party will have average sales of $200 to $250, and the local AFS chapter receives a 25 percent commission on all sales. In this way, the ISEDC is providing a meaningful alternative to bake sales, car washes, and candy sales often used as fundraising efforts. Importantly, with this marketing channel, the ISEDC is helping AFS fulfill its goals while simultaneously helping fulfill its own nonprofit goal of assisting producers in the less developed world to market their products.

Source: Adapted from George Miaoulis and Chris E. Meyer. "Alternative Marketing Channels: An Emerging Approach to Third World Development," in Michael G. Harvey and Robert F. Lusch (eds.), *Marketing Channels: Domestic and International Perspectives* (Norman, OK: Center for Economic and Management Research, University of Oklahoma, 1982), pp. 30–36.

involved in international business developed a marketing channel to distribute arts and crafts from less developed countries to the United States.

Promotion. Many nonprofit organizations seem unaware that marketing comprises more than promotion aspects, such as advertising, public relations, sales promotions, and personal selling. This is unfortunate because it prevents them from having an effective marketing mix. The promotion efforts of many nonprofit organizations are often inefficient as well. Few nonprofit firms pretest advertisements, scientifically determine their advertising budgets, train their salespeople, and so on.

Advertisements by nonprofit organizations are often **public service advertisements** *that the media* (TV, radio, newspapers, and so on) *broadcast or run at no cost to the organization.* Unfortunately, these ads frequently are ineffective,[20] as they tend to be produced on a very tight budget by in-house staff. In addition, the nonprofit organization has no control over the placement or frequency of the advertisements. Some public service advertisements are well designed, such as the Food Stamps advertisement.

Half the people suffering from unemployment aren't old enough to work.

You may be out of work, but your kids don't have to be out of food. Call for a free brochure that tells you how to get Food Stamps in your area. And how to find out if you qualify. We don't want anyone in the American family to be hungry.

FOOD STAMPS
MEALTIMES DON'T HAVE TO BE TOUGH TIMES.
1-800-453-4000

Public service advertisements are often run by the media at no cost to help promote the social causes of nonprofit organizations.

Most salespeople in nonprofit organizations are called by another name. For example, when the U.S. Navy sets up an office on a college campus to provide career information, the personnel are called *recruiters*. Similarly, when the Ohio State University coaching staff visits high school athletes and their parents, they are also referred to as *recruiters*, but again, they are primarily performing a selling function. When personnel attempt to solicit donations from target donor publics, they are referred to as *fund raisers*. The University of Texas at Austin (as most universities) has a large staff employed to raise money, and in so doing, they must be able to sell potential donors on the benefits of giving.

Many recruiters and fund raisers are, themselves, volunteers and are thus donating their time and skills: Jehovah Witness Church members actively recruit new members, and community volunteers are the primary source of fund raisers for the United Way. Volunteer workers are always difficult to control and manage, since they are not employees of the organization and can refuse to cooperate or follow instructions and there is little the manager can do to change their behavior. Managers don't fire volunteers, but volunteers essentially fire managers by deciding to ignore them! Predictably, this is a big problem with no easy solution.

Price.   When establishing price, most nonprofit firms have some type of financial objective in mind, although it is not profit oriented. The objective may be to break even or to cover a certain percentage of the costs. For example, a major state university may set tuition rates to cover 30 percent of the total costs of operating the university, with the other 70 percent coming from taxpayers and charitable donations. The price often is not set to cover total costs, because nonprofit firms provide goods or services that would be too expensive for their target client publics if full costs were charged. For example, if public transit systems charged full costs, the very poor could not afford to ride them.

When setting price, a nonprofit organization should consider the time

Note that *Newsweek* contributed space for this American Red Cross ad.

costs, travel costs, and psychic costs the potential client must spend in acquiring the product. **Time costs** represent *the value of the time it takes to acquire a product,* which essentially adds to the price paid because, if a client does not take the time to purchase a product, the time saved could be used in an alternative fashion. Consider a city symphony that gives free concerts. Is the price zero? No. Let's say the music hall is downtown, and it takes you one hour to reach downtown by car. In this case, you must invest two hours of travel time. There are also **travel costs,** which are *your direct outlays for transportation.* In our example, your car consumed oil and gas and you probably had to pay for several hours of downtown parking, which could have easily totaled $10 to $20. Finally, there are **psychic costs,** which are *the frustrations and tensions you encounter in purchasing the product.* Again, using the symphony example, assume you had to travel on congested highways at ten to twenty miles per hour and then had to drive through some rundown areas to reach the music hall; these are psychic costs. Psychic and time costs are unique to each individual, since people experience different degrees of frustration and tension and place different values on their time.

Finally, we should emphasize that no organization, not even a nonprofit organization, is free from competition. The U.S. Army must compete with other employers since military service is not mandatory; the U.S. postal service must compete with Federal Express, UPS, MCI, and other mail carriers; the American Cancer Society must compete with other organizations seeking donations; colleges must compete for students; and so on. Competition should not be ignored in setting prices.

Evaluating and Controlling Performance

Most nonprofit organizations have poor evaluation and control procedures, one reason being that they use volunteers or attract employees who are strongly committed to the organization's mission or purpose. It is incorrectly assumed that these people do not need to be evaluated and controlled because they will naturally do what is best for the organization. Another false assumption is that financial control is unnecessary since these organizations are not profit oriented. Neither of these reasons is an acceptable excuse for a poorly developed evaluation and control system.

Control cannot be exercised unless a plan exists, because control is the process of comparing expected performance with actual performance and taking corrective action where necessary. If nonprofit organizations plan activities in terms of dollars and cents, then a budget control system can easily be developed. Such a system would compare budgeted or planned revenues and costs with actual revenues and costs.

To plan revenues, an organization should develop a revenue function that shows the sources and determinants of revenues. Figure 20.3 shows a church revenue function; a church receives revenue from regular religious services, facility rental, and other sources such as special donations. Each of these should be planned, and the development of the marketing mix naturally will influence the revenue plans. The organization should also prepare a budget for expenses such as salaries, heat, rent, telephone, and insurance.

Nonprofit firms can develop other types of control besides financial or budget control. For example, some hospitals send questionnaires to patients after they are discharged asking them questions about the quality of nursing, food, and physician care. Some colleges send questionnaires to recent graduates so that they can evaluate the quality of their education. These questionnaires are good nonfinancial control tools.

The marketing manager should be prepared to use the performance evaluation and control system to decide when to take corrective action. This is a key part of control; problems that are uncovered must be corrected, and this often involves a change in the organization's marketing mix. For example, if revenues are below what was planned, then perhaps more pro-

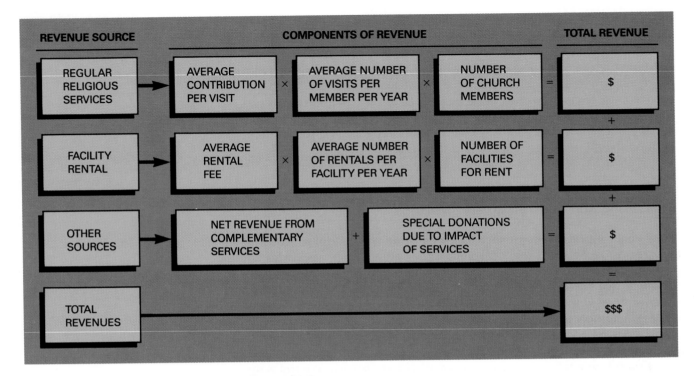

Figure 20.3

Church Revenue Function

Source: Based on ideas presented in Philip Kotler. *Marketing for Nonprofit Organizations* (Englewood Cliffs, NJ: Prentice Hall, 1982), p. 273. Used by permission.

motion needs to occur, new products need to be added, prices need to be altered, or distribution needs to be improved.

ETHICS OF NONPROFIT MARKETING

How ethical is nonprofit marketing? Is it acceptable to sell presidential candidates or religion in the same way that we sell toothpaste? Is it ethical to promote the acceptability of nuclear power? Is it ethical for the American Heart Association to sponsor a sweepstakes to raise money for heart research? Although these questions are difficult and are likely to cause disagreement, they cannot be ignored.

People often have difficulty in separating the ethics of the social cause or idea from the ethics of the marketing practices themselves. For example, some individuals would say that it is not acceptable to use marketing to promote abortions. Their objection may be based on religious beliefs rather than the marketing practice per se.

We have no answers to this ethical dilemma, but we do challenge you to think about it. Is the marketer guilty or unethical for developing advertising campaigns or marketing programs to promote controversial social ideas such as euthanasia, abortion, or public school prayer?

SUMMARY

This chapter explained how nonprofit organizations use marketing principles to solve their special problems. Nonprofit marketing is the marketing effort conducted by firms or individuals in order to accomplish nonfinancial goals. It is practiced by various religious, educational, government, health, social cause, political, and cultural groups, which may be involved in the marketing of people, places, and causes, as well as goods and services.

Nonprofit organizations have some unique problems that differentiate them from profit-oriented organizations and that require special marketing tools and procedures. Since the product is often a person, place, or social issue, marketing strategies need to be modified to fit the situation. In addition, nonprofit organizations cannot be evaluated on the usual profit-oriented scales. Because it is often difficult to obtain the necessary resources or generate enough revenue to cover expenses, these groups must seek volunteer labor, special tax considerations, and donations. Two other special problems confronting the nonprofit organization are the difficulties involved in applying the marketing concept and coping with the political pressures of nonmarket groups, such as political parties and professional and industry trade associations.

The marketing plan for nonprofit organizations consists of identifying and analyzing target donor publics and target client publics and developing and implementing a marketing mix. The target donor publics are those people who give time, money, or other resources to a nonprofit organization. On the other hand, the target client publics are those people who receive the output or benefits the nonprofit organization has to offer. It is difficult for the nonprofit marketing manager to get information about both of these target markets because little research has been done on segmenting nonprofit client and donor publics. In addition, if marketing managers decide to do marketing research, they may have difficulty getting the donor and client publics to express their views or feelings.

When developing a marketing mix, the nonprofit marketing manager should analyze competition and identify the organization's desire competitors, generic competitors, service form competitors, and enterprise competitors. The various concepts that were discussed in Chapters 8 and 9, such as product mix and product addition and deletion, are applicable and should be used to help make decisions. The distribution decisions usually focus on developing short or direct marketing channels that have the goal of convenience. The easier it is for people to donate to an organization or use its services, the more likely they are to do so. The nonprofit organization needs an especially efficient promotion plan since it usually must rely on volunteers and donations for survival. This often means using public service advertisements, volunteer recruiters, and fund raisers who are not always effective. Finally, the price of the product includes not only the actual dollar amount, but also the time costs, travel costs, and psychic costs involved in obtaining the product.

The chapter also touched on the control of nonprofit organizations and the ethics of their marketing activities. Control is a major problem because of the number of volunteer workers and the amount of public participation involved. It is difficult to turn down volunteer help and even harder to turn down donations from illegitimate sources. When such help is accepted, control becomes difficult because the volunteers may be doing more harm than good and the givers may want to have a say in the policies of the organization.

The ethics of nonprofit marketing is difficult to assess. There are many sides to this question, and the debate on it is often quite loud and emotional. However, it is an important question for you to ponder as you continue your studies and move into a career in business for either a profit or nonprofit organization.

KEY CONCEPTS

nonprofit marketing (p. 616)
social marketing (p. 620)
target donor publics (p. 622)
target client publics (p. 622)
desire competitors (p. 625)
generic competitors (p. 625)

service form competitors (p. 625)
enterprise competitors (p. 625)
public service advertisements (p. 628)
time costs (p. 630)
travel costs (p. 630)
psychic costs (p. 630)

REVIEW AND DISCUSSION QUESTIONS

1. How does nonprofit marketing differ from profit-oriented marketing?
2. What is the scope of nonprofit marketing?
3. What are some of the unique marketing problems that face nonprofit firms?
4. The marketing concept is equally applicable to profit and nonprofit firms. Agree or disagree with this statement, and explain your position.
5. What are the two types of target markets that most nonprofit firms must identify?
6. How can nonprofit organizations use marketing research? Identify some of the problems that nonprofit organizations have with using marketing research.
7. Why have nonprofit firms resisted the use of marketing tools and techniques?
8. What are four types of competition that confront nonprofit organizations?
9. Name some of the distribution and marketing channel decisions that the following nonprofit organizations must make: hospital, university, church, art museum, zoo.
10. What is a public service advertisement? Why are they often ineffective?
11. What do time costs, travel costs, and psychic costs have to do with the pricing policies of nonprofit organizations?
12. Why do many nonprofit organizations find control an especially difficult problem?

ACTION PROBLEMS

1. You are chief of police for a large city in the midwestern United States. Define the mission of your police department. Define some possible objectives. Can marketing play a role in helping to attain any of these objectives?

2. List possible target client publics and target donor publics for the following nonprofit organizations:
   a. Right-to-Life
   b. Sierra Club
   c. United Way
   d. Smithsonian Institute

3. Write a brief paragraph on your views about the use of marketing to promote each of the following causes:
   a. Abortion
   b. Gun control
   c. Antismoking
   d. Christianity
   e. Atheism
   f. Mainstreaming

4. Plan a marketing program for one of the causes listed in question 3.

NOTES

1. Christopher H. Lovelock and Charles B. Weinberg, "Public and Nonprofit Marketing Comes of Age," in Gerald Zaltman and Thomas V. Bonoma (eds.), *Review of Marketing 1978* (Chicago: American Marketing Association, 1978), pp. 413–452.

2. Philip Kotler and Sidney J. Levy, "Broadening the Concept of Marketing," *Journal of Marketing* 33(January 1969), pp. 10–15.

3. Some of the following articles were contained in the July 1971 (vol. 35) issue of the *Journal of Marketing:* William A. Mindak and H. Malcolm Bybee, "Marketing's Application to Fund Raising," pp. 13–18; John U. Farley and Theodore J. Leavitt, "Marketing and Population Problems," pp. 28–33; Harold H. Kassarjian, "Incorporating Ecology into Marketing Strategy: The Case of Air Pollution," pp. 61–65.

4. David J. Luck, "Broadening the Concept of Marketing—Too Far," *Journal of Marketing* 33(July 1969), pp. 53–55.

5. This section is adapted from Christopher H. Lovelock and Charles B. Weinberg, *Marketing for Public and Nonprofit Managers* (New York: John Wiley & Sons, 1984), pp. 31–37.

6. Philip Kotler, *Marketing for Nonprofit Organizations,* second edition (Englewood Cliffs, NJ: Prentice-Hall, 1982), p. 462. Used by permission.

7. Ibid., p. 490. Used by permission.

8. In this regard, an interesting article is Adel I. El-Ansary and Oscar E. Kramer, Jr., "Social Marketing: The Family Planning Experience," *Journal of Marketing* 37(July 1973), pp. 1–7.

9. "Ad Campaign Urges Citizens To Speak Against Nuclear Weapons," *Marketing News* (August 30, 1985), p. 1.

10. Marketing as an agent of social change is discussed in Philip Kotler and Gerald Zaltman, "Social Marketing: An Approach to Planned Social Change," *Journal of Marketing* 35(July 1971), pp. 3–12.

11. A pair of good articles on the development and future of social marketing are Karen F.A. Fox and Philip Kotler, "The Marketing of Social Causes: The First 10 Years," *Journal of Marketing* 44(Fall 1980), pp. 24–33; Paul N. Bloom and William D. Novelli, "Problems and Challenges in Social Marketing," *Journal of Marketing* 45(Spring 1981), pp. 79–88.

12. "When Should the Profits of Nonprofits Be Taxed?" *BusinessWeek* (December 5, 1983), pp. 191–192.

13. Marketing in not-for-profit firms is discussed more completely in Benson Shapiro, "Marketing for Nonprofit Organizations," *Harvard Business Review* (September–October 1973), pp. 123–132; Lovelock and Weinberg, *Marketing for Public and Nonprofit Managers.*

14. An example of research that uses many of these variables can be found in Alan R. Andreasen and Russell W. Belk, "Predictions of Attendance at the Performing Arts," *Journal of Consumer Research* 7(September 1980), pp. 112–120.

15. For an additional segmentation approach for political candidates, see Lovelock and Weinberg, *Marketing for Public and Nonprofit Managers,* pp. 103–105.

16. Some other problems are discussed by Bloom and Novelli, "Problems and Challenges in Social Marketing," pp. 79–88.

17. John J. Burnett, "Psychographics and Demographic Characteristics of Blood Donors," *Journal of Consumer Research* 8(June 1981), pp. 62–66.

18. See, for example, Imran S. Currim, Charles B. Weinberg, Dick R. Wittink, "Design of Subscription Programs for a Performing Arts Series," *Journal of Consumer Research* 8(June 1981), pp. 67–75; Charles B. Weinberg, "Marketing Mix Decisions for Nonprofit Organizations: An Analytical Approach," in Christopher H. Lovelock and Charles B. Weinberg (eds.), *Public and Nonprofit Marketing: Cases and Readings* (Palo Alto, CA; New York: The Scientific Press and John Wiley & Sons, 1984), pp. 261–269.

19. Adapted from Kotler, *Marketing for Nonprofit Organizations,* p. 55. Used by permission.

20. Joe Adams, "Why Public Service Advertising Doesn't Work," *Ad Week* (November 17, 1980), p. 72.

36.

The Motorcycle Glut

In spring 1983, many of the 6,000 independent motorcycle dealers in the United States had a twelve- to eighteen-month supply of motorcycles. Most of these were 1982 Japanese models. In fact, many dealers sold more 1982 models than 1983 models in 1983.

In 1980 and 1981, when auto industry sales were declining, the sales of motorcycles were remaining steady. Consequently, motorcycle manufacturers began to believe their industry was recession proof. Although many industry analysts believed that 1982 would bring 5 to 10 percent growth in industry sales, industry sales fell 15 percent. The recession continued in 1982, and unemployment among blue collar workers was above 20 percent in many large cities. In short, the target market could not afford to buy.

Since the market was flooded with bikes, Honda and Yamaha began to engage in an aggressive marketing battle. Collectively, Honda and Yamaha had a 65 percent share of the U.S. market. They increased their advertising and began to offer rebates and dealer incentives. In 1982, Honda doubled its advertising to $40 million, while Yamaha had twenty-four-page advertising inserts in magazines such as *Cycle World* and *Playboy.*

The Japanese manufacturers also forced dealers to order more bikes and tried to push the bikes through the marketing channel. "There was horrendous pressure [on the dealers] from Yamaha," says Ed Lemco, a former dealer and now head of the newly formed Motorcycle Dealers of America (MDA). "Regional managers were told to have so many orders or they'd lose their jobs. It was the same for district managers." A Yamaha spokesperson, however, described this charge as "insane."

According to Lemco, the culmination was Yamaha's national meeting with its dealers in Anaheim, California, in September of 1981. "District managers said to the dealers, 'I need a big order, but you can cancel it later.' So, some dealers ordered two, three, or four times what they needed," he says.

Some industry experts believed the problem was in Japan. Scott Brown, a former Yamaha executive, concedes that the dealers were pressured to overorder, but, he places much of the blame on the fact that Japanese manufacturers make all decisions about the U.S. market in Japan, often disregarding feedback from the United States. "Sales and marketing managers here were all puppets," Brown says. "We had no communications with Japan; only upper management did. We had told them for four years about the growing glut, but they didn't listen."

Brown, now a regional manager for BMW, a West German maker of top-of-the-line bikes, asserts that when Japanese managers are sent to the United States, "Market share is everything. Managers have to produce and go back heroes."

In part, as a result of this fierce foreign competition and oversupply of motorcycles, Harley-Davidson Motor Co. was able to lobby successfully to increase the import tariffs on imported heavyweight motorcycles (those with a 700 cc displacement or greater). The tariff went from 4.4 percent to 49.4 percent in 1983 and is set up to return incrementally to 4.4 percent in five years.

Questions

1. How could the Japanese motorcycle manufacturers improve their forecasting ability?
2. Should Japanese motorcycle manufacturers modify any part of their marketing program?

Source: Based in part on Bob Woods. "Wheeling & Reeling," *Sales & Marketing Management* (May 16, 1983), pp. 43–50.

37.

Political Uncertainty on Hong Kong Island

China ceded Hong Kong Island to Britain in 1842, when it lost the opium wars. In 1860, it further ceded to Britain a tiny strip of mainland China that flanks Hong Kong Island's harbor. Britain did not actually gain ownership of this land but got a 100-year lease that began in 1898. The lease is due to expire in 1997, a situation that is causing widespread fear and uncertainty.

Hong Kong's economy is based on capitalism and free enterprise. It has low taxes, cheap labor, and little government regulation of business. Hong Kong is the third largest financial center in the world, and its harbor is world class—ranking as the third largest container port in the world. It is also the home of a thriving electronics industry (over $3 billion in sales annually in the early 1980s). The most popular electronics products manufactured in Hong Kong are radios, watches, clocks, microcomputers, and integrated circuits. Such well-known U.S. firms as Atari, IBM, NCR, and Data General have production facilities on the island.

Will the People's Republic of China take control of the island in 1997, or will it renew Britain's lease? The unknown consequences for foreign firms operating in Hong Kong should China take control have already started to soften real estate prices and stock prices. A major run on the banks occurred in 1983 as the public lost faith in the banking system. In addition, the brightest young engineers and professional people are attempting to move to the United States to establish residency. Since almost all of them have been trained or educated in the United States, they find this move relatively easy as they are familiar with the U.S. culture. Also, jobs are plentiful in the United States for computer experts, especially in the Silicon Valley in California and in the Boston area.

Questions

1. Should firms like IBM and NCR divest themselves of their investments in Hong Kong?
2. Suppose that you are president of a small U.S. manufacturer of microcomputers and you estimate that you would manufacture your product at a cost 30 percent below your U.S. manufacturing cost if you had a plant in Hong Kong. Should you set up a manufacturing facility there? Should it be a joint venture or directly owned?

Source: Based on Louis Kraar. "Confidence Is Building in Hong Kong," *Fortune* (June 11, 1984), pp. 140–148; "Big Business Sees Profit in Chinese Flag Over Hong Kong," *BusinessWeek* (October 8, 1984), p. 55; Vonnie Bishop. "Hong Kong: Business as Usual in the Midst of Uncertainty," *Electronic Business* (March 1984), pp. 172–185; Joshua Hyatt. "Hong Kong: One Order of Sweet and Sour Takeover," *Inc.* (November 1984), p. 29.

38.

Henry and Richard Block of H & R Block, Inc.

Henry and Richard Block started United Business Company, a bookkeeping service in Kansas City for small businesses in 1946. From the start, both brothers firmly

believed that customer service was the key to operating a successful business. Consequently, they offered to prepare income tax returns for their clients free of charge. This free service created a lot of word-of-mouth advertising that drew more customers to the Block brothers for tax preparation services—business the brothers welcomed.

By 1954, they were the biggest bookkeeping service in town. There was simply too much work for the brothers to handle and they gave up the tax business. Their customers strongly protested this decision, however, so they decided to discard the bookkeeping business and concentrate on tax preparation. On January 25, 1955, United Business Company was dissolved and H & R Block, Inc., was formed. On that day, Henry and Richard Block not only started a new business, they also created an industry.

On H & R Block's first day of operation, it ran two small newspaper ads, "Income Taxes Prepared, $5 and Up." Their pricing strategy was to price on the basis of the complexity of the return, not upon the client's income or refund. The response was phenomenal. By 1957, there were seventeen offices in three states. In 1958, the company began franchising its business format and by 1965, it used television advertising for the first time and prepared a million tax returns in a single season.

Recognizing that convenience is critical, H & R Block created an intensive distribution strategy. By the early 1980s, it had opened over 9,000 tax preparation offices in the United States, Canada, and ten foreign countries. Included are satellite franchises in communities as small as 20,000, where local business people are trained to prepare tax returns. H & R Block also has offices in over 800 Sears stores and over 400 other department stores. To further emphasize convenience, a customer can either make an appointment, drop off receipts and records at a Block office, or for an added charge have the return prepared at his or her home or office.

A comprehensive policy and procedures manual helps to make certain that office procedures are designed for the comfort of clients and staff, and that they allow for an efficient and effective operation. Training of employees is also an important success ingredient. Collectively, the policies, procedures, and training help to reinforce the fact that H & R Block is selling a "feeling." This philosophy is best summarized by Thomas M. Block

(Henry's son): "Even though we deliver a tangible product to our clients, what we sell is a feeling—a feeling that begins to develop from the time a client walks in the door of our office until the completed tax return is signed and dropped in the mail. It begins with a friendly greeting by our receptionist, a cup of fresh coffee, and a complete and thorough interview by a trained preparer. It includes the peace of mind offered by our guarantee and the assurance that at H & R Block, we stand behind our work and our clients."

Questions

1. Discuss the role of price, promotion, distribution, product, and people in H & R Block's marketing mix.
2. Why has H & R Block been so successful? Is their success threatened by any environmental trends?

Source: Based upon information provided in Thomas M. Block, "Innovations in Services Marketing," in Leonard L. Berry, G. Lynn Shostack, and Gregory D. Upah (eds.), *Emerging Perspectives on Services Marketing* (Chicago: American Marketing Association 1983), pp. 22–24. Direct quote used by permission.

39.

Willoughby Realty Inc. and Willoughby/Gendell Commercial Real Estate Services (by Martin Meyers)

Shirley Gendell converted the den of her home into a small real estate office in 1970. Her home is located in Skokie, Illinois, population 70,000, an upper middle class suburb north of Chicago. Mrs. Gendell brings together clients who wish to buy or sell a home in the Skokie area.

In 1972, her business grew and she opened a small office in town, where she employed four full-time salespersons. In 1975, as her business continued to expand, her husband Henry joined the business. He represented purchasers and sellers interested in vacant land in Skokie, Morton Grove, and other neighboring suburbs. In 1982, their son Scott received his law degree and joined the business. He had a real estate law practice in addition to his responsibilities with his parents' business.

In 1984, Gendell Realty merged with Willoughby, a real estate firm founded by Florence Bubes, to form Willoughby Realty Inc. The new company handles residential property. A division of Willoughby Realty, Willoughby/Gendell Commercial Real Estate Services, handles commercial property. Today there are six offices—two in Skokie and one each in Chicago and the suburbs of Niles, Buffalo Grove, and Northbrook.

Willoughby Realty controls 25 percent of the Skokie home market, which is the largest single resale market in any Chicago suburb. They control a lower percentage in the neighboring suburbs.

Willoughby Realty recently added a mortgage division. A client can obtain a mortgage through Willoughby instead of a savings and loan or other financial institution. Willoughby Realty acts as a middleman for the mortgage, rather than directly financing it. Approximately 15 percent of their clients take out mortgages through Willoughby Realty. Their goal is to increase this figure to 50 percent.

Approximately 90 percent of Willoughby Realty's customers purchase residential properties, generally a home within a three-mile radius of one of Willoughby Realty's offices. Approximately 10 percent of their customers are purchasers of commercial property. Willoughby/Gendell Commercial Real Estate Services represents purchasers who acquire and develop shopping centers and who purchase or sell established shopping centers.

The residential division's peak season is between January and August with their busiest months being March through July. The commercial business is less cyclical and can carry the residential business during the slack season. In the slack season, residential salespeople develop the Florida market for retirement or relocation—Florida is a popular retirement area for people living in the Midwest.

Willoughby Realty recently started a real estate school. They offer a six-week course in Skokie and in Buffalo Grove. The course meets twice a week and costs $105. It prepares students for the test required to obtain a real estate license. There are twenty students enrolled in the Skokie division and ten students enrolled in Buffalo Grove. Willoughby Realty hires many of the course's graduates to fill vacancies in their sales force of 105. In the residential division there are ninety-nine: fifty-four full-time, and forty-five part-time. There are six full-time salespersons in the commercial division. The sales staffs for the two divisions operate out of different offices. In the commercial division, salespersons are required to wear business suits, but in the residential division, the salespersons can dress more casually.

Willoughby Realty advertises their inventory in the suburban newspapers and the *Chicago Tribune*. They also utilize *Real Estate News* and *Realty and Building,* which are trade magazines. A trade magazine is a publication targeted to people employed in a certain business. Articles about Willoughby/Gendell Commercial Real Estate Services are published in the trade magazines. The articles typically explain the services provided by Willoughby/Gendell and discuss their latest projects. Approximately one third of their residential and commercial customers are derived from their advertising. The remainder are derived from referrals and word-of-mouth advertising.

Questions

1. How do their clients learn about Willoughby Realty and Willoughby/Gendell Commercial Real Estate Services? Is it typical for service firms? How might the firm's promotion be improved?

2. Comment on Willoughby Realty's marketing activities during the slack season. How might they be modified to improve the firm's performance?

40.

Northridge Methodist Church

James Larson is the minister at Northridge Methodist Church. Northridge is in a community of approximately 100,000 and is served by nine additional churches. There is only one Methodist church, however. Recently, Reverend Larson and Erin England (the assistant minister) were discussing their church's dismal financial situation. The most recent annual statement of revenues and expenses is shown in Table 1.

The major revenue sources are pledges and worship service offerings. Northridge has 800 members who pledge an average weekly contribution of $3.12. The average total nonpledge offering per week is $797.67. Attendance at worship services is low (the average member attends 18 Sundays per year). In 1986, Jim and Erin performed twenty-one weddings and seventy-three funerals. Twenty of the twenty-one weddings were for church members, however, only twenty-eight of the funeral services were for church members. The other funeral services were the result of referrals from two local funeral homes that recommended Northridge to families who wished to have a church funeral service but did not belong to a local church. During 1986, Northridge also had seventeen special donations or pledges for a total of $8,160. A final source of revenue is its bimonthly rental of a meeting room to a local civic organization.

These revenue sources, when contrasted with expenses, resulted in a surplus of only $15,896 in 1986. Both ministers believe that this amount is far below what is necessary because of several large, anticipated future expenses. The heating and cooling system needs to be replaced at an estimated cost of $27,000. The church also needs a new organ, which would cost approximately $35,000. Finally, a major interior renovation of the church is necessary, and this is estimated to require $125,000 to $140,000. Thus, Northridge needs to spend $187,000 to $202,000 to put the church facilities in top condition. At year-end 1986, the church had cash or investible funds of $41,909, of which $20,000 was in a certificate of deposit that matures in July 1987 and the remainder was in an interest-bearing checking account.

Northridge Methodist Church has a finance committee composed of the two ministers and three appointed church members: Rodney Churchill, a widower and retired dentist; Richard Hancock, a 36-year-old high school biology teacher; and Sandra Noble, a 26-year-old married woman who owns a local consulting firm. At a recent finance committee meeting, Rev. Larson asked for suggestions on how to improve Northridge's financial performance. Many of the suggestions were of the typical "cut your costs and control expenses" variety. Only Sandra concentrated her suggestions on the revenue rather than the expense structure of the church. For example, she argued that if average annual Sunday attendance could be increased, revenues would rise with little or no increase in expenses. Sandra also felt that the average pledge of $3.12 could be increased to $4.00 and that more members could be encouraged to pledge. She also suggested that special donations should be a vehicle to fund certain projects such as the new organ. For example, thirty-five $1,000 special donations could fund the purchase of the new organ. In addition, she thought that more space could be rented to local clubs and organizations for their meetings and that space could also be rented to nursery schools.

Both ministers were interested in Sandra's ideas, but the other lay members of the committee were rather negative. They believed that people gave money to the church based on what they felt was appropriate and could afford and that giving was a sensitive issue. Attempts to increase membership support could backfire and result in less revenue because of the possibility of losing members. They believed that the best way to manage the church's finances was to better control costs. This position angered Sandra, who insisted that running a church is not that different from operating any business. She stated that she could not try to improve the

financial performance of her firm by cutting costs such as locating her office in a tent; she argued that it was often necessary to increase costs in order to generate more revenue and make higher profits.

At the conclusion of the meeting, she urged both ministers to think seriously about developing a strategic marketing plan for Northridge Methodist Church. As Rodney Churchill left the meeting, he disgustedly said, "God doesn't need to be marketed or sold!"

Questions

1. If Northridge Methodist Church develops a marketing plan, what marketing research might be useful?
2. What are some of the aspects of a marketing mix for a church? How should these be related to developing a marketing plan for Northridge Methodist? How would this plan increase revenues?

Table 1 Northridge Methodist Church: Revenues and Expenses (1986)

Revenues		
Sunday church service offerings	$ 41,479	
Pledges	129,792	
Weddings	5,250	
Funerals	13,708	
Hall rental	2,300	
Special donations	8,160	
Total revenues		$200,689
Expenses		
Mortgage payments	$ 23,515	
Utilities and phone	13,113	
Maintenance and cleaning supplies	20,424	
Insurance	3,500	
Equipment rental	5,992	
Salaries and wages	81,900	
Outreach	25,500	
Advertising	4,000	
Miscellaneous	6,849	
Total expenses		184,793
Year-end surplus		$ 15,896

PART VIII

EXECUTION, EVALUATION, AND THE FUTURE OF MARKETING

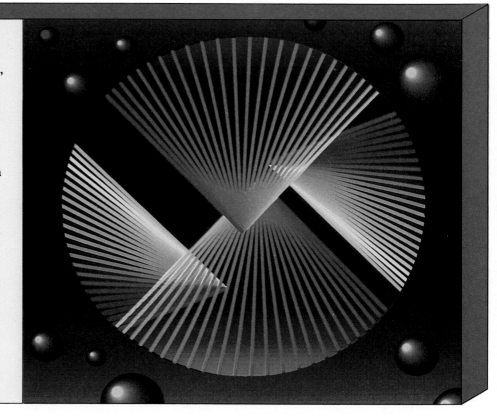

Part VIII concludes our discussion of marketing. Chapter 21, "Executing the Marketing Plan," describes the two major steps in executing a marketing plan: implementation and control. Chapter 22, "Evaluation, Ethics, and the Future of Marketing," reflects on the performance of marketing on a societal level, the ethical behavior of marketers, and what marketing might be like in the mid-1990s.

EXECUTING THE MARKETING PLAN

MARKETER PROFILE

Stanley C. Gault of Rubbermaid

Stanley C. Gault is the chairman of Rubbermaid—a manufacturer of rubber and plastic products for the consumer and institutional markets. Gault came to Rubbermaid in 1980 after losing a bid for the chairmanship at General Electric, where he started as a salesperson and moved on to become a marketing executive and senior vice president and sector executive.

When Gault joined Rubbermaid, his assignment was challenging: to improve significantly his firm's financial performance. Stanley Gault has succeeded in meeting this challenge: between 1980 and 1983, the firm's net profit nearly doubled. One of the major changes that Gault instituted within the Home Products Division was the implementation of the product management concept combined with the restructuring of the sales force. In the past, the sales force sold every product category to all channels of distribution (i.e., sinkware, household containers, space organizers). "But, because of rapidly expanding product lines and changed distribution patterns, specialty sales organizations now concentrate on such outlets as supermarkets or mass merchandisers. Last year's restructuring of the sales force, both in the field and headquarters, will provide a more intense level of management involvement with customers," says Gault, adding that, "Contented retailers are a byproduct of the reorganization." Rubbermaid also eliminated a home party sales program within the housewares area of this business.

Stanley Gault has also opted to aggressively pursue expansion into new markets, such as microwave cookware and food storage containers on the consumer housewares side of the business, and agriculture, commercial horticulture, and health care on the commercial side. The company has also acquired ConTact brand self-adhesive decorative coverings; Little Tikes, a traditional high-quality toy manufacturer; the Gott Corporation, a manufacturer of plastic insulated products; and Seco, a manufacturer of floor care products.

Source: "Putting Rubbermaid's House in Order," *Sales and Marketing Management* (January 16, 1984), p. 14; corporate annual reports.

INTRODUCTION

In Chapter 1, we defined marketing as the process of planning and executing the conception, pricing, promotion, and distribution of ideas, goods, and services to create exchanges that satisfy individual and organizational objectives. The first twenty chapters of this book concentrated on the planning phase. This chapter will detail how a firm can execute its marketing plans and will show that properly organizing a firm's resources, as Rubbermaid's Stanley Gault did in the Marketer Profile, is one of the necessary steps in executing a marketing plan.

Once the organization has developed a plan, it must execute that plan. (It may be helpful to refer to Figure 3.1, which shows the planning and execution steps in the strategic marketing management process.) The first step in execution is implementation (or putting the plan into practice). Charles Schwab, founder of Charles Schwab and Co., the largest discount stockbroker in the United States, believes that failure to properly implement a plan is the major reason why many businesses and marketing programs fail.[1] The second step in executing a marketing plan is control. A plan cannot be executed properly unless there are good control procedures to keep the plan working well and help the firm achieve its objectives.

IMPLEMENTING THE PLAN

Implementation of plans consists of (1) acquiring the necessary financial and human resources, (2) organizing the personnel so that they can be properly managed to execute the plan, and (3) using resources by coordinating efforts, motivating personnel, and communicating the assignment of tasks, scheduling of activities, and deadlines, so that the plan can be carried out on a day-to-day basis.

Resource Acquisition

All marketing plans require an organization to commit financial and human resources to achieve some stated objectives. Financial resources are necessary for the acquisition of capital assets, such as new plant and equipment, to produce new products; accounts receivable, to finance purchases by customers; and inventory, to have products available for distribution or sale. Human resources are necessary because most growth-oriented marketing plans create a need for more marketing personnel (i.e., product managers, sales force managers, salespeople, warehouse managers, transportation managers, or marketing research staff). An increased work load may lead to an increase in the number of employees or the need for a different mix of personnel. For example, a company planning to enter a new, unfamiliar market may hire personnel from other industries in order to gain the necessary expertise.

Financial resources can be obtained either internally or externally. Many organizations have sufficient capital to finance expansion into new markets or to develop new products internally on their own. Frequently, however, a firm must raise funds externally by such methods as selling bonds, borrowing from banks, selling stock, or otherwise getting outsiders to put capital into the organization. Human resources also can be obtained internally or externally. An organization can promote existing employees and assign other employees new marketing responsibilities, or it may decide to hire experienced personnel from competitors. For example, Apple Computer hired John Scully, president of PepsiCo., to be its president. In addition, Apple hired William V. Campbell from Eastman Kodak to be its vice president of marketing.[2]

Resource Organization

If a company is committed to the marketing concept, the first requirement for organizing marketing resources is to accord marketing equal status with other key areas in the firm. This will also help facilitate the execution of marketing plans, as shown in Figure 21.1, where the top marketing person has vice presidential status and reports directly to the chief executive officer. Table 21.1 provides some examples of primary responsibilities of marketing vice presidents in different types of U.S. corporations.

We also see in Figure 21.1 that the vice president of marketing is on the same level as the vice presidents of human resources, production, finance, and research and development, all of whom report directly to the chief executive officer (CEO). These five vice presidents all participate in top-level decision making with the CEO. If the CEO is doing a good job, then decisions will be made that are beneficial to the organization as a whole and that do not favor any functional area to the detriment of other areas. The CEO must develop a spirit of cooperation among the various vice presidents so that they can collectively help the firm fulfill its mission and achieve its objectives.

A cooperative attitude is often difficult to develop because each vice president will be evaluated on his or her ability to accomplish certain objectives. For example, the vice president of human resources may be evaluated on the rate of employee turnover, employee relations, and the

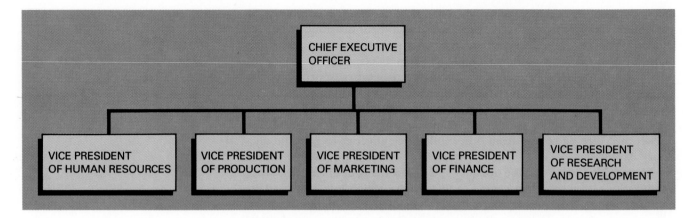

Figure 21.1

An Organization That Accords Equal Status to Marketing

recruitment of high-quality employees. The production vice president may be evaluated on the basis of unit production costs, ability to keep on schedule, and quality control. The financial vice president is likely to be evaluated on his or her ability to maintain adequate liquidity, limit bad debts expense, prepare accurate budgets, use working capital productively, and minimize corporate income taxes. Because the research and development vice president's performance is difficult to evaluate in the short run, he or she usually is judged on the ability to stay within the budget. In the long run, however, the research and development vice president is evaluated on the quantity and quality of new products developed. The vice president of marketing will be evaluated on such things as growth in sales, market share, and control of marketing costs.

A key problem that arises in all organizations is that each vice president may try to achieve his or her objectives at the expense of the other vice presidents' objectives. This is referred to as *suboptimization.* Consider the following conflicts that may arise:

1. The production vice president can lower unit production costs by producing fewer model variations (i.e., color, style, size), which will mean larger production runs; however, the job of selling is easier if the firm has lots of model variations.
2. The marketing vice president can increase the products' market shares if buyers are offered liberal credit. Unfortunately, this will lower working capital productivity and increase bad debt expense, which will make the finance vice president look inept.
3. The vice president of human resources can look good if tight control is maintained on salaries and wages, which means not allowing them to increase at a rate faster than the industry average. If the vice president of marketing can pay higher than competitive wages, however, a more productive sales force can be attracted, which will allow the firm to increase sales more rapidly.

Table 21.1   Primary Responsibilities of Corporate Marketing Vice Presidents in Selected Companies

Vice President of Marketing of a Specialty Chemicals Producer
  · Coordination and development of overall marketing strategies
  · Training and development of first-line marketing managers
  · Providing a corporate marketing service of information systems
  · Pricing and distribution policies and practices
  · Evaluating opportunities for new products and new businesses

Senior Vice President of Marketing of a Consumer Products Manufacturer
  · Overall planning and establishment of strategic priorities within marketing
  · Integration of the marketing function
  · Creative stimulation of marketing innovation

Senior Vice President of Marketing and Sales of an Aircraft Manufacturer
  · To improve and develop the distribution system, both domestic and international
  · To direct the advertising program
  · To ensure a good product-support system
  · To provide good marketing information to the company
  · To suggest product improvements
  · To help develop long-range plans
  · To prepare short-range and long-range forecasts
  · To recommend product pricing

Vice President of Marketing for a Manufacturer of Electrical and Electronic Products
  · Planning for the long term
  · Forecasting for the short term
  · Work on new product and market opportunities
  · Management of the marketing and sales efforts of the divisions

Source: David S. Hopkins and Earl L. Bailey. *Organizing Corporate Marketing*
(New York: The Conference Board, 1984), p. 10. Used by permission.

4. The vice president of research and development will look best in the long run if he or she concentrates on developing a few major innovations rather than a series of minor product modifications. However, the marketing vice president needs a regular series of minor product changes in order to compete with the other firms' marketing efforts. The marketing vice president does need major product introductions, but for short-term survival in the marketplace, something new must be offered, even if it is only a minor modification.

The preceding are only a few of the possible types of conflicts that can develop between marketing and other departments and harm an organization. Somehow the vice presidents must be made to see that they are all working for the same ultimate goal. Actions should only be taken that benefit the organization as a whole, which implies that one or more areas in the firm can be harmed only if the benefit to the entire organization is positive. This is why, as was stated in Chapter 3, a CEO must clearly state and communicate to all managers the firm's mission and objectives, which should guide all important management decisions.

The extent to which the marketing vice-president or top marketing executive is able to effectively execute the marketing plan depends on cooperation not only with other senior managers in the firm, but also with other marketing personnel. Although the senior marketing executive has the authority to tell all other marketing personnel what to do, in most organizations, these employees do not report directly to the senior marketing person. Thus, the organizational structure of the marketing unit will be used to establish who has the authority and responsibility to make certain decisions and perform certain marketing tasks and activities and who reports to whom.

Marketing activities can be organized in several ways, depending on such factors as the size of the firm, the environment in which it operates, the breadth of its product mix, and the number of market segments it serves. Even if two firms are similar with respect to these factors, they may decide to organize the marketing unit differently, and both may be successfully managed firms. We will now explore four major ways firms organize their marketing departments: (1) by function, (2) by geographic region, (3) by product, and (4) by market segment.

Organizing by Function.   **Functional organization** of marketing efforts consists of *having a key manager responsible for each major marketing function.* These managers typically report to the senior marketing manager and/or vice president of marketing, as is illustrated in Figure 21.2.

When a firm serves a single market and sells only a few products, then functional organization can be advantageous because the firm becomes very

Figure 21.2

Organizing the Marketing Unit by Function

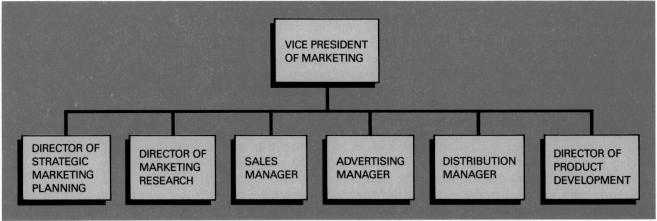

efficient at performing the necessary functions. However, coordination problems arise once the firm develops a large product mix or decides to serve more than one market.

Organizing by Geographic Region. Often when a firm begins to grow, it expands its base of operations to other geographic areas—first domestic and then international. Since it is difficult to manage and coordinate operations over a wide geographic region from one location, firms may begin to organize their marketing efforts on a regional basis. **Geographic organization** consists of *organizing marketing efforts by the major geographic areas the firm serves.*

Figure 21.3 shows how a firm might organize its marketing unit by geographic region. Reporting to the vice president of marketing is a corporate marketing manager, and reporting to him or her are three regional marketing managers. At the corporate headquarters, there is a marketing research staff, a strategic marketing planning staff, a customer service staff, an advertising and sales promotion staff, and a new product development staff. Each of these reports directly to the vice president of marketing. The various corporate staffs, by offering their expertise and skills, will help each regional marketing manager develop an effective marketing program.

If the company is large, each region might also have various functional managers. For example, in Figure 21.3 we see that for the area west of the Mississippi River an advertising manager, a sales manager, and a distribution manager report directly to the regional marketing manager. These regional functional managers will work with the regional marketing manager to develop effective marketing programs. Generally, the geographic mode of organizing is most effective when the firm's customers are geographically varied and when the geographic scope of a firm's operations is diverse.

Organizing by Product. If a company produces or sells highly diverse products, functional and geographic approaches to organizing the marketing unit may prove ineffective. The problems of managing advertising or some other function may differ depending on the product. For example, if a company is selling such diverse products as electronic cash registers, personal computers, and electronic security alarms, then it may need to organize its marketing effort around these distinct product lines.

Product organization consists of *organizing marketing efforts by the firm's major product lines.* General Motors Company traditionally has organized its marketing efforts by its five major product groups—Pontiac, Chevrolet, Oldsmobile, Buick, and Cadillac. In 1984, the company reorganized. It still has a product organization, but with only two groups: the big car group consists of Cadillac, Oldsmobile, and Buick, and the small car group consists of Chevrolet and Pontiac. In a separate move, GM created a company to produce a new small car called *Saturn.*[3]

Figure 21.4 shows how a firm might organize a marketing unit by product lines. The marketing managers for the different product lines report

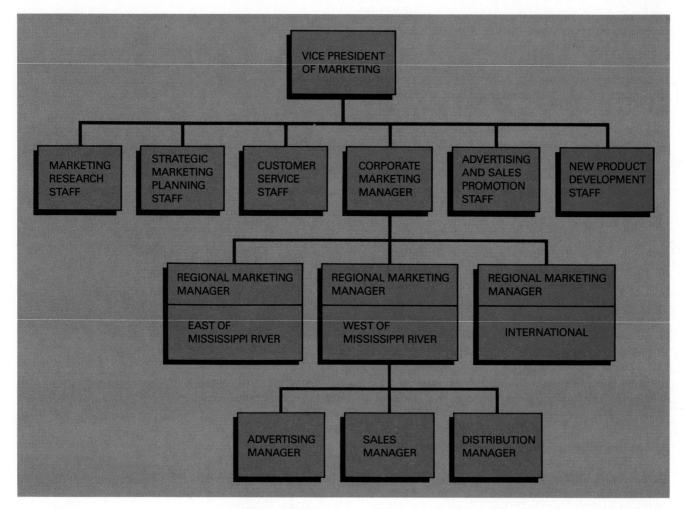

Figure 21.3
Organizing the Marketing Unit by Geographic Region

directly to the vice president of marketing. Each of these managers is responsible for developing an effective marketing mix for the products under his or her control. One of the advantages of this type of organization is that it gives the firm flexibility in developing appropriate marketing mixes for different product lines. The product manager can draw on the expertise of various staff people at headquarters, such as specialists in marketing research, advertising, planning, and customer service. In addition, if the company is quite large and each product line manager is responsible for numerous products, then each product manager may have a director of marketing research, an advertising manager, a sales manager, and a distribution manager.

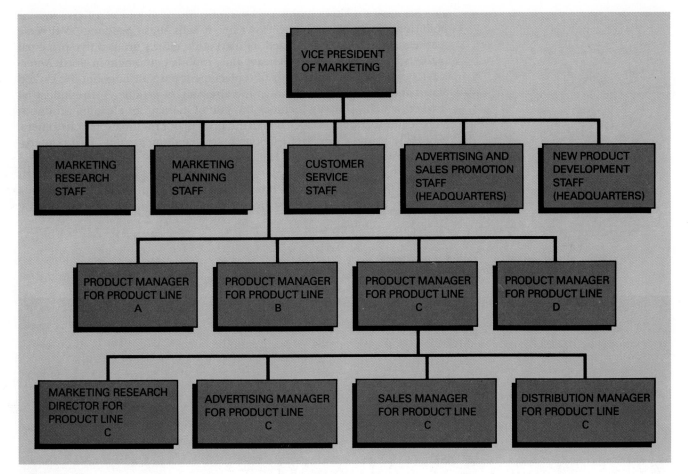

Figure 21.4

Organizing the Marketing Unit by Product Lines

One of the disadvantages of a product line approach is that a lot of duplication in personnel and effort occurs. For example, if each product group has its own sales manager and sales force, it is possible for a single customer to be called on by several different salespeople, all representing the same selling organization.

Organizing by Market Segment. A firm may find that its marketing effort is directed at several diverse market segments.[4] Because each of these market segments or customer groups may have different needs and purchase requirements, marketing managers who are in charge of each segment must make sure these diverse groups are well served. **Market segment organization** consists of *organizing marketing efforts around a firm's major market segments.* For example, the Donaldson Company, Inc. manufactures air cleaners, air filters, mufflers, hydraulic filters, liquid clarifiers, and air pollution control equipment. However, it sells these products to diverse markets and thus has organized its marketing efforts around five principal markets: (1) manufacturers of heavy-duty mobile equipment in North America; (2) warehouse distributors of replacement parts throughout the United States and Canada, referred to as the aftermarket group; (3) the industrial market, which primarily includes the sale of in-plant air cleaning products; (4) the international market, which includes major multinational customers, especially manufacturers of truck and farm equipment; and (5) the micro-filtration/defense products market, which includes specialized filters for the computer disk drive and copier markets and traditional engine filtration products for the military and other defense-related products.[5]

Figure 21.5 shows how a firm might organize its marketing unit by

Figure 21.5

Organizing the Marketing Unit by Market Segments

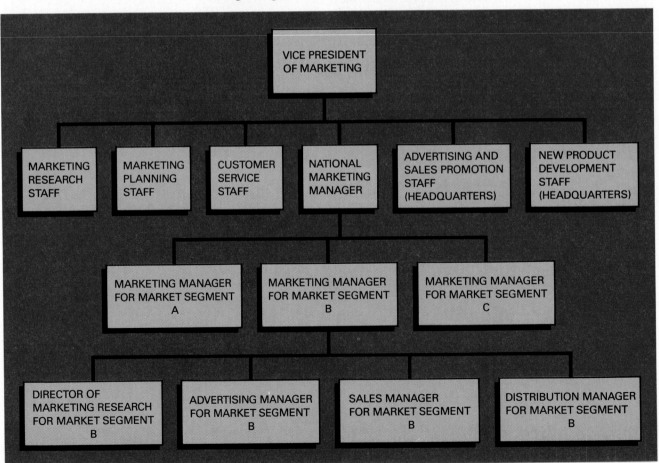

MARKETING IN ACTION

One of the industry leaders in the manufacture of paper bags and containers is St. Regis Corp. In 1983, it restructured its marketing efforts by segmenting its business to improve response time for handling customer inquiries and complaints. The paper bag packaging business is in the mature stage of the product life cycle, which means that excess capacity leads customers to expect faster response from manufacturers.

To accomplish its objectives, the company combined consumer and industrial products and then divided them into the following five autonomous strategic business units based on different market segments: (1) consumer goods, (2) retail packaging, (3) specialty packaging (for example, stretch film), (4) multi-

Reorganization at St. Regis

wall packaging—east region, (5) multiwall packaging—west region. Each strategic business unit has a sales manager, four area or regional managers, and twenty-five to thirty salespeople. Each SBU also has its own financial and engineering personnel. When the reorganization occurred, St. Regis took the opportunity to realign sales regions to better respond to major customers.

Each of the five SBUs are responsible for marketing, sales, and production. Consequently, they are also responsible for profits and planning for growth. This high degree of au-

tonomy and responsibility creates a spirit of entrepreneurship and concern for bottom-line results within each business unit.

With this new organization, St. Regis can now respond to customer inquiries, complaints, and demands for product modification or new product development much more quickly. Also, if a St. Regis salesperson wants to bid on an account, he or she can get a bid approved within minutes whereas it once took days to go through all the layers of management.

Source: Corporate annual reports; Rayna Skolnik. "St. Regis Divides to Conquer," *Sales & Marketing Management* (October 10, 1983), pp. 39–42.

market segments. Reporting to the vice president of marketing are various corporate marketing staff personnel and a national marketing manager. In turn, three different marketing managers for three different market segments report to the national marketing manager. If the firm is quite large, it may have functional managers for marketing research, advertising, sales, and distribution reporting to the manager of a market segment. They will work with the marketing manager and various corporate staff personnel to develop an effective marketing program for the market segment. A major advantage of this organization mode is that it allows managers to get close to customers and better understand them. This method of organizing also facilitates the development of a strategy for each target market.

The Marketing in Action on this page highlights the efforts of the St. Regis Corp. to reorganize its paper bag business around market segments.

Multiple Modes.   Du Pont's textile fibers division has product line managers and market segment managers. The five product line managers are for rayon, acetate, nylon, orlon, and dacron; the four market segment managers are for menswear, womenswear, home furnishings, and industrial markets. This allows Du Pont to have product and market expertise in its organization.[6] Most firms, such as Du Pont, employ a hybrid form of organizing, combining function, geographic region, product line, and market segmentation approaches. A very large firm may use several approaches, whereas a smaller firm may just use one or two. For example, a firm could first organize around regions and then have product or market segment managers, or, functional managers for advertising, sales, distribution, and marketing research, within each region.

A guiding principle is to match the method of organization to the firm's marketing environment.[7] Thus, a firm operating in a single city, selling one product, and serving one market segment can prosper with a simple functional organization. If the firm begins to expand geographically, increase its product mix, and serve multiple market segments, then its marketing environment will become more complex, thus requiring a more complex marketing organization.

Resource Utilization

Once the personnel resources have been properly organized, steps must be taken to obtain good resource utilization if the plan is to be implemented effectively. In this regard, the efforts of the personnel must be coordinated, the personnel must be motivated, and communication with the personnel must be effective.

Coordination.　A marketing plan is doomed to failure unless all personnel are coordinated to assist in carrying out the plan. Three types of coordination must be developed. First, personnel in the marketing department must coordinate their activities. The advertising personnel, salespeople, transportation and distribution people, marketing research staff, and so on must all work to develop an integrated marketing mix that offers benefits to a well-defined target market. Second, marketing personnel must coordinate their efforts with personnel in accounting, finance, and production. A marketing plan cannot be implemented effectively if the support of these personnel is not obtained. Third, efforts must be coordinated with other organizations that will play a critical role in implementing the marketing plan. For example, the support of wholesalers and retailers in stocking the firm's products is needed; the support of an advertising agency may be necessary; the support of motor carriers may be required; and the support of bankers to help finance the marketing plan is usually mandatory.

Motivation.　In Chapter 15, we discussed motivating salespeople; however, all personnel must be motivated to perform at a high level if the plan is to be implemented effectively. Motivation occurs by offering the right package of rewards to personnel. This package should consist of extrinsic rewards, such as monetary inducements, and intrinsic rewards, such as personal recognition and esteem of colleagues.

Communication.　The final ingredient in implementing the plan is communicating to the respective personnel their tasks, the schedule of activities necessary to implement the plan, and the necessary deadlines, so that the plan can be carried out on a day-to-day basis.

BEFORE YOU PUSH HERE,

PUSH HERE.

To get the most sales, a salesman has to be pushy in the right way.

Using New England Telephone for making appointments is a perfect example.

A call ahead not only gives the customer a chance to schedule your meeting, it gives you a chance to pre-sell your product. You can determine a sales prospect's needs, so you're better prepared to give the right answers. And you can save steps by eliminating trips to those who aren't sales prospects at all.

To make matters even better, New England Telephone lets you do it all for less money than any other kind of sales call.

Use New England Telephone to turn cold calls into hot prospects, and watch what happens.

We're the one for you New England.

New England Telephone
A **NYNEX** Company

Personnel involved in the marketing plan have to coordinate their efforts, and New England Telephone wants to make the sales representative's part in the plan that much easier.

Open lines of communication must exist among the different functional areas in the organization. One effective method for facilitating communication among different functional areas is to have open-door planning meetings. This does not mean that anyone in the organization can attend any meeting, but that senior managers can sit in on meetings conducted by other senior managers that may not pertain directly to their areas of responsibility. If the production vice president has weekly meetings to discuss production planning and scheduling, the marketing vice president should be allowed to attend. If the vice president of finance has a quarterly meeting with the CEO on the next period's budget, the other vice presidents (including marketing) should be welcome. An open-door policy creates an aura of openness and cooperation, as well as allows input from the other senior managers.

Another method for fostering open communication across functional areas is to set up a task force. A **task force** is *a special group of people organized on a temporary basis to solve a particular problem.* Each task force should have representatives from all the functional areas of the firm that might be affected by the problem. For example, a task force established to evaluate the feasibility of building an automated warehouse that is called for in the marketing plan should include representatives from finance, because this is a major capital expenditure; representatives from personnel, because labor contracts may need to be renegotiated; marketing representatives, because the size of packages shipped to customers may need to be considered; and representatives from distribution, since this is essentially a physical distribution decision. Joint participation on task forces allows for the views of all interested parties to be heard and facilitates open communication.

CONTROLLING THE MARKETING PLAN

Importance of Control

Control is *the process of comparing expected performance with actual performance and taking corrective action where necessary.* Assume, for illustration purposes, that your plan projects sales of your product to be $1.5 million annually. After three months, sales are running at the rate of $1.2 million annually. Based on this finding, you should reassess your marketing mix and target market plans and ask questions such as: Is the price too high? Is advertising expenditure too low? Is there a quality defect in the product? Has the appropriate target market been selected? For example, in 1982 Grid Systems, Inc. introduced a portable personal computer called *Compass* targeted at the senior executive.[8] Sales were far below expectations, and the company found that few top executives were ready to accept personal computers. A better target probably would have been middle managers.

The Marketing in Action on page 659 shows how the senior management at Shaklee Corporation explained to stockholders the firm's disappointing 1984 financial performance. Pay particular attention to their comments on marketing-related causes of poor performance.

Most marketing managers don't like the idea of controlling their expenditures.[9] Many believe that the cost of creating a customer cannot be forecast accurately because marketing operates in an open environment and is influenced by such uncontrollable phenomena as competitor behavior, changing consumer tastes, and the economy. Some of this uneasiness about control is reasonable—after all, they do operate in an open and largely

MARKETING IN ACTION

Many times, the best marketing plans do not produce the financial results envisioned. The following quote from the senior management of Shaklee Corporation attempts to explain to stockholders the firm's disappointing financial performance.

"Fiscal 1984 was a difficult and challenging year for Shaklee Corporation and for the entire direct-selling industry. Our sales for the year were $459.1 million, or 15 percent below the $538.7 million reported a year ago, and our net income fell to $13.2 million, or $1.01 per share compared to $35.1 million or $2.71 per share, last year. The number of our Sales Leaders worldwide also declined to 12,100 at September 30, 1984 compared to 13,400 a year ago.

As we reported last year, we began to experience—in both domestic and international markets—increased competition in the nutritional products and direct-selling industries. In addition, direct-selling companies began to face difficulties in recruiting and retaining new distributors as the economy improved and some individuals returned to their previous occupations or found that they no longer needed the supplemental income provided by direct selling.

This trend continued throughout 1984. It had a significant impact on Shaklee—and on direct selling in

Shaklee Corporation Experiences a Disappointing Year

general—and has led to a contraction in the ranks of our field sales force.

During the past year we took several major steps to establish a framework necessary to improve our Sales Leader base and to increase our sales in the future. We concluded that we had to provide our sales organization—and potential Sales Leaders—with the two things they needed most: an improved business opportunity and even stronger product and marketing support.

More than a year ago we began to work with members of our sales force to restructure the basic Shaklee sales plan and to create new incentive programs which would meet their needs and provide them with an even more rewarding business opportunity. Several new incentive programs were introduced during the latter part of fiscal 1984, and major improvements to our basic sales plan were implemented in October 1984. These changes were well received by our Field and are expected to have a positive effect on our domestic sales and Sales Leader growth over the long term. We are returning

a greater percentage of each sales dollar to our Field than ever before. Our sales plan is the most rewarding of any major company in the direct-selling industry—and is even more attractive for those individuals who remain with us over the long term.

We have also taken additional steps to make the public more familiar with Shaklee and Shaklee products. Our visibility has been increased by the establishment of a Scientific Advisory Board and the targeting of the Shaklee message directly to members of the scientific and medical communities. We have been heavily involved in supporting the U.S. Ski Team. These activities are helping the general public to more closely associate Shaklee with nutrition, fitness and well-being. We have aggressively promoted our products through increased advertising and marketing campaigns so that Shaklee will become a more familiar name to millions of potential consumers. Finally we have improved the quality of the support materials we provide our Field so that Sales Leaders will be even more knowledgeable about Shaklee and Shaklee products, and more efficient in their own business building."

Source: *Shaklee Corporation 1984 Annual Report,* letter to shareholders, p. 2. Used by permission.

unpredictable environment. Also, most traditional corporate controllers lack the background to report and evaluate the financial impact of promotion and media policies, physical distribution policies, and marketing strategies. They usually are schooled in factory cost accounting techniques, which are

31 million adults went shopping today...in the Yellow Pages

(New independent usage study proves it)

1985 National Yellow Pages Usage Study Highlights

76.5% of all adults referred to the Yellow Pages in the typical month during 1985.

55.7% of all adults in the U.S. referred to the Yellow Pages in a typical week.

3.29 references to the Yellow Pages were made, on the average, by adult users in the average week, or 45 million references on the typical day.

17.8% of all adults used the Yellow Pages on the typical day during 1985. That's a total of 30.7 million people!

This just-published study will open your eyes to the profitable selling potential of National Yellow Pages as a major advertising medium.

Statistical Research, Inc., a respected and independent national research firm, is conducting a continuous study of Consumer Yellow Pages usage. The first year of results (which covers over 12,000 interviews) is completed and summarized in a new report that is now available to you.

Order your free copy of this revealing research study today. Discover the new power that National Yellow Pages advertising can bring to your product or service. Call or write National Yellow Pages Service Association or ask your advertising agency to contact us.

National Yellow Pages Service Association

nypsa®

888 W. Big Beaver Road
Troy, Michigan 48084
Telephone: (313) 362-3300

The medium that puts the "closing touch" on your marketing/media plan.

With its 1985 usage study, the National Yellow Pages Service Association appeals to marketing managers' desire to be able to forecast potential customers.

largely inappropriate for evaluating and controlling marketing efforts. For this reason, Sam Goodman, former controller of Nestle, has suggested that firms employ a marketing controller in addition to a traditional controller.[10] A **marketing controller** is *a financial officer who has a good understanding of accounting, finance, and marketing and who is specifically charged with evaluating, budgeting, and controlling marketing and distribution expenditures.*

Tools for Evaluating and Controlling Marketing Performance

We will discuss three tools that can be used to evaluate and control marketing efforts: sales analysis, sales performance analysis, and marketing profitability analysis.[11]

Sales Analysis.   **Sales analysis** is *the process of breaking down aggregate sales data to determine the firm's strengths and potential problem areas.* A marketing manager who knows that the company had sales of $10 million last year actually knows little that is useful. Aggregate sales statistics hide most of the useful information that a detailed sales analysis provides. Similarly, if the controller gave the marketing manager 30,000 sales invoices and said, "Here is the data on sales trends or sales breakdowns you need," again, not much information would be provided. Although these sales invoices represent an enormous amount of data, they are useless unless they are properly categorized and summarized to provide meaningful information.

If properly designed, the sales invoice can represent an excellent vehicle for collecting sales data, and if these data are properly processed, it can shed light on several marketing areas. A well-designed sales invoice should have the following information recorded:

1. Customer information (name, address, zip, phone)
2. Method of payment (cash or charge)
3. Name of salesperson
4. Method of selling (mail, phone, personal selling)
5. Products purchased (type, size, order quantity)
6. Price or discount category
7. Date of sale

If this information is recorded on a form that can be processed by a computer, then all types of useful sales analysis reports can be generated relatively quickly. Recall the example of the company with $10 million in annual sales. If the company computerized all its sales invoices, it could easily generate reports such as the following:

❑ Weekly, monthly, and quarterly sales reports

❑ Territory and product line sales reports

❑ Sales reports for each salesperson

❑ Sales analysis reports for phone, mail, and direct personal selling sales

❑ Sales reports for cash versus credit sales

Other reports also could be generated, depending on which questions the marketing manager wants answered.

One type of report that is quite informative is a **20/80 rule** report. With this type of report, one decides *which 20 percent of which particular* *category accounts for the highest percentage of sales*—frequently, 80 percent of sales—thus, the 20/80 notation. For example, a marketing manager may like to know:

❏ Which 20 percent of salespeople produce the highest sales, and what percentage of sales they account for.

❏ Which 20 percent of customers buy the most from the firm, and what percentage of total sales they account for.

❏ Which 20 percent of products produce the highest sales, and what percentage of total sales they account for.

Because the best 20 percent usually will account for a disproportionate volume of sales, the firm should keep a close watch over this sacred 20 percent.

The major advantage of sales analysis as a control tool is that it is easy and inexpensive to implement because sales data are readily available in most firms. It also has some major disadvantages: (1) it does not show the whole picture because profits are ignored and (2) the sales analyses are not compared with any standard or goal.

Sales Performance Analysis. Sales performance analysis is *the process of analyzing actual sales data and comparing them with planned or budgeted sales to determine strengths and potential problem areas in the organization.* Those areas where sales are significantly below plan or budget are identified for special management attention in hopes of correcting the poor performance. An area that does markedly better than expected also will be investigated to learn why the firm is doing so well in this area and how the knowledge gained might be applied elsewhere.

Once again, we will consider the firm that had $10 million in annual sales. Table 21.2 shows how this sales figure was generated in seven different sales territories. All of these sales territories had a sales budget, or quota, for a total of $10,400,000. By comparing actual with budgeted sales, we see that the firm fell $400,000 short of its budget. Importantly, most of this shortfall was in the Northeast region where sales were $300,000, or 11.1 percent, less than planned.

The firm, however, has not yet identified the cause of the poor performance. To help provide the answer, the analyst might examine the sales performance of the salespeople in the Northeast territory. This analysis is provided in Table 21.3. A careful study of this table reveals that the problem resides with two salespeople—Fred Smith and Joyce Eisel.

To shed additional light on the problem, the analyst next looks at each of three product lines that each salesperson sells. This analysis is provided in Table 21.4. Fred Smith and Joyce Eisel experienced the most difficulty in selling product line A. After consulting with Fred and Joyce, who have New York City and Boston as their respective territories, the analyst finds that a leading competitor recently introduced a new product in these two cities that competes with product line A. Because rumor has it that the

Table 21.2   Sales Performance by Territory

Sales Territory	Sales Budget	Actual Sales	(Actual − Budget)	Variance As Percentage of Budget
Midwest	$1,875,000	$1,900,000	$25,000	1.3%
Northeast	2,700,000	2,400,000	− 300,000	−11.1
South	1,150,000	1,100,000	− 50,000	− 4.3
Northwest	375,000	400,000	25,000	6.7
West	3,100,000	3,000,000	− 100,000	− 3.2
Southwest	690,000	700,000	10,000	1.4
North central	510,000	500,000	− 10,000	− 2.0
Total	$10,400,000	$10,000,000	$− 400,000	3.8%

Table 21.3   Salesperson Performance in Northeast

Salesperson	Quota	Actual Sales	(Actual − Budget)	Variance As Percentage of Quota
Bill Coleman	$ 600,000	$ 610,000	10,000	1.7%
Fred Smith	750,000	630,000	− 120,000	−16.0%
Sally Hoover	475,000	460,000	− 15,000	− 3.2%
Joyce Eisel	875,000	700,000	− 175,000	−20.0%
Total	$2,700,000	$2,400,000	− 300,000	−11.1%

Table 21.4   Product Line Analysis

Salesperson	Quota	Actual Sales	(Actual − Budget)	Variance As Percentage of Quota
FRED SMITH				
Product line A	$350,000	$240,000	$− 110,000	−31.4%
Product line B	200,000	210,000	10,000	5.0
Product line C	200,000	180,000	− 20,000	−10.0
	$750,000	$630,000	$− 120,000	−16.0%
JOYCE EISEL				
Product line A	$400,000	$270,000	$− 130,000	−32.5%
Product line B	240,000	225,000	− 15,000	− 6.3%
Product line C	$235,000	205,000	− 30,000	−12.8%
	$875,000	$700,000	$− 175,000	−20.0%

competitor will soon introduce this product nationally, the firm must immediately begin to develop a plan to cope with this increased competition.

As the prior example illustrated, sales performance analysis can be a sequential process. Typically, a variety of performance reports need to be examined before the true problem can be identified. Often, other data such as personal interviews with those parties most directly responsible for performance need to be obtained, but eventually the cause of poor performance can be isolated and corrective action taken.

Marketing Profitability Analysis.   Sales analysis and sales performance analysis are only partial appraisals of marketing control, since they do not consider the cost side of marketing and thus ignore profitability. **Marketing profitability analysis** *determines the profitability of particular products, sales territories, market segments, salespeople, and/or marketing channels.*[12]

Marketing profitability analysis has several important uses or purposes:

1. To show not only overall profit or loss, but also the profitability of various divisions of the business. Significant losses can be hidden in aggregate financial statistics.
2. To control the efficiency and performance of the firm's divisions.
3. To facilitate pricing decisions. Pricing decisions can be made more accurate by adding the costs of distribution/marketing to the manufacturing costs.
4. To help direct promotional effort to areas where it is most needed and will do the most good.
5. To aid in managing marketing channel relations. When the most profitable channel has been determined, the firm should attempt to have good relations with the wholesale and retail institutions that are part of it.

To conduct a marketing profitability analysis, the marketing manager must first be familiar with the different types of marketing costs that exist. A general classification of marketing costs is provided in Figure 21.6. Marketing costs are divided into order generation costs and order filling costs. **Order generation costs,** *the costs of obtaining orders, consist of advertising, personal selling, and sales promotion costs.* **Order filling costs,** *the costs of filling orders, consist of warehousing, transportation, order processing, and billing and collecting costs.*

Although order filling and order generation costs are drawn in Figure 21.6 separately for the purposes of classification, in reality they are closely connected. The higher the order generating costs, the higher are the order filling costs in most situations. Conversely, if order filling costs are high in order to provide a high level of customer service (i.e., quick deliveries and most items in stock), then the job of generating orders will be easier because customers will be satisfied.

The first approach to marketing profitability analysis that we will discuss is the **full cost analysis** approach, in which *all costs are identified with*

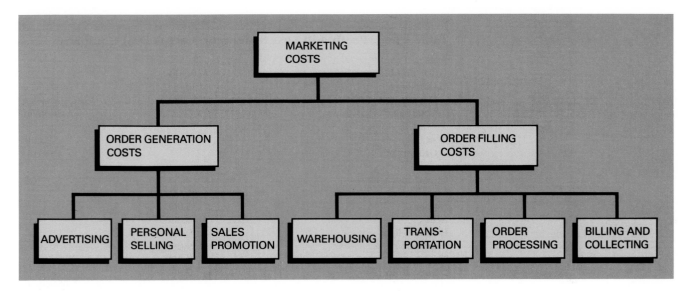

Figure 21.6
Classifying Marketing Costs

a particular area, such as a product line, channel of distribution, or geographic territory. There are several steps in full cost analysis, and we will illustrate them by using the example of the Cactus Doll Company.

Cactus Doll Company, which makes only one product, a doll in the form of a saguaro cactus plant, sells its dolls through three retail marketing channels: (1) toy and hobby stores, (2) gift shops, and (3) department stores. Cactus Doll's marketing manager wants to know how profitable these different marketing channels are, but the aggregate profit and loss statement (Table 21.5) does not reveal this. A **profit and loss statement** *takes the firm's sales for a stated period and subtracts the concomitant expenses to yield a profit or a loss.* (For a more detailed discussion of a profit and loss statement, see Appendix A, "Marketing Math, Finance, Accounting.") Although Cactus Doll Company is making a profit of $15,800 annually, this does not mean that all marketing channels are profitable or equally profitable. The firm knows the amount of sales generated through each channel: $300,000 in toy and hobby stores, $180,000 in gift shops, and $120,000 in department stores. However, these figures do not tell the marketing manager anything about the profitability of the different channels.

Table 21.6 identifies the four major steps in conducting a full cost marketing profitability analysis. We will now illustrate the necessary steps in order to determine the profitability of the three marketing channels that Cactus Doll Company uses.

The first step in a full cost marketing profitability analysis is to allocate or map the natural expenses (those that occur in the profit and loss statement) into functional expenses. **Functional expenses** are *the costs of performing various marketing tasks, namely, various order getting and*

Table 21.5 Profit and Loss Statement: Cactus Doll Company

Sales

Toy and hobby stores	$300,000	
Gift shops	180,000	
Department stores	120,000	
Total sales		$600,000
Cost of goods sold		390,000
Gross profit		$210,000

Operating Expenses

Payroll	$ 90,000	
Supplies	35,000	
Rent	30,000	
Heat and light	9,000	
Insurance	9,000	
Telephone	5,400	
Depreciation	2,800	
Other	13,000	
Total operation expenses		$194,200
Net profit		$ 15,800

order filling functions. Table 21.7 shows how the natural expenses of the Cactus Doll Company were allocated to various functional accounts.

To allocate natural expenses to functional expenses, good accounting records need to be maintained. Let's take the $90,000 payroll expense as an example. The company's payroll records should note which employees worked in advertising, personal selling, warehousing, order processing, and billing and collecting. These records would allow the firm to determine which of the $90,000 should be identified with each functional expense category. How might the company allocate the $30,000 rent to the various functions? One method would be to assign costs based on the proportion of space each function occupies in the building.

When this analysis is completed, the total functional expenses will equal the total natural expenses. The benefit of this analysis is that the total cost of performing certain marketing functions will be known. For example, the cost of personal selling for the Cactus Doll Company is $58,000, and the cost of warehousing is $39,300.

The second step in conducting the full cost marketing profitability analysis is to determine the allocation bases to be used to allocate the functional expenses to the different areas of the firm, which in this example are the three marketing channels (see Table 21.8). An **allocation base** is *something that helps to explain the variation in an expense item and can be used to assign expenses to segments.* For example, one might ask which

Table 21.6　Steps in Conducting a Full Cost Marketing Profitability Analysis

Step	What Needs To Be Done?	What Will It Tell The Marketing Manager?	Table to Study
1	Allocate or map natural expenses into functional expenses.	The total cost of performing marketing functions such as personal selling and advertising.	21.7
2	Determine (1) allocation bases for mapping functional expenses to areas of the firm and (2) the number of allocation units each area of the firm used.	Which things help to explain the behavior of functional expenses, and which areas of the firm account for most of the functional activity.	21.8
3	Determine the functional expense per allocation unit.	How much it costs per allocation unit to perform each function.	21.9
4	Determine the profit and loss statement by area.	The relative profitability or unprofitability of different areas of the firm.	21.10

single item helps to explain why personal selling costs are high or low. The answer might be the number of sales calls; as the number of sales calls rise, personal selling costs would be expected to rise.

Table 21.8 shows the different allocation bases that will be used for the Cactus Doll Company example and provides information on the number

Table 21.7　Mapping the Natural Expenses of Cactus Doll Company into Functional Expenses

	Functional Expenses							
	Order Getting Expenses			Order Filling Expenses				Total Natural Expenses
Natural Expenses	Advertising	Personal Selling	Total Order Getting Expenses	Warehousing	Order Processing	Billing and Collecting	Total Order Filling Expenses	
Payroll	$16,000	$40,000	$56,000	$12,000	$ 7,500	$14,500	$34,000	$90,000
Supplies	9,000	6,000	15,000	1,000	8,000	11,000	20,000	35,000
Rent	5,000	2,000	7,000	15,000	4,000	4,000	23,000	30,000
Heat and light	1,500	600	2,100	4,500	1,200	1,200	6,900	9,000
Insurance	900	3,100	4,000	3,000	800	1,200	5,000	9,000
Telephone	500	2,000	2,500	800	500	1,600	2,900	5,400
Depreciation	500	400	900	400	1,200	300	1,900	2,800
Other	2,400	3,900	6,300	2,600	1,600	2,500	6,700	13,000
Total functional expenses	35,800	58,000	93,800	39,300	24,800	36,300	100,400	194,200

Table 21.8   Allocation Bases for Mapping Functional Expenses to Areas of Firm: Cactus Doll Company

Functional Expense and Allocation Base Channel	Advertising (Number of Direct Mail Pieces)	Personal Selling (Number of Sales Calls)	Warehousing (Sales in Pounds)	Order Processing (Orders Placed)	Billing and Collecting (Orders Placed)
Toy and hobby stores	20,000	1,100	250,000	1,600	1,600
Gift shops	10,000	500	150,000	400	400
Department stores	7,000	400	100,000	200	200
Total allocation units	37,000	2,000	500,000	2,200	2,200

of allocation units each channel type used. For example, toy and hobby stores received 1,100 sales calls and 20,000 direct mail advertisements, purchased 250,000 pounds of dolls, and placed 1,600 orders. Which channel do you think is the most profitable at this stage of the analysis?

Step three consists of determining the functional expense per allocation unit. Table 21.9 computes the functional expense per allocation unit. For example, we see that there were 37,000 direct mail advertisements sent last year, and when this is divided into the total advertising cost of $35,800 we get a cost per direct mail advertising piece of 96.8¢. Using a similar procedure, we see that the cost per sales call was $29, the warehousing cost per pound of sales was 7.9¢, the order processing cost per order placed was $11.27, and the billing and collecting cost per order placed was $16.50.

Our final step is to determine the profit and loss statement for each

Table 21.9   Determining the Functional Expense per Unit: Cactus Doll Company

	Advertising	Personal Selling	Warehousing	Order Processing	Billing and Collecting
(A) Total functional expense (see Table 21.7)	$35,800	$58,000	$39,300	$24,800	$36,300
(B) Total allocation units (see Table 21.8)	37,000 direct mail pieces	2,000 sales calls	500,000 pounds	2,200 orders	2,200 orders
(C) Functional expense per allocation unit (A ÷ B)	96.8¢ per direct mail piece	$29.00 per sales call	7.9¢ per pound	$11.27 per order	$16.50 per order

marketing channel. Since we already know the sales for each marketing channel, we must determine what amount of functional expenses each marketing channel should be assigned. How might this be done? If we take the number of allocation units each channel type used and multiply this figure by the functional expenses per allocation unit, we obtain the functional expenses to be assigned to a channel. For example, toy and hobby stores received 1,100 sales calls, and the cost per sales call was $29. Therefore, the personal selling costs assigned to toy and hobby stores is $31,900 or ($29 × 1,100).

Table 21.10 presents a profit and loss statement by each channel type for the Cactus Doll Company. Since the firm produces only one product, all segments are assigned manufacturing costs of 65 percent of sales, which is the average for the entire firm (see Table 21.5 cost of goods sold). The bottom line results indicate that the toy and hobby store channel is losing $10,337; the gift store channel is the most profitable with $15,925; and the department store channel generates $10,212 in profit. If the analyst adds these three bottom-line figures, he or she will obtain a profit of $15,800, which is the overall profit of the Cactus Doll Company. This relationship occurs because all costs have been fully allocated to each of the three segments being analyzed.

What decision did you make about the three different marketing channels on the basis of the financial results in Table 21.10? Would you recommend that the company stop selling to toy and hobby stores? Consider what would happen to Cactus Doll's overall profits if it decides not to sell to toy and hobby stores. Shouldn't profits go up by $10,337 because that loss will be prevented? The answer, unfortunately, is no. If Cactus Doll does not sell to toy and hobby stores, it will lose $300,000 in sales. Furthermore,

Table 21.10   Profit and Loss Statement (Full Costing) by Channel Type: Cactus Doll Company

	Toy and Hobby Stores	Gift Shops	Department Stores	Total Company
Sales	$300,000	$180,000	$120,000	$600,000
Less: Standard manufacturing costs	195,000	117,000	78,000	390,000
Marketing revenues generated	$105,000	$ 63,000	$ 42,000	$210,000
Less: Order getting costs				
Advertising	19,351	9,676	6,773	35,800
Personal selling	31,900	14,500	11,600	58,000
Promotional profit	$ 53,749	$ 38,824	$ 23,627	$116,200
Less: Order filling costs				
Warehousing	19,650	11,790	7,860	39,300
Order processing	18,036	4,509	2,255	24,800
Billing and collecting	26,400	6,600	3,300	36,300
Net profit	($ 10,337)	$ 15,925	$ 10,212	$ 15,800

all of the costs and expenses shown in Table 21.10 that are identified with toy and hobby stores will not be eliminated if this channel is eliminated because some of these costs are fixed. For example, some of the manufacturing costs are for fixed factory overhead, which stays the same, and some of the warehousing cost is for rent, which also stays the same. If the toy and hobby store channel is eliminated, then the other two channels will need to absorb more of these fixed costs, and consequently, they will be less profitable.

In short, a full cost approach to marketing profitability analysis can be misleading and, if taken literally, can lead management to unwise decisions. Nonetheless, this approach can be used to send up red flags to investigate certain areas of the business. Obviously, something is wrong with the toy and hobby store channel. A careful analysis of the segmental profit and loss statement shows that this channel uses a disproportionate amount of order processing and billing and collecting costs. They have half the sales but over 70 percent of order processing and billing and collecting costs. Therefore, these stores tend to place small orders, which are just as expensive to handle as large orders. Further analysis shows that toy and hobby stores have an average order size of $187.50, whereas the average order for gift stores is $450 and for department stores is $600. Clearly, a program needs to be developed to induce toy and hobby stores to place larger orders.

With a **contribution margin** approach to marketing profitability analysis, *only those costs that can be traced directly to an area of the firm are assigned to that area.* These costs are called *direct costs*; all others are *indirect costs* and thus are not assigned to a specific area. An area's contribution margin is the dollars it contributes to company profitability and all indirect costs. Many experts claim that contribution margin analysis, or the direct cost approach to marketing profitability, is better for management decision making than is the full cost approach.

Without going into considerable detail, we present a contribution margin statement for the Cactus Doll Company and its three channels in Table 21.11. The statement reveals that all three channels have a positive contribution margin. The toy and hobby store channel has a contribution margin of $48,635, so that it does not create a loss for the company, as the full cost analysis suggested. Note, however, that the contribution margin analysis still reveals some potential problems with toy and hobby stores. Contribution margin as a percentage of sales for this channel is 16.2 percent versus 24 percent for gift stores and 23.6 percent for department stores. Once again, a more detailed analysis reveals that toy and hobby stores have order sizes that are smaller than those of the other channel types.

A final glance at Table 21.11 will show how the net profit for the firm can be determined by adding up the contribution margins for each channel and subtracting the indirect costs. For the Cactus Doll Company, the total contribution margin for the three channels is $120,170 and indirect costs

Table 21.11   Area Contribution Margin Statement by Type of Channel: Cactus Doll Company

	Toy and Hobby Stores	Gift Shops	Department Stores	Total Company
Sales	$300,000	$180,000	$120,000	$600,000
Less: Direct manufacturing costs	180,000	108,000	72,000	360,000
Marketing revenues generated	$120,000	$ 72,000	$ 48,000	$240,000
Less: Direct order getting costs				
Advertising	14,513	7,257	5,080	26,850
Personal selling	22,330	10,150	8,120	40,600
Promotional profit contribution	$ 83,157	$ 54,593	$ 34,800	$172,550
Less: Direct order filling costs				
Warehousing	7,860	4,716	3,144	15,720
Order processing	10,822	2,705	1,353	14,880
Billing and collecting	15,840	3,960	1,980	21,780
Marketing profit contribution	$ 48,635	$ 43,212	$ 28,323	$120,170
Less: Indirect costs				104,370
Net profit				$ 15,800

are $104,370. The difference between these is the net profit of $15,800, which we first saw in Table 21.5.

SUMMARY

This chapter focused on executing the marketing plan. Execution involves implementation and control of the plan. If a firm is to be able to effectively implement its marketing plan and practice the marketing concept, then marketing managers and executives must be put on an equal organizational status with other key managers in the organization. Conflicts may arise between marketing executives and executives in other functional areas of the firm even if they have equal status, but if the firm can develop a marketing-oriented corporate mission, other functional managers should be more willing to cooperate with the marketing vice president.

Implementation requires resource acquisition, resource organization, and resource utilization. All marketing plans require that financial and human resources be acquired and committed to achieve stated objectives. These resources can be obtained internally or externally.

There is no single best way to organize marketing activity; each firm needs to decide the best way to organize depending on its size, the environment in which it operates, the breadth of its product mix, and the number of market segments it serves. Some of the more popular ways of organizing marketing resources are by function, by geographic region, by product line, and by market segment. Most large organizations use a combination of these modes to organize marketing effort.

Good resource utilization is obtained by coordinating all personnel in marketing, in other departments in the firm, and in external organizations that are necessary to carry out the plan. Next, all the personnel in the firm must be motivated with intrinsic and extrinsic rewards to get them to perform at a high level. The final ingredient in implementing the plan is communicating to the respective personnel their tasks, the schedule of activities necessary to implement the plan, and the necessary deadlines so that the plan can be carried out on a day-to-day basis.

Marketing resources and efforts must be effectively organized as well as properly controlled. Control is the process of comparing ongoing plans with actual results in order to determine if the plan is working and what, if any, corrective action needs to be taken. Some large organizations are beginning to employ marketing controllers, whose job is to evaluate, budget, and control marketing and distribution expenditures.

Three popular tools that are useful for evaluating and controlling marketing efforts are sales analysis, sales performance analysis, and marketing profitability analysis. Sales analysis involves taking the results of a past period's sales (usually a month or quarter of a year) and analyzing where sales are coming from; that is, which products, salespeople, or territories account for the majority of a firm's sales.

Sales performance analysis is similar to sales analysis, except that sales are compared with planned sales or some standard of performance. When a product, salesperson, or territory is significantly below standard, the causes for the poor performance should be identified so that management can help correct the poor performance. It is also good practice to identify the areas where performance is significantly better than expected, so that management can learn why the firm is performing so well in these areas.

Finally, the firm can conduct a marketing profitability analysis, which determines the profit of particular products, salespeople, and so on. In a marketing profitability analysis, marketing costs need to be classified as order generation and order filling costs. These costs are then fully allocated or traced directly to the segments being evaluated. When costs are fully allocated, the net profit or loss of a segment can be determined. On the other hand, when csots are traced directly to segments, some costs will not be allocated, and thus the analyst will only be able to determine the contribution margin of a segment. A segment's contribution margin is the dollars it contributes to company profitability and all indirect costs.

KEY CONCEPTS

functional organization (p. 650)
geographic organization (p. 651)
product organization (p. 651)
market segment organization (p. 653)
task force (p. 658)
control (p. 658)
marketing controller (p. 660)
sales analysis (p. 661)
20/80 rule (pp. 661–662)

sales performance analysis (p. 662)
marketing profitability analysis (p. 664)
order generation costs (p. 664)
order filling costs (p. 664)
full cost analysis (pp. 664–665)
profit and loss statement (p. 665)
functional expenses (pp. 665–666)
allocation base (p. 666)
contribution margin (p. 670)

REVIEW AND DISCUSSION QUESTIONS

1. Explain why an organization's chief marketing officer and chief financial and production officer should be accorded equal status.

2. Discuss some of the conflicts that can arise between marketing and other functional areas in the firm.

3. Identify and define the different ways to organize the marketing unit of a firm. What is the principal advantage and disadvantage of each of these methods?

4. When should a purely functional approach to organizing the marketing unit be used?

5. What three ingredients of effective resource utilization are necessary to implement a marketing plan?

6. Marketers operate in an open and largely unpredictable environment, and thus attempts to control their efforts are largely a waste of time and money. Agree or disagree with this statement, and defend your position.

7. What is a marketing controller? Why should firms employ a marketing controller in addition to a traditional controller?

8. What are the shortcomings of the sales analysis approach in evaluating marketing efforts?

9. What is the 20/80 rule? How can it be used to analyze the effectiveness of marketing resources?

10. If sales performance analysis reveals that a salesperson is 30 percent below quota, then he or she should be fired and replaced with a more productive salesperson. Agree or disagree with this statement, and defend your position.

11. How might the director of marketing at Chevrolet use marketing profitability analysis to make better marketing decisions?

12. What are the problems with a full cost approach to marketing profitability analysis? Should the full cost approach be avoided?

ACTION PROBLEMS

1. You have been retained as a consultant to advise a book publisher on how to organize its marketing efforts. The publisher has annual sales of $11 million and net profits (after taxes) of $814,000. Below is some pertinent information on the company:

   - A total of 174 titles were published in the disciplines of mathematics, chemistry, biology, physics, psychology, and sociology.

   - Approximately 40 percent of sales are to high schools and 60 percent are to colleges.

   - Eighteen salespeople are in the United States, and three are in Canada.

   - All warehousing and distribution functions are subcontracted to others.

- Thirty-five titles are due to be added over the next five years in the disciplines of accounting, finance, economics, management, and marketing.
- Advertising is slated to become very aggressive, and the advertising budget will be tripled over the next two years. The budget is currently $340,000.

Suggest three ways in which the publisher might organize its marketing efforts. Which do you prefer? Why?

2. What would be the most useful way for the publishing company described in the preceding problem to identify areas for reporting marketing profitability?

3. As the national sales manager for a manufacturer of industrial building alarm systems, you are excited about the recently released year-end sales results. Total sales for the year were $3.61 million, which was substantially above the forecast, or budgeted, sales of $3.25 million. You want to know more about the causes that contributed to this excellent performance. To help you in this task, you have requested and received the following reports via your IBM PC, which can tap into the companywide accounting data system.

Table 1   Sales by Geographic Region

Territory	Budget	Actual
East	$1,100,000	$1,300,000
Central	750,000	700,000
West	1,400,000	1,610,000

Table 2   Sales by Salesperson

Salesperson by Territory	Budget (Quota)	Actual
East		
June Furr	$600,000	$805,000
Fred Jones	500,000	495,000
Central		
Sally Smythe	400,000	350,000
Kris Kasulis	350,000	350,000
West		
Paul Hays	800,000	910,000
David Greenhut	600,000	700,000

Which areas helped the firm achieve its recent success? Where are the potential problem areas? What additional data might you wish to examine? Why?

NOTES

1. Lisa R. Sheeran, "Sadder But Wiser," *Inc.* (October 1985), pp. 139–140, 144.

2. Philip Maher, "Apple Bolsters Marketing Staff," *Business Marketing* (Summer 1983), p. 28.

3. Anne B. Fisher, "GM's Unlikely Revolutionist," *Fortune* (March 19, 1984), pp. 106–112.

4. Mack Hanon, "Reorganize Your Company Around Its Markets," *Harvard Business Review* (November–December 1974), pp. 63–74.

5. *Donaldson Company, Inc. 1984 Annual Report.*

6. Philip Kotler, *Principles of Marketing* (Englewood Cliffs, NJ: Prentice-Hall, 1980), p. 181.

7. Barton Weitz and Erin Anderson, "Organizing and Controlling the Marketing Function," in Ben M. Enis and Kenneth J. Roering (eds.), *Review of Marketing* (Chicago: American Marketing Association, 1981), pp. 134–142.

8. "Ironing Out Grid's Marketing Mistakes," *BusinessWeek* (February 28, 1983), pp. 66, 71.

9. An excellent book on controlling marketing costs is Frank H. Mossman, W.J.E. Crissy, and Paul M. Fischer, *Financial Dimensions of Marketing Management* (New York: John Wiley & Sons, 1978).

10. Sam R. Goodman, *Techniques of Profitability Analysis* (New York: John Wiley & Sons, 1970).

11. An excellent model for marketing control that we will not discuss is the STETCOM model; see Subhash Sharma and Dale D. Achabal, "STETCOM: An Analytical Model for Marketing Control," *Journal of Marketing* 45(Spring 1982), pp. 104–113.

12. Leland L. Beik and Stephen L. Buzby, "Profitability Analysis by Market Segments," *Journal of Marketing* (July 1973), pp. 48–53; Patrick M. Dunne and Henry I. Wolk, "Marketing Cost Analysis: A Modularized Contribution Approach," *Journal of Marketing* (July 1977), pp. 83–94; Donald W. Jackson, Jr., and Lonnie L. Ostrom, "Grouping Segments for Profitability Analysis," *MSU Business Topics* (Spring 1980), pp. 39–44.

LEARNING OBJECTIVES

After you complete this chapter, you should be able to:

- **List** and **discuss** the five common criticisms of marketing

- **Explain** the concept of social responsibility and **discuss** how marketers can become more socially responsible

- **List** the four basic rights of consumers and **evaluate** whether these rights are being provided in the marketplace

- **Identify** five ethical frameworks and use them to **analyze** the ethics of various marketing decisions

- **Assess** the future of marketing

EVALUATION, ETHICS, AND THE FUTURE OF MARKETING

MARKETER PROFILE

Ron Schultz of Medicine for Children, Inc.

Ron Schultz is the founder of Medicine for Children, Inc., the ultimate in altruistic firms. This company contributes not 5 or 10 percent of its profits to charity, but 100 percent. Why and how did this company develop?

With several successful careers behind him in academia, the army, and business, Schultz wanted to combine entrepreneurship with charity. He wanted to use his skills to develop a product at a fair market value, form a company to market the product, and then use the profits in a socially responsible manner to support a worthy charity. When Schultz learned about Lalmba Association, a nonprofit charitable organization that sends volun-

teer medical professionals and medicines to Sudan, Africa, he contacted its founders, Hugh and Marty Downey. At first the Downeys were predictably suspicious about his desire to start a company to market a product whose profits would go entirely to the Lalmba Association, but after Ron had detailed discussions with the husband-wife team, they accepted his offer.

The product Ron developed was Christmas Spice Tea. During the 1983 Christmas season, 45,000 bags of the spicy, sweet blended tea made it to market. The tea package proclaims that the buyers are "no ordinary customers," because Medicine for Children is "no ordinary company." However, the message on the package also urges the buyer to purchase the tea "because you like it— not because the profits go to charity." Schultz does this because he wants the product to stand on its own, recognizing that the market segment for those sympathetic to a particular charity or cause is limited.

Source: Based on Susan Buchabaum. "Tea and Sympathy," *Inc.* (June 1984), pp. 97– 100. Reprinted with permission, INC. magazine, June 1984. Copyright © 1984 by INC. Publishing Company, 38 Commercial Wharf, Boston, Mass. 02110.

INTRODUCTION

As we have noted throughout this book, marketing is prevalent in our daily lives and plays an important role in both business and nonbusiness organizations. Marketing is not without its critics, however, and their criticisms should not be ignored. One purpose of this chapter is to discuss some of the common criticisms of marketing and to stress the need for marketers to behave in a socially responsible manner and to respect the rights of consumers. The ultimate example of social responsibility was portrayed in the Marketer Profile on Ron Schultz, who marketed a product for the sole benefit of a charity. Granted, it would not be economically feasible for all companies to donate all their profits to charity; however, many charitable organizations, like those discussed in prior chapters, rely on the help of socially responsible businesspeople. This chapter concludes with a discussion of ethics in marketing and a glimpse at the future of marketing as envisioned by a group of Fortune 500 business executives.

COMMON CRITICISMS OF MARKETING

Because marketing is the aspect of business that most of us regularly come in contact with, it is the obvious target for the majority of complaints against business. In fact, it would be surprising if you have not had occasion to criticize the practice of marketing. Following are some of the main criticisms of marketing.[1]

Marketing Costs Too Much

Approximately 50 percent of the final price that the consumer pays for a product will go to cover marketing costs. This includes things like the cost of promotion, such as advertising and personal selling; supply-related costs, such as transportation and warehousing; and marketing administration costs, such as salaries for marketing managers and marketing researchers.

Frequently, when the costs of marketing in the United States are criticized as too high, comparisons are made to other economies, such as the Soviet Union, where the percentage of the final price due to marketing expenditures is considerably lower. The conclusion is often erroneously drawn that marketing is more efficient in these other economies. Consumers do not care what percentage of the price is due to production or marketing costs as long as the final price is acceptable. Consider, for example, that a nation such as the United States could design a marketing system for automobiles in which almost all the costs were for production rather than marketing. This could be accomplished by having custom auto builders in each community, even if the community had only a few thousand people. In this scenario, everyone would be able to travel to a nearby auto builder and have a car custom built. The cars would not need to be shipped to an auto dealer because they could be bought directly from the manufacturer. Also, little advertising or personal selling would be necessary because the cars could be built to your exact specifications, which would be the ultimate in satisfying your needs and wants. Unfortunately, this auto could cost you $250,000. When comparing the effectiveness of marketing in the United States with that in another country, you should assess which system can deliver reliable, reasonably priced products that are needed and wanted.

Marketing Encourages Materialism

Marketing is sometimes criticized for making people materialistic. For example, in extremely poor areas of the United States, such as Appalachia, households are more likely to have modern television sets than modern bathrooms. You could conclude from this that excessive advertising and promotion have warped the minds of the poor to prefer television to sanitary living. Is this a fair conclusion? Again, we must look at it from the consumer's vantage point. If you were living in one of the poorest areas of the United States, with few forms of cheap entertainment available, which would you rather have, a new television or a modern bathroom? I think most of us would prefer the television. In short, what may appear to be manipulated behavior from the social critic's perspective may, in fact, be rational behavior from the consumer's perspective.

Another way to look at this criticism is to recognize that people are materialistic. Marketing is a phenomenon created by humans so that we can have more material wealth. Marketing does not create materialism; materialistic people created the practice of marketing.

Marketing Does Not Create Value

Marketers are sometimes viewed as parasites who wedge themselves between producers and final buyers in order to create profits for their own selfish interests. Some critics think that marketers (especially wholesalers and retailers) are unnecessary because they do not create value but merely add to costs. As we discussed in Chapter 1, marketing does create value by developing time, place, and possession utilities. Products are worth little if they cannot be possessed at the time and place where they are most needed.

Marketing Practitioners Are Unscrupulous

Many people view marketers with suspicion because they believe that marketers will do anything to make a sale. There are unscrupulous marketers, and you probably remember a time when a salesperson twisted your arm into buying something you didn't want or need, but, unfortunately, this is true of all professions. Society has unscrupulous members, and they are not any more likely to be in marketing than in other professions. We probably notice marketers' unethical activity because we confront them on a daily basis. A strong set of ethical principles is important in any profession, whether it is marketing or something else.[2]

Marketing Is Unresponsive to Consumer Wants

As consumers, we have all found occasion to complain that we cannot find the brand that best suits our wants and desires. Clothes and shoes may not fit properly, autos may not perform as we would like, household appliances may break too frequently, and our favorite products may be discontinued. Although these complaints are legitimate, they are mostly due to the nature of the mass marketing system we live in.

To benefit from the economies and resulting lower prices of mass production, we, as a society, must accept mass marketing. Men's dress shirts will be produced in neck sizes of half-inch increments; if a $14\frac{1}{2}$-inch size is too tight, you might go to a 15-inch neck size, but this could be too loose. There is the option of having a tailor make your shirts, but the cost would be excessive for most of us. Many products fail because they are engineered for the typical user. If you are a hard or heavy user of a product, it will not last as long. Teenage boy drivers often get only one-third the wear from a set of tires that a seasoned adult driver can obtain.

The U.S. market economy is very competitive and is characterized by few international trade barriers and relative ease of entry for new firms. We open our markets to companies from around the globe. Consequently, if a business firm is unresponsive to consumer wants, it makes itself vulnerable to a competitive onslaught from other organizations. Because U.S. auto manufacturers did not give a large segment of the U.S. auto buying public what they wanted in the 1960s and 1970s, Japanese auto manufacturers, such as Nissan, Honda, and Toyota, exploited a market niche for high-quality, small, affordable cars.

If you frequently complain that marketing is unresponsive to your wants, you might consider becoming an entrepreneur and starting a business to fill this need. If there really is an unmet need, you can serve society, have a rewarding career, and possibly get rich at the same time!

Five common criticisms of marketing have been aired that you will hear throughout your career in marketing or business. Be prepared to respond, but don't be too defensive. The practice of marketing is not perfect because the people who practice it are not perfect. Some firms have excessive and unnecessary marketing costs, some advertising may encourage us to value materialism, some firms' marketing activity may not create value, some unscrupulous marketers exist, and sometimes marketing is unresponsive to consumer wants. On average, however, marketing in the United States performs well and helps to provide a high degree of consumer choice and a high standard of living.

SOCIAL RESPONSIBILITY

Without a doubt, marketing is a powerful tool for many organizations. Power, however, must be used responsibly. **Social responsibility** in a business is defined as *taking actions and making marketing decisions that do not have any significant negative consequences for society.* Obviously, there will always be some negative consequences, but they should not result in an overall deterioration of societal well-being.[3]

Some Problem Areas

We will examine several areas where marketing decisions are being made that arguably create major concerns about social responsibility: advertising to children, ecology, and product safety.

Children's Advertising.   Is advertising that is directed at children a socially responsible action? Advertising that encourages children to desire sugar-coated cereals, fast-food hamburgers and french fries, toys, and other things is preying on the innocent, uneducated, and unsophisticated. Can children make intelligent decisions concerning these products? Children's opinions and values will be shaped as they grow, but the central question is, who should be allowed to influence this shaping process—parents, relatives, churches, schools, friends, advertisers? Some people would argue that being exposed to advertising and other marketing tools and techniques allows children to learn how to become good consumers. They learn that there is misleading advertising, that choices need to be made among many alternative products, that wrong decisions can be made, and that past purchase dissatisfactions must be coped with. The problem is in knowing whether or not society, in the long run, would be better off if advertising to children was abolished.

Ecology. Whose responsibility is it to protect the physical environment? Who should insist on such things as returnable bottles for beverages, autos with low pollution levels, and products that are biodegradable? Business? The consumer? The government? If valuable natural resources such as oil, water, metals, and timber are in short supply, whose job is it to conserve their use—individuals, businesses, or the government? A major problem is that it takes money and effort to conserve our natural resources, and sometimes the effort is perceived as or actually is more costly than the benefit obtained. If copper is selling for 75¢ a pound, then salvaging a pound of copper from old household appliances or other obsolete or nonuseful products may cost more than 75¢. Many consumers do not recycle their used aluminum beverage cans for this reason; they believe that the low price of a pound of aluminum is an insufficient incentive. Should the government intercede and pass laws requiring returnable beverage containers? Consumers often want benefits without paying the cost. They want clean energy and thus wish to avoid coal burning power plants, but on the other hand, they are unwilling to pay the cost of nuclear energy.

It would be foolish to argue that business has no obligation to protect the physical environment, since all tangible products are derived from matter in the physical environment. Marketers and consumers must recognize their dependence on the physical environment and behave responsibly.

Product Safety. Marketers should design products that are safe. When we discuss product safety, we are talking about service safety as well as the safety of tangible goods, since products can be either goods or services. For example, consumers have a right to expect properly trained and rested airline pilots and bus drivers, safe child care centers, ethical and careful physicians, and clean, sanitary restaurants.

Tangible product safety should include safe design, especially in regard to product usage. Safety in use is often difficult to anticipate. For example, some consumers may use a lawn mower to cut grass (as the manufacturer intended), whereas others may attempt to use the lawn mower to trim a hedge and cut off all their fingers in the process. It is the responsibility of the manufacturers to anticipate how their products can be misused and either to warn the consumers of the danger of such use (as the caution labels on curling irons and blow dryers warn the user of possible hazards) or to actually design the products so they will not operate under certain misuse applications (most food processors will not start unless all parts are assembled correctly). Sometimes, the federal government must step in and require manufacturers to build safety features into their products. For example, the federal government requires all lawn mowers produced after 1982 to stop running when they are lifted off the ground, which prevents the consumer from trying to trim hedges with the mower.

Packaging also needs to be designed with safety in mind. This issue became more recognized when Tylenol brand acetaminophen was tampered

Boise Cascade promotes their social responsibility to the physical environment with this ad about their conservation program.

Firms that are socially responsible recognize their obligation to product safety, as Mercedes-Benz shows with their ad about the Supplemental Restraint System.

with in 1982, which resulted in several deaths in the Chicago area. Today most over-the-counter drugs are sold in virtually tamper-proof packages. Packages also need to be designed to safely hold the contents of the package. For instance, if the consumer purchases a computer in a shipping carton with handles on the carton, the handles need to be durable enough to allow the package to be safely lifted by the handles.

If a firm is socially responsible, it will do its best to design safe products, as Mercedes-Benz has done with its supplemental restraint system. Mercedes spent fifteen years developing this system, which incorporates an airbag with an electronic emergency tensioning retractor in the seat belt mechanism. This system is available on Mercedes autos and is expected to increase the safety of passengers in those autos.

Products can be introduced to the market that prove to be defective or poorly designed. A socially responsible firm should not be on the defensive when such a problem is discovered but should be ready to modify the product, as Sears was willing to do in the advertisement concerning Brawny Beds, or withdraw it from the market until the problem is rectified. The Marketing in Action on page 685 illustrates the different responses of firms that have been confronted with information about a product defect.

A Statement To Owners Of
SEARS BRAWNY BEDS

You may have seen recent news reports about the fatal accident of a Denver boy in December 1983 involving a Brawny Bed.

Here are some facts you should know:

- Three separate investigations—by Sears, the Consumer Product Safety Commission and the manufacturer—all determined that there is no defect in the bed and a recall is not warranted.

- The Sears Brawny Bed meets or exceeds all industry standards.

- There are over one million similarly designed beds in use today, of which Sears has sold about 100,000.

Despite these facts, some Brawny Bed owners have expressed concern about the safety of the bed.

To alleviate this concern, a modification kit has been developed as an additional safeguard. The kit consists of four metal tie-wires and screws to be securely fastened to the side rails of the beds.

If your Brawny Bed does not already contain tie-wires that are securely fastened to the side rails, you can order the free modification kit through your nearest Sears store, or directly from the manufacturer by calling one of the following toll-free numbers:

(800) 831-5551—Continental U.S. (except Illinois), Alaska, Hawaii and Puerto Rico

(800) 323-0366—Illinois only

SEARS
MERCHANDISE GROUP

Once a product already in the marketplace is found to be defective, a socially responsible firm will take action to modify the product and ensure its safety.

Benefits and Costs

As a general rule, all purported acts of social responsibility by business firms will be viewed as benefits by some and as costs or punishments by others. Witness the following examples:

❑ Emission control devices on autos create cleaner air, which especially benefits those with respiratory diseases, but cost auto purchasers an extra $800 to $1,200 per auto.

❑ Minority employment quotas help minorities get a foothold in business but discriminate against other qualified applicants.

❑ Special price discounts offered to senior citizens help them manage better during retirement years but result in higher prices for other customer groups.

MARKETING IN ACTION

Social Responsibility and Product Safety

When Procter & Gamble became aware that its Rely brand tampons were linked to an illness known as *toxic shock syndrome*, it reacted very responsibly. Although P & G had spent $75 million and twenty years developing this product, it removed all of the Rely brand tampons from distribution and offered to repurchase from consumers those already bought. The firm also undertook a program to educate women about the link between toxic shock syndrome and tampon use, especially use of the Rely brand.

On the other hand, Firestone reacted defensively when it was accused of producing defectively designed Firestone 500 steel-belted radials. These tires were prone to blowouts, tread separations, and other dangerous deformities and had twice the failure rate of comparable brands. Firestone contended that there was nothing wrong with their tire design; rather it claimed consumers misused the tires, causing them to fail. Generally, the company was very uncooperative with the Traffic Safety Administration in their investigation of the safety of the Firestone 500.

Another example of a defensive versus a responsible reaction toward product safety involves Ford Motor Company and their Pinto automobile, which had a poorly designed fuel tank. Critics claimed that when a Pinto was involved in a rear end collision, the probability that the fuel tank would explode was too high. For more than eight years, Ford successfully lobbied against federal authorities and delayed redesigning the Pinto fuel tank because cost-benefit analysis suggested a redesign was not profitable.

Source: Arthur M. Louis. "Lessons from the Firestone Fracas," *Fortune* (August 28, 1978), pp. 44–48; Mark Dowei. "How Ford Put Two Million Firetraps on Wheels," *Business and Society Review* 23(Fall 1977), pp. 26–55; Elizabeth Gatewood and Archie B. Carroll. "The Anatomy of Corporate Social Response: The Rely, Firestone 500, and Pinto Cases," *Business Horizons* (September–October 1981), pp. 9–16.

Because of the inherent difficulty in weighing these types of tradeoffs, some business commentators suggest that the only socially responsible thing for business to do is to make as much profit as possible.[4] In a free economy, consumers vote with their dollars, and those firms that best serve society make the most profit. This view is obviously debatable.

CONSUMER RIGHTS

Consumers must be provided with certain rights if they are to have fair bargaining power with sellers. In Chapter 2, we described consumerism as a social movement that attempts to foster programs that give consumers more power. The first piece of U.S. consumer protection legislation, which was passed in 1872, made it a federal crime to use the mails to defraud customers.[5] The National Consumers League was formed in 1899 to help protect consumers and has recently focused its efforts on the health care industry.

As consumers, what rights do we have? In 1962, President John F. Kennedy delineated the following four **consumer rights** that businesses and government should help guarantee[6]:

> 1. *The right to safety*—to be protected against the marketing of goods [and services] that are hazardous to health or life.
> 2. *The right to be informed*—to be protected against fraudulent, deceitful, or grossly misleading information, advertising, labeling, or other practices, and to be given the facts needed to make an informed choice.
> 3. *The right to choose*—to be assured access (wherever possible) to a variety of goods and services at competitive prices; and in those industries in which competition is not workable and government regulation is substituted, an assurance of satisfactory quality and service at fair prices.
> 4. *The right to be heard*—to be assured that consumer interests will receive full and sympathetic consideration in the formulation of government policy, and fair and expeditious treatment in its administrative tribunals.

Ten years after John F. Kennedy enunciated these consumer rights to Congress, they were duplicated by the European Economic Commission to help protect European consumers.

The federal government responded to Kennedy's Bill of Consumer Rights and the consumerism movement by passing the Truth-in-Lending Act (1968), the Fair Packaging and Labeling Act (1966), the Consumer Product Safety Act (1972), the Magnuson-Moss Warranty Federal Trade Commission Act (1975), and a variety of other laws to give consumers more power in their dealings with sellers. Many businesses have responded to the consumerism movement by establishing consumer affairs departments in their organizations.[7] A **consumer affairs department** is *responsible for advocating the consumer's interest in marketing decisions and programs.* Most consumer affairs departments began as complaint handling departments, but they now have a much broader set of consumer-related responsibilities and duties. Table 22.1 shows some of the major decision areas influenced by consumer affairs officers. Eastman Kodak, Whirlpool, General Foods, and J.C. Penney all have active consumer affairs departments. A professional organization called the Society of Consumer Affairs Professionals in Business (SOCAP) promotes professionalism among consumer affairs executives. The Marketing in Action on page 688 discusses the elements in consumer affairs programming.

Table 22.1   Level of Influence Indicated by Chief Consumer Affairs Officers for Eighteen Decision Areas

Decision Area	Individuals Indicating Decision Area Is Applicable to Consumer Affairs Department		Individuals from Total Sample Indicating Decision Area Is Not Applicable to Consumer Affairs Department	
	Number (and Percentage) Indicating Much Influence	Number (and Percentage) Indicating Little or No Influence	Number	Percentage
Handling consumer inquiries	140 (93.3)	10 (6.7)	3	2.0
Processing consumer complaints	125 (86.8)	19 (13.2)	6	4.0
Consumer education programs	108 (79.4)	28 (20.6)	13	8.7
Researching consumer satisfaction	107 (74.3)	37 (25.7)	4	2.7
Developing consumer orientation among executives	103 (72.5)	39 (27.5)	7	4.7
Improving employee attitudes toward consumers	104 (72.2)	40 (27.8)	4	2.7
Public relations programs	90 (65.7)	47 (34.3)	10	6.8
Product safety	46 (51.1)	44 (48.9)	56	38.3
Developing consumer orientation among dealers and distributors	39 (46.4)	45 (53.6)	60	41.6
Developing warranties and guarantees	34 (44.2)	43 (55.8)	70	47.7
Advertisements	60 (43.5)	78 (56.5)	11	7.4
Packaging and labeling	39 (40.2)	58 (59.8)	54	35.8
Quality control	39 (38.2)	63 (61.8)	42	29.1
Training service personnel	33 (31.4)	72 (68.6)	44	29.5
Establishing industry standards	27 (23.8)	86 (76.2)	35	23.6
Product design	22 (22.9)	74 (77.1)	50	33.8
Training sales personnel	22 (22.0)	78 (78.0)	47	31.8
Selecting suppliers	16 (17.8)	74 (82.2)	60	39.9

Source: Richard T. Hise, Peter L. Gillett, J. Patrick Kelly. "The Corporate Consumer Affairs Effort," *MSU Business Topics* (Summer 1978), p. 22. Used by permission.

BUSINESS ETHICS

Business ethics is concerned with *the moral choices between "right" and "wrong" conduct that a business executive must make in his or her position in a business organization.* The issues we have dealt with in this chapter—criticisms of marketing, social responsibility, consumer rights, and consumerism—are essentially ethical questions that the marketer must face. Questions of what is right or wrong (i.e., what is ethical behavior) are difficult to answer.[8]

All marketing managers inevitably will find themselves in situations in which their decisions will have ethical overtones. Consider, for example, the six marketing scenarios in Table 22.2, which raise ethical questions for the marketing manager.

MARKETING IN ACTION

Consumer Affairs Programming

Ronald W. Stampfl, a professor of marketing and consumer education at the University of Wisconsin—Madison, is a well respected authority on consumer affairs. Professor Stampfl has suggested that business firms take a more active role in consumer affairs programming because doing so is consistent with the marketing concept. He defines consumer affairs programming as all business activities designed to increase consumer satisfaction through implementation of consumer rights and business performance.

Three components of consumer affairs programming are consumer complaint management, consumer communication programming, and consumer advocacy programming. These three components, if properly designed and implemented collectively, will deliver the four consumer rights identified by President Kennedy.

Consumer complaint management should be viewed as a form of marketing research. Complaints are sources of information that can guide corrective action. Perhaps, for instance sales losses caused by brand or store switching can be minimized. *Consumer communications programming* includes providing consumers with the information they need to make intelligent purchasing decisions. It also includes listening to consumers to understand their wants and desires. *Consumer advocacy programming* involves establishing policies that put the firm in the position of purchasing agent for the consumer. The firm then becomes consumers' first-line defense in the marketplace. J.C. Penney Company, for example, has a consumer advocate in the formal organization of the firm. The consumer advocate presents and argues the consumer viewpoint on all significant issues related to the firm and its marketing actions.

Source: Based on Ronald W. Stampfl. "Building Retail Patronage Through Consumer Affairs Programming," in Robert F. Lusch and William R. Darden (eds.), *Retail Patronage Theory 1981 Workshop Proceedings* (Norman, OK.: Center for Economic and Management Research, School of Business Administration, the University of Oklahoma 1981), pp. 76–81.

In deciding how you should handle marketing decisions with ethical overtones, consider the following five ethical frameworks[9]:

❑ *Golden rule.* You should act in a manner that you would expect others to act toward you.

❑ *Moral idealism.* You would, regardless of the circumstances, always view certain acts or decisions as bad (unethical) and others as good (ethical).

Table 22.2 Marketing Scenarios That Raise Ethical Questions

Scenario 1

The Thrifty Supermarket Chain has 12 stores in the city of Gotham, U.S.A. The company's policy is to maintain the same prices for all items at all stores. However, the distribution manager knowingly sends the poorest cuts of meat and the lowest quality produce to the store located in the low-income section of town. He justifies this action based on the fact that this store has the highest overhead due to factors such as employee turnover, pilferage, and vandalism. *Is the distribution manager's economic rationale sufficient justification for his allocation method?*

Scenario 2

The Independent Chevy Dealers of Metropolis, U.S.A. have undertaken an advertising campaign headlined by the slogan: "Is your family's life worth 45 MPG?" The ads admit that while Chevy subcompacts are *not* as fuel efficient as foreign imports and cost more to maintain, they are safer according to government-sponsored crash tests. The ads implicitly ask if responsible parents, when purchasing a car, should trade off fuel efficiency for safety? *Is it ethical for the dealers association to use a fear appeal to offset an economic disadvantage?*

Scenario 3

A few recent studies have linked the presence of the artificial sweetener, subsugural, to cancer in laboratory rats. While the validity of these findings has been hotly debated by medical experts, the Food and Drug Administration has ordered products containing the ingredient banned from sale in the U.S. The Jones Company sends all of its sugar-free J. C. Cola (which contains subsugural) to European supermarkets because the sweetener has not been banned there. *Is it acceptable for the Jones Company to send an arguably unsafe product to another market without waiting for further evidence?*

Scenario 4

The Acme Company sells industrial supplies through its own sales force, which calls on company purchasing agents. Acme has found that providing the purchasing agent with small gifts helps cement a cordial relationship and creates goodwill. Acme follows the policy that the bigger the order, the bigger the gift to the purchasing agent. The gifts range from a pair of tickets to a sporting event to outboard motors and snowmobiles. Acme does not give gifts to personnel at companies which they know have an explicit policy prohibiting the acceptance of such gifts. *Assuming no laws are violated, is Acme's policy of providing gifts to purchasing agents morally proper?*

Scenario 5

The Buy American Electronics Company has been selling its highly rated System X Color TV sets (21″, 19″, 12″) for $700, $500 and $300 respectively. These prices have been relatively uncompetitive in the market. After some study, Buy American substitutes several cheaper components (which engineering says may reduce the quality of performance slightly) and passes on the savings to the consumer in the form of a $100 price reduction on each model. Buy American institutes a price-oriented promotional campaign which neglects to mention that the second generation System X sets are different from the first. *Is the company's competitive strategy ethical?*

Scenario 6

The Smith and Smith Advertising Agency has been struggling financially. Mr. Smith is approached by the representative of a small South American country which is on good terms with the U.S. Department of State. He wants S and S to create a multimillion dollar advertising and public relations campaign which will bolster the image of the country and increase the likelihood that it will receive U.S. foreign aid assistance and attract investment capital. Smith knows the country is a dictatorship which has been accused of numerous human rights violations. *Is it ethical for the Smith and Smith Agency to undertake the proposed campaign?*

Source: Gene R. Laczniak. "Framework for Analyzing Marketing Ethics," *Journal of Macromarketing* 3(Spring 1983), p. 8. Used by permission.

❑ *Intuitionism.*   You would focus on your motives for a certain act; if they are good and you do not intend to hurt anyone, then the act is ethical.

❑ *Utilitarianism.*   You would examine the expected outcome of an act, and if it creates more good than bad (i.e., the well-being of society is increased), then the act is ethical.

❑ *The TV test.*   You would simply ask yourself if you would feel comfortable explaining to a national TV audience why you took this action.

MARKETING IN THE FUTURE

On a final note, we will discuss the future of marketing as it is influenced by major environmental trends and the intensification of competition. We will also predict how the marketing concept will be altered and recommend an increased use of strategic market planning to deal with these environmental changes.

Environmental Trends

What will the practice of marketing be like in the mid-1990s? A careful assessment of the external environments would be helpful in trying to answer this question, since it is these environments that influence the firm's threats and opportunities. Recently, a group of senior executives from various Fortune 500 companies responded to a research questionnaire on "business and its environments—1995." The results of this survey showed that this group of executives feels that ten major environmental trends are likely to have occurred by the mid-1990s and have a major impact on business and marketing. These trends deal with the technological, social, political, and physical environments and are summarized in Table 22.3.[10]

Technological Environment.   Three trends in the technological environment relate to the continued proliferation of information/computer-based technologies:

1. Increasingly powerful and relatively inexpensive microcomputers will make possible inexpensive and highly comprehensive interlocking data banks.
2. The telecommunications, information, and electronics industries will continue their ascendancy.
3. The majority of American manufacturing facilities will have moved to significantly greater automation through computerized machine tools, robotic systems, and computer-aided design and manufacturing (CAD/CAM).

The major implication of these trends will be in the new types of goods and services that will be marketed. Services such as electronic in-home

Table 22.3   Ten Major Trends in the External Environments

Development	Likelihood That It Will Substantially Occur by 1995
Technological Environment	
1. Increasingly powerful and relatively inexpensive microcomputers will make possible inexpensive and highly comprehensive interlocking data banks.	73%
2. The telecommunications, information and electronics industries will continue their ascendance.	73%
3. The majority of American manufacturing facilities will have moved to significantly greater automation via computerized machine tools, robotic systems and CAD/CAM.	62%
Political Environment	
4. The elderly will accrue increased political power.	62%
5. Labor unions will lose political power.	63%
Social Environment	
6. The quality of public education at the primary, secondary, and tertiary levels will be a major concern throughout the 1990s.	67%
7. Eighty percent of married households will be two-income households.	64%
8. There will be a significantly increased life span in developed countries.	61%
Physical Environment	
9. The oceans will be a frontier for major scientific developments.	55%
10. Space will be a frontier for major scientific developments.	61%

Source: Gene Laczniak and Robert F. Lusch. "Environment and Strategy in 1995: A Survey of High-Level Executives," *The Journal of Consumer Marketing* 3(Spring 1986), pp. 27–45.

banking and in-home retailing are likely to be common. In addition, because of the increased use of CAD/CAM, firms will be able to modify and design products more quickly. Robotics will enable the types of products produced to be changed on short notice. A car manufacturer could easily switch to manufacturing lawn mowers because it would only need new software for the robots. Finally, because the information/computer-based technologies will grow, firms selling computer hardware and software will witness a major growth opportunity.

Political Environment.   The primary development in the political environment will be a restructuring of power relationships in society. The power of the elderly and labor unions will be altered significantly, and you may already have seen signs of these developments. Our group of senior executives predicted the following events as very likely to occur:

4. The elderly will accrue increased political power.
5. Labor unions will lose political power.

The survey group sees increased political power on behalf of the elderly. The elderly population is growing: by 1995, approximately 18 million people will be over 60 years of age. People are living longer and, in many cases, receiving good retirement incomes. Senior citizens will continue to fight for social security increases, medicare, and other favorable tax benefits and government programs. Because of their growing numbers and purchasing power, senior citizens represent a growth market for retirement housing, travel, recreational vehicles, dining out, medication, and so on.

Many labor unions have been more moderate in their wage and fringe benefit demands, and in some cases, employees have taken wage cuts. As most union members are blue collar workers, this will result in lost income and purchasing power. Predictably, this will have a negative impact on firms whose target market is blue collar workers.

Social Environment.   Three major trends are emerging in the social environment, each of which is quite independent of the others:

6. The quality of public education at the primary, secondary, and university levels will be a major concern throughout the 1990s.
7. Eighty percent of married households will be two-income households.
8. Life span will increase significantly in developed countries.

Already the quality of public education is an issue of national debate, and this debate will intensify and result in a renewed economic commitment to public education on behalf of local, state, and federal governments. Firms that sell goods and services to educational institutions face an opportunity if they can increase the "quality" of their offerings.

We also are witnessing the proliferation of two-income households, and this trend will continue strongly into the mid-1990s. Households in which both husband and wife are employed will have more time constraints and thus will be seeking time-saving goods and services. Also, since people tend to marry those with similar educational and social class backgrounds, the incomes of the two-income households will be relatively low or high. A household in which husband and wife are blue collar workers may make $35,000, whereas a household in which both husband and wife are white collar workers may have an income of $125,000. The market for luxury goods targeted at this latter type of household is likely to grow in size.

Another trend is increased longevity, and this trend reinforces our prior statement on the growth in power of the elderly. The increased longevity of the population is due both to advanced medical technology and to "cleaner and safer" living. The physical fitness craze of the 1970s was more than a fad. The U.S. population is increasingly concerned with wellness and preventive medicine, and consequently this represents a growth market.

Physical Environment.   Two major trends forecast for the physical environment are:

9. The oceans will be a frontier for major scientific developments.
10. Space will be a frontier for major scientific developments.

The possibilities of new products based on developments in the frontiers of space and oceans are limitless. For example, pharmaceutical companies are already experimenting with production methods in a zero gravity environment, and results indicate substantially more pure and perfect drugs can be manufactured in space.

Intensification of Competition

Table 22.4 shows how our survey group of senior executives perceived the degree of competitive intensity their firms will experience in 1995. Essentially, they agree that competition will intensify and that firms will be spending more of each sales dollar on marketing because of increased competition. The executives also foresee firms aggressively fighting to hold onto their market share. This is likely due to a stabilizing of population in the United States and in many highly developed countries, such as France, West Germany, and Switzerland, and the resultant inability to count on automatic increases in the population as a means of market growth. In the mid-1990s, executives also agree that international competition will have increased significantly.

The Marketing Concept

What will become of the marketing concept in the mid-1990s? Based on our survey of Fortune 500 executives, firms that practice the traditional marketing concept will continue to be consumer oriented, to be profit rather than sales oriented, and to integrate efforts across departments (see Table 22.5). However, the marketing concept will be expanded to include publics

Table 22.4   The Intensification of Competition by 1995

Item	Mean Response[a]
Firms in our industry will be aggressively fighting to hold onto their share of the market.	4.6
Competition will be more intense.	4.3
International competition will have increased significantly in our industry.	3.9
Firms will be spending more of each sales dollar on marketing due to increased competition.	3.8

[a]Strongly disagree (1) to strongly agree (5).

Source: Gene Laczniak and Robert F. Lusch. "Environment and Strategy in 1995: A Survey of High-Level Executives," *The Journal of Consumer Marketing* 3(Spring 1986), pp. 27–45.

Table 22.5 The Predicted Expanded Marketing Concept in 1995

Item	Mean Response[a]
The Traditional Marketing Concept	
Firms will be more consumer oriented.	4.3
Firms will concentrate their efforts more on profits than on sales volume.	4.2
Marketers will work together more with other functional departments in the firm in order to achieve total company objectives.	4.2
The Expanded Marketing Concept	
Firms will be more concerned with developing good relations with employees.	4.1
Firms will be more concerned with developing good relations with their agents and/or distributors.	4.0
Firms will be more concerned with developing good relations with suppliers.	4.0

[a]Strongly disagree (1) to strongly agree (5).

Source: Gene Laczniak and Robert F. Lusch. "Environment and Strategy in 1995: A Survey of High-Level Executives," *The Journal of Consumer Marketing* 3(Spring 1986), pp. 27–45.

beyond the consuming public that a firm serves. Senior executives expressed agreement with the following statements:

1. Firms will be more concerned with developing good relations with employees.
2. Firms will be more concerned with developing good relations with their agents and/or distributors.
3. Firms will be more concerned with developing good relations with suppliers.

In short, the marketing concept of the 1990s will continue to be concerned with the consumer public, with profit orientation, with integrated effort across departments in the firm, but there will also be increased emphasis on input publics (employees and suppliers) and intermediary publics (agents and/or distributors).

A Recommendation

You might find yourself questioning some of the preceding conclusions. That is good. It is impossible to accurately predict the future of marketing, but you can anticipate the future of marketing by assessing external environments and attempting to identify the consequences of major environmental trends on the firm, industry, or marketing in general.

One thing that is definite, however, is the constant change occurring in the environment and the consequent change in marketing practices. Because of this, firms are increasingly engaging in strategic marketing planning, as we have discussed throughout this book. Clearly in the future, firms must spend considerable effort anticipating changes in the environment well before they occur so that they can acquire or redirect resources to capitalize on these trends.

As you complete your study of marketing and other business topics you will most likely begin a career in the world of business and, perhaps, marketing. What you experience in the world of business throughout your career will be influenced largely by the forces and trends we have reviewed. It will undoubtedly be an exciting time as advancing technology brings forth bionic body parts, computers that write their own software, daily travel into space, and so on. With these advances, business will have a major responsibility to behave in a socially responsible and ethical manner, and we hope you will assist in this regard. Have fun on your journey, and thanks for exploring the world of marketing with us.

SUMMARY

This chapter dealt with some criticisms of marketing, social responsibility, consumer rights, business ethics, and the future of marketing. Some of the most frequent criticisms of marketing are that it costs too much, it fosters materialism, it does not create value, its practitioners are unscrupulous, and it is unresponsive to consumer wants. We presented arguments as to why these criticisms are mostly unfounded. Clearly, most criticisms of marketing can be minimized if the firm is socially responsible. Social responsibility is taking actions and making decisions that do not have significant negative consequences for society. Three areas were discussed: advertising to children, ecology, and product safety. It is safe to say that what is considered socially responsible by one probably will not be considered so by all.

The protection of consumer rights has been a concern in the United States for over 100 years. In that time, many laws have been passed to help ensure the rights of consumers to safety, to be informed, to choose, and to be heard. In addition, many businesses have responded by establishing their own consumer affairs departments.

In dealing with the criticisms of marketing, social responsibility, and consumer rights, the marketer is essentially confronted with ethical questions. We considered five frameworks for dealing with ethical questions: the golden rule, moral idealism, intuitionism, utilitarianism, and the TV test.

On a final note, we discussed the future of marketing by using the responses of a group of Fortune 500 firm senior executives to predict future trends. The results indicated that at least ten environmental trends will gain importance by the mid-1990s, such as new information and computer technology, longer life spans, increased emphasis on education, and major new uses of the ocean and space. The senior executives also predicted that competition will intensify and that the marketing concept will expand to include multiple publics. Finally, it was pointed out that in order to survive in the future, firms must study their external environments and try to plan strategically how to profit from predicted long-range trends.

KEY CONCEPTS

social responsibility (p. 680)   consumer affairs department (p. 686)
consumer rights (p. 686)   business ethics (p. 687)

REVIEW AND DISCUSSION QUESTIONS

1. List the five common criticisms of marketing. Which one of these do you agree with most strongly and why?

2. Recommend how the costs of marketing could be reduced. What are the consequences of your recommendations for business? Society? Consumers?

3. Do you agree that social responsibility and profit maximization go together? Why or why not?

4. Outdoor billboard advertising often clutters the physical environment and scenery. Would a socially responsible firm use outdoor billboard advertising? Why or why not?

5. If consumers have the freedom to refuse to purchase from socially irresponsible firms, then why does the government need to police the actions of business?

6. What are the four basic rights of consumers? Do you feel the U.S. marketing system does a good job of providing these rights?

7. As long as it is legal in business, it is ethical. Agree or disagree with this statement, and defend your position.

8. In assessing the ethics of marketing decisions, the marketer often needs to examine the consequences of the decision on various publics: stockholders, consumers, society, employees, suppliers, intermediaries. Which public is most important in this regard?

9. Identify one external environment and discuss how it will change over the next ten years. Explain how these changes will influence marketing in general and an industry that you are familiar with.

ACTION PROBLEMS

1. On pages 688 and 690 there are five different ethical frameworks: the golden rule, moral idealism, intuitionism, utilitarianism, and the TV test. Select one framework and use it to assess the ethics of the six marketing scenarios in Table 22.2.

2. Consider the following environmental trend that was presented in Table 22.3: "Increasingly powerful and relatively inexpensive microcomputers will make possible inexpensive and highly comprehensive interlocking data banks." What impact will this development have on the following industries or products?
   a. Hospitals and health care
   b. College education
   c. Department stores

  d. Automobiles

  e. Travel agents

  f. Internal Revenue Service

3. Watch several Saturday morning children's television shows and take notes on the advertisments. For each advertisement answer the following:

  a. What product was being promoted?

  b. What claims were being made or benefits offered about the product?

  c. Was the product shown in use or demonstrated?

  d. Do you believe the advertisement was truthful, or do you believe it had a tendency to mislead children?

  e. Was the advertisement socially responsible? Why or why not?

NOTES

1. These criticisms are discussed in more detail in Ronald R. Gist, *Marketing and Society* (New York: Holt, Rinehart and Winston, 1971), pp. 25–41.

2. Gene R. Laczniak, "Framework for Analyzing Marketing Ethics," *Journal of Macromarketing* 3(Spring 1983), pp. 7–18; Gene R. Laczniak, "Business Ethics: A Manager's Primer," *Business* (January–March 1983), pp. 23–29.

3. For a complete discussion of social responsibility, see Keith Davis, "Five Propositions for Social Responsibility," *Business Horizons* (June 1975), pp. 19–24; Dan R. Dalton and Richard A. Cosier, "The Four Faces of Social Responsibility," *Business Horizons* (May–June 1982), pp. 19–27.

4. For one opinion, see Theodore Levitt, "The Dangers of Social Responsibility," *Harvard Business Review* (September–October 1958), pp. 41–50.

5. Ralph Gaedeke, "The Muckraking Era," in Ralph Gaedeke and Warren Etcheson (eds.), *Consumerism: Viewpoints from Business, Government, and the Public Interest* (San Francisco: Harper & Row, 1972), pp. 57–59.

6. The preceding four points are from "Message from the President of the United States Relative to Consumers' Protection and Interest Program," Document No. 364, House of Representatives, 87th Congress, 2nd Session, March 15, 1962, reprinted in Robert J. Halloway and Robert S. Hancock (eds.), *The Environment of Marketing Behavior,* second edition (New York: John Wiley & Sons, 1969), p. 174.

7. The trend toward consumer affairs departments is further discussed in Richard T. Hise, Peter L. Gillett, J. Patrick Kelly, "The Corporate Consumer Affairs Effort," *MSU Business Topics* (Summer 1978), pp. 17–26.

8. Several insightful articles dealing with marketing ethics are Robert Bartels, "A Model for Ethics in Marketing," *Journal of Marketing* (January 1967), pp. 20–26; O.C. Ferrell and K. Mark Weaver, "Ethical Beliefs of Marketing Managers," *Journal of Marketing* (July 1978), pp. 69–73; Patrick E. Murphy and Gene R. Laczniak, "Marketing Ethics: A Review with Implications for Managers, Educators and Researchers," in Ben M. Enis and Kenneth J. Roering (eds.), *Review of Marketing* (Chicago: American Marketing Association, 1981), pp. 251–266.

9. These five frameworks are adapted from Laczniak, "Framework for Analyzing Marketing Ethics," p. 7; Philip Kotler, *Marketing Management: Analysis, Planning, and Control* (Englewood Cliffs, NJ: Prentice-Hall, 1980), pp. 705–708.

10. Gene R. Laczniak and Robert F. Lusch, "Environment and Strategy in 1995: A Survey of High-Level Executives," *The Journal of Consumer Marketing* 3(Spring 1986), pp. 27–45.

41.

Maxwell Uniform Company

Richard Maxwell began working as a janitor at Memorial Hospital shortly after returning home from World War II. Within ten months, he was promoted to night supervisor of maintenance, and fourteen months later he became director of maintenance for the 400-bed hospital. During May of 1950, Alpha Uniforms, Memorial's janitorial uniform supplier, went bankrupt. Alpha sold or rented uniforms and also provided laundry and cleaning services for its uniforms. Maxwell had been looking for an opportunity to start his own business, so when he heard of the Alpha bankruptcy, he made a proposal to Dr. Michelle Barnes, the hospital administrator, and she accepted. This proposal essentially suggested that Memorial Hospital continue to purchase uniform and cleaning services from a new firm that Maxwell would form. The new firm would be called *Maxwell Uniform Company.*

Dr. Barnes was concerned about losing a valued employee, but Maxwell assured her that he could still hold down his old job at Memorial. Nonetheless, Dr. Barnes realized that Maxwell would be successful in business and eventually would quit his position at the hospital. Reluctantly, she agreed to Maxwell's proposal.

Maxwell Uniform Co. quickly became successful, and Maxwell decided to quit his job at the hospital. Although Maxwell Uniform Company had sales of only $92,000 in 1951, it generated a net profit of $18,000, and this was after Maxwell paid himself a $6,000 salary.

Maxwell Uniform Company sold uniform and laundry services locally to three hospitals, six auto dealerships, a large regional bakery, and forty other small businesses. By 1960, annual sales had reached $720,000 and net profits were $47,000. In 1960, Richard Maxwell received a $14,000 annual salary.

During these early years, Maxwell, Ted Zolbert, and Fred Smith ran the company while ten additional employees did everything from bookkeeping and delivery to uniform repair. Zolbert was the only salesperson, although Maxwell still called on a few key accounts. Smith was responsible for the laundry and cleaning operations.

In 1961, Maxwell decided to get out of the low-margin laundry and cleaning business, which limited the company's growth because the company could not enter a new geographic market when it needed to offer the laundry and cleaning services as well as uniform sales. At the same time, Maxwell noticed that he was missing the opportunity to expand into the manufacture and sale of other types of uniforms including police, nurse, and food service uniforms. The company had myopically focused on janitorial uniforms.

Maxwell decided that the key to growth was to design and manufacture uniforms in a single geographic location but to sell them regionally or even nationally. Previously, Maxwell had purchased janitorial uniforms from a leading apparel manufacturer.

This strategic redirection took place between 1961 and 1980, and 1980 witnessed sales of $15 million and net profits of $730,000. In addition, Maxwell paid himself a salary of $125,000, had an $18,000 expense allowance, and drove the company Cadillac. Sales were national, and the four major product lines were nursing uniforms, janitorial uniforms, security/police uniforms, and food service uniforms. Maxwell helped develop each of these lines with the aid of a consulting designer retained by the company.

Beginning in the early 1980s, the business began to experience declining sales and profits for several reasons. Richard Maxwell, now in his sixties, was no longer excited about entering new markets or giving his input on uniform design. Thus, some of the styles in the product mix had not been updated since 1976. This was a serious problem requiring immediate attention because workers, just as society in general, were becoming more fashion conscious.

More conflict was also occurring in the organization. When sales began to stabilize, Maxwell became concerned with cost containment and control. Encouraged to reduce distribution costs, Janna Haynes, the director of distribution, did so successfully. In fact, she was given a $10,000 annual bonus for cutting distribution costs by $50,000. In a recent meeting with Fred Smith, Maxwell expressed disappointment in rising production costs.

Although Zolbert successfully convinced Maxwell to avoid cutting advertising and selling costs, the sales force was finding it increasingly difficult to retain customers because of an outdated product mix and slow delivery of orders. Customers were also increasingly reluctant to pay prices that were 10 to 13 percent higher than competitors' prices. Many competitors had their uniforms made in Taiwan and Korea and were able to pass savings on to their customers in the form of lower prices.

Another source of conflict was over who was to succeed Richard Maxwell as president when he retired in 1988. Richard had not made his plans clear; in fact, it wasn't clear whether or not he had a plan.

In early 1986, a professor of business administration from a local university contacted Richard Maxwell about the possibility of using Maxwell Uniform Company as a classroom project for a group of MBA students. The students would be responsible for conducting a thorough investigation of the firm's strengths and weaknesses. Maxwell thought this would be an excellent opportunity to get some ideas on improving his firm's performance; however, he was skeptical that students could have the insights and practical experience to help him. The professor requested a copy of the firm's organization chart and some background information on the management personnel, which Maxwell willingly provided (see Table 1).

Table 1   Maxwell Uniform Company Management Personnel, December 31, 1985

Employee	Title	Age (years)	Years in Company	Education	Primary Responsibility
Richard Maxwell	President and chief executive officer	62	34 (founder)	High school	1. Planning and control 2. Pricing and product development 3. Financial management
Tom Badgewell	Vice president of operations	43	15	BS industrial engineering	1. Production planning and cost control 2. Distribution planning and cost control
Ted Zolbert	Vice president of sales	59	21	High school	1. Sales force planning and control 2. Sales training 3. Advertising
Fred Smith	Director of production	52	25	High school	1. Production line scheduling 2. Managing production labor
Janna Haynes	Director of distribution	34	2	BS economics; MBA	1. Warehousing 2. Transportation 3. Customer service 4. Management of warehouse and transportation personnel
Jim Brown	Sales force manager—West	55	18	High school	1. Supervision and control of 8 salespeople 2. Sales forecasting 3. Sales force motivation
Etta Selski	Sales force manager—South	36	10	BS marketing; MBA	1. Supervision and control of 8 salespeople 2. Sales forecasting 3. Sales force motivation
Robert Stock	Sales force manager—Midwest	38	8	BS marketing	1. Supervision and control of 8 salespeople 2. Sales forecasting 3. Sales force motivation
Jim Halpern	Sales force manager—Northeast	57	19	High school	1. Supervision and control of 8 salespeople 2. Sales forecasting 3. Sales force motivation

Questions

1. How would you go about assessing the strengths and weaknesses of Maxwell Uniform Company?
2. What is wrong with Maxwell Uniform Company's current organization structure? How would you redesign the organization to allow it to grow and prosper in the future?

42.

Jet Tire Company

Harold Iman received a bachelor's degree in accounting from a midwestern university in 1962 and, upon graduation, went to work in the accounting department of a Detroit auto manufacturer. He soon discovered that the confinement of sitting behind a desk all day poring over accounting records was not the type of work he enjoyed. One day in the company cafeteria, he ran into a salesperson with ABC Tire who was in Detroit to conduct business with Iman's employer. They exchanged business cards, and in the weeks to come, Iman decided to quit his job and go to work for ABC as a salesperson calling on wholesale and retail tire dealers in Michigan.

Iman did well in sales with ABC and stayed with the company ten years before quitting in the fall of 1973 to go into business for himself. He had found a small wholesale tire dealership in Flint, Michigan, that the owner, Tom Petrini, wished to sell. Petrini was 58 years old and wanted to retire and move to Florida. Because Petrini was anxious to sell, he offered the business to Iman for $20,000 payable over twenty years at 8 percent annual interest.

Iman became very active in the National Tire Dealers and Retreaders Association (NTDRA) and was able to meet many wholesale and retail tire dealers across the United States. He found that his concerns were similar to those of many other small dealers: (1) being able to purchase tires at attractive prices and (2) getting good quality products with few defects, thus avoiding warranty problems.

Iman was cognizant of the trend toward private branding in the tire industry. Private branding occurs when an independent party, such as Sears, contracts with a manufacturer to produce tires to Sears' specifications and with a trademark owned by Sears. Private branding was also occurring at the wholesale level, where a group of wholesale dealers would pool their purchasing power and contract with a manufacturer to produce tires for them under a trademark owned by the dealers. This type of arrangement gave the dealers the power to negotiate extremely attractive prices.

In 1982, Iman decided to form Jet Tire Company, which would contract with tire manufacturers to produce private label tires. Over the next two years, Iman was able to convince thirteen wholesale tire dealers across the United States, whom he had met at NTDRA conventions, to purchase stock in Jet Tire and agree to concentrate their purchases through Jet. Because he was the major organizer and investor, he controlled 51 percent of Jet's stock, and the thirteen dealers owned the remaining 49 percent. Figure 1 presents the organizational chart for Jet Tire Company. The company negotiated a contract with Dayton Tire & Rubber Company, and 1985 was the first year of full operation for Jet Tire Company.

In general, the participating dealers were very happy with their first year of selling Jet Tires. The dealers were able to purchase the tires at roughly 15 to 20 percent less than prices charged by comparable tire companies, and each dealer also received a year-end rebate based on cumulative purchases for the year. By policy, Jet Tire Company was committed to paying out one-half of its profits as rebates to its dealers.

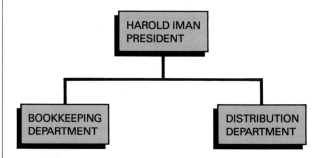

Figure 1

Organizational Chart: Jet Tire Company

To improve his understanding of Jet's performance during 1985, Iman prepared the data in Tables 1 to 3. Table 1 provides information on planned and actual sales for three major types of tires. Note that in 1985 the company only sold passenger car tires and not truck or off-road tires, which it planned to begin selling as soon as its passenger car tires proved to be successful. Table 2 provides unit planned and actual sales figures for six regions of the United States. Jet had one dealer each in the Northeast and Southwest, two dealers in the Midwest, three dealers each in the West and Southeast, and four dealers in the Central region. Table 3 is a profit and loss statement for the firm for 1985. Iman planned to study the data in these tables in order to make a report to the stockholders on the company's status. He also wanted to use the data to help generate some ideas for a marketing strategy, which the firm currently does not have.

Table 1   Unit Sales Performance by Type of Tire, Jet Tire Company, Year Ended December 31, 1985

Type of Tire	Units Sold	
	Planned	**Actual**
Bias ply	140,000	143,980
Bias belt	111,000	121,312
Radial	67,500	49,334
Total	318,500	314,626

Table 2   Unit Sales Performance by Region, Jet Tire Company, Year Ended December 31, 1985

Region	Units Sold	
	Planned	**Actual**
Northeast	44,300	38,334
Southeast	64,000	56,764
Midwest	46,400	46,800
Southwest	28,100	30,412
Central	52,000	53,102
West	83,700	89,214
Total	318,500	314,626

Table 3   Profit and Loss Statement, Jet Tire Company, Year Ended December 31, 1985

Income Statement Item	Dollars
Sales	$9,698,481
Cost of goods sold	8,728,633
Gross profit	$ 969,848
Operating expenses	
Warehousing	289,714
Transportation[a]	412,308
Salaries	78,000
Office rent	16,000
Utilities	4,311
Phone	10,704
Insurance	5,750
Professional services	7,240
Miscellaneous	4,379
Total expenses	828,406
Net profit before rebates	141,442
Rebates to dealers	70,721
Net profit before taxes	$ 70,721
Taxes	24,349
Net profit after taxes	$ 46,372

[a]Transportation is from the factory to Jet's warehouse (which is a public warehouse where Jet leases space); dealers pay transportation from the warehouse to their places of business.

Questions

1. Analyze Jet's sales performance for 1985. Where is it doing especially well, and where is it experiencing difficulties? What additional data would be helpful to Harold Iman in analyzing Jet's performance in 1985?

2. Develop a marketing strategy for Jet. What are the implications of this strategy for Jet's organizational chart?

43.

R.J. Reynolds Tobacco Company: Advertising, Children, and Smoking

In early 1984, R.J. Reynolds Tobacco Company ran an advertisement in *Better Homes and Gardens* entitled "Can we have an open debate about smoking?". In this advertisement, they desired to debate with the public such topics as relations between smokers and nonsmokers, smoking and health, smoking by children, and the role of advertising in influencing children to smoke.

Another advertisment prepared by R.J. Reynolds discusses the issue of children smoking. These advertisements appeared in magazines such as *Seventeen* and *Good Housekeeping.*

Questions

1. Evaluate R.J. Reynolds' decision to have an open debate with the public on such sensitive topics as smoking and health and children smoking.

44.

Nestle's Infant Formula (by Jeannie Akhter)

On May 21, 1981, the World Health Organization (WHO) voted 118 to 1 in favor of establishing an International Code of Marketing of Breast-milk Substitutes. This code was prompted by growing concern over the aggressive marketing activities by multinational infant formula manufacturers in less developed countries (LDCs). Formula producers maintained that their target audience was high-income, well-educated women; however, promotional reach went far beyond the target audience. As a result, low-income, illiterate women were also purchasing formula and improperly preparing the mixture: they overdiluted the infant formula and fed their children using bacteria-filled bottles.

More than 96 percent of the Nestle Company's total business is conducted outside of its home country, Switzerland. In the late 1800s, Nestle introduced its first infant food product under the bird's nest trademark. Infant food products represent approximately 8 percent of Nestle's total sales.

Worldwide infant formula industry sales in 1981 were \$1.4 billion, of which Nestle's share was \$300 to \$400 million. Over 50 percent of the infant food market is in developing countries, where the annual market growth is 15 to 20 percent, compared with 5 to 10 percent in advanced countries.

A WHO report grouped infant formula users into four categories: (1) urban economically advantaged, (2) urban middle income, (3) urban poor, and (4) rural. Literacy rates in LDCs are generally low; there is more than one recognized national language in many LDCs, and other provincial languages and dialects are commonly used. This literacy and language condition created serious problems for companies marketing their products in LDCs.

Two of Nestle's infant formula products are Neslac (which was replaced by a newer product called *Nan*) and Lactogen. Neslac and Nan were designed for infants up to the age of 5 months, and Lactogen was generally for infants over 5 months old.

Prices varied from country to country and from region to region within a country. For most families in LDCs, the price of infant formula is extremely high. The WHO determined the cost of feeding an infant with formula for six months as a percentage of per capita gross national product (GNP). In the Philippines, the cost was between 15 and 30 percent of per capita GNP, in India it was 40 to 60 percent, and in Ethiopia it was 50 to 140 percent (cost is shown as a range between the lowest and highest priced products).

Nestle's used a combination of push and pull promotional strategies in developing countries. The push consisted of promotional appeals to retailers and intensive use of health professionals and medical facilities.

Retail establishments were reached through advertisements in local retail magazines. These ads encouraged store owners to increase profitability by stocking a wide variety of Nestle infant products. Health professionals were given free supplies of infant formula for professional as well as personal use. To supplement promotional campaigns, Nestle sponsored medical conferences and provided educational materials, posters, medical equipment, personal gifts, and awards for outstanding medical students.

Nestle's pull promotional efforts reached customers directly through advertising, public relations activities, and extensive sales promotions. The advertising media used in LDCs varied from country to country depending on availability and reach. Nestle's advertising objective was to communicate its image as an infant care specialist, "Nestle—We Help Babies Grow into People."

Before the creation of the WHO code, Nestle product labels displayed a woman (usually white) holding a healthy, happy baby. Labels and instructions for the use of the product often were written in English, even in countries where English was not the national language. For instance, in Zimbabwe, only 4 percent of the people understand English; however, the products were marketed nationally with instructions given in English.

Nestle's public relations and sales promotion activities included in-store displays and company-sponsored baby shows, but the most controversial activity involved the use of "mothercraft nurses." Mothercraft nurses were company representatives dressed in nurse uniforms (not all were qualified nurses) who visited new mothers after they were released from the hospital. These mothercraft nurses weighed infants, gave helpful information on child care, demonstrated infant formula preparation and bottle feeding, and left free samples for the mother. If free samples were not allowed in a given country, the mothercraft nurse left a coupon redeemable at a local retail outlet.

In 1973, the results of an interview with tropical medical experts, Drs. Hendrickse and Morley, were published. The article, "The Baby Food Tragedy," indicated that aggressive promotion of infant products and an increase in the number of working mothers contributed to high rates of infant malnutrition.

In 1974, a London organization called *War on Want* issued a report, "The Baby Killer." War on Want's publication was translated into several languages, but the title was changed to "Nestle Kills Babies" when the report was translated into German. Nestle filed a lawsuit against the offenders in 1974. In 1976, the judge ruled in favor of Nestle; the thirteen members of the group who were found guilty were fined $120 each plus a contribution of $160 toward Nestle's legal expenses.

Following the War on Want publication, Peter Kreig, a German filmmaker, shot a film in Kenya dramatizing the problems created by formula feeding children. These activities culminated in a boycott of all Nestle products by the Infant Formula Action Coalition (INFACT) in July 1977. This U.S.-based boycott later spread to nine other countries and resulted in the largest nonunion boycott in history.

When opposition began to surface in 1973, Nestle ignored the problem. In 1974, Nestle initiated the lawsuit against the activists who published "Nestle Kills Babies," and in 1975, Nestle and other infant formula producers organized the International Council of Infant Food Industry (ICIFI) in an effort to curb mounting public criticism. This council established a voluntary code of marketing infant formula products; however, the code was not enforced, and the industry failed in its attempt to self-regulate. In 1977, when the U.S. boycott began, Nestle again chose to ignore the situation.

In winter 1979, Ernest W. Lefever, head of the nonprofit organization Ethics and Public Policy Center (EPPC), met with *Fortune*'s Washington editor, Herman Nickel. Lefever commissioned Nickel to write an article on the Nestle boycott. The contract specified that Nickel would receive half of the agreed price of $5,000 on submission of the first draft, which was targeted for March 1980; the balance would be paid on publication of the article.

Nestle admitted, through the Daniel J. Edelman public relations firm, that it did not know of the EPPC before the center commissioned Nickel to write the Nestle boycott article. Nestle donated $5,000 to EPPC in March of 1980 and an additional $20,000 in the summer of 1980. Both Nestle and Lefever strongly assert that there was no connection between the donations and the June 1980 *Fortune* article, "The Corporation Haters."

Following the publication of "The Corporation Haters," a Nestle vice president, E.W. Saunders, wrote an intracompany memo that was leaked to the *Washington*

Post. The memo indicated that "third party rebuttals" like the *Fortune* article are important to Nestle because of the lack of credibility in the United States for any company that overtly tries to sell itself after it has been attacked. Later in the memo Saunders said, "The basic strategy for dealing with the boycott, i.e., containment of the awareness of the activists' campaign, without being responsible for escalating awareness levels is working." Nestle mailed out additional copies of the *Fortune* article to gain support against the activists. The Nickel article and the leaked Nestle memo created further public relations difficulties for Nestle.

Before and during the 34th WHO assembly, Nestle joined industry opposition to the WHO code of marketing. After the WHO code was instituted, however, Nestle announced its agreement with the "aim" of the code. On July 16, 1981, Nestle issued a press release stating that it fully supported the WHO code and was taking steps to abide by the code. Furthermore, in February 1982, Nestle issued its interpretation of the WHO International Code of Marketing of Breast-milk Substitutes to all its companies, agents, and distributors who market infant formula under the Nestle trademarks. The purpose of this move was to apply WHO recommendations to countries that had not established the Nestle Infant Formula Audit Commission as an autonomous body to investigate allegations of noncompliance with the WHO code. Nestle appointed Edmund Muskie chairman of its commission, which was composed of prominent clergy members, pediatricians, and health scientists who advised the company quarterly of its findings and also made recommendations for changes. Nestle accepted many of the commission's recommendations.

By the end of 1982, Nestle had made changes in its upper-level management, including the replacement of its chief executive officer. The new leadership worked with church organizations and other concerned groups toward compliance with the WHO code.

In the winter of 1983, Carl L. Angst, executive vice president of Nestle, stated that the company would be in compliance with the WHO code by the end of 1983 at a cost to Nestle of $10 to $20 million. However, the cost to Nestle in goodwill and sales cannot be measured.

Questions

1. When opposition to Nestle's activities in LDCs first surfaced in 1973, what options did Nestle have available and what should Nestle's response have been?

2. Nestle's social response spanned a ten-year period and cost the firm in profits and public esteem. If history could be changed, how should Nestle have solved its public relations problems?

Sources: Based on information in Timothy B. Blodgett and Pamela Banks. "Nestle—At Home Abroad," *Harvard Business Review* (November–December), p. 84; Robert Ball. "Nestle Revs Up Its U.S. Campaign," *Fortune* (February 1978), p. 83; Michael de Courcy Hinds. "Nestle's New Formula Policy," *New York Times* (March 1982), p. C10; Government of Zimbabwe, Ministry of Health, *Baby Feeding—Behind & Towards a Health Model for Zimbabwe* (Zimbabwe: Government Printers, Harare/Salisbury, 1981), p. 16; James E. Post and Edward Baer. "The International Code of Marketing for Breast-milk Substitutes: Consensus, Compromise, and Conflict in the Infant Formula Controversy," *Bulletin of the International Commission of Jurists Review* (December 1980), p. 53; United Nations, World Health Organization. *Contemporary Patterns of Breast-Feeding—Report on the WHO Collaborative Study on Breast-Feeding* (Geneva: World Health Organization, 1981), p. 53; United Nations, United Nations International Children's Emergency Fund. *UNICEF Information—Questions and Answers on Infant Feeding* (April 1981), p. 5; Douglas Clement. "The African Experience: A New Nestle," *INFACT Newsletter* (Winter 1980), p. 6; Stephen Solomon. "The Controversy Over Infant Formula," *New York Times Magazine* (December 1981), p. 102; "News Formula," *National Review* (August 1981), p. 942; Morton Mintz. "Infant-Formula Market Battles Boycotters by Painting Them Red," *Washington Post* (January 1981), p. A2; Nestle press release (June 1981), in *The Nestle Case* (Washington, DC: Nestle Coordination Center for Nutrition, Inc., April 1983); "Nestle Puts Curbs on Marketing—Infant Formula Policy at Issue," *New York Times* (October 1983), p. D16(L). Used by permission of Jeannie Akhter.

LEARNING OBJECTIVES

After you complete this appendix,
you should be able to:

• **Analyze** an income statement and
balance sheet

• **Compute** markup percentages

• **Define** some important accounting terms

MARKETING MATH, FINANCE, AND ACCOUNTING

INTRODUCTION

Accounting is the basic language of business; a firm's financial successes and failures are communicated through its accounting records. Since marketing efforts will have a major influence on a firm's financial situation, marketers must understand accounting concepts.

Both marketing and accounting deal with exchange. Marketing is responsible for creating economic exchanges with supplier publics, intermediary publics, and customers (or output public), while accounting records document the monetary aspects of these exchanges. For example, if a salesperson for Xerox sells a copy machine for $7,500, then this transaction is recorded in the accounting books of Xerox. Similarly, the company purchasing the copier will record the purchase of the machine in its accounting books.

All marketing managers should be able to readily interpret a firm's two basic accounting statements—the income statement and the balance sheet. The **income statement** reports *the results of the enterprise's profit-directed activities for a specified period.* The **balance sheet** *summarizes the financial position of a business at a particular point in time.*[1]

UNDERSTANDING THE INCOME STATEMENT

A firm's income statement must have a minimum of three components: (1) sales, (2) expenses or costs, and (3) profit. The basic income statement equation is:

Sales − expenses = profit

Sales represent economic exchanges with an output public (i.e., customers), and expenses represent exchanges with input publics (i.e., employees and suppliers). When the value of economic exchanges with output publics is greater than that with input publics, then a net positive benefit accrues to the enterprise. This benefit is referred to as *profit.* Accounting for nonprofit firms (i.e., Boy Scouts) is essentially the same, except that profit is termed *surplus generated.* If the value of economic exchanges with output publics is less than the value of exchanges with input publics, a negative result, called *loss,* occurs.

To illustrate these concepts more concretely, consider the following simplified income statement for the RST Company for the most recent calendar year.

Sales	$725,000
Less: Expenses	701,000
PROFIT	$ 24,000

Although this income statement contains the three essential elements, it is not very helpful except in communicating that RST Company was successful because it generated a profit of $24,000.

The usefulness of an income statement expands with the amount of detail it contains. Consider the following, more detailed income statement for the RST Company:

Gross sales	$750,000
Less: Returns and allowances	25,000
Net sales	$725,000
Less: Cost of goods sold	420,500
Gross profit	$304,500
Less: Operating expenses	280,500
NET PROFIT	$ 24,000

This income statement introduces several new concepts or terms that you should become familiar with. At the top of the statement, we have **gross sales,** which is *the total dollar amount of all sales to customers during a specified period.* Predictably, some of these sales will be unsuccessful because customers become dissatisfied and thus may *return* the merchandise and get a refund of the purchase price, or the customer and RST may negotiate a settlement in terms of what is called an *allowance.* For example, RST may convince the customer to keep the merchandise in exchange for a refund of 25 percent of the purchase price. The RST Company, with gross sales of $750,000, had to absorb $25,000 in returns and allowances, which yielded net sales of $725,000. **Net sales** is simply *gross sales less returns and allowances.*

Subtracted from net sales is cost of goods or merchandise sold. **Cost of goods** or merchandise sold *represents the prices paid by a firm for the products it sells to customers.* For a wholesale or retail firm, cost of goods sold is simply the amount paid to the manufacturers or wholesalers for merchandise, plus the cost of getting that merchandise to the firm's place of operation. For a manufacturing enterprise, cost of goods sold represents all the prices a manufacturer paid to manufacture the goods, including such things as material costs, labor costs, and factory overhead (e.g., electricity, insurance, property taxes, janitorial services). **Gross profit,** which is *sales minus cost of goods sold,* is the dollar amount available to cover all operating expenses and provide a profit for the enterprise or its owners.

Next, we come to **operating expenses,** which represent *all the expenses incurred in carrying out the day-to-day operations of the enterprise.* These include marketing expenses, such as advertising, sales force salaries, and distribution expenses, as well as office expenses and administrative salaries. When *operating expenses are subtracted from gross profit,* we obtain the **net profit** for the enterprise. Note that net profit comes before the firm has paid any local, state, or federal income taxes. Net profit is what remains from a firm's sales dollars after all expenses incurred to generate the sales have been subtracted.

Table A.1   Income Statement: The RST Company

Income Statement Element	Dollars	Percentage of Net Sales
Gross Sales	$750,000	103.33%
Less: Returns and allowances	25,000	3.33
Net Sales	$725,000	100.00%
Less: Cost of goods or merchandise sold	420,500	58.00
Gross Profit	$304,500	42.00%
Less: Operating Expenses		
Selling expenses		
Advertising	20,000	2.76%
Sales force salaries	69,000	9.52
Delivery	24,000	3.31
Bad debts	7,500	1.03
Total	$120,500	16.62%
Administrative expenses		
Office salaries	94,000	12.97%
Office supplies	12,000	1.65
Miscellaneous	1,000	.13
Total	$107,000	14.76%
General expenses		
Building occupancy	26,000	3.59%
Depreciation	10,000	1.38
Miscellaneous	1,000	.13
Other wages	16,000	2.21
Total	$ 53,000	7.31%
Total Operating Expenses	$280,500	38.69%
Net Profit (before taxes)	$ 24,000	3.31%

The key income statement computations are illustrated in Table A.1, which presents a detailed income statement for the RST Company. Operating expenses are placed into three broad categories: selling, general, and administrative expenses. Note that this income statement communicates in terms of dollars and percentages. Net sales is given a base of 100.0 percent, and everything is stated in percentage terms in relation to this base. The relationship between expenses and sales can be more easily conveyed with a percentile income statement. For example, advertising was 2.76 percent of net sales for the RST Company.

UNDERSTANDING THE BALANCE SHEET

A balance sheet includes at least three essential elements: (1) assets, (2) liabilities, and (3) owner's equity. An **asset** is *an item of value to which the firm has ownership rights and that is expected to generate future benefits to the organization.* Assets include such things as buildings, inventory, equipment, and cash. A **liability** is *any obligation to pay money or provide goods and services to an output or input public.* A loan from a bank or credit from suppliers represents a liability—these are obligations to pay input publics at some future date. If a firm receives deposits from customers on merchandise or services to be performed in the future, this would be a liability due to an output public (i.e., customers). Finally, **equity** is *assets less liabilities.* Equity represents what would be left in assets if all liabilities were paid. Equity is sometimes referred to as *net worth* or *owner's capital.*

The balance sheet, as its name implies, involves a balancing relationship. The balancing relationship is referred to as the *basic accounting equation.* It has the formula:

Assets = liabilities + equity

Stated alternatively, it can be said that:

Resources = creditors' share + owner's share

A simplified balance sheet for the RST Company might look like this:

Balance Sheet: The RST Company

Assets	$250,000	Liabilities	$125,000
		Equity	125,000
Total Assets	$250,000	Total Liabilities and Equity	$250,000

Note that the assets are on the left side of the balance sheet and liabilities and equity are on the right side. The left side must equal the total of the right side: total assets must equal the sum of liabilities and equity. More specific information can be provided by identifying the composition of assets, liabilities, and equity.

Asset Composition

The assets of an organization can be referred to as *current assets* and *long-term* or *fixed assets.* A **current asset** is *cash or any other asset that can be converted to cash in the normal course of operating the business over a one-year period.* The most frequently used current assets in business are cash, inventory, and accounts receivable. **Accounts receivable** is *what customers owe the firm because they purchase on credit.* A **fixed asset** is *any asset that is expected to provide benefits to the firm for a period greater than one year.* Some common fixed assets are land, buildings, and equipment.

Returning to the RST Company, we see the following composition of assets:

Asset Composition: The RST Company

Cash	$ 7,500	
Inventory	100,000	
Accounts receivable	42,500	
Current Assets		$150,000
Building and land	$ 75,000	
Equipment	25,000	
Fixed Assets		$100,000
Total Assets		$250,000

Liability and Equity Composition

An organization's liabilities and equity can be classified meaningfully into several categories. First, liabilities can be classified as long term or current. A **long-term liability** is *a liability that is due and payable beyond a one-year period.* Bonds and long-term notes payable are common long-term liabilities. A **current liability** is *any obligation to pay an input or output public that becomes due within a one-year period.* The most common current liabilities are accounts payable—what a firm owes its suppliers—and notes payable—what a firm owes banks, financial institutions, or others for money they have loaned to the firm. Another common current liability is taxes payable, which are taxes due within the year to the local, county, state, or federal government.

The equity section of the balance sheet can be divided into two major parts: paid-in capital and retained earnings, or earned surplus. **Paid-in capital** is *the monetary value of capital contributed to the organization by the owners of the enterprise.* On the other hand, **retained earnings** is *the profit the enterprise has earned since its inception that has not been paid out to the owners.* Retained earnings are essentially the profits that the owners are reinvesting in the enterprise.

Coming back to the RST Company, we see the following composition of liabilities and equity:

Composition of Liabilities and Equity: The RST Company

Acccounts payable	$50,000	
Notes payable	20,000	
Taxes payable	5,000	
Current Liabilities		$ 75,000
Bonds	$40,000	
Notes payable	10,000	
Long-Term Liabilities		$ 50,000
Total Liabilities		$125,000
Paid-in capital	$90,000	
Retained earnings	35,000	
Total Equity		$125,000
Total Liabilities and Equity		$250,000

Analyzing the Complete Balance Sheet

Table A.2 presents a detailed balance sheet for the RST Company, which is stated in terms of dollars and percentages. The percentile balance sheet states all balance sheet elements as a percentage of total assets or total liabilities and equity. For example, inventory is 36.0 percent, which means that inventory is 36 percent of total assets. Retained earnings of 14 percent means that 14 percent of all capital has been provided by retained earnings.

Table A.2   Balance Sheet: The RST Company

Assets				Liabilities and Equity			
Current assets	**Dollars**		**Percent**	Current liabilities	**Dollars**		**Percent**
Cash	$10,000		4.0%	Accounts payable	$50,000		20.0%
Inventory	90,000		36.0	Notes payable	20,000		8.0
Accounts receivable	50,000		20.0	Taxes payable	5,000		2.0
Total		$150,000	60.0%	Total		$ 75,000	30.0%
Fixed assets				Long-term liabilities			
Building and land	$75,000		30.0%	Bonds	$40,000		16.0%
Equipment	25,000		10.0	Long-term notes	10,000		4.0
Total		$100,000	40.0%	Total		$ 50,000	20.0
Total assets		$250,000	100.0%	Equity			
				Paid-in capital	$90,000		36.0%
				Retained earnings	35,000		14.0
				Total equity		$125,000	50.0
				Total liabilities and equity		$250,000	100.0%

Useful information can be obtained by analyzing different components of the balance sheet. For example, the analyst can systematically examine the extent to which the organization is using debt in its total capital structure. The higher the proportion of the debt, the more leveraged is the firm; that is, it is using other people's money to finance the enterprise. One popular measure of **financial leverage** is *total assets divided by total equity.* This ratio helps to depict the extent to which the organization is using debt in its total capital structure. The low end of this ratio is 1.0× and depicts a situation in which the firm is using no debt in its capital structure. As the ratio moves beyond 1.0, the firm is using a heavier mix of debt versus equity. In the case of the RST Company, the ratio is 2.0×; thus, the firm has two dollars in assets for every dollar in equity.

The balance sheet can also be analyzed to evaluate a firm's liquidity. **Liquidity** represents *the firm's ability to meet its current payment obligations.* Liquidity is crucial for two reasons. On the one hand, if an enterprise has too much liquidity, then capital is not being fully used. Thus, attractive options for using capital probably are being ignored or discarded to minimize the risks of insolvency. Having too much liquidity can be just as risky as not having enough. On the other hand, not enough liquidity can mean that a retailer may not be able to take advantage of opportunities to develop or market new products, enter new markets on short notice, or to pay all the bills. In general, sufficient liquidity is important because it protects the company from economic downturns and potential insolvency and also provides the needed flexibility to capitalize on unexpected marketing opportunities.

Financial analysts generally use three financial ratios to evaluate liquidity. The most popular is the ratio of current assets to current liabilities, which is often called the **current ratio.** This ratio is *the basic measurement of a firm's solvency.* The conventional wisdom of finance suggests that a firm should maintain a current ratio of approximately 2.0×, which happens to be the value of the current ratio for the RST Company.

A second ratio is called the **quick ratio** and is computed as *current assets less inventory divided by current liabilities.* The quick ratio is a more stringent measure of a firm's ability to pay its current liabilities. Again, the conventional wisdom of finance suggests that firms should maintain a quick ratio of 1.0×. The RST Company has a quick ratio of 0.8×.

The third liquidity ratio is the **acid-test ratio** and is computed as *cash divided by current liabilities.* This ratio received considerable attention during the 1969 to 1970, 1974 to 1975, and 1981 to 1982 credit crises. Analysts contend that U.S. firms should have a supply of cash that is equal to 15 to 20 percent of current liabilities. The RST Company has cash that is equal to 13 percent of current liabilities.

To provide you with a frame of reference, Table A.3 shows average liquidity ratios for manufacturing, wholesaling, and retailing firms for the year 1984. Why do you think wholesale and retail firms have lower liquidity ratios than do manufacturers?

Table A.3   Liquidity Ratios for U.S. Firms (1984)

Liquidity Ratio	Manufacturers	Wholesalers	Retailers
Current ratio	1.6×	1.4×	1.7×
Quick ratio	0.9×	0.8×	0.8×
Acid-test ratio	22.0%	17.6%	15.2%

Sources: U.S. Bureau of the Census. *Quarterly Financial Report for Manufacturing, Mining, and Trade Corporations,* second quarter, 1985, series QFR-85-2 (Washington, DC: U.S. Government Printing Office, 1985); authors' computations.

THE STRATEGIC PROFIT MODEL

As stated at the outset, the two basic financial statements of an enterprise are the income statement and balance sheet. These statements can be analyzed individually or collectively. If you want to analyze them together to see how they interact and determine a firm's performance, you will need some type of framework or model. One useful and very popular framework is the strategic profit model, which is displayed in Figure A.1.

An organization's profit performance can be clearly specified using the **strategic profit model.** This model *multiplies a firm's net profit margin by its rate of asset turnover to arrive at its return on assets and this figure is then multiplied by financial leverage to obtain return on equity.* (The formulas are shown in Figure A.1.) Thus, if a firm has a profit margin of 2 percent and a rate of asset turnover of 3.0×, then it automatically will have a return on assets of 6 percent (2% × 3.0 = 6%). **Return on assets** *depicts*

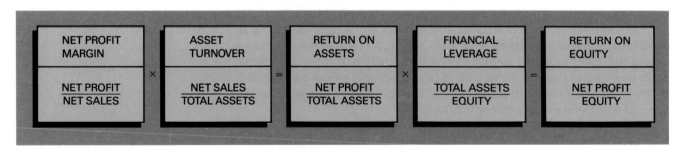

Figure A.1
Strategic Profit Model

the profit return the organization achieved on all assets invested in the enterprise regardless of whether the assets were financed by debt or equity.

The return on asset figure is multiplied by the firm's financial leverage to yield return on equity. In the preceding example, if the firm had financial leverage of 2.0× and this figure was multiplied by the return on assets of 6 percent, the result would be a return on equity of 12 percent (6% × 2.0 = 12%). **Return on equity** depicts *the profit the owners of the enterprise achieved on the dollars they had invested in the enterprise.*

As is readily evident, the strategic profit model focuses on three important financial ratios: (1) net profit margin, (2) asset turnover, and (3) financial leverage. We will examine each ratio.

Net Profit Margin

The **net profit margin** is *the ratio of net profit to net sales.* This ratio comes solely from the income statement, and it shows how much profit a firm makes on each dollar of sales after all expenses have been taken into account. For example, we see in Table A.1 that the RST Company has a net profit margin of 3.31 percent; it is making 3.31¢ on each dollar of sales. Since this ratio comes solely from the income statement, it does not show how effectively a firm is using the capital (i.e., assets) at its disposal.

Asset Turnover

The **asset turnover** is computed by *dividing net sales by total assets.* This ratio reveals how many dollars of sales a firm can generate on an annual basis with each dollar invested in assets. The RST Company has an asset turnover of 2.9× ($725,000/$250,000), which suggests that this company is generating $2.90 in sales for each dollar in assets. The asset turnover ratio incorporates key measures from the income statement (net sales) and the balance sheet (total assets) and, as such, shows how well the firm is using its capital to generate sales.

Financial Leverage

Financial leverage, which we discussed earlier, is defined as total assets divided by equity and shows the extent to which the firm uses debt in its total capital structure. The RST Company has a financial leverage ratio of 2.0×, which suggests that RST has two dollars of assets for each dollar of equity.

RST Strategic Profit Model

Figure A.2 portrays the RST Company's strategic profit model. The RST Company has a net profit margin of 3.31 percent, which, when multiplied by an asset turnover of 2.9×, results in a return on assets of 9.6 percent. When the return on assets of 9.6 percent is multiplied by financial leverage of 2.0×, the result is 19.2 percent return on equity.

OTHER MEASURES OF FINANCIAL PERFORMANCE

There are two other important measures of financial performance in marketing management with which you should be familiar: markup and inventory turnover.

Markup

Both retailers and wholesalers purchase merchandise from other organizations and in turn sell it to other firms or individuals. Since retailers and wholesalers incur business expenses, they must markup the merchandise they sell.

A basic markup equation is as follows:

$$P = C + M$$

where:

C = dollar cost of merchandise per unit
M = dollar markup per unit
P = selling price per unit

If a retail or wholesale firm has a cost per unit of $10 and a dollar markup of $5, then the selling price per unit is $15.

NET PROFIT MARGIN		ASSET TURNOVER		RETURN ON ASSETS		FINANCIAL LEVERAGE		RETURN ON EQUITY
3.31%	×	2.9x	=	9.6%	×	2.0x	=	19.2%

Figure A.2

The RST Company's Strategic Profit Model

In the retail and wholesale trades, markup typically is discussed in terms of percentages rather than dollars. Two methods exist for computing markup percentages that differ in terms of the base on which the markup is computed: the cost-based markup method and the selling price–based markup method.

Cost-Based Markup.   The cost-based markup method uses the following formula:

Percent markup on cost $= (P-C) / C$

Using the previous example in which P was \$15 and C was \$10, the markup would be 50 percent.

Price-Based Markup.   The formula for finding the price-based markup is:

Percent markup on selling price $= (P-C) / P$

If P is \$15 and C is \$10, the markup on price would be 33.3 percent. Since price (P) is always higher than cost (C), the percentage of markup on cost will always be greater than the percentage of markup on price. In actual practice, most retailers and wholesalers use a price-based markup.

Relating Price-Based and Cost-Based Markups.   Both methods of computing markup percentages use the same two pieces of information: price per unit (P) and cost per unit (C). The formula for relating these two methods of computing markup is:

Percent markup on price

$$= \left(\begin{matrix} \text{percent markup} \\ \text{on cost} \end{matrix} \right) \times \left(\cfrac{1}{\begin{matrix} 1 + \text{percent markup} \\ \text{on cost} \end{matrix}} \right)$$

If you have a 50 percent markup on cost, the preceding formula would yield the following percentage of markup on price:

$(0.5) \times [1/(1 + 0.5)] = 0.333$ or 33.3%

Similarly, the formula for relating percent markup on cost to percent markup on price is as follows:

Percent markup on cost

$$= \left(\begin{matrix} \text{percent markup} \\ \text{on price} \end{matrix} \right) \times \left(\cfrac{1}{\begin{matrix} 1 - \text{percent markup} \\ \text{on price} \end{matrix}} \right)$$

If you have a price markup of 33.3 percent, the preceding formula would yield this markup on cost:

$$(0.333) \times [1/(1 - 0.333)] = 0.50 \text{ or } 50\%$$

Table A.4 converts markup on price to markup on cost. Note that markup on cost grows rapidly as the markup on price gets closer to 100 percent. It is important to be able to relate the price-based and cost-based markup methods because sellers may quote a certain markup percent, and it is useful to know how this figure translates to the alternative method of computing markups. For example, a seller may state that a product has a markup of 50 percent. If you question the seller and determine that the 50 percent is a markup on price, then you could translate this figure into the markup on cost and find out that the markup on cost is 100 percent (see Table A.4). These figures can then be used as a basis for bargaining.

Inventory Turnover

Inventory turnover is a key to profitability in retail and wholesale organizations. **Inventory turnover** represents *the average number of times per year that inventory is sold.* Inventory turnover is determined by taking the cost of merchandise sold during a one-year period and dividing it by average inventory investment. For example, if a grocery retailer had an annual cost of merchandise of $6,500,000 and an average inventory investment of $500,000, then the inventory turnover would be thirteen times ($6,500,000/ $500,000 = 13). In retailing and wholesaling, the higher the inventory turnover, holding all else constant, the higher is the profitability of the organization.

Table A.4   Markup on Price Converted to Markup on Cost

Percent Markup on Price	Percent Markup on Cost
10	11
20	25
30	43
33	50
40	67
50	100
60	150
70	233
80	400
90	900

SUMMARY

This appendix reviewed some basic accounting and finance concepts that marketers need to know. It is important that the marketing manager understand and interpret a firm's income statement and balance sheet. The income statement reports the results of the enterprise's profit-directed activities for a specified period. The balance sheet summarizes the financial position of a business at a particular point in time.

A useful framework that ties together important items from the income statement and balance sheet is the strategic profit model. The strategic profit model begins with the net profit margin, which is net profit divided by net sales. This net profit margin is multiplied by asset turnover, which is net sales divided by total assets, and the result is return on assets. Return on assets is defined as net profit divided by total assets. The return on assets is then multiplied by financial leverage, which is total assets divided by equity, and the outcome is return on equity. Return on equity is net profit divided by equity.

A marketing manager should also understand the concepts of markup and inventory turnover. A markup percent can be computed based on cost or selling price of a product, and the marketer should be proficient at computing markups using either approach. The markup computed on the basis of cost is always higher than the markup based on selling price. Inventory turnover represents the average number of times per year an inventory is sold. If all else is held constant, then higher inventory turnover leads to higher profitability.

KEY CONCEPTS

income statement (p. 705)
balance sheet (p. 705)
gross sales (p. 706)
net sales (p. 706)
cost of goods (p. 706)
gross profit (p. 707)
operating expenses (p. 707)
net profit (p. 707)
asset (p. 708)
liability (p. 708)
equity (p. 708)
current asset (p. 709)
accounts receivable (p. 709)
fixed asset (p. 709)
long-term liability (p. 709)

current liability (p. 709)
paid-in capital (p. 709)
retained earnings (p. 709)
financial leverage (p. 711)
liquidity (p. 711)
current ratio (p. 711)
quick ratio (p. 711)
acid-test ratio (p. 711)
strategic profit model (p. 712)
return on assets (pp. 712–713)
return on equity (p. 713)
net profit margin (p. 713)
asset turnover (p. 713)
inventory turnover (p. 716)

QUESTIONS, PROBLEMS, AND EXERCISES

1. Classify the following items into assets, liabilities, and equity.
   a. Computer
   b. Inventory

    c. Certificate of deposit for $10,000

    d. Prepaid insurance (i.e., an insurance policy paid on January 1, which provides insurance for 12 months)

    e. A $200 deposit that a customer gives to a retailer to order a carpet

    f. A bank note for $100,000

    g. $1,000,000 that a company receives after issuing new stock: 100,000 shares at $10 per share

2. Are gross profit as a percent of net sales and markup percent different or the same?

3. Why are liquidity and profitability important to a firm? Can a firm have too much liquidity?

4. What types of marketing decisions or policies might influence liquidity?

5. The Alpha Hardware Store completed fiscal 1984 with the following results:

Net sales	$1,500,000
Net profit	30,000
Current assets	80,000
Gross profit as percent of net sales	15%
Cash on hand	30,000
Average inventory	100,000
Current liabilities	120,000
Accounts payable	60,000
Equity	100,000
Fixed assets	70,000

Develop an income statement and balance sheet and evaluate the firm's financial performance. Compute the strategic profit model.

6. Convert the following markups on cost to markup on selling price:

    a. 21%   d. 43%

    b. 28%   e. 54%

    c. 39%   f. 79%

7. Reconsider the data for Alpha Hardware. If management expects sales to be $1,800,000 next year and inventory turnover remains the same, how much will average inventory need to increase?

NOTES

1. J. Owne Cherrington, *Accounting Basics* (Boston: Kent Publishing Company, 1981), pp. 7, 24.

APPENDIX B

MARKETING CAREERS AND MARKETING PROFESSIONALISM

INTRODUCTION

No matter what your interests and skills, there is a career in marketing for you. This point will become evident as you learn about the many career opportunities in marketing in this appendix. Marketing careers are open to all kinds of people—men and women; blacks, whites, Hispanics, and other ethnic groups; physically strong and disabled or handicapped persons.

If your job is to be a career, not just a place to work, you must develop a sense of professionalism. Therefore, we conclude this appendix by discussing the three fundamental qualifications of a marketing professional.

CAREER OPPORTUNITIES IN MARKETING

The American economic system is dependent on sales generation and the distribution of products over large geographic areas. Consequently, marketing jobs exist worldwide in organizations ranging from aerospace firms to zoos.

Marketing is also a common career path to the chief executive offices of major U.S. corporations. According to a study conducted by a major executive search firm, over 30 percent of chief executive officers in the survey spent most of their careers in marketing.[1] Accounting and finance was the next most common background. If you refer back to Table 1.1 in Chapter 1, you will see that the top compensation levels in marketing can match those in any career field. Compensation levels for the ten best-paid sales and marketing executives in 1984 ranged from approximately $400,000 to over $1,200,000 per year.

It is not unusual for someone involved in a career search to be concerned about which jobs are the best paying. Marketers can earn a high level of compensation, but these high levels are not the norm. In fact, norms or averages are misleading because wide variations exist for all careers in marketing. For example, the average industrial salesperson makes more than the average market research analyst, but the best market research analysts receive better compensation than the average industrial salesperson. For this reason, you should not be overly concerned about comparing starting compensation for different careers in marketing. You should select the career that best fits your interests and skills. This is especially important because most entry-level positions in marketing are merely stepping stones to higher level positions. Therefore, you should start in a field, geographic area, and industry that fit your needs; perform well, and the opportunities for career change and geographic mobility will be endless.

We will explore some career possibilities in marketing by profiling eighteen popular marketing careers. The brief career descriptions are intended only to provide an introduction to each career option. Most management level positions require several years of experience that is gained in less prestigious entry-level positions. In addition, you might want to consult the list of career information sources at the end of this appendix. All of these sources should be available in your campus library or at the college or campus career placement office. Additional sources of information on careers in marketing are available from the many professional and trade associations in marketing. Some of the more well-known associations and their addresses are also listed at the end of this appendix.

Business-to-Business Technical Sales

This type of salesperson is responsible for interacting with managers, engineers, and decision makers in business firms in order to sell them technologically sophisticated products, such as computers, robots, or airplanes. An understanding of the technology of the product is required. Extensive travel over a well-defined geographic sales territory is common, but some selling by phone may be required.

Typical employers of college graduates for business-to-business technical sales are Dow Chemical, Satellite Business Systems, General Electric Corp., and Teledyne.

Business-to-Business Nontechnical Sales

This type of salesperson is responsible for interacting with managers and purchasing agents in business firms in order to sell these firms frequently purchased supplies, raw materials, or business services. Travel over a well-defined geographic sales territory may be necessary, but usually a major amount of selling is done by phone.

Typical employers of college graduates for business-to-business non-technical sales are Cooper Tire & Rubber, Citicorp, Olin Corp., and Brockway Inc.

Consumer Sales

A consumer salesperson is responsible for making sales to final consumers. Employment could be with a retail store, insurance company, realtor, stock brokerage, or other firm that sells to the ultimate consumer. Generally, entry-level positions require little experience or formal training, although in times of high unemployment, this may not be the case.

Sales Manager

A sales manager is primarily responsible for supervising the sales force. Common duties include recruiting, selecting, training, motivating, and evaluating the sales personnel. Another responsibility includes controlling the cost of supporting the sales force.

College graduates can move into a sales management position after they gain several years of experience in sales. Most major organizations employ sales managers, but several examples are IBM Corp., Quaker Oats, Aetna Life and Casualty, and Maytag Corp.

Advertising Manager

An advertising manager is responsible for directing a firm's total advertising program, including selection of the firm's advertising agency. The advertising manager is responsible for advertising budgeting/media selection, decisions on timing and frequency of advertising, and approval of advertising copy. Therefore, course work or experience in journalism, accounting, and sociology may be helpful.

Many organizations recruit college graduates for advertising management positions. Some of the typical employers are Procter & Gamble, Genesco, Fisher's Big Wheel, Inc., and Tenneco.

Advertising Account Executive

An advertising account executive works for an advertising agency and is responsible for maintaining good client relationships. Typical duties include studying the client's promotion objectives and assisting the client in developing an advertising program. The account executive may also recommend the budget, message, layout, media, and timing of advertisements.

Because of the glamour of working in advertising, there is much competition for the relatively limited number of jobs. Some of the large agencies such as Ogilvy and Mather, Leo Burnett Co., Inc., Young & Rubicam, Saatchi & Saatchi, and Doyle Dane Bernbach, as well as many smaller local agencies, are typical employers.

Public Relations Manager

A public relations manager is responsible for maintaining a positive image with a firm's publics. The public relations manager also makes an effort to minimize negative reactions to an organization's activities and policies. One of their duties may be to perform surveys to gauge public opinion of the organization.

Competition among students of marketing, management, journalism, and psychology is strong for public relations positions. Typical employers include Philip Morris, Teledyne, Ford Motor Company, and Blue Cross and Blue Shield of America.

Product Manager

Product managers are also often called *brand managers.* Product, or brand, managers are responsible for planning and supervising the complete marketing program for a particular product or brand. Because this manager must do a considerable amount of coordination with various departments in the organization such as advertising, physical distribution, legal, and finance, a background including course work and experience in these departments is helpful.

Some typical employers of product and brand managers are Campbell Soup Co., Colgate-Palmolive Co., the Crocker Bank, and S.C. Johnson & Son, Inc.

Market Research Analyst

A market research analyst performs marketing research functions such as questionnaire design, sampling plan, data analysis, and interpretation of results. This person may also help write up the results in the form of a management report.

Many organizations employ market research analysts. Some typical employers are Mead Corp., General Motors, Amtrak-National Railroad, and Du Pont E.I. Nemours & Co.

Purchasing Manager

A purchasing manager is responsible for purchasing an organization's operating supplies and equipment and, in the case of a manufacturing organization, the raw materials and other items needed to manufacture products. This person seeks reliable vendors and negotiates favorable terms of trade. The purchasing manager may help set product specifications to help screen which items to purchase.

Predictably, all organizations need purchasing managers. Some of the firms that employ recent college graduates for purchasing manager positions are NCR, Clorox Co., GTE, and McDermott, Inc.

Customer Service Manager

A customer service manager is responsible for coordinating supply and demand generation activities in order to maintain good customer relations. Typical responsibilities include ensuring that orders are processed, promised delivery dates are kept, defective products are returned to the company, warranty service is quick and courteous, and products are properly installed.

Inventory Control Manager

An inventory control manager is primarily responsible for optimizing a firm's investment in inventory. Duties include maintaining the proper quantity of units in inventory, helping the organization offer good customer service through control of out-of-stock items, and maintaining inventory turnover objectives.

Examples of organizations that employ college graduates for inventory control managers are J.C. Penney, Scrivner, American Hospital Supply, and Anixter Bros.

Warehouse Manager

A warehouse manager is responsible for the safe storage and movement of merchandise in a firm's warehouse. Duties include effective use of warehouse space, control of warehouse labor expenses and staffing, and purchase and maintenance of warehouse equipment such as forklifts.

Some examples of organizations that recruit business college graduates for warehouse managers are Fleming Companies, R.H. Macy & Co., American Hospital Supply, and Malone & Hyde.

Transportation Manager

A transportation manager is responsible for directing a firm's inbound and outbound transportation activities. This manager evaluates costs and benefits of different types of transportation. The transportation manager also routes and schedules shipments and, if the firm has its own fleet of vehicles, is responsible for the maintenance of the transportation fleet.

Examples of organizations that recruit college graduates for positions in transportation management are Frito-Lay, Inc., Sunoco Products, Inc., Ralston Purina Co., Inc., and Woodward & Lothrop, Inc.

Retail Buyer

A retail buyer is responsible for purchasing items to be resold at retail. The buyer decides which vendors are the best to purchase from and negotiates terms of sale. A buyer usually concentrates on a particular merchandise category (such as housewares) and must plan the proper product assortment in this area. The buyer is given a dollar budget for purchases for a given period and must spend these dollars effectively.

Large retail chains and department stores often recruit college graduates for retail buyer positions. Some typical employers are Foley's, Mervyns, Famous Barr Co., the Limited, and Sears.

Retail Manager

Opportunities in retail management are in one of three areas: (1) department manager, (2) merchandise manager, and (3) store manager. A *department manager* supervises one retail department in a store (this is often the first job a college graduate assumes with a retail firm). A *merchandise manager* supervises several retail buyers and allocates budget dollars to them. A *store manager* supervises all day-to-day activities in a store. All department managers and other supervisory personnel report to the store manager.

Some of the typical firms that recruit business college graduates for positions in retail management are K mart, Gimbels, Marshall Field, Joske's, the May Company, and Neiman-Marcus.

Bank Marketing Manager

A bank marketing manager is responsible for developing solid relationships with the bank's customers. Duties may include the development of new banking services, advertising budgeting, and establishment of the proper loan and investment rates. The bank marketing manager also is responsible for buying marketing research and may assist in site selection decisions for new branch bank locations.

Some of the banks that have recruited college graduates with a background in marketing include Fidelity Bank, Citicorp, BankAmerica Corp., and the Crocker Bank.

International Marketing

A person employed in international marketing works in a foreign office of a domestic firm or in the international department of a domestic firm. Positions available relate to all areas of marketing previously discussed.

Part of your preparation for a career in marketing should consist of learning about professionalism. All successful marketers have a high degree of professionalism. Clearly, therefore, if you are to be successful in marketing, you must develop the status, methods, standards, and character of a professional.

The nature of professionalism has at least three major dimensions: commitment, competence, and conduct.[2]

BECOMING A MARKETING PROFESSIONAL

Commitment

A marketing professional should be able to make an emotional and an intellectual pledge that includes:

1. A commitment and appreciation of the necessary role that marketing plays in the economic system of capitalism.
2. A commitment to the ethical standards necessary for marketing to fulfill its responsibility.
3. A commitment to his or her employer and to the publics of that organization.
4. A commitment to the successful completion of tasks that are undertaken.
5. A commitment to setting personal and professional goals and working toward reaching these goals.

Competence

To become a professional, you must also develop the skill level necessary to be competent in the practice of marketing. Much of your formal education will occur at the university, but this is only part of your education. To truly become competent, you should try to apply what you are learning by (1) seeking part-time or summer employment in marketing, (2) applying your marketing knowledge in volunteer efforts with clubs and organizations you belong to, and (3) reading the business trade publications, such as, *BusinessWeek, Wall Street Journal, Advertising Age, Sales & Marketing Management,* and *Marketing News.*

Conduct

To be a professional, you must act and behave like a professional.

When recruiters come to campus looking for candidates that seem to possess "professionalism," what will they look for? When students graduate and enter the workplace, what will their business associates' basis be for perceiving them as "professional" or "unprofessional"? These judgements will probably be made based on the individual's dress, speech, and verbal ability, ethics, and mannerisms.[3]

CAREER INFORMATION SOURCES

Professional Marketing Organizations

Marketers have many professional trade associations that have useful member benefits, such as newsletters, magazines and journals, educational conferences, and library facilities. The following is a list of the names and addresses of most of the top marketing-related professional trade associations. Useful career information is available from most of these associations.

❏ American Advertising Federation (AAF)
 1225 Connecticut Avenue, NW
 Washington, DC 20036
 (202) 659-1800

❏ American Association of Advertising Agencies (AAAA)
 666 Third Avenue, 13th Floor
 New York, NY 10017
 (212) 682-2500

❑ American Financial Services Association (Credit) (AFSA)
(Formerly [1983] National Consumer Finance Association)
1101 14th Street, NW
Washington, DC 20005
(202) 289-0400

❑ American Marketing Association (AMA)
250 S. Wacker Drive, Suite 200
Chicago, IL 60606
(312) 648-0536

❑ Business/Professional Advertising Association (B/PAA)
(Formerly [1959] National Industrial Advertisers Association and [1976]
Association of Industrial Advertisers)
205 E. 42nd Street
New York, NY 10017
(212) 661-0222

❑ Direct Marketing Association (DMA)
Six E. 43rd Street
New York, NY 10017
(212) 689-4977

❑ Industrial Marketing Associates (IMA)
520 Pleasant Street
St. Joseph, MO 49085
(616) 983-3926

❑ Marketing Research Association (MRA)
221 N. LaSalle Street
Chicago, IL 60601
(312) 346-1600

❑ National Association of Wholesaler-Distributors (NAW)
(Formerly [1970] National Association of Wholesalers)
1725 K Street, NW
Washington, DC 20006
(202) 872-0885

❑ National Council of Physical Distribution Management (NCPDM)
2803 Butterfield Road, Suite 380
Oak Brook, IL 60521
(312) 655-0985

❑ National Retail Merchants Association (NRMA)
100 W. 31st Street
New York, NY 10001
(212) 244-8780

❑ Sales and Marketing Executives International (SMEI)
330 W. 42nd Street
New York, NY 10036
(212) 986-9300

Library Resources on Careers in Marketing

Career Fields.

❏ *BusinessWeek's Guide to Careers* (New York: McGraw-Hill, 1986).

❏ *National Business Employment Weekly: College Career Edition* (New York: Dow Jones & Company, 1986).

❏ U.S. Department of Labor, Bureau of Labor Statistics, *Occupational Outlook Handbook,* 1986–1987 edition (Washington, DC: U.S. Government Printing Office).

❏ *Occupational Outlook Quarterly,* published quarterly by the U.S. Department of Labor, Bureau of Labor Statistics.

❏ David W. Rosenthal and Michael A. Powell, *Careers in Marketing* (Englewood Cliffs, NJ: Prentice Hall, 1984).

Potential Employers Directories.

❏ Career Research Systems' *Career Opportunity Index.*

❏ College Placement Council's *College Placement Annual.*

❏ *Directory of Corporate Affiliations.*

❏ Dun & Bradstreet's *Million Dollar Directory.*

❏ Dun & Bradstreet's *Middle Market Directory.*

❏ *Moody's Manual.*

❏ *Peterson's Annual Guide to Careers and Employment for Engineers, Computer Scientists, and Physical Scientists.*

❏ Standard & Poor's *Register of Corporations, Directors, and Executives.*

❏ *Thomas Register of American Manufacturers.*

Miscellaneous Resources.

❏ *Business Periodicals Index.*

❏ Companies' annual financial reports.

❏ Company literature.

❏ *The Encyclopedia of Associations.*

❏ *F&S Index for Corporations and Industries.*

❏ *Guide to American Directories.*

❏ Standard & Poor's *Standard Corporation Records.*

❏ Standard & Poor's *Industry Surveys.*

❏ State and local occupational information available from state employment agencies. For a listing of state employment agencies' names and addresses, see the most recent edition of U.S. Department of Labor,

Bureau of Labor Statistics, *Occupational Outlook* (Washington, DC: U.S. Government Printing Office), Bulletin 2205.

❑ Telephone directories.

SUMMARY

This appendix introduced you to the career opportunities available in marketing and helped you to understand the importance of professionalism in marketing. There are marketing career opportunities in all industries, all cities, all regions, and at most salary levels, ranging from jobs in consumer sales to the chief executive officer of a major corporation. The section on career descriptions profiled the duties of eighteen popular marketing careers.

Because the business world differs from the world of the student, you will need to develop an attitude of professionalism. Professionalism is composed of three dimensions: commitment, competence, and conduct. All are necessary ingredients of success.

QUESTIONS AND PROBLEMS

1. Perform a written self-assessment as a prerequisite to identifying the marketing careers that best fit your talents and limitations. This self-assessment should include an inventory of your education, abilities, limitations or weaknesses, past work experience, interests and hobbies, and goals.

2. Of the eighteen careers in marketing that were profiled in this appendix, which ones most appeal to you? Why? Which careers would you least prefer? Why?

3. List and describe the three dimensions of a marketing professional. Which of these qualities are you most lacking? How can you improve your performance in this area?

NOTES

1. "What Is the Fastest Track to the Executive Suite? Sales/Marketing," *Marketing News* (July 6, 1984), p. 7.

2. James A. Muncy, "Professionalism and Marketing Education," in Russell W. Belk et al. (eds.), *1984 AMA Educators Proceedings* (Chicago: American Marketing Association, 1984), pp. 110–112.

3. Ibid.

GLOSSARY

ABC inventory analysis Inventory is divided into three groups based on sales volume: A products are those sold most frequently and get the highest customer service; B products have moderate sales rates and get moderate customer service; C products sell slowly and get low customer service.

accounts receivable What customers owe the firm because they purchase on credit.

acid-test ratio Cash divided by current liabilities.

administered vertical marketing system A vertical marketing system in which one of the channel members uses the principles of interorganizational management to become channel captain.

adoption process The series of steps a buyer goes through in deciding to try and then regularly use a new product innovation. The five steps are awareness, knowledge, evaluation, trial, and adoption.

advertising Any paid form of nonpersonal presentation of ideas, goods, or services by an identified sponsor.

advertising agency An independent firm that specializes in developing advertising programs or plans for a fee or commission for client firms.

advertising target The part of a firm's target market that the firm wishes to attract.

agent or intermediary publics A public of an organization that helps the firm sell and distribute its output.

AIDA An acronym for the steps through which a buyer progresses on the way to purchasing a product. The steps are awareness, interest, desire, and action.

AIDAS An acronym for the steps through which a buyer progresses on the way to purchasing a product and evaluating it after purchase. The steps are awareness, interest, desire, action, and satisfaction.

allocation base Something that helps to explain the variation in an expense item and can be used to assign expenses to segments.

assemblers Independent wholesale institutions that primarily purchase farm products in small quantities to accumulate large quantities to sell to other firms.

asset An item of value to which the firm has ownership rights and that is expected to generate future benefits to the organization.

asset turnover Net sales divided by total assets.

atmospherics The conscious design of retail space and its various dimensions to evoke certain effects in buyers.

attitude A learned predisposition to respond in a consistently favorable or unfavorable manner with respect to a given object.

bait and switch Advertising or promoting an item at an unrealistically low price to serve as "bait" and then attempting to steer the customers away from the low-priced item to a higher priced model.

balance of payments The total outflow of currency (or its equivalent) contrasted to the inflow of foreign currency (or its equivalent). A favorable balance of payments occurs when inflows exceed outflows, and an unfavorable balance of payments occurs when outflows exceed inflows.

balance of trade The difference between exports and imports in a country. When exports are greater than imports, a surplus or favorable balance of trade exists. When imports are greater than exports, the balance of trade is in deficit or unfavorable.

balance sheet A statement that summarizes a firm's financial position at a particular point in time.

BCG product portfolio matrix A planning device for classifying products by their market share and market growth rate. Products can be cash cows, dogs, question marks, or stars.

behavioristic segmentation Segmenting the market by using variables that reflect how consumers behave or act toward particular products. The more common of these variables are benefits sought, usage rate, and user loyalty.

bidding Multiple sellers submit proposals to a buyer, and the lowest price is accepted.

brand A symbol, design, name, term, or combination of the preceding that uniquely identifies a seller's product and distinguishes it from the competition.

brand licensing The authorized use of a brand, brand name, brand mark, trademark, or trade name in conjunction with a good, service, or promotion that the brand was not initially designed for in return for a royalty.

brand manager The manager who is responsible for the profitability of a particular brand.

brand mark The part of a brand that can be seen but not voiced (usually a symbol or design; i.e., the hood ornament on a Mercedes Benz).

brand name The part of a brand (including numbers, letters, and words) that can be voiced (i.e., Crest or Geritol).

breakeven analysis A method of determining the number of units that must be sold at a given price to recover costs.

business cycles The changing patterns of economic growth over time. A business cycle consists of three stages: (1) prosperity, (2) recession, and (3) recovery.

business ethics The moral choices between "right" and "wrong" conduct that a business executive must make in his or her position in a business organization.

business screen An analytical device used to evaluate the strengths, weaknesses, opportunities, and threats of each SBU in order to determine if it is a candidate for growth or retrenchment.

business strength A firm's ability to compete effectively in its industry or market.

buyer-intention forecast Asks potential buyers about their purchasing plans in order to forecast sales.

buying center All members in an organization who have an impact on the buying decision (e.g., users, influencers, buyers, deciders, and gatekeepers).

cannibalism The extent to which a new product robs its sales from existing products the firm sells.

cash cows Products in a low-growth market but that have a high relative market share.

catalog showroom A retail store with a relatively large physical facility that is partitioned into a warehouse and showroom. The showroom displays one item of each product the retailer sells.

central business district The geographic point where most cities originated and from which they grew.

chain-store retailer A retailer with eleven or more units operating under the same name.

channel captain A member of the marketing channel who attempts to organize and lead the efforts of the institutions in the channel in order to obtain system-wide economies and maximum market impact.

closed system A system that is not affected by outside forces.

cognitive dissonance Doubt that occurs when the consumer becomes aware that unchosen alternatives have desirable attributes, leading the consumer to wonder whether he or she made the right decision.

communication process A process that includes a sender who encodes a message, which is then transmitted through a message channel, and the receiver who decodes the message and provides feedback to the sender.

comparative advertising Advertising in which a firm's brand is compared with competing brands on a set of product attributes.

competitive environment An external environment of a firm that consists of all other sellers who are vying for the patronage of the same consumers or market the firm is seeking.

concentrated segmentation A segmentation strategy in which the firm focuses its efforts on a single target market with a single marketing mix.

concept testing A tool for assessing the feasibility of a new product idea by presenting a group of potential buyers with a word description and/or drawing of the proposed product.

confiscation When a foreign investment is taken over by a government without any payment.

conglomerate diversification A diversification strategy that consists of adding products and serving markets that are totally unrelated to the firm's current business.

consumer affairs department A department in an organization that is responsible for advocating the consumer's interest in marketing decisions and programs.

consumerism movement A social movement that seeks to protect the rights and safety of consumers.

consumer market A market consisting of all buyers and potential buyers for goods and services that are acquired for personal or household use.

consumer orientation The dimension of the marketing concept that argues that a firm can be more successful if it determines consumer needs and wants before it decides what product to produce and/or sell.

consumer rights The four basic consumer rights are the right to safety, the right to be informed, the right to choose, and the right to be heard.

consumer sales promotions Sales promotions that are intended to motivate customers to pull the product through the marketing channel.

consuming publics Those groups in a society that use or consume a firm's output (also called *customers*).

contests A type of consumer sales promotion in which customers compete for prizes based on skill.

contractual vertical marketing system A vertical marketing system in which the channel captain has a contract with one or more channel members. Contractual systems include wholesaler-sponsored voluntary groups, retailer-owned cooperatives, and franchise organizations.

contribution margin An approach to marketing profitability analysis in which only those costs that can be traced directly to an area of the firm are assigned to that area.

convenience product A product that is purchased by the consumer with a minimum of time and effort.

convenience store A relatively small store that stocks frequently purchased items such as bread, tobacco, and milk. These stores are generally small (2,000 to 4,000 square feet) and serve the surrounding neighborhood of about 0.5 to 1 mile from the store.

conventional marketing channel A

marketing channel in which each member is loosely aligned with the others.

convergent diversification Sometimes called *concentric diversification.* A diversification strategy in which a firm attempts to diversify into products and markets that use a firm's existing production or marketing knowledge.

corporate vertical marketing system A vertical marketing system typically consisting of either a manufacturer who has integrated forward in the channel to reach the consumer or a retailer who has integrated backward into the channel to create a self-supply network.

cost-based markup A pricing method that computes a percent markup by taking the price minus the cost of the product and dividing this by cost.

cost of goods The prices paid by a firm for the products it sells to customers.

cost per thousand method The cost of one exposure unit divided by (the number of people reached divided by 1,000).

cost tradeoffs Things done to reduce the cost of one distribution activity may increase the cost of another distribution activity.

countertrade A form of international trade that is not transacted totally in cash, although cash can be partially used.

coupon A type of consumer sales promotion in which the customer is most often offered cents off on the next purchase of the item. Coupons are distributed in the package of the product, by direct mail, or in newspapers and magazines.

culture A set of beliefs, attitudes, customs, and institutions created by people to help them explain and cope with their environment.

cumulative quantity discount A type of quantity discount that is given for accumulating a certain quantity of purchases over a stated period.

current asset Cash or any other asset that can be converted to cash in the normal course of operating the business over a one-year period.

current liability Any obligation to pay an input or output public that becomes due within a one-year period.

current ratio The basic measurement of a firm's solvency.

customer service Getting the right products to the right places at the right time.

decision tree model A graphical model in which the alternative decisions a manager can select from are portrayed as branches of a tree.

decoding A step in the communication process in which a receiver receives and interprets the message transmitted.

demographic variables The general characteristics of a population, such as age, sex, income, education, and family life cycle.

department store A large-scale retail organization with a broad product mix consisting of many different product lines with above-average depth in each of them.

derived demand A demand in a producer market that is based on or derived from the demand for consumer products.

desire competitors Other immediate desires that the consumer might want to satisfy.

direct costs Costs that can be traced specifically to a particular product.

direct ownership A foreign market entry strategy in which a firm establishes a wholly owned subsidiary in a foreign country.

discount department store A department store with a strong price emphasis.

discretionary income The income remaining after the basic necessities of life and fixed commitments, such as auto and house payments or rent, are paid.

disposable personal income Per-

sonal income less taxes and social security levies.

distribution The marketing channel used and the physical movement of a product to market.

diversification A growth strategy that involves taking a company into new products and new markets.

dogs Products that have a low relative market share in a low-growth market.

drive A motivating force that directs behavior.

drop error When a company decides to drop an idea that, if introduced to the marketplace, would have been a winning new product.

dual distribution A manufacturer that resells to independent retailers and through its own retail or wholesale outlets.

dumping A pricing strategy in which a firm ignores fixed costs and merely assesses marginal or variable costs, so that the resulting foreign price is lower than the domestic price.

durable good A manufactured product capable of a long, useful life, such as furniture, household appliances, and automobiles.

economic environment An external environment of a firm that includes the factors that determine the income and wealth-generating ability of the economy.

economic factors Factors concerned with the influence of a person's income and other economic resources on purchasing behavior.

economic order quantity The quantity to order that will minimize the sum of inventory ordering costs and inventory carrying costs.

employee publics A public of an organization that consists of individuals who perform jobs and activities within the firm.

encoding A step in the communication process in which the sender puts a thought or idea into words, actions, or symbols.

enterprise competitors Similar organizations competing for a consumer's business.

environmental scanner A person who collects and analyzes data and information on the firm's external environments.

equity Assets less liabilities.

ethical environment An external environment of the firm that is composed of the norms or moral behavior that society imposes on business and marketers.

ethnocentrism An orientation toward international marketing in which an operation in a foreign country is viewed as secondary or as a child of the domestic operation.

exclusive dealing The practice of a seller giving a reseller the exclusive right to sell a product in a particular geographic area.

exclusive distribution A distribution pattern for which there is only one reseller of a product in each geographic area.

execution Making things happen, and consists of implementation and control.

experimental method A procedure in which the researcher assesses how changes in manipulated variables affect other variables. The factor to be assessed is called the *dependent variable,* and the factors that affect it are called the *independent variables.*

export-import agent An agent that brings buyers and sellers from different countries together and collects a commission on all sales transacted.

exporting When a firm, government, or individual from one country sells a product to a firm, government, or individual in another country.

express warranty A warranty that is the outcome of negotiations between the seller and the buyer and may be given either in writing or orally.

expropriation When a foreign investment is taken over by a government, but some form of payment is made.

extended problem solving A type of

problem solving in which the consumer recognizes a problem but has decided on neither the brand nor the store.

external environments The set of forces outside the organization that affect the organization's survival potential and influence its decision-making process.

extrinsic rewards Job-related rewards that are external to the individual, such as wages, bonuses, fringe benefits, job promotions, and so on.

facilitating channel institution A channel participant who does not take title to the product but makes the marketing process easier by specializing in the performance of certain marketing activities.

family branding The practice of using a single brand name (usually the organization's name) for all products in the product mix.

family life cycle The stages and substages a person may go through from being young and single to being married to being old and unmarried.

financial leverage Total assets divided by total equity.

fixed asset Any asset that is expected to provide benefits to the firm for a period greater than one year.

FOB origin (A geographic pricing policy) the product is placed free on board (FOB) at a certain geographic point. The buyer pays for the transportation costs from the point of origin.

foreign currency exchange rate The price of one country's money in terms of another country's money (i.e., 1 U.S. dollar equals 5 French francs, or a franc costs 20¢).

form utility Separate materials are combined and transformed into a finished product that has higher value than the separate materials composing it.

forward buy When a retailer or wholesaler buys inventory more weeks in advance than it normally would.

franchise A contractual vertical marketing system in which an entire business format is licensed.

free merchandise A form of trade promotion that is usually tied to some unit purchase volume.

freight absorption pricing A geographic pricing policy in which a seller who is located far from buyers (who are located near competing suppliers) will charge a reduced freight rate to those buyers. The distant seller can thus compete with the nearby seller.

frequency The average number of exposures to a firm's advertising by those who were reached within a given period.

full cost analysis An approach to marketing profitability analysis in which all costs are identified with a particular area, such as a product line, channel of distribution, or geographic territory.

full-service wholesaler Wholesalers that perform part or most of the marketing functions for either manufacturers or their customers.

functional discount A price break given to one who performs certain marketing activities for other channel members.

functional expenses The costs of performing various marketing tasks, namely, various order getting and order filling functions.

functional organization A method of organizing marketing activities in which a key manager is responsible for each major marketing function.

general public The totality of society on which a firm is dependent for support and freedom to function or operate.

generic branding Identifying a product by its generic contents: soap, coffee, sugar, catsup, and so on.

generic competition Competition between all products capable of satisfying the same basic need.

generic market A market that consists

of all products capable of satisfying the same basic needs.

geocentrism An orientation toward international marketing in which the world is viewed as a single market.

geographic organization A method of organizing marketing activities in which marketing efforts are organized by the major geographic areas the firm serves.

geographic variables The areas where buyers reside, such as the east, west, north, or south, and the physical characteristics of these areas, such as population density, climate, and city size.

go error When a company decides to go ahead with an idea that is not worth pursuing and, if developed into a product, would meet with failure in the marketplace.

government market A market that consists of federal, state, and local government agencies and the goods and services they purchase to conduct operations and serve the public.

gross margin How much gross profit (sales less cost of goods sold) the reseller makes as a percentage of sales.

gross profit Sales minus cost of goods sold.

gross rating points (GRP) A number used in developing a media schedule that is obtained by multiplying reach times frequency.

gross sales The total dollar amount of all sales to customers during a specified period.

growth strategies Strategies that attempt to close a strategic gap by sales growth. Four common growth strategies are market penetration, market development, product development, and diversification.

habitual problem solving A type of problem solving in which the consumer relies on past experience and learning to convert a problem into a situation that requires no decision.

horizontal cooperative advertising Advertising for which several firms at the same level of distribution share the cost.

horizontal price fixing When a group of competing sellers establishes a fixed price at which to sell their products.

implied warranty A warranty that is not verbalized by the seller but is based on custom, norms, or reasonable buyer expectations.

importance-performance analysis A method that organizations can use to have their customers rate the job the organization is doing (i.e., performance) on a set of evaluative criteria; it also shows how important the criteria are to customers in their purchasing decisions.

importing When a firm, government, or individual in one country purchases a product from a firm, government, or individual in another country.

income statement A statement that reports the results of the enterprise's profit-directed activities for a specified period.

incremental approach To determine the size of the sales force, the expected gross profit an additional sales person would generate is computed and compared with the cost of supporting the salesperson.

individual branding The practice of giving each product in the product mix a distinct brand name.

informative advertising Advertising that attempts to provide customers with objective information about the product's attributes and does not try to persuade.

institutional advertising Advertising that tries to enhance the image of the firm or organization rather than sell a specific product. This type of advertising can be aimed at any of the organization's seven key publics.

integrated effort Departments within the organization work together toward the common goal of satisfying the customer.

intensive distribution A distribution pattern in which most of the available resellers in a geographic area sell the product.

intermodal transportation Using two or more modes to transport a product.

international marketing The marketing of goods and services between countries.

interorganizational behavior The process of human interaction between organizations, such as how a representative from Eli Lily (a pharmaceutical company) interacts with the pharmacist at a local Walgreens drugstore.

interpersonal communication Communication between sender and receiver where each can query the other directly.

intrinsic rewards Job-related rewards that are internal to the individual and consist of personal feelings such as job satisfaction, sense of worth, and freedom.

inventory The quantity of a product that is available to sell or use at any given time.

inventory carrying cost The expense of holding inventory, including the costs of space, capital, insurance, and spoilage or obsolescence.

inventory productivity Sales or gross profit divided by average inventory investment.

inventory turnover The average number of times per year that inventory is sold.

joint costs Costs that cannot be uniquely identified with a particular product but are common to two or more products.

joint demand When the demand for two or more products is interdependent because the products must be used together.

joint venture A foreign market entry strategy in which the firm becomes partners with a foreign firm and they share in financing, management, and decision-making responsibilities.

jury of expert opinion A sales forecasting method that gathers the opinions of various experts in an area in order to forecast company or industry sales for a given period, usually a year.

learning The more or less permanent acquisition of tendencies to behave in particular ways in response to particular situations or stimuli.

learning curve Also referred to as an *experience curve,* it shows the percentage reduction in average costs per unit as cumulative output doubles.

lease A contract that grants use of a product during a specified period in exchange for a rental payment.

legal/political environment An external environment of an organization that consists of the rules and regulations society has imposed on business firms and the political interest groups that affect it.

liability Any obligation to pay money or provide goods and services to an output or input public.

licensing Granting a firm in another country the right to produce and/or market your products for a fee. Also, the authorized use of a brand, brand name, brand mark, trademark, or trade name in conjunction with a good, service, or promotion in return for a royalty.

life-style segmentation Often used to help refine a firm's promotional efforts by showing how a product will fit into a consumer's life. Life-style is usually measured in terms of activities, interests, and opinions.

limited problem solving A type of problem solving in which the consumer has a strong preference for either the brand or the store, but not both.

limited-service wholesaler A wholesaler that performs only a small number of marketing functions for manufacturers or for its customers.

liquidity The firm's ability to meet its current payment obligations.

logistical costs The costs of moving supplies and raw materials to manufacturing and processing plants and subsequently moving the finished product to the final customers or buyers.

long-term liability A liability that is due and payable beyond a one-year period.

make or buy A term used in organizational buying to indicate the decision an organization must make between making a product or component or purchasing it from an outside supplier.

manufacturer's brand A brand that is owned by the manufacturer.

manufacturer's sales branches Sales outlets of the manufacturer usually located in areas of high demand that serve as a base of operation for the sales staff. These outlets may or may not carry inventories.

marginal cost The change in total costs as a result of a change in one unit of output.

marginal revenue The change in total sales revenue divided by the change in one unit of quantity.

market All potential buyers with a similar need and the purchasing power to fill this need, and all firms or sellers offering to satisfy that need.

market attractiveness An uncontrollable dimension of the business screen that includes market size, market growth rate, competitive intensity, legal constraints, and a host of other things that represent the opportunities and threats emanating from the SBU's external environments.

market development A growth strategy in which the firm attempts to sell existing products in new markets.

market forecast The expected sales for the market as a whole during a specified period under assumed environmental conditions with expected industry marketing effort.

marketing The process of planning and executing the conception, pricing, promotion, and distribution of ideas, goods, and services to create exchanges that satisfy individual and organizational objectives.

marketing channel The set of institutions or people that participate in moving goods and services from point of initial source or production to point of final consumption or use.

marketing concept A marketing philosophy in which firms study the consumer to determine consumer needs and wants and organize and integrate all activities within the firm toward helping the consumer fulfill these needs and wants while simultaneously achieving organizational goals.

marketing controller A financial officer who has a good understanding of accounting, finance, and marketing and who is specifically charged with evaluating, budgeting, and controlling marketing and distribution expenditures.

marketing information system (MIS) A blueprint for the continual and periodic systematic collection, analysis, and reporting of relevant data about past, present, or future developments that could or already have influenced the firm's marketing performance.

marketing intelligence system A part of the marketing information system that continually monitors relevant data about an organization's external environments and publics.

marketing mix The four controllable marketing variables: product, distribution (or place), promotion, and price.

marketing model An abstraction of some real marketing phenomena to be used as a frame of reference to facilitate decision making.

marketing profitability analysis The process of determining the profitability of particular products, sales territories, market segments, salespeople, and/or marketing channels.

marketing research The systematic

collection, recording, and analyzing of data that deal with the marketing of goods and services.

market opportunity When there is an unmet or unsatisfied need or want in the marketplace that the firm has an interest in and capability of satisfying.

market penetration A growth strategy that involves concentrating on existing markets and products.

market potential The maximum amount of product that could be sold by all firms in a market during a given period with a maximum level of industry marketing activity under an assumed set of environmental conditions.

market segmentation The process of dividing a heterogeneous group of buyers or potential buyers into more homogeneous groups with relatively similar product needs.

market segment organization A method for organizing marketing activities in which marketing efforts are organized around the firm's major market segments.

market share A firm's sales in a particular market divided by total market sales.

markup pricing Taking the dollar cost of merchandise and adding it to a dollar markup, which is intended to cover the wholesaler's or retailer's cost of doing business and allow for a profit.

mass communication A sender communicating in a impersonal way with a large number of receivers, with no direct feedback from the receivers.

materials handling The actual physical handling of goods in a warehouse, retail store, or production facility.

materials management The management of all activities that bring to the manufacturing or processing plant all the necessary materials to produce a product.

mathematical function model A model that specifies a quantitative relationship between a dependent variable and independent variable(s).

media mix The combination of media types (radio, television, magazine, newspaper, direct mail, and outdoor displays) that is used to communicate a message.

media plan The part of the advertising plan that establishes the media mix and specific media vehicles and develops the media schedule.

media schedule A plan that details how often and when to advertise.

media vehicle A specific device for carrying advertising messages, such as *Time* magazine or the television show "Dallas."

merchant wholesalers Independent wholesalers that purchase a product, take title to it, and then resell it to another firm, but not to the ultimate consumer.

message channel The medium through which a messsage is carried.

mission A firm's overall justification for existing.

missionary salesperson A salesperson who attempts to create goodwill in the marketing channel by providing potential or existing product informatin, advice, or assistance on product use. This type of salesperson does not obtain or take orders.

modified rebuy The organizational buyer is dissatisfied because the current supplier and/or product is not performing up to standard with respect to some evaluative criteria. Therefore the buyer must reevaluate the supplier and/or product.

monopolistic competition A competitive structure in which many sellers sell similar but not necessarily identical products. Each firm has differentiated its product somewhat and thus has some degree of control over the prices it can charge.

monopoly A competitive structure in which there is only one seller of a product.

motivation An internal force that directs people to act in a particular way to satisfy a particular need.

multinational corporation (MNC) An enterprise with direct investment in manufacturing and/or marketing facilities in multiple countries (usually 4 or more), with the parent company located in a single country that serves as its base for coordinating worldwide operations.

multiple segmentation A segmentation strategy in which the firm focuses on several distinct market segments and develops a separate marketing mix for each.

negotiated contract bidding A type of bidding in government markets in which a government agency will directly negotiate a contract with a limited number of firms and will then award the contract to one of them.

net profit Gross profit less operating expenses.

net profit margin The ratio of net profit to net sales.

net sales Gross sales less returns and allowances.

new product committee A group of personnel from all departments in the organization who are responsible for developing a new product.

new product department A department in an organization that is responsible for evaluating new product ideas and developing them into marketable products.

new product development process A normative process for developing new products that consists of six steps: exploration, screening, business analysis, development, test marketing and commercialization.

new product venture team An organizational unit that is established specifically to develop product innovations.

new task buying A term used in organizational buying to indicate a situation in which the organization has a new problem to solve and is not certain which product and/or supplier to use.

noise Any interference that distorts a message in the communication process.

noncumulative quantity discount A quantity discount that is a one-time discount based on the number of units purchased or dollar volume purchased.

nondurable good A manufactured or processed product with a relatively short life span, such as food, clothing, gasoline, beverages, and paper goods.

nonprice competition Competition that occurs between firms based on product, distribution, or promotion factors and not price.

nonprobability sample A sampling plan in which the probability of a person being included in the sample is unknown.

nonprofit marketing All marketing effort that is conducted by firms or individuals to accomplish nonfinancial goals.

objectives Specific, quantifiable results that a firm wants to achieve in a given period.

observation method A method for collecting primary data in which data are obtained by watching human behavior.

odd-even pricing Using a numbering system that gives the impression of a lower price.

off-premise buying When wholesalers and retailers have buying offices geographically removed from the location of their headquarters.

oligopoly A competitive structure in which there are only a few sellers and each firm's sales are a high percentage of the total market. Each brand has unique characteristics but can be substituted easily. Sellers cannot ignore each other's actions.

open bid A type of bidding in government markets in which the government procurement office invites bids from qualified suppliers.

open system A firm that is affected by outside forces.

open-to-buy The dollar amount that a retailer or wholesaler can spend on inventory at any given time.

operating expenses All the expenses incurred in carrying out the day-to-day operations of the enterprise.

opinion leader Someone who actively espouses his or her opinions about products or from whom others seek out the views and opinions of products.

order filling costs The costs of filling orders, which usually consist of warehousing, transportation, order processing, and billing and collecting costs.

order generation costs The costs of obtaining orders, which usually consists of advertising, personal selling, and sales promotion costs.

order getter A salesperson who finds or creates new customers and also tries to get present customers to purchase more.

order processing All activities performed to gather, check, and transmit sales orders.

order taker A type of salesperson who only writes up sales and is not actively involved in persuading customers to purchase.

organizational buyer A professional who is employed solely to buy goods and services for the organization.

organizational markets Markets that are composed of business units and organizations that purchase goods and services to be used, directly or indirectly, in the production of other goods and services or to be resold to governments, resellers (retailers and wholesalers), and producers.

paid-in capital The monetary value of capital contributed to the organization by the owners of the enterprise.

penetration price strategy A price strategy that involves setting price low at the outset of the product life cycle and using it as a wedge to enter a market.

perception The process of receiving and deriving meaning from stimuli present in the environment.

personal income An individual's total before-tax income.

personal selling An oral presentation in a conversation with one or more prospective purchasers for the purpose of making sales.

persuasive advertising Advertisements that incorporate a high proportion of subjective statements and claims and attempt to convince consumers that a particular product is the best one for them.

physical distribution management The management of all activities that deal with the movement of finished products from the end of the production process to the final consumer or buyer.

physical environment An external environment of the organization that consists of the geographic and raw material characteristics of the country or part of the country where a firm operates.

place utility The value created by having a product at the place you desire it.

planning Deciding today what to do in the future and consists of analysis and strategy.

point-of purchase display A special presentation of merchandise or signing in a store that communicates a message, which is usually "buy me."

polycentrism An orientation toward international marketing that is host country oriented. A firm establishes an autonomous subsidiary in each foreign country where it markets its products.

possession utility The value created from having the legal right to possess and freely use a product.

postpurchase evaluation Assesses how satisfied or dissatisfied the consumer is with the purchase.

predatory pricing When a business firm charges different prices in different geographical areas in order to eliminate competition in selected areas.

premiums A type of consumer sales promotion in which the customer is offered free or lower priced merchandise if the customer makes a certain purchase or a store visit.

prestige pricing A pricing tactic that recognizes that a product's quality image may be directly associated with price. If the price is set too low, the sales may be lower than with a higher price because of the poor quality inferences associated with a low price.

price Something of value that is exchanged for something else.

price-based markup A method of pricing in which a markup is computed by taking the price minus the cost of the product and dividing this by the price.

price discrimination When two business firms buy identical merchandise and/or services from the same supplier but pay different prices.

price elasticity of demand The percentage change in quantity demand divided by the percentage change in the price of a product. This statistic is stated as an absolute value.

price lining A firm has multiple products in a product line, and each product is given a different price.

price objectives The firm's pricing goals.

price policies A set of guiding principles for price setting. These policies include price lining, geographic pricing, negotiation policies, leasing, credit policies, and discounts.

pricing strategies Where a firm wants to position its product's price in relation to the prices of competing products. For existing products there are three price strategies, pricing above, below, and at the market.

pricing tool A mechanical method, often a mathematical formula, used to help set prices in day-to-day business.

primary channel institution A channel participant who takes title to the product.

primary data Research data that are collected explicitly to solve a particular problem.

primary demand Demand for a product class rather than for a particular brand within that class.

private warehouse A storage facility that a company owns and uses exclusively for its products.

probability sample A sampling plan in which each individual in the population has a known probability of being selected.

producer markets A market that consists of firms that purchase goods and services for the production of other goods and services.

product A bundle of tangible and intangible attributes that a seller offers the potential buyer and that satisfies the buyer's needs or wants.

product advertising Advertising that attempts to sell a good or service for a particular organization.

product audit A regulary scheduled evaluation of all existing products in the product mix in terms of their strengths, weaknesses, and potential.

product development A growth strategy in which the firm develops new products or modifies existing products to better serve its existing markets.

production orientation A firm whose primary concern is to produce as much as possible, with high efficiency.

product life cycle The stages a product moves through from its introduction to the market to its disappearance from the market. The stages are introduction, growth, maturity, and decline.

product line A group of products that are closely related because they are intended for the same end use (all televisions), are sold to the same customer group (junior miss womenswear), or fall within a given price range (budget womenswear).

product manager The person responsible for the profitability of a single product or group of products.

product markets Product groups that serve narrow customer needs.

product mix The total set of products that a company sells.

product modification Modifying an existing product by changing product features, changing product quality, restyling, or any combination of these.

product organization A method of organizing marketing activities in which marketing efforts are organized by the firm's major product lines.

product position The place the product occupies in the consumer's mind with respect to a small number of key attributes, which can be tangible or intangible.

product positioning The process marketers go through in manipulating the marketing mix to achieve a particular product position.

product positioning map Shows how consumers perceive competing products that serve a particular need based on a set of key attributes.

product use testing A research process in which a few customers are selected to borrow or to be given a new product if they will use it under normal conditions and give the company feedback on its performance.

profit and loss statement A statement that takes a firm's sales for a stated period and subtracts the concomitant expenses to yield a profit or a loss.

profit center The part of an organization that is responsible for sales, expenses, and investments and is accountable for the profits it generates.

profit maximization When prices are set as high as possible to get "all the traffic will bear."

promotion Communication by marketers that attempts to inform, persuade, and influence potential buyers of a product in order to elicit a response.

promotional allowance A type of trade sales promotion in which marketing channel members are provided with some monetary incentive to promote the manufacturer's products. It is often some type of vertical cooperative advertising.

promotion mix The mix of advertising, personal selling, sales promotion, and publicity that composes the firm's promotional tools.

prototype development The building or production of a model or sample of a new product.

psychic costs The frustrations and tensions encountered in purchasing a product.

psychological factors Variables such as attitudes, learning processes, motivation, and perceptual processes that are internal to the individual's thought processes.

psychological pricing Pertains to customers' perception of price rather than the actual price.

public Any group that has an actual or potential interest or impact on an organization's ability to achieve its objectives.

publicity Nonpersonal stimulation of demand for goods, services, or business units by generating commercially significant news about them in the mass media. It is not paid for directly by a sponsor.

public relations director The head of a firm's public relations department who is responsible for planning publicity.

public service advertisements Advertisements by nonprofit organizations that the media broadcast or run at no cost to the nonprofit organization.

public warehouse An independently owned and operated storage facility that stores goods for a fee.

pull strategy A promotion strategy in which the manufacturer directs the majority of its promotional effort toward the ultimate consumer in an attempt to get them to pull the products through the marketing channel.

pure competition A competitive market structure in which a large number of sellers sell an undifferentiated product, such as wheat, corn, or hogs.

push money Also frequently called

spiff. A direct payment by a manufacturer to the reseller's salespeople to get them to push a particular product or group of products.

push strategy A promotion strategy in which the bulk of promotional effort is directed at the members of the marketing channel to get them to push the products forward in the marketing channel.

quantity discount Selling products at a lower cost per unit if the buyer purchases a given quantity.

question marks Products that have a low relative market share in a high-growth market.

quick ratio Current assets less inventory divided by current liabilities.

reach The percentage of the advertising target that is exposed to at least one of the firm's advertisements within a given period.

reference groups The groups with which an individual identifies; thus, the group becomes a standard, a norm, or a point of reference for the consumer.

regression analysis A sales forecasting method using the functional relationship between a dependent variable and an independent variable or set of independent variables.

reminder advertising Advertising that has the objectives of keeping a firm's brand name(s) well entrenched in the customer's mind and reinforcing previous promotional efforts.

research design A blueprint or map for obtaining and collecting the primary data needed to test a hypothesis.

reseller market A market that consists of business organizations that purchase products for resale to other business organizations or individuals.

reseller's brand A brand that is owned by a retailer or wholesaler. The reseller assumes major responsibility for the design of the marketing mix.

retailers Individuals or organizations

that purchase from wholesalers or manufacturers and in turn sell to the final consumers.

retailing The activities involved in selling products to the final consumer.

retail life cycle A theory of retail evolution in which retail institutions pass through four stages: (1) innovation, (2) accelerated development, (3) maturity, and (4) decline.

retained earnings The profit the enterprise has earned since its inception that has not been paid out to the owners.

retrenchment strategies Strategies that attempt to close a strategic gap by a planned reduction in the size of the organization. Two popular retrenchment strategies are liquidation and cost containment.

return on assets The profit return a firm achieved on all assets invested in the enterprise regardless of whether the assets were financed by debt or equity.

return on equity The profits the owners of the enterprise achieved on the dollars they had invested in the enterprise.

sales analysis The process of breaking down aggregate sales data to determine a firm's strengths and potential problem areas.

sales force composite forecast Enlists the members of the sales force to forecast sales.

sales forecast The amount of the product that a firm expects to sell in a given period with a given level of marketing activity under an assumed set of environmental conditions.

sales orientation A firm aggressively uses promotional tools, such as advertising and salespeople, to convince the customer to purchase the firm's product(s).

sales performance analysis The process of analyzing actual sales data and comparing them with planned or budgeted sales to determine strengths and potential problem areas in the organization.

sales promotion Any promotional activity—other than personal selling, advertising, and publicity—that stimulates consumer purchasing and dealer effectiveness.

samples A type of consumer sales promotion in which the customer is given a free sample of a product to try or use. Most often samples are used to introduce a new, nondurable consumer product.

scale economies The change in output per unit of resource input (e.g., labor and materials).

scrambled merchandising Handling merchandise lines based solely on the profitability and without regard to the consistency of the merchandise mix. This results in unrelated lines of merchandise being carried by a single retailer (i.e., gas and milk).

seasonal discount A special discount given to purchasers that buy during a period of nonpeak demand or off-season.

secondary data Data that has already been collected or published for purposes other than the one immediately at hand.

selective demand Demand for a particular brand in a product class.

selective distortion The alteration or modification of the information received by consumers to make it consistent with their values, beliefs, attitudes, and prior experiences.

selective distribution A distribution pattern for which most suitable resellers in a geographic area sell the product, but selling through all available resellers is avoided.

selective exposure The process of screening out excessive stimuli so that they don't reach our awareness level.

selective retention A perceptual process in which some or most of the information received is forgotten and thus what is retained is selective.

SELECT model Describes the six steps in marketing research: situation analysis, explicitly stating problem, laying out the research design and collecting data, evaluating research results and making a decision, creating a plan to implement the decision, testing the correctness of the decision.

selling process A six-step process used by salespeople: (1) prospect for customers, (2) plan the approach, (3) make the presentation and/or demonstration, (4) handle objections, (5) close the sale, (6) follow up.

service form competitors The different types of organizations that can help fulfill a particular desire.

services Intangible tasks that satisfy buyer or user needs.

services marketing The application of marketing principles to the development, distribution, and sale of products that are primarily intangible (services).

shared frame of reference The point at which words, actions, and symbols are understood in the same fashion by both sender and receiver in the communication process.

shopping product A product that is purchased after the consumer shops around to find the best deal based on comparisons of price, quality, style, durability, and other product attributes that are felt to be important.

sink-or-swim training New sales recruits are thrust into the field and have to learn in any way possible or quit or get fired.

situation analysis A stage of the marketing research process in which an investigation of the factors internal and external to the firm that potentially relate to the problem area is performed.

skimming price strategy A price strategy that involves setting prices high at the introduction stage of the product life cycle and then lowering prices in later stages.

social class A group of people with similar levels of prestige and esteem who also share a set of related beliefs, attitudes, and values that they express in their thinking and behavior.

social environment An external environment of the firm that consists of the behavior of individuals and groups of individuals in society.

social marketing The design, implementation, and control of programs seeking to increase the acceptability of a social idea or cause in a target group.

social responsibility When business takes actions and makes marketing decisions that do not have any significant negative consequences for society.

societal marketing concept A business philosophy in which the firm determines consumer needs and wants and then integrates all activities in the firm to serve these needs while simultaneously enhancing societal well-being and achieving organizational goals.

sociological factors Factors that deal with the influence of other persons and groups on the consumer's decisions.

sorting process A process that is performed by retailers and wholesalers and other marketing channel institutions and that consists of four steps: sorting out, accumulation, allocation, and assortment.

space productivity Sales or gross profit per square foot of retail or wholesale space.

specialty product A product that the consumer desires and is willing to make a special effort to find and purchase, sometimes traveling long distances.

specialty store A small-scale retail establishment with a narrow assortment of merchandise but high depth in the lines carried.

sponsorship training Assigning the new sales recruit to one of the more successful salespersons in the firm, who directs, guides, advises, and watches over the new recruit until the tasks and techniques associated with selling are learned.

standard industrial classification

(SIC) A system for categorizing all U.S. businesses by product or market segment. The SIC code has seven digits; the first four deal with industry groups, the fifth shows the product class, while the sixth and seventh denote specific products.

star A product in a high-growth market for which the company has a high relative market share.

stimulus The first component of the learning process, often called the *cue*; any object or phenomenon in the environment that is capable of eliciting a response.

stockholder and investor publics A public of an organization that provides the firm with the financial resources it needs to operate.

straight rebuy The prior purchase of a product was satisfactory and that no new information is needed for subsequent purchases.

strategic business units (SBUs) Profit centers in an organization that serve broad customer needs.

strategic gap The extent to which a firm's required financial performance for some future period is greater than the projected financial performance.

strategic marketing management The analysis, strategy, implementation, and control of marketing activities in order to achieve organization's objectives.

strategic profit model Multiplies a firm's net profit margin by its rate of asset turnover to arrive at its return on assets and this figure is then multiplied by financial leverage to obtain return on equity.

supermarket concept This concept has five points: (1) self-service and self-selection displays, (2) centralization of customer services, (3) large-scale, low-cost physical facilities, (4) a strong price emphasis, (5) a broad assortment of merchandise to obtain multiple-item purchases.

superstore A large-scale store that uses the concept of supermarket retailing but sells products that meet most of the consumer's needs.

supplier publics One of a firm's publics that consist of organizations that provide a firm with raw materials, services, machinery, and other items needed to produce a product and operate its business.

support personnel Personnel that support the work of order takers and order getters to help ensure the viability of selling efforts.

survey method A primary data collection method in which people are questioned directly by telephone, mail, or personal interviews.

sweepstakes A type of consumer sales promotion in which consumers win prizes based solely on chance.

SWOT analysis Studying a firm's performance trends, resources, and capabilities to assess a firm's strengths and weaknesses, explicitly stating a firm's mission and objectives, and scanning the external environments to identify opportunities and threats.

system objectives Those goals that are best for the entire company and that are more important than those that are best for any subfunction or single activity.

systems selling A method of selling to organizations that recognizes the organization's total problem and attempts to sell a set of interrelated products and/or services that will solve this problem.

target client publics Those people who will receive the output or benefits of a nonprofit organization.

target donor publics Those people who give time, money, or other resources to a nonprofit organization.

target market A portion of a total market, which consists of buyers with similar traits that the organization wants to attract.

TARGET model A six-step process used to select a target market: target a generic market, analyze benefits desired in the generic market, remove qualifying benefits, group remaining benefits into segments, enumerate customer characteristics of segments, and target a market segment for cultivation.

target return A firm sets a specific profit goal for a particular period, which is usually stated as a target return on investment.

target return pricing An approach to pricing that calculates the price required for the firm to make a specified profit or rate of return on investment.

task force A special group of people organized on a temporary basis to solve a particular problem.

technological environment An external environment of the firm that consists of the application of science to develop new methods or ways of doing things.

territorial restrictions Attempts by a supplier, usually a manufacturer, to limit the geographic area in which a reseller may resell its merchandise.

test market The introduction of a new product into a limited number of representative communities in order to assess potential product demand and the marketing mix.

theory-in-use model A model that includes a set of "if I do A, then B will occur" statements.

time costs The value of the time it takes to acquire a product.

time series analysis A sales forecasting method that examines the pattern of sales that has occurred over time.

time utility The value created from having a product available at the time you desire it.

total cost orientation Minimizing total costs rather than the costs of a single distribution activity.

total fixed cost The sum of all costs for a particular period that will not change as output volume rises or falls.

total sales revenue The price per unit multiplied by the total units sold during a specified period.

trademark The brand name and/or

brand mark that the seller has an exclusive legal right to use.

trade name The legal name of an organization rather than a specific product (i.e., Firestone Tire Company).

trade sales promotions A sales promotion tool that gets dealers to push products.

trade show An industry convention where manufacturers, resellers, and sometimes consumers meet to discuss, study, and observe industry trends.

trading stamps A consumer sales promotion that is a form of coupon distributed by retailers in proportion to the amount of the consumer's purchase. The trading stamps can then be traded at redemption centers for free merchandise.

transportation The physical movement of goods by air, rail, water, truck, pipeline, or some combination of these from one geographic location to another.

travel costs The consumer's direct outlays for transportation incurred in the purchase of a product.

20/80 rule Which 20 percent of which particular category accounts for the highest percentage of sales.

tying arrangement When a seller with a strong product forces a buyer to purchase a weak product as a condition for getting the strong product.

undifferentiated marketing A segmentation strategy that ignores the heterogeneity of buyers in the market and instead focuses on what all or most buyers have in common.

uniform delivered pricing A geographic pricing policy in which all buyers pay an identical price regardless of where they are located. This is also referred to as *postage stamp pricing*.

unit pricing A pricing tactic in which the price is stated in some common unit of measurement, such as the price per ounce or price per pound.

unsought product A product that the consumer does not yet want or know he or she can purchase.

value analysis The process of dividing a product into its most basic components and then identifying parts of the product that could be modified, substituted, or eliminated to reduce costs or increase product performance.

variable cost Any costs that rise or fall in direct relation to changes in output level.

vertical cooperative advertising Advertising for which a supplier (usually a manufacturer or wholesaler) picks up part or all of the cost of advertising.

vertical marketing system A type of marketing channel that is professionally managed and centrally programmed networks that are preengineered to achieve significant operating economies and maximum market impact.

vertical price fixing When a retailer or wholesaler agrees with a manufacturer or other supplier to resell a product at an agreed-on price. Also often referred to as *resale price maintenance*.

warehousing The placement of products in a storage facility to (1) store them, (2) consolidate them with other, similar products, (3) break them down into smaller quantities, (4) build up assortments of products.

wheel of retailing A theory of retail evolution in which retailers enter the market as low-margin, low-cost operators, meet with success, and gradually upgrade their stores, resulting in higher prices, at which time new retailers enter the market with low margins and prices.

wholesalers Individuals or organizations that purchase from manufacturers or other wholesalers and in turn sell to retailers, manufacturers, service organizations, or other wholesalers.

wholesaling The activities of those persons or establishments that sell to retailers and other merchants, and/or to industrial, institutional, and commercial users, but do not sell in significant amounts to ultimate consumers.

word-of-mouth advertising When consumers engage in conversation about a marketer's products.

workload approach To establish the size of the sales force, the sales manager estimates how many hours each salesperson works per year and the total number of hours required to serve the customer.

zone pricing A geographic pricing policy in which a seller's territory is divided into two or more zones, and within each zone, all buyers pay an identical freight charge regardless of where they are located in the zone.

CREDITS

Photos and advertisements were provided courtesy of the companies, organizations, and individuals listed below.

Chapter 1

Page 3: Chrysler Corporation.
Page 8: Du Pont Company.
Page 11, right: Julie O'Neil, photographer.
Page 15: The Procter & Gamble Company.
Page 17: American Cancer Society, Inc.
Page 19: Sears Financial Network.
Page 20: Caterpillar Tractor Co.

Chapter 2

Page 25: Henderson Industries.
Page 33, left: Renaissance Center Venture.
Page 33, right: Wal-Mart Stores Inc.
Page 35: Shapes-Boston.
Page 45: Anheuser-Busch Companies.

Chapter 3

Page 52: Leslie Jean-Bart, photographer.
Page 63: Filene's.

Chapter 4

Page 91: Information Resources Inc.
Page 101: Research International.
Page 103: Anderson, Niebuhr & Associates, Inc.
Page 107: Sophisticated Data Research, Inc.

Chapter 5

Page 120: NameLab, Inc.
Page 130: Bally, Inc.
Page 135: Trans World Airlines, Inc.
Page 136: Lever Bros.

Chapter 6

Page 148: R.C. Auletta and Company, Inc.
Page 150: RCA Corporate Staff Materials.
Page 153: General Electric, Robotics & Vision Systems Dept.
Page 157: Glass Packaging Institute.
Page 159: RCA.
Page 162, left: Mark Joseph-Chicago, photographer.

Page 162, right: Gibson Greeting Cards, Inc.
Page 170: Cahners Exposition Group.

Chapter 7

Page 180: Goya Foods.
Page 182: Beecham Cosmetics.
Page 187: Radio Advertising Bureau.
Page 190: Gerber Products Company.
Page 192: *Inc.* Magazine.
Page 193: U.S. Bureau of Census.
Page 195: Outdoor Life Book Club, Book Div., Times Mirror Magazine.

Chapter 8

Page 235: King Karpen, Aireloom Bedding Company.
Page 238: Sears, Roebuck and Co.
Page 242: American Home Products.
Page 244: Canon USA.
Page 250: Thomas J. Lipton Inc.
Page 258: Wallace Berrie Licensing.
Page 260, left: Reprinted by permission of Hershey Foods Corporation. HERSHEY'S KISSES is a registered trademark of Hershey Foods Corporation.
Page 260, right: Colgate Palmolive Co.
Page 264: Polaroid.

Chapter 9

Page 270: Associated Mills Inc.
Page 276: Commercial Office Supply Division/3M.
Page 281: Underwriters Laboratories Inc.

Chapter 10

Page 301: L.P. Bucklin.
Page 311: The Hartford Insurance Group.
Page 314: Digital Equipment Corporation.
Page 319: Ace Hardware Corporation.
Page 320: The Seven-Up Company.

Chapter 11

Page 332: Marnette Perry, Kroger Company.
Page 342: Rapistan, A Lear Siegler Company.
Page 347: American Association of Railroads.

Page 348: Yellow Freight System, Inc.
Page 350: IU International.

Chapter 12

Page 359: The Limited, Inc.
Page 362: Sears, Roebuck and Co.
Page 365, left, top: Toys "R" Us.
Page 365, left, middle and bottom: Service Merchandise Company, Inc.
Page 365, right, top: CVS.
Page 365, right, bottom: The Athlete's Foot.
Page 366: Circle K Corporation.
Page 369: Faneuil Hall Marketplace, Inc.
Page 371: CompuServe.
Page 383: Chevron U.S.A. Inc.

Chapter 13

Page 399: Julian Wasser, photographer/ Gamma-Liaison.
Page 411, left: Jenn-Air Company.
Page 411, right: SAAB-Scania of America.
Page 412, left: L.L. Bean, Inc.
Page 412, right: The Ohio Art Co.
Page 417: Reproduced with permission of the American Library Association. copyright © 1985 by ALA.

Chapter 14

Page 424: Proctor & Gardner Advertising Inc.
Page 428: *Endless Vacation.*
Page 429: Retail Fragrance Division/Cosmair, Inc./Bruce Weber, photographer.
Page 430: The Procter & Gamble Company.
Page 431: John Deere Company; IBM; Merrill Lynch & Co., Inc.; Beatrice Companies, Inc.
Page 436: Julie O'Neil, photographer.
Page 438: Norcliff Thayer Inc.

Chapter 15

Page 459: Kraft Inc.
Page 470: Princess Cruises.
Page 472: Eastman Kodak Company.

Chapter 16

Page 491: American TV Company.
Page 496, far left, top: Entertainment Inc.

Page 496, far left, center: Balloons
    Delivered.
Page 496, far left, bottom: Salon
    Internationale.
Page 496, center: For Eyes.
Page 496, far right: Black & Decker U.S.
    Household Products Group.
Page 505: Julie O'Neil, photographer.
Page 509: Carole Frohlich, photographer.
Page 512: Herman Geist.

Chapter 17

Page 518: Price Corporation/Karl Ferron,
    photographer.
Page 537: Mazda Motors of America.
Page 538: Julie O'Neil, photographer.

Chapter 18

Page 549: Ito Yokado Co., Ltd.
Page 556, top: Aerospatiale.

Page 556, bottom: General Electric
    Corporation.
Page 562: World Bank Photo.
Page 573: McDonald's.

Chapter 19

Page 586: Jo-Ann Friedman, Health
    Marketing Systems, Inc.
Page 595: Wellesley Chiropractic Office,
    © Val-Pak, 1986.
Page 599: After Six, Inc.
Page 603: The Williamsburg/Four Seasons
    Nursing Center.
Page 606: Metropolitan Life Insurance
    Company.

Chapter 20

Page 615: Decision/Making/Information.
Page 619: Bahamas Tourist Office.
Page 621, left: The Beef Industry Council.

Page 621, right: U.S. Committee for Energy
    Awareness.
Page 629: The Advertising Council Inc.
Page 630: American Red Cross.

Chapter 21

Page 645: Rubbermaid Incorporated.
Page 657: New England Telephone.
Page 660: National Yellow Pages Service
    Assn.

Chapter 22

Page 676: Ron Schultz, Medicine for
    Children, Inc.
Page 682: Boise Cascade Corporation.
Page 683: Mercedes Benz.
Page 684: Sears, Roebuck and Co.

SUBJECT INDEX

NAME AND COMPANY INDEX